SPACES OF LAW IN AMERICAN FOREIGN RELATIONS

Extradition and Extraterritoriality

in the Borderlands and Beyond,

1877–1898

DANIEL S. MARGOLIES

The University of Georgia Press
Athens and London

© 2011 by the University of Georgia Press

Athens, Georgia 30602

www.ugapress.org

All rights reserved

Set in 10/14 Minion Pro by Graphic Composition, Inc.

Printed digitally in the United States of America

Library of Congress Cataloging-in-Publication Data

Margolies, Daniel S., 1969–

Spaces of law in American foreign relations :

extradition and extraterritoriality in the borderlands

and beyond, 1877–1898 / Daniel S. Margolies.

    p.   cm.

Includes bibliographical references and index.

ISBN-13: 978-0-8203-3092-1 (hardcover : alk. paper)

ISBN-10: 0-8203-3092-2 (hardcover : alk. paper)

ISBN-13: 978-0-8203-3871-2 (pbk. : alk. paper)

ISBN-10: 0-8203-3871-0 (pbk. : alk. paper)

1. Extradition—United States. 2. Criminal jurisdiction—United States.

3. Exterritoriality. 4. United States—Foreign relations—Mexico.

5. United States—Foreign relations—19th century. I. Title.

KF9635.M37 2011

345.73′052—dc22   2010039376

British Library Cataloging-in-Publication Data available

CONTENTS

ILLUSTRATIONS

ACKNOWLEDGMENTS

I received a lot of assistance and encouragement while traveling across the country to research and later write this book, and I racked up debts to a wide array of people.

My research on U.S. foreign relations and my conception of the objectives of American power strive to meet the standard set by Tom McCormick. If he alone finds some value in this book, I will be satisfied. I remain continually challenged and graciously assisted by Andy Fry. His suggestion, offered at a Society for Historians of American Foreign Relations meeting a couple of years ago, that I focus more directly on the policy relevance of the legal abstractions that interested me spurred me to tighten my work significantly. I hope to be able to repay him sufficiently for his ideas and help over the years.

I originally became interested in the borderlands not through history but through a long-standing passion for the Conjunto and Norteño music of South Texas. I intend for this book to reflect the accomplishments of pioneers like Narciso Martínez, Santiago Jiménez Sr., Santiago Almeida, Eugenio Abrego, Tomás Ortiz (Los Alegres de Teran), Tony de la Rosa, Mario Montes, and Ramiro Cavazos (Los Donneños), all of whom continue to inspire me to understand the region and the lives and culture of the people there.

I began writing this book as a visiting scholar at the Center for the Study of Law and Society at the University of California–Berkeley and cannot imagine a better-situated or more supportive environment in which to think and write. I am grateful for the opportunity and for the support and friendly assistance of Calvin Morrill, Rosann Greenspan, and Meg Gentes. I valued my interactions with Ely Aharonson, Kurt Pärli, Chris Roberts, and especially Françoise Briegel and the ever-interesting Jinee Lokaneeta.

I would not have been able to spend a fall writing this book in San Francisco without the expansive and idiosyncratic generosity of the Fellowship Desk at Bad Co. Films and especially the friendship and support (in that order) of *jefe de jefes*, Raub Shapiro. If there is a more generous or better person, I have yet to meet him.

As I researched and wrote this book, I received support from Virginia Wesleyan College in the form of a Batten Professorship, various summer development grants, and a very welcome sabbatical. Students in my foreign relations and globalization classes have provided challenging discussion of many of these topics over the years. Arianne Avery was extremely helpful as she speedily tracked down every interlibrary loan request I made (and remained graciously unconcerned when I returned the material late). I am grateful to Rich Bond for his sardonic and insightful comments concerning my work whenever I asked for them, which was always at inconvenient times and at the last minute. My biggest supporter at Virginia Wesleyan remains Craig Wansink, and I am thankful for his kind friendship.

Many of the ideas in this book regarding legal spatiality were shaped during my time as a Fulbright Senior Scholar/Lecturer at Sogang University in Seoul, Korea. I appreciate the input of my students in my U.S. in the World class in the History Department and in my globalization seminar in the Graduate School of International Studies, as well as the opportunity to present my research at the annual meeting of the American Studies Association of Korea. I am grateful for the support of Yoon Byong Nam and the Fulbright Korean-American Educational Commission in Seoul and for the collegiality and insight of Donald Bellomy. Though I did not end up including a chapter on U.S. extraterritoriality in Korea as I had originally planned, I look forward to returning to this topic—and especially to getting back to Korea as soon as possible!

I appreciate the critical readings of Ben Coates, who has an exacting analytical mind and the enviable ability to cut directly to the meaning and implications of U.S. foreign relations law. Paul Kramer and Chris Capozzola offered perceptive suggestions on the manuscript which have been helpful in making my argument clearer. I could not have finished revising this book during my stay in Ulaanbaatar, Mongolia, in summer 2010 without the friendship and help of Milo Silva, who not only lent me his computer but did not complain when I broke it!

I appreciate the assistance of numerous archivists and librarians at the National Archives I and II, the Library of Congress Manuscript Division, the Benson Latin American Collection at the University of Texas–Austin, and the C. L. Sonnichsen Special Collections at the University of Texas–El Paso. I appreciate the permission to quote from the collections of the Bancroft Library at the University of California–Berkeley.

I presented my work at a number of conferences over the years and appreciate the thoughtful critiques of Ed Crapol, Bat Sparrow, Peter Spiro, Greg Downs, Sven Beckert, Elizabeth Sanders, Elizabeth Kelly Gray, Curt Cardwell, and Van Mobley. Austen Parrish has generously shared his ideas and research and helped me to better understand how extraterritoriality has operated in contemporary international and environmental legal disputes. Of course, any mistakes in this book are purely my own.

When I was considering a publisher for this book, I immediately sought the advice of Scott Nelson, who is among the most accomplished historians I know. His advice was very helpful and much appreciated. My experience working with Derek Krissoff at the University of Georgia Press has been effortless from the beginning, and I look forward to the opportunity for future collaboration.

I am grateful for the support, advice, and friendship of Rise Delmar Ochsner, Alexi and Julie Margolies, David Stagman, Arnu Pless Farm, Rio Hackford, Sam Dylan, Rick Donner, Brett McNeil, Arök Miksys, Bill Maltarich, Steve McGuirl, Slim Jim Mathews, Cindy Miller, Jim Andres, James Ruchala, Chip Landrum, Bradley Tatar, F. Chuck Hornemann, Bob Schwartz, Allen Shelton, Dan Roth, Ben Duff, Jeff Engel, Gloria Goodwin Raheja, Hiroshi Kitamura, Ben Dobrin, Bob Albertson, and Wayne Willis. I first became interested in extraterritoriality in graduate school, when I worked alongside Jeff Gayton at the University of Wisconsin–Madison's Memorial Library. His political science dissertation on sovereignty and extraterritoriality intrigued me, and I looked deeper at the historical issues involved in questions of legal spatiality.

It helps to have ready legal advice in the family, and I appreciate my sister Allison's willingness to read and critique the manuscript and answer even my most basic legal questions. I value our deep friendship. My parents are my most loving supporters, and I have enjoyed sharing my ideas with them, even if my dad still does not listen to my beekeeping advice.

My lovely wife, Skye, is unsurpassed in her support for everything I do, even as she completes her own significant research on sleep treatment for posttraumatic stress disorder in U.S. veterans. No matter what harebrained scheme I have come up with—from going to California to write this book right before she started a new job to traveling to Mongolia to study music just as she was beginning a different job—she smiles. She is the best friend a person could have. Our daughter, Lark June, the little Buddha, came into our lives as I have worked on this book, and nothing I write can fully express the love that she simply is. This book is dedicated to them.

SPACES OF LAW IN AMERICAN FOREIGN RELATIONS

Introduction

A stick dressed up does not look like a stick.
Don Quixote

For decades, the task of determining jurisdiction and clarifying governance at the U.S.-Mexican border was termed, simply and wistfully, "impossible." Responding to a State Department request to report on the borderlands situation on June 15, 1879, Warner P. Sutton, the garrulous U.S. consul in Matamoros, argued that this impossibility grew directly out of the ongoing jurisdictional snarls on the border. These in turn were rooted in the failures of diplomacy, the persistent lack of clarity on the geographic boundary line, the cascading failures of the extradition system to limit fugitive flight across the border, and the basic nature of the population that lived in the region, which he characterized as "a large floating class of lawless men on both sides of the river." The state, federal, and transnational systems in place to grapple with these challenges were at best unwieldy and inadequate, if not actually broken. When regular channels did not work or were perceived as insufficient for the task at hand, authorities simply stepped outside of the system.[1]

People also stepped outside of the law, literally. After committing a crime, they simply fled for the inadequately defined border and put themselves beyond surrender. Sutton, expressing typical U.S. borderland attitudes, emphasized the racial aspect of this jurisdictional escape hatch:

> There is a class of low Mexicans, negroes, and mixed races generally, who are now residents of our side and again of the other. . . . [T]hey change the name, nationality, and residence like a garment. If they commit a crime in one place they flee to the opposite shore. The sympathies of their own class and often the difficulty of determining their rightful nationality operates as a bar to their extradition.[2]

Sutton pleaded for a "prompt, contractual, and inexpensive plan" to address "the vexational question of the extradition of criminals" and the question of "rightful nationality." The major objective of a new effort would be to surrender all fugitives in an efficient fashion, "not to exhaust the technicalities of the law and treaties to retain the accused, but to employ all these agencies to get the man out of the country of refuge and into court for trial." Sutton wanted reform to produce a watertight system whereby escape was impossible and jurisdiction was not muddied by geography, politics, or the "sympathies of class" that seemed so troubling to him. New as the consul in Matamoros, he clearly did not sense how truly impossible his reforms would prove to be in the ensuing years.[3]

More than a decade later, Sutton—who had become the Consul General stationed at Nuevo Laredo—wrote the State Department yet again about the same problems, which had only intensified over the years. There was an even more "urgent necessity of relocating the boundary line" since "it is impossible to tell now definitely in very many places, what is the true boundary line." The local, state, and federal officials charged with keeping order hesitated to pursue criminals into territories at the boundary on the Rio Grande, especially onto islands, because of uncertain jurisdiction. Train robbers frequently fled and hid on "the cut-offs along the river above Brownsville and Matamoros," where they could not "be legally arrested as it is almost impossible to tell where the boundary line . . . now is." Their fellow robbers were often Mexicans who fled to Mexico and could not be extradited because of their citizenship. Sutton thought this "put almost a premium on crime" as "any Mexican or Mexicans . . . can cross over to the Texas side and there commit any crime and if they succeed in getting back to Mexico cannot be extradited." The Mexican military was no help because he suspected that, upon grabbing "men of known bad antecedents . . . [it] would be likely to shoot them" instead of bringing them to trial. Alternatively, if captured by American forces, the criminals could claim "illegal capture." Informal illegality in confused jurisdictional spaces offered no solution.[4]

The same was true at the river crossings at El Paso and at Laredo, where "questions of customs jurisdiction are constantly arising" and the spaces of law were so unclear that there was no "true boundary." Nor had Sutton changed his estimation of the 200,000 people on the lower Rio Grande between Rio Grande City and the Gulf, for "the population is of such a character that it is extremely important for the officers of both countries to know the exact dividing line. . . . Many of the lower classes here, when jealous or intoxicated, use knife or pistol, and then resort to the other side. This makes a bad state of affairs and hinders the peaceful development of this border."[5]

This question of economic development and the increasingly settled character of the Texas-Mexico borderlands had intensified the need for clear jurisdictions. While the border used to be an easy refuge for troublemakers, Sutton now saw a new population of "enterprising business men" who were being "hampered in the peaceful development of this section of the country because no one can tell where the jurisdiction of our sovereign ends and that of the other begins."[6] Sutton continued to write so many long discussions focused on the linkage of "boundary and extradition" with different permutations of the phrases "hampering development" and "putting a premium on crime" that the State Department eventually cautioned him that it well understood his perspective, and it was not necessary to continue sending in his views on these matters. However, Sutton persisted, convinced that the failure to address the unclear jurisdictional, interdiction, and extradition regimes in the region put "a premium on crimes along this border, and [was] exceedingly detrimental to the peaceful development of this frontier."[7]

This book traces the sometimes torturous course of these territorial issues raised by Sutton as well as many other officials, judges, and politicians at the state and federal levels, and links them to the overall U.S. approach to a very wide array of jurisdictional disputes in foreign relations during the critical period from the 1870s through the 1890s, when the United States pushed assertively toward global power. At this time, policymakers responded to new slippages of jurisdiction around the globe by defining the space of law in foreign relations in terms of strict sovereign territoriality and unilateralist control.[8] This response was directed to the Mexican borderlands as well as other transnational systems the United States structured with dozens of other countries around the world.

American foreign policy formation and implementation during this time occurred in response to a new and constant stream of unpredictable and explosive challenges to sovereignty, territoriality, socioeconomic order, and jurisdiction. This book examines extraterritorial criminal claims, treaty negotiations, trade conflicts, boundary line disputes, extradition controversies, transborder abductions, and interdiction efforts to map the unilateralism of American foreign relations power as it was deployed, shaped, and resisted in jurisdictional assertions. Countering old views of U.S. foreign relations as reactive, weak, or indistinct in this era, and introducing a key frame of legal analysis into the history of U.S. foreign relations, this book reveals how the stridently sovereigntist reshaping of jurisdiction was used to construct global influence and imperial power in novel ways.

United States hegemonic power was built in the spaces of law, not simply attained by war, trade, or imperial absentmindedness. This book examines these spaces during their formative era. To understand the tenor of rising global power requires carefully tracing the legal decisions, structures, ideologies, and jurisdictional assertions that attended its creation. This book redirects needed attention to the period between 1877 and 1898, when power was articulated in the legal spaces that later undergirded the formal imperial state.

Among the most important and interesting of these spaces of law in late nineteenth-century foreign relations were American extradition regimes and the exceptions carved within them. Extradition of fugitives reflected critical questions of federal sovereignty and the foreign affairs power under the Constitution during the often-mischaracterized period before the turn to overseas empire.[9] This book explores the construction and operation of U.S. extradition relations around the globe during this time. It argues that these structures and the jurisdictional approaches they represented served both an evolving foreign policy emphasis on unilateralism and sovereign exception and a formative emphasis on foreign market expansionism, all while deftly attending to American legal idiosyncrasies. This book is not exclusively a study of extradition policy. Rather, it uses a variety of American extradition regimes as critical and unique lenses by which to examine the rich embeddedness of questions of sovereignty, legality, spatiality, citizenship, and exception in the U.S. approach to global order and governance.[10]

Close examination of U.S. extradition relations as foreign policy offers historians an unusually effective way of gauging and assessing the nation's ongoing pursuit of unilateral governance of transnational concerns as it moved toward formal imperial modes of governance. This is a new emphasis in the historical study of U.S. foreign relations. Extradition has been studied exhaustively as a legal system, but it has been almost wholly ignored by historians of American foreign relations despite its profound importance as a policy, its reflection of activist and globally oriented state power, and its systemic implications.[11]

This book freshly presents the ways American extradition regimes inserted new elements of sovereign exception into transnational jurisdiction questions. Exception broadly can be considered the power of the sovereign to exclude itself from its own law or alternatively to elide or even suspend law entirely. Peter Fitzpatrick and Richard Joyce call it "the intrinsic ability of law to become other to itself . . . [where] even the most seemingly stable law carries with it a power of being radically revised or reversed." John Marshall, as discussed later, identified the power of exception as a core attribute of sovereignty itself.[12] Exception played a critical role in the creation of the spaces of law in American foreign relations.

This book also explains the expansion of the activist state in foreign relations during this time. The tenor of governance as revealed in extradition relations can be found in its creative embeddedness *between* and *within* established territorial jurisdictions and sovereignties. The system of extradition relationships as created by treaty and exercised by the executive branch was an aspect of foreign policy in which state power was designed to be relatively autonomous of the rule of law it was serving. And this power experienced increasingly fewer constraints over time. Considering the governance of legal spatiality through extradition and jurisdictional regimes opens a critical window into the nature and implications of state action as it connected to ideological, judicial, regional, and global interests.

American extradition policy in the latter period of the nineteenth century was the product of confident policymakers who had a clear vision of national interests and a sophisticated understanding of the utilities of legal spatiality. Extradition as a formal political process was newly emergent as a diplomatic form among "civilized" countries at the time. The United States did not hesitate to adapt it to the broader thrust of its increasingly assertive foreign policy and territorial consolidation in the era between the Civil War and the Spanish-American War of 1898. It led the world in the creation of new extradition agreements in both number and variety. U.S. policymakers understood that shaping the mechanics of international fugitive exchange through a distributed network of treaties had a critical role to play in bringing global interactions into congruence with American unilateralist impulses and interests. This period saw varied efforts to clarify and project American interests in the spaces of law as an efficient and convenient way to expand security, market access, and jurisdictional dominance. Extradition was a certain step in this effort to shape global legal structures to best reflect U.S. interests and policy goals.

If sovereignty and the exercise of power were at all compatible with abstractions of justice and order in late nineteenth-century American foreign relations, extradition might have been the ideal solvent. Extradition resonated within and reaffirmed late nineteenth-century sovereign territoriality. Though seemingly simple, the surrender of a fugitive evoked the full panoply of questions about the malleable ends of state power. Extradition regimes encouraged the establishment of fluid legal and extralegal spaces within nineteenth-century international relations. They were carefully calibrated to interest, attuned to expedience, and larded with protections of state autonomy.

This introduction presents the core theoretical concepts that shape this book and that guide the study of legal spatiality in late nineteenth-century U.S. foreign relations. It begins with a brief consideration of territoriality in U.S. policy and practice and continues with a detailed explanation of how to conceptualize extradition as a foreign policy and in terms of governance and borderlands.

TERRITORIALITY, EXTRATERRITORIALITY, AND THE QUESTION OF JURISDICTION

The study of jurisdiction in U.S. foreign relations begins with the core principles of sovereign territoriality, which has been the organizing feature of international state formation and relations since the peace of Westphalia in 1648.[13] In American terms, and of great utility for jurists and policymakers throughout the nineteenth century, there was no clearer or more profound statement of strict territoriality than Chief Justice John Marshall's foundational decision in *Exchange v. McFaddon*. This decision was the basic touchstone for all subsequent approaches to questions of territoriality until the sea changes brought by hegemony and modern globalization in the twentieth century. The development of strict territoriality was historically contingent, and the United States stood among the most strident and constant defenders of it in principle and practice, despite numerous manipulations of it—and more than occasional deviations from a steady path when interest demanded.

The 1812 case of *Exchange v. McFaddon* concerned the sovereignty of a ship owned by Americans that had been nationalized by France. Marshall wrote his decision, as he put it, "exploring an unbeaten path with few if any aids from precedents or written law." But he was sensitive to the centrality of the issue in the core structures of interstate relations and subsequently offered a clear definition of sovereign territoriality that became emblazoned on nineteenth-century jurisprudence and foreign policy. A section of the decision is worth reading in some detail in order to become attuned to the ideas, as they echo throughout the case law discussed in the rest of this book:

> The jurisdiction of the nation within its own territory is necessarily exclusive and absolute. It is susceptible of no limitation not imposed by itself. Any

restriction upon it deriving validity from an external source would imply a diminution of its sovereignty to the extent of the restriction and an investment of that sovereignty to the same extent in that power which could impose such restriction. All exceptions, therefore, to the full and complete power of a nation within its own territories must be traced up to the consent of the nation itself. They can flow from no other legitimate source. . . . This full and absolute territorial jurisdiction, being alike the attribute of every sovereign and being incapable of conferring extraterritorial power, would not seem to contemplate foreign sovereigns nor their sovereign rights as its objects.[14]

In defending the "perfect equality and absolute independence of sovereigns," Marshall highlighted the importance of territoriality in the structuring of state power. Sovereign territoriality was the hallmark of a self-defined "civilized" regime and of a properly functioning state system that respected the rights of such civilized powers. Jurisdiction was constrained, and the state liberated, from both limitation on action and unsought responsibility abroad. In the strict sense clarified by Marshall, sovereignty, territory, and jurisdiction were one. Significantly, the only exceptions were created by the sovereign itself.

It followed that the sanctity of territoriality forbade extraterritoriality, which is the assertion of sovereignty within other sovereignties. Extraterritorial power derived from the artful creation of an "*imperium in imperio*" and indicated sharp divisions of jurisdiction and power. The term was, as nineteenth-century State Department diplomat and international law expert John Bassett Moore clarified it, "peculiarly metaphorical and misleading" and perhaps best understood "in reality merely [as] an *exemption from process*."[15]

Extraterritoriality was a key attribute of nineteenth-century imperial control, achieved legally rather than exclusively by force, usually as a result of unequal treaties. It highlighted the imperialist manipulation of legal spatiality for maximum latitude and exploitation. Turan Kayaoğlu calls it plainly "quintessential legal imperialism," which required both "a legal framework to deny non-Western law and sovereignty" and the power to support this denial. To President Grover Cleveland, extraterritoriality may have been merely an "ill-defined fiction," but it was also embraced by U.S. policymakers as an extremely useful exception in certain circumstances.[16]

Three forms of jurisdiction formed the paradoxical U.S. framework of legal spatiality throughout the nineteenth century: the bedrock claims of sovereign territoriality, the rejection of all extraterritorial claims as a function of this same absolute sovereignty (referred to as the presumption against extraterritoriality), and the deliberate assertions of extraterritorial jurisdiction in selected cases. Between these opposing applications of law lay a vast and complex field of practice, policy, and experimentation. This contradictory approach to legal spatiality persisted in U.S. policy in a wide variety of ways. Legal scholar Kal Raustiala argues that "rules of legal spatiality in American law derive from configurations of power and interest, not from any overarching normative theory of legal geography."[17] The ease with which the United States stepped outside the law—in the cases of legalized extraterritorial abduction in lieu of extradition, for example— clearly marked the centrality of power as the single most dominant feature.

American formal extraterritorial claims in the nineteenth century were relatively limited in scope but very significant, especially considering how stridently extraterritoriality was rejected in other ways. The only assertions of extraterritoriality considered appropriate were in states deemed to be either "uncivilized or semi-civilized" or "other places where Pagan and Mohammedan law prevail[ed]."[18] In those states, for a variety of reasons pioneered in long-standing European imperialist practice, extraterritorial jurisdiction could be asserted by a state powerful enough to force this invasion of local sovereignty upon a weaker state.

In the best-known and most widely studied examples, the United States claimed extraterritorial consular court jurisdiction in thousands of cases in dozens of countries around the world, most notably and lastingly in China and also in Korea, Japan, the Ottoman Empire, and numerous other states. This was the most blatant form of extraterritorial jurisdictional imperialism, a system of control over sojourning nationals that catalyzed variable "citizenship regimes" in the dynamics of American imperial dominance. These court systems, so thoroughly explored by recent scholars like Eileen P. Scully and Teemu Ruskola, are not the focus here.[19] There were other, less overt but more expansive and durable ways in which the United States unrolled extraterritorial jurisdictional claims in its foreign policy. These ways are explored throughout this book in such critical issues as borderlands crime and interdiction, water usage, diplomatic asylum, and the definition and response to terrorism.

How could the stridently territorial United States so facilely insert its sovereignty within other sovereignties? Extraterritorial claims were generally justified on the basis of both necessity and expedience. The claims reflected the ways policymakers divided the world into civilized states of sovereign power and uncivilized systems, where zones of extraterritorial exception necessarily held sway. The differences between the two were developmental, cultural, and religious. As Moore explained it, "those exceptions are barbarous lands, in which local law does not exist, and to which the doctrine of the sovereignty of each nation over all persons within its territory does not completely apply; and Mohammedan and other non-Christian countries, in which the citizens of many states enjoy a conventional immunity from the local law. In such places it is *not only proper but necessary* for many states to subject [their] citizens to [their] own regulations." The exquisite irony of this explanation (especially with its echoes of the language in the Constitution) is that Moore expressed it while fulminating at book length against Mexico's assertion of extraterritorial juris- diction over an American newspaper editor's act of libel in Texas. This 1886 in- cident, called the Cutting case, was enormously controversial, almost produced armed conflict, and was never fully resolved, as is explored fully in chapter 1.[20]

Extradition represented a unique connection of sovereignties for the limited purpose of fugitive surrender that did not unsettle basic asymmetries of power. The United States constructed different, often contradictory, systems for each extradition agreement in order to achieve this central goal of surrender. The differences in bilateral relationships reflected the relative position of the treaty nation within the hierarchical American constellation of ethnic, legal, and po- litical development and civilization. Diversity of treaty regimes was conse- quently of enormous significance; part 2 of this book demonstrates these stark differences in the structuring of relations around the world.

Particular attention in this book is given to relations with Mexico, which the United States treated as a "civilized" power only begrudgingly and with many exceptions that were marbled with claims of extraterritorial jurisdiction. One of the most overt assertions of this kind of extraterritoriality, and one illustra- tive of the nature of power along the border, was the infamous June 1, 1877, "Ord Order," named after General E. O. C. Ord, who commanded the Army Department of Texas. This order authorized U.S. troops to enter Mexican ter- ritory as they saw fit in order to pursue and capture Indian raiders, and confis- cate property, on the basis of a "duty" to suppress "lawless incursions." The Ord Order read,

the president desires that the utmost vigilance on the part of the military forces in Texas be exercised for the suppression of these raids. It is very desir- able that efforts to this end, in so far at least as they necessarily involve opera- tions on both sides of the border, be made with the cooperation of the Mexican authorities; and you will instruct General Ord, commanding in Texas, to invite such co-operation on the part of the local Mexican authorities, and to inform them that while the President is anxious to avoid giving offense to Mexico, he is nevertheless convinced that the invasion of our territory by armed and organized bodies of thieves and robbers, to prey upon our citizens, should not be longer endured. General Ord will at once notify the Mexican authorities along the Texas border of the great desire of the President to unite with them in efforts to suppress this long continued lawlessness. At the same time he will inform those authorities that if the Government of Mexico shall continue to neglect the duty of suppressing these outrages, that duty will devolve upon this Government, and will be performed, even if its performance should render necessary the occasional crossing of the border by our troops. You will, therefore, direct General Ord that in case the lawless incursions continue he will be at liberty, in the use of his own discretion, when in pursuit of a band of the marauders, and when his troops are either in sight of them or upon a fresh trail, to follow them across the Rio Grande, and to overtake and punish them, as well as retake stolen property taken from our citizens and found in their hands on the Mexican side of the line.[21]

This was a significant "legal" and military assertion of extraterritorial jurisdiction in pursuit of "lawless" elements. Mexico was "invited" to assist, but in the absence of full American satisfaction, the policy would "devolve" and U.S. troops could cross the border at will. This unabashed assertion of extraterritorial sovereignty resonated in the borderland region for more than a decade, long after the order was officially rescinded. Numerous other acts of incursion and exception are detailed throughout this book.

Clearly, even operating under Marshall's stark definition of "necessarily exclusive and absolute" sovereignty based on territoriality, state interest in the pursuit of fugitives triggered multiple and often elastic definitions of jurisdiction and assertions of sovereign exception. As Paul Schiff Berman writes, "the exercise of jurisdiction has always been part of the way in which societies demarcate space, delineate communities, and draw both physical and symbolic boundaries."[22] There are a variety of specific forms of jurisdiction codified today such as legislative, judicial, and enforcement jurisdiction, which are self-explanatory. Jurisdiction specifically over crime can be further subdivided into several categories such as territorial, protective, nationality, universal, and passive personality. Christopher L. Blakesley has clearly defined each of these categories:

The "territorial theory" allows for jurisdiction over conduct that takes place within the territorial boundaries of the state. The "nationality theory" bases jurisdiction on the allegiance of nationality of the perpetrator . . . no matter where the offenses take place. The "protective principle" . . . emphasizes the effect or possible effect of the offense and provides for jurisdiction over conduct deemed harmful to specific national interests of the forum state. The "passive personality principle" extends jurisdiction over offenses where the victims are nationals of the forum state. The "universal theory" allows jurisdiction in any forum that obtains jurisdiction over the person of the perpetrator of certain offenses considered particularly heinous or harmful to mankind generally.[23]

In the nineteenth century, the United States rejected all of these forms except territorial jurisdiction, though in extradition relations it engaged other nations, which had broader or alternative readings of these different jurisdictional forms. The language of the treaties differed on the point that fugitives could be returned from the "jurisdiction" or the "territories" of other powers, but Moore pointed out that "as the term 'jurisdiction' is construed by the government of the United States, no additional words are necessary to confine the operation of the treaties to offences committed within the territorial jurisdiction of the contracting parties."[24] Jurisdiction and territory, fused and inseparable, were the beginning and the end of it, most of the time.

EXTRADITION AS A FOREIGN POLICY

Nineteenth-century diplomatic and legal wrangles over transnational extradition and interdiction issues developed out of the confusing and constant movement of criminals, fugitives, anarchists, revolutionaries, smugglers, "illegal aliens," and illicit goods throughout the world system. United States extradition diplomacy formed a singular component of the country's global efforts to systematize a coherent response to transnational crime in the latter half of the nineteenth century just as American foreign economic policy fitfully (and unsuccessfully, at the time) attempted to reshape global political economy in line with distinct American interests. Both efforts were founded on a unilateralist footing, a confident and sometimes aggressive heritage of ideological and legal exceptionalism, and a rapidly developing awareness of the nation's power and its potential uses in both suasion and coercion. The exchange of fugitives was viewed as a means of exercising authority at least as much as a means of establishing a regime of justice. Furtherance of national power and wealth, along with sustenance of jurisdiction, were the primary objectives.

Extradition was founded on two broad conjoined concepts. One was inviolable territorial jurisdiction, with an emphasis on executive power. The other was the creation of a limited connection between sovereign jurisdictions via a treaty designed for the single delineated purpose of surrendering fugitives. Such international connections of criminal enforcement, pursuit, and exchange served each state's interest while also reinforcing the territorial jurisdiction so treasured by policymakers at the time. They did not imply future collaboration, deeper connection, or a true regime of international justice. These approaches could be seen as contradictory in conception, and were in many respects, but they proved to be mutually reinforcing in practice.

Familiar and formal as the process might seem today, extradition has had a slippery development and a fitful lineage. Fugitive surrender appears as a requirement of the states in Article IV, Section 2 of the U.S. Constitution, but it is couched in an austere statement: "A person charged in any state with treason, felony, or other crime, who shall flee from justice, and be found in another state, shall on demand of the executive authority of the state from which he fled, be delivered up, to be removed to the state having jurisdiction of the crime." The Constitution does not mention international surrender of fugitives or provide guidance for structuring the links between U.S. sovereignty and other sovereignties in this regard.

Extradition policies were created by treaty and diplomatic precedent as a matter of foreign policy (and only later, to a lesser extent, by federal statute), and the system that evolved directly reflected a fungible array of political, regional, economic, and other interests that were often quite removed from abstractions of justice. One of the most interesting benefits of examining extradition as a foreign policy is that it allows historians to examine how each aspect of fugitive exchange functioned on so many systemic levels.

As both a system and an ideal, extradition developed slowly. Scholars disagree about the precise origin of the term "extradition" as it is understood in modern usage. The word extradition referring to the broader surrender of fugitives from justice to a foreign government for trial was not even finally sanctioned for official American usage by statute until 1848. The clearest basic definition of extradition as finally regularized by the United States by the 1890s came from the indefatigable John Bassett Moore, who stood as the State Department's central expert on extradition at the end of the nineteenth century. He had a special interest in the subject, wrote several long works on it as both policy and practice, and helped to define and defend the embrace of strict territoriality involved in the process of fugitive surrender. Moore defined extradition straightforwardly as "the act by which one nation delivers up an individual, accused or convicted of an offence outside of its own territory, to another nation which demands him, and which is competent to try and punish him."[25]

Fugitive surrender based on treaty constraints was the core component of extradition, and Moore's emphasis on the national *competence* to extradite was significant. Competence within the international state system was relative, related to legal standing grounded in territoriality and jurisdiction and reflective of culture, power, and region. American policymakers believed certain baseline competencies trumped all others. Albert Billot defined three cornerstones of extradition in his classic and influential 1874 work *Traité de L'Extradition*: "secur[ing] the application of the territorial competence"; "the conservation of order, the observation of justice, and the repression of crime," and "secur[ing] reciprocity." Moore relied on Billot heavily but emphasized only one of the cornerstones: "the superiority of the territorial competence over every other is now universally accepted." Moore cited as proof his own recent and very strident work detailing the sanctity of American notions on territoriality, the *Report on Extraterritorial Crime and the Cutting Case!*[26] The unilateralist underpinnings of American policy may have seemed ragged and fitfully applied, but they were coherent in the minds of the policymakers themselves.

There were of course many varying definitions of legal competency common throughout the late nineteenth century relating to hierarchies within the space of law for everything from individuals to corporations.[27] But in the American construction of extradition relationships, the devil was in the details of situating another nation's competence within a hierarchy of national attributes. "Competence" was related directly to sovereignty and jurisdiction and thus to civilization itself. Evoking competence also evoked the division of the world into civilized and barbarous nations, into discrete, defined territorial sovereignties and looser areas of extraterritorial authority. States with competence were granted the right to extraterritorial claims; states without were not. Incompetence, like disorder or barbarism, invited exception. Real or imagined incompetence in any area would change the relationship and thus the flow of extradition.

M. Cherif Bassiouni, the modern expert on extradition procedure and policy, argues that the surrender of a fugitive should more properly be called "rendition," a concept that "did not always derive from the process of extradition, but was more a gesture of friendship and cooperation between sovereigns. The individual in these early days of the practice was deemed an object and not a subject of the process." Extradition had a more complicated origin related to the operations of state power:

> [T]he surrender of a person who has been granted the privilege of presence or refuge in the requested state was deemed an exceptional measure running against the traditions of asylum and hospitality of the requesting state. This gave rise to a speculation about the origin of the term extradition, i.e. "extra-tradition," which ultimately evolved into "extradition." A more commonly accepted explanation for the term 'extradition' is its Latin original *extradere*, which means forceful return of a person to his sovereign.[28]

The key was that the "process of extradition" required the "forceful return" of the fugitive. Extradition was a structured political act linked to express treaty requirements rather than a required function of interstate relations. It was "neither the product of sound legislative policy nor the outgrowth of judicious doctrinal thinking."[29] Extradition as a formalized treaty system requiring state action was actually something of a novelty in nineteenth-century international relations, and the United States had a pioneering impact upon it.

In U.S. practice, distinctions between extradition and rendition regimes had much more than mere semantic weight since the act of extradition reflected core constitutional issues and the system of intersecting and sometimes competing jurisdictions. Moore distinguished between rendition and extradition. In his view, rendition occurred only between the states of the Union whereas extradition was properly viewed as an international act. He argued that rendition "proceeds upon a principle precisely antipodal to that from which are derived the leading doctrines of extradition, *its true and international sense*." Fugitive surrender in policy terms was rooted paradoxically in "the right, in strict law, of every sovereign power to grant asylum to fugitives from justice." There was no right to such interstate asylum under the Constitution. A rendition request required only criminal charges, not evidence, and all crimes were included, "however frivolous."[30] Importantly, there existed no explicit political offense exception to interstate rendition as there was to extradition, as is discussed in chapter 6.

Rendition was a required duty of states, but international extradition was a tool of foreign policy utterly open to interpretation and modification by the federal government through treaties. There was "no positive obligation" for extradition and no compelling international authority. As an important early (1823) extradition case, *Commonwealth v. Deacon*, phrased it, "no state has an *absolute and perfect right to demand* of another the delivery a fugitive criminal, though it has what is called an *imperfect right*, that is a right to ask it as a matter of courtesy, good-will and mutual convenience." While sovereigns may have had "an undoubted right to surrender fugitives" in European practice, in the American context, the latitude of the president to act at all in the absence of an express grant of law was disputed.[31]

Indeed, in the absence of authority derived from a treaty, extradition simply did not exist. There were no essential guidelines to the evolving structures of international extradition; it was created piecemeal by treaties. American extradition was set wholly in a national policy realm governed by executive authority rooted in an extremely flexible treaty power.[32] This left the meaning of extradition both potentially limitless and perpetually contested. The United States never produced a single coherent "substantive statute" of extradition like Great Britain did in its landmark Act of 1870, which was one of the most important nineteenth-century pieces of legislation governing extradition. The United States preferred to create different, finely tuned protocols of extradition with each country through separate treaty negotiations.

The process of extradition originated in an official request between the United States and a foreign government for the return of a fugitive accused of a crime identified in a treaty. The entire process was authorized and constrained by this formal agreement. When a request was made, U.S. statutes provided that "any justice of the Supreme Court, circuit judge, district judge, [or] commissioner authorized so to do by any of the courts of the United States, or judge of a court of record of general jurisdiction of any state" could issue a warrant for the arrest of the fugitive. After a hearing that simply established jurisdiction over the case and certified the validity and sufficiency of the evidence to match treaty obligations, the secretary of state could (but was not required to) issue an extradition warrant. The guilt of the accused was a matter for the requesting state to determine.[33]

Extradition was fundamentally a diplomatic act, but it produced unique interactions between the highest level of foreign policy creation and the most local points of police power throughout the world. It was not an easy or quick process. Extradition for even seemingly minor crimes or uncontested surrenders required very large amounts of material, including full criminal proceedings, official warrants, sworn testimony, agreements of authority, photographs, authentications, translations of the documents and the cases, orders to surrender the individuals to the proper authorities of each country involved, certificates of complaint, official documentation of treaty compliance, and the involvement of a very large network of individuals at the local, state, and national level in at least two countries.[34]

Form followed function in extradition. The political conception of extradition derived in part from the need to define and structure fugitive exchange and to create mechanisms for surrender. This required a novel and clearly defined relationship between the states in addition to internal administrative clarity *within* each state. An administrative apparatus had to be invented "which enable[d] the requested State to accede to the request of the latter" in light of the judicial, ideological, and political implications of such a surrender.[35] Extradition did not signal an end to inviolable territorial sovereignty in part because the surrendering state alone—not the requesting state—determined the outcome of an exchange according to the treaty stipulations.

Though sustained by the sovereign territorial system, nineteenth-century international extradition relationships were inherently reciprocal by design. Moore put it directly and succinctly: "[A]s a rule, reciprocity is strictly required."[36] In this sense, it was similar to trade policy of the same era, which was designed to maximize national economic advantage through protectionism but still moved toward reciprocity as a policy tool for focused regional and sectoral objectives. The United States adopted a great number of extradition treaties at the same time it sought trade reciprocity agreements, which signaled a shift in its relationship to the world system.[37] Reciprocity in extradition relations was a slippery concept, made more so by the proliferation of theories of jurisdiction and the existence of exceptions. The citizenship exception, for example, which allowed states to refuse to extradite their citizens in some treaty relations, had a directly corrosive effect on the reciprocity inherent in extradition, as chapters 3 and 5 explain. In practice, it is essential to recognize that reciprocity was inherent but thoroughly amenable to adjustment.

The United States was not alone in requiring that extradition relations be reciprocal; this was an international standard followed by a great many countries. The Anglo-American extradition tradition emphasized express, delineated treaty requirements very strongly, and Great Britain and the United States projected their approach as a global example. Mexico considered reciprocity to be an "essential" component of the extradition process. Mexican foreign minister Ignacio Mariscal noted that "the promise of reciprocity is always required." On the other hand, France and some other civil law countries often accepted a looser standard.[38]

One striking element of extradition as a foreign policy rather than as foremost a judicial process is how very little issues of habeas corpus were discussed by the foreign policymakers in their internal and official writings and negotiations over treaty language, definitions of crimes, procedures, and extradition controversies. The judiciary had an essential role to play in the process, but it was not a causal or plenary one. Extradition was an act of foreign policy that produced domestic habeas corpus issues simply by bringing an individual into the justice system, where the accused had a right to a hearing on the jurisdictional authority of his or her restraint. But there was an extremely neat—even stark—separation of the legal questions from political and diplomatic policy in the creation of the extradition regime and its execution. Extradition surrenders were primarily conceived of in political terms. As Augustus Hill Garland of the Senate Committee on the Judiciary wrote in 1882, "the judiciary cannot surrender him, and the President cannot do it until the judiciary has decided that the case is a proper one for delivery, and even then he may revise and reject that decision."[39] The details may have been left to lawyers and judges, but the power was created and exercised by the state, shaped by the politicians for their own policy ends, and ultimately therefore controlled by them.

Studying extradition as policy over process helps deepen the understanding of the mechanics of state power. Cary Federman has argued (looking at domestic cases) that the state must be brought back directly into the study of habeas corpus so that issues of federalism do not obscure the actual interests behind the exercise of state power. "Jurisdictional niceties" tended to fall by the wayside when the state found it had a specific (usually economic) interest involved.[40] Yet habeas corpus was not, and could not be, ignored in any detention of an accused criminal under American jurisdiction. Further, habeas petitions formed a standard part of the extradition proceedings for fugitive surrenders. All manner of policymakers, courts, and extradition agents and others involved in the system grappled with petitions, responded to them, and certified them. But the discussion remained extremely and deliberately limited.

This issue was finally resolved in *Benson v. McMahon*, an 1888 Supreme Court case that regularized the status quo in judicial oversight over extradition that had developed over the previous half century and in so doing reaffirmed executive power. This case decided that the judiciary was constrained within the narrow limits of the treaty language and the statutes dealing with treaty implementation. Indeed, the Court seemed rather dismissive of any other claim:

> We are not sitting in this Court on the trial of the prisoner, with power to pronounce him guilty and punish him or declare him innocent and acquit him. We are now engaged simply in an inquiry as to whether, under the construction of the act of Congress and the treaty entered into between this country and Mexico, there was legal evidence before the commissioner to justify him in exercising his power to commit the person accused to custody to await the requisition.[41]

Questions relating to guilt or other issues outside the treaty were irrelevant.

The United States relied on flourishes of its own to define global extradition standards and regularize lists of extraditable crime. It established extradition with Great Britain in the 1794 Jay Treaty but only extradited one person under it in the very controversial case of Thomas Nash, alias Jonathan Robbins, before stopping extradition altogether. The Robbins case remained a poisoned experience so tightly intertwined with sharp partisanship and Anglophobia, critiques of executive power, and memories of national humiliation that extradition effectively vanished from the national political realm as a matter of policy.[42] As the United States increased in wealth, power, and confidence, its willingness to acquiesce to subordinating or unsatisfactory extradition relations, particularly with Great Britain, faded as rapidly as its unilateralism and power grew. Amazingly, for the first half century of its existence, the United States extradited only this single person.

Crime itself might not have stopped, but it ceased to have foreign policy relevance for decades. Between 1794 and 1842, no extradition treaties were signed. The United States created no legislation concerning international extradition until 1848. There were no definitions of offenses, formal federal procedures for the capture or surrender of fugitives, or rules for authentication of evidence. Extradition effectively did not exist, regardless of the crime. Not until the era of the Civil War was a standardized practice rooted in a varied and global array of treaties and implementing legislation established.

In 1842, the United States signed the first extradition treaty with Great Britain in the limited form of Article X of the Webster-Ashburton Treaty. This is generally considered to be the start of modern extradition in international relations. As one observer wrote in retrospect at the start of the twentieth century, "the treaty mark[ed] the close of one period . . . and the opening of another."[43]

Article X was a calibrated and very limited grant of jurisdictional connection between the two countries. The treaty did not even provide a clear statement as to *how* extradition was to operate, just that it would. In delivering the treaty to the Senate, President John Tyler stressed its limits. He promised in particular that the United States could unilaterally abrogate Article X at any time "lest some unforeseen inconvenience or unexpected abuse should arise from the stipulation rendering its continuance in the opinion of one or both of the parties not longer desirable." The United States was not embracing a new order so much as structuring a limited new exchange. Tyler told the Senate that maintaining the "present state of civilization and intercourse" along a very long and permeable boundary line needed such a new order. Absence of an extradition regime had invited disorder, with grave foreign relations implications: "A consciousness of immunity from the power of avoiding justice in this way instigates the unprincipled and reckless to the commission of offenses, and the peace and good neighborhood of the border are consequently often disturbed."[44]

Of great significance in the 1842 treaty was the fact that citizens were not exempt from extradition. The treaty referred only to "persons," a deliberate usage that meant that citizenship did not afford an individual any exemption.[45] Given the strenuous U.S. emphasis on exacting treaty language, this distinction was significant. The United States later carefully constructed certain extradition treaties specifically to exempt citizens and in other instances argued unrelentingly to keep *out* such a provision. The willingness to extradite citizens in all cases to some countries and only some or no individuals to other nations was a key zone of exception in the U.S. regime.

Soon after the passage of the Webster-Ashburton Treaty, the United States sought similar extradition treaties with a wide variety of other nations, starting with France in November 9, 1843. This treaty was notably more detailed and robust in establishing an extradition relationship than was the spartan Article X in the British agreement. It was the French treaty, in its coverage, structure, and utility, that became the utilitarian model for the later U.S. extradition agreements that are considered throughout this book.[46]

With remarkable speed, U.S. policymakers transformed (or, more precisely, reversed) their concept of the foreign policy utility of extradition. They did this without attenuating a strong emphasis on strict territoriality or strong, unilateralist executive action in foreign relations. The means were independently negotiated, bilateral treaties featuring varied exceptions rather than systematic legislation. Each agreement was held up by American policymakers as a model of diplomatic grace and effectiveness combined with respect for international law and sovereign territoriality. This book explores the meaning of this move to an elaborate network of treaties covering a wide array of crimes with all of the strongest and many of the smaller nations of the world.

Within two decades, the United States created seventeen new extradition agreements operating independently according to an array of approaches. In contrast, Great Britain, which had the preponderance of international interests as the global hegemonic leader, only signed three. By the end of the nineteenth century, the United States close to doubled the number of its treaty-based extradition regimes and extradited and surrendered an unprecedented number of people under these agreements. Clearly, something was going on to motivate American policymakers to act with such speed and commitment.

This speed and scale would have seemed shocking if it were not so characteristic of U.S. actions at the time. Considering the role of law in late nineteenth-century American development, James Willard Hurst characterized domestic legal culture in terms of a "release-of-energy policy." As Hurst writes, "on the whole, the nineteenth-century United States valued change more than stability and valued stability most often where it helped create a framework for change."[47] U.S. extradition policy stood at the heart of the desire to adapt a policy coordinating the Constitution, broad notions of sovereignty and jurisdiction, and the pursuit of unilateral power within this still quite unformed (and hence wide-open) realm of international fugitive exchange. The United States was drawn to it through interest in enhancing state power and for practical purposes that were especially valuable to a raucous, dynamic, immigrant-rich nation uniquely suitable for (and vulnerable to) fugitive flight.

The new extradition regimes both challenged and reinforced boundaries by linking sovereignties in a system progressively shaped according to U.S. values, procedures, concepts of jurisdiction, and world systemic interests. Through extradition regimes, American policymakers increasingly sensed the advantages of "the idea of sovereignty as an expansive power in networks."[48] Networks erode boundaries, and the United States sought to carefully control this erosion along distinctly unilateralist lines. Treaties and fugitive exchange were key structural means of driving this overall transformation. The change they represented or produced was determined by both a very diverse, flexible, and sometimes contradictory set of agreements and a style of implementation and governance being newly developed alongside it.

VIEWING EXTRADITION IN TERMS OF GOVERNANCE

The implementation of extradition regimes can be fruitfully viewed within a broader appreciation of its relation to American foreign policy governance. Most discussions of American governance systems focus on the connections among policy creation, political choices, and economic interests and constraints. As Miles Kahler and David A. Lake directly phrase it, "governance is politics by other means."[49]

In vital ways, extradition served as a laboratory for the governance of transnational concerns. It was a novel but cobbled-together system of clearly enunciated jurisdictional territoriality and related U.S. case law, international legal tradition, and police power, all stitched with important exceptions to make governance more effective. It was expandable and malleable.

It was not an accident of history that extradition emerged at this time as a new, or newly applied, representation of American governance. The United States was undergoing a rapid and unprecedented transformation in governance throughout the polity in the second half of the nineteenth century. This great transformation tracked with the changes produced by industrialization and nascent globalization, and in many respects amounted to the first of several governance revolutions that emerged in the era after the Civil War. The transformation of governance occurred across all sectors of the economy, founded upon a reimagination of the role and vitality of the state in its relation to economic policy, regional interests and development, corporate structures and behaviors, and the market itself.[50] The relatively weak executive at this time additionally located new avenues for assertion through foreign relations. This revolution had an impact on the scale, scope, and jurisdiction of the federal government; the intensified global orientation of politicians and business leaders; and the emerging experimentation with overseas economic expansionism and later, empire. Despite it being a protectionist era, unimpeded expansion into foreign markets through bilateral and reciprocal trade agreements was a fundamental, even relentless policy objective at this time, and it developed out of a very similar approach to governance.

The modern American system of extradition developed alongside the accelerating global interconnections of the nineteenth century and was designed to carve space within it as well as create new jurisdictional inroads for the future. Extradition regimes serve as an effective microcosm of state reaction to the challenges of early globalization. This was a period of explosive national growth and prosperity, newfound mobility and transnational movement, increased social complexity, and intensified political dispute. The rapid internationalization of criminal escape and the increased range of state actions therefore highlighted core transformations of early globalization. The extradition system that American policymakers created in response was regionally varied and even graceful. In an era in which jurisdiction in global terms was often subject to political, imperial, and extraterritorial limitation, extradition provided a clear way of erecting discrete and definable connections within the system.[51]

Extradition should not be viewed as a mitigation of territorial distinctions or the rush to a new order based on the borderless expansion of legal and enforcement structures. It did not signal hybridization of legal systems, global legal plurality, or a move toward global governance regimes in the late nineteenth century. During that key formative era, extradition did not carry the freight of reforming international relations or ushering in liberalized rights regimes. The global pursuit of criminals had at its heart a concern with the smooth operation of justice and the end of fugitive criminality; citizenship and assertions of state power were but two complicating factors out of many swirling around the linkage of international jurisdictions. It was at times difficult to assess the relevance of notions of justice in American extradition relations.[52]

Extradition helped to produce a definite but limited equality in sovereign jurisdictions but by design did nothing to address the inequality of states in terms of wealth, power, or reach. It remained a tool of unilateralist, exclusionary states that were faced with newly globalized networks of criminality and fugitive escape but that were as ever interested in enhancing their own power. Extradition was a function of unilateral power rather than an act of international comity, sovereign responsibility, or abstract right. It was convenient and even appealing but entirely constructed. It could just as easily be dismantled as applied or so riddled with exceptions as to be rendered meaningless.

There was one particularly unusual exception in the extradition relations created with Mexico. Along the border, the state executive and other officers were specially empowered by the so-called "border states clause" in Article II of the 1861 U.S.-Mexico Extradition Treaty to handle the whole process of extradition surrenders and demands that elsewhere were a purely national function of the executive branch.[53] This extreme localization of a foreign affairs process, and the great deal of autonomy and extralegal abuses it created, uniquely structured jurisdictional questions in the borderlands. The borderlands exception and the other exceptions based on citizenship and the political nature of extraditable crime are a major focus of this book. So too are the numerous ways in which these policies were inscribed across this diverse, defiant, and difficult landscape. Jurisdictional assertions and sovereign exceptions were linked with a regional style of governance in which the lines between the foreign and the domestic were contested daily.

Exceptions to jurisdiction and process made extradition at least potentially more reflective of American governance, and they slowly but significantly transformed notions of illegality, the reach of sovereign power, the nature of political crime, and the meaning of asylum. These issues underlay and sustained what M. Cherif Bassiouni identified as the matrix of "exceptions, exemptions, exclusions, and defenses" that paradoxically both served and undermined extradition.[54] Exceptions within and to extradition relations represented ever-finer gradations of distinction in jurisdiction as well as ever-finer expressions of sovereign power. Exceptions created means for the alternative exercise of state power.

As Linda Kerber argues, in this era "the nation experimented with the creation of ambiguous spaces between the domestic and the foreign, between the national and the international, between sovereignty and subjugation."[55] As a transnational exchange connected in essential ways to foreign policy ambitions, domestic ideals, and understandings of sovereignty, extradition was a unique addition to this project of revising American governance along new lines of exception. Gerald L. Neuman has identified exceptions in the "anomalous zones" under U.S. governance, which he defines as "a geographical area in which certain legal rules, otherwise regarded as embodying fundamental policies of the larger legal system, are locally suspended."[56]

Exceptions loomed large in the service of unilateral governance. United States extradition regimes created functional abstractions of these "anomalous zones" by forming jurisdictional exceptions within extradition regimes and international state relations. Exceptions provided a significant reversal or denial of the very act of connection, opening, and exchange at the heart of extradition exchanges. They formed an essential part of the broader American approach to spatial governance, to extradition, and to the exercise of sovereignty itself.

CONSIDERING BORDERLANDS WITHIN JURISDICTIONAL AND FOREIGN AFFAIRS FRAMEWORKS

Neither international boundary lines nor jurisdictional limits nor the global socioeconomic order were naturally occurring; they were artificial constructions conjured upon the map by force or diplomacy for specific policy purposes. Richard Ford notes that "lines on a map may anticipate a jurisdiction, but a jurisdiction itself consists of the practices that make the abstract space depicted on a map significant."[57] How could American jurisdiction, and thus its conception of order, be conclusively defined in this world system of borders in which all aspects were contested and complicated as a basic structural and geographic reality? Even the geographic border between the United States and Mexico was so lightly policed, it was in practical terms "more symbolic than real," even if it was viewed as a distinct legal reality.[58]

As solid as sovereignty and the concept of jurisdiction may have seemed and felt to policymakers, in the borderlands it was not and could not be unilaterally applied. In the borderlands—a region long treated as an exception to U.S. policy in many ways—unclear jurisdictions, local autonomy, endemic crime, transborder incursions, casual violence, water disputes, and periodic revolution invited diverse approaches. Karl Jacoby defined borderlands as "by their very nature undergirded by the countervailing impulses of separation and linkage, of political division and the myriad continuities—ecological, economic, familial, and other—that persist across national boundaries."[59] These connections did not, however, stop U.S. and Texas officials from embracing unilateralism, exclusion, and the threat of violence and from extravagantly opposing any challenges to jurisdiction. Even within regional constraints, the exercise of national power through sovereign exception hewed closely to the cherished lines of unilateral governance. Policymakers utilized these approaches in everything from strident assertions of sovereignty in water-use controversies to increasingly enhanced interdiction and surveillance systems.

Attempting to realize a specific vision of order and implement the vision within the dynamic, transnational system on the U.S.-Mexican boundary required policymakers to directly confront the other federal state that shared the same spaces. Juan Mora-Torres notes that "Mexico was the first formally legitimated nation that the United States encountered as it began to disseminate its values, doctrines, and practices in less economically and technologically advanced nations." The border "had become more than just an international boundary separating two countries. The border was the meeting point between a northern neighbor in the process of becoming an industrial power and a country that, after fifty years of economic chaos and political disorder, was beginning to chart a path of economic development based on exports."[60] It is no wonder then that the sovereigntist United States felt so challenged by a Mexico it considered recalcitrant and that relations in this era with regard to jurisdictional questions careened from crisis to crisis.

At all points, the challenges of transnationality invited scalding expressions of sovereign assertion on both sides of the border. A significant focus of this book is thus the shifting and often chaotic coordination of power, interest, and jurisdiction in foreign relations that congealed in this transnational region during an intense period at the end of the nineteenth century. This system of authority and power is also considered in a comparative framework with the global articulation of these interests by the United States.

Studying the U.S.-Mexico borderland reveals how state power was implemented, evaded, and contested on a local scale by military officials; state and municipal officials like sheriffs, consuls, generals, judges, and extradition commissioners; and transnational actors like smugglers, thieves, murderers, and fugitives. The actions of these individuals demonstrate the exercise of the strong and supple state in nineteenth-century America. As William Novak has argued in his study of the reality of the strong state in this era, "this American state grew by developing effective mechanisms for policing an ever-expanding and diverse territory. Coming to terms with the American state requires a better understanding of this power on the periphery." Nowhere was this clearer than on the most important periphery of the state in this era: the U.S.-Mexico border. According to Novak, "the American system of government, with its peculiar array of distributive technologies of state action—divided sovereignty, separation of powers, federalism, delegation, incorporation, and the rule of law—allows for an extraordinary penetration of the state through civil society to the periphery."[61] In the borderlands, the infrastructural power that Novak highlights was implemented and contested on a daily basis. Extradition, interdiction, and the response to extraterritorial crime in the borderlands signaled the governance of legal space as an aspect of foreign policy in this region.

This book concentrates on these experiences because they not only are illustrative of the system of power and law but are rare views of moments when the fates of fugitives hung in the balance and local questions of rights, evidence, justice, and culture were continually tested. This book unearths a great variety of forgotten events and in so doing explores the innumerable ways in which the power of the state and transnational connections of sovereign jurisdiction were inscribed upon individual lives. The nature and tenor of state power can be fruitfully explored in these cases. This book details these stories without overlooking the implications of each request and surrender in terms of deeper issues of sovereignty and governance. Policy ends should never be obscured or diminished; it is at the level of policy creation that the significance and intent of state power are best observed.

In comprehending the power of the state, nothing becomes more important than studying the law. "One of the distinctive attributes of American governance is the central place of law in state formation and policy development," Novak argues.[62] The law is sovereign power made manifest, and assertions of jurisdictions and exception are demonstrations of this power.

It follows that studies of borderlands extradition, interdiction, and the response to extraterritorial crime as reflections of foreign policy are among the best ways to examine the operations of power in terms of both abstract conceptualization and real-world implementation and governance. Nowhere was state policy more directly or clearly articulated. The constant thrum of borderland jurisdictional disputes helped produce the need for the profound enhancement and exercise of state authority.

While seeking to project order upon the fluid borderland region, American officials grappled with a stunning array of political and strategic interests, economic ambitions, and administrative and environmental constraints grounded in an abiding sense of unilateralist state sovereignty and an urgent desire for legal and economic supremacy. The system of extradition in the borderlands was especially fascinating since the exceptions to it were explicitly and deliberately articulated in a relationship already rich in attenuations of sovereignty and jurisdiction. As a uniquely malleable foreign policy act geared toward projecting sovereign power, extradition fit well into this blend of approaches. So too did American efforts to amplify its sovereignty by clarifying the geographic border, intensifying interdiction campaigns, tightening the citizenship and racial regimes, and generally attempting to convince or coerce Mexico into obeying its wishes and legal models.

Examination of the various ways in which the United States handled issues of extraterritorial and transborder crime at the boundary line as well as interdiction of smugglers and illegal migrants serves as an interesting complement to the study of extradition as a foreign policy. Borderlands exclusion and interdiction efforts created a tightening and clarification of sovereignty in pursuit of racial purity and federal authority. Racial stratifications and categorizations saturated absolutely every action taken in the borderlands and were as constructed as jurisdictional assertions. The control and exclusion of a wide variety of categories of both peoples and goods tracked with the expansion of extradition relations. Both were at least equally sourced in the American emphasis on unilateral governance of transnational concerns. There remained an indelicate balance between sovereignty and rights in which the former was emphasized and strengthened but the latter were not entirely absent.[63]

Observing borderlands extradition and interdiction regimes as they related to the mechanics of governance helps clarify the broader spaces of law in American foreign relations. This approach mirrors the way in which the application of legal studies to the mechanics of globalization brings clarity and creativity to more traditional state studies. This emphasis on the contested spaces and uses of law at all levels, as Berman argues, "allows us to expand our conception of what counts as law." Concentrating on the slippery character of *jurisdiction* rather than merely state power also "can turn the legal gaze to the insights of interdisciplinary scholarship concerning people's relationships to concepts such as space, place, borders, distance, and community affiliation."[64]

All of these issues demonstrate the real-world connections between relatively abstract assertions of state sovereign territoriality at the federal level and the spaces of law as they were articulated in varying form as "local matters being left to local authorities." As Justice Stephen Field framed it in the 1889 Chinese Exclusion case *Chae Chan Ping v. United States*, "for national purposes, embracing our relations with foreign nations, we are but one people, one nation, one power."[65] Yet on the border, local actions and decisions were crucial ways in which unilateralist territoriality sought and gained material consequence. Tracing this implementation is one of the best ways of understanding how power and policy operated and were made manifest.

PLAN OF THE BOOK

This book is organized thematically but proceeds roughly chronologically, with each chapter covering a significant aspect of U.S. involvement in extradition, territorial, and jurisdictional matters in the period between 1877 and 1898.

Part 1 focuses on the U.S.-Mexican borderlands in order to evaluate American responses to a cascading series of jurisdictional, geographic, criminal, and interdiction challenges. Within the muddied disputes that flourished in the region, there remained a clear sense that extradition disputes, water-use controversies, trade competition, Chinese migration, boundary line confusion, and challenges of extraterritorial jurisdictional claims such as the 1886 Cutting case were all directly connected. American and Texas politicians considered the *Zona Libre*, a unique and unilateral Mexican free trade zone along the border, as the bone in the throat of the region, which simultaneously triggered and hampered all other borderland controversies. Within this jurisdictional snarl and amid socioeconomic anxiety and borderland violence, the United States strongly sought unilateral governance of the legal spaces of this transnational system in a variety of ways.

Part 2 broadens the scope significantly and builds on the abstractions of this introduction in order to explore extradition as a foreign policy in a wide variety of international relations. The chapters in this section closely examine the governance of the U.S. extradition system from a number of perspectives, including the surprisingly variant development of definitions of extraditable crime for violent and financial transgressions, terrorism, and dynamite bombing, among other crimes. These chapters consider extradition surrenders and controversies in terms of the challenges of extraterritorial jurisdiction, the rules of double criminality and specialty, and the impact of a wide array of critical state and U.S. Supreme Court decisions. Special attention is directed to the politics of extradition regimes in terms of the meaning of citizenship and naturalization in sharp disputes such as that which developed between the United States and Italy in the 1880s. This section concludes with an examination of the role of asylum and sovereign exception in the construction of the legal spatiality of American foreign relations in response to political offenses and revolution.

This study of exception returns us to some significant cases from the borderlands at the end of the century. In those cases, the citizenship exception to extradition carved out unique challenges to extradition and order. The invocation of the political offense exception in important cases such as that of Catarino Garza Revolutionaries like Francisco Benavides and Inez Ruiz offered models to American policymakers who learned (or invented) lessons for application in revolutionary disputes here and in other far-afield regions throughout the twentieth century. The issues and challenges of the borderlands produced a series of profound political and philosophical interrogations of sovereignty and territoriality, which in turn continued to shape the nature of power in the borderlands and beyond well into the imperial century that was inaugurated in 1898.

PART ONE

The Geography of Dispute

CHAPTER ONE

Outrage and Order

There is the *Zona Libre*, the nest and nurturing-place, the home and residence of thieves and robbers and smugglers, created right upon our border. . . . Why, Mr. President, to create the *Zona Libre* there was to place the
wolf within the sheep-fold. . . . The principles and courtesies of international law have never been carried to the romantic extent of surrendering
the great natural right of self-defense against the constant infliction of serious, permanent and wrongful injury upon the people of one nation by those
of another, although the acts may be unauthorized by the government of the
country from which they come.
> Senator Richard Coke of Texas, "Mexican Outrages on the Texas Border,"
> U.S. Senate, November 14, 1877

O n a ferry crossing from the Mexican side of the Rio Grande on November 26, 1877, Zeferino Avalos, a second sergeant in the Mexican Army
Corps of Military Colonies, carelessly shot his pistol twice toward some women
washing clothing on the bank. When "rebuked" by the people around him that
he should stop since he might kill someone, Avalos announced that "when he
wished to kill a man he killed him." With that remark, Avalos crossed the Rio
Grande into Eagle Pass, Texas, and proved his words by murdering in cold
blood a blind man named Antonio Muñoz with a single shot to the face.[1]

The details of the incident and the language of the subsequent trial seem
tailor-made for a borderlands *corrido*. Witnesses at the trial in the Superior Tribunal of Coahuila described Avalos as "a vicious, incorrigible man, a very bad
husband, a deadly, passionate, and cruel enemy" who "while intoxicated, [was]
a provoking, quarrelsome, and cruel and treacherous man, which detestable
qualities caused him to be feared by the people." In contrast, his victim, "the unfortunate blind man, Antonio Muñoz," was "of a prudent and peaceable character, and had an unimpeachable name." He was "docile . . . and of an agreeable

and beneficent character." The contrast presented between the murderer Avalos and the peaceable Muñoz seems almost too terrible to bear.[2]

Before shooting, Avalos told the blind man to say a prayer. Muñoz refused, "saying that he did not know how to say prayers; that he lived by his work, so as not to ask alms." As Muñoz stood his ground proudly, "the murderer fired the shot which deprived him of his life." Miguel Ruelas, Mexican Minister of Foreign Affairs, wrote to John W. Foster in Mexico that it was the particular "circumstance of the murdered man being blind [that] imparted to the crime a character of notable atrocity."[3]

The tragic and poetic story of Muñoz's death produced an almost iconic example of the jurisdictional complexities of the borderlands at the time despite the clear-cut territoriality of the murder. Even the most local acts of random violence on the U.S.-Mexican border rapidly became issues of great diplomatic and legal interest. The murder, committed while Avalos was standing on U.S. soil, raised no inherent question as to jurisdiction. It was a well-established maxim of territorial jurisdiction that an individual was liable where the crime was committed. If Avalos had remained on Mexico soil, or even on the ferry, and shot Muñoz over the national boundary, the affair would have been entirely different under the law.[4] While it seems straightforward that Avalos should have been tried in Texas for the murder of Muñoz, instead the story took an interesting direction that revealed much about the shape and limits of conceptions of legal authority and national responsibility in the region.

Following the shooting, Avalos forced a skiff owner at gunpoint to take him back to Mexico and to, presumably, freedom from American criminal jurisdiction. According to the 1861 U.S.-Mexico Extradition Treaty, Mexican citizens were not extraditable, so Avalos was beyond the reach of American courts.[5] Yet when he reached the bank of Mexico, the chief of the customshouse guard turned Avalos over to the local Piedras Negras judicial authorities, who tried and sentenced him to twelve years in prison. Because Avalos's crime was considered by the Superior Tribunal of Coahuila to be "premeditated, with advantage and treacherously," the initial prison term was changed to a death sentence. The court decided that "it is a badly applied compassion to preserve the lives of such criminals as Avalos." He was more dangerous than just a regular murderer. According to the court,

if the criminal Zeferino Avalos, thirsting for human blood, should attack, without any cause whatever, a passer-by, who being opportunely warned of

the danger, should make use of his arms, defend himself, and be killed in
the fight [that would be one thing]; but if the said Avalos, with no other motive than his ferocious pleasure, should arm himself with a knife, go into the
streets of a city, and commence to cut the throats of the women, children,
blind men, cripples, and all other defenseless persons, to qualify those acts
as simple homicide, thus freeing from the death penalty that savage beast in
human shape, would be contrary to common sense, and it should not be supposed that the legislator desired to decree such an absurdity.

On March 25, 1879, Avalos was executed at Piedras Negras for the murder he
had committed in Texas.[6]

Though this killing occurred on the "left bank" of the river, Mexico claimed
jurisdiction over Avalos's act in "the United States of the North" under Article
186 of its penal code, which apparently was not previously known to the State
Department or the American ministers in Mexico. With four brief conditions,
Article 186 presented a broad assertion of extraterritorial authority over any "offenses committed in foreign countries by a Mexican against Mexicans or foreigners, or by a foreigner against Mexicans." Any such offense was to be tried in
a Mexican court according to Mexican law as long as the accused was brought
to justice voluntarily or by extradition (presumably abduction was not authorized) and "the complaint be made from a legitimate quarter." The offense had
to be considered a crime in both Mexico and the foreign jurisdiction, and no
acquittal could have been made previously.[7] Under this standard, Mexico had
full jurisdiction over the Avalos murder in Texas.

Minister Ruelas happily impressed upon Foster that the Avalos decision was
"evidence of the efficiency and energy with which his government proceeds when
convinced of the justice demanded."[8] This, perhaps, was the kind of vigorous action that had been so emphasized over the past decade by a United States seeking
order and jurisdictional clarity in the borderlands. Foster agreed that a positive
precedent was set by newly applying Article 186, and he approvingly sent along
the first translation of this Mexican law to the State Department at the end of
1879. The Superior Tribunal of the State of Coahuila found no fault in the claim
of Mexican jurisdiction, and neither did he. Writing to Secretary of State William Evarts, Foster noted the novelty of this act:

[T]he execution of Avalos in Mexico, by sentence of a Mexican tribunal, for a
murder committed in American territory, is the first instance on record in this
legation of punishment having been inflicted for a crime perpetrated under

the same circumstances. This precedent is considered valuable in showing that Mexican law provides for such punishment, and that it can be enforced when the Mexican authorities are disposed, as in this instance, to execute it. Although the murdered man was a Mexican, the article of the penal code invoked by the tribunal already referred to is equally applicable to foreigners.[9]

Foster was not confused at all about the issues involved or their broad implications. This was a new application of a broad extraterritorial claim by the Mexican state. It was "valuable" because Mexico seemed to be doing its part to stop transborder violence. And Foster clearly was comfortable, if not actually welcoming, of the application of Article 186 extraterritoriality to non-Mexican foreigners. Back in Washington, Evarts agreed. He raised no question of Mexico's claim of jurisdiction over this murder on American soil or the possible future implications of Mexican extraterritoriality. Evarts told Foster that "the Department agrees with you as to the value of the precedent thus established under the operation of the Mexican penal code."[10] No further action was taken. The broad extraterritorial claims of Article 186 were definitely unchallenged, and even seemingly welcomed, as a means of creating at least temporary calm on the border. Yet more than Mexican judicial vigor was involved.

The Avalos case only briefly grabbed the attention of the U.S. Department of State because it was not significantly different than the hundreds of other Mexican "outrages" along the border during the 1870s and 1880s. Transborder conflicts and wrangles consumed U.S.-Mexican relations for years and subsequently produced diplomatic froth and a stunning series of violations of territorial sovereignty, security, and honor on both sides of the line. Among numerous "border-troubles," crimes, and other "outrages" that consumed policymakers, a long-anticipated comprehensive report in April 1878 from the House of Representatives included widespread smuggling, cattle and horse stealing, arson, murders, shootings, kidnappings, desertions, fugitive escape, and problems with extradition for criminals. All of these transborder acts continued—and some flourished—for the next two decades. Of particular attention in the 1870s was the hot pursuit of bandits and Indians and a prolonged series of transborder punitive army incursions into Mexico in pursuit of hostile Indian tribes that culminated in the capture of Geronimo in 1886.[11]

Yet even situated amidst this stunning array of borderlands concerns with local, regional, and international impact, this random murder of a blind man and execution of the killer were significant. In 1877, the invocation of the extraterritorial Article 186 to try and execute Avalos garnered praise and only slight notice. In 1886, another Mexican assertion of extraterritorial jurisdiction to arrest and imprison a newspaper editor named A. K. Cutting in Paso Del Norte, Mexico, produced sharp diplomatic conflict, a war scare, and, in the end, no satisfactory resolution. The politics, tensions, and jurisdictional irregularities of the Texas-Mexico borderlands regime crystallized in the years between these two events. A matrix of regional, federal, national, transnational, and global interests injected unexpected significance into the issue of jurisdiction over crime. To begin to unravel the meaning of these interests, it is essential first to situate the crisis within a broader consideration of the evolution of American definitions of jurisdiction and imperial and economic order in the borderlands in the 1870s and 1880s.

The Avalos case revealed the idiosyncratic arc of the State Department's conception of borderlands legal spatiality that this chapter explores in the context of a wide variety of circumstances. Concerns regarding territoriality, jurisdiction, and lawlessness oscillated at the center of U.S.-Mexican relations. In situations in which order was elusive or seemed disorganized or loose, the United States sought structure and assertive territoriality. It seemed to U.S. policymakers that the borderlands needed delineated and tight control of the economic, military, and legal systems on both sides of the river, rooted in American principles and reflective of American interests. This chapter traces these interconnected and extremely complicated borderlands issues in American foreign relations in order to clarify the policy interests and territorial questions involved at this key moment when the United States began to exercise its growing economic, military, and legal dominance. In so doing, this chapter explores the way in which numerous assertions of territorial and extraterritorial jurisdiction sat at the core of the idealized American order on the Mexican border and expressed the broader goal of unilateral control of transnational concerns.

A big challenge in this regard for American policymakers was having to share the power to define the legal order with Mexico. This concern was made explicit in the way the 1878 House report presented the issues the United States faced in the borderlands. The report's analysis was clear-eyed about power but was not a reasoned discussion of the anticipated outcomes and implications of foreign policy in the Rio Grande borderlands. It was saturated with bald assertions of U.S. interests, sweeping disregard for Mexican interests, and sharp distinctions on jurisdictional regimes. The report deliberately fused together the disparate threads that had come to define the previous decade of policy at ex-

actly the moment when American dominance in the region began to acceler-
ate. Given the huge geographic area of operations under consideration and the
great diversity of interests that were folded into policymaking at both the federal and state levels in this region, this report deftly cut through the chatter to
lay out a particular vision of the challenges and opportunities of U.S.-Mexican
relations in this critical era of conflict over legal spatiality. The most prominent issues the report focused on are the subject of much of this book: "the
border-troubles" as well as what the report called, "the collateral questions, the
Free Zone, and the subject of extradition."[12]

Starting in the late 1870s and continuing for more than two decades, American
policymakers turned their attention to grappling in a comprehensive way with
the territorial questions on the Rio Grande boundary for a variety of reasons only
partially due to the seemingly never-ending series of issues and conflicts. The
many points of competition and conflict were grounded fundamentally upon
disputes over territoriality with grave and complicated implications. These territorial disputes incorporated a broad array of jurisdictional conflicts on land,
crime, and national security questions, which were also considered in terms
of more abstract and important wrangles over the governance of transnational
economic concerns. U.S. policy in the borderlands reflected the core uses of
governance as a means of subduing and further incorporating the borderlands
into the broader American political economic system.

Borderlands territorial conflicts were viewed as an impediment to the long-
standing and now newly resurgent national imperative of expanding foreign
market opportunities. "We have arrived at a turning point in the industrial and
commercial development of our country," the 1878 report intoned in the increasingly common emphasis of the time:

> Heretofore we appeared, as was natural, in the trade of the world, only as ex-
> porters of raw products and importers of the products of foreign manufac-
> turing industry. The leading features of our interior policy, our questions of
> tariff, and other economical issues, turned upon the struggle between our
> own manufactures and foreign manufactures for our own home market. That
> period has passed and we are entering upon a new contest. . . . The immense
> importance to us of foreign markets is therefore so clear that it is now uni-
> versally admitted.[13]

The focus of American foreign policy shifted to this pressing need for new foreign markets. Issues of territorial and extraterritorial jurisdiction were directly,

though not simply, harnessed to this project. The establishment of order was the precondition for expansion into new foreign markets.

Mexico provided the closest and most immediately promising field of investment, and realization of that promise required directed attention and new policy. It was only a neat half step from controlling security and jurisdictional concerns on the northern side of the border to seeking to shape the commercial interests that ran alongside them. Thus did the introduction to the report note straightforwardly that "the times seem to demand *a full and clear understanding* of our relations with Mexico; for, on the one hand, the constant border troubles, and the evils consequent on them, imperatively call for measures to prevent their continuance; while, on the other hand, the productions of our manufacturing industries have increased to such an extent that our country has become fully alive to the necessity of foreign markets." Nowhere were these markets more important than in Mexico, the most promising new focus of investment among the nations of Central and South America. These nations were "especially fields into which our commerce should extend, and our relations with those countries have, therefore, become, more than ever, matters of public interest."[14]

Congressional leaders claimed a special American interest in, and responsibility for, the stability and prosperity of Mexico, a neighbor that could not be viewed with the detached "philosophical equanimity" that prevailed in isolationist U.S. relations with Europe. The United States needed a prosperous southern neighbor, "one in which law and order prevails and the people are peaceably engaged in the pursuits of commerce and industry" to prevent "the offscourings of a disordered society collect[ing] to threaten the lives and prey upon the substance of our people." The word "offscourings," indicative of the language throughout this report and its documentary support, is suggestive of the ways in which Mexican transgressions were couched in terms of disgust.[15]

Faced with this major challenge, American assertions of authority could not be limited merely to interests of the territorial United States; they had to be expanded to include protection for commercial interests outside national borders. "So, also, in examining into the condition of our commerce with Mexico, our attention was at once drawn to the consideration of the position of our merchants in that country, to their need of protection, and to the unavoidable duty which rests upon our government of affording them such protection," the report noted.[16]

This need to protect citizens abroad as a precondition for commercial success was of such importance that the exact phrase was repeated several times in this report. American merchants abroad were on the advance edge of America's inexorable rise to wealth and power. Expansion of markets required an equal effort to secure their position. "With the great importance which the securing of foreign markets has assumed at this present time the question of the protection of our citizens is equally rising in importance," concluded the report. In an unsurprising but extremely interesting analogy, the report situated merchants at the heart of the outward thrust of American power: "Commerce cannot move without merchants and agents any more than war can be made without armies, or the frontier be settled without pioneers." At the border frontier of the Rio Grande, a region of armies and pioneers, this analysis elevated merchants to a privileged position in rapidly transforming foreign relations that needed to be reorganized around new sensitivity and responsiveness to structures outside national boundaries: "With the increase of our commerce, this duty will impress itself of necessity more and more on our government." The report continues,

> Not long since our citizens in Mexico were told that every American leaving the United States for the purpose of trading in a foreign country, went there with his eyes open, took all the risks, and could not look for protection to his own country. This theory must be entirely discarded or we must not expect that our commerce will ever rival that of England, which has never entertained this timid and short-sighted doctrine. We must rather look upon the enterprising men who go forth to gather the advantages of trade for their country as one of the most useful classes of citizens, as the pioneers of our commerce who undergo special risks, and are entitled to special consideration. If, on the contrary, we act upon the theory that the merchant who leaves the United States severs his connection with us and must not look for protection from his government against any wrongs he may have to endure, we must make up our mind that none but men of desperate fortunes will embark in a business involving such extraordinary risks. We cannot expect an extended commerce when it can only be carried on by such men. We must either resign ourselves to do what little trade we may obtain through the medium of other nations who have a clearer perception of the value of a definite and decided policy, or we must adopt such a policy ourselves.[17]

When coupled with a new and pressing (if not irresistible) set of market imperatives and the interests of extraterritorial commercial interests, border concerns required transborder state action.

This transformative moment in the final decades of the century seemed to these policymakers to go beyond merely securing the borders on a basis of strict territorial sovereignty to a broader redesign of the balance of power, authority, and trade along the Rio Grande boundary. But as the committee studied the issues, it became clear that there were a great many interests at stake that required an expansive assertion of American authority over transnational questions. The central, traditional issues were territorial sovereignty and security: protecting life and property in South Texas from incursions, encroachment, and crime and securing the borders themselves. Importantly, the security question was founded on broader economic and legal questions in which the lines of control were muddier and less satisfying—not least because Mexico seemed to be making the guiding decisions and to have the momentum.

Mexico posed a specific and unique set of problems for U.S. policymakers since it was not so subordinate, weak, or dismissible a nation that the United States could dictate policy and questions of law as it did in its extraterritorial relations with "uncivilized" nations around the world. But at the same time, in ways that American policymakers expressed both explicitly and implicitly, Mexico was seen as not quite civilized. It needed American guidance in questions of sovereignty and order. The 1878 House report claimed that "the trade with barbarous people has risks which cannot be avoided. But a civilized country, or *one which claims in its intercourse with other civilized nations the privileges of a civilized country, like Mexico*, must as a necessary consequence of that claim, give to the citizens of other nations the protection of its laws or become responsible if it does not. It cannot sustain the claim without complying with the duties implied by it."[18] If Mexico wanted to be considered civilized or to continue to *claim* the rights of civilized nations, it had to acquiesce to a system of geopolitical and economic order articulated by the United States in line with its own interests. If not, Mexico would be reduced to the ranks of uncivilized nations, where extraterritoriality was assumed as a matter of course and sovereign right.

The United States was particularly concerned about Mexico's unilateral embrace of free trade along its northern border, which was seen as corrosive of territoriality as well as economically harmful. This seemingly innocuous policy (it was after all, a Mexican trade policy with effect only in Mexico) seemed instead to invite a lifting of restrictions on all actions—economic, legal, and criminal—on both sides of the border. The mere act of one Mexican state suspending tariff duties in the creation of the *Zona Libre* ("Free Zone") in Tamaulipas was framed as being akin to unleashing the forces of chaos, crime, and cross-border raids along the entire Rio Grande. The *Zona Libre*, controversial and widely reviled in Texas and national politics for decades, as is explored later in this chapter, produced extraterritorial effects and seemed to require a similarly expansive response in 1878: "We could not go far in this inquiry without perceiving the intimate connection of the raids from Mexican territory with the condition of the Free Zone on the Mexican side of the Rio Grande, free alike from duties on importations, from which it derives its name, and from punishment for crime, as we find to be the remarkable fact."[19] The *Zona Libre* seemed to create an atmosphere of looseness and lawlessness that in turn catalyzed American desires for greater assertions of control projected from its own ordered side of the river. It is thus impossible to consider legality along the river separate from the overall American critique of Mexican trade policy, coupled with the questions of jurisdiction and order.

THE CHALLENGE OF ORDER IN EL PASO

El Paso, Texas, in the 1880s was a raucous, rapidly growing trading town clustered along a very changeable Rio Grande and integrated economically, though unequally, with its neighboring city of Paso del Norte. The conflicts produced by the search for legal order, prosperity, and social peace in El Paso occurred precisely at the time when the city became more economically and culturally integrated into the national political economy by the arrival of the railroad in 1881. The railroads linking the city to critical trade routes in both the southwestern United States and throughout Mexico seemed to guarantee, in the minds of its boosters like *The Lone Star* newspaper, that "El Paso will become the great metropolis of the southwest because all the great southwestern railroads will contribute to its growth." J. Harvey Brigham, the generally excitable U.S. consul in Paso del Norte, called El Paso "one of the most enterprising and progressive cities of the southwest which is rapidly pushing its business into the interior of Mexico."[20]

That sense of developing greatness was surprisingly new, and it characterized the boomtown mentality of the city. Prior to the arrival of the Southern Pacific Railway on May 19, 1881, there were only 800 people living in El Paso. In short order, over the next two years, the Atchison-Topeka-Santa Fe line was connected from the north and the transcontinental railroad lines in the region were completed at nearby Sierra Blanca when the Southern Pacific joined the Texas and Pacific Railroad seven months later. Within a decade of the establishment of these critical railroads, commercial advantage that formerly was centered south of the Rio Grande switched to El Paso, and the population had grown a hundredfold to eight thousand. The population was an amazing twenty-five thousand by 1900. The city, which lacked even a church before the railroad arrived, had by 1882 "a street railway, two banks, three newspapers, four churches, an established city government, and the largest hotel in the state." One historian characterizes the arrival of the railways in the 1880s as "the defining moment for border commerce and urban development along the frontier." The two cities were now "firmly enmeshed within the modern economic network of the continent," and El Paso was the essential nexus point for transportation in all directions.[21]

The population of El Paso remained overwhelmingly of Mexican origin. One revealing and commonly cited demographic statistic is that of approximately twelve thousand people living on both sides of the Rio Grande near the city of El Paso (including the thirty-seven hundred people in El Paso County, Texas); in 1877, only eighty were of other than Mexican descent.[22] America's urge to strongly exercise power and establish its jurisdictional hegemony should not and cannot be considered separately from this demographic reality. Along most of the borderlands region, the population was relatively small, even as the conflicts loomed large: "In 1880 the country between El Paso and San Antonio encompassed 43,726 square miles of land but numbered less than 20,000 inhabitants."[23]

Dedicated to and dependent upon trade, El Paso was a growing city with energy and a strong sense of drive that gave little credence to a sense of limitation from any quarter—regional, federal, or Mexican. As the railroad linkages between cities in the borderlands shrank space (Laredo and San Antonio were now linked in five hours rather than five days), it is not hard to understand why there was a move for clear assertions of sovereignty, definition of jurisdictions, and more broadly still, the construction of clear limits.[24] Speed, connection, development, and change encouraged or even demanded fresh articulations of power.

It became clear then that the establishment of American hegemony over both local and transnational issues in El Paso required more than the actions of local or Texas officials. Incorporating this hybrid borderlands region fully into the American system demanded acceptance of the abstractions of power in the form of American legal structures through deepened consciousness of uncontested American sovereignty. It also required overt expression of American power in the form of an assertive federal presence and a more robust military garrison. Diplomacy was a key attribute of this effort, clarifying questions of jurisdiction and territoriality as the consciousness of American sovereignty was increasingly expressed. At issue was nothing less than the establishment of unchallenged American order along the entire border with Mexico. El Paso was a short-term focal point in the establishment of American regional hegemony that had been ongoing since the Civil War. Local issues were subsumed in this effort. "The border region is always a function of somewhere else," argues Victor M. Ortíz-González. "This pervasive subordination of the local to the nonlocal has given place to the alienated instrumentality of the border for centuries."[25]

In El Paso, power and authority were constantly considered arrayed against questions of partisanship, legitimacy, order, and citizenship. The city nourished its own regional variant on the racial tensions common along the U.S.-Mexican divide amidst the emerging prosperity. One scholar of the region noted, "it benefited local Anglos to recognize the border population's citizenship during a political campaign, whereas it was to their advantage to deny the border population U.S. citizenship during incidents of economic exploitation or military suppression . . . citizenship was a distinction that was socially meaningful only to Anglos."[26]

As in many frontier cities, the rule of law in El Paso was cherished rhetorically but fitfully implemented—and often discarded entirely when convenient. El Paso followed the pattern of the rest of the frontier West, about which one historian has written, "in no state or region did the establishment of a system of justice under duly enacted law come easy or with steady and uninterrupted progress."[27] Indeed, the concept of the "rule of law" was still a hotly contingent one in El Paso, as unchallenged U.S. jurisdiction had not yet been fully asserted or implemented in the local area. Hegemonic control of the territory bequeathed by treaty in 1848 was only partially realized in legal terms forty years later, following local political and cultural contestation catalyzed by rapid economic development. As had been manifest across the Rio Grande frontier since the U.S. Civil War, the establishment of American order emerged finally as the result of an ongoing and dynamic process and not from a neat unilateralist declaration. The American rule of law remained singularly hard to establish during this time, given the structural realities and incomplete settlement of the boundary region.

El Paso was an American city in a territorial sense and in terms of basic sovereignty, but it also lay astride a borderlands region experiencing continuing legal formation. The question of a solidly American rule of law can be framed as push for "increasing hegemony of the Anglo-American legal system in the borderlands." In this era, the city operated with a "hybrid legal system," which meant an evolving system that included "remnants of a Spanish legal system and elements of the newly arrived Anglo-American system." Within this hybrid system, the underpinnings of U.S. hegemony remained unfocused and newly sought. This hegemony derived from the structure and implementation of the law itself in criminal and property matters and from the sense of "legal consciousness" operating as an ideology of American order for the citizens of El Paso. This situation "foreshadowed the coming twentieth century, during which the once-fluid border would become increasingly calcified as the U.S. government deployed the law to prevent the continued development of a cross-border community."[28]

Legal consciousness at the popular level operated in conjunction with larger ideological constructions of order and understandings of the spatiality of legal and political power. As Mari J. Matsuda asserts in the case of legal consciousness and American hegemony in Hawaii around the same time, the establishment of "law and legal consciousness [worked] in concert with other forces to alter culture" and to make it more suitable for incorporation into the American political economy. In Hawaii, she found that "while capitalists will venture wherever there is money to be made, the presence of a familiar legal system reduces business risks, or perhaps more significantly, the perception of risk, and thus encourages investment."[29] In El Paso, the system served the same function. The American rule of law at first reflected local forms but soon reshaped them to make them more amenable to the new order and to U.S. economic interests.

One example of the fitful process of civic formation that dominated El Paso throughout the 1880s during the years of growth can be seen in the oddities of the law enforcement system of the city and of El Paso County more broadly. The system was increasingly, if inconsistently, harsh on Mexican-Americans. Mexican-Americans and Mexican sojourners faced differential treatment in El Paso courts, and Mexican nationals in particular often found themselves the subjects of arbitrary arrest, mistreatment, and deportation. J. Escobar y Armendariz, the Mexican consul in El Paso, complained repeatedly about all of these matters, arguing "Mexicans who arrive looking for work in this area have no rights."[30]

Some of the character of the fitful legal regime in El Paso is evident in the jail records for common crimes, which have not received much attention from historians. These records reveal the city to have been a fluid, international place where local law enforcement attempted (with limited success) to create order. The legal system confronted the expected matrix of small crimes such as robbery, assault, prostitution, vagrancy, and drunkenness, combined with complex transborder issues and questions of race, ethnicity, and power. These latter issues in many cases might have been better handled at the diplomatic level but on the border, they were the stuff of daily business. This same set of often-contradictory issues came to a head in the Cutting case, and it is almost certain that the crisis produced at the local level would have been significantly different in another city, even if the diplomatic and legal principles involved were the same.

El Paso saw crime like all border communities, but it handled it in a distracted and inconsistent fashion.[31] One interesting indication of the chaotic nature of El Paso in the early 1880s is that the county jail register printed column categories noting if prisoners had "escaped or [been] discharged" and what actions were taken following either escape or discharge. Clearly, this was not a place where the rule of law was ironclad since escape from jail was common enough to warrant its own official category. On some single pages of the docket, about half of the prisoners are listed as escapees.[32] Crime and enforcement in Texas cannot be analyzed separately from the reality of persistent violence and lawlessness in the region. In the West, violent conflict developed from the "rapid convergence of diverse cultures, industrialization, and differing social systems." Within the subregion of West Texas, violence had a localized geography. The borderlands had a particular quality that pushed them beyond the realm of American myth-making that has coated West Texas violence so thoroughly. What made the situation in the borderlands interesting and complex was the layer of racialized transnationality atop the political economic concerns of the region.[33]

Establishing the new order was not free of difficulty. As was common through-out the frontier cities of the borderlands region (and the West generally), El Paso–Paso del Norte experienced swings of instability, jurisdictional disputes, spurts of violence, and general excitability alongside a sense of dynamism and promise. The same factors produced conflict here as elsewhere along the border. There was a bare-knuckled political style rooted in strong partisan affiliation, racial discrimination, economic exploitation, rampant illegality, and an easy resort to violence. An ever-present and occasionally flaring racial divide among

Mexicans, Mexican-Americans, and Anglo-Americans in the city was not re-solved by the 1880s, though an uneasy truce was settled.

It is useful in this regard to consider the El Paso Salt War of 1877, which was a very significant upheaval in the formation of the borderlands jurisdictional re-gime, if perhaps not quite the "bloodiest civil disorder in the country's history" as one historian of El Paso has rather grandly characterized it. The Salt War was part of a series of jurisdictional struggles that flourished in the late nineteenth century as "both a product of and a challenge to [El Paso's] hybrid legal system" and as an example of the ways in which a local dispute often could mushroom out of control because of its transnational character. Historian Paul Cool has called the Salt War an "insurgency" based on "a deliberate, community-based decision squarely in the tradition of the American nation's original fight for self-government." The Salt War created significant tension and disorder in the region shortly before the Cutting case. Both incidents were similarly triggered by jurisdictional disputes in which questions of race, class, law, and power rap-idly became manifest. One important way to interpret the Salt War is to view it as the result of Mexican-American "fear of American colonization" and a well-developed sense of mistrust of the justice system.[34]

The Salt War was a community uprising in response to systemic social and economic concerns and specifically a struggle over resources triggered by an American enclosure effort. Salt was an essential commodity in frontier El Paso, and it had been treated as a shared, open community resource since at least Spanish colonial rule. Sol Schutz, the U.S. commercial agent at Paso del Norte, told the State Department at the beginning of the crisis that people had "from time immemorial procured the salt, not only for their own use but also for trade & export into the state of Chihuahua" and have "long looked upon these Salt Lakes as public property."[35]

The conflict began when Charles H. Howard, a county judge already disliked locally, claimed salt ponds outside town as his own by filing a "location" on them and then "notified the people that he required a certain payment for every cart-load of salt." Two men, Macedonio Gandara and José María Juárez, were arrested merely for "saying they intended to go get salt" without paying How-ard. This unwise arrest by the county justice of the peace, Gregoria N. Garcia, on Howard's request soon prompted "an armed mob numbering fifty or sixty men" from both sides of the Rio Grande to revolt. Schutz reported, "a most in-tense and bitter feeling has manifested itself since that day among the Mexicans on both side of the river against the Americans which is likely to break forth at any moment, in which event it is my opinion, not a single American would be spared."[36]

Louis Cardis dissuaded the crowd from killing Howard. According to W. M. Dunn, the judge advocate general of the U.S. War Department who investigated the matter, Cardis was "revered by the Spanish people on both sides of the river" and his "word was [considered] little less than law." In conjunction with four others, Cardis persuaded Howard to accept five terms of release, which included denying the earlier claims, setting bond, and leaving town. Howard willingly left the county, still alive but apparently not satisfied. Peacemaking did Cardis little good. Howard soon returned to town, and on October 10, 1877, found Cardis and "shot him dead in cold blood." In the majority report of the official U.S. investigation run by the War Department, Howard's shooting of Cardis was called "premeditated murder." Howard hid with a customs agent and later some Texas Rangers. The region meanwhile exploded in violence, rape, and murder on the part of citizens and civil authorities alike.[37]

The majority report of the War Department concluded that the problems that produced such violent conflict derived at least as much from a failure of local governance as from a style of violent dispute that was "the fashion of an ignorant and hot-blooded race." It found that the "civil law in this country is loosely administered" and that during the siege, there was evidence of excessive use of force that bordered on extralegal, state-directed murder. The Rangers in particular were excoriated for their failure to make "wise discrimination in the choice of material" in recruiting. The result was that the Rangers who were involved contained "an adventurous and lawless element, which, though not predominant, was yet strong enough to make its evil influence felt in deeds of violence and outrage matched only by the mob itself." The Rangers, in fact, acted murderously. The report details that among other acts, they shot unarmed and bound Mexican prisoners and in another incident, fired into the closed door of a house fifteen times, resulting in the death of two people inside. The Rangers sowed death and helped fuel the conflict, while it was the U.S. Army (according to the official army report) that finally restored order and "the confidence of the people [who] had fled into Mexico."[38]

The War Department was certain that local authorities had made matters worse. The investigating Board of Officers excoriated the El Paso County judge for his actions and accused him of being "though an educated man . . . addicted to drink . . . and frequently unfitted for business by reason of intemperance." The four local justices of the peace could not speak English, and the Board concluded that "in any other community, more civilized than this, they would be regarded as ignorant men." The minority report, written by Jonathan B. Jones, a major in the Frontier Battalion of the State Troops and an appointee of the Texas governor, emphasized instead the supposedly excessive violence of the Mexicans involved in the dispute. Most of the trouble, according to this account, was caused by Mexicans from across the border and their coconspirators in Texas. This report radically increased the estimates of the number of Mexican nationals involved in the trouble and defended the local officials and Texas Rangers. It also presented an elevated overall cost of damages. The Salt War caused property damage of between twelve thousand and thirty-one thousand dollars, depending on which federal government report one chooses to believe.[39]

Despite the differing interpretations of the causes, catalysts, and cycles of the Salt War, both the majority and minority reports sought swift extradition of all those involved from Mexico. The extradition question was a significant one following the conflict and helped connect this crisis to one of the most potent transborder issues of the time. Not only had there been a riot that some chose to interpret as a large-scale "Mexican outrage" but the Mexican state was blamed for harboring the alleged criminals involved. In this way, a frontier jurisdictional and racial conflict was propelled into the realm of foreign policy, where it found a well-exercised set of concepts and complaints that U.S. and Texas policymakers had long employed in grappling with jurisdictional questions. The language was similar, as were the demands for Mexico to turn over its citizens despite the lack of a requirement to do so in the extradition treaty. Mexico's refusal to step outside these requirements was held up as a form of intransigence, or worse.

Schutz told the State Department that the "property stolen from the murdered Americans" was brought over the Rio Grande and the thieves hidden from justice. "It is easy to judge what their [Mexico's] course will be in the Extradition of those who committed the cold blooded murders and other outrages in San Elizano," he wrote. Texas extradition judge Allen Black had requested the return of seventeen people. Schutz, sure that the state extradition request would be ignored, argued that a federal request "with a sufficient force of troops near at hand to cause just demands to be respected" would be necessary. Mexico was employing what Schutz called "the old excuse of the lower Rio Grande" by claiming it could not locate the criminals, but the threat of force might just jog official memories. El Paso officials were eager to use such a threat of force. Schutz reported the city had available "a force of from 200 to 300 men to assist in executing the law," but these local forces, some with blood on their hands from the Salt War, were not utilized. Extradition efforts were stymied.[40]

The situation remained tense for some time. Although the Salt War officially ended in 1877, Paul Cool argues that for more than a year after overt hostilities ended, lawlessness continued, constituting a "new phase" of the war.[41] The lessons learned or imagined by both sides, including the turn to federal power and the dramatic positioning of troops, were not forgotten at the time of the Cutting case a few years later.

Perhaps the most significant conclusion of the investigating Board of Officers assembled at Fort Bliss by the War Department was that the problems in the borderlands were the result of inadequate U.S. military power presence and movement on the frontier. Assertive and apparent force was necessary to maintain the American understanding of order in the region. Only the federal government had the power, authority, and wherewithal to apply this force correctly and sufficiently. Focused militarization of the borderlands would help restrain the Mexican-American population in El Paso and keep jurisdictional disputes from escalating into anarchy, systemic violence, or other transnational dangers. American law and moral order—sovereignty in its fullest form—would be established and operationalized at this conjunction of hierarchical social peace and display of power.

Mexico briefly stopped grain exports to Texas in protest of the conflict, which the consul at Paso del Norte took as something of an attack on the United States, especially given the newly increased grain needs of the enhanced American forces now stationed at Fort Bliss.[42] Thus the situation reflected the interlocked but conflicted situation on the boundary line. Increased militarism on the border on the U.S. side to sustain an assertion of sovereignty and secure appropriate order also required a certain level of support and even complicity from the Mexican side. The unwillingness of Mexico to directly support this action was in turn considered an affront by the United States. It was considered necessary for Mexico to not only recognize and accept American terms of borderlands security but even help sustain it logistically.

It is significant that the officers on the ground in El Paso who completed the Board majority report stressed the need for more troops, as by now there was a well-established tendency for U.S. troops in Texas to lobby for additional reinforcements to occupy the borderlands. In part, this move was necessary in order to offset the fitful, violent, and unacceptable conduct of the state troops (Rangers), which had so often and persistently complicated jurisdictional questions along the boundary. The majority report concluded that even "a small force of United States troops" would have prevented such "deplorable events." But the War Department was not thinking small. The report in fact called for not just a few additional troops but "the immediate establishment of a strong military post at El Paso."[43]

The need to stop this neglect of the border was imperative, the Board of Officers concluded, not because of the danger of another Salt War but because of the great likelihood of continued conflict in the region. Schutz told the State Department a story he called "laughable" but still very instructive of the mood along the border: Two companies of U.S. troops were redeployed from Fort Bliss to Fort Bayard, New Mexico. The Mexican army understood these troop movements to be an indication of an impending American invasion and within half a day posted 200 soldiers on the border. This reaction was what amused Schutz.[44]

But clearly the United States had to be prepared for future conflict, and the army sensed that it would stem from a bigger issue than just border skirmishes. The report concluded that "the questions [most] likely to spring from the present constitution of society, that of *water*, as to its division and distribution, the Board regards as serious." The Board thought the water question in this rapidly developing area was sure to be of central concern to the governance and control of the region, and it directly foresaw a role for the War Department to play. "As time progresses and the country is opened by accessions to its populations, sure to come—for it is a most fertile region and gloriously rewards the labor spent in irrigation—the question must grow in importance, and may occasion trouble beyond the reach of diplomacy to settle," the Board concluded. Only the army could supply the necessary persuasion. The region therefore needed at least "the moral effect of a single battalion."[45]

It is worth noting that State Department personnel also saw the expansion of the U.S. diplomatic presence on the frontier in the same terms as the moral effects of state power. All of the Rio Grande commercial agencies had been elevated into consular posts in November 1879. U.S. Consul (and later Consul General) Warner P. Sutton in Matamoros toured these consulates and reinforced the need for a diplomatic presence as a means of pacifying and securing the borderlands as representatives of state interest. He equated the establishment of a consulate at Camargo, Mexico, with the "carrying of arms on this frontier—you may not need them often, but when they are needed the matter is decidedly urgent. Also, carrying arms here implies that you know how and are

willing to use them when needed on the road, and is a sort of moral protection."
Perhaps exaggerating his own and others' power as metaphorical weapons of
the state, he called the mere presence of a consul a "restraining moral force" for
"peace and security" of such fortitude and power that it "would be worth, as
a place measure, [as much as] a company of United States troops at Ringgold
Barracks near Rio Grande City."[46]

Sutton called for competent consuls to serve as "a firm and intelligent guard"
who could in turn reassure both "capital and well disposed citizens" to "fill
up this fertile land and render property and human life more secure." Such a
change in the American stance on the border would be expensive, but it was
worth the nation making an investment in soft power: "The War Department
spends a good deal and if the Department of State spent more it would do more
good." If the state were to increase its spending, not only would the War Department be able to spend less, the peace would be more secure and U.S. order
more clearly inscribed.[47]

The reinvigorated diplomatic effort would give a means of dealing with the
issues of "the always important boundary matters, Indian Raids, outrages on
citizens of the United States, the varying phase of the civil government of Mexico and the large subjects of extradition and smuggling." So the State Department "need[ed], and urgently need[ed], more and more each year, a good man
in that office." Sutton emphasized the opportunity to transform the ways things
were being done on the border. He referred to overly high War Department expenditures for the troops at the frontier. "Not too much money," he added, "although I might criticize the manner in which a part is spent."[48]

Sutton had an alternative vision for the borderlands, one in which the State
Department would take the lead by expanding its operations into fully creden-
tialed consulates using new men of high standards and strong skills, "independent, efficient representatives . . . with authority to expend money for certain
purposes occasionally." He stressed the importance of new consuls, fresh and
bright and energetic. In contrast, he wrote that "as a general thing, officers of
the United States Army are quite dull on such subjects" relating to Mexican internal affairs. Sutton was fond of pointing out how many multiples of a salary a
competent consular officer could return to public coffers. As he toured the consulates, Sutton pushed the case for fresh blood. He urged the State Department
to bring in "some person wholly outside the Texan frontier . . . because in this
case utter ignorance is sometimes better than half knowledge."[49]

Reinvigorating the frontier diplomatic service in this way "would save the

United States much in money and much in added peace on the border while at the same time the interests of American trade could be zealously fostered." Sutton's prolonged discussion of the replacement of War Department spending with State Department practices is interesting in that it highlights the alternative, if not actually competing, visions at the time over the best way to structure a stable system of imperial rule on the U.S.-Mexican border. This system required clear sovereign control in the form of trade protection and expansion, social peace, stable borders, Indian control, and the assertion of order in the form of the rule of (American) law. The War Department's imperative in this regard was rather simple in the sense that it was limited and demarcated: to occupy and pacify the border region and thereby secure it. Order, security, calm, and control were its objectives, and force, mobility, and superior firepower were the main tools. Whereas the army may have served as a tool of social policy and political rehabilitation during Reconstruction, on the borderlands, it was restored to its core functionality as the instrument of state-directed violence.[50]

Given these objectives and its own predilections and orders, the army was selectively insensitive to the jurisdictional constraints of the borderlands region and the potential for political dispute. This attitude dated back to at least the 1877 Ord Order authorizing at-will transborder incursion. Indeed, the mechanics of life, trade, and crime on the border seemed to invite or even require invasions of sovereignty in pursuit of the primary objective of territorial security and control. Perhaps most importantly, the army was not concerned with facilitating trade between the two countries—and definitely not with zealously fostering it. This expansion of trade was, however, the central goal of the consulates that stretched across the river. The fact that Mexican trade was so riddled with smuggling on the south side of the Rio Grande seemed like a matter of great involvement for diplomats in Sutton's estimation, not a call for extraterritorial police action. More sensitive and competent leadership on the part of State Department officials would yield ever-greater results. "The hand may safely be gloved, but the grip should be maintained intact," Sutton added with a bit of dramatic flair.[51]

JURISDICTION AND ARMY BASING STRATEGY

It was at this time in the early 1880s that the War Department moved to consolidate control of the borderlands and firmly establish clear jurisdiction over bases in Texas. It took some time for the new military stance to be established on a basis entirely satisfactory to the federal government. The War Department wanted clarified and unchallenged jurisdiction over its expanded fort system and no competition or conflict with state authorities.

Fort Bliss in El Paso was created in 1849 after the Mexican War but soon deactivated. After 1854, the fort was put back into service, but it received little attention for decades. The fort was of marginal utility given its isolation from most of the settlement in Texas before the coming of the railroad and distance from the zone of conflict along the border toward the mouth of the Rio Grande. For most of this time, Fort Bliss was used loosely to protect long-distance mail service and watch over the border.[52] The Salt War in 1877 and the arrival of the railroad in the region in 1881 helped to change all the calculations. Revised American policy in the region demanded a new fort with unchallenged jurisdiction for the United States as a way of projecting certitudes of power. At issue was less simply expanding the fort and more the establishment of unrestricted jurisdiction over it and the region through occupation.

Texas ceded "exclusive jurisdiction" over Fort Bliss in El Paso to the War Department on March 9, 1880, but the fine-grained jurisdictional questions involved in securing both title beyond challenge and true exclusivity took several years. On October 4, 1883, the adjutant general referred the governor's proclamation to the Department of Texas, which in turn triggered a series of communications between Washington, Austin, and El Paso County as well as strong legal argumentation from the War Department in defense of a permanent establishment of unrestricted federal authority. The troops were welcomed to the area, but the jurisdictional structuring of their deployment was contested.[53]

J. W. Clous, judge advocate of the Department of Texas, was tasked to clarify the department's jurisdictional stance. His May 1, 1884, report was released as War Department General Order number 8 on June 5, 1884. The department based its claim to exclusive jurisdiction over the bases on Article I, Section 8 of the Constitution, which stated Congress's power "to exercise exclusive Legislation in all Cases whatsoever, over such District (not exceeding ten Miles square) as may, by Cession of particular States, and the acceptance of Congress, become the Seat of the Government of the United States, and to exercise like Authority over all Places purchased by the Consent of the Legislature of the State in which the Same shall be, for the Erection of Forts, Magazines, Arsenals, dock-Yards, and other needful Buildings." The Constitution seemed to admit no limit or exceptions to federal jurisdiction on such property. The War Department therefore flatly rejected the attempt by Texas to maintain zones of exclusive authority within these base grants as the state had attempted to do on the basis of Article 334 from the 1879 Revised Statutes of Texas.[54]

Clous demonstrated how once U.S. jurisdiction was established in these base territories in Texas, it was exclusive and there could be no challenge and no recognition of state claims even to legal process within the ceded areas. He cited a large body of case law starting with the 1819 case *U.S. vs. Cornell*, which decided that cessation of land based upon consent of the legislature of the state created exclusive federal jurisdiction. The report argued that Texas had no claim to jurisdiction "by the very terms of the Constitution, by which all the States are bound and to which all are parties, a virtual surrender and cession of its sovereignty over the place." In a ringing phrase from the Cornell case, Clous concluded that "such a place [the base territories] is to the State as much a foreign territory as if it had been occupied by a foreign sovereign."[55] In keeping with the basic U.S. conception of sovereign territoriality, there was no room for competing or shared jurisdictions.

The question of jurisdiction over these bases as zones of dominion and sovereignty gained in significance in Texas and throughout the West because the systemics of this sovereignty on the imperial frontier were still in the process of formation. The army had a key role in this process both as an institutional actor and as locus of policy innovation. Fresh determination had to accompany the expansion of this institution westward. The establishment of American hegemony on the western frontier should then be viewed as a process of imperial consolidation—a process that had long-term resonance in the forthcoming era of overseas hegemonic power. Robert Wooster, a historian of the army in Texas during the latter half of the nineteenth century, calls the movement of the army westward the "march of empire across the continent." He argues that "in the absence of any other federal bureaucracy large enough to handle the myriad tasks associated with conquering a nation the size of the United States, Americans repeatedly turned to the army."[56]

The army had many crucial roles in connecting the West to national sinews of investment, commerce, and development. Of course, it fulfilled its core role by bringing force to bear when necessary, facilitating the ethnic cleansing of the region, and encouraging and protecting settlement. It also acted as a significant catalyst of economic development. The army oversaw telegraph-line construction and the gathering of scientific, geographical, and geological data. Indeed, Wooster argues "the Army was too busy doing other things, including nation building, to devote much attention to fighting." In an exhaustive study of the political economy of the frontier army, Thomas T. Smith has demonstrated the enormous impact of millions of dollars of army expenditures on the developing economy of Texas. In addition to changing the markets for land, animals, construction materials, and transportation, "the army dollar was an important economic multiplier in many Texas agricultural commodity markets."[57]

Economic development clearly ranked alongside fighting as an important component of the army function on the imperial frontier. Many factors went into the basing strategy of the army of this period, such as strategic placement, availability of water and forage, communication requirements, and land size. But the jurisdictional aspects of American basing on the frontier has been largely ignored, despite the great interest in this topic in later eras and other areas, particularly overseas. In many important respects, the establishment of sovereignty in military installations in the West raised jurisdictional and territorial questions that were related to those involved in the overseas basing of American military forces. Understanding the army's imperial role must include consideration of the establishment of hegemony in law and the exercise of authority in jurisdictional disputes. Though less dramatic than some of its other actions like Indian fighting, this effort was centrally important to the overall project of incorporating these areas into the American system.

Constructing the forts and clearing jurisdictional space for them functioned as a test of the way the United States approached inserting sovereignty into other sovereignties overall. Clearly, the domestic case is different because of the structured nature of the Constitutional republic in which the states were subordinated on this issue. But it is worth observing the ways Washington conceived of the clearly delineated architecture of power and authority in the areas it was in the process of incorporating fully into the broader political economic system. Historians have demonstrated that the perceived lessons and analogies of Indian warfare served as tools in later imperial expansionism and overseas wars.[58] In a similar way, the pursuit of exclusive jurisdiction served the interests of the state in establishing authority in the West and the borderlands as well as in later imperial overseas base structure agreements. If anything, as power was more completely contested in the international realm than within the nation, the pursuit of exclusive jurisdiction became that much more pressing.

The domestic military base jurisdiction questions became almost as complicated as the boundary-line jurisdictional questions had continued to be in Texas in part because they were so similar. Both questions reflected efforts of the federal government to pursue unilateralist power within bilateral or multilateral relations. The structure of the polity was a boon in this case since federal power was often supreme.

As the Supreme Court explained in the 1885 case *Fort Leavenworth R. R. v. Lowe*, "it is for the protection and interests of the states, their people and property, as well as for the protection and interests of the people generally of the United States, that forts, arsenals, and other buildings for public uses are constructed within the states." The Court called these military installations "instrumentalities for the execution of the powers of the general government" and as such declared they were "exempt from such control of the states as would defeat or impair their use for those purposes." The Court held (rather wishfully it seems in retrospect) that these grants of property and jurisdiction were "necessarily temporary, to be exercised only so long as the places continue to be used for the public purposes for which the property was acquired or reserved from sale. When they cease to be thus used, the jurisdiction reverts to the state."[59]

The question of exclusive jurisdiction triggered an important area of case law since it involved the sudden need to deal with coiled lines of state and federal jurisdiction in areas that had grown jurisdictionally indistinct for a variety of reasons. This need for clarity developed precisely as a result of the expanded role of the "instrumentalities for the execution of the powers of the general government." The situation in the West was fluid because change was so dramatic in the region, and the position and operating stance of the army changed accordingly. Some areas that were suddenly under jurisdictional dispute emerged when territories moved from their relatively suspended status to full sovereign statehood (Montana, Washington, South Dakota, and North Dakota became states in 1889; Wyoming and Idaho, in 1890). Other areas, such as El Paso, were being transformed because of capitalist development, and still others were being newly established as military reservations as the Indian wars progressed and American sovereignty was more fully determined. The U.S. Army continued to rapidly expand its scope, reach, and activity in the region in terms of basing and deployments. Lastly, industrialization and the mechanics of economic development, infrastructure growth, and the expansion of transportation and communication networks radically increased controversies over property, access, taxation, and jurisdiction. The cessions of land for army bases had different characteristics and different jurisdictional arrangements depending on a fine network of decisions and precedents, but they always intersected with different territorial realities, economic structures, and local arrangements.

Fort Leavenworth R. R. v. Lowe unraveled many of the issues raised in the search for the exclusive jurisdiction of the federal government on military reserves. The case held that if the land was bought or was carried over from the territorial stage without restrictions, the states could continue to exercise certain types of authority within the grant of federal jurisdiction. "When the United States acquires lands within the limits of a state by purchase, with the consent of the legislature of the state, for the erection of forts, magazines, arsenals, dockyards, and other needful buildings, the Constitution confers upon them exclusive jurisdiction of the tract so acquired." But following any other kind of acquisition meant federal "exclusive jurisdiction" was "confined to the erections, buildings, and land used for the public purposes of the federal government." The state could, however, choose to cede exclusive jurisdiction, or it could prescribe conditions to the cession as long as the federal use of the property was not affected. The only power a state could *not* reserve was a "cession of sovereignty or political jurisdiction . . . to a foreign country" since that was an entirely federal power.

The specific issue in this case was Kansas's state taxation of railroads within the Fort Leavenworth Military Reservation. Kansas had no such power to tax in this area when it was a territory. In the words of Justice Stephen Field, "the United States possessed the rights of a proprietor and had political dominion and sovereignty over it," and federal jurisdiction "was necessarily paramount." But upon becoming a state and gaining the full rights of states, Kansas obtained the "same rights of political dominion and sovereignty, subject like them only to the Constitution." Kansas thereby gained the right of limited jurisdiction over taxation at Fort Leavenworth. Though the Fort Leavenworth Military Reservation was not purchased but ceded from France in the Louisiana Purchase, Congress had never clarified it as a zone of exclusive jurisdiction. Field noted that this may have been "from some cause, inadvertence, perhaps, or overconfidence that a recession of such jurisdiction could be had whenever desired." But he argued nevertheless that the failure to carve an exception created a "defect in the jurisdiction of the United States." Once Kansas gained its statehood, there was no power to force it to yield exclusive jurisdiction unless the legislature so decided. However, the Kansas legislature in fact declared that it retained quite a bit of jurisdiction such as the "right to serve civil or criminal process within said reservation" and "the right to tax railroad, bridge, and other corporations, their franchises and property, on said reservation." Criminal jurisdiction and taxation were indeed powerful reservations of authority.[60]

In the case of El Paso, the process and reasoning of the federal government in setting up its exclusive jurisdiction over the army base territories ceded by Texas revealed much about the conception of authority, jurisdiction, and territoriality in the region. It was not until early 1886 that the Department of Texas moved to perfect the title of Fort Bliss, and the task was not actually completed until April 27, 1887. In Texas, the War Department was clearly taking no chances and even argued for exclusive jurisdiction over a cemetery that had accidentally been put into the Fort Bliss reservation as far back as 1874.[61] The bases were not just areas of military control for strategic forward operations. They were also conceived of as islands of federal power in oceans of contested terrain nestled on an international boundary in a region that was sparsely settled at best. The basing strategy of the War Department mirrored an archipelagic structure, encompassing a network of forts, posts, subposts, picket stations, and signal stations. The relatively small size of the army required a creative network of these installations coupled with high mobility achieved on horseback or, increasingly, railroads.[62]

The territories themselves, as zones of federal power and authority, were also symbols of the federal regime designed, as suggested by the Salt War investigating board, to have an outward directed "moral effect." Absolute sovereignty was essential within these zones of control since it was ultimately the goal. The radiating moral effect was one of unchallenged and unassailable authority. There was to be no jurisdictional confusion. Thus did Fort Bliss and other forts stand as interesting microcosms of the overall rejection of extraterritoriality by the United States and its emphasis on clear lines of sovereignty within interlocked systems. It is significant to note that this stridency was directed toward bases within the states of the Union. Bases in the territories were already under direct congressional control. Bases that later would be created in the era of overseas formal imperialism were based on the standard of exclusive jurisdiction originally enshrined in the control of the borderlands.

ZONES OF EXCEPTION

Like El Paso, the bigger and historically more dynamic city of Paso del Norte across the river (renamed Ciudad Juárez in 1888) experienced a transformation with the arrival of the railroads. Prior to 1881, Paso del Norte was considered the dominant city in terms of population, economy, and connectivity to the markets of the Mexican interior. Brigham, the U.S. Consul in Paso del Norte, wrote an effusive consular report touting the city as having "grown in a few years from a frontier city of no commercial importance to be the leading city commercially in the entire Republic as a port of entry and distribution of foreign merchandise and as a point of exports to the United States." Of great influence was the Mexican Central Railroad, built by American investors, which was one of the principal rail lines facilitating American investment and trade in Mexico. The railroad brought "the commercial centers of the United States into close connection with the business circle of nearly the entire Republic." Yet the orientation and reach of the newly connected rail network in the United States ultimately favored El Paso because Paso del Norte lacked an independent east-west railroad, and it consequently took an "auxiliary role."[63]

Though he touted the burgeoning economy of the area, Brigham had less pleasant things to say about the inhabitants of Paso del Note. This sentiment reflected a common pairing of economic interest and racial dismissiveness. Brigham wrote of the Mexican population with striking disdain. Citizens of the city were "not remarkable for intellectual culture," he said, but were instead "a hardy race, of lazy, idle habits, without principle" who "live in the most primitive style, and in many instances in squalid poverty." Although the economy was doing well with American investment, Brigham did not think that American ways were having an impact or "any marked change in these people. They adhere with great tenacity to their ancient customs and habits, both in a business and social way that are obsolete and belonging to an era long since passed."[64] Brigham's attitudes were not uncommon. This kind of perspective helped fuel the conflict in the Cutting case and color the understanding of the issues involved.

A major reason why Paso del Norte began again to flourish economically after the advent of the railroads was that the *Zona Libre* recently had been extended to include it. Indeed, agitation in the state of Chihuahua for this change was based upon concern over El Paso's newfound prosperity and growth. The *Zona Libre* was an area of "fiscal exception" where all goods could enter free of all duties except for municipal taxes. It was nearly but not fully a free-trade zone. Goods imported to or manufactured in the *Zona Libre* could enter the rest of Mexico only if the high Mexican tariffs were paid; this exchange was called the internation trade. The *Zona Libre* was originally established on March 17, 1858, by Ramón Guerra, the acting governor of Tamaulipas, in an effort to regain Mexican control over cross-border trade and stem outmigration. Guerra proposed the *Zona Libre* because the contrast between the high Mexican tariff and the supposedly free situation on the U.S. side had reduced the northern border region to "a true state of decadence." The establishment of fiscal exception was meant to serve as a counterbalance both to the growing, asymmetric dominance of U.S. commerce and to the unsatisfactory economic relations between the northern Mexican border states and the internal economy. The intention was to restore prosperity and vibrancy to the northern border and thereby encourage further development and settlement. Guerra's original decree was not entirely clear, but it did include Matamoros, Reynosa, Camargo, Mier, Guerrero, Monterrey, and Laredo.[65]

Throughout Tamaulipas, the *Zona Libre* was credited as being the source of prosperity, a huge increase in trade, and a major reason why the state did not succumb economically to the United States—facts that were increasingly observed with envy in the other states of the northern Mexican border and that were a source of agitation in the United States. Americans blamed the *Zona Libre* for increased lawlessness, smuggling, loss of markets, and, at various times, virtually every other concern of the time that could possibly be produced by a unilateralist assertion of Mexican authority.

Though the *Zona Libre* at first only touched a small area (approximately twelve miles along the Rio Grande), it immediately created intense controversy in the United States, which considered the establishment of even a limited free-trade area on the border to be an unacceptable assault on territorial sovereignty and prosperity. Even if the position was not quite logical, it was strongly supported, and the controversy only increased over time. What especially galled American officials and business interests was that Mexico had made this policy without first consulting them.

Peter Seuzeneau, the U.S. Consul in Matamoros in 1858, reported immediately upon its creation that the *Zona Libre* produced "bold attempts which our merchants on the left bank of the Rio Grande are making to evade the revenue laws of the U. States and of Mexico." Other consuls complained about the need for direct action to repeal the Zona "else our commercial prosperity declines at once on the Rio Grande." Within six months of the zone's formation, the new U.S. consul in Matamoros, Richard Fitzpatrick, found that people taking advantage of the *Zona Libre* on the Mexican side could "undersell the fair trade in any market in the United States, and I am certain, that goods of foreign manufacture can be purchased cheaper in the small towns of the Rio Grande than they can be in New Orleans or New York." This manner of complaint was constant for twenty years.[66]

In 1871, U.S. Consul Thomas F. Wilson in Matamoros complained that "the continuance of the *Zona Libre* appears to indicate a settled determination of the

Mexican Government to afford exceptional advantages to the merchants doing business on this side of the line and which are especially injurious to the legitimate commercial and industrial interests of the citizens of the United States on the Texas border." Somehow the Mexican trade policy was "exceptional" because it worked for the benefit of its own citizens. In 1879, the Foreign Affairs Committee of the U.S. House of Representatives called for a new commercial treaty relation with Mexico since "the Republic of Mexico lies almost in the lap of this country, bordering on us for over a thousand miles, with all her wealth and products . . . [but] it is cheaper for Mexico to trade with Europe."[67]

The State Department asked Sutton on July 14, 1879, to report if the *Zona Libre* was indeed "avowedly hostile to American interests." Sutton responded that it was not actually hostile but was certainly "avowedly averse," though his position on this matter would soon change dramatically. Alternatively, Mexican Minister Matías Romero, who actually opposed the *Zona Libre* as bad for Mexico, argued that its establishment "was a step taken in what was then thought to be the duty of self-preservation, so to speak, and imitating similar measures adopted by the Congress of the United States, and that it was by no means a measure approved in a spirit of unfriendliness, much less of hostility, towards the United States, as has been generally believed in this country."[68]

But this was not how the *Zona Libre* was viewed at the time of its creation or at any time in the following half century except by a handful of U.S. officials. The trade issue was connected with Mexican revolutionary activity on the border in terms of "disastrous effects of these two radical evils" on peace and security. John W. Foster, U.S. minister to Mexico, was one of the few who rather undramatically concluded that though he could not

> regard the continuance of the *Zona Libre* as a friendly act toward the United States, my recent visit satisfied me that it was a much greater evil to Mexico itself than to our country. The existence of such a discriminating territory most always be a source of annoyance, and ought to be abolished if we are ever to have a legitimate and cordial commercial intercourse between the two countries, but at present it is the occasion of greater damage to the government and people who created it than to its neighbors.[69]

Coming from its controversial origins, the expansion of the *Zona Libre* was among the most significant political and economic changes in this section of the borderlands since the building of the railroads, and it produced an enormous cascade of criticism, fear, and political action in the United States. As of

March 29, 1884, Paso del Norte was made a free port of first entry for all foreign goods. The customshouse was moved to the city of Chihuahua, and the full advantages of the *Zona Libre* were extended into this region of the border for the first time. The expanded *Zona Libre* now included a narrow strip twenty kilometers wide that ran along the entire frontier from Matamoros through the states of Tamaulipas, Coahuila, Chihuahua, Sonora, and Lower California to the Pacific.[70] This change dramatically transformed Paso del Norte's relationship to the flow of goods from the United States and Europe. It now stood as a central conduit for distribution through the rest of Mexico. When the *Zona Libre* was extended, Brigham was certain that this change would "have a most important effect upon the commercial routes between the United States and Mexico." He wrote the State Department that this would certainly make the city "the most important entry point on the Rio Grande."[71]

Brigham reported that property values shot up in Paso del Norte, and some businesses moved from Texas to the south bank of the river based merely on the rumor that change was going to be enacted. Sutton, the U.S. consul at Matamoros, reported "great rejoicing" across northern Mexico at the moment when the *Zona Libre* was extended. In Paso del Norte, he wrote, "bells were rung, cannon fired, and the price of real estate went up a hundred per cent." Conversely, at the same time, El Paso saw "vigorous protests" and a lot of fear. The *Lone Star* newspaper in El Paso reported that the "'*Zona Libre*' has been the principal theme of conversation in business circles this week. Several El Paso business men [already] propose to open up large stores on the other side of the river."[72]

The *Zona Libre* had long been saddled with an unprovoked assortment of anger and fear by merchants in Texas and politicians in Washington, and its expansion further west consequently carried with it a great deal of controversy. The consciously anti-American origins of the policy back in 1858 had not been forgotten, and such sinister original motivations persisted in tainting the *Zona Libre* in American eyes. From the perspective of many in Texas, this strip of duty-free territory had a corrosive impact on order and prosperity along the entire length of the frontier, threatened the functionality of the transnational trade system, and perhaps even eliminated that crucial line separating wealth and power in El Paso and Paso del Norte. Simply put, by expanding the *Zona Libre*, Mexico seemed suddenly to have grabbed the initiative along the frontier.

This attitude might have been surprising given that virtually none of the similar fears of the previous three decades that the *Zona Libre* in Tamaulipas would destroy the borderlands economy had actually materialized. Yet old prejudices died hard on the Texas frontier. The political culture in the borderlands sustained a predisposition to hysteria on this issue. Easy connections between the *Zona Libre* and all other issues continued to be made. El Paso residents had in fact been funneling their concerns about *Zona Libre* expansion to Senator Samuel Bell Maxey and successive Texas governors over several years.[73] The howls of protest from El Paso in 1884 stressed the belief that the *Zona Libre* was an aggressive extraterritorial act projected in order to damage the American and Texas economies. There was particular fear that it was the forward wedge of *total* Mexican control of the transnational economy on the Rio Grande.

On April 10, 1884, only a week after the *Zona Libre* was extended, forty prominent citizens from El Paso wrote a protest memorial to Richard Coke, the U.S. senator from Texas, and to S. W. T. Lanham, representative of the Eleventh District of Texas. This memorial was in turn duly forwarded to the secretary of state, who launched another round of inquiry into the ramifications of the *Zona Libre*. The protest was signed by the mayor, Joseph Magoffin; C. R. Morehead, president of the State National Bank (the first bank in El Paso); and other luminaries from the city. At least a quarter of the signatures were the names of local businesses rather than individuals. The memorialists characterized the expansion of the *Zona Libre* as "the destruction of our property and commercial interests by the Mexican Government." The *zona* was not just an economic policy but a transborder assault at once "unfriendly and unwise."[74]

Oddly for something produced by a group of business-minded elites in a trading city on the border, the memorial bemoaned the "unrestricted commerce" produced by the *Zona Libre*. Echoing decades of complaints about the *zona*, the memorial claimed that making Paso del Norte a free port "greatly increased opportunities for smuggling, and the utter demoralization of legitimate business." It engendered "sharp and unequal competition with foreign merchants and industries wholly unprotected." The El Paso group feared lower property values and a stagnant economy while the newly empowered capitalists of Paso del Norte in turn penetrated the United States by turning the railroad system against itself— the agent of market penetration now a commandeered route of contraband and corruption. The *Zona Libre* promised "an organized and extensive system of smuggling far into the interior of the United States on account of the various railways extending in every direction from El Paso."[75]

The memorial called for the *Zona Libre* to "be overthrown if possible," a choice phrase that indicates that the economic policy was very much interpreted in politicized, even militarized, terms. It was a yoke that needed to be cast off, a system of power that needed to be toppled. If such an overthrow was not possible, then the United States should consider retaliation in the form of "the immediate establishment of a 'Free Zone' on our own borders."[76] The El Paso memorialists clearly understood that trade policy was politics by other means. The complaints in the memorial lay well within the established arsenal of anti–*Zona Libre* agitation in the United States, but the call for potentially arming El Paso with its own "Free Zone" revealed a sense of what was at stake.

Despite the dire predictions, the expansion of the *Zona Libre* did not in fact destroy the El Paso economy overnight. The *Lone Star* reported that in its first couple months of operation, "the '*Zona Libre*' [had] not yet injured the business of this city to any perceptible extent, nor helped that of Paso del Norte."[77] Nevertheless, Morehead, the State National Bank president, was sufficiently incited by the dangers to American market penetration of Mexico to write a pamphlet titled *The Free Zone of Mexico, Its Baneful Effects on the Commercial Interests of that Republic and those of the United States* as well as his own memorial to Lanham. Morehead fast gained the reputation as "one of the most determined opponents of the Free Zone." In his memorial, he calmly batted aside the idea that Mexico sought "to create a certain and easy opportunity for wholesale smuggling into the United States" but found a far graver and more realistic threat to the movement of U.S. goods into the Mexican interior. Articles 17 and 18 of the *Zona Libre* allowed for reimportation of goods free of every duty on ships of any nation or by land, whether shipped through the United States to Mexico or through Mexico to the United States, in what was known as the bonded goods trade. These goods were luxury, high-value, high-duty items like French liquor and Cuban cigars as well as rugs, silks, linen, and other items. There was also a class of "drawback" American bonded goods produced in Mexico for sale in the United States, particularly liquor. Morehead was certain that this bonded goods policy meant that goods would merely be "transported across our Territory and landed into their free cities free of all duties" and from there pass through to the international markets. "By that means," he warned, Mexico would "cut off all trade from the interior of Mexico from the towns and cities of the United States, thus giving the merchandise of all out countries a decided advantage over us."[78]

By the summer of 1885, a year after the *Zona Libre* was expanded, the issues remained a constant topic of discussion among El Paso business interests. The *Lone Star* said the crisis was "better understood and is still more felt by our businessmen than ever before." It urged its readers to "study the *Zona*

Libre question. . . . [E]veryone interested in our future prosperity and perma-
nency should lend their personal aid in securing justice for El Paso." The price
of goods had dropped so significantly in Mexico that American merchants had
begun discounting their own goods by up to 10 percent. "So much for our high
tariff," the paper chimed. Everything could be bought cheaper in Mexico than
in the United States, and protectionism was doing more harm than good. Con-
troversially, the *Lone Star* led the charge to create a movement supporting El
Paso as a "Free City in order to place us upon an equality with our neighbors."
It supported the effort to send petitions to all the Texas towns across the border
as well as to the boards of trade in New York, Philadelphia, Boston, Chicago,
St. Louis, and Galveston and the senators and congressmen in Washington. The
State Department was urged to protest. But this plan for creating a zone of ex-
ception from U.S. tariff law in El Paso in order to compete with the Mexican
Zona Libre did not sit well with all members of the business community.[79]

Morehead, working now with a well-honed sense of injustice, articulated to
the American consul at Paso del Norte what was fast becoming the standard
Texan critique of the *Zona Libre*. This was based upon the unique (and rather
bizarre) belief that Mexican trade policy should be more reflective of American
and particularly Texas interests. He wrote, "the will of the majority having enacted our laws our government should protect her merchants trading under her
to the full extent of her power and the Mexican government should not be permitted to trifle with the dignity and good faith of the United States by creating
free towns on her borders in open violation in spirit and in fact of the late [and
unratified] reciprocity treaty." He moved neatly between the idea that the U.S.
government was required to defend domestic economic interests and the idea
that the Mexican state should be equally as sensitive to the same interests. He
even thought it appropriate that Mexico concede points to the United States in
the never-ratified Reciprocity Treaty of 1883, apparently out of comity alone.[80]

This kind of direct connectivity was a widespread idea across Texas. In an
article titled "The *Zona Libre* and How It Injures Texas Interests," the *Galveston Daily News* wrote, "under the privileges granted to the Mexican border by
virtue of the operation of the free zone the prosperity of Mexican merchants is
materially enhanced at the sacrifice of the commercial interests of Texas along
the Rio Grande." The paper, a longtime critic of the *Zona Libre*, noted that the
problem was especially sharp in El Paso, with "the Rio Grande being narrow
and fordable, and crossing by bridges and street railways at El Paso being easily affected."[81]

Morehead decided that the Mexican policy was "a discrimination in favor of foreign commerce, which must create an unfriendliness between the two Republics in time," as if American exports to Mexico were not also foreign commerce. Here is the interesting linkage of the borderlands commercial relationship. Morehead expressed the U.S. sense that the transborder trade existed for American benefit and therefore should be operated on regionally exceptional rules that recognized this special relationship. The border was not a division but a connection in this mindset. It bestowed a special set of interests and responsibilities. At the same time, however, the boundary line was considered inviolable in every other way. Morehead was also disturbed by the idea that the *Zona Libre* would begin to have broader policy effects in the United States. He opposed the floated idea that the United States set up "a like free territory" because it would discriminate against other areas. He argued that "to create free towns and cities on the American border to the same extent as that as exists on the Mexican side . . . would afford relief only to the merchants in said towns." Such a move would discriminate against other borderlands area. Given the "immense profits" at stake, Morehead instead believed the answer was "a large additional force and expense on the American border to suppress smuggling."[82]

Newspaper attention to the *Zona Libre* issue is important to note if only because the Cutting case in the summer of 1886 was in part also a media-driven affair. While the issues raised by the *Zona Libre* and later by the arrest of Cutting did garner the attention of policymakers up to the highest levels of government, the emotional crises of both of these almost entirely regional issues started in Texas and thereafter spread to more hot-headed areas in the South. With this crisis, the corrosive dangers of the *Zona Libre* fit neatly into a longstanding discussion and far deeper narrative of Mexican overreach and Mexican "outrages" that made for entertaining news, effective politics, and good theatre.

Critics of the *Zona Libre* in Texas and U.S. politics were correct about one thing: this freshly assertive enunciation of Mexican trade policy had broader political objectives. As economic historian Richard J. Salvucci has written, "commercial policy was, and is, a weapon. . . . Mexico employed the weapon, sometimes successfully and sometimes less so, but always in reaction to enormous pressures on its sovereignty. In Mexican eyes, the flag followed trade."[83] The policy choices Mexico made regarding the trade relationship with the United States were at heart rational responses to the challenges of the exchange coupled with a desire to protect its sovereignty in addition to its prosperity.

The United States had become Mexico's largest trading partner by the end of the 1870s. The increased productivity of American manufacturing made it competitive in the Mexican market for the first time. "Virtually all of Mexico's trade growth 1880–1910 was with the United States, not with England, Germany or France," and its bilateral trade structure continued to favor the United States in the period from 1880 until the Revolution.[84] Such developments in the regional political economy helped to produce new questions and areas of conflict in the borderlands. The focal point of trade shifted constantly, and directly reflecting this dynamic situation, sovereignty and jurisdiction continued to be contested. Describing economic changes in other areas of Mexico, Salvucci has noted how relative advantage shifted place as "one port's prostration was another's prosperity."[85] A similar dynamic was at work across the region. Americans, and particularly business interests in Texas and their political representatives, tended to blame all disputes as well as the newly arising problems in the commercial relationship on Mexico. They correspondingly ignored the "enormous pressures" on the nation brought by increased American economic dominance or directly helped to increase the pressures by countenancing smuggling.

This attitude was reflected well in Congress by Texas senator Richard Coke, a former Texas governor back in the tumultuous 1870s who was well attuned and responsive to the peculiarities and regional interests of the Texas political economy. On January 18, 1886, Coke announced in the Senate that "a large number of merchants of El Paso" were "praying for the intervention of the Government of the United States" because the *Zona Libre* made it "impossible for Americans on the American side of the Rio Grande to do a legitimate business." This group in fact considered the Mexican trade policy to be directed aggressively against the United States. Coke said the U.S. government believed "the establishment of the *Zona Libre* to be an unfriendly act on the part of the Mexican Government, and [asked] some relief from this Government." The *Zona Libre* did not represent just a loosening of tariff restrictions; it could be viewed as a positive creation. Coke said the *zona* "create[d] a depot on the bank of the Rio Grande, from its mouth to its source, from which smugglers [could] introduce their goods free of duty into the United States."[86]

Exact figures on the legal and contraband trade between the United States and Mexico during this time were difficult to ascertain. William Eleroy Curtis, the executive officer of the International American Conference, wrote in a report to Congress on Latin American trade around this time that "the statistics of our trade with Mexico are very defective" since they only revealed "the amount carried on by water." Specific amounts carried on other trade routes were unavailable since there was not a law written that allowed for the "collection of statistics concerning transportation in cars."[87] And of course smuggling was not officially calculated, despite its massive role in exchange between the two countries. Citing Mexican sources, historian David Pletcher describes the share of American goods in the Mexican trade as increasing from 36 percent in 1872–1873 to 72 percent by 1892–1893.[88] The change was also evident in local returns on trade that were kept by the U.S. Consul on the frontier at Nuevo Laredo. Transborder trade strongly increased in quantity and value every quarter each year at the beginning of the 1880s.[89]

Considering the trade as a whole along the frontier in Texas from his perch in Matamoros, U.S. Consul Sutton provided a clear perspective on how American manufactured goods came to ever increasingly dominate the trade with Mexico by 1880. He reported that between 1874 and 1880, the total value of European and American goods brought into Matamoros, Nuevo Laredo, and Piedras Negras (which lay outside the *Zona Libre* until it was expanded) was $2.7 million, of which two million dollars worth came from the United States. Sutton noted that only one quarter of the population of the *Zona Libre* even had sufficient money to consume imported European goods. Also, importantly, it was almost certain that an additional one million dollars of goods crossed annually, in Sutton's delicate words, "without the formality of written documents." This meant the goods were transported illegally and outside the system of accountability in Mexico. Sutton estimated that this illicit trade was made up "entirely of American goods." The smuggling trade was worth almost a quarter of the entire value of trade along the border, and if any smuggling "depot" was indeed created by the *Zona Libre*, it seemed to be one that favored American interests. Nevertheless, the many issues raised by the *Zona Libre* were not insignificant in shaping popular and official attitudes toward the meaning of order in this region.[90]

American transportation interests also saw increases as a result of the situation with Mexico. European goods were brought in on only one of two bonded routes through the United States to Mexico before the expansion of the *Zona Libre*. A quarter to a third of the bonded goods passed through the "large importers in New York and New Orleans" on their way through Texas to Mexico. The bonded goods system was designed so that these firms could import goods and hold them in bond, warehousing them free of duty for a prescribed time and then re-warehousing them for export. Some of the goods also came through Brazos de Santiago (a transshipment point for oceangoing ships at the mouth of the Rio Grande) to Brownsville to Matamoros, and the others came through Corpus Christi to Laredo, Texas, and on to Nuevo Laredo. Cities such as Piedras Negras or Paso del Norte had hitherto seen none of this trade since they lay outside the *Zona Libre* and therefore were useless for American profit-taking on the bonded goods routes. There was money to be made in this trade, and any changes to the system threatened American profitability.[91]

The bonded goods trade itself signaled an interesting little zone of exception carved into the U.S. trading regime that allowed merchants to squeeze profit from transactions without endangering the overall integrity of the U.S. protectionist system. It demonstrated the utility of the very notion of exception. There was no reason why strident defense of markets could not coexist with profitable activity if it occurred only within this tightly constrained zone. The exception was designed to enrich commercial interests that otherwise would be cut out of the trade system, and the system also "implied a considerable transportation either by land or water and by American carriers exclusively." All of the profit for transport and any associated commissions would be collected by the shippers.[92]

The relevance and utility of bonded routes was in the process of changing, wrote Sutton, because of "the changed condition of American manufacturers which are now eagerly seeking markets all over the world. In the nature of things this search for markets must steadily increase." Sutton was convinced that American goods could continue to outcompete foreign goods, so why eliminate the profits accrued from the carrying trade in bonded goods? The bigger concern was in ensuring that the borderlands trade environment was tied into global carrying trade networks in the most profitable way possible. High freight rates between New York or New Orleans and Brazos de Santiago or Corpus Christi would mean that shippers would find it more convenient to ship directly from Europe at Liverpool or Hamburg (both of which were also free ports). While these ships would still land at American ports in Texas, the carrying profits would be greatly diminished since the distance to the Matamoros ferry would be only about twenty-five miles.[93]

Sutton thought there was no way to be certain how many bonded goods actually were smuggled into the United States, but he did not think smuggling was a large problem. He never saw evidence of the smuggling, though he would not have been surprised to see it. After all, a smuggler from Mexico to the United States could be hired in less than 30 minutes. "I have been surprised by other things here and am liable to be again," he wrote. Sutton's solution to this problem was simply tighter surveillance among customs inspectors and better paperwork, whereas the call for "the abolition of the *Zona Libre* would destroy the retail, local, and contraband trade of the zone, throwing this all to the American side." His underlined conclusion was that *"to abolish the* Zona Libre *is to make the same a comparative desert."*[94]

Sutton wrote that "the control of this foreign trade, which *should be* in the hands of New York and New Orleans wholesale importers, has passed to Europe and these goods come direct only using for convenience this small section of the United States." Despite this change and the loss of the carrying trade for some commercial houses, Sutton thought that most of the focus on the U.S. trade to Mexico should be directed to the expansion of markets for American goods rather than to maintaining a death grip on the bonded goods routes: "When it is considered that three-fourths of all this bonded trade between the United States and Mexico is done here [at Matamoros] and that at least two-thirds of this is from Europe direct, it will be seen that the bonded system as regards the Mexican trade is of *comparatively* small benefit to American business."[95]

It seems logical (though it did not follow in practice) that at this time, American commercial interests along the frontier should have been more focused on their own business models than on the structuring of global trade routes to Mexico, which the Mexican state sought to influence by expanding the *Zona Libre*. First, Americans had no possibility of changing Mexican policy or global trade assemblages, and second, these routes in fact did not interfere with the legal or contraband trade to Mexico dominated by the United States. It is true that since European bonded goods were increasingly going directly into Mexico, the change would be viewed with trepidation. But it was curious that American businessmen were so concerned with the unilateral liberalization of trade by Mexico when in fact it portended increased opportunity to the nation already dominant in the markets and poised for rapid exploitation of the new opportunity. Clearly, the loosening of restraints in the borderlands system of trade was viewed with concern because it disrupted the balance and seemed to give Mexico greater governing power within it. Any shift in the trade along the U.S.-Mexico frontier could be interpreted as a zero-sum loss with significant repercussions.

In his report to Congress about the trade, Curtis, of the International American Conference, noted that arrogance and laziness on the part of American merchants impeded the market and encouraged a variety of Mexican reactions. "Our trade in cottons might be very much increased if the manufacturers in the United States would study the peculiar demands of the market, and comply with them," he wrote. Mexicans instead sought European manufacturers for the goods they desired rather than buying the ones Americans thought they should desire. Accordingly, they sought to reshape the system for receiving these European goods. "If our manufacturers desire this trade they must send competent men to Mexico to make a careful study of the whims and peculiarities of the people," Curtis wrote. "The disposition of the French and Germans is to gratify the local taste, while the manufacturers of the United States attempt to force upon the market goods that are popular at home, but are not suited to foreign buyers." Curtis saw other problems with the U.S. approach to the Mexican trade, including an unwillingness of "the commission men" to send desired goods rather than to "send what they happen to have in stock" and the inadequate preparation of goods for the Mexican market. American merchants sent oversized and heavy-weight goods that incurred greater duties. In contrast, European suppliers sought to "economize weight" in ways more suitable to the unique mule- or hand-carried transportation system of much of Mexico.[96]

Curtis thus argued that American merchants failed to meet market conditions and demand in Mexico in many ways. Yet like so many American policymakers, he could not shake the belief that the core problem was the Mexican system itself. His report concluded that "the chief obstacle in the way of an increased trade with Mexico is the annoying and oppressive regulations imposed at the customhouses, particularly on the Rio Grande, which are intended to prevent smuggling, but practically prohibit trade, as the fines imposed for this unintentional violation eat up the profits on the sales."[97]

It happened that the United States had an important defender of the expanded *Zona Libre* in Warner P. Sutton. He was required to report regularly on the commercial situation along the borderlands, and his understanding of the order, power, and interaction along the border were rooted in consideration of the simmering unhappiness of American commercial interests that colored the whole system. Sutton found that most questions from businessmen all over the United States returned unerringly to the *Zona Libre*: "Owing to the anomalous conditions caused by the workings of the '*Zona Libre*' this information is necessarily of value to those interested in Mexican Trade. I presume that I have explained various conditions of the '*Zona*' to American merchants on an average of fifty times a year." He observed, "this is the only '*Zona Libre*' in the civilized world and as such it is an object of curiosity."[98]

For some time, Sutton had not reported his generally positive view of the *Zona Libre* because he did not wish to express an opinion that would "perhaps, be more favorable than the opinion previously expressed by others" or that was divergent from State Department policy. "I had feared that my views on the subject might not be approved and I had not felt quite secure enough in them to care to run counter to the general view of the matter," he remarked. He believed the *Zona Libre* supplied "elasticity." He was confident that merchants in America "are more advantageously situated than merchants enjoying all the benefits of the *Zona.*" There had been "rigorous, even tyrannical, enforcement of the laws" on the part of the Mexicans, which is why smuggling was down. Sutton believed Canada's low tariff was just as much a danger to American business interests as Mexico's, and the same was true for France, England, and Cuba.[99]

The real difference—in fact the whole key—in all trade relations was that the U.S. governance structure was so much more stable and business friendly than elsewhere that U.S. trade would dominate no matter what. This was true even if the *Zona Libre* seemed, at the simplest level of understanding, to unfairly shape the protocols of exchange. American productivity was key since manufacturers could increasingly offer very competitive prices for goods. "Under all circumstances it will be seen that the American merchant with his secure government, low taxes and liberal and honorable treatment in the custom-house and courts, has an immense advantage over the *Zona* merchant in every thing except in those goods which are in demand on this frontier and which pay heavy import duties in the United States." And those goods were "fancy articles": wine, Havana cigars, lace, rugs, French gaiters, and sardines. It was in fact the *American* tariff laws that were creating the barriers to prosperity, not the free trade of the *Zona Libre*. Sutton urged the State Department to orient its policy around an understanding of American strengths in this setting rather than an exaggerated sense of the challenges and inequalities the United States faced. Suffice it to say, Sutton's perspective was not as persuasive as more strident and simplistic defenses of American interests.[100]

Sutton understood why Mexico would want to extend the *Zona Libre* since it was "its only chance of anything like even handed competition with the left bank. Without that or some great change in the Mexican tariff laws the contrast between the two sides of the river will be as great as between a brick block and a *jacal.*" But in Sutton's view, American wholesalers and manufacturers should also welcome the change—and not just the business interests clustered in Texas. Sutton referred to the wholesale dealers of all the major trading cities in the United States like St. Louis, Chicago, Cincinnati, New York, and New Orleans. They would profit "because the moving back of the *Zona* limits [would be] like opening a gate." The local merchants might see a short-term loss, but the economic situation would soon rebound: "The mutual interests of the two banks are many and the increased prosperity and values on the Mexican side, the impetus it would give to mining, agriculture, &c, &c, would in turn greatly benefit all classes on the American bank." If, on the other hand, the *Zona* was ended, Sutton argued seriously, "life here [in Mexico] would, so to speak, be hardly worth living" because things would become so expensive.

Sutton described what Piedras Negras looked like in 1879, outside the *Zona Libre*. Buildings were falling down, there was "no movement, no energy, and no commerce." There developed a "universal" smuggling system for all articles needed. Mixing his metaphors, Sutton stressed that, if ended, "the *Zona* would thus be a thorn in the side of good government and a wedge." Indeed, Sutton said he had "many times wished, in pity" that the *Zona Libre* would be extended all the way to the Pacific. This is an amazing comment from a public official of a government that decried this very policy.[101]

Upon first hearing of the official expansion of the *Zona Libre*, Sutton quite optimistically argued that Mexico had not changed the terms of trade so much as opened up the terms for greater opportunity. He telegraphed back to the State Department that the *Zona Libre* "will be an important benefit to our manufactories as it increases the buying capacity of the towns affected [in Mexico] and in which three-fourths of the goods now used are American." Sutton was confident that the *Zona Libre* promised special advantages for the frontier communities as well as a burst of new market opportunities. He was certain that expansion of the *Zona Libre* would have a "considerable" and immediate impact on both Piedras Negras and Paso del Norte and would "render life possible there under more favorable conditions than heretofore." Americans stood ready to expand business there, and "many Mexicans [would] also come in from the interior to enjoy the advantages of the *Zona Libre*" at the frontier, meaning an entirely new group of potential customers. Freed from the restrictive Mexican tariff, "all residents of the territory of the newly established *Zona Libre* [could] legally buy two dollars' worth of goods where they formally bought one dollars' worth."[102]

The careful and limited expansion of this zone of exception for trade along the boundary promised regionally specific advantages that American business interests could exploit. Indeed, the limited reach of the *Zona Libre* made it even more appealing. U.S. trade represented three-quarters of all goods crossing the border while it amounted to only half of the imports at Vera Cruz. "Hence," wrote Sutton, "we should be in favor of a *Zona Libre* for the frontier but not in favor of one for the Gulf Coast."[103] The limited scope of the Mexican policy was, in fact, its strength rather than an indication of worrisome arbitrariness. Sutton understood that the *Zona* was an exception not only to the impassable Mexican tariff but also to the constraints of the global competition for Mexican markets.

At the request of Secretary of State Frederick Frelinghuysen to respond to the memorials written by the El Paso citizens and by Morehead, Sutton employed his signature thoroughness and long-windedness to issue a fresh report on the expanded *Zona Libre* in Paso del Norte. This report echoed many of the themes in his first full-length analysis of the *Zona* in 1882 but included a new appreciation of its specific benefits for El Paso. In this report, Sutton utterly rejected citizens' fear that the *Zona Libre* would release "unrestricted commerce" below the Rio Grande. "Mexican commercial legislation is based upon far different ideas," he wrote with great emphasis. "Everything is restricted, and so much so that doing a profitable business nowadays in Matamoros or Nuevo Laredo is almost impossible." If anything, Sutton thought American businessmen could count on the enhanced inadequacy of the Mexican state to interfere with their markets. He promised there would be no "utter demoralization of legitimate business" in El Paso any more than there had been in Brownsville or Laredo, just an expansion of new access. "The merchant on the American side can thus compete fairly with the merchant on the Mexican side on more than three-fourths of all frontier trade, even with the *Zona*."[104]

The American emphasis on business friendly law and the maintenance of social and legal order meant the country had a natural advantage. At one point, Sutton referred to this advantage as the ever-present calculation of "freights, risk, and time" in the Mexican trade. Not only could Americans compete effectively against Mexican merchants, Sutton was certain they actually had the "positive advantage" because taxes were "so high, so oppressive, and the risks of living and doing business [were] so many on the Mexican side" that the elimination of tariff restrictions meant business flowed to the northern bank. He considered this point important enough that he repeated it three times in a twenty-seven page report.[105]

Sutton's understanding of the *Zona Libre* in frontier terms was that it made each cross-border city relationship balanced, symbiotic, and profitable, in effect creating the interlinked "imagined economies" recently theorized by Angus Cameron and Ronen O. Palan. In this way, "the imagined community of the

territorial nation-state" became "a series of imagined economies which maintain the fiction of the state—and indeed perpetuate it as a legal entity—but
situate it within [a] radically different set of boundaries and notions of social
space."[106] This pattern had been demonstrated in Matamoros-Brownsville and
Laredo–Nuevo Laredo. Rather than disrupting the power balance between the
United States and Mexico, the *Zona Libre* ensured that the commercial relations
between the two sides of the river would be "mutually dependent," which Sutton thought desirable along the frontier. He did not question the right of Mexico to assert "free trade if she chooses" on only one side of the line. Furthermore, the *Zona Libre* kept the population happy, stable, and situated. Without
it, Sutton was certain there would be mass migration north, whereas the *Zona
Libre* drew Mexicans from the interior to the border cities and simply produced
customers for U.S. interests without the nation having to accept broader responsibilities for Mexicans' well-being.[107]

El Paso business and civic interests had strong concerns about the possible
corrosive effects of the *Zona Libre* on the rule of law in their city, particularly
relating to smuggling. Assessing this supposed threat of an expansion of smuggling or lawlessness, Sutton was firm that it would be impossible. "It will be right
difficult to increase" smuggling into Mexico, he wrote, because "it is now down
on a gigantic scale." Sutton was aware of "carloads" of contraband American
goods being secreted across the river and loaded onto mules for distribution in
the Mexican interior. Smuggling into Mexico by Americans was in fact "notorious" and was occurring "at a greater rate than [Sutton had] ever known before."
Animals, mezcal, and European luxury goods that were bought duty free in
Mexico might be smuggled in turn back into the United States, but Sutton was
sanguine about the ability of the customshouses to control this trade, except for
an insignificant trickle.[108]

Surely part of this reassurance was wishful thinking on the part of Sutton—
or at least an effort to allay fears. How, after all, could the U.S. customshouses
suddenly be so effective along the river boundary in ways that the Mexican
force and U.S. authorities found impossible before the expansion of the *Zona
Libre*? Sutton's claim that American authorities could handle any new crime or
disorder was a key aspect of his fanciful contrast between the two systems on
the Rio Grande. Sutton's emphasis on a superior and more orderly system of
surveillance, documentation, and control that would solve any new problems
might have seemed reassuring to some and certainly created a useful contrast

to the widely held belief that Mexican customs enforcement, like the country's legal system, was lax, corrupt, incompetent, and not to be trusted.

The one consideration Sutton was most sensitive to was Morehead's criticism of the competition of European bonded goods with American goods. In this case, Sutton's response simply detailed the developmentalist logic behind the bonded transit laws in the first place. These laws were, of course, a sop to national commercial interests across the United States and themselves delineated a zone of exception on the American side of the border. The bonded transit laws essentially created a small-scale, portable, and nationwide network of *Zona Libres* established wherever the bonded goods traveled or were warehoused. Sutton noted that while bonded goods flowed freely into Mexico, they were also being distributed throughout the nation in "our principal cities" and transshipped to Cuba and in even greater part to Canada, all at a profit to American companies, small merchant houses, and railroad interests. He conceded that in the areas of Mexico served by direct rail lines from the United States like Matamoros, Saltillo, and Chihuahua, "the bonded and transit laws of the United States are unquestionably hostile to our manufacturing interests." But Sutton claimed that most shippers to Mexico did not have much of a choice. They did not want to have to wean Mexican consumers off "European styles and qualities," and they did not want to be "forced to buy American goods" or European goods from Mexican suppliers.[109]

It was clear that the trade in European bonded goods was going to continue both within and through the United States, observed Sutton, so the only sensible option was to carve out a profitable and preferential position within it. The route through the United States to Mexico was going to remain attractive despite the *Zona Libre*, so one essential goal was to obtain especially low rates on the bonded goods from Europe as a way to ensure profits. Since global shipping prices were steadily dropping, this was a promising development. Sutton also stressed that thinking of the bonded goods system in terms of regional profitability lost sight of the reality that these issues had to be addressed at the national level of tariff policy, where the U.S. Treasury should begin to "charge a fairer price for important entries, warehouse fees, and the various charges upon such goods . . . so as to make the system self-supporting." Here Sutton encouraged the memorialists to think systemically about American foreign economic policy rather than focus on Mexican policy as the sole and most decisive casual factor in the borderlands.[110]

Perhaps the protest over the *Zona Libre* should be viewed less as a controversy over the establishment of a duty free zone and subsequent lifting of restrictions and instead in terms of how Mexico created new restrictions on American illegality. Smugglers of American goods might have been a bit disadvantaged because in economic terms, the boundary effectively had been moved to the south side of the *Zona Libre*. The borderline that now mattered was not the Rio Grande but the line *in* Mexico itself, between the *Zona Libre* and the interior. To smuggle goods into Mexico now meant leaving a "*Zona* town," which posed a whole new set of considerations and constraints for smugglers.[111]

Sutton recognized that "a considerable share of the prosperity of El Paso [was] due to the sale of goods to be smuggled into Mexico." He included a long section on smuggling, which was bracketed and marked "omit" by hand in the margin, presumably so that the State Department would not distribute or print the document if it chose to distribute the overall *Zona Libre* report. This omitted section discussed in detail how the smuggling system for bonded goods actually operated and especially how El Paso smugglers could be sure to avoid all customs guards in the *Zona Libre*. Sutton wrote of "one old smuggler" from the United States who had treasured his freedom to smuggle. He thought the *Zona* towns were too expensive to buy out of but that the Rio Grande was a snap: "As long as the river lay between his goods and the guards he could laugh and take his ease," looking for the right place to cross with a guard with "speculation in [his] eyes." Now this form of smuggling was suddenly gone. But smugglers of bonded goods could theoretically do better, Sutton asserted in this omitted section, as the "profits of the 'negotiation' [would] accrue largely to the operator who [was] on American soil." Smugglers of bonded goods would still find the American side, where most of the smuggling originated and would continue to originate, as congenial to their interests.[112]

FAILURES OF RECIPROCITY

The U.S. share of goods in the Mexican economy had increased enormously in the 1880s, and Mexico was very accommodating to U.S. investment by "twisting ancient laws and granting generous concessions to attract the desired capital." Yet total dominance of Mexico's economy and, perhaps more importantly, of the structure of the trade itself, proved frustratingly elusive. The United States did not accept the situation or falter in its drive to expand into and shape Mexican markets. Salvucci argues, "like all good campaigners, U.S. officials wanted complete victory (or unconditional surrender). For a variety of reasons, they did not get it, at least before 1884. One explanation was the changing terms of trade."[113] The terms changed precisely because Mexico began to assert its interests with more vigor. Quite manifestly, these changing terms of trade were linked in numerous ways to sovereignty and jurisdiction on the borderlands. The definitions of these terms were in a constant and dynamic state of testing, challenge, and reaffirmation.

One reason why Mexico unilaterally established a zone of free-trade exception along its northern border in 1884 was not just to try to undercut this profitable smuggling system but to mitigate the effects of the changing balances of the entire system of trade with the United States. Mexico's own high tariff system choked trade and encouraged smuggling and had helped unbalance trade along the northern frontier. This was, in the words of Mexican Secretary of Finance and Minister to the United States Matías Romero, "an almost impassable tariff wall . . . against [which]. . . the operations of the Free Zone are thrown into strong relief." A second consideration was the unbalanced flow of Mexican silver into the United States, which was a result of the massive contraband trade out of Texas as well as capital flight on the part of Mexican elites finding themselves squeezed by swings in Mexican revenue policy.[114] In these senses, the *Zona Libre* could be viewed as a practical economic solution to structural inadequacies bordering at times on crisis.

The third reason may have been the most important as it more clearly demonstrates the political edge of the *Zona Libre* and its direct relation to questions of jurisdiction, authority, and power along the border. The expansion of the *Zona Libre* revealed Mexico's renewed reliance upon unilateralist exception as a response to the loose structuring and lack of maneuverability in the borderlands trading system. Both the United States and Mexico maintained highly protectionist trading systems that reflected the challenges of this system and global trade networks, but these barriers were inflexible and undesirable with regard to the specific situation of the borderlands. To force the issue, Mexico unilaterally terminated the 1831 trade treaty and thereafter pursued readjustment to its commercial relationship in a Reciprocity Agreement of 1883.[115]

Both Mexico and the United States were interested in reciprocity, though it was the latter that pushed it most. Reciprocity is usually understood as a tool of American foreign market expansionism, regional and global ambitions, and political expediency. It was eagerly sought by the tariff reform movement in the United States. President Chester Arthur, in bemoaning the congressional failure to pass the commercial treaty with Mexico in his third annual message in 1883, announced that "at no time in our national history has there been more manifest need of close and lasting relations with a neighboring state than now exists with respect to Mexico. The rapid influx of our capital and enterprise into that country shows, by what has already been accomplished, the vast reciprocal advantages which must attend the progress of its internal development."[116]

Mexico likewise desired reciprocity as a way of balancing its trading inter-action with the increasingly dominant, industrializing, export-oriented United States. But Mexico was at least as interested in breaking down American tariff barriers as in opening internal investment fields. It was presumed, too, that im-proved trade would streamline other relations. Speaking to the Manufacturers' Association in Chicago about reducing the impediments to trade, Romero de-clared easier commerce to be "the most powerful and beneficent means of pre-serving peace on the frontier, of furthering and establishing political and social friendship between Mexico and the United States, and of helping both nations to mutually maintain Republican institutions."[117]

Mexican policymakers harbored no illusions that the United States struc-tured its reciprocal agreements in order to gain the most unilateral benefits from them. They remembered the aggressive negotiation of the Ocampo-MacLane treaty signed but not ratified in 1859, wherein the United States pushed hard for territorial as well as trade concessions. Mexico viewed the recent 1875 signing of the U.S. reciprocity treaty with Hawaii as slightly more fair but still a caution-ary example. Especially noteworthy in that effort was the deft way the United States carved a unilateralist exception out of the Most Favored Nation clause in order to keep its hard-won reciprocity exclusive. Reciprocity was itself an ex-ceptional system within trade policy, and creating further pockets of exception within this exception indicated just how wily American negotiators could be in structuring reciprocal trade relations. Mexico would be sure to avoid being saddled with a system of "reciprocity in no more than name," which the United States often pursued.[118]

Nevertheless, in considering the best way to increase trade and undercut if not eliminate smuggling, Romero believed that reciprocity with the United States could very possibly have "truly prodigious results" when approached with care so as not to be exploited or cornered by exceptions. Mexico would be careful in this regard not to endanger its commerce with European nations. He concluded "that even though a reciprocity treaty may be looked upon in Mexico on the part of many with marked suspicion, springing from the fear that the United States [would take] advantage of [its] power . . . there is no fear that this will operate to impede the celebration of a treaty, because the reasons militating in favor of it are so clear and of such notorious public convenience that they cannot be objected to on any good foundation."[119]

Though signed and ratified, the Reciprocity Treaty never actually became law. The actions of the United States in negotiating, ratifying, but ultimately refusing to implement it were a sign that bilateral accommodation was truly unattainable at that moment. It failed in the United States because of procedural tricks in Congress. Though the treaty actually passed with the required two-thirds majority, there was an added-on requirement of "implementing legislation," which effectively killed it. Looking back at the failure of reciprocity a few years later, Romero decided the problem was that American "public opinion [was] not yet prepared" to adopt a policy that mitigated its powerful streak of unilateral territoriality in the form of still-vibrant protectionism. This was particularly true in the continued emphasis on protecting the sugar interests. "The subject of reciprocity is far more complicated than it appears to be," Romero wrote, "since it has become connected with the protection and free-trade questions which are now so earnestly agitated in this country." He understood that "reciprocity treaties [would] represent the transition between these two stages, and until the second [was] fully attained there [would] be many difficulties in the way." Though he was optimistic about the eventual outcome, Romero was convinced that the failure of the Mexican reciprocity treaty in 1883 was a sign that change would be very slow in developing.[120]

But the logic of the two nations becoming seamlessly linked was inexorable if only because the systems were already so interdependent in basic structural terms, even if the United States refused to recognize it yet. Romero contrasted the productive United States with Mexico, "a country contiguous to it for nearly two thousand miles, inhabited by twelve millions of people, who produce, in proportion to their population, very few manufactured articles, but who have all the elements of soil, climate, and labor necessary to produce the raw materials needed by the manufacturing industries of the United States." Transportation, proximity, and economic interdependence demanded reciprocity. If it could not be established between these two countries, there was no hope for reciprocity anywhere.[121]

Following this treaty failure, Mexico adopted the attractive solution of further forcing the issue by increasing its other tariff rates and signing "favorable commercial treaties with France, Britain, and Japan" in the next three years.[122] Mexico also used the carving of a unilateral exception through the expansion of the *Zona Libre* to act as a catalyst for systemic change to the borderlands relationship.

Mexico's unilateralist trade policy stood as a prime example of independent governance of what otherwise might just have been accelerated U.S. domination of the borderlands economy.[123] The expansion of the *Zona Libre* to all of the northern states further accentuated this independence by "thereby placing it [the *Zona*] on a better footing than it had been before, when it appeared as a privilege confined to a single State and denied to others which were in exactly the same condition," as Romero phrased it.[124]

The fluctuating terms of commerce, jurisdiction, and sovereignty produced a great deal of fluidity in the fortunes and mindsets of the towns in the borderlands. With this fluidity came uncomfortable uncertainty and fear of rapid economic decline. People chose to focus on the potential negative implications. The *Zona Libra* seemed so free of restraint from the Mexican state, and so impervious to negotiation or threat from the United States, that it was difficult for many in Texas to view it as anything other than an anarchistic assault on order and prosperity, not to mention neighborliness. Mexican states seemed to act only in their own narrow, short-term economic interests in a style that threatened economic order and even the concept of legitimate governance.

This impact was also directly related to the basic mechanics of structuring commercial policy, which was far more localized (and seemingly more chaotic) in Mexico than it was in the United States. In the United States, trade policy and uniform tariff rates were set and enforced by Washington and subject to sectoral pressures, partisan constraints, and other systemic considerations that often were resisted in Texas and the free-trade Democratic South more broadly. Trapped as they were behind the American protectionist wall, these same free-trade interests were infuriated when Mexico dared to loosen the terms of trade unilaterally. The *San Francisco Daily Evening Bulletin*, a free-trade paper that often discussed the *Zona Libre*, argued this point that Mexican trade policy was not constrained by the appropriate governance structures common in the United States. "In our Union, the State that wants the recognition of a particular policy agitates till it secures practical unanimity at home. Then it watches its opportunity in national politics. . . . But in Mexico they usually begin at the other end, set up first the regulation which they want, defy the General Government and afterwards secure the concession, whatever it may be." This kind of latitude undermined the entire system of order. For example, the paper reported (using John W. Foster as the support) that through "the strangest of commercial mutations," the *Zona Libre* was now in fact helping American manufacturers. That served as just "another illustration of the fact that unwise interference with natural laws is a two-edged sword, which should not be hastily picked up."[125]

Clearly, logic was not the main factor in American opposition. Romero remained a bit aghast at the opposition to the *Zona Libre* in the United States since it manifestly did not threaten American trade. Romero felt badly enough about the mushrooming controversy over the extension of the *Zona Libre* that he reminded Secretary of State Frelinghuysen of his longstanding opposition to the *Zona Libre* stretching back to a multiday speech he gave to the Mexican Congress in 1870.[126] Romero considered it "absurd" for Americans to consider the *Zona Libre* a hostile act when it created open opportunity for them in a market untainted by taxation or other restraints of trade. He confessed that it "was for some time a matter of wonder to me that public opinion in this country could have been so grossly misled on the subject of the Free Zone; and that a measure which allowed a free market for all kinds of products and manufactures of this country into a large section of Mexican territory could be misunderstood to the extent of considering it as an offence to the United States."[127] While American merchants were focusing on the new advantages of European goods in the opened Mexican market, they seemed to be losing sight of the reality that it was in fact the United States that dominated the market share south of the border:

If the Free Zone has inconveniences for this country, although much less serious ones than those which it has for Mexico, it possesses, in my judgment, a decided advantage which has remained hitherto unnoticed. It practically makes a portion of Mexico a free market for all the products and manufactures of the United States, since merchandise of all kinds from this country may be imported into and consumed in Mexican territory almost duty free, and be warehoused in the region of the Zone for an unlimited time. No greater privilege can be asked for the commerce of a nation, and the only drawback in this respect that I can see to the Free Zone, in so far as the

United States is concerned, is that it does not embrace the whole of Mexico. Supposing its privileges were extended to the whole of Mexico, would the United States consider the free admission of their products into that country as prejudicial to their interests? How strange, under this view of the question, does the idea prevailing here appear, that the Free Zone brings only injury to the United States and has been established to the advantage of European goods only, when ninety-five per cent of the goods imported there under its franchises are from the United States.[128]

What Romero did not fully explore was the idea that expanding the *Zona Libre* as a zone of exception along the border seemed the equivalent of spreading Mexican *control* in the abstract across the borderline. American goods could enter the market, but only on terms created by Mexico in the constrained area that it defined. The *Zona Libre* was no longer a contained expression of Mexican autonomy functioning along a tiny slice of the boundary line in Tamaulipas; it was a long band of uncertainty that lay just out of reach of American authority. It was difficult to understand how the impact of it might in fact be limited or beneficial. Suddenly, elites in El Paso, a newly reinvigorated commercial city with much to lose, faced an obvious expression of the limits of their power wrapped in a seeming assault on their wealth and position. They knew that the impact of the shifting structures of trade functioned such that some areas flourished at the expense of others. Cities in Mexico that originally were left outside the newly carved zone of exclusion had withered. This had been seen in the border cities formerly excluded from the *Zona Libre* like Piedras Negras. El Paso's business interests did not want their city to be transformed into a decaying bypass. They wanted the zones of exception to stop and for American order to be forthrightly implemented.

THE POLITICS OF EXTRATERRITORIAL CLAIMS

The summer of 1886 was "unusually hot" in El Paso. As the temperature climbed to 110 degrees, the *El Paso Daily Times* even felt compelled to ask, "is it hot enough for you?"[129] But the *Cutting* crisis cannot be blamed on intemperance triggered by the heat. The El Paso–Paso del Norte region was essentially quiet and undisturbed at the moment. Brigham sent significantly fewer reports back to the State Department than other U.S. consuls in border cities, and the situa-

Figure 1. The editor A. K. Cutting at the time of his controversial arrest in Mexico. *El Paso Daily Times,* September 11, 1886.

tion in 1886 was no different. Most of the news of "Mexican outrages" seemed to be coming from elsewhere like the border counties between Laredo and Corpus Christi.[130]

It all changed on June 23, when an American newspaper editor, A. K. Cutting (fig. 1) was arrested in Paso del Norte, Mexico, for a libelous ad (or "card") he published in the *El Paso Herald* about a Mexican editor named Emigdio Medina. Cutting had only just finished retracting a libelous statement he had placed in his Paso del Norte newspaper, *El Centinela,* which he edited. In that statement, Cutting had called Medina a "fraud" and termed his desire to start a rival newspaper in town "a scheme to swindle advertisers, etc., etc." Medina took Cutting to Mexican court, and under court orders in a "reconciliation" agreement, Cutting had published a retraction of his initial libel. According to one Mexican writer, Cutting had retracted his libel in *El Centinela* only "in dreadful and incorrect Spanish and in microscopic letters." He did not make that mistake twice.[131]

On June 18, the same day he printed the retraction in Mexico, Cutting published his card about Medina, which elaborated on his multiple failings: "Now, I do hereby reiterate my original assertions that said Emigdio Medina is a 'fraud,' and add 'deadbeat' to the name." Cutting termed the reconciliation "contemptible and cowardly," and he vaguely threatened Medina with violence: "And should said Emigdio Medina desire 'American' satisfactions for this reiteration, I will be pleased to grant him all he may desire, at any time, in any manner." Clearly, fearing no consequences for publishing the card, Cutting crossed back into Mexico and distributed it. A few days later, he was arrested under jurisdiction of the extraterritorial Article 186 of the Mexican penal code. Cutting was tried without counsel or interpreter in the Paso del Norte Second Court "behind closed doors." He was locked up without bail, and U.S. Consul Brigham began what was to become a rocky series of negotiations for Cutting's release that started locally but soon exploded into a full fledged crisis with diplomatic threats and troops massed on both sides of the border poised for conflict.[132]

After a series of delays because of a legal holiday, Brigham's agitation for Cutting's release was denied a few days after his arrest. The consul began to suspect that there was no intent "to do Mr. Cutting justice" and began blaming the local judicial authorities, particularly the overseeing Judge Zubia and the prosecuting attorney José Maria Siena, for a conspiracy to keep Cutting locked up out of a hatred for Americans. Cutting's experience, even at this early stage, confirmed Brigham's "observation . . . that the Mexican authorities have not the slightest regard for the rights of American citizens and they will only respect them when made to do so. Their courts are a mockery of justice and presided over by judges for the most part ignorant of the law." Brigham thought they were all "corrupt, prejudiced, and utterly dead to every sense of right or equity." The Cutting arrest was symptomatic of what he thought plagued the entire country: "With our immense territory bordering on this so-called Republic, there is ample opportunity given to these petty officials to oppress and cruelly treat American citizens and they rarely ever fail to avail themselves of the privileges of doing so." This was merely one in a series of "such cases of outrage and oppression," many of which Washington never heard about. Nevertheless, Brigham claimed that he had "demeaned himself throughout with every proper courtesy and respect to the authorities, and urged Cutting to do likewise." He concluded that despite the abuse he felt he was receiving, he claimed he would "be prepared intelligently to act."[133]

The court in Paso del Norte refused to release Cutting or even to discuss the case, and a long series of recriminations began.[134] The Cutting case was propelled to the highest ranks of crisis in large part by the efforts of Brigham and the local press to make the issue a major crisis. From the start of this affair, the tone was different than that associated with other outrages. This case turned locally on personalities, prominently Cutting and Brigham and U.S. special envoy A. G. Sedgwick, who was sent to press the U.S. case in Paso Del Norte (though with little chance of success; in an interview, when asked if he was "conversant with the Spanish language," he replied "only very slightly").[135]

But the real divisive issues involved jurisdictional and philosophical questions that became aired on a national political stage. In the U.S. perspective, the arrest of Cutting raised a very serious threat to national sovereignty and territorial integrity based upon what is termed the "passive personality theory of jurisdiction." The categorical rejection of "any assertion of jurisdiction by foreign courts over acts of United States nationals committed against nationals of the forum state outside that state's territory" was one of the core legacies of the Cutting case.[136]

The Cutting case was covered daily, sometimes multiple times, in the *El Paso Daily Times*, which started out calling it "[a]nother Mexican Outrage" but soon sensed its unique character and sought increasingly more caustic descriptors than the well-worn "outrage." The paper not only helped gin up hysteria over Cutting's arrest, it also directly crystallized the anxieties in El Paso over the broader questions of social order and jurisdictional inviolability. Whereas the libel issue was a minor one, the jurisdictional one was extremely significant and easily couched in the racialist terms used to characterize assertions of American legal spatiality in other regions. Cutting's libel was entirely beside the point:

Occurring as this Cutting-Medina case did, on the "dead line" of the *Zona Hostil*, it has assumed an importance which it did not intrinsically deserve. However it is well enough that it did occur at this time. This claim which the Mexicans are setting up, of extra-territorial jurisdiction, ought to be disposed of right now, once and forever. . . . It is no use mincing matters at this late date. Mexico is too near to us and too closely related commercially, politically, and socially to be allowed the luxury of antiquated feudal laws that would disgrace even China in the palmy days of the great wall. She must assimilate her laws and their execution to the forward march of the nineteenth century. . . . There seems to be absolutely no more check on state authorities, on minor officials, on anybody vested with "a little brief authority" than there is in China. . . . No civilized nation laying claim to be abreast with the progress of the nineteenth century makes any claim to extra-territorial jurisdiction. . . . It is reserved to an insignificant canton in the border state of Chihuahua to spring this question upon a civilized world.[137]

The contrast of American civilized order and the faintly Chinese ("canton in the border state") uncivilized disorder produced by the Mexican claim of extraterritorial jurisdiction was a key distinction. The paper was, in fact, fixated on comparing the U.S. experience in the case with the extraterritorial treatment of the Chinese. A couple days later, it argued, "Cutting's case is not the only outrage that has been perpetrated on American citizens in Mexico. A man had better be a Chinaman than an American if he does business there." If the United States was to trade with an equal partner, it could not be subjected to this kind of jurisdictional claim best suited for the uncivilized (and therefore open to extraterritoriality) nether regions of the globe, such as that which the United States exercised in China. Nor should the country stand for the *Zona Libre*, a similarly destabilizing fiction. At the same time it discussed the Cutting case, the *Daily Times* urged U.S. envoy Sedgwick to get active and "post himself about the 'zona libre,' that little trick that was intended to ruin El Paso, Laredo, and Eagle Pass, but luckily didn't do it. El Paso is too far ahead to be ruined by any sour little *zona libre* hocus pocus."[138]

The correspondence between the United States and Mexico on the *Cutting* affair continued well beyond the case itself because of the gravity of the issues involved. Yet in many ways, as the rest of this book will demonstrate, the challenge to sovereign jurisdiction that this case came to represent above all actually paled in comparison to the range of incidents large and small that consumed the attention of the two countries. Nevertheless, both nations remained committed to their positions and published documentation and long treatises defending them. Mexico even had choice selections from the diplomatic correspondence in the case published (including an edition in English) and distributed to schools and newspapers in the United States through 1888, as the lingering issues continued to be debated.[139] But the only true resolution in the case came years later when both countries (still insisting that their interpretation was correct) finally dropped the discussion without conceding an inch.

The immense diplomatic correspondence circled unrelentingly around the unresolved question of extraterritorial jurisdiction over noncitizens. The United States officially complained and demanded both restitution and contrition, and the Mexican response to these demands argued a series of interlinked points, which deflected any calls for the government to reverse itself. The main point was that Article 186 gave Mexico full authority over Cutting's crimes. Related to that was the strong assertion that in so doing, Mexico "act[ed] according to the precepts of international law," which allowed for such personal jurisdiction, and encouraged "the trend of modern civilization [which] is not to let crimes go unpunished." Another key part of the Mexican argument was that the federal state simply did not have the authority to override local jurisdiction in Chihuahua. Foreign Minister Ignacio Mariscal advised that this kind of delay was "inevitable in a country ruled by institutions like ours, where the federal executive cannot communicate directly with local officials in the states, much less . . . give orders." Mariscal noted that "doing so would constitute a real attack" and would be unfair both to the interested party (Cutting) and to the whole idea of an independent judiciary—just like it would be in the U.S. judicial system, he noted.[140]

The structuring of Secretary of State Thomas F. Bayard's complaint was interesting because he framed it initially in terms of the protection of borderlands business and free speech interests and only later expanded it to incorporate the much more focused jurisdictional complaint that dominated the exchange. At first he simply rejected Mexico's right to arrest Cutting as "wholly inadmissible" because it was

> equivalent to asserting that Mexico can take jurisdiction over the authors of the various criticisms of Mexican business operations which appear in the newspapers of the United States. If Mr. Cutting can be tried and imprisoned in Mexico for publishing in the United States a criticism on a Mexican business transaction in which he was concerned, there is not an editor or publisher of a newspaper in the United States who could not, were he found in Mexico, be subjected to like indignities and injuries on the same ground.

Since Cutting's acts could be claimed only obliquely as "business criticism," Bayard's mindset was telling. Mexico's actions threatened the free atmosphere in which business was conducted. Each state of the United States would also protect "the exclusiveness of [its] jurisdiction over acts done within [its] own boundaries."[141]

Bayard also found Cutting's arrest to undermine the rule of civilized law: "By the law of nations no punishment can be inflicted by a sovereign on citizens of other countries unless in conformity with those sanctions of justice which all civilized nations hold in common." The treatment of Cutting was not in accordance with these standards, especially the manner in which his trial was held. These were, to be sure, common complaints about the Mexican justice system, though in this case it was given unusually strong condemnation in the long missive from the consul on the ground, from which Bayard borrowed freely.[142]

It was not until July 27 that Bayard organized his complaint around the Mexican application of Article 186, a translated copy of which he received from Romero in Washington. Bayard flatly told Romero that "the United States would not assent to or permit the existence of such extraterritorial force to be given to Mexican law, nor their own jurisdiction to be so usurped, nor their own local justice to be so vicariously executed by a foreign government. . . . The existence of such power was and is denied by the United States." A bit gently, and with the express reservation that it was an unofficial discussion, Romero later reminded Bayard that in fact Article 186 had been known to the United States for several years, since its application in the Avalos case. While the key difference was that Avalos was a citizen and Cutting was not, the issue of extraterritorial jurisdiction was clearly the same and "demonstrate[d] that the law had been applied long ago with the knowledge, and one can say with the satisfaction" of the United States.[143]

Cutting's continued imprisonment meanwhile had erupted into a national crisis. It was discussed in Congress, debated in the press, and mentioned on the campaign trail. James G. Blaine condemned Bayard's handling in the opening speech of his congressional campaign, saying he "blustered most egregiously in his imperative demand for the release of Cutting, with the implied menace of war in the event of noncompliance, and deserves, as he has received, the just criticism of the press. He acted without adequate knowledge of either the law or the facts in the case."[144]

Perhaps spurred by the fact that Cutting was an editor, papers from the *Galveston Daily News* to the *New York Times* and the *Washington Post* featured discussions about his fate. Large crowds gathered on the streets of El Paso calling for war and cheering when the band played "Dixie." Newspapers around the country heavily stressed the possibility of war. The *El Paso Daily Times* stressed troop movements to Fort Bliss, and headlines asked, "Is it War?" The *New York Times* declared "Texans ready for war" on its front page and reported "the rumor that batteries of cannon were planted on the American side of the river, and that the Alcalde of El Paso Del Norte had been ordered to release the American editor or that the town would be bombarded, spread rapidly through the city and soon became the talk of the people." According to the paper, "all the native hatred of the Mexicans is aroused and the veterans who fought against Santa Anna under Houston, and those younger ones who went to Monterrey, Buena Vista, and the City of Mexico with Scott and Taylor, find interested audiences when telling of those campaigns and the treachery of the 'greasers'. . . . Texas is aroused, and a strong war feeling is apparent. Citizens of Texas meet the lower classes of Mexicans daily, and heartily hate them. The cattlemen, cowboys, and frontiersmen all tell of the encroachments on the border, of their stealing, and the murders committed by marauding bands."[145]

The *Galveston Daily News* made the most direct connection between the issues of legal spatiality in the borderlands and the deeper meaning of the Cutting case. The intensity of the feeling this situation produced grew out of the unstable and indistinct jurisdictional regime that persisted in the area. Of particular concern was that the United States had to treat Mexico's assertions of sovereign jurisdiction with respect on equal rather than on the unequal terms that marked extraterritorial relations in other regions. The *News* expressed this sentiment clearly in a front-page editorial that called for the use of force:

Relying upon their own estimate of Mexican prowess and gringo inferiority, they seem to be contemptuous toward any reasoning; therefore it is thrown away upon. With such miscreants the only decisive arguments are rifles and Gatling guns. In the interest of future peace and the maintenance of safety for Americans the time has come when the alternative of instant submission or unsparing retribution must be presented. . . . Because Mexico is a republic she has been indulgently treated. But tolerance of indignities and ruthless crimes has borne its inevitable fruit. Unless a severe example is made of the murderers of Rasures [discussed in chapter 3] and the persecutors of Cutting . . . and in a manner to show that this is not a Mexican but an American dictate, the persecutions and murders will certainly be tenfold aggravated and nothing will be gained, for war must follow such a state of things if war is the only means of finally convincing the Mexicans that the outages have to be stopped. Short diplomacy and long range guns, gatlings and plenty of them, are therefore the truest common sense and the tenderest mercy the case will admit. The News has not faith in the willingness of the Mexican local vampires to humiliate themselves by hanging or shooting the murderers and heavily fining their fraudulent and impudent judges. But it would like to see them govern a brief space of time in which to make full reparation, eye for eye and tooth for tooth. And then it would like to see the American people vindicate themselves with the calm severity needed to make our national name a terror for the next twenty years in that particular region. Thus only can the reptile officials of the miscalled republican states of northern Mexico be made to realize that our people are in earnest and intend to be respected and decently treated.[146]

This was no mere statement against Mexican outrages; it was an explicit call for twenty years of "terror" to correct the perceived indulgences and lack of jurisdictional clarity that had allowed the situation in the borderlands to become so indistinct. Obviously, the many jurisdictional implications of the Cutting case engaged the live wires of borderlands political, economic, and legal formation.

The United States did not go to war, of course, but the diplomatic line did harden significantly. In a report submitted to the Senate on August 2, Bayard noted that the "conflict of laws is even more profound than the literal difference of corresponding statutes, for it affects the underlying principles of security to personal liberty and freedom of speech or expression, which are among the main objects sought to be secured by our framework of Government." What was at stake in the Cutting case was nothing less than the overall security of the U.S. legal system: "The safety of our citizens and all others lawfully within our jurisdiction would be greatly impaired, if not wholly destroyed, by admitting the power of a foreign state to define offenses and apply penalties to acts committed within the jurisdiction of the United States."[147]

Cutting was eventually sentenced to one year in prison, but it was commuted, and in late August he was freed. Inevitably, he immediately demanded reparations and read his manifesto, which read in part, "I am satisfied that the United States can never yield the point involved in my imprisonment and sentence. With a frontier extending over fifteen hundred miles between Mexico and the United States, and the business relations of the two countries continually growing more intimate, our government can never allow the claim of Mexico to punish American citizens for offenses committed within the United States."[148]

The strident U.S. rejection of Mexican extraterritoriality helped to clarify a key attribute of the U.S. approach to territoriality and the treatment of crime. All histories of the role of extraterritorial jurisdiction in the United States at least mention the Cutting case because it embodied the strident American defense of territoriality that was considered a hallmark of the era. The year 1886 has been called "the height of strict territoriality," and the Cutting case stood in the diplomatic record and in subsequent scholarship as one of the purest and seemingly most straightforward expressions of territoriality from the time. Oddly, the case has been ignored by diplomatic historians and does not appear in histories of Texas or standard accounts of El Paso. The broader context of the Cutting controversy in diplomacy, politics, law, and borderlands idiosyncrasies, so intensely felt in 1886, has remained obscured.[149]

The Cutting case occurred at a moment when the borderlands issues became viewed directly through the prism of the urgent global political and economic ambitions that increasingly were being embraced and touted by American policymakers. The specific legal issues at stake in the Cutting case thus took on a far greater potential significance than the mere task of clarifying territorial jurisdiction or seeing to the establishment of a short-term fix to the perpetually unstable borderlands order in the case of a soon-forgotten troublemaker. The crisis signaled a reinvigorated American push for systemic order in state relations. This order was constructed upon a specific regime of unilateral governance and delineated, constrained jurisdiction that could be carefully applied when expedient—or just as easily ignored when not.

At its heart, the controversy of the Cutting case turned on a question of jurisdiction over extraterritorial acts.[150] Bayard was not exaggerating when he said that the implications of the Cutting case were that legal citizenship regimes would be "wholly destroyed," since the presumption against extraterritoriality in fact reflected the basic U.S. sense of legal order. To American policymakers, the mere fact of nationality outside the boundaries of the sovereign territory did not signal a concurrent extension of jurisdiction or of rights. John Bassett Moore clarified this position in his scathing exegesis on the controversy titled *Report on Extraterritorial Crime and the Cutting Case*. This book, in which Moore marshaled all possible arguments to deny Mexico's extraterritorial claims, contained the most commonly cited articulations of strict American territoriality by the State Department up until World War II, and the work is still considered the definitive statement of the era.

Moore had no doubt that every nation, "in the exercise of its sovereignty," had a right to jurisdiction rooted in strict territoriality. He described jurisdictional claims over acts by nationals in three significant and interconnected ways. Claims over all acts within national territory were clearly acceptable. So too were acts on seagoing vessels "national or private, which for most purposes are considered as part of the national territory," including issues involving any merchant ship that found itself within the jurisdiction of another sovereignty such as in a port. In some rarer but important cases, sovereigns also had jurisdiction over "offenses committed within [their] territory by persons corporeally outside" the territory. These offenses took the form of egregious transnational acts with territorial effects, including an act like firing a gun into a territory from without or the use of an "infernal machine, swindling letter, poisonous food, [or] counterfeit money, &c, sent into [a] country from outside." In all of these cases, jurisdiction lay with the territory where the law was violated or the injury was committed.[151]

Moore also reflected on the acceptable category of "non-territorial," or extraterritorial jurisdiction. In this category, Moore summarized international legal opinion as including personal jurisdiction over national citizens in "barbarous lands" in the classic extraterritorial sense as well as perpetrators of crimes of piracy and crimes that had been defined by international conventions, such as agreements covering suppression of the slave trade. Crimes against the state and some of its core monopolies, particularly crimes involving counterfeiting of currency and securities and the police power, also enjoyed special status within this category.[152] These crimes were also almost always extraditable crimes, which further established their acceptance under international law and their consequent universality in international relations.

Given these basic definitions, it is clear that other claims of extraterritorial jurisdiction had no standing in the international law tradition that Moore emphasized and that the United States sought to perpetuate for reasons that went beyond simply preserving its prerogative for all three major forms of jurisdiction. Under this perspective, such basic understandings of the inherent territoriality of jurisdiction were essential for the smooth operation of the entire international state system.

Desire for rationalization and stability in integrating international relations was at least as significant as the unilateralist urges underpinning territoriality in U.S. policy. In reviewing the meaning of the Cutting case, for example, arch expansionist and imperialist Hannis Taylor wrote that "the contention of the United States which prevailed in that case embodies a clear and positive statement of the views of those who are prepared to maintain the ancient principle as to the territoriality of crime against the dangerous innovation which assumes 'that the principle is not founded on reason, and that as intercourse grows closer in the world nations will the more readily aid general justice."[153] Confronted with such "dangerous innovations," the United States reacted with a notoriously clear expression of its policy and interest.

Territorial jurisdiction was a key marker of sovereignty and a linchpin in the system of global order and peace that was facing new transnational challenges in the latter part of the nineteenth century. As the international system moved toward tighter integration, questions of territoriality became keen. Moore recognized some key factors that were helping "to diminish extraterritorial pretensions in criminal matters" protecting the purity and dominance of American-style territoriality. One such factor was the ever-increasing "idea of nationality and national equality." Though some nations still considered themselves more equal than others in the state system, as "the idea" of equality increased, so too did the desire for increased systemic order in which to embed the weaker nations. The language of state equality outside imperialist frameworks begat self-control and respect for limits on jurisdictional claims, and stronger assertions of territoriality provided this manner of framework for the system without actually producing—or requiring—equality.[154]

Moore believed that international economic interdependence and "the development and extension of commercial intercourse" increased the need for clear lines of jurisdictional authority in which to embed these relations. Significantly, so too did the increasing spread of the principles of international law in foreign relations and "more general recognition and performance by independent states of their rights and duties under [this] international law" increase the need for clear lines. In summarizing these three interrelated concepts, Moore argued "the first cause [of equality] has operated to produce a clearer apprehension of the objects of national existence and of the bounds of national authority; the second [globalization] has rendered more apparent the necessity of personal immunity from vexatious and unjust prosecutions under foreign and unknown laws; the third [international law] has made governments more ready to abandon assumptions of authority which infringe the rights of other sovereign powers."[155] International law was no more a solvent of sovereignty or territoriality than was global trade or growing notions of state equality. Quite the opposite in fact.

One more related crucial factor of globalization clearly played a role in the strong American reaction to the Cutting case. Mexican extraterritorial claims over the actions of American citizens having an impact on Mexican nationals in the United States raised the uncomfortable specter of all the nations of the earth claiming jurisdiction over the actions affecting their own citizens. In a world of increasingly globalized labor flows, migration, emigration, and movement, this type of jurisdictional explosion (and especially of extraterritorial penal claims) spelled potentially catastrophic trouble for an immigrant destination like the United States. Not only could such precedents open the citizens up to danger in arbitrary foreign legal systems, but these types of jurisdictional intrusions on the American polity would challenge the very essence of hierarchy that underlay Americans' cherished notions of limited, divided, and competitive governance. This was the *imperium in imperio* enshrined in the structure of the polity itself: the divided jurisdictions of federalism that created a proper territorial place for each level and variety of jurisdiction. Foreign extraterritorial claims on American actions could conceivably challenge a multinational socioeconomic order quite literally built by and upon millions of immigrant laborers.

As Moore stated it, "a state may, if it see fit, tie its criminal law about the neck of its citizen and hold him answerable for its violation everywhere. But even this power of control has its limitations." He warned that "such a pretension is an assertion not only of an *imperium in imperio*, but of *imperia in imperio*. It would expose citizens and all other persons in the United States to liability to as many penal systems as there happened to be nationalities represented in the foreign population."[156] And, according to Moore and his contemporaries, no American citizen should live in fear of being the arbitrary object of jurisdictional overreach. Secretary of State Thomas F. Bayard, in his August 2, 1886, report to President Grover Cleveland on the Cutting case crisis, noted that the "conflict of laws is even more profound than the literal difference of corresponding statutes, for it affects the underlying principles of security to personal liberty and freedom of speech or expression, which are among the main objects sought to be secured by our framework of Government."[157] The Cutting case presented a challenge to basic notions of governance, order, and rights not just in the borderlands but within the entire global system of exchange in which the United States intended to become dominant quite soon.

CHAPTER TWO

Jurisdiction, Sovereignty, and Space

There is, of course, a vast amount of lawlessness on this frontier. . . . [T]he criminals from each side escape to the other where they are safe from arrest. . . . Laredo, Texas is becoming thoroughly Americanized and law and order should prevail. These can only be secured by prompt punishment of criminals. As long as these cities are harbors for law violation, and immunity secured by crossing a fordable river, just so long life and property are in danger.

John F. Jenne, U.S. Vice-Consul, Nuevo Laredo, 1880

The ease of migration, incursion, smuggling, and fugitive escape in the borderlands made extradition and interdiction important and especially difficult issues between the United States and Mexico. The ever-contested boundary line between the two nations made the interconnection between the criminal legal systems, as between the states themselves, a thornier and more daily contest than was the case in U.S. relations with other nations. Policymakers also generally believed the region to be more lawless and violent than others, rooted in a racialized understanding of Mexican justice that colored the U.S. perception of virtually every discussion of establishing order on the border. There was a pronounced sense that the justice system in Mexico was inherently corrupt and flawed, if not actually inoperable. American policymakers at all levels of authority stressed the lawlessness of this system and its arbitrary treatment of Americans below the border. They also did not trust Mexican authorities to seek out or pursue fugitives, to treat innocent Americans with respect or lawfulness, or to execute extradition warrants faithfully.

The rugged geography of the border had a pronounced impact on the trajectory of politics and governance of jurisdiction in the region. In Texas, the Rio

Grande boundary presented everything from a formidable barrier to an easily fordable crossing, depending on the area, and it was the river itself that fundamentally shaped all future considerations. Making matters more interesting and difficult—and ensuring snarled jurisdictions—the river boundary moved significantly and often. Further west at a place like Nogales, border-crossing simply meant crossing the street. The desert boundary was inhospitable but wide open, and the national boundary was simply not always clear. Secretary of State John Sherman once dismissed some of the labor put into boundary definitions as having "but small intrinsic worth" and "generally of little value" since some of the borderlands was "hopeless desert."[1] Nevertheless the lines in this "hopeless desert" mattered mightily in determining jurisdiction and power.

Under the broad guidance of U.S. foreign policymakers, there existed strikingly different legal regimes across the entire length of the border, determined by local officials, the size, nature, and distribution of the local populace, the basis of economic exchange, the distribution of U.S. troops and local law enforcement, and the level and variety of criminality and revolutionary behavior of the populace. This chapter considers these varying jurisdictional regimes in the region as they were enacted across this vast space and in conjunction with the systems of movement, governance, and illegality that operated within it.

THE GEOPOLITICS OF EXTRADITION AND INTERDICTION IN ARIZONA

One of the basic difficulties of maintaining clear jurisdictional lines along the U.S.-Mexico border in the Arizona and New Mexico territories was determining the exact boundary line. Strict territoriality in jurisdiction demanded a similar effort on the map. In 1881, John J. Gosper, the acting governor of Arizona wrote Secretary of the Interior S. J. Kirkwood that it was essential to clearly determine the national boundaries, as "connected with the grand march of events, looking toward rapid settlements and a better civilization for Mexico from the American side, many efforts will be made by unscrupulous men to take advantage of unguarded lines and laws." Even though there were stones marking the boundary in some spots, "in many instances, [they were] so far between as to make it very difficult to distinguish with any definiteness where the line [ran]." The material, size, "thickness," placement, number, and location of these monument stones demarcating the border were a persistent focus of discussion throughout this period. The same year, Secretary of State James G. Blaine also wrote Kirkwood a long correspondence "touching certain difficulties and disturbances alleged to arise from the absence of distinct marks on the boundary line between the United States and Mexico."[2]

Following an agreement with Mexico in July 1882, the boundary was to be resurveyed and then freshly marked with monuments all the way from the Pacific to the Rio Grande in order to (in President Chester Arthur's words) end uncertainty "as to jurisdiction in criminal and municipal affairs." But it took Congress a full two years to appropriate $100,000 for this purpose, and "some embarrassment [had] been occasioned by the failure," as Arthur noted in his annual message in 1884.[3]

The maps used tended to be inadequate and sometimes incompetently produced. In 1886, one of the delays in implementing yet another boundary agreement came from mistakes in the Spanish translation that placed the Gila River on the boundary line and omitted the Colorado River entirely. There was yet another signed convention in February 1889 to revive the essentially orphaned 1882 convention and extend the boundary survey and marking effort. But still, U.S. Consul Delos H. Smith in Nogales reported as late as 1890 that "the monuments along this part of the line are insufficient to enable the increasing population along the border to readily determine where the line is." The monuments were five to forty miles apart, whereas the convention within Mexico stipulated they be eight thousand meters (about five miles) apart. Smith wrote, "I am told that our Customs Officers along the border—not being positive as to where the line is—are often at a disadvantage in apprehending smugglers" (fig. 2).[4]

Within this landscape of sometimes-indistinct jurisdictional lines, both criminal and incidental territorial incursions flourished in the Arizona borderlands in the last two decades of the nineteenth century. All manner of goods were smuggled in both directions along the boundary, but one item that particularly raised American hackles was mezcal.[5] This illicit traffic was almost entirely a local issue in subregions on the frontier—the federal government soon determined officially (and wrongly) that "occasional smuggling in mescal and stock is detected, but smuggling *as a business* no longer exists to any extent"—but it was intensely felt. There was actually significant production of the liquor along the boundary line of Arizona and Sonora, often from agave grown in Arizona (or "gathered on the soil of the United States," as the U.S. consul more ominously put it) and carried back into Mexico. Along a seventy-five-mile stretch on the Mexican side of the border south of San Pedro, Arizona, there were found seven stills. Delos H. Smith estimated that 90 percent of their output was

Figure 2. Smugglers cross the Rio Grande as U.S. customs agents hide in the reeds in this 1886 illustration by P. Frenzeny. *Harper's Weekly*, September 4, 1886. Library of Congress Prints and Photographs Division, LC-USZ62-119617.

smuggled back into the United States. Mezcal was also produced in Sinaloa and sent north. Smith explained that the illicit trade was a major concern because "these stills are harbors for all kinds of dissolute characters" and the drink was "about as strong a stimulant as can be produced." If the United States fought mezcal smuggling, argued Smith in calling for action, "the cause of temperance [would] be advanced and much of the crime caused by its use [would] be avoided." And if the country did not, it would just continue to face violation of revenue laws and invite lawlessness in the region.[6]

In 1887, Lowell H. Jerome, special agent of the Treasury Department, argued against any compromise for a group of mezcal smugglers, including Manuel Valtaris, José Olivas, Sacramento Granillo, and Sacramento Granillo Jr. Jerome had "not the slightest doubt of their guilt and that [it was] their regular business," and he lobbied at great length to stop any deal that would set them free. He "earnestly protest[ed] against any compromise being made." It was no easy task to catch mezcal smugglers: "the Customs officers of the District deserve great praise for the seizure they have made. The wonder is that they ever make any owing to the smallness of the force and the long line of territory to be guarded." Since it was "next to impossible to catch them," the men should be jailed as long as possible. Jerome hoped to hurt the owners of the operation across the border, who ran "three or four distilleries of Mescal in full blast just over the line in Mexico and the product all comes to this country." Jerome felt that to lock up the workers would be better than "the single seizure for sale of a thousand gallons of mescal." For, "as long as the 'tools' of these men escape punishment, they lose nothing and are willing to go back and try it over again, being more careful." Jerome wanted to jail these "tools" to drive the price of making mezcal up and presumably (no doubt wishfully) destroy the market. "There have been too many compromises on this border," he declared, speaking from "the experience of several years on the Southern border as Special Inspector, Collector, and Special Agent." Local interdiction efforts aimed at low-level traffickers as the policy choice to try to staunch a supply of illicit controlled substances for an insatiable domestic market clearly had long historical roots—as did the failure of this policy.[7]

Many other goods crossed the line illegally. Horses and cattle pastured near the boundary line often wandered over the line or were targets for cattle thieves and seizures from customs officials. Cattleman sought to graze their animals directly astride the line while asserting the right to cross the border to retrieve their stray cattle. Consul Smith wrote that "the cattle interests along the border are becoming quite extensive and it frequently [happens] that stockmen from both sides crowd their cattle across the line for the purpose of grazing and if confronted make the excuse that they did not know where the line begins and ends." The problem of straying cattle was large and increasing on the Sonora frontier because of the lack of "natural or other barrier at the international boundary line" to prevent their movement. In 1878, the consul at Guaymas was happy to report that the government of Sonora and "the full approbation of all good citizens on both sides of the boundary line" made cattle theft uncommon. "The disorders that exist on the Texas border are not complained of on the Arizona frontier," he wrote in his annual report, which was certainly not the case for long, as the population of people and cattle increased on the frontier. Soon the cattlemen deemed it "practically impossible" to keep track of the cattle, particularly in the winter or during storms. They were "confident" that the cattle were stolen and rebranded while the cattlemen were kept from pursuing them.[8] This issue was a constant source of irritation between the nations and continued long after many of the criminal and revolutionary border issues had been resolved.

Protection of branded cattle along the fluid and indistinct international border required a strong assertion of jurisdiction and authority along a wide network in a way similar to the protection of brand names in today's more abstract but equally fluid and sometimes lawless global economy. One of the biggest problems was the scale of the problem and sheer number of different aspects of it to consider and control. "This has always been a difficult matter to treat satisfactorily," a correspondent told the consul. "Remember perfectly well the trouble we had some years ago on the Texas border in relation to estray cattle." A July 11, 1888, agreement between the United States and Mexico regulated the legitimate crossing of cattle as well as the retrieval of stray and stolen cattle, but it was never finally ratified. There were local arrangements made for reciprocal crossings, but consuls at Nogales, Guaymas, and elsewhere complained about the arbitrary application of these local agreements. The cattlemen were "anxiously awaiting permission to cross the line in search of their cattle," but when they attempted to avail themselves of a promised local reciprocity, they were denied. Sometimes their horses or cattle were confiscated and then sold at auction by Mexicans, as happened repeatedly in Sonora. Sometimes, too, American cattlemen were suspected of crossing and then selling stock themselves. This was a large enough concern to be expressly forbidden in agreements with Mexico and for a bond to be required for entry. In June 1891, Smith warned that "this is getting to be a serious question" and that there was increased talk of cattlemen arming themselves unless certain reciprocity could be established. This issue simmered in various permutations with little resolution for the entire decade. The United States passed a law in 1894 allowing American cattlemen to graze their cattle in Mexico and reimport them free of duties within twelve months, but Mexico understandably "did not regard the resolution in question as embracing any real reciprocity in favor of the Mexican stock raisers."[9]

The criminal flow worked both ways, as transborder thieves created a profitable exchange in stealing horses in Arizona and New Mexico for sale in Mexico and stealing cattle in Mexico for sale back in the United States. Mexico complained to the United States because the crimes were suppressing legitimate economic exchange on the border. An official Mexican report declared that "the thieves and desperadoes who rondez-vous on the American side have become unendurable. They are described as being worse than the Apaches in the heyday of their career." Most pointedly, the report asked, "is it possible that within the boundaries of the best organized Government on the planet a few outlaws, the whole number probably not exceeding one hundred, can band together, defy the civil authorities, and while taking advantage of the security our soil affords reach out and paralyze the industries of a neighboring state?"[10]

Arizona officials of course complained in turn about Mexican lawlessness and about fugitive escape across the border. They complained about Mexican laws being applied fitfully and about new ones being invented or discovered. In February 1879, territorial governor John C. Fremont complained about the refusal of the Mexican government to surrender two murderers. This refusal would "undoubtedly make serious trouble on our frontier," though he was committed to "prevent[ing] reprisals and disorders that are likely to bring about serious tensions between the two governments." By this time, most of the criminal "outrages" occurring on the border were coming from the U.S. side, and the perpetrators remained unpunished. And indeed by 1881, cattle thefts produced "bad blood between the cow-boys and the citizens of Sonora," and a series of reprisal attacks and killings made it "unsafe for any person to travel across the border."[11] It was striking though that in Arizona the complaints of lawlessness, depredation, and an uncivilized rejection of the rule of law tended to be coming from Mexico and directed toward the United States instead of the usual litany being heard just east in Texas, where the opposite was the norm.

Some of the cattle crimes on the border were dramatic in scale and audacity; most were less so. Treasury Department special agent R. U. Moore reported that 3,544 head of cattle were smuggled into the United States in July 1880, 3,444 of which were purchased in Mexico by Zadok Staab of New York City and then smuggled into Arizona and sold as beef in order to fulfill U.S.-Indian contracts at the San Carlos Agency. But most of Moore's cases involved the movement and undervaluation of cattle across the border rather than large-scale illegal movement. No record appears in the Treasury Department special agent files about the irony of an agent named R. U. Moore reporting on cattle undervaluations.[12]

In August 1881, a mining cashier, named Eugene H. Hathaway, wrote to the secretary of the interior from the St. Helena gold mine in Las Delicias in Sonora to complain about the "depredations of bandits and marauders in Arizona" from the American side and to call for action:

These robberies and murders have been generally, on good evidence, committed by "Cow Boys" from the U.S. who continually run over the line in Mexico + back; and large bands of them are continually lying in wait for every merchant and courier who is sent up from here is waylaid and robbed or murdered. The Mexicans especially are sufferers and are in continual terror for fear of them; it seems important that immediate measures should be taken by the Government of the U. States to have the disturbances put down in [their] beginnings else the property and lives of the many Americans in Sonora and other portions of Mexico will be endangered and much jealousy caused.[13]

Hathaway's estimation of the American origins and probable transnational impact of the gang of "Cow Boys" was widely shared. This criminal group terrorized the southeastern frontier in Arizona for years, and the conflict they produced (some criminal, some political) underlay such famous incidents of frontier violence as the shoot-out at the O.K. Corral in Tombstone.[14] They also preyed extensively on the Mexican side of the border. The Cow Boys were incorrigible criminals, many from "the utterly abandoned class," but there was also "a much larger" group made up of "the 'Good Lord and good devil' kind who 'carry water on both shoulders'" who were as difficult to deal with as the "*extreme* criminals class."[15]

Acting Governor John J. Gosper of Arizona noted in his annual report to the secretary of the interior in 1881 that crime in the territory was "far more frequent and appalling in the Territories than elsewhere, because of the less regard generally paid to virtue and the rights of property, but more generally because of the fact that criminals—fugitives from justice—from thickly settled sections of the East, flee to the wild and unsettled portions of our territories, where they can form in bands for mutual protection against arrest and punishment." He noted huge lawless areas and chaos in the borderlands, where "most of the common property stolen is taken from Mexicans near or on either side of the boundary line dividing Mexico from the United States."[16] In this way, 1880s Arizona evoked the chaos and attendant jurisdictional scrum of Texas in the 1870s, though the precise causal differences were important.

Gosper was one of several Arizona governors and officials who requested (and periodically demanded) the suspension of the new *posse comitatus* act passed in the wake of Reconstruction that forbad military involvement in civil policing. While President Chester Arthur was sympathetic to it and asked Congress to amend the law on April 26, 1882, a gun-shy Congress was not eager to violate the new act and unleash the army in this way. Gosper fretted that "the arm of the military being paralyzed by unwise congressional legislation in the matter of aiding in certain civil processes," all that Arizona had left were underfunded U.S. marshals. Although disorder was rampant and U.S. and territorial authority were consequently weakened, criminality did not invite a fully militarized response. Arthur found an end run in declaring the area under rebellion, and the U.S. marshals were able to draw on military assistance.[17]

The ongoing crisis fell between administrative responsibilities at the federal level between the Departments of State and Interior. Blaine sent a note to Secretary of the Interior Kirkwood about "the present unfortunate condition of affairs on the frontier" and the fact that "the territorial authorities are unable to prevent the lawlessness which is manifest in that quarter." Blaine wanted the Department of the Interior to get control of the situation because the crimes and incompetence of the local authorities were creating problems with large diplomatic impact. When Kirkwood investigated, the acting governor reported back that "a bitter hatred exists between the 'cowboys' and the Mexicans generally." J. W. Evans, the U.S. marshal for Arizona Territory, told the governor of Sonora that he understood "the great and irreparable injury the people of Sonora, Mexico are suffering and have been for more than a year past at the hands of marauders invading Sonora from Arizona," but he did not think the Department of Justice was fully aware of what was going on.[18]

Since order had not been established in the southern counties, there was no extradition of criminals for a time. But there *was* transborder pursuit of fugitives, especially of Indians into Mexico, some of it legal and some of it not. Unlike so many other border incursions in this era, these incidents on the Arizona-U.S. border caused only mild diplomatic controversies. This relative calm was aided by a common national interest in fighting the Apaches as well as the settlement of a reciprocal agreement for border-crossing in the hot pursuit of Indians on May 11, 1882.[19]

One notorious incursion was led by Captain W. J. Ross, deputy sheriff of Pima County, Arizona, and his posse in July 1882, who for two months penetrated "hundreds of miles" into the Mexican countryside and killed "thirty-seven Apaches in Mexico, mostly women and children." This clearly was not an opportunistic hot pursuit over the border. Ross was caught, disarmed, and expelled from Mexican territory by General Bernado Reyes of Sonora. Secretary of State Frederick T. Frelinghuysen dealt with this incident on an informal basis, asking Matías Romero to contact Sonora directly and get the weapons shipped back so that the request did not have to go through the U.S. legation at Mexico City. He wanted to "dispose of the matter frankly and amicably" and even "refrain[ed] from any criticism of General Reyes' course on disarming and exposing to the dangers of a tedious march through wild country a body of men on a mission of justice and good will."[20]

The United States was much more apologetic a year later when another Pima County deputy sheriff, W. H. Daniels, pursued American fugitives from a murder charge as far as 110 miles south of the boundary line into Chihuahua. Daniels defended his actions because the murders had been "most atrocious and [the fugitive's] speedy trial and execution [would] rid the border of an assassin and serve to deter the commission of a like crime by those of his gang who are yet at large." He claimed to have the support of Mexican officials in the pursuit, but Mexico disagreed.[21]

The chaos, violence, and lawlessness of both criminals and officials subsided by the mid-1880s, and with the establishment of legal order came a greater emphasis on extradition. In his second biennial message, Governor F. A. Tritle recognized that the border between Arizona and Sonora and Chihuahua was still the "only marked exception to the peace and order of the Territory." He stressed the need to strengthen extradition relations as a sure way to lessen tensions: "at times differences have arisen over the pursuit and arrest of criminals by one people upon the soil of the other, and questions relating to extradition. For the welfare of our citizens along the border it is of the utmost importance that our relations with Mexico do not become strained in this respect, and that the most liberal facilities be afforded for the detection and punishment of crime, which might at times unjustly be ascribed by the citizens of one country to those of the other." He called for "modification of the treaty relations . . . as will provide for greater security to residents near the border, and reduce the difficulties and delays of extradition," implying that the problems of extradition were ones of speed and accessibility more than anything else.[22]

By 1888 there seemed to be less of an issue with returning citizens to Mexico and receiving them on the Arizona-Mexico border, and a spirit of relative reciprocity blossomed. It started in the summer of 1888, when Arizona officials surrendered to Sonora an American railroad robber, Conrad Rohling, along with a Canadian, Jean Fallier (a.k.a. J. J. Taylor), for thefts on the passenger and express train of the Sonora Railroad. The body of a third member of this gang, who had been killed by the sheriff's posse at Tombstone, was left in Nogales after being identified. Just a week later, a cattle thief named Edwards Lopez (alias "Pluma Blanca") and a murderer named Manuel Grijabra were "immediately" extradited from Mexico on the basis of a requisition from the Arizona governor, which the U.S. Consul at Guaymas, Alexander Willard, celebrated as "the first time that the State Government of Sonora has delivered Mexican citizens to be tried and punished in the United States." He attributed this change to "the delivery of J. J. Taylor and Conrad Rohling, the Sonora train robbers and assassins." Willard considered these exchanges "proof of friendly relations which exists between the American and Mexican Authorities of Arizona (U.S.) and Sonora (Mexico)." He called it, more clearly, the "first time . . . in a formal manner" that such an exchange had occurred.[23] Nonetheless, other extralegal methods continued apace.

THE "MONGOLIAN IRRUPTION"

A different kind of fugitive escape suddenly appeared as a significant and po-litically resonant problem on the border. Much of the jurisdictional energy in Arizona in the mid-1880s became directed toward control of the Chinese popu-lation, which had newly become such an important aspect of the transnational migrant and labor system in the region. Of particular concern was illegal Chi-nese border-crossing from Sonora that started as a result of the Chinese Exclu-sion Act of 1882 and increased steadily. Representative Herman Lehlbach, chair of the House Select Committee on Immigration and Naturalization tasked with handling the Chinese question in 1890, called the route through Mexico a "mode of invasion." More dramatically (if erroneously), the *El Paso Daily Times* called it the "Mongolian irruption."[24]

The Chinese issue was one in which U.S. policies of strict territoriality in the borderlands began to be seriously tested in a sustained way on the subject of migration, which presented far different constraints and quandaries than did the more common criminal, Native American, smuggling, and revolutionary issues dominating the era. As Erika Lee has argued, the creation of institutional structures to enforce this exclusion provides a key consideration of "the role of race in the state building processes of the nineteenth and twentieth centu-ries." And state action produced unintended effects. Chinese movement across the U.S.-Mexican line was in fact ironically produced as "a direct consequence of successful border enforcement in the north," on the Canadian border. The combination of racial exclusion and enhanced borderlands security triggered in the southern borderlands what Samuel Truett termed "a fugitive landscape of smuggling rings, border crossings, and border patrols."[25]

At the federal level, the process of Chinese exclusion at the Sonora-Arizona boundary was a microcosm of the expansion of unrestrained governance over immigrant movement at the borders. Gerald Neuman has punctured the "pleas-ant" myth of open immigrant borders, revealing how they were in fact not quan-titatively closed but closed only to targeted populations. This was a Hobbesian variant of U.S. power directed against aliens paradoxically operating within an "anti-Hobbesian constitutional tradition."²⁶ This trick was accomplished through legislation, executive action in interdiction, and expansive Supreme Court cases (often grouped as "the Chinese Exclusion Cases") like *Chae Chan Ping v. United States* in 1889, which settled the absolute sovereignty of the federal government in immigration cases. As Justice Field wrote in a crystalline expression of his view on sovereign territoriality as applied to the case:

> [T]hat the government of the United States, through the action of the legislative department, can exclude aliens from its territory is a proposition which we do not think open to controversy. *Jurisdiction over its own territory to that extent is an incident of every independent nation. It is a part of its independence....* While under our Constitution and form of government the great mass of local matters is controlled by local authorities, the United States, in their relation to foreign countries and their subjects or citizens, are one nation, invested with powers which belong to independent nations, the exercise of which can be invoked for the maintenance of its absolute independence and security throughout its entire territory.²⁷

Field of course here cited Marshall's *Exchange v. McFaddon*, and *Chae Chan Ping* was indeed a strong reaffirmation of this venerable decision. Territoriality was applied to Chinese exclusion but directly congruent with the Supreme Court decisions on sovereignty and unitary federal authority (many of which were written by Field) that governed the approach to other issues explored in this book such as extradition and extraterritorial jurisdiction. Of particular relevance to the borderlands was Field's strident, and even joyful, statement of federal plenary power:

> The control of local matters being left to local authorities, and national matters being entrusted to the government of the union, the problem of free institutions existing over a widely extended country, having different climates and varied interests, has been happily solved. For local interests, the several states of the union exist, but for national purposes, embracing our relations with foreign nations, we are but one people, one nation, one power. To preserve its independence, and give security against foreign aggression and encroachment, is the highest duty of every nation, and to attain these ends nearly all other considerations are to be subordinated. It matters not in what form such aggression and encroachment come, whether from the foreign na-

tion acting in its national character, or from vast hordes of its people crowd-
ing in upon us.[28]

In Field's view, the division between local and federal preserved the jurisdiction of both and freed the latter for unrestricted pursuit of its "highest duty"
in foreign relations through the protection of sovereign territoriality. Chinese
immigrants were as legitimate a focus of this foreign relations power as was an
invading nation, and this allowed the foreign policy power to be applied quite
close to home, at the border where these "vast hordes" crowded.

In considering the significance of the Supreme Court Chinese exclusion
cases, T. Alexander Aleinikoff emphasizes a policy approach based on "federal
unilateralism," which he defines as "the authority of the national government to
impose governing structures and substantive legal norms as it deems appropriate," importantly though not exclusively through the Supreme Court. The Chinese Exclusion Cases were an example of how the Supreme Court viewed territoriality as a basis for "virtually unlimited congressional power" over borders
and admissions of people rooted in "mystical notions of sovereignty." Aleinikoff
argues that "behind these cases lay a vision of the United States as a *nation-state*:
a *state* endowed with the power to control its territory and take its place as an
equal among other foreign states and a *nation* that defined itself in ethno-racial
terms as Anglo-Saxon." Different ethnic groups got access to the legal spaces of
the nation depending on their relative level of "civilization."[29] This was a strikingly similar variant of the approach to global legal spatiality underlying U.S.
foreign relations in this period.

Exclusion in fact invited territorial incursion and made the border a loose
space, as illegal Chinese migration through Mexico across the permeable U.S.
border became strikingly common. In an unintentionally ironic phrase, U.S.
Consul Willard in Guaymas first denied but slowly came to see that the Chinese were attempting to use his consular district as a "stepping stone" into the
United States. P. J. Dowling, part owner of the El Rosario Mine on the boundary line near Quitobaquito, reported "large numbers of Chinamen are crossing at, and in the vicinity of his place, into Arizona and California" at the start
of 1890. U.S. Consul Delos H. Smith in Nogales reported that he "hardly know
whether or not I am right in reporting this matter, but the 'Exclusion Act' seems
to justify it."[30]

Soon thereafter, the consuls along this section of the boundary line became focused on the numbers, patterns, and significance of this illicit movement of Chinese across the line, and significant state bureaucracy was oriented to gain control of it.[31] Willard assiduously counted the ships and numbers of passengers and reported the numbers leaving for El Paso and Nogales "so that we can be prepared to intercept them, should they endeavor to cross the boundary line into the United States." On May 8, 1890, he reported counting fifty-nine who left for the border and was happy to discover that "six of said Chinamen a few days after were captured at Nogales."[32]

The next month, Warner P. Sutton, now at Nuevo Laredo, reported approximately one hundred Chinese being brought in bond through the United States to Piedras Negras and then Nogales, Arizona, and Eagle Pass. Sutton's travels had shown him that "considerable numbers were coming to Ensenada . . . Guaymas, Mazatlan, and other ports on the West coast" and from there into California, Arizona, New Mexico, or Texas. He warned (though his numbers were guesses) that "unless extreme care is taken, several thousand will find their way across the border within a year." The desire to come was strong, and the "geographical conditions [provided that] this can be easily done."[33]

This Chinese migration eventually did involve very large numbers of individuals (including approximately one thousand through Guaymas in 1890 alone) arriving in a variety of ways from a variety of points. Only after a 1899 agreement could Chinese arrive directly into Mexico. Direct steamer service was not established until 1902, so the most common route was to land in the United States and then travel in bond to Mexico. Ships commonly arrived in the Mexican port of Guaymas from San Francisco carrying dozens to hundreds of people, many of whom upon landing made their way to the Sonora-Arizona border and to the California border north of Ensenada. T. J. Phelps, a customs collector in California, found "there was undoubtedly a scheme on foot to send great numbers around through Mexico into Arizona and New Mexico and California, etc." Representative Lehlbach thought this bonded trade could be "promptly suppressed by a recent order of the Secretary of the Treasury directing the collector of customs to refuse a transit permit to any Chinese bound to a Mexican port, whereupon they were denied a landing and returned to China." As it happened, however, the Treasury Department directive was not sufficient to stop crossings at the Mexican border in the least; all that changed was the route as Chinese headed directly into Mexican ports like Guaymas.[34]

By 1895, consuls were reporting that "it appears there is a steady migration of Chinese from Havana to Tampico with through tickets to El Paso. As no Chinaman stays in Mexico who can by hook or crook make his way into the United States, the inquiry is pertinent what becomes of those thus ticketed through to El Paso." The next year, the *El Paso Times* reported "five hundred Chinaman are idle in this city [Ciudad Juárez] and watching for an opportunity to gain entrance to the United States." But Consul Charles W. Kindrick thought this was an exaggeration, though "it is undoubtedly true there are a great many and that their object in remaining here is to gain admission to the United States."[35]

George Pattison, collector of customs in San Francisco, testified to Congress that he rode with a bonded group to Ensenada in 1890, where fifteen of the fifty Chinese aboard went ashore. These same individuals were then soon captured in San Diego. The rest were caught in Arizona, which "fully demonstrated the fact that they used the Republic of Mexico simply as a ruse to get in here." Pattison repeated this journey several times, always with the same outcome.[36]

The scale of the movement made efforts to control it difficult to conceive fully, let alone implement. Testifying before the House Select Committee on Immigration and Naturalization tasked to rationalize Chinese exclusion, John Leary (a Washington mayor) perfectly captured the challenge: "How to enforce the exclusion act is another thing. With the northern portion of Mexico and the Sandwich Islands it would be impossible for this Government to enforce the act, as the extent of territory is such that it would be impossible almost to keep out the Chinese. We have thousands of miles to protect." Leary's idea was that "a commercial treaty or treaty of some kind would not be a bad thing" as a way to embed the immigration issue into more persuasive topics. He also called for what was emerging as an increasingly appealing solution for control: an organized system of government surveillance and control. He called for "a complete record of these Chinese . . . with their photographs attached, [so] that you could control or in a measure protect not only the Chinese who have a right to be here, but control the coming in of others. I would give those who are entitled to be here, a certificate, and a Chinaman without any certificate would not have any right to be here and I would enforce the law against him."[37]

Combination of surveillance and identification was a popular approach to the problem of control in this vast endeavor. It was the establishment of clear state sovereignty calibrated to the individual level. In California's first ports of entry, inspectors dealing with Chinese traveling in bond through the United States to Mexico were sometimes deeply suspicious and even hostile, and they embraced novel controls. Chinese Inspector J. D. Putnam, headquartered in Los Angeles, saw such controls as the answer to the problem of Chinese entering fraudulently and claiming the bonded travel to Mexico merely as a means of returning north by sneaking across the border. Putnam testified that in addition to bonded travelers en route to San Diego, he was personally aware of three boat loads of Chinese from Mexico who had landed on the coast near L.A., with nineteen to twenty-six people each time, in the space of five months. Both bonded returnees and illegals were aided, he said, "through the different ports by connivance with so-called Chinese attorneys, who are allowed to appear and argue cases before the several collectors of customs, presenting Chinese evidence which is wholly unreliable, and often backing such evidence by that of Jews or hangers-on about Chinese quarters, or others seeking the trade of Chinese." Putnam had a low opinion of this legal assistance: "The general standing and character of attorneys who represent the Chinese immigrant become very low after a considerable time is devoted to the work in that line. I believe that they, as a rule, become perfectly unscrupulous, and are ready to wink at or connive to introduce perjured evidence of the rankest Mud."[38]

Putnam's solution was two part: a government surveillance and control bureaucracy reinforced by a public program of surveillance. He called for the creation of a sophisticated and thorough identification system wherein photographs and identifying information on bonded Chinese travelers were gathered: "as accurate a description [should] be taken of them as is taken of a soldier who enlists in the United States Regular Army, and a description and photograph of these passing in bond [should] be forwarded to ports of entry along the Mexican border." The analogy with the lot of a soldier—a subject under complete control of the state—was an interesting one, and scholars of modern surveillance indeed date most U.S. practices to those developed expressly out of the imperatives of control in the governance of Chinese exclusion.[39] Putnam's other solution was to encourage public vigilance with "a reward of $5 for each person, Chinese or others, who will give information leading to the arrest and deportation of Chinese illegally within the United States, to be paid after deportation." This payment, he believed, would be more effective at "detecting frauds than the addition of twenty new inspectors, as Chinese and those engaged in the business make it their business to know the whereabouts of the officers of the Government, and when attempting to cross the line or land a party they have their signs and signals."[40] A combination of an intrusive state and a suspicious citizenry could produce tight social control.

The exclusion of Chinese nationals, and especially the borderland interdiction efforts, invited this kind of jurisdictional innovation. The United States responded to Chinese illicit border-crossing by refracting the new laws through existing jurisdictions and creating new structures and positions to handle the work. Some of these were more impressive in name than in impact on the ground. Each customs district appointed a special "Chinese Inspector" who was acquainted with the complicated law. A special agent of the Treasury Department, L. S. Irwin, was sent to Sonora to grapple with the issue of extraterritorially. Sutton called for the Treasury Department to send "a good man" to Ensenada and not an "indiscreet" one and for the numbers of special agents operating within other parts of Mexico as far away as Tampico to be increased. "Vigorous action is necessary to enforce the law," he warned. Consul Willard felt confident that "the precautions taken and vigilance exercised along the U.S. boundary by our Government officials will make the clandestine crossing to U.S. territory of this class of persons somewhat difficult." A month later, he rejoiced that this increased interdiction was indeed working, as "the recent capture of 20 odd Chinamen by the U.S. officials prove this fact."[41]

Yet this border force remained small and inadequate considering the size of the task and territory involved, as was so common in borderland jurisdictional issues. The border force was also a good indication of the disconnect between national policy and ambitions and regional realities that encouraged local variations in implementation.[42] George Pattison, the collector of customs, testified that he was "sorry to say" that the force on the Arizona-Sonora line was "not sufficient to guard anything or scarcely anything." It was too small and widely dispersed in this difficult area with such a long and sometimes forbidding border: "Our custom-house in Tombstone, Arizona, is 30 or 35 miles from the borderline, and there is only one man guarding a line of something like 80 miles long, and that is not sufficient to prevent anything from coming in. . . . He may accidentally stumble onto a Chinaman or something else, but it would be an accident." But he did not think it was worth it to invest much money expressly for anti-Chinese interdiction efforts or to try to staunch the flow unless perhaps such action was coupled with a broader effort to stop the smuggling of goods like cattle, cigars, and "a drink known to the Mexicans as mescal."[43] Given the consistent lack of success on these fronts (a later 1898 report on the *Zona Libre* noted bluntly that "this individual smuggling will exist forever"), it was certainly extremely difficult to conceive how the border could be secured against migrants who were determined to cross.[44]

There was also a strong effort made to govern the locales where captured Chinese were sent, since there was confusion about whether the law required they be sent back to China or Mexico. Representative Herman Stump's idea was that "it was presumable that the Chinaman came from China." As T. J. Phelps, a collector of customs, testified to the House, the Chinese should only be sent back to Mexico if they had become Mexican citizens. Otherwise, when sent back across the border, a fugitive "would sit down on his haunches and wait till the marshal came back here, and then he would follow him back across the line."[45]

Competent or not in illegal interdiction, the apparatus of state control did have an impact on Chinese merchants in Nogales who tried to enter the country *legally* in order to travel through the United States to other parts of Mexico. Since a large number of Chinese settled in Sonora and some even became Mexican citizens, Consul Willard raised "an interesting question" about what would happen "as to their entering the United States, not as a Chinaman, but as citizens of a sister Republic." Willard did not raise here (or elsewhere) the equally "interesting question" about revising the status of *Mexican* citizens crossing the border, so the emphasis was on Chinese ethnicity trumping all citizenship distinctions created by law. In Willard's view of the process, in becoming Mexican citizens, the Chinese did not necessarily gain a whole new standing by moving up the sliding scale of civilization. Nor did they really become "Mexican." (Though by law, as citizens, they had become relatively free of extradition, if the Mexican state so desired.[46])

Josiah E. Stone, vice consul at Nogales, was unclear about how to handle individuals "considered . . . as Mexican subjects under Mexican law," whom he apparently could not bring himself to simply call "Mexicans." Stone wanted to understand exactly which obstacles were appropriate to construct when they tried to cross the border. He wrote to the State Department on February 11, 1892, for guidance about a particular case, which was merely "one of a number of instances in which Chinese merchants established in business in Mexico desiring to pass through the United States to point beyond and to return later on by the same way."[47]

This case involved twenty-seven-year-old businessman Lau Chy, who was permanently in business in Sonora and bought a great deal of supplies from the United States. He was not a transient migrant but an established businessman earning two thousand dollars a year as a shoe manufacturer and was considered, according to his affidavits from Mexican municipal officials, to be of good character and reputation. He merely wanted to travel the fastest route to Mexico City through Nogales and El Paso. Willis P. Haynes, the acting collector at Nogales, refused to let him go without a bond and a passel of identification documents "in view of the increasing stringency of the Department regulations governing the entry of the prohibited classes." He told Chy to follow the requirements that were suggested by the local Chinese Inspector, Emile Solignac. When Chy met these requirements the next day, Haynes found yet another technicality in the law and denied him entry. But Haynes professed to have rejected Chy repeatedly while "not wishing however to act otherwise than in strict conformity to the letter and spirit of the laws relating to Chinese exclusion or in any manner work an injustice to those lawfully entitled to the privilege of entry or transit."[48]

These cases appeared regularly and increased as the Chinese business presence grew significantly in Sonora.[49] Mexican citizens were subjected to a variety of requirements for passage. In another case, in order to travel through the United States on the way to China, Tang Leung submitted "a photographic likeness and full description" as well as "certificates signed by the most prominent citizens and capitalists of Nogales Arizona neither of whom is Chinese." This exact language was repeated in several cases. In order to cross at Nogales in October 1898, Lau Chi, Lau Chan, and Chin Chan Jin, businessmen from Magdalena, Hermosilla, and Guaymas, respectively, had to provide "testimony of representative business men (not Chinese) of Magdalena" and detailed accounting of the amount invested in their firms *six* years prior to travel.[50] Thus, clearly the pure racialism of exclusion produced complexities in the treatment of citizenship as well as intrusive and bizarre regimes of control in the same borderlands that were so given to disorder and exception in other respects discussed in this chapter.

It was no coincidence that given its treatment of Chinese immigrants and notion of the application of legality within the process, the United States did not recognize the need to create extradition relations with China, which of course fell under U.S. extraterritorial jurisdiction. It was not necessary to establish formal extradition treaties with states with which the United States had extraterritorial status. There were no jurisdictional impediments to the arrest of U.S. nationals in extraterritorial relations and no corresponding recognition of Chinese jurisdiction. Neither was there a push or need to create reciprocal obligations as an exception to the decidedly anti-reciprocal extraterritorial agreement. During a thorough survey of U.S. global extradition relations in 1889, Charles Denby told the State Department that no extradition treaty was sought or thought necessary with China. Although the American legation in China did itself practice extradition with European extraterritorial states in China, Denby wrote that "it has been held in this legation and by the consuls that an American who is charged with being an absconding criminal from any country with which we have extradition treaties can be arrested in China by our consuls and delivered up after the proof required by the treaties has been made." China, should it desire the return of a fugitive, was left without a formal option. Denby wrote that for "the arrest and delivery of Chinese subjects who are charged with crime committed in the United States, the only course now available is an appeal to the comity of this Government." He did not doubt that the United States would comply with such a request, but there was none on file.[51]

SERIO-COMEDIES OF JURISDICTION

Aside from the reprehensible Chinese exclusion regime, some territorial jurisdiction issues in the Arizona borderlands at the end of the 1890s were comical, even if they did also engage critical issues. These episodes of local disorder demonstrated how the legal spatiality at the borderline helped to cement the sensibilities of Americans eager to prove their suspicions of Mexican malfeasance. A couple of examples demonstrate this clearly.

One bizarre crisis was created by Jesus Garcia on a drunken night in July 1893 in Nogales, Arizona. While out on a bender, Garcia fought another Mexican national named Celedonio Carrillo and was then arrested for disturbing the peace. He was arrested by an American deputy sheriff, John Roberts, who had been on the Mexican side of the boundary when he observed the fight break out and ran back into the United States to grab the troublemaker. Garcia managed to break away and ran back for the borderline, which bisected the town, and Roberts and another man (an American citizen) named Alfonso Bachelier tackled him. Bachelier thereafter struck Garcia on the head at least once, which became the grounds for much dispute, as did the later blow on the head Roberts delivered with a "leather walking stick" as Garcia was being brought to jail.

The Garcia case produced immediate and intense local controversy, and this spilled over not just into calls for political action but into acts of violence. Arrest warrants were put out for Roberts and Bachelier, a baker who made regular deliveries on both sides of the border, so as "long as the order of arrest remain[ed] in force his business [was] handicapped." Meanwhile, the now-free Garcia assaulted Mr. Wylie, the postmaster of Nogales, Arizona, when he crossed into Mexico to buy a cigar. It was reported that "[f]or this outrage he [Garcia] was arrested by Mexican authorities and sent as a convict to the army, which is the same as the penitentiary with us."[52] Though he might have been physically removed from the picture, the issues remained and filtered up to the diplomatic level. Thus did the arrest of a local drunk (and his place of falling) easily become magnified into a typically broad dispute over territorial sanctity, with the added twist that it was an *American* outrage that caused it.

A dispute immediately arose that captivated the authorities along the border and simmered locally before becoming a matter of diplomatic controversy. There were quite a few questions about exactly how much of Garcia's body landed in Mexico when he was tackled, where Roberts was standing when he tackled Garcia, whether Bachelier pushed Garcia back into the United States before tackling him, and how much damage Bachelier did to Garcia's face when striking him. The United States claimed there was nary a mark on him, and Mexico insisted he was "cruelly beaten." Both inevitably had different theories of his location at the time of the arrest (or, more specifically, of how and where his body landed after being tackled).

American officials in Nogales, Sonora, for reasons that took years to emerge, sought an informal solution to the problem that would sidestep a political firestorm. This kind of transnational deal was a common if not daily means of adjusting relations in this bifurcated town. As part of a secret, unwritten deal between Manuel Masearenas, president (mayor) of Nogales, Sonora, and U.S. Vice-Consul Reuben D. George, Garcia was returned, and everybody agreed to hush up the deal and not pursue the jurisdictional question at the federal level in Mexico. Masearenas did not fulfill this pledge, and the ensuing controversy dragged on for an astounding three-and-a-half years.[53]

There was some later dispute about the origins of the George-Masearenas deal, but a letter George sent to the U.S. legation at Mexico City in December 1893 noted that he had investigated and decided that Bachelier had indeed pushed Garcia back into the United States from Mexican territory and that Mexico had "just cause for complaint." George told the State Department he did not want to "burden [it] with useless correspondence," so he took matters into his own hands and arranged, privately, to have the Arizona justice of the peace remit the fine and release Garcia and deliver him to the Mexican officials, who in turn agreed to drop the matter. He thought "peace and goodwill [were] apparently restored" with this. But this piece of private diplomacy quickly soured, and to cover his actions, George later stressed that he had been encouraged to make this move. He was especially frustrated because "the man over which all this trouble occurred was not of good standing, but one of those individuals who are more or less of a disturbing element on the frontier."[54]

Mexico made a surprisingly strong official protest to the arrest because the Garcia arrest, small as it was, seemed to be part of a renewed pattern of aggressive U.S. cross-border incursions. The usually conciliatory Matías Romero wrote Secretary of State Walter Q. Gresham on September 6, 1893, that "my Government instructs me, furthermore, to call the serious attention of your Department to the frequency with which violations of Mexican territory have recently been committed by United States officers, an instance of which is afforded by the entrance into Mexico of Texas rangers, who advanced as far as the town of Tres Jacales, in the State of Chihuahua, for the purpose of arresting Jesus Holguin." Romero wrote, in phrasing that must have been satisfying given the regular expression of "outrage" in U.S. complaints to Mexico, that it was time that the United States "put a stop to these outrages and . . . prevent their occurrence in the future."[55]

The Jesus Holguin pursuit of June 30, 1893, was a far more significant incident in which Captain Frank C. Jones of the Texas Rangers crossed the border in an area where the Texas governor claimed "the boundary line between the United States and Mexico has never been so definitely settled as to be known except by citizens of long residence on the border" because "the old river-bed, the true boundary line between Mexico and the United States has become filled up and so obliterated that it is practically impossible for it to be recognized." This was a much more typical (and more profound) jurisdictional problem than was the arrest of Garcia in Nogales, where no such boundary confusion existed.[56]

Back in Nogales, the United States continued to insist on Sheriff Robert's jurisdiction and rectitude based in part on Robert's affidavit sent by the Arizona governor two and a half years after the incident, a self-serving move that Mexico considered both a sham and an affront. Mexican Chargé d'Affaires Miguel Covarrubias was also appalled to have learned that Vice-Consul George had attempted to make a secret, even shady deal with the local authorities to end the case. It was a cover-up for an illegal arrest that was really more like an abduction coupled with a territorial invasion of sovereignty:

> Setting aside what there is untenable in the pretensions of the vice consul, since invasions of territory are very serious offenses which are always the occasions of claims between government and government through their re-

spective diplomatic agents, and can not be settled by confidential agreement between subordinate authorities and simple consular agents, the fact that the aforesaid vice-consul proposed this arrangement by asking the local authorities if they were disposed to overlook the matter provided he should return their man to them ("if they would drop the matter if I turned their man over to them") shows that the arrest was not effected in the Territory of Arizona. This confession of culpability and the proposal of reparation could only have been made in view of the results of the investigation which he conducted— that is to say, that the unfortunate Garcia was arrested and beaten in Mexican territory by the sheriff Roberts and Bachelier, and taken by force to the territory of the United States.[57] Mexico demanded reparations but the U.S. instead sent R. Hughes Long to Nogales for the first time, "fresh upon the ground and altogether unbiased, and . . . fair-minded" and it was his report that they based a strong rejection of Mexico's claim.

Long fought vigorously to prevent the State Department from accepting blame for the incident or for paying reparations to Garcia or to Mexico and produced evidence to support his point, including a map of the Garcia arrest notable for its attention to detail. Long thought it was "possible that [Garcia's] head and a small portion of his body were on the Mexican side" but that his feet and "part, if not all of his body were on the American side of the International Boundary Line." To Long, although he was "fresh upon the ground," Garcia represented more than simply a troublesome drunk; he was a sign of all the difficulty American law faced on the border. He determined that there was "no question but [t]hat Jesus Garcia is a low down Mexican desperado" and that the "most prominent citizens" described Garcia as "a general drunk bulldozing the saloons." Long wrote that he felt "that it is an imposition that our Government is called on to pay a cent to such a man as Jesus Garcia, not alone because [he] is a low down Mexican tough, but a desperado of the overbearing kind that have given so much trouble along the frontier." Long's report was scathing and determined, and his language was clearly strong, though he (or some later editor in the State Department) did ask that his statements that specifically identified Garcia as a Mexican (such as the phrases "low down Mexican desperado" and "low down Mexican tough") be for officials' eyes only and omitted from the final report. This language was removed from the copy of the official report that was printed and forwarded to Mexico in November 1896.[58]

Long also argued that Vice-Consul George did the right thing in creating the secret deal, not least because he had apparently received a telegram (which had been mysteriously lost) from the State Department at the time of the arrest, which read "if this man is a reputable citizen, fight the case, and if not drop it." Long felt that the reason George was being pilloried was because the former mayor of Sonora who agreed to the deal was now the Mexican consul in Nogales, Arizona, and was trying to bury the issue. "Knowing the peculiar conditions along the frontier and the peculiar location of the International Boundary Line in these two towns," Long felt that George made a prudent decision in order to maintain good relations. Mexico, for reasons not entirely clear, aside from accepting that Roberts "had no intention of violating the territory of Mexico," dropped the case after Long's investigation. Perhaps the hand-drawn map and the consciously moderated racial language of the report helped end the three-year ordeal.[59]

Another case of the extradition of James Temple in 1898 was more serious in potential impact since it mirrored the Cutting case quite exactly in the assertion of Mexican extraterritorial jurisdiction but was something of a constructed farce before being easily resolved in an extradition surrender. The reason it had more potential to endanger the peace was, simply, that the outrage was felt this time on the U.S. side of the border, and as was not uncommon, tempers and rhetoric ran hot. This case not only exhibited in fact the typical trajectory of a borderlands outrage but also revealed how readily an extradition decision would squelch concerns over the corrosions of extraterritoriality.

Temple was arrested in Mexico for carrying concealed weapons shortly after the killing of a Mexican citizen named Juan Arvallo in Nogales, Arizona. When the charge in Arizona was changed to murder (perhaps in self-defense) the arrest charge in Sonora was correspondingly updated, and Temple was charged in a state court under the extraterritorial provisions of the Mexican penal code, Article 186.[60]

Temple's situation was clearly laid out to U.S. Consul J. F. Darnall by Ramon Corral, governor of Sonora, on November 9, 1898. Despite (or perhaps because of) the clear provisions of Article 186, which Corral detailed and which he knew were still contested even more than a decade after the Cutting case, Corral indicated that since this was a homicide case, he was "desiring to serve [Darnall]" to resolve it without Temple having to face justice in Mexico. Corral said he would inquire with the secretary of foreign relations whether Temple could be extradited to Arizona instead. Darnall seemed poised to be outraged, and he was. Incredibly, the next day after being informed of this process by the governor, Darnall complained to Washington that Corral "refuses to recognize my protest" and that Temple's trial was progressing. In a series of telegrams and dispatches conveying increasing alarm, Darnall ramped up fear that Temple's trial in Sonora was unfair and that the Mexican government was unresponsive but never let on that he had actually been informed of the process in place. Darnall claimed that Temple was being forced to sign confessions and was being bundled off to undisclosed locations. The trouble was, he had no evidence of either charge other than being "satisfied in my own mind" that this was the case. Darnall also detailed (and one suspects, encouraged) the popular agitation brewing among railroad workers with whom Temple worked, who were "much excited over it." On November 11, 1898, he claimed that he could "only hold American citizens from outbreak by promising active measures" since "they believe Temple will be shot without prompt interference."[61]

But this whole (non)crisis was defused quite easily when Powell Clayton, acting as envoy extraordinary and minister plenipotentiary, requested and readily received Temple's extradition to Arizona. Mariscal readily extradited Temple despite the fact that, as he noted in the surrender statement, the 1861 extradition treaty had been terminated on January 24, 1898. Clayton and Mariscal would sign the new U.S.-Mexican extradition convention on April 24, 1899.[62] If the experience of such cases revealed anything certain, it was that the refracted spaces of law in the borderlands allowed the principles of sovereign territoriality and the sanctity of jurisdiction to at times seem the most threatened when in fact the issues at stake were the least meaningful.[63]

THE GEOGRAPHY OF DISPUTE AT THE TEXAS-MEXICO BOUNDARY

One might think that the border was clearer in Texas given that the Rio Grande was not a trackless desert, but this boundary was itself extremely dynamic and for more than a century, was therefore even more problematic than the landed barrier to the west. Each shift in the shape and direction of the river brought changes to the land that in turn created jurisdictional confusion and snarls in governance. One historian calls the successive attempts to clarify the boundary line through ever-underfunded surveys "a nightmare." Because the Rio Grande "irritatingly shifted its channel from time to time transferring land from one nation to the other," the survey could never "be considered finished."[64] This geographic reality where territory actually switched sides of the river in turn stymied efforts to construct uniform jurisdictions, undercut property values, encouraged lawlessness, smuggling, and raids, and engendered diplomatic conflict. Without a clear geographic boundary, the decidedly contingent nature of legal spatiality in the Texas borderlands was strengthened enormously.

The U.S.-Mexican border that had been set by the 1848 Treaty of Guadalupe Hidalgo followed the middle of the Rio Grande. As Paula Rebert has explained, the treaty stipulated a line that existed both "up the middle of that river" and "following the deepest channel," and so the "delimitation was ambiguous" at best.[65] This channel is what remained in dispute for more than a century, and there were new boundary treaties and conventions signed in 1853, 1882, 1884, 1885, and 1888, with numerous extensions thereafter, to attempt to uncoil this jurisdictional snarl. The issue was finally given some teeth with the formation of the International Boundary Commission by treaty on March 1, 1889, granting it exclusive jurisdiction to resolve the issues.[66]

The use of water was an issue that grew over time into a crisis as agriculture and population grew along the river and irrigation use increased enormously on the American side. Nevertheless, in June 1880, Secretary of State Willam M. Evarts complained to Phillip H. Morgan at the embassy in Mexico City about what had been reported as the misuse of water by Mexicans living across the river from El Paso County: "The ground of the complaint, as alleged is that the Mexicans engaged in agricultural pursuits on the western short of the river, are in the habit of diverting all the water that comes down the river during the dry season into their ditches, thereby preventing our citizens from getting sufficient water to irrigate their crops." Evarts argued that this "if true, would be in direct opposition to the recognized rights of riparian owners and, if persisted in, must result in disaster and ruin to our faming population on the line of the Rio Grande, and might eventually, if not amicably adjusted through the medium of diplomatic intervention, be productive of constant strife and breaches of the peace between the inhabitants of either shore." This was only three years after the army commission investigating the Salt War had presciently forecasted that water would be the great borderlands conflict of the future, as it became in the twentieth century with complexities of jurisdiction and usage that Evarts would have had difficulty imagining.[67]

By 1889, General D. S. Stanley, the commander of the Department of Texas, wrote in the annual report to the secretary of war that this type of jurisdictional dispute could only be resolved by political action. The old assertions were no longer relevant: "Our relations with our Mexican neighbors upon the long line of the Rio Grande have been kindly, although they are a good deal excited over what they deem the violation of their riparian rights, through our people taking all the water of the Rio Grande for the irrigation of the San Luis Valley, which leaves the Rio Grande a dry bed for 500 miles. *The question is one that must be settled by the State Department, and thus far there has been no call for military force.*"[68] In the following years, water issues would become a topic of negotiation that would outshine many other borderland wrangles in terms of scale but minus the drama, violence, and overall tensions. The emphasis by 1900 was on politically adjusting the "violation of the spirit" of the treaty of 1848 and "equitable distribution of the waters."[69]

One of the largest jurisdictional problems, and certainly the one that produced the most intense disputes for a time, concerned *bancos*, which were islands or river cut-offs created by shifts in the course of the Rio Grande, erosion, and avulsion. The river could shift quite dramatically and very quickly, and as a result the islands, boundary, main river channel, and both territorial and riparian jurisdictions were in a constant state of flux. These pieces of territory varied in size but could be massive, with up to two hundred acres changing sides of the river or reforming within forty-eight hours. As the U.S. consul at Mier, Enrique Vizcaya, exclaimed, "changes have transferred portions several miles long containing often hundreds of acres of valuable land."[70] The riverbed itself could be dry, or there could be several channels that made it impossible to tell exactly where the border was. Anson Mills, the U.S. commissioner on the International Boundary Commission that "eliminated" the *bancos* in 1905, described the process of their formation:

Where the river passes through low alluvial bottoms with banks of fragile consistency and slight fall the channel continually changes from right to left, eroding the concave bank and depositing on the convex. This occurs in low as well as high water, though the changes are more marked during high water stages. . . . When the curve forms a circle the radius of which is dependent on the consistency of the earth and the volume and velocity of the water, erosions practically cease and the river turns upon itself in a circle and forms a "cut-off," leaving the land thus separated (called a *banco*) somewhat in the form of a pear or gourd, with the stem cut by the river's current at the moment of separation.[71]

Geographer James E. Hill Jr. characterized *bancos* as "political bridgeheads," a designation indicating an "extension of a nation's boundary and territorial control across a river."[72] This was precisely how they were seen by policymakers and locals at the time—as territorial invasions within an already-complicated political, economic, and legal context.

Because they constantly changed shape, sides of the rivers, and jurisdictions, *bancos* were themselves literally transnational places. The people who lived on them, permanently or not, also faced the reality of a changed national context for their lives and property with each shift of the river. Warner P. Sutton, indicating that changes of several miles were not uncommon, asked the State Department to visualize six particularly egregious examples of the dangers the moving river could potentially produce. He thought it was conceivable that "the national boundary at Fort Brown" could be shifted to Mexico, while Matamoros would transfer to the United States, and near Bagdad, a seven-by-ten-mile section could shift to Mexico, cutting through the Arroyo Colorado, leaving "2,000 square miles of this lower valley on the Mexican side." And all of this could just as easily be reversed. This exact problem was particularly serious in El Paso, where the consul observed that changes in the river brought new claims of jurisdiction and "[threw] public buildings and valuable property into Mexico. Citizens much excited."[73]

Jurisdiction over the *bancos* was governed by a stunning array of officials, from sheriffs, rangers, customs collectors, soldiers, cattlemen, departments, judges, governors, and the people who lived on them to the politicians and diplomats in the Departments of State, Interior, and War and the staff of the International Boundary Commission. A citizen named Juan Armendariz wrote Anson Mills, noting that "in 1896 or 1897 I called your attention to a piece or parcel of land, right in front of my house in Socorro, Texas, which belongs to me and is now on the Mexican side of the Rio Grande." Armendariz had been referred to the Mexican commissioner and to the Mexican authorities in the "little town" of Zaragoza, but nothing was accomplished for three years. He wrote in 1899 seeking closure to "see what can be done now in regard to this case, as I would like to know whether it is mine or not, as I am still paying taxes in this County for it."[74]

Jurisdiction over the *bancos* thus can be seen as a matter of significant state attention with regard to clarifying borders, stopping smuggling, securing and protecting property and taxation rights, and protecting cattle, timber, agriculture, and other pursuits. A very important objective was to establish and maintain clear and unilateral jurisdiction in these loose spaces of the borderlands as a way of bolstering the authority of the state in control of citizens. Sutton wrote that "it is not reasonable to presume that residents along such a boundary will assent to the idea that their citizenship and the nationality of their home shall vary with so variable a line. It is not practicable, nor right, nor in accord with the provisions of the treaty of 1848." With quite a bit less sympathy to the feelings of the individuals involved, W. W. Follet, the consulting engineer of the International Boundary Commission, wrote to Anson Mills in November 1899, as they prepared to create the final boundary settlement after decades of conflict: "it seems to me considering the ignorant population along the lower river that the sooner it is forgotten that a piece of land once belonged on the opposite side of the river—the better it will be for all parties."[75]

In very significant respects, *bancos* were not governed spaces at all. They had become significantly ungovernable because of uncertain nationality; they lay outside jurisdiction, were contested in ownership, and so were malleable or loose spaces. This stopped neither the states nor the two nations from asserting sovereignty over them. Individuals also saw opportunities on these newly formed lands. A. D. McCabe, the proprietor of the Zapata Drug Company, wrote the secretary of state that "there [are] two ilands in the Rio Grande in front of Carrizo, Texas that do not belong to Mexico. I wish to ask if they belong to the state of Texas or are they the property of the Federal Government. And which has criminal jurisdiction over the ilands, Texas or the United States government? [sic]"[76] *Bancos*, especially newly created ones, became independent, attractive nodes squatting between the national delineations on either side.

Smuggling from these *bancos* was a major activity and thus was also a major concern. Robert R. Hitt, chair of the House Committee on Foreign Affairs, stated in 1884 that "these *bancos* with their uncertain boundaries afford retreats from smugglers, thieves, kidnappers, murderers, and every class of criminals, as well as bases of supplied from which to carry on their operations free from interference by either Government. Liquors, tobacco, and all kinds of dutiable merchandise are taken there and smuggled into the United States as opportunity offers." Smugglers were essentially impossible to catch and if caught, were almost impossible to convict because of the difficulty of proving jurisdiction. The customs collector at Brownsville, who called the smuggling operations "nests," reported that two of his inspectors at Santa Maria found one hundred gallons of mezcal on the Balsa *banco* but "while they were on one side the liquor went out on the other, and was consumed at some big Christmas *bailes* about fifteen miles in the country." Hitt was mortified to learn that "at the last term of the United States district court at Brownsville, the most noted smuggling case was lost by the Government for want of that accurate knowledge that would satisfy the court" about jurisdiction of the *bancos*. It is interesting to note that the Brownsville inspector (and the whole report) did not necessarily agitate for the expansion of U.S. jurisdictional reach, just its clarification. The way to resolve the *bancos* issue was to give each side control of the cut-offs that appeared on their side of the main channel of the Rio Grande.[77]

Only very slowly did bilateral agreement emerge to permanently assign sovereignty in this fashion. The *bancos* issue resisted efforts to define, control, and govern it until fifty-eight identified *bancos* were at long last "eliminated" by a 1905 convention that gave the International Boundary Commission the means of fulfilling the terms of the treaty signed back in November 1884 (and each subsequent reaffirmation and extension over twenty years). Under the 1884 treaty, the dividing line was "forever" set at the 1853 determination, following "the center of the normal channel of the rivers named, notwithstanding any alterations in the banks or in the course of those rivers." The changes could include "slow and gradual erosion and deposit of alluvium," and as long as the river did not open an entirely new riverbed the line would remain the same. Article 2 of the treaty dealt fairly directly with *bancos* by deciding that "any other change wrought by the force of the current, whether by the cutting of a new bed, or when there is more than one channel by the deepening of another channel than that which marked the boundary at the time of the survey . . . shall produce no change in the dividing line as fixed by the surveys of the International Boundary Commission in 1884." The boundary line would remain and would "follow the middle of the original channel bed, even though this should become wholly dry or be obstructed by deposits."[78] This did not end *bancos* or the problems they produced, but it did systematize the core dispute. It certainly was no wonder that before this settlement, smuggling, crime, cattle theft and seizures, and other marginal activities flourished in these micro *bancos* borderlands within the borderlands.

Following the well-established pattern in Texas politics of linking all jurisdictional and territorial questions to the effervescent effort to end the *Zona Libre* for supposedly inhibiting regional development and encouraging crime, it is worth observing the ways in which the *bancos* issue was also harnessed to this project. In 1882, after Senator John Tyler Morgan introduced a resolution supporting reciprocity between the United States and Mexico, the discussion of the Texas senators quickly turned to *bancos* and the *Zona Libre* instead. This was not a leap; all of the issues were related, and all reflected the core need for assertive state action in the uncertain spaces of the borderlands. Even Senator Morrill of Vermont came to agree that reciprocity should be negotiated in light of the *Zona Libre* and the question of smuggling across the border. Texas Senator Samuel Bell Maxey thought a reciprocity treaty was "an actual necessity" and had been agitating for one since at least 1877. At this time, however, he was more interested in pursuing the issues that together provided the matrix for all interaction in the region. In so doing, he provided a succinct example of the ability of Texas politicians of the era to link all questions into one broad consideration of aggrieved borderlands jurisdiction:

> Living in a State bordering Mexico it has been my duty to investigate very closely and thoroughly this question of a treaty with Mexico. In addition to the great question of reciprocity, now so important, in addition to the great purpose which the Government ought to have in view to secure to the people of the United States the trade of Mexico, if possible, there are other and many reasons why a treaty should be made. The question of extradition comes in, the question of the *Zona Libre*, and the question of the present boundary, which, according to the treaty of 1848, is the main channel of the Rio Grande. That river is constantly changing its position. . . . [I]n all the troubles we have had down there, smugglers and others, citizens of Mexico, could come over on their own soil lying on our side of the river and prepare their raids upon our people. That question should be taken into consideration.[79]

Richard Coke, the other senator from Texas, also viewed Mexican reciprocity through the same lenses and as being bundled with the same concerns. He thought the boundary and *Zona Libre* issues should be the main subjects of U.S.-Mexican negotiation: "There are to-day large tracts of land in Texas, as the Rio Grande runs, that formerly were in Mexico; and *vice versa* large bodies of land in Mexico that formerly were in Texas," he said. The biggest problem was that shifts of the river were "throwing citizens of Texas into Mexico, and again throwing people of Mexico into Texas. The local courts on the Rio Grande have to deal with these questions and find them very troublesome." Only the federal government could solve the problem "in a way that would preclude further trouble." There were few evident concerns about federal overreach but many about the lack of power judiciously applied. And "again, there is the *Zona Libre*," said Coke, "a breeding nest for smugglers. It promotes smuggling upon that border to an extent that is not known, not appreciated, not believed, by those who are distant from that country."[80]

Both Maxey and Coke had heard rumors that the *Zona Libre* was to be extended, and both feared for the future as a result. Maxey was sure it "would be a curse to our entire frontier." Coke argued that "it should be insisted on that the establishment of the Free Zone upon the opposite bank of the Rio Grande is detrimental to the interests of the United States in every possible way. When the State authorities of Texas had so much trouble on the Rio Grande with marauders from Mexico it was produced almost entirely by the congregation of desperate and bad men in the *Zona Libre* who were congregated there for smuggling purposes and who made their raids into Texas from there." Coke wanted a different kind of liberalized economy in the region. Instead of expanding the *Zona*, Mexico should be opening its markets, legalizing American ownership of property in Mexico, and seeking to stabilize in order to attract investment. "The insecurity of person and property in Mexico heretofore has been such as virtually to exclude our people from the commerce of that country," Coke said. But "we are now establishing intimate relations with Mexico. Our railroad system is penetrating that country, and it becomes necessary that we should have a new agreement with Mexico in order to adapt our relations to existing and changing conditions."[81]

It was clear that the borderlands operated like a system wherein looseness in any aspect had a holistic impact. In considering disputes over *bancos* and other boundary jurisdictional questions, additional areas of looseness in the U.S.-Mexican relationship were brought into stronger relief: property ownership, citizenship, reciprocal trade, and the always-fascinating *Zona Libre*. Broad Mexican assertions of jurisdictional authority on U.S. territory (*bancos*) or on their own were met with near-equal interest in reversing them and gaining control of the space.

There were as many of these jurisdictional disputes as there were *bancos*, but one of the most important, which led to the 1884 treaty, was the issue of Morteritos Island in 1884. A dispute over ownership of it surfaced in March of that year when U.S. customs agents started collecting import duties on the island. Mexico, which based its general jurisdictional claims first on surveying the "deepest flow" of the river and then on property rights, declared that the island "has always been considered as Mexican territory" and that the border in fact was the dry riverbed running alongside it. Mexico claimed Morteritos as "Mexican Territory, with its accretions, and [protested] against any attempt on the part of the United States to exercise authority over that Island." Mexico also claimed jurisdiction over Sabinitos Island and other nearby small islands in the Rio Grande between Ringgold Barracks and Roma, Texas. The governor of Tamaulipas and the mayor of Mier both described American moves on Morteritos as "invading," "robbing," and "expelling" the proper inhabitants. The investigating Mexican engineer, Ignacio Garfias, determined this scientifically and through explanation of the longtime Mexican use of the island. He reported that "before the drawing of the dividing line, the islands were used interchangeably by the inhabitants of both banks of the river," especially during the dry season. He reported that the locals on Sabinitos "appeared genuinely amazed" that there was a question about sovereignty over the islands. Following this logic, in June of that year, Mexican customshouse officers crossed from Mier and "seized and conveyed to Mexican territory twenty-five head of cattle" from a number of American citizens.[82]

Adding to the confusion and helping to fuel the dispute was that these islands, and some smaller ones, had multiple names, such as islands No. 12 and 13 and the Beaver Islands. The U.S. Secretary of War claimed solid jurisdiction going back to 1848 but launched a new investigation under Brigadier General William H. Emory (who as a major in 1856 had been the chief of the U.S. Boundary Commission) to solidify the claim. J. L. Haynes, the customs collector at Brownsville, argued that the jurisdiction over the "two islands about which the Mexican local authorities are still raising questions" had been settled by the Boundary Commission, while they continued to "claim not only the Islands but also some 1,200 to 1,500 acres of land as accretion to the islands, in face of the fact that Islands and accretions are wholly attached to the Texas shore, and that there now exists only one Channel to the river and that the one made the boundary between the two Countries, by the Boundary Commission." Haynes asked for the military to be deployed to "protect our territory and jurisdiction from invasion" and stop the clearly impending bloodshed. In fact, calling out military forces to assert and enforce jurisdiction on *bancos* was a regular policy.[83]

Secretary of State Frelinghuysen discussed and met with Romero many times, and the correspondence and evidence submitted between the two countries on this issue was commensurately enormous. Through a combination of will, relentless discussion, and eventually some hard evidence, Frelinghuysen convinced Romero of the justice of the American claim. The secretary argued that the jurisdiction question was "appearing to be one of simply fact" that U.S. control of the island dated to 1848, and he believed that General Emory's report conclusively supported this. Sabinitos, or Sabinos, "is a large single island" and now indeed seemed like it was Mexico.

Then there was another set of islands, called the Beaver Islands, or Island No. 13 (which was also known as Morteritos), paired with a smaller island that "may or may not be locally known as Sabinos" as well. In any case, despite the confusing double names, Frelinghuysen argued that the nomenclature was all "wholly immaterial, for both [of] the islands are by the two [boundary] Commissioners assigned to the United States." His point was that no matter what kind of claims of channels had been made or appeals to "the allegiance of the reputed Mexican owners of the land," the fact was that jurisdiction and ownership had been set by the treaties and boundary conventions and no alluvial changes could alter the realities.[84]

The inhabitants might claim "territorial jurisdiction of Mexico also" but "*annexation of U.S. territory by accretion or by change of channel could not be recognized.*" Also, the United States did "not admit . . . the right of alien owners of land to transfer, under color of any judicial agreement whatsoever, the territorial domain over their estates to the jurisdiction and sovereignty of the nation to whom such individuals owe allegiance." The Mexican claim of authority actually meant by extension that "the Mexican authorities at Mier [had] assumed to exercise territorial jurisdiction, not merely over the island of Moreteritos, but over part of the territory of the United States which [had] since accidentally been joined to that island by the closing of a water-way." Thus did Frelinghuysen cast the *bancos* issue in broader terms of defense of the overall territorial integrity of the United States and its "effort to assert the jurisdictional power belonging to us of right."[85]

The United States did tell its border troops to stand down until the jurisdictional dispute was resolved and to "avoid forcible assumption of jurisdiction." Frelinghuysen told Philip H. Morgan that after the Mexicans backed off, the State Department would consider a new set of negotiations over fixing the boundary permanently, but not before. The issue of cattle seizures on the *bancos* eked along for some time, in part because Mexico insisted exclusively on its own jurisdictional rulings for guidance.[86]

Mexico suggested that the American citizens involved apply to Mexican courts for relief, an idea that bewildered and outraged Frelinghuysen considering how thoroughly he thought he had laid out the case for unquestionable American jurisdiction over the island. The U.S. Congress had paid off Albino Giron and Romulo Lucero, two Mexicans who had had their cattle seized and sold by U.S. customs and thereafter won judgments in Mexican court that had been recognized by the United States. But still, the reciprocal payments to Americans with seized cattle were not forthcoming. This confirmed Frelinghuysen's growing sense that territoriality and legality were both the real victims in the case. "This being the case, it is difficult to understand the reasoning of the Mexican Government in these claims with all the facts before it, except upon the hypothesis that there was no desire to accord our citizens fair and just treatment. I regret to believe this is so. But the conviction necessarily forces itself upon me," he told Morgan.

However, he did concede that the whole problem was not due to Mexican lawlessness, as some of the claims over the island were a function of the basic lack of clarity of conditions on the border. Romero proposed to restart the boundary negotiations that Mariscal and Fish had carried on in 1875, but Frelinghuysen only slowly moved to accept a new formal treaty negotiation.[87]

The territorial issue was centrally important and quite serious, but Frelinghuysen sensed other opportunities. He felt that the process of tightening jurisdiction in this kind of dispute in which the United States had the strongest hand would provide a lever to force long-desired concessions in other areas of the relationship between the two nations, particularly regarding more abstract jurisdictional questions and the pressing issues of trade and market access. In this respect, Frelinghuysen's attitudes sat perfectly in line with the understanding of the interconnectedness of issues felt by the Texas senatorial delegation. As always, the United States felt that economic relations with Mexico needed adjustment toward greater pliability, openness, and opportunity for American investment and commerce. In particular, Frelinghuysen wanted to use the leverage built up from the Morteritos jurisdictional dispute to open a new connection between the nations on American terms and to link a number of issues together that were not necessarily the most obviously connected. But everything in the borderlands was connected.

Writing Morgan confidentially (a fact that he stressed twice in the letter), the secretary said that "the most important" issue was "the conclusion of a new commercial treaty between Mexico and the U.S. to replace the lately terminated Convention of 1831," which Mexico had abrogated against the wishes of the United States. Though he thought the actual construction of a treaty would have to wait for a time, he had secretly told Romero all of the conditions the United States wanted to achieve and conveyed his hope that Mexico would change its policy orientation before even coming to the table. This was the middle of the decade in which commerce between the United States and Mexico doubled, and Frelinghuysen sensed the promise of explosive growth.[88]

Frelinghuysen wanted a treaty, but one built especially for a unique coupling of the nations that was reflective of growing American dominance and of American structures and ideals. He therefore called for a complicated series of openings and closings in the Mexican economic and jurisdictional system structured according to U.S. interests. Some of these proposed changes were directed toward specific structures and others to approaches and the Mexican mindset.

The first issue was trade. "While the late commercial treaty between Germany and Mexico might serve in many respects as a model to be followed in any negotiation now to be entered upon, it does not meet the peculiar conditions which exist by reason of the coterminous inland boundary between Mexico and the United States," he wrote. Of particular concern was that "the present laws of Mexico concerning the domicile of citizens of the United States in the twenty-league strip of Mexican territory along the frontier would doubtless . . . [have] to *be obliterated or so changed* by the treaty [so] as not to impede the free communication between the two countries which is so desirable."[89] He was referring to the law preventing foreign ownership of land along the border, a nationalist barrier that was seen as a major impediment to American profits. Frelinghuysen's harsh choice of words indicates the view of the U.S. government in this regard, and the demand that the law not just be changed but be changed by a treaty indicates a clear desire to have this transformation enshrined in a bilateral agreement that would presumably prevent Mexico from unprofitable nationalist posturing of this sort in the future.

This restriction on property ownership was one discrete issue, but Frelinghuysen also wanted to end the whole range of exceptions over which the United States had no control. The biggest example in this regard was, unsurprisingly, the *Zona Libre*. Frelinghuysen asserted that "the existence, too, of a free zone is anomalous and interposes unnecessary restrictions upon intercourse by changing new conditions which it is difficult to maintain except by vexatious and restrictive measures often of harsh application, and any treaty between the two countries which recognized and confirmed such a state of things would fall short of its true object."[90]

Again Frelinghuysen called for a bilateral treaty to enforce an agreement, this time to end the hated *Zona Libre*. A treaty would presumably be much more effective than the failed diplomacy of the previous three decades. His convoluted statement also implied that the absence of trade restrictions was in itself a form of trade restriction because it forced the United States to shape its policy to it. It was almost a vacuum of policy that demanded new policies. Both countries consequently had to adopt "vexatious and restrictive measures often of harsh application" rather than a more appropriate model of exchange. Clearly, Frelinghuysen was not opposed so much to "changing new conditions" as to those changes and conditions the United States could not control because they were unilateral Mexican decisions.[91]

In a related way, Frelinghuysen also sought to use this opportunity to carve a special status for American diplomatic interests in the border region. Consular officials represented the forward wedge of state interests in the region. Reform meant reorienting and strengthening the standing of the U.S. presence on the border by obtaining more authority and recognition for consuls who were daily grappling with the fine-grained details of disputed jurisdictions on every issue from cattle to drunks to smuggling. Thus, Frelinghuysen argued that the "rights and functions of Consuls on this inland frontier needed to be much more carefully and fully defined than in the case of the sea-port consuls of a distant nation with which such direct connections of intercourse do not prevail."

He also very much wanted to increase the security of sojourning American citizens and safeguard American sovereignty in the process by ending the Mexican requirement of "matriculation." In this process, foreigners who purchased property in Mexico, or had a son there, without first expressing their interest in retaining their original citizenship and obtaining a certificate of matriculation unwittingly, automatically, and irreversibly became citizens of Mexico under Article 13 of the Mexican Constitution. These newly minted Mexican citizens were then unable to claim protection of their home country. A contemporary law book geared toward sojourning Americans warned, "*no act performed prior to the fact of matriculation can be remedied or benefited by subsequent matriculation*. Hence the protection awarded by this law must be sought, before any business is transacted by a foreign resident in the Republic."[92]

The odd matriculation policy had been a known and controversial issue for a while and was a particular irritant to Frelinghuysen. Two years earlier, he had quite firmly argued against it. Though he saw no grounds to question Mexico's sovereign right to determine "civil and domiciliary rights" for foreigners in Mexico, he was greatly disturbed by what Mexico viewed as debarring a person from protection of his or her own government, a unilateral stripping of citizenship. The foreign status of an individual should not be so susceptible to control by a municipal law, in his view. In this way, the matriculation issue was related to the U.S. denial of Mexican extraterritoriality since it had a direct impact on the sovereign power of the United States to act on its citizens abroad and on the bounds of passive personality jurisdiction. According to Frelinghuysen,

We hold, under the general principles of international law, that the right of an American citizen to claim the protection of his own Government while in a foreign land, and the duty of this Government to exercise such protection, are reciprocal, and are inherent in the allegiance if the citizen under the constitution of his own land, and that, inasmuch as this reciprocal right on the part of the citizen and duty on the part of his Government is not created by the laws of any foreign country, it cannot on the other hand be denied by the municipal law of a foreign state. Holding thus, it is impossible for this Government to accept the proposition that its right to intervene for the protection of one of its citizens in Mexico can only begin with, and be created by the matriculation of such a citizen as a foreign sojourner in Mexico, and can only exist and be exercised with respect to the redress of wrongs which such a citizen may suffer there after his name shall have been inscribed on the books of the foreign office in the city of Mexico.[93]

There was no question that citizens in other territories were under foreign jurisdiction, but to accept the Mexican construction of matriculation would mean extraterritorially submitting to a foreign decision-making process before taking state actions to protect American citizens. It was less a citizenship issue at heart than one of interference in sovereign foreign relations. This was a notably strong assertion of territorial authority as well as a unilateral absorption of nationality.

Frelinghuysen viewed matriculation as an absorption of sovereignty. It interfered unilaterally with the rights of the United States to step into disputes involving one of its unwittingly unmatriculated citizens. While the United States could simply ignore the Mexican citizenship assertions, it wanted the policy eliminated. There were other possible complications as well. For instance, if a citizen was forced into military service after failing to be matriculated, Morgan warned that this individual would in fact forever "be debarred from the right of claiming the protection of the United States." The matriculation issue was a regular one offering no promise of resolution since Mexico showed no sign of change. Most recently, it had been triggered in the 1883 case of William Lewis Zuber, who unwittingly became a citizen by buying a piece of property in Mazatlan. Morgan guessed "there are not a few Americans in the country who have become citizens thereof without knowing it."[94]

In 1884, Frelinghuysen realized that forcing a decision by treaty might be the best way of ending the notorious system. He made it clear that the United States intended to become much firmer: "When the Mexican Government, however, by domestic act undertakes to sever the relations of dependence and protection which exist between the citizens of a foreign state and their own government, it is clear that it goes beyond legitimate bounds and that acquiescence in such measure is not to be expected from the government whose constitutional and international rights are so infringed."[95]

Overall, Frelinghuysen wanted Romero to begin laying the groundwork for a comprehensive settlement that would solve all of the extant problems and at the same time elevate the U.S.-Mexico relationship not just above such squabbles but above the complicated provinciality of the borderlands disputes. Mexico no longer had to fear U.S. territorial invasion or "even the remotest desire on the part of the U.S. to interfere with the absolute independence of Mexico." Instead, the new relationship would be built on a decidedly modern framework of jurisdictional purity combined with economic interdependence—almost a federal structure: "The aim of the new treaty should be to assimilate the general conditions as far as possible to those of domestic intercourse in either country between its several districts." The two nations should become economically linked and mutually respectful. "Such a guarantee is not to be afforded by municipal measures framed in a spirit of distrust. The aim should be to remove distrust, not to increase it."[96]

In fascinating and perhaps unconscious ways, Frelinghuysen followed his defensive move on Morteritos sovereignty with a counterpunch, attempting to destroy any vestiges of Mexican unilateralism in the transnational spaces of the borderlands. The pleas for mutual respect and an end to disputes on idiosyncratic legal decisions was optimistic and did not yield anything beyond the boundary treaty of 1884 which, as noted, did not solve the problems of the boundary, the *bancos*, or the jurisdictional confusion.

Indeed, the problem of the *bancos* might have even worsened. On December 31, 1887, J. J. Cocke, the inspector from the customshouse in Brownsville, reiterated his request to the Treasury Department for more mounted inspectors for the District of Brazos Santiago and equally for a solution to the river problem. He thought "the so-called Morteritos Treaty of Nov. 12, 1884 proclaimed Sept 14, 1886, [was] perfectly worthless" because it offered no precision in the definition of the old riverbed's middle. If something were not done to get more inspectors, "the business men of all South Western Texas would be [under] mined and the people generally become demoralized through continuous violations of law." While "honest importers would continue to make entry according to law, until they found it did not pay," most would turn to "the 'Free Town' of Tamaulipas, where everything is cheaper." Smuggling would also increase. But Cocke thought the same task could be accomplished with fewer mounted inspectors if there were "a decrease of the distance to be traveled" through elimination of the *bancos*, or what he called "the anomalous condition of the boundary between the two countries along the Lower Rio Grande." He thought that "this would be a partial remedy for the evil but would be of great advantage in the administration of the criminal as well as the custom laws."[97]

The problem was that the "*bancos*, with their uncertain boundaries, offered safe retreats for smugglers, thieves, kidnappers, murderers, and every class of criminals, as well as bases of supplies from which to carry on their operations free from interference from with Government," Cocke wrote. Of particular concern was liquor smuggling. There were "a hundred gallons of Mescoe [sic] ready to be brought over." And he thought the solution was simply a matter of extending U.S. and Texas jurisdiction over the *bancos* and leaving the still-thorny issue of "ownership of the land to be settled by other provisions of treaty or courts."[98]

Cocke's plea for jurisdictional and geographical clarity was one of dozens of similar complaints from across the frontier that were also being increasingly aired in Washington. In January 1888, Secretary of the Treasury Charles S. Fairchild wrote the secretary of state calling for an International River Commission to properly apply the Boundary Convention of November 12, 1884, since "the difficulties constantly experienced in enforcing the revenue laws on the Mexican frontier [were owed] in a great measure to the present uncertainty as to the boundary line between the two countries." The same month, William H. Crain, a House member from Brownsville, Texas, asked about "the need of practically determining the boundary between the United States and Mexico where it follows the channel of the Rio Grande or Bravo." He also wanted to know what Mexico was doing about implementing the Convention of 1884. At the end of the month, Bayard was considering Fairchild's proposal for an International River Commission to solve this problem, but at the same time, he had decided that Mexico did not seem interested in implementing the boundary agreement.[99]

Continued conflict took the place of agreement under the treaty, and people continued to find themselves and their property to be in the opposite jurisdiction. In March 1890, G. S. Smith of Ebanito Ranch in Cameron County, Texas, built a fence on Banco de Surron, which produced a ruckus because Mexico also claimed the territory. Smith called in U.S. troops and Texas Rangers, but, he claimed, only "for purposes of moral support and in the intent of peace, and that no act of aggression or defence [be] performed by them." He claimed that Banco de Surron was a well-known "place of refuge for outlaws from both sides." Property owners across from Camargo, Tamaulipas, on land "first formed on the American side of the river" found their property moved to the Mexican side in the summer of 1893 which, the United States claimed, left "the land within the jurisdiction of the United States of America and the property of the claimants."[100]

Ten years after Morteritos seemed to have opened a new direction, the truly degraded state of the *bancos* issue was evident. This was the year that Captain Frank C. Jones of the Texas Rangers pursued Jesus Holguin onto a *banco* well beyond the Mexican border, as discussed earlier in the context of the Garcia arrest at the same time. It was also the year of armed conflict on "El Banco de Vela" (called Banco Cuauhtémoc in Mexico), where Americans used to pasture three thousand sheep until Mexico claimed jurisdiction over the *banco*, jailed the herders, and confiscated the sheep. Troops were called to a tense standoff, and in the words of Anson Mills, then a colonel of the 3rd Cavalry who was sent to guard the *banco*, "the shedding of blood was probably only prevented by a compromise between the State Departments of each government." The feelings remained "bitter and difficulties [were] likely to break out anew at any time." The Banco Vela dispute, though submitted for decision to the International Boundary Commission, continued to generate controversy for years as Mexico complained "the authorities of Texas [were] performing acts of jurisdiction" on it.[101]

But Mills's involvement was an important development. He was soon thereafter appointed the U.S. Commissioner on the International Boundary Commission, where he had a profound influence on the final settlement of the *bancos* issue, development of El Paso, and management of water resources of the Rio Grande. As Mills later recalled, he accepted because he thought it would take a year or two to straighten out. But,

> the origin of these *bancos* was so different from our expectations that both the Mexican Commissioner and I, after deliberate consideration, concluded that their process of formation, their form and constantly changing character, could not have been contemplated by the conventions creating the treaties of 1884 and 1889. We both suggested to our governments the reconsideration of Articles I and II of the treaty of 1884, as far as they related to these *bancos*,

to the end that provision might be made for transferring all such *bancos* to the sovereignty of the United States or Mexico according as they lay on the American or Mexican side of the present river channel, without disturbing the private ownership as it might be ascertained.[102]

This happy and graceful solution to the issue took years and mountains of paperwork, and it did push the thorny El Chamizal issue into the atomic age. The end of *bancos* as an issue did have the unintended consequence of shifting much of the animosity in the jurisdictional dispute to the use of the water in the river. To this problem, a quintessentially transnational one, the United States responded with the most stridently territorial assertion of riparian rights ever articulated by a modern state. This was a rule so strident and clear that the United States itself only implemented it on rare occasion, and water rights scholars look back on it with a mixture of wonderment and disdain as "the most notorious theory in all of international natural resources law."[103] Nevertheless, this statement perfectly reflected the U.S. approach to all transnational issues and to the question of sovereign territoriality and should be properly viewed in the context of nineteenth-century unilateralism in foreign relations as well as in terms of the international water diplomacy it helped to launch.

WATER AND SOVEREIGNTY

In October 1894, José Zayas Guarneros, the Mexican consul in El Paso, wrote Matías Romero to express his fear that very "existence or the disappearance of the frontier towns" was at stake because of an ongoing water supply crisis. Agriculture in the region faced "total destruction" and would bring "infant industries" with it. This was not a natural problem but rather an economic one, for Americans were draining of the river for their "own exclusive use." Romero in turn wrote Secretary of State Gresham to inform him of this "urgent necessity" for a decision on water usage, as problems had developed to the point around Paso del Norte that there was "the danger lest otherwise these communities may be annihilated." Gresham predictably denied that the lack of water was due to U.S. irrigation and noted that water supply had long been an issue in the region. But he forwarded this issue to the Department of Agriculture for clarification, and after a full year and another urging from Romero, it went to Attorney General Judson Harmon for a ruling on the nature of U.S. jurisdiction over the waters of the Rio Grande.[104]

Harmon released his famous decision on December 12, 1895, and began by examining the water issues in the Treaty of Guadalupe Hildago in which he found only discussion of navigation and no discussion or stipulation of water usage or agricultural interests. Even the free navigation guaranteed by the treaty was only relevant to the point of the river below New Mexico. He reviewed the status of Rio Grande water in 1894 and found that indeed, the United States was using the bulk of it in irrigation in Colorado and New Mexico, where the river flowed entirely through U.S. territory. El Paso as a result was starved for water between June and March. In 1894, he noted, "the river was entirely dry by June 15 so that no crop could be raised and even fruit trees began to wither." He recognized that these conditions resulted in "great hardships to the people" in Paso del Norte, Zaragoza, Tres Jacales, Guadalupe, and San Ignacio as well as a population drop of fifty percent.[105]

Most of Harmon's decision involved analysis of the severe limits of the 1848 treaty language, but at the end of the document, he considered the idea of "natural international servitude" regarding international waterways. Harmon found no such servitude. He rejected what he said was "really contended for [which was] a servitude which makes the lower country dominant and subjects the upper country to the burden on arresting its development and denying to its inhabitants the use of a provision which nature has supplied entirely within its territory." Framed this way, the issue was not about agriculture; it was about sovereignty. And Harmon, like Justice Fields and so many others, drew upon John Marshall's understanding of sovereignty that "the fundamental principle of international law is the absolute sovereignty of every nation, as against all others, within its own territory."[106]

Harmon quoted Marshall and then found the principle so perfectly stated that he thought "it would be entirely useless to multiply authorities." There was no way an international servitude could pierce this perfect sovereignty on the basis of self-preservation if nothing else. Harmon saw the Mexican claim as not just injurious to sovereignty but an attempt to cause very real harm to the American economy and actually reverse its current growth: "The claim involves not only the arrest of further settlement and development of large regions of country, but the abandonment, in great measure at least of what has already been accomplished." It was sad but true, Harmon concluded, "the water is simply insufficient to supply the needs of the great stretch of arid country," but it was not an issue that involved "liability or obligation upon the United States."[107]

The Harmon decision was as searing an assertion of territoriality as was

Chae Chan Ping v. United States or *In Re Ross,* because, of course, it stated the same position on strict, absolute sovereignty in the exact same strong language American policymakers had used since it first appeared in *Exchange v. McFaddon.* Stephen C. McCaffrey, a major scholar on international war law, notes that "what is known as the 'Harmon Doctrine' thus consists of a few rather short paragraphs in an opinion of some nine pages. And those paragraphs consist chiefly of a quotation from an opinion of the Supreme Court in a sovereign immunity case decided over eighty years earlier." McCaffrey demonstrates persuasively that the Harmon Doctrine was not applied in *future* water diplomacy with the same vigor or clarity it was enunciated in 1895, and in some ways, he believes it was even purposefully ignored. He argues that it should be seen as "a piece of advocacy that might be useful as a negotiating device."¹⁰⁸

This perspective on Harmon merely as a negotiating device considers the microcosm of borderlands water diplomacy as it developed under the reciprocity-minded Anson Mills. On approaching the water issue when he became American Commissioner for the International Boundary Commission, Mills wrote that

> "it at once occurred to me that as the Rio Grande was the joint property of the two nations, and especially as the Mexicans had used its waters since time when 'the memory of man runneth not to the contrary,' *that any plan to be acceptable and satisfactory must be international in character,* and the works, both before and after completion, under the joint federal control of the two nations, the more so as riparian rights in this country, so far as regards irrigation, are not well defined by law, and could be best brought about in this instance by treaty stipulations between the two countries."¹⁰⁹

But sovereignty was not negotiable in nineteenth-century American foreign relations; it was the bedrock underlying any negotiation. While the American position on water usage later pivoted toward reciprocal cooperation (a fitful and slow process that is too complex and belabored to detail here), it is vital to consider the significance of the Harmon statement in terms of virtually every other decision that touched on jurisdictional issues in complicated transnational cases of this era. The same assertion of strict sovereign unilateralism and reaffirmation of territoriality appeared repeatedly in numerous district court and Supreme Court decisions, in diplomatic extradition wrangles, in the political responses to the expansion of the *Zona Libre,* and in a wide array of other forms. Anticipating how the United States moved *away* from the Harmon Doctrine in the future is an ahistorical approach to its actual significance as a foreign policy in response to these types of issues in 1895.

As the record laid out in this book demonstrates, there were plenty of exceptions to this dominant strand in U.S. foreign relations at this time but no denial of it or real turn away from it. Likewise, the Harmon Doctrine was never actually repudiated; it was merely moderated within a broadly consistent reaffirmed series of foreign policy choices until sovereign territoriality was imaginatively recast in some transboundary instances in the twentieth century.[110] The territorial Harmon Doctrine remained a live opinion not just because it was potentially useful but because it directly reflected the sovereigntist approach taken by late nineteenth-century policymakers to seek unilateral governance of transnational concerns.

CHAPTER THREE

Borderlands Exceptions

There seems no good reason why the man who has committed any major
crime should go unwhipped of justice because he has fled to another
sovereign.

Warner P. Sutton, U.S. consul at Matamoros, March 19, 1888

At 11:00 a.m. on March 3, 1888, a group of disguised Mexican soldiers
under Captain Francisco A. Muñoz crossed the Rio Grande at Eagle Pass
to grab a deserter named Atanacio Luis. The bungled kidnapping ended with
a gunfight that left several dead and wounded. It was, the local *Eagle Pass Press
Telegram* intoned, a "coolly planned" and "deplorable incident" that stood as
"one of the foulest outrages upon international law and friendship" to occur
along the border. According to Warner P. Sutton, the U.S. consul at Matamoros,
it was "all in all . . . the most flagrant and glaring outrage I have ever known on
this border."[1] And Sutton, readers of the previous chapters will recall, was no
stranger to feeling outraged in this era of perpetual borderlands outrage.

This kind of language, though excessive even by the inflated standards set
along the border, reflected the seriousness of the crossing and shoot-out at
Eagle Pass and the sharp inadequacies of and slippages within the legal regime
along the border. This looseness was produced as much by the physical realities
of geography as by the abstractions of legal spatiality. It was intensified by the
local political culture. Jurisdictional issues became particularly stark in cases of
legal and extralegal transborder pursuit of criminals, smugglers, deserters, and
other fugitives, though they were also troublesome in all other relations from
trade to property ownership (fig. 3). The aftermath to the Eagle Pass affair, one
of many similar incidents that occurred in the borderlands with regularity during the last three decades of the nineteenth century, demonstrated how U.S. foreign policy and especially extradition policy in the region was a servant first to
interest, power, and theories of state sovereignty and territoriality at the federal,

Figure 3. "Los charros contrabandistas. Juego de dados," a dice game about cowboy smugglers, created by the legendary Mexico City engraver José Posada between 1890 and 1913. Library of Congress Prints and Photographs Division, LC-DIG-ppmsc-03448.

state, and local levels. Only thereafter (if ever) did it attend to the less compelling if oft-cited abstractions of justice.

Central to the troublesome operation of the borderlands extradition system and the issues of legal spatiality within it was a reliance on exceptions—exceptions to process, structures, jurisdiction, territoriality, and even legality itself. This chapter focuses on the political significance and governance implications of the borderlands clause to the U.S.-Mexico Extradition Treaty of 1861 as an excellent way of exploring exceptions and the place of law as they were implemented in the late nineteenth-century borderlands.

Sovereignty can be understood in part as the power to create exceptions in the furtherance of its own ends, or placing sovereignty outside of the law.[2] The unusual border states clause stood as a marked exception to all American extradition relations, including those involving the states of the U.S.-Canadian borderlands. The system of exception at the border undergirded the search for other such exceptions and exclusions as a function of the wider structuring of U.S. power and jurisdiction during the critical time in the last two decades of the nineteenth century. Rogers M. Smith characterized this period as "the mounting repudiation of Reconstruction egalitarianism and inclusiveness in favor on an extraordinarily broad political, intellectual, and legal embrace of renewed ascriptive hierarchies" that were manifest in social relations, racial exclusion and oppression, and imperialism.[3] This chapter explores the function of exceptions in fulfilling and sustaining these systemic divisions through the foreign policymaking of extradition. It situates the carving of exceptions where they sat in policy terms, at the linkages between domestic and foreign policies, in which local lawlessness often projected incoherence upon expressions of sovereignty and transnational power.

In 1888, the soldiers crossed out of frustration over Mexico's half-hearted and failed official attempts to compel Luis's return. Luis, who had committed no crime except desertion, was not surrendered to Mexico by Texas officials because desertion was not considered an extraditable offense according to the existing U.S.-Mexico Extradition Treaty signed in 1861. This situation rankled the soldiers in the Mexican 3rd Cavalry, and they took matters into their own hands, following the pattern where failures of clear legality in the borderlands invited extralegal action even by officials or military officers.

Luis had deserted the army on February 26 after serving ten months. He later carefully noted that he had come "across the river naked, and brought nothing with me" because even the "clothes that I was wearing that day belonged to the Mexican government," and he did not want to invite a charge of theft. His desertion was no secret in the area and had even been reported about in the *Eagle Pass Press Telegram* during the week before the Muñoz crossing. Luis had been met with a waiting set of clothes and a job, and his crossing of the border had somehow legitimated his desertion in the local and official mindset in Texas. American officials always described the episode as an attempted kidnapping and his job in Eagle Pass as lawful, which indicates some amount of sympathy for Luis's desertion and a belief in his secure position in Texas. In reconsidering the whole series of events, his desertion was later described by a contemporary observer as a search for his "right of sanctuary."[4]

Mexican Lieutenant Miguel Cabrera had reconnoitered the situation the night before in preparation for the direct action. Muñoz and Cabrera crossed the Rio Grande along with two noncommissioned officers and a private under the pretense of looking at some horses. The whole group was disguised in civilian clothing and carried concealed weapons. A "chance word" and a request for directions made U.S. customs agent Frank H. Dillon suspicious that the men wanted to travel further than Eagle Pass, so he told them to get the necessary permission for such movement from the customshouse, which was up the hill in town and a distance from the border. Instead of following these instructions, upon landing on the American bank, the soldiers headed for the edge of town toward the Sunset Railway depot a half mile further, where the deserter was working. When Luis tried to escape and hide, he was grabbed, whipped with pistols, stabbed repeatedly in the legs, and threatened with death. The soldiers, according to the detailed and understated report written by U.S. Consul Allen at Piedras Negras across the river from Eagle Pass, "violently proceeded to compel the deserter to return with them to Piedras Negras."[5]

At this point, Shadrack White, the Maverick County sheriff's deputy, came upon the soldiers "brutally maltreating Luis" and ordered them to stop or they would be arrested. He told them "if they wished to take that man they would have to take him by law." Cabrera responded, "Chingado la ley" ("fuck the law"), which was a phrase that could in fact stand as a fair characterization of the prevailing attitude along both sides of the border throughout the entire period.[6]

Muñoz and the soldiers leveled their pistols at the deputy and Cabrera said "they intended to take that man or die right there." Rather incredibly for a Texas lawman in this era, White was unarmed at this time. "I told them it was not necessary for any one to die, and turned off and rode back to the jail and procured my Winchester rifle," he later recalled. White also got Sheriff W. N. Cook and other reinforcements, and this group intercepted the Mexican soldiers near the river. Cabrera started firing. When the sheriff and deputies reached the soldiers, White identified his group as the law and told them to halt ("matters were too urgent for exchange of courtesies").

An intense firefight broke out. White, who though armed now had initially failed to load his gun at the start of the shooting, managed to kill one of the horses of the fleeing soldiers. He was shot in the left arm and right hand at such close range that it set "fire to my clothing and badly powder-burn[ed] my flesh." Two of the enlisted Mexican soldiers were wounded. A third, a sergeant named Poliaorpe Garcia, was wounded and disappeared into the Rio Grande during the escape back into Mexico; his body was never found. Luis, the deserter, was left behind on the American side, bloody and insensible. According to news reports by the U.S. consul, the entire Mexican company supposedly lined the shore of the river ready to shoot or invade at the slightest aggressive move from the American side, but as in so many other instances, this intensely violent episode soon ended and was converted into a diplomatic issue attendant to broader national interests.[7]

Mexico refused extradition for the soldiers, as was its undisputed right under Article VI of the 1861 U.S.-Mexico Extradition Treaty, which stated that "neither of the contracting parties shall be bound to deliver up its own citizens."[8] The treaty did not expressly forbid the extradition of citizens, but it was rarely mentioned and even less often exercised by either country. Mexico and the United States both had the option to do so, though neither nation ever manifested a compulsion to extradite its citizens. This refusal to extradite Muñoz, though politically unpopular in Texas at this time as it was in other incidences considered later in this chapter, was not disputed by the United States.

Mexico quickly resolved the Eagle Pass controversy much as it had in the Avalos case (though not to the extreme of execution) by rapidly trying and convicting the men for their actions. Mariscal, the Mexican foreign minister, called the crossing and the gunfight "disagreeable incidents" but did not consider extraditing Muñoz or his men. U.S. chargé H. Remsen Whitehouse attempted to whip up a sense of fervor in his urgings to the State Department about the "outrage," but the United States clearly found the Muñoz action less compelling than other outrages—and the options fewer. Mexico asserted jurisdiction over Muñoz's acts based on the active personality principle, an extraterritorial legal fiction that was a key underpinning of Article 186 of its penal code and had just recently created so much controversy in the Cutting case. Yet it was not critiqued in the slightest in this case by the usually vigilant and often touchy United States. As was not uncommon in this type of case, which was regularly if not constantly occurring, the United States adopted a flexible and expedient position.

Although the State Department did not see it necessary or useful to conflate the Cutting case with the Muñoz incursion, Mexican president Porfirio Díaz himself observed the connections in a retrospective speech on his actions in office between 1884 and 1888, a period almost bookended by these two events. He noted that Mexico based its policy on "the feelings of national dignity as well as the healthy aims of justice" and for this reason felt no obligation and refused to change its penal code or offer indemnity "in the case of an American journalist at Paso del Norte." Díaz commended the United States for "closing its ears to the exalted passions which endeavored to influence this affair." At the same time, Díaz argued that the United States clearly understood the Mexican commitment to justice when Muñoz and his coconspirators were sentenced to death, and in fact, he interceded to get their sentence commuted.[9]

A diplomatic flurry resulted over the Muñoz case as would be expected, but it was quickly resolved and reasonably free of the heated language that so often was a result of transboundary conflicts. Indeed, diplomatic exchanges with Mexico over extradition often lacked the wounded and outraged tone that was a hallmark of American diplomacy in other transborder issues during the time from the tumultuous 1870s through the end of the century. There was a noticeable loosening of tension in matters related to the extradition system that was absent in the controversies over border incursions, extraterritorial criminal jurisdiction, and creations of zones of legal and economic exceptions even though similar issues were involved. At least part of the reason for this mellower approach was that the delineated responsibilities under the extradition treaty were few, and many issues were dealt with on a local level. This did not mean that some inchoate justice prevailed but that local issues not uncommonly stayed local and were handled in unofficial or even extralegal ways that did not filter up to Washington or Mexico City. And, no less importantly, the exceptions (particularly pertaining to citizenship) were flexible enough that what reigned at all levels was interest and pragmatism unleavened with subordination on either side of the border. A certain kind of order was maintained along the border with respect to these issues, though it was not what could be described as an entirely legal one.

The State Department officially focused its efforts only on the task of securing reparations for Deputy Sheriff White, whose right hand had been permanently disabled in the shooting. These negotiations continued for a couple of years. White had asked for $775 in lost wages and medical costs and his lawyer, James A. Ware, argued that "insult and outraged feelings are as much a subject of compensation in damages as the permanent injuries to his body." Mexico ultimately paid him the enormous sum of $7,000 in U.S. gold coin. U.S. consul at Piedras Negras, Eugene O. Fechét, wrote to Thomas Ryan in Mexico City on May 11, 1890, that "I shall rejoice when this claim shall have been paid and we can make it public, for the actual money payment of a frontier claim by Mexico will have an immense and most beneficial effect on the ignorant frontier class, and markedly upon the petty local authorities."[10] The money had the expected mollifying effect, but there was no shortage of future incidents.

This incident, involving duplicity, transboundary incursion, and violence, logically might have been considered a significant event and certainly was graver than the Cutting case. This was after all precisely the kind of borderlands outrage that had consumed so much attention for years, made even more egregious by the involvement of soldiers, even if they were loose cannons. Although agitation over extradition was sidestepped, the Muñoz incursion was still interpreted as a stark and premeditated violation of American sovereignty. It not unimportantly marked an incursion from Mexico into the United States, instead of the more common reverse, and it differed in significant ways from the more familiar borderlands issues relating to Indian depredations, smuggling, border crime, invasion, and assertions of extraterritorial authority. Yet as an issue, it only momentarily flared and then disappeared. Surely this at least in part indicated a robust embrace of the inherent and consciously designed limits to borderlands extradition.

The events at Eagle Pass highlighted a key facet of the ongoing contestation of jurisdiction and exception at the border. A critical twist in this instance was that both nations were neatly freed from having even to consider questions of law and lawlessness because of the uncommon—if even outright bizarre at times, in practice—citizenship exemption to extradition that prevailed on the U.S.-Mexican border. What did the rule of law really mean in the region with this exception in such a case? And where could it ever be applied if the borderlands were allowed to remain an insurmountable barrier to justice as well as a ready escape hatch for citizens of either state no matter what their criminal acts?

The official responses of the United States changed dramatically with each episode, sometimes reflecting a strict territoriality that the crime should be tried where it was committed and sometimes welcoming the exercise of speedy state power if it meant a seemingly easy death sentence in Mexico and administrative clarity at home. The United States readily suppressed its outrage at yet another border "outrage" in order to preserve its own latitude for action in the region by judicious use of the very useful citizenship exception in Mexican extradition relations. This was emblematic of the period and the region but also notably unlike the situation in almost all of the other extradition relations that the United States maintained at the time. The further implications of the citizenship exception outside the borderlands are considered in chapter 5.

The Muñoz affair, although merely one of many similar events over the last third of the nineteenth century, encouraged renewed questioning about the system of legal exchange on the border. It was a thorny problem to conceptualize the absence of legal recourse for troublesome acts like desertion, let alone a wide range of other currently non-extraditable crimes including extralegal cross-border incursion, smuggling, and revolutionary acts. The Muñoz affair raised questions particularly about the exceptions to extradition no matter what the nature of the crime and about the overall nature of exception in the region. Particularly, it raised concerns about the need to reform the extradition relations that helped to produce it.

The most clear-eyed contextualization of the meaning of this controversy within the broader question of state power along the border came not surprisingly from U.S. Consul Sutton in Matamoros, who was less given to excitability than Whitehouse but still flabbergasted and disturbed by the implications of Muñoz's acts. Framing his understanding was a similar incursion that had just recently happened further west in Nogales, which Sutton felt should be rightfully excoriated as a volitional Mexican act. Whereas the Muñoz affair revealed core weaknesses of the interstate system along the Texas-Mexico Rio Grande boundary, the Nogales incident was less surprising. Perhaps, Sutton noted in his critique, if the Mexicans who crossed into Nogales actually "had been shot the example might have [later] deterred Muñoz and Cabrera."[11]

Very similar to the Eagle Pass events in many ways, the Nogales affair had occurred the previous fall and was, inevitably, described by most American observers as an "outrage." It had in fact become a major topic of diplomatic exchange, in interesting contrast to some other incidents. This was another case of territorial invasion and violence on the street in Nogales, which served as the dividing line between the nations. It involved two Mexican army officers, Colonel Arvizú and Lieutenant Gutierrez, and someone variously described as a citizen or a sergeant named R. [Rincon] Valenzuela who crossed into Nogales and started a gun battle.

The affair apparently started when Arvizú's mistress fled to the United States and was pursued, perhaps to be kidnapped or perhaps just for a conversation as was claimed, by a "well-known Mexican named Rincon." He failed to compel her to return, and she called for assistance from local law enforcement. Three officials, a constable named Littlejohn, a deputy sheriff, and a doctor, "induced Rincon to desist" and escorted him away. It was at this time that Gutierrez "emerged from concealment" and compelled the release of Rincon at gunpoint. Littlejohn convinced Gutierrez to holster his gun since Rincon was not actually a prisoner and then managed to draw his own gun. Now arrested, Gutierrez was marched forward until Arvizú appeared to free him. "Promiscuous firing then commenced," with the death of one Mexican soldier. The soldiers fled to Mexico, and Gutierrez vanished for a time until he was captured.[12]

There were all the makings of a major crisis, and Sonora governor Luis E. Torres arrived quickly at the scene to try to alleviate the tension by personally overseeing the arrest of the soldiers. Mexico did not return Gutierrez to Arizona authorities as requested, but it did bring Arvizú to trial under Mexican military jurisdiction and the "very severe . . . and especially rigorous character of that code in Mexico," as the Mexican foreign minister, Mariscal, explained. He promised speed and severity in the punishment, which pleased the State Department. U.S. officials did not dispute this action because of the "provision of our extradition treaty," as Secretary of State Thomas F. Bayard told Mariscal, so "I refrained from formal demand for the surrender of those Mexican solider who had invaded our territory and forcibly rescued a prisoner there in legal custody." Mariscal apparently took Bayard's comments to mean that he was "given the option to deliver the offenders at Nogales to the American authorities for punishment, or for the Mexican Government itself to inflict adequate punishment." American minister T. C. Manning told Bayard that Mariscal was indeed going to exercise this supposed option and that "as the Mexican Government had determined to avail itself of this option, I presumed it would feel the more incumbent to make the punishment so severe that the United States would have no reason to complain, and I added that this was a good opportunity to punish such an offense as this so rigorously as to act as a deterrent to others in the future."[13]

One of the reasons Mexico had shown such eagerness to try Arvizú itself is because extradition was a complicated hassle in general and because this case in particular was so freighted with potential political complications in the northern states, as all border surrenders tended to be. The sense of "outrage" was alive on both sides of the border. Mariscal told Manning that, of course, Mexico was "by no means obliged" to deliver its citizen under the treaty, and so it would not. But he averred that in any case, "Mr. Bayard should view [that decision] with satisfaction and an elevated judgment, worthy of praise, the practicability of terminating the matter without extraditing a Mexican, a process involving many difficulties." Mariscal was especially interested in avoiding "the irritation, even though unfounded, which that extradition would cause in the Mexican town upon the frontier as contrasted with the spirit of conciliation and harmony which should be cultivated." The State Department did not dispute the utility of having Arvizú subjected to military justice, but it was very firm on demanding the return of Gutierrez as a "restoration of the status quo."[14]

Thus the United States sidestepped the prosecution of the incursion and the difficulties of extradition while also demanding with some vigor that there be recognition of the "very different basis" of the "questions of international jurisdiction" between the invading soldiers and the prisoners. Bayard was firm, though, that even if Mexico did not have to give up the solider, "armed invasion of our territory and rescue of a prisoner from our lawful jurisdiction could confer upon the rescued person no asylum in Mexico, nor bring him within the formalities of extradition." It was instead "the simple international duty of the Mexican Government to undo the wrong committed by its own soldiery" and return him. This never happened, though Mexico did not in fact contest the point that the extradition request and the surrender of Gutierrez were indeed different. It was simply uninterested in complying, especially given the possibility for political complication.

After a month, Bayard gave up protesting. He regretted to Manning that Mariscal had "understood as coupling a request for non-insistence upon that right [of extradition] with an explicit disclaimer of desire or intention to fall short of the full measure of friendly international obligation in the premises." Bayard accepted the realities of Mexico's refusal in light of the promised deterrence effect of the "severity" of the punishment. But at the same time, Bayard took pains to detail that "this Government can not, even by implication, permit this case to become a precedent for any assumption that forcible rescue can create any right of asylum or that the Mexican Government is not under the obligation to undo the unlawful act of its own officers and return the rescued party to the jurisdiction of the United States."[15]

Mexico was true to its word, as it sentenced Arvizú and Gutierrez to death and the others to prison. Mariscal seemed to have estimated correctly that not extraditing the accused was politically popular in Sonora. There was a public ball for Governor Torres to celebrate this event, as the invitations indicated: "the distinguished services of Governor Luis E. Torres, lent to the country in general and to the State of Sonora in particular, intervening with singular tact in the disagreeable occurrences at Nogales and ably avoiding an international conflict, has inspired us to make him this public manifestation of our gratitude." Manning was very pleased at this type of public recognition of an official who brought "offenders against our territorial and judicial jurisdiction to justice." On May 11, 1887, Manning sent a telegram declaring "the three officers of the Nogales outrage have been shot." But this turned out to be a rumor, and the process dragged on for some time. The United States, apparently with a change of heart, soon officially requested that the death sentences be commuted to prison terms. A long process followed during which the men were jailed, and Díaz was supposedly "teaching a lesson to his people, and particularly to his army" while also "preserv[ing] the *entente cordiale* between the two countries." The U.S. consul at Guaymas expected Díaz to pardon the men.[16]

It was at this stage in the late fall of 1887 that Sutton had visited the area en route for Chihuahua on a tour of the borderlands U.S. consulates. He thought the men were suffering without actually being executed: "Life inside the jail is almost as bad as shooting. Indeed, they are said to prefer being shot to passing another summer in jail." Though the United States had requested a reduced sentence, it was to no avail. Nevertheless, Sutton thought "it was a graceful act on our part and was highly appreciated by the Mexican authorities. It will enable them, if they choose, to shoot one or all of them without being in any way morally bound to it." Sutton thought two of the men should just receive a few years, but that "Arvizú ought to be shot and buried. Anything which would save his life would be a misfortune." Sutton reported that based on what he had heard "indirectly, I am inclined to think that the Mexican Government would be glad of this good excuse to be forever rid of him. I would not be surprised if he were led out some midnight and shot to death." Of Arvizú, Sutton found nothing redeeming that should save him from execution: "my acquaintance, personally and by repute, with Mexican desperadoes is rather extensive, but I have never known one worse than he."[17]

But despite these strong words, Sutton still found something even more ominous in the aftermath of the Muñoz incident at Eagle Pass: "At Nogales an imaginary line was passed and that at night and when the party had been drinking. This at Eagle Pass was deliberately planned; permission to pass the river, a well known boundary, was obtained under false pretenses and the outrageous act done defiantly and in broad daylight."[18] The imaginary border might not have existed in Texas, but the different jurisdictions certainly did. Sutton was as concerned about the brazen violation of territoriality as he was about the failure of law in the wake of the incident.

As both of these events happened when Congress was getting ready to consider a new commission working on clarifying the forever-complicated boundary lines, Sutton decided to again discourse upon "two subjects which are so intimately connected that I treat them in the same dispatch—Boundary and Extradition." If an extradition system was to provide for the focused international pursuit of criminal activity and therefore strengthen the rule of law, Sutton thought the only way to properly structure it was by simultaneously clarifying and marking the boundary line, defining the status of fugitives, refining the list of extraditable offenses, and regularizing the very questions of illegality and punishment.

Sutton proposed a clear effort to define nationality of residence and jurisdiction on the *bancos* and thereby to "line up citizenship, taxation, and titles to lands." He was confident that this effort would greatly clear up jurisdictional questions and criminal and civil jurisdiction would no longer be so changeable and instead would follow "the actual channel of the river" or the main channel, except if it was within five miles of an incorporated village or city. Importation to *bancos* would be governed by the state whose banks the goods left from, while there would be a new transnational effort to regulate commerce in the banks. The lawless zones would be eliminated. Of course, these issues emphasized by Sutton had been the focus of a great deal of international bargaining for some time. The boundary rules had been laid down with seeming (but as it turned out, still elusive) finality after the resolution of the Morteritos *banco* issue in the Boundary Convention of 1884. Sutton forecast a real need to implement this agreement at long last and get the boundary monument markers up and to "relocate the boundary on the lower river" and "demand certain regulations to insure peace and good order." The river, it went without saying, had shifted a good deal and continued to change. The Mexican *bancos* remained zones where there simply was no operative jurisdiction and wherein the whole notion of law was suspended. The result was, simply, that these *bancos* had created along the river "a lawless region [which was] the menace and dread of all well disposed citizens."[19]

As he had been doing since the 1870s, Sutton linked the geographic issue to broader considerations of crime, race, and citizenship into a single nexus of concern. He informed the State Department that the problem was that "along the border [lived] a considerable population of the lower class of Mexicans among whom such crimes are naturally very frequent." The ease with which they could cross the border meant that this supposed criminal class was "less restrained." And it was not only Mexicans who were committing crimes, for the "lawless American element" also made use of the border for escape. This prevented the "peaceful settlement and development of the country." Americans who committed crimes in Mexico could not be extradited or tried for their crimes back in the United States. Sutton also found it extremely worrisome that it was "impossible to prove the American citizenship of persons of Mexican blood," which allowed people to seek shelter in Mexico. The border seemed to invite crime, and the cultural geography of the region provided easy cover for individuals seeking to commit them without consequence.[20]

How did these issues connect to extradition in Sutton's analysis? At heart, borderlands geography and demographics offered a particular hazard in the pursuit of criminals and required a systemic response. The central concern as he saw it was clarifying the reach of law and the spaces of law. Sutton called for both an extradition commission and a border commission to straighten out the problems of fugitive escape and surrender along the border and to fix the fundamental jurisdictional confusions. Why should criminals of any sort go unpunished because of the arbitrary and limited negotiated definitions of a treaty? "There seems no good reason why the man who has committed any major crime should go unwhipped of justice because he has fled to another sovereign," Sutton wrote.[21]

This simple act of bringing people to justice by clarifying the reach of sovereignty was, of course, the principal logic of constructing extradition systems in the first place. But in practice, such matters of justice and its relative merits were never clear in the borderlands, where each nation assiduously safeguarded its sovereignty and jurisdiction in whatever shifting forms they were manifest. The ease of fleeing from sovereign jurisdiction, let alone justice, was a central concern on the U.S.-Mexican border. Sutton wishfully suggested a zero-tolerance approach to crime and fugitive flight: "This is particularly true here where the line is at best only a narrow river and in many cases an unknown imaginary line. Its provision would greatly simplify matters and further justice."[22]

One of these defects of great concern that prevented the return of fugitives and was considered to be particularly troublesome along the Mexican border was the citizenship exception in Article VI of the 1861 U.S.-Mexico Extradition Treaty. As he had in the past, Sutton urged that extradition be allowed "without regard being had to citizenship" unless there was an explicit adoption of active and passive personality principles of jurisdiction wherein the nation in whose territory the fugitives were found could punish such crimes as were committed in whole or in part beyond its limits, depending on the citizenship of the offender and victim, as Mexico had done in the Nogales incident. In such a system as viewed from the perspective of international law, "jurisdiction can . . . be exclusive to one state or concurrent with that of another state or states."[23] If the asylum nation did not punish the criminal, Sutton argued that within ten to thirty days of the incident, a request should be made to the "chief executive authority" for rendition or an appeal.

Sutton even rejected the principle of specialty holding that criminals could only be tried for crimes for which they had been specifically extradited. If tried but not yet sentenced, a criminal could escape and then not be extraditable again because of double jeopardy. Sutton, interested in capturing fugitives and successfully trying criminals no matter where they hid, feared that justice was not being sufficiently attended to in the exceptions erected within the legal spaces of the borderlands. The Nogales and Muñoz incursions were just the most recent examples of the kind of extralegal violence, transboundary adventurism, and criminal escape that resulted from a system so riddled with loopholes.

The rest of this chapter considers these loopholes, inadequacies, and incompletely applied policies as they were manifest in the borderlands extradition system and situates them within both the search for order in U.S.-Mexican relations and the fuller sweep of U.S. foreign relations at this time. With complete borderlands security no longer the concern it was in the 1870s, U.S. policymakers turned their attention to expressing and furthering national dominance in the region in ways large and small, including an interest in regularizing the trade system and reforming the *Zona Libre*. This region experienced development, violence, and varying revolutionary activity unlike anywhere else in the country. It was within this transnational context of dynamic action, violence, and crime that U.S. policymakers solidified power and simultaneously crafted exceptions as a core aspect of legal spatiality in the region.

THE "BORDER STATES CLAUSE"

Situated in the unique borderlands, the extradition relations between the United States and Mexico stood as an exception to the system developed for all other countries because of the ways geography and governance invited (or depending on one's view, necessitated) local control. Article II of the 1861 extradition treaty included what was called a border states clause, which was an exception allowing for utterly unmatched local control of all aspects of extradition from requisition to surrender. It was a major exception to the foreign affairs power in general. John Bassett Moore described it, with a bit of wonderment, as "the only instance in which power has been conferred by the Federal government, either by law or by treaty, upon the authorities of a State or a Territory of the United States, to practise extradition with foreign countries."[24] Article II of the treaty read,

> In the case of crimes committed in the frontier States or Territories of the two contracting parties, requisitions may be made through their respective diplomatic agents, or through the chief civil authority of said States or Territories,

or through such chief civil or judicial authority of the districts or counties bordering on the frontier as may for this purpose be duly authorized by the said chief civil authority of the said frontier States or Territories, or when, from any cause, the civil authority of such State or Territory shall be suspended, through the chief military officer in command of such State or Territory.[25]

Thus, extradition could be accomplished through local magistrates and sheriffs as the governor of the territory or state so appointed, which meant a structure much more attuned to local interests and political realities as well as regional and local prejudices and agendas. Federal diplomatic personnel were also allowed to be involved in extradition, and the president had final authority over surrenders, of course. This created a situation in which two tracks of extradition emerged.

Within each of these tracks, the relative power of different components of the system had an impact on the governance of extradition. The executive remained the centerpiece of decision making at the state and federal levels, but the judiciary retained a role. It is interesting that it was only the treaty with Mexico that empowered the Texas governor to act as a foreign policy agent for the purposes of extradition. As *Ex parte McCabe*, one of the very few court cases to consider the border states clause directly, argued, "the state executive officer, under the treaty with Mexico, is indebted solely to the treaty for whatever power or authority he may possess, and his rights and corresponding duties are plainly limited and prescribed by its stipulations."[26]

Fugitive surrender as an act of foreign policy could be conversely realized or thwarted, as state or territorial issues on both sides of the border were structurally folded into what was elsewhere a purely national, executive-driven foreign relations act. The acknowledged role for the local chief military officer to handle extraditions in times of unrest had significant meaning for the entire heavily militarized border along the intermittently revolutionary Mexican frontier. State civilian officials often refused to comply with surrender requests deemed inoffensive by federal officials at further remove from local sensitivities. In turn, federal policymakers sometimes claimed an inability to intercede in state extradition decisions, especially if Mexico appealed to Texas instead of to the United States for the surrender of a fugitive. This was the case in the 1887 request for the surrender of an embezzling Mexican soldier named Paulino Preciado. The extradition was rejected on very narrow technical grounds regarding the certification procedures by E. C. Forto, a county judge and extradition agent in Cameron County, Texas. When Mexico complained about the absurdity of this rejection, Secretary of State Bayard simply denied any power to intercede since "no application for his surrender [had] been through the diplomatic agents of Mexico" but through the "authorities in Texas . . . and now that these proceedings are at an end, I have no power to review the decision of local magistrate."[27] This kind of dodge effectively handed plenary foreign policy power to Texas.

The border states exception was more than just a political concession to realities in the borderlands. It in fact allowed for almost total autonomy of policymakers in the region to run their own foreign policy and extradition system. Moore could not compile statistics from extradition cases on the U.S.-Mexico border because "information has not been obtainable as to the surrenders granted under the border states clause in the treaty between the United States and Mexico. It is very seldom that a case arising under that clause is brought to the attention of the Department of State."[28] Free of federal oversight, the space of extradition law gathered as many meanings and possible applications as there were local, state, and national jurisdictions on both sides of the border. The borderlands were truly different.

It is important to note that appellate power was reserved to the federal government through writs of error and writs of habeas corpus brought to the federal courts, so despite the local control, theoretically, no extradition request was allowed to violate federal law. But the evolution of this clarity in extradition proceedings was slowed by the context of the border clause exception, and the connection between local governance and federal executive plenary oversight did not become clearly enunciated until 1884 in the controversial Trimble extradition case that is discussed in chapter 5.

Virtually every extradition case of this era reflected these issues of border exception in some way. Not all of them were problematic. In some cases, the local extradition agents proved to be more responsive—and quicker—than their counterparts in federally directed extradition proceedings. Local and state officials sometimes produced surrender of fugitives to the other jurisdictions that might not have occurred in other circumstances. The system took a surprisingly long time to evolve. Judges acted as Texas extradition agents along the Rio Grande border, but it took twenty years for them to begin to get paid for their acts. Texas Governor O. M. Roberts, in introducing a state constitutional amendment to have the judge/extradition agents compensated in 1881, said, "it has often been difficult to get this service performed, and those officers, who have been patriotic enough to act promptly, have had to do so without any compensation. The duties are often onerous. I, therefore, recommend that some provision be made to compensate all of the officers concerned in this business for the actual services performed therein." Two years prior, Roberts had overseen a massive expansion of the state extradition system. "On account of the facility of criminals in crossing the Rio Grande from either side, to avoid arrests and prosecutions," he said, "it became necessary to appoint *all* of the county judges and district judges whose jurisdictions reached that river, extradition agents in behalf of Texas." Texas was not lacking in local officials capable of overseeing transboundary fugitive exchanges.[29]

In some cases, local control created concerns about the abuse of power, triggered transnational disputes, and even prompted extralegal killing, as discussed later in this chapter. Having the power to extradite locally sometimes encouraged bypass of the exchange system entirely. The status of fugitives as themselves outside the law seemed to invite lawless behavior that differed sharply from all other U.S. extradition relations—except perhaps those on the Canadian-U.S. borderlands in the 1840s.[30]

A much more decentralized reality on the southern border made extradition relations there utterly unlike the tightly defined extradition relations with Great Britain. Canada's proximity was comparable in terms of geography, ease of movement, and flight, and as might be expected, the extradition relations with both the Canadian and British regimes had been often strained and rife with conflict, challenges, excesses, and intimations of violence. But the British imperial context was a critical becalming element missing from the relationship with Mexico. While transborder extradition relations could be episodically intense at the Canadian border, the stability and uniformity of that dominion did not present the same array of contingency and chaos that so repeatedly (and for so long) characterized the Rio Grande Valley. Ultimately, extradition relations were about power more than justice. The relationship with Canada was embedded in the extradition system with Great Britain, where power was more regularized and constrained. The relations with Mexico provided a great deal of leeway for federal and state officials to exercise authority and limit the exposure of American citizens to the arbitrariness that policymakers believed defined Mexican justice.

While local control of extradition was common in Texas under the border states clauses, it was in fact further complicated in the Arizona and New Mexico territories given the realities of the governance structure and federal authority over the administration of territorial affairs. Furthermore, Arizona extradition statutes allowed even greater latitude by granting power to "any justice of the Supreme Court of the Territory" to "make requisition upon the executive or other principal authority of any State or province of the Mexican Republic adjoining the boundaries of the Territory, agreeably to the stipulations of the treaty."[31]

The ease of crossing into Mexico from the Arizona Territory coupled with an intense burst of illegality and violence in the region seemed especially to invite abuses of the space for action provided by the border clause exception. Territorial status also added a level of complexity since the governance system was already highly stratified at the same time it remained in a process of formation. As Katherine Benton-Choen argues, "maintaining a border, then as now, required navigating carefully between local and federal governments and between civil and military authority and along the fine line between law enforcement and vigilantism."[32]

In February 1881, an Arizona sheriff and three others crossed into Mexico from Tombstone and grabbed a fugitive criminal "without complying with the formalities prescribed by the extradition treaty." Manuel de Zamacona, the head of the Mexican legation in the United States, told Secretary of State James G. Blaine that the men had to be punished and changes in the legal system made immediately. He called for "the adoption of penal and repressive measures [which] is inspired not only by sentiment of wounded national dignity, but by the solicitude for the reestablishment of respect for law and treaty in the frontier districts of both countries, this being a matter in which both Republics are equally interested."[33] But this mutual interest was not actually entirely clear.

In a case soon after in the fall of 1881, the same unwillingness to call through legal procedures occurred again, this time in the summary hanging of two horse thieves, one of whom was a Mexican citizen named José Ordiña. John J. Gosper, the acting governor of Arizona, spoke with V. Morales, the Mexican consul in Tucson, who was informed of the event by, among others, R. H. Paul, the sheriff of Pima County, who was involved in the hanging. These sources revealed (or claimed) that Ordiña was only going to be hanged long enough to give up information about the whereabouts of the stolen horses, but then they accidentally hanged him too long! Gosper was unmoved at this so-called accidental death, and he told Morales that while "the illegal and unfortunate hanging of these two men without due process of law" was indeed unfortunate, "the two men were probably outlaws" anyway, and witnesses in court would have been hard to find to testify against them. Extradition almost certainly would not have worked and was not locally accepted. And even if Gosper had wanted to intervene, as he later explained to Blaine, the "Executive of the territory cannot legally interfere with the local affairs of any county," unless the laws were declared not enforceable. Since he was "simply the Acting Governor of the Territory," Gosper did not feel "justified in inaugurating radical measures" to force changes in the ways local authorities handled crime.[34]

In a truly blinkered statement, Gosper also intimated to Blaine that Mexicans were just overly sensitive. Both governments should be proactive, he wrote, but Mexico is "sometimes perhaps more sensitive over crimes committed by Americans than the circumstances in particular cases would justify." He agreed that the legal system was fraying, but this was only a current reality. "While it is true Americans on our side of the line are often guilty of murder and theft upon the citizens of Mexico it is equally true that Mexicans on their side of said line are equally guilty with Americans in the matter of murder and theft and until recently—since the cow-boy combinations along the border for common plunder, the crimes committed against citizens of both the Governments of the U.S. and Mexico along the borders were, in most part, committed by citizens of Mexico."[35]

Gosper continually agitated for more authority as governor and more force through the U.S. marshals or the military to bring order to the region: "If I could be assured that I would be sustained by the *General Government* and that I should remain as Acting Governor long enough to make the effort, I would find some legal authority and the proper civil officers to bring about a different state of affairs in the present disturbed portions of the Territory." The collapse of the local legal system as far as extradition was concerned was near total, and the territorial government was unable to compel action.[36] Order was a long time in coming, especially in an Arizona Territory teetering into chaos, violence, and bloodshed betwixt "Cowboy" crimes and Apache warfare in which local governance remained nonfunctional or nonexistent.

New Mexico provided a similar situation where local authorities governed extradition as though the legal order in the territory was not fully established for decades. In 1882, Territorial Governor Lionel A. Sheldon told the Legislative Assembly of New Mexico, "organized, vigorous States adjacent to us are driving the bad elements from their borders, and they naturally come to New Mexico as a promising theatre in which to prolong a carnival of crime," and unfortunately "the Jurisprudence of this Territory is not certain nor well defined."[37] Given their relative emptiness and loose judicial systems, Arizona and New Mexico Territories were themselves attractive draws to fugitives from justice in Texas and to a lesser extent, other parts of the West. Surrenders of fugitives to other states were very common, and the relative fluidity of this process presents an interesting contrast to the (non-)surrenders of fugitives to Mexico.[38]

It was in Texas where the problems of the border clause exceptions were the most troublesome for international relations and borderlands peace. Sometimes it just meant a general devolution of extradition into a local matter handled in the same way so many local legal issues were handled in the interests of a broader peace and stability—informally, unofficially, independently, and often extralegally. Other times, the motivations were darker and the results were more problematic, more violent, and more emblematic of the confused jurisdictional spaces of the region.

An example of local treatment was the surrender of John H. Aufdemorte, "the defaulting Redemption Clerk of the Sub Treasury at New Orleans," who embezzled thirteen thousand dollars and fled to Monterrey, Mexico, in 1885, where he changed his appearance and hid for three months. Robert C. Campbell, the U.S. consul there, discovered his whereabouts, made all of the appropriate reports on both sides of the Rio Grande, and managed to get Aufdemorte arrested. On August 20, Deputy U.S. Marshal Henry C. Parker and Lovell H. Jerome, the collector of customs at Corpus Christi, came to collect Aufdemorte with some extradition papers that were found to be "not correct" by the Mexican authorities. This led to a scramble to get the proper papers and approvals, as Aufdemorte was entitled by Mexican law to be released within 48 hours. This problem was not at all an issue of Mexican intransigence ("Governor Canuto Garcia of this state is very kindly disposed towards the United States and has rendered every assistance possible to expedite matters in the extradition of Criminals," Campbell reported) but rather of simple American disorganization.[39]

Meanwhile, the marshal visited Aufdemorte in prison, and Aufdemorte promised "that he would go quietly with the Marshal to the United States." Since no response was forthcoming from Mexico City, Governor Garcia was amenable, and the border was so easily reachable, the men set off with the prisoner to Laredo accompanied by the Monterrey chief of police and two Mexican soldiers. Campbell reported that the trip was "very pleasant," even though Aufdemorte had some stomach pain. He was so cooperative that they did not even handcuff him. There was no intent for them to violate the extradition treaty or cause a jurisdictional headache in allowing the Monterrey police chief to bring

Aufdemorte into Laredo, but this was the functional result in the eyes of the two unhappy sovereignties involved. Campbell claimed that he thought it was his "duty to save the Government further trouble and additional expense" by running this semiprivate surrender. In the end, after a reserved and apologetic report, the issue was resolved and Aufdemorte was tried.[40]

Other cases were not so easily resolved or so benign. For instance, there was the series of events culminating in the murder of Francisco Resures (also called Francisco Arresures and sometimes Erresuris), a Mexican citizen wrongly extradited to Mexico without sufficient cause by local Texas authorities in Eagle Pass in the summer of 1886. This happened at the same time the Cutting case was brewing, and this context of extraterritorial reach was significant. The United States became particularly attendant to and exercised about the incident because it believed Arresures was an American citizen, when in fact it turned out that his name was Resures and he was a Mexican citizen who had deserted the army and fled to Texas.

But his citizenship mattered less than the total failure of the legality of the extradition system and what was seen as corrosive and invasive Mexican illegality because of the heightened sensitivity of that period. The outrage surpassed considerations of citizenship. The whole affair was presented initially as, in the words of a *San Antonio Daily Express* headline, "another Mexican outrage," but even more it was in fact a failure of the entire extradition system in the local involvement on both sides of the border.[41]

As Sutton wrote the State Department, "[Arresures] was a 'bad man' who was wanted in Piedras Negras for several acts contrary to the laws," though he gave no evidence that Arresures was more than a deserter who had some enemies, and the rest of the record provides none. "By what is supposed to have been a private agreement between the officials of the two sides an exchange of men wanted was made," Sutton reported. Arresures was arrested "without sufficient cause" in Eagle Pass by the sheriff, Y. L. Oglesby, and the deputy sheriff, Bonifacio Diaz, acting on the basis of a warrant issued by Maverick County judge and extradition agent Joseph Hoffstetter. After "a farcical examination" of fifteen minutes, Arresures was "rendered up to Mondragon," the Coahuila chief of police who Sutton said had "a personal grudge against him." The prisoner was handcuffed only until reaching the Mexican side of the bridge, when he was unshackled. Supposedly he "took flight" and "in any rate he [Mondragon] shot him [Arresures] while ostensibly moving him at night from the Piedras Negras to the Zaragoza jail." Though the local consul complained that Arresures was an American citizen, Sutton "was unable to find good evidence to prove this claim and believ[ed] him to have been legally what he was at heart, a Mexican citizen."[42]

Sutton was distressed that "his extradition, if not abduction, was at the best a pitiless farce," and he argued that "the Texas officers, County Judge Hoffstetter and Sheriff Oglesby, who were responsible there should be severely punished." They had been indicted but not tried, which often meant quiet acquittal on the border in such cases.[43] Secretary of State Bayard put it even more bluntly, saying that Arresures was "simply kidnapped on Texan soil by the complicity of the sheriff and county judge" and the incident was in no way an extradition under the terms of the treaty. He condemned the "collusion of officers of the State of Coahuila and of Maverick County, Texas under circumstances which leave no reasonable doubt that a brutal murder was the object and result of the successful attempt of the Coahuila officials to get unlawful possession of Arresures." Bayard remarked that his sensitivity to this issue was certainly intensified by the ongoing Cutting crisis, and as a result he focused on the crime of extralegal murder in Mexico rather than on the nature of the so-called extradition process on the Texas side. In a statement of jurisdiction in which territory mattered more than citizenship, Bayard wrote,

> The citizenship of Arresures is not material. He appears to have resided for some years in the United States, and there to have declared his intention to become its citizen. He was therefore not merely under the protection which the laws of the United States and of the State of Texas, where he had his residence, throw over him as an alien resident, but entitled to the peculiar protection, as against any unlawful exercise of authority emanating from the land of his origin, with which our laws invest those aliens lawfully within their jurisdiction who have acquired rights of inchoate citizenship by duly making declaration of intention to become citizens.[44]

Bayard also rejected the idea that Arresures was killed while escaping as a standby Mexican claim. "This plea is one of unhappily familiar repetition," he wrote. "This Government has never met with so conclusive an instance as this where a solitary and unarmed man, taken from his bed at dead of night by a body of armed men, conducted just outside the town limits, and while pinioned and blindfolded had been alleged to have attempted flight from his guard. Such a statement mocks the moral sense and defies credulity."[45]

Mondragon was overheard saying he had ordered Arresures killed, and according to the local consul, he was supposedly responsible for many other such summary executions. Nevertheless, he was very quickly acquitted of the murder. This rapid decision of the Mexican courts made Bayard fume since it was in such contrast with the ongoing proceedings in the comparatively interminable trial of A. K. Cutting in Paso del Norte.[46]

It was almost certainly because of the Cutting case that this episode was not simply buried, as the fervor over territoriality and jurisdiction on the border was historically intense at that moment. As such, Bayard stressed less the culpability of Texas officials and more the lawlessness and jurisdictional overstretch of the Mexicans. The collected diplomatic correspondence over it, with supporting documentation, made it seem like an enormously significant case that was out of proportion to its actual effect on the course of extradition policy.

Alternatively, Sutton, writing several months later and not ever as caught up in the Cutting case frenzy, firmly blamed the episode almost entirely on the actions of local officials and the inadequacies of the overall system. He expected execution of prisoners in Mexico and was not surprised by Mondragon's extralegal acts. "His powers were rather full and indefinite and he only received his prisoner on Mexican soil," wrote Sutton, pointing out that the "outrage" was not one accomplished in American territory. "Whether it is legal or not, these summary executions are quite common in Mexico and not a matter of general regret," he added. But the officials in Texas revealed the problems with the current extradition system. Sutton argued that illegal prisoner exchange and summary execution were in fact the logical endpoint of the extradition regime on the border: "Owning to the restrictions of the present extradition treaty with Mexico and the difficulty of getting criminals across the border to answer for the crimes alleged against them, this sort of unlawful action is tolerated by the law abiding element as the only way to get rid of this class of people." Indeed, it did appear from the documentation that Hoffstetter used the opportunity of the extradition request not just to order his arrest but to expel him immediately. This act occurred entirely in U.S. jurisdiction. Mariscal therefore blamed the killing on "an officious manner by the American authorities, who, not content with his arrest, but influenced by his criminal reputation, ordered that he be forthwith conducted to Mexican territory."[47]

This extradition case revealed the ways in which extradition on the border could be easily harnessed to local issues and interest in personal, extralegal deals made possible by Article II of the treaty. The State Department quickly moved on from this issue. A handwritten note attached to Sutton's final report in the

State Department file (which seems to have been signed by Moore), reads, "this is all doubtless true. We presented claim, and there I think the matter will end. We may ack. + file" and then, written in a different hand (probably that of Assistant Secretary of State George C. Rives), "so ordered, 19 December 1887."[48] Only the simultaneous explosion of the Cutting case, perhaps the most significant jurisdictional dispute of the era, helped to keep Resures/Arresures from an utterly obscure and forgotten death.

There were a great many of these cases on the border, where local involvement in extradition proceedings verged into transboundary abduction or extralegal murder. These cases are really only known in full because occasionally an American consul became incensed at the lawlessness and corruption that prevailed on both sides of the river and chose to write about them, or the local press sought to cover news of another Mexican outrage. While the tonalities of outrage toward perceived Mexican illegality varied, there was not uncommonly a certain amount of shock over how implicated Texas officialdom was in this system. In some ways, this feeling mirrored the irritation and disdain various consuls felt for Texan incursions across the border during the tumultuous days of the 1870s.

This kind of outrage and activism on the part of a U.S. consul is exemplified in a situation involving Joseph G. Donnelly, consul general at Nuevo Laredo, who single-mindedly pursued justice on both sides of the Rio Grande in the name of a murdered Mexican deserter named Atilano Mata in the fall of 1894. "A great crime has been committed here, not only against an individual entitled to the right of asylum in our land and the protection of our laws, but a crime in violation of the sovereignty of the United States," wrote Donnelly. He told Judge Matias Guerra of the Court of First Instance in Nuevo Laredo that he was "convinced that this great crime . . . was the result of a conspiracy." Even worse, what Donnelly felt made it a "tragic outrage" was that "American officials sworn to execute the law [were] the paid accessories of such crimes." Donnelly found this to be an endemic problem all along the border, where American officials often illegally delivered Mexican nationals accused of crime and especially desertion rather than engage the often bulky extradition system or let deserters live in peace: "It is freely claimed that in nearly every border county there are men playing the double role of American officer and Mexican spy—a part well rewarded when well acted—who are retained to run down refugees from Mexico, and without mercy and without legal process, disregarding humanity and law, deliver up their victims."[49]

The story that so outraged and energized Donnelly concerned Atilano Mata, a deserter from the Mexican army who had crossed the river to go live with his mother in Laredo, Texas, for eight months. On September 15, 1894, Mata was arrested without any legal process by Antonio Magnon, chief deputy sheriff of Webb County. Mata was released the next day, or so the official story went. In fact, he was tied up and thrown in the back of a wagon by Magnon and another deputy sheriff. At the same time, a Mexican skiff owner, Ricardo Hernandez, was forced at gunpoint to take Pedro Hernandez (no relation) of the Mexican Rurales along with some other Rurales and a couple of soldiers over the river into Laredo. The two groups met at 2:00 a.m. on the Laredo side of the Rio Grande. The bound Mata was handed over to Hernandez and his men, who carried him back to the skiff. As it crossed back to the Mexican side, there was a struggle and the boat capsized. The Rurales fired some shots. One of them, Sixto Perez, made it back to the American side, and Pedro Hernandez escaped. "The corpse of the boatman Ricardo Hernandez was taken from the river two days later." Mata's body was found on September 19, his skull showing "a deep dent," apparently from a pistol blow.[50]

This story would have almost certainly not been noticed, considering the involvement of local law enforcement, had Donnelly not made it his personal cause throughout the following several months. As it was, there was little official interest in it in either Mexico or the United States. It became something of a one-man crusade. Donnelly managed to successfully lobby the Nuevo Laredo government to arrest Hernandez, after which the consul personally took the sworn statements of every witness he could find. It was made his task to substantiate the charges he brought, which he said was "no easy task" since witnesses were afraid to talk to him in Mexico as they "fear[ed] to cross the border or enter a Mexican court intimidated by dread of the military." Guadalupe Estrada, a skiffman who saw the transfer of Mata and was the man who saved Sixto Perez's life, told Donnelley, "I am afraid that Magnon or Hernandez will kill me. I am still afraid for others have been killed by him." Despite all of his hard work, which filled many pages of testimony, Donnelly sensed that "military terrorism and subornation of perjury seemed likely to defeat the ends of justice."[51]

Donnelly considered it his duty to force this issue for at least two reasons: to bring order and the rule of law to the region and to expose the lax system that had developed there and that undermined what he understood to be broader U.S. objectives. "That minor County officers of Texas were corruptly concerned does not lessen the outrage but rather aggravates it," he stated. He was sure that this kind of transfer was common, and all officials on the border were implicated: "I am now compelled to the belief that consular officers in the past could not have been altogether ignorant of the practice; and knowledge thereof not communicated to the Department, could only have been concealed through cowardice or worse." Loose legality on the border did not fit comfortably into the American narrative of order, power, and civilization being broadcast in the region, and it did not fit into the accepted operations of state power. "The people feel that life and liberty on the border will be more secure if the perpetrators of this outrage are exposed and punished and they look to the Government I represent to secure justice and assert the dignity and sovereignty of the United States," he wrote, perhaps a bit grandly. Certainly it did not look like "the people" were seeking this justice. The two deputy sheriffs "seem[ed] not unlikely to escape the just consequences of their crimes." They were given very light bail and went to visit Hernandez in jail in Nuevo Laredo "almost daily."[52]

The subject of Donnelly's mini-crusade ultimately devolved into another variant of Mexican incursion, and his narrative concerning local corruption was lost. Donnelly did not write again to detail what happened to the officers on either side, and the criminality that so disturbed him seemed to have dissipated. The next year, when some American hunters near Carrizo, Texas, were fired on by men apparently in Mexican military uniforms (they may have been customs officers) and, according to them, had their boat and other property stolen (it may have been confiscated), Donnelly reported that he would have been surprised if the attackers actually had been the military. "Since the Mata incident . . . the Mexican military authorities along the border [have] shown a wholesome respect for boundary lines and due consideration of the rights of American citizens," he wrote.[53]

While the record offers a huge array of cases that highlighted the dubious legalities prevalent on the border, it is worth noting that toward the end of the nineteenth century, the system in place often operated just as it was designed, with little interference from the federal governments of either state and efficient fugitive surrenders produced by local officials acting in concert with governors and consuls communicating at the local level. For example, in the case of John Keeton, wanted in Coleman County, Texas, for train robbery, Mexico City and the State Department were informed, but since it was not a controversial case, it was handled as a purely local matter. And handled very rapidly too. Keeton was arrested in Ciudad Juárez on order of the deputy sheriff of Coleman County, on May 10, 1899. Charles W. Kindrick, the U.S. consul, certified the papers and "requested the local authorities to hold Keeton pending the institution of extradition proceedings in the regular way." Texas governor Joseph D. Savers asked for his extradition from the Mexican government on May 11, 1899. The whole process took less than a day.[54]

A FINAL STAB AT THE *ZONA LIBRE*

Exception may have reigned in local control of extradition through the border states clause, but this did not mean that all jurisdictional exceptions were tolerated at this time. Seemingly on a relentless drive to increase the jurisdictional tensions at the boundary, politicians in Texas and Washington launched a newly intensified campaign against the *Zona Libre* on the idea that Mexico had no sovereign right to determine its own economic policy along the boundary. It was utterly without irony that this was done at the same time the Harmon Doctrine declared the inviolability of all American sovereign decisions on Rio Grande water usage and, by extension, reaffirmed strict territoriality on the boundary. The *Zona Libre* should in fact be seen as a related movement for borderlands autonomy. Precious few Americans saw any dissonance in decrying an action that only potentially had a negative result (a bordering free trade zone, which actually had a positive impact on Texas) while embracing a policy with an undeniably negative impact (excessive irrigation from the Rio Grande) as the wages of sovereignty. The issues were connected in the way that policymakers sought to tighten the border system by redefining jurisdiction and maximizing U.S. unilateralism, even in issues of extraterritorial importance.

Critics of the *Zona Libre* in the 1890s, most of them in Texas, did not consider it to be a legitimate policy, fundamentally because of its strong cross-border impact, which they believe lent it a much greater significance than a mere trade policy decision. They viewed it as somehow acting as more than the elimination of a tariff barrier, though it was unclear how. The details did not matter. At an El Paso City Council meeting to discuss whether to send a mission to Washington to push for an American free zone or to fight against the *Zona Libre*, Charles Merrick put it baldly: "there were two distinct interests and classes here—those on this side of the river and those on the other. Those who are not for us are against us."[55]

Surely a free trade policy that seemed to advantage one side of the trade equation must have been unfair and an affront to prosperity and sovereignty.

The *Zona Libre* was bizarrely associated with extraterritorial force in a way that other trade decisions were not. Changes to the *Zona Libre* that were intended to improve its operation for the Mexican economy were especially viewed with fear, each change often being interpreted as a search for a new death grip on the Texas border economy. In a wide variety of ways, policymakers described the free trade zone as not just a bad, held-over system comparable to the matriculation policy, for example, but as a total exception to acceptable trade relations because of its transnational effect.

The issue of smuggling remained a concern and was a focus of much of the discussion, although there were no clear answers as to how much revenue it produced or whether it was increasing or whether it was even really a problem at all. In 1888, Secretary of the Treasury C. S. Fairchild was less sure, writing that "there is no doubt that the existence of the Free Zone of Mexico furnishes *an opportunity* for smuggling into the United States," but he could not estimate what the actual impact was. Whereas the usual claim was that the bonded goods that were shipped into Mexico were smuggled back into the United States, Fairchild wrote that "this Department has no means of ascertaining to what extent this is true." Since the United States maintained a protectionist system, he did not believe that ending the *Zona Libre* would at all change the number or expense of the customs officers on the border.[56]

Warner P. Sutton, now the consul in Nuevo Laredo, continued to wage his battle against ignorant views of the *Zona Libre*. Knowing the issue was being discussed anew in Congress, he sent a pamphlet by "my friend Mr. Pedro Argüelles Collector of Customs here and a very able man," which "lays [out] the whole truth of the matter" by detailing specifically how beneficial the *Zona Libre* had been for the United States.[57] Sutton provided a strongly worded introduction to his translation, starting with an attempt to clarify the realities of smuggling. He wrote that before the zone was extended, he used to eat entire meals where everything on the table had been smuggled into Mexico from the United States. The *Zona Libre* had arrested this massive smuggling economy and enabled Mexicans to buy twice as many goods. Now, any goods smuggled into the United States would be three-quarters Mexican and perhaps one-quarter European goods. Meanwhile, three-quarters of all spending in the zone was on U.S. goods.[58]

The *Zona Libre* was now 13 miles wide and 2,248 miles deep, with the Rio Grande forming 1,308 miles of it, and the border towns of the United States almost across the board had benefited from its continuance, as Sutton had predicted at the time of its expansion. The dual river towns "were really rivals, yet they [were] also to a considerable extent mutually dependent on each other." Sutton noted that Brownsville (opposite Matamoros) and Rio Grande City (opposite Camargo) had both been advancing under the *zona* compared with the Mexican cities: "In Laredo-Nuevo-Laredo, the American side has gone forward wonderfully and is, to day, the first town in commercial importance on either side of the whole border." He argued "a considerable share of the prosperity of Laredo, Texas results from the factories now established there and this location of the railway shops" carrying the bonded goods. In Nogales, the main commercial action was on the American side of the line despite the ease of crossing the border. The United States had no reason to complain about the *Zona Libre* except out of fear and misunderstanding since this system was not a threat to U.S. prosperity or sovereignty. By contrast, Sutton reported, "there is and has been a strong Mexican opposition to the *Zona Libre* . . . [and] it is not too much to say that its bitterest and most influential enemies are in Mexico."[59]

The revitalized movement to end the *Zona Libre* reflected all of the same issues as the reaction since its expansion, but with a new emphasis on ending the bonded routes for European goods. This was seen as the more controllable aspect by the United States. Sutton called the suggestion to end the bonded routes a "radical change," especially since the routes were a core part of the economy. More bonded goods passed through Nuevo Laredo than "any other consular office in the whole foreign service." And Paso del Norte and Piedras Negras were second and third, respectively.[60]

This renewed outrage at the bonded system was strange and unexpected because it was a long-standing U.S. policy considered profitable and much enjoyed by commercial shipping and warehousing firms taking advantage of this exception to strict protectionism.[61] John F. Valls, also at Nuevo Laredo, wrote that "the proposal to take from American railroads the privilege they now have of transporting foreign goods in bond into the *Zona Libre* seemed so preposterous that none of the merchants here took it seriously" when it was first mentioned. But to the critics of the *Zona Libre*, given to hysteria as they tended to be, the sense that the goods could travel freely through the United States and then be equally free in Mexico was unnerving and repugnant. The free goods were, simply, a reward to a nation stubbornly holding on to its own damaging policy. As the century drew to a close, the issue intensified.[62]

A congressional report in 1890 covered the gamut of borderlands problems with Mexico but cheerily noted that they were solvable because both republics were "mutually interested in maintaining supremacy in the territory over which their respective flags float[ed]." But problems persisted ranging from crime to a "certain class of alien immigration" (meaning Chinese) coming up through Mexico:

Another cause of irritation arises from the fact that foreign dutiable goods destined to points of consignment or delivery in Mexico entered at ports of the United States, are permitted by our laws to pass over American lines of transportation into Mexico free from payment of import duty to this country. By an abuse of a Mexican law known as the *Zona Libre*, designed for beneficial purposes, foreign dutiable goods arriving in Mexico over American transportation lines and destined to any part of Mexico may be detained within the *Zona Libre*, or free zone of Mexico, without payment of customs duty to Mexico, having previously passed free through this country.[63]

Somehow, the Mexican usage of the system was deemed an "abuse" although it did not have a negative impact on the American economy. Indeed, Octavio Herrera Pérez argues that "another paradox that added to the trail of nonsense of the American challenges to the *Zona Libre* was that promoting the suspension of the bounded routes favored their rivals: the European commercial interests in Mexico." The irritating point to *Zona Libre* critics seemed to be that the goods passed freely and remained free, which indicated that this connected into something close to a fully free trading system for this specific set of goods. The United States did not tax them, and the failure of Mexico to do the same was unacceptable. Added to that, of course, was the long-standing idea that the goods were supposedly being smuggled back into the United States, with a subsequently "demoralization of trade [that extended] along the whole border from the Gulf of Mexico to the Pacific Ocean."[64]

A joint resolution followed requesting seven reforms, including "the establishment and maintenance of liberal commercial relations," which was an odd choice of phraseology given the rejection of the liberal free flow of goods into and out of the *Zona Libre*. The committee also wanted new "regulations for the fair administration of the customs laws of the two countries at points of interchange on the line of the coterminous boundary" and a new agreement on the "regulation and distribution" of river waters. The call for "adjustment and reform of existing boundaries on the Rio Grande and Colorado Rivers" was especially pointed, since the committee was far more interested in getting navigation rights on the Colorado, which it considered restricted since the mouth of it lay fully in Mexico. "It is not unreasonable to expect such an adjustment as will guaranty to this country security in the free use of the mouth of that river for the future," the report noted.[65]

Another impetus for the reintensified concern over the *Zona Libre* at this time was the evolution of its regulations brought by developments in the Mexican economy. Eugene O. Fechét, consul in Piedras Negras, characterized the zone in 1891 as almost an independent entity, especially since the goods manufactured in the *Zona Libre* had no special status within the Mexican economy. The towns of the *Zona Libre* were up to this point "merely trade centers.... It can be seen that the narrow strip of country extending from the mouth of the Rio Grande to the Pacific Ocean, constituting the *Zona Libre*, is, in respect to the Republic of Mexico, a foreign country as far as privileges of market for manufactured products is concerned." The fall of the price of silver helped convince Mexico in 1891 to establish "internation" duties on manufactured goods leaving the *zona* for the interior, which meant it would remain a trade center. This was considered to be an increased benefit for the United States by those who tracked the regional trade but was still viewed as a conspiracy by others. J. Bielenberg, the vice consul at Matamoros, considered the new law "a crushing blow to the privileges which [Mexico had] so far enjoyed" in the *Zona Libre*, while conversely it was "of great benefit to the commerce of the United States." *Zona Libre* goods could just as cheaply travel into the United States as into the Mexican interior, and American goods no longer faced competition in this same interior. Mexicans in the *Zona Libre* complained loudly but were in fact overshouted by their American counterparts.[66]

There developed a political movement in Washington that mirrored the debate in Texas. Senator John H. Reagan of Texas had pushed hard but unsuccessfully in 1890 to get the bonded routes suspended. The *El Paso Herald* could not figure out why it should support Reagan's bill since it had little chance of passing and it was clear the bill would definitely hurt El Paso. The paper believed a unilateral suspension of the bonded routes would actually "retard the abolishment of the free zone" because it "aroused the pride of the Mexicans." The *Herald* thought Mexicans were "peculiarly sensitive—probably foolishly so—upon any question touching the management of their own affairs, and particularly so if the suggestions or recommendations come from the United States and is sought to be enforced by retaliatory measures." Though the paper wished to see the *Zona Libre* killed, it was sensitive to the reality that attempting to force this change upon Mexico could easily backfire.[67]

Five years later, the successful effort came from Texas, where the state Senate and House of Representatives passed a joint resolution in 1895 urging the federal government to discontinue the system of the United States "so long as said *Zona Libre* shall be maintained by said Republic." The original Texas resolution erroneously claimed that in the *Zona Libre*, "no tariff laws are in force," but this was amended by striking out the words "no tariff laws exist" and inserting "the tariff existing is so low as to make a ruinous discrimination against the business of American towns on our Mexican frontier." This sentence was not bizarre in the context of Texas anti–*Zona Libre* politics although the idea of a ruinous discrimination through a *low* tariff was certainly manifestly strange.

The resolution declared, "the effect of free trade in said free zone is disastrous to the commerce and material prosperity of that portion of Texas adjacent thereto," with particularly devastating effect on the "honest importers in the State of Texas and other parts of the United States." Clearly, the Texas politicians saw the problem with the *Zona Libre* to be that Mexico was insisting on setting its own tariff laws according to its own interests (or at least those of the northern border states) rather than shaping its national policy to the current ends of Americans.[68]

This reborn movement led some proponents of the zone to redouble their lobbying against the Texas legislation. J. B. Gorman, the consul from Matamoros in 1895, sent a long report on "such a contingency, showing its disastrous effects upon American commerce and trade with Northern Mexico." He included a clipping from the *Galveston Daily News*, which argued "that instead of seeking the abolition of the free zone we should ask Mexico to extend it." He believed that the end of the bonded system would mean "the total abolishon [sic] of the *Zona Libre*." All the rail traffic and steamship traffic via New Orleans would be redirected to the Mexican ports. New Orleans and Galveston would be replaced by Bagdad, which would "awake from its 30 years of deathless sleep and Tampico and Vera Cruz grow to greater wealth and importance." Gorman detailed a long list of things bought in the United States, all "necessities of life" bought by *Zona Libre* inhabitants who did not seek to buy European finery. Gorman argued that smuggling was greatly reduced from "former years" and consisted only of cigarettes, mezcal, needle work, and other such items that could be easily handled by the full array of U.S. interdiction agents in the region: U.S. military, state troops, marshals, special treasury agents, and customs officers.[69]

Gorman presented a lot of figures in support of his argument, many of which were later determined to be a bit off and were later corrected by Joseph G. Connelly, the consul general at Nuevo Laredo. But Connelly seconded Gorman's passion, noting that the agitation in Texas against the *Zona Libre* was "by the same parties on the Texas border who have carried [it] for the past ten years." He was amazed that Reagan's failed bid had been revived and warned "Mexico was and is unmoved" by this current threat. "In fact the main thing which maintains the Zone is Texas agitation to suppress it," he argued. "Let that agitation cease [and] the Mexican policy of gradually increasing duties here would speedily prevail. The Free Zone is a good thing in a small way but it isn't big enough nor free enough. Its extensions, not its abolitions would benefit the United States."[70]

The consulates were unified in support of the *Zona Libre* and actually had been for decades, led by Sutton, but policymakers pushing the change in bonded routes policy apparently did not read these reports. The State Department forwarded this information to the Treasury Department, and it was made publicly available, but the key to the 1890s anti–*Zona Libre* movement was that it was not responding to facts on the ground but rather to the concepts regarding Mexican liberalized trade that lived in the minds of agitators along the border. It was the potential there, perceived to be coiling like a snake ready to strike, rather than the reality of increased trade that focused the minds of policymakers.

The Texas resolution produced results in Congress, though not without debate. Not every member of the Texas delegation was against the *Zona Libre*. In debate on February 27, 1895, William H. Crain (a representative from pro–*Zona Libre* Brownsville) quoted some "leading citizens" saying, "the arguments favoring the abolition of the *Zona Libre* do not apply here." Crain alone cut directly to the oddity and paradox of the U.S. position in a statement that minced no words:

> I cannot understand, Mr. Speaker, how Democrats who are theoretically and who are assumed to be practically free traders can favor a measure which has for its ultimate effect, as stated in the body of it, the coercion of a sister Republic into the disestablishment of free trade and the establishment in lieu thereof of a protective tariff system. I can readily understand how logically and consistently our Republican brethren can support such a proposition, but I fail to understand how gentlemen claiming to be Democrats and who are willing to put wool upon the free list and sugar upon the free list and iron upon the free list, and other raw materials upon the free list, can support a measure which declares to the Mexican Government that it must discontinue free trade along our frontier and substitute in place of it a protective tariff sys-

tem. . . . Now, Mexican wool comes into Texas free. Why? Because we have established a *Zona Libre*, not three miles in extent, but coextensive with the limits of the United States, because we have made wool free. . . . It is said that the Mexican Government wants this Free Zone disestablished. It is within their own province. It is within their own territorial jurisdiction, and if they desire to have it abolished, why does not the Mexican Congress, acting with the Mexican President, abolish it? Is it possible that in order to accomplish this result they appeal to the American Congress? We might as well say that until Great Britain does away with comparative free trade we will keep up our high protective tariff system. We repel the idea of coercion on the part of European Governments, and yet we attempt to establish a similar policy by our legislative enactment.[71]

Crain was especially exercised that any American politician could demand that a foreign nation obey American dictates since no one would conceive of the United States doing so in terms of its own politics of trade. And this trade policy provided a contradictory example at best. Crain negatively cast the attempt to control Mexican trade policy in terms of foreign market interests and domestic partisanship as well as the strong emphasis on U.S. sovereignty emphasized in so many other ways. Nevertheless, Congress did end up passing a law preventing bonded goods from going to the *Zona Libre*, though they were still allowed to be shipped through the United States to the rest of Mexico.[72]

Sutton, in his usual role as advocate of the mutual advantages of the *Zona Libre* for both Mexico and Texas, was widely interviewed about the new law and the fresh attacks on the zone in the United States. No doubt to tweak the Texans who were so opposed to it, he told the *Lower Rio Grande* newspaper in Brownsville that the *Zona Libre* was an "extraordinary exhibition of State rights." He called the anti–bonded route law "the most hostilely offensive legislation passed by our Government in many a year. It is, in effect, a threat, and an effort to compel Mexico to change her domestic arrangements under foreign pressure. She herself has struggled with the question for years and would gladly embrace any good plan to get rid of the anomaly if this could be done without serious injury to her own people." Sutton made a telling contrast between American sovereign practice and that in Mexico:

We in Colorado have, since 1880, taken away the waters of the Rio Grande which for hundreds of years have irrigated the Mexican valley at Paso del Norte, so that her agriculture there is ruined and her people living in misery except the few foreigners who are in commercial pursuits. We have not yet seen our way to restore this water either by means of dams or otherwise, notwithstanding the great annual loss which this entails. We have recently put on an absurd quarantine against all Mexican cattle when the most that was justified was as to certain districts. Our Agricultural Department has also, within a few months, requested the State of Texas to pass a law against an alleged cotton insect said to [be] found in Mexico, an action which is as useless as it is hostile.[73]

Sutton found not irony but hostility in the U.S. attempt to force a change in the Mexican *Zona Libre* policy, especially given all of these numerous other instances in which the United States asserted unilateral actions over transnational affairs to the detriment of Mexico. And these were all matters that did not have the proven benefits for both sides of the border like the *Zona Libre*. Tightening jurisdiction and improving the interstate system, which he had advocated throughout a long career on the border, did not necessitate this type of action. Borderlands calm and prosperity could only be produced by transnational agreement, not unilateral assertion. And Sutton cautioned that if the *Zona Libre* was ended, then bonded trade would shift to Mexican ports, and railroads in Texas would be left with "the unprofitable task of holding the empty sacks."[74]

In the U.S. Congress and in Texas, there had been a wishful belief that this change would "probably be welcomed by the Mexican Government," but reports after its passage from consuls like John F. Valls indicated that there was "intense feeling here against [the] measure in Congress taking bonded privileges from *Zona Libre*, [which is] regarded as an unbecoming attempt to force Mexico to increase her protective duties and injurious to best interests of both countries. . . . The impression is general that no good can come from the measure." Valls predicted that "should [the United States] fail to abolish the *Zona Libre*, as seems probable, then the business now done by American roads of carrying bonded goods via United States ports will be transferred to Mexican roads via Tampico."[75] This last point, that Mexican free ports could be opened for European bonded goods, had been the subject of more wishful thinking. The anti–*Zona Libre El Paso Times* claimed it was a "a bug-a-boo connection," but it was mistaken.[76]

The Mexican response was "blunt" and quick and, unsurprisingly, very much opposed to the hostile American legislation. In response, Mexico indeed opened these "bug-a-boo" specialized transportation routes for foreign bonded goods to supply the *Zona Libre* running through Tampico, Veracruz, and Guaymas.[77] Since this was precisely the replacement feared by bonded routes advocates in the United States, the movement to repeal the legislation began almost immediately, though it took some years to finally do so.[78]

The *Zona Libre* catalyzed a system of border-crossing in which bonded goods, smugglers, criminals, and legal commercial interests stood in sharp contrast to the protectionist U.S. border. It also continued to unnerve Texas and federal policymakers, as the total failure of the state response was a reminder of the limits of power in the absence of true jurisdiction. The nation simply could not always compel compliance in such a transnational quandary. The *Zona Libre* transformed the commercial relationship into a more profound and wide-reaching borderlands governance relationship in ways that American merchants and policymakers were left to respond to but could not control.

But there were other, more profound ways for state power to be exercised and for the system to be inexorably turned toward service to American interests. It was this very instability in trade relations that invited (or even required) establishment of new orders in other realms, particularly in jurisdictional questions related to extradition and interdiction, where governance was easier to construct. In these questions, U.S. policy built on strict territoriality, exclusion, exception, and a drive for unilateral solutions to quintessentially transnational problems could still yield results.

PART TWO

Unwhipped of Justice

CHAPTER FOUR

Crime, Pure and Simple

Why this specific enumeration of the crimes,—this proviso? Does not this enumeration evidently exclude crimes not named therein? If not, why enumerate? If the maxim *"expressio unius est exclusio alterius"* does not apply here, it can never be applied to any act either of Congress or the State Legislatures. It would be a useless, antiquated maxim and should be expunged from legal literature. To hold that it has no application in this treaty would render treaties a snare and a delusion, a farce and a solemn fraud.

R. A. Blandford v. The State, Texas Court of Appeals, 1881

Extradition did not knit the world together but rather linked it into discrete chains of exchange. The extradition network that emerged roughly realized by the 1890s was a decentralized, loosely arrayed series of bilateral arrangements similar in design and intent but never completely replicated. Constrained through precise treaty language, extradition arrangements operated independently and free of competition between jurisdictions. The few truly shared aspects of extradition, which were the elements that made it a global phenomenon, were rooted upon finely drawn definitions of political crime and terrorism. Aside from these, extradition relations remained exclusive and idiosyncratic, a transnational system created by the state to cement jurisdiction and strict territoriality.

Sir Edward Clarke, a British nineteenth-century expert on extradition, wrote, "in the matter of extradition, the American law was, until 1870, better than that of any other country in the world."[1] By "better," he meant not just coherent but more integrated with policy and procedure. But Clarke's evaluation of the best law changed after Great Britain created its systematic Extradition Act of 1870. Considered inflexible and a threat to sovereignty by the United States, this act remained basic British law for over a century and provided a significant model for global procedures. The British government liked to grandiosely consider the act (as Secretary of State Hamilton Fish phrased it) "the embodiment of what was the general opinion of all countries on the subject of extradition."[2] Great Britain sought to rationalize and codify all extradition processes and have treaties (including ones already signed) tightly constrained by the Act of 1870. These strictures were principally a strictly delineated list of extraditable crimes that largely excluded "fiscal offences," an emphasis on the rule of specialty, and especially the political offense exception to extradition.[3]

But this approach was not held by the unilateralist United States, and the contrast between the two approaches to establishing extradition relations and defining jurisdictions after 1870 was sharp and headed for conflict. The United States refused to recognize the act as anything other than a statement of British policy irrelevant to U.S. practices. Fish told British minister Sir Edward Thornton that the United States could not accede to the Act of 1870 and consider extradition "for crimes which may be created or changed in their definition by foreign legislation by enactments subsequent to our entering into the arrangements. For the United States to do this would be to abdicate to that extent their sovereignty."[4]

Viewed as a whole, the series of American extradition relations with other states formed a unique system in which foreign policy interests were safeguarded without many (or any) significant concessions being made in return. No agreement was made that truly challenged the particularistic U.S. understanding of territoriality or the nation's existing sense of judicial purity or ideological exceptionalism. None required the United States to change its procedures or definitions of crimes. Indeed, the diversity across the different extradition treaties had the opposite effect. Rather than change any aspect of U.S. interests, policymakers simply changed the terms of extradition they were willing to accept in each specific circumstance.

The United States proved to be powerfully intransigent when its unilateralist efforts failed and often continued diplomatic disputes for decades rather than concede a point. When confronted with challenges to the U.S. unilateral definition of appropriate extradition structures, policymakers tended to demand total compliance with their view or refused to create an agreement.

It is important to recognize that as unilateralist as American motivations were, the treaty-making process was a bilateral diplomatic exchange in which both sides had agency. There were necessarily distinctions "drawn between what a state *wishes* to do in terms of applying its law to disputes involving foreign elements, and what a state is *entitled* to do." Sometimes extradition negotiations and systems broke down over major policy differences, such as the controversy over the exclusion of citizens in U.S.-Italian extradition, and sometimes over trifling matters, such as an unwillingness of Denmark to accept a clause "providing that each nation should pay the expense of the arrest of the persons whose extradition it asks."[5] The United States did not dictate extradition treaties, and it dealt with numerous states from imperial powers to small states, which were all also highly protective of their own interests. But policymakers did very assertively seek to create extradition agreements to reflect American interests first and foremost as much as possible without accommodation to foreign interests.

In some instances, the United States simply eliminated crimes from the list of extraditable offenses in the treaty. In cases of negotiating treaties and modifications of extradition relations with powers like Britain, Italy, and very small states like the Orange Free State in Africa, the United States preferred to suspend the system of fugitive surrender entirely than to concede an important point.

For example, when the Orange Free State initiated renegotiation of the decade-old "General Convention of Friendship, Commerce, and Extradition" in 1894, the United States used the opportunity to insist on the adoption of two different treaties, one on friendship and commerce and a separate one purely on extradition. It invited the Orange Free State to propose the draft commercial treaty based upon the nation's "changed situation" as it saw fit, but the U.S. claimed for itself the authority to draft (and really to dictate) an extradition treaty based on the U.S.-Switzerland agreement since these two tiny states seemed similar in American eyes. This divided effort was seen as an opportunity to de-link, clarify, and control the extradition relationship. After years of detailed negotiation and continued insistence on not accepting the Orange Free State's suggestions of modifications to the treaty, the United States was willing to sign this treaty at last in 1896, though final ratification did not come until 1899.[6] Such an unyielding stance was not infrequent or the result of happenstance; intransigence was standard.

Nor did the United States cultivate much of an awareness of the extradition interests or procedures of other states. The State Department did not even inquire into foreign extradition practices in a formal, systematic way until November 1888, when it sent a ten-part circular asking the consular service for reports on the practice of extradition. This was the same period when the U.S. Supreme Court quite suddenly decided a series of extradition cases (discussed throughout part 2) that limited foreign influence, reinforced territoriality, and expanded the reach of American power beyond borders unrestrained by legal or international comity restrictions.[7] The judicial and political wings worked in conjunction to clarify and strengthen U.S. territoriality and unilateralism.

Following the 1843 treaty with France, and signaling an avid interest in restructuring U.S. jurisdictional reach, the United States rapidly created extradition relations with nations all over the world. The treaties the United States signed, with supplemental and replacement treaty dates included, were as follows:[8]

Great Britain	1794, 1842, 1889
France	1843, 1845, 1858
Hawaii	1849
Swiss Confederation	1850
Prussia and German Confederation	1852
Bavaria	1853
Bremen	1853
Mecklenburg-Schwerin	1853
Mecklenburg-Strelitz	1853
Oldenburg	1853
Würtemberg	1853, 1868
Schaumburg-Lippe	1854
Two Sicilies	1855
Hanover	1855
Austria	1856
Baden	1857
Sweden and Norway	1860
Venezuela	1860
Mexico	1861, 1899
Haiti	1864
Dominican Republic	1867
Italy	1868, 1869, 1884
North German Union	1868
Nicaragua	1870
San Salvador	1870
Peru	1870
Orange Free State	1871
Ecuador	1872
Belgium	1874, 1882

Ottoman Empire	1874
Spain	1877, 1882
Netherlands	1880, 1887
Luxembourg	1883
Japan	1886
Colombia	1891
Russia	1893

The dates of these agreements demonstrated how quickly the United States moved to create a network of extradition relations after the hiatus in the early nineteenth century. To enter into thirty-five treaties in this short period (not even including various revisions and restatements) was an incredible accomplishment as well as a major focus of foreign policy. Crafting each treaty was an involved process requiring diplomatic coordination, consideration of the judicial apparatus of each state, and the input of a wide array of variant interests and international definitions of criminality, evidence, punishment, and politics. This process was eased by having the 1843 French treaty serve as an initial mode for a robust system, though only rarely was this expressly stated by American policymakers seeking to secure agreements.

Each successive agreement built upon the previous ones, replicating a basic structure on which the new terms were overlaid. The agreements were founded on a series of rules that were recognized in international law and practice and embedded, often for the first time, in treaties. These principles were then combined with terms reached only through diplomatic exchanges. Extradition rapidly became a standard component of the world system, an unremarkable and functional requirement of international relations and legal space. As John Bassett Moore later characterized it (while trying to convince the United States to accept a controversial treaty with ill-liberal Russia), "extradition has become one of the ordinary incidents of international intercourse, and a nation which refused both to surrender such fugitives and to enter into treaties for that purpose would become an object of general aversion and would be the recipient of impressive remonstrances."[9]

American treaties had a very similar structure detailing the types of extraditable crimes, the exceptions or limitations, and the procedures for surrender. The structure and language in each varied in small but very significant ways. This chapter is a full examination of the tenor and governance of the American extradition treaty system as it emerged between the Civil War and the end of the nineteenth century, with a focus on the definition of extraditable crime, assertion of jurisdiction, and the rules of double criminality and specialty.

The following thematic discussion will consider the core features and the shape and limitations of this system based on examples drawn from the full range of U.S. relations throughout the formative period of modern extradition in the nineteenth century. The focus in this chapter is on governance, policy, and choice rather than procedural concerns such as treaty negotiation, provisional arrest and detention procedures, regulations on paperwork, and the other mechanics of fugitive exchange. The court cases of the era recapitulated U.S. governance in a series of unilateralist expressions that continue to have an enormous impact on legal doctrine and foreign policy today.

CRIME AS EXTRADITABLE CRIME

One of the most striking things about the system of extradition treaties created by American policymakers is the distribution and sheer diversity of extraditable crimes in each treaty. These offenses differed regionally, economically, and systemically. This extreme range of difference in agreements was a function of geography, reciprocal state interest, diplomatic feasibility, and, one suspects in some cases, a certain amount of chance. Certainly one of the most important differences was the period when the treaty was signed. The development of U.S. ideas about order, governance, and the ends of extradition policy were clearly wrought in each successive treaty as they evolved significantly between 1865 and 1900.

There were patterns of interest and intent in the spatiality of the extraditable crimes but not a single rule. Since the treaties tended to share so many characteristics, this was an interesting development. Some crimes were of merely local concern, and some had definite international application. Crimes that fell below a certain threshold were never included. Sensitivity to new crimes developed over time as criminal patterns shifted, and the extradition treaties reflected these changes. Different countries were also concerned with specific transgressions either because of their commonality or for economic or cultural reasons. It is useful to consider some of the crimes listed in the treaties by the end of the nineteenth century. Some of the groupings are surprising.[10]

The most commonly listed extraditable crimes went far beyond the earlier British and French treaty lists from the early 1840s to include financial crimes like various kinds of embezzlement, forgery and utterance of forged paper, and fabrication and circulation of counterfeit money as well as violent crimes like assassination, piracy, murder, arson, rape, and robbery.[11] Parricide was extraditable to eighteen countries and poisoning to nineteen. These were crimes of traditional state interest, and all of them tended to meet with the "infamous punishment" standard, but their distribution was not necessarily logical. There was a strong effort to avoid "laws beneath the dignity of an international compact, or which, owing to their different definitions and degree under different statutes, might not be readily capable of general interpretation," as in the case of the 1886 treaty with Japan.[12]

There were inherent difficulties in many of these categories since the meaning of each crime was so different in various countries, and the definition of crime itself was perpetually in a state of development in the United States. All such loose standards in the definitions of extraditable crime and thus in the extradition system were matters of public concern in the United States, but it often took a long time for these concerns to appear in policy. A good example was kidnapping. "What is legally understood by 'Kidnapping' or 'Abduction' it is very difficult to state. . . . In the criminal law of some States they are probably unknown," complained E. J. Phelps, the U.S. minister to Great Britain during the ten-year-long treaty renegotiations of the mid-1880s. "The term 'Kidnapping' is most frequently applied to arrests that are claimed to be illegal. That of 'abduction' is often used as substantially equivalent to seduction. And quite as often refers to the efforts of parties in divorce suits to obtain from each other possession of children in contempt of judicial orders," he explained. In contrast, in the treaties with Mexico and Peru, kidnapping meant "'the taking and carrying away of a person' (or 'a free person') 'by force or deception.'"[13]

Phelps also did not like the proposed crime of "obtaining by false pretenses money or goods of the value of fifty dollars, or ten pounds and upwards" because it did not appear in other extradition treaties and because it received "different definitions in different jurisdictions" that likely would have given "rise to vexatious and doubtful questions on the point whether the facts relied on are really criminal or only fraudulent." Moreover, it might be construed as offensive to Americans that extraditable crimes would be illegal in Great Britain but not in *all* of the United States. There simply was too much variation: "Yet if resort is had to American Law to define a crime that depends altogether upon Statute provisions for its existence, to the Statutes of what State among the thirty-eight is it to be made?" There was such wide difference between the laws of the states that felonies in some were misdemeanors in others. "It seems to me that any crime less than felony is below the dignity of an Extradition treaty, or of International proceedings," he concluded.[14]

Also at issue with the list of extraditable crimes was the fact that abstractions did not do actions, meaning that "acts" and "crimes" had to be considered separately.[15] Naming a crime was one thing; defining it "within the terms of the statute" entirely another. Secretary of State Thomas F. Bayard told the British minister in 1886 that the multiple meanings of any particular "extradition crime" made the problem one of clarification: "a crime may be complex, made up of allied criminal acts. To illustrate, one may break into an inhabited dwelling by night, violate a female inmate, murder her, and after plundering the dwelling set it on fire to conceal the several crimes. Here would be combined burglary, robbery, rape, murder, and arson, five distinct crimes, four of which would be embraced in the proposed extradition arrangement with Great Britain."[16] Which crime would be appropriate grounds for surrender and also for trial?

Another crime that emerged as a new problem and was exceedingly difficult to define was the complex and deceptively slippery concept of embezzlement. This crime gained a new significance and resonance in the late nineteenth century, and it suddenly started appearing in extradition treaties, though the inclusion of specifically private embezzlement was slower to appear. Calls for uniform extradition rules for both public and private financial crimes of embezzlement were increasingly common from the business and banking classes, reflecting a growth in these crimes, the ease of global movement of the criminals, and the odd inconsistencies in extradition regimes that prevented their persecution. Mexico and Canada were especially ripe destinations for criminals fleeing the United States because of their proximity, and both offered a bewildering set of possibilities for criminals of all stripes. Germany and Italy were also considered to be major attractive nuisances. While crimes of forgery were already in many extradition treaties, this crime had no set standard of definition and was increasingly seen as a private issue contrasted with the bigger and more costly crimes directed against institutions and public financial trust.

Speaking to the 1882 Convention of the American Bankers Association, which featured a long session on the need to lobby for concentrated extradition reform, banker C. C. Bonney said, "the great pecuniary crime of the age is the embezzlement of trust funds [of a bank] . . . which multiplies a thousand-fold the enormity of the offense." He referred dramatically to "the stupendous wrong of a practical international license to rob banks with a piratical audacity, and find a safe asylum under the sheltering flag of some friendly power." The problem was that these piratical crimes were not being included in the proliferating extradition agreements. "Yet strange to say," Bonney told the gathered bankers, "the civilized nations of the nineteenth century, in too many cases, offer an asylum to criminals of that class and refuse to surrender them for trial and punishment, because the present state of international law does not so authorize and require." He thought the United States overly accommodated the lack of uniformity in extradition treaties and allowed dangerous inconsistencies. Embezzlement of public funds was extraditable from Mexico (the same was true of France after 1843) but not Great Britain. On the other hand, "the offense of embezzling private or corporate funds by hired or salaried persons, to the detriment of their employers" was excluded from Great Britain, Mexico, Germany, and several other countries.[17]

In the same vein, E. R. Olmsted argued at the bankers' meeting that "it seems like trifling to provide the machinery of treaties for the rendition of thieves and forgers of petty degrees, while criminals of a hundred-fold deeper dye are assured a sacred right of asylum." Instead, he wanted uniform extradition across all treaty relations for financial crimes like embezzlement and "fraudulent breaches of trust by men in fiduciary positions, so common of late, [which] carry disaster to classes helpless to protect themselves, and at the same time create widespread demoralization."[18] Another speaker, Washington B. Williams, warned that at the moment,

> [i]t thus appears that the fugitive clerk or cashier who absconds with his employer's funds, whether public or private, may take up his abode and enjoy his plunder in peace, so far as criminal procedure is concerned, anywhere in the vast extent of the British and Russian empires, Greece, Portugal and Denmark, and in nearly the whole expanse of the South American continent, without referring to more remote or uncivilized portions of the earth. If he were not a public official, but has only betrayed private or commercial trusts, his empire is far more extensive. He may expatiate at will in all of the countries last mentioned, and also in Germany and Austria, by which the domain of civilized existence for him is agreeably enlarged.[19]

Williams and other speakers called for clear, new reciprocal agreements enshrining embezzlement of public and private funds as extraditable crimes to end what they viewed as this extensive, open empire of crime. The Banker's Association unanimously adopted a vague resolution calling in the broadest possible terms "to procure such amendments to existing extradition treaties as will secure the return of fugitives from justice who at present are at large on account of what are considered defects in the existing treaties."[20]

The ability to interpret each crime so differently brought George H. Adams to conclude in the *American Law Review* in 1886 that "the mere fact of the enumeration of these five crimes [in the 1842 British Treaty] has tended to make extradition more difficult than it commonly is between countries which have *no* such treaty." For example, including "murder" may seem straightforward but did not inherently include all deaths caused by an individual "however heinous and unjustifiable," and it excluded attempted murder. Indeed, "attempted murder" was included in fewer than half (fourteen) as many treaties as was murder (thirty-three). Similar problems were to be had with forgery, which was exceedingly undefined in international practice. In 1886, the *Nation* intoned, "diplomacy has sometimes aided in the escape of rascals of high degree."[21] And indeed, this was the key point. No matter how each nation defined the crimes, these definitions were always susceptible to manipulation by diplomats. There were no irrefutable standards, but there were plenty of alternative understandings, political interests, and legal fictions to change the meaning of virtually any act.

Some uncommon extraditable crimes appeared only in a single or a handful of extradition agreements but nevertheless spoke volumes about the spreading horizons of the legal constellation of American policy. Great Britain and Peru were the only countries where abduction appeared in the treaty. Abortion was extraditable in relations with three countries—Belgium, Luxemburg, and the Netherlands—and bigamy to those three plus, unexpectedly, Peru. Some newly arising inclusions of crimes were simply unusual choices, but others had clear political intent. The former category included "mutilation" in Mexico, "child-stealing" and "shop-breaking" in Great Britain, and "breaking and entering the house of another in the day or night with intent to commit felony" in Japan. A clearly political inclusion was the crime of "malicious destruction of or attempt to destroy railways, public edifices, etc., when the act endangers human life," which was also an extraditable offense in the treaty with Japan.[22]

Political criminals would have been advised to avoid Peru entirely, as its agreements with the United States seemed to lead the world in having singular extraditable crimes that were not granted political immunity. It was the only country that sought extradition for fraudulent bankruptcy, fraudulent barratry, highway robbery, "willful injuries to telegraph line," and "intentional explosion of mines or steam-boilers, causing severe injuries."[23] The inclusion of abduction in the American treaty with Peru had a deeply ironic result in a situation involving American extraterritorial abduction, which is examined at the end of this book. All of these inclusions indicate that the exclusion of political crimes from extradition was attenuated quite graphically.

Other excluded crimes were "offenses against customs laws . . . laws relating to religion or to matters of peculiarly local concern, growing out of [a] particular national polity."[24] An example of this type of peculiar law was one pushed hard by the Orange Free State against "larceny of a diamond or diamonds knowing the same to have been stolen or being the property of another person." The United States rejected the inclusion of diamond crime as too oddball since in that country, the theft of diamonds was not made distinct from the theft of any other property. While this was a major concern for the Orange Free State, the United States insisted on folding diamond crime into the broader larceny category. Acting Secretary of State W. W. Rockhill opined that "as the receiving of diamonds which are the property of other persons is doubtless of daily occurrence and probably the legitimate business of many persons connected with the diamond industry in the Orange Free State, it would be unfortunate if the language of this treaty were permitted to describe such transactions as crimes." The United States knew this was not the intent of the suggestion, and said so, but nevertheless refused to add the crime onto the list. However, it did not object to having the value of goods listed under larceny designated in dollars. The crimes might not have been shared, but the value of the dollar was universal.[25]

The clamor for other similar changes in the enumeration of extraditable crime came from numerous sources. The most obvious source was during the time extradition treaties were initiated or renegotiated, as in the case of the Orange Free State. Other pushes for change came from the public and from a wide array of private and public figures as new crimes were identified or became the focus of public attention, as in the wake of a particularly egregious event like a bombing or assassination. Crimes were not removed from extraditable status unless they were heavily politicized, and even then this was rare. The sheer volume of crime and fugitive flight was often a motivation for a more expansive but focused list of extraditable crimes. This was particularly the case along the borders, where jurisdictions bled into each other and crime was embedded in the local economies.

Canada agitated strongly for the expansion of the extraditable crimes list with the United States (and for general extradition revision) because it handled the brunt of fugitive flight from its more populous and more criminal southern neighbor. So many fugitives escaped on a "thieves highway" to Canada because of its territorial proximity and cultural similarity with so little judicial response that it seemed like the "British courts and society . . . [had] strong prejudice against the rendition of criminals, if not a secret liking for those who run away with other people's money."[26]

The lobbying for change was an internal British Empire matter, of course, because Canada had no more autonomy in making extradition relations than did Vermont. The Canadian perspective was that the Webster-Ashburton Treaty limitations were really inviting a dual evil: "the evil of making the United States a harbour of refuge for the criminals of this country, and the evil of making Canada the resort of runaway criminals from the other side of the line." The reason for this, according to Edward Blake, president of the Privy Council of Ontario and the chief voice of extradition reform of the time, was that the very short list of crimes in the treaty essentially gave "practical immunity" to "the rascals of over forty millions of people." Canada was becoming a "safe refuge" for criminals because too many new or financial crimes were not considered extraditable crimes.

Blake gave a summertime speech to a "pic-nic" of fellow politicians bemoaning the powerlessness of the Dominion to negotiate new extradition standards. "The old Ashburton Treaty . . . is altogether too limited," he announced. It omitted "many serious crimes against the person . . . and a still greater number of that unfortunately increasing class which may be called commercial crimes. In all these omitted cases the offender finds a safe refuge in the neighbouring country. Between two States whose border of 3,000 miles is in many places unmarked by any natural line of demarcation, and where every facility exists for escape from one country to the other, the absence of fuller provision for the surrender of fugitive criminals is simply shameful."[27]

Virtually the same language calling for expansion of the list of extraditable crimes was being used to describe the situation on the Mexican border by American officials. These complaints were well exercised over a period of many years by Warner P. Sutton when he was the consul at Matamoros. He provided a constant and detailed critique of the extradition system with Mexico for years, starting in the early 1880s.[28]

Crimes large and small were a daily phenomenon in the region, and escape to the opposite side of the Rio Grande was so common and "the limitations of the present treaty [were] so great" that Sutton predicted "that not one offense in ten is extraditable." In particular, he wanted expansion of the approach, terms, reach, and mechanisms of extradition relations between the two countries. Sutton really wanted "all crimes, excepting minor or petty offences" to be extraditable. He called for the addition of embezzlement, swindling of money or property of more than twenty-five dollars in value, defection from the armed forces, and for all other crimes that were subject to infamous punishment ("one which imposes absolute imprisonment") according to the laws of both countries.[29]

Regarding embezzlement as an extraditable crime, Sutton argued plainly that he saw "no reason why the money of an individual is not as sacred as that of a government." He called smuggling "as bad as stealing," and he marveled that American sailors could be extradited for desertion but that soldiers were immune. Desertion was an endemic and unique problem along the border and had become the centerpiece of many dramatic and important diplomatic incidents. Desertion was a big problem since the United States "had posts and must continue to have [them] all along this border" while the ease of escape into Mexico was "a demoralizing temptation to [soldiers]." The same could not be said for sailors, though a few were on duty on the Rio Grande and they did occasionally show up as deserters on the Mexican shore. Indeed, desertion was a common phenomenon that went on in both directions across the border, and it was considered a serious policy problem in the region. The borderland post–Civil War desertion rate was the highest in American history, with rates upward of thirty percent at its highpoint in the 1870s.[30] Once in Mexico, Sutton wrote, the soldiers "live wretchedly and as vagabonds" and were a "nuisance." It was better to create a formal mechanism by which to send them back. Conversely, Mexican deserters were "great gainers by the change, but usually at the expense of the community where they may resort. They are of the lowest grades and largely ignorant Indians or laborers or criminals" who had been conscripted. Sutton thought "they are not desirable citizens and should not be encouraged to come" by not facing clear consequences.[31]

The appeal to justice was not mere idealism since it did have a strong connection to material concerns. Many of Sutton's suggestions had in fact recently had wide circulation in American business and diplomatic circles. American capital interests had a heightened awareness of the global dimensions of their interests and of the slippage inherent in the patchwork of the U.S. global extradition regimes for a wide variety of crimes. Most nineteenth-century considerations of extradition mentioned the increased ease of criminal flight and communication in the new technologically advancing modern age. This was not a mere borderlands problem; criminal flight was a truly international concern. Some calls for revisions were meant to address core weaknesses rather than to expand or cherry pick from among the list of extraditable crimes. Theodore Dwight Woolsey, author of one of the standard works on U.S. and international law at the time and the president of Yale, simply stated that the extradition system was flawed because the treaties were "framed on no uniform plan, and need extensive revision." Woolsey saw the problem as purely one of careful consideration since he interpreted extradition as a relatively straightforward, even mechanical process. Revising the treaties "would not be difficult for no part of the intercourse of nations can be brought under general forms more easily than this," he concluded.[32]

Technological changes also produced calls for changes in the extradition standards and procedures. For example, in the 1886 treaty negotiated with Japan, policymakers in the Senate were very concerned that the treaty-mandated two-month detention period would not be long enough to process extradition in the case of "a criminal whose extradition has been demanded by telegraph." This problem was corrected by the simple addition in the legality of "other written communications" in extradition proceedings.[33]

DYNAMITE CRIME AND EXTRATERRITORIALITY

The most alarmist, and most global, agitation came in support of strengthening the provisions for dealing with new violent crime such as terrorism and especially the exotic and terrifying new "dynamite crime." Explosive attacks, assassinations, and other such terrorist acts became prevalent after the invention of dynamite in 1866 (and its further refinement in 1875) and the rise of international anarchist terrorism in the early 1880s. Most anarchist violence such as bombings and assassinations of political leaders occurred in Europe, and a campaign of violence culminated between 1892 and 1901 into an unprecedented bloodbath for world leaders, which one historian called "the Decade of Regicide." The reverberations of this violence had a big influence in the United States, especially following the May 4, 1886, Haymarket bombing in Chicago, "the most famous act of anarchist terrorism connected to a labor act."[34]

Though the United States had refused to recognize separate categories within crimes, such as larceny of diamonds as a separate category, anarchist killing by dynamite unnerved people so thoroughly that there was a strong movement for its inclusion in treaties as a special category of crime. Rather than being placed under the political exception to extradition, it was expressly declared both too criminal to be political and too political not to be a crime.

In an 1885 forum in the influential *North American Review* considering the treatment of so-called dynamite criminals, James B. Angell stated, "no enlightened state can refuse to recognize the importance of having justice maintained everywhere, and the duty of states to strengthen one another in proper attempts."[35] George Ticknor Curtis called dynamiting an individualist usurpation of the nation's power to wage war, or the harnessing of a political act to a purely individualist criminal end. This view of terrorist violence was added to calls for a combination of approaches that combined local, state, national, and transnational action and carved new exceptions for unrestricted police power against this most political of crimes. Dynamite crimes were thus made a double exception, an inherently political form of murder that could be both included in the list of extraditable crimes and excluded from the citizenship or political exceptions that were features of the treaties.

Angell did not doubt that no matter how political a bombing might have been, the essence of it was criminal. "Take the crime that can with most plausibility be called political, the assassination by dynamite of the sovereign," he argued. "This may be committed with a political aim, and may have a political effect. But in all civilized lands assassination has been considered utterly unjustifiable, even in time of open war." In the case of terrorist violence, the political exception was removed for political reasons since this means of expression simply was not acceptable: "It is incompatible with the safety of society that a political end should be sought by such means."[36]

One argument made by those interested in establishing the criminality of dynamite bombing was that even political acts could be seen as criminal in the proper context. All criminals would use political motivations as an excuse to escape punishment. "A political offense, like any other crime, is an offense against sovereignty; but it is peculiar in this, that it is either an act done in furtherance of an attempt to overthrow an existing government, or an act done in defense of a government that proves unable to maintain itself against revolution," Curtis wrote. Therefore, "every political question must be considered in the light of probable consequences." Since terrorism evinced such disdain for all civilized society, it clearly had to be treated as a crime to protect basic social and legal stability.

Both Angell and Curtis were not above using emotional reasoning to argue that simply seeing politics in such criminal acts was akin to supporting them. Both insisted that a failure to treat terrorism as a nonpolitical crime would open the United States up to freeing future assassins of presidents. "Would any govern-

ment have declined to surrender the assassin of President Garfield?" asked Angell. Curtis followed with an argument that "if we refuse to extradite the slayer of
one of these [foreign sovereigns], on the ground that his act was political, other
countries must on the same ground refuse to return any assassin that may escape to them after killing a President. This is self-evident; no one country can
concede to another a protection for rulers that is not reciprocated."[37]

It is worth noting as a brief aside that the United States had in fact already
experienced the difficulty of obtaining the surrender of a presidential assassin
escaping into another sovereignty in one of the strangest cases of the nineteenth
century. This was the pursuit of John Surratt, one of the conspirators with John
Wilkes Booth in the assassination of Abraham Lincoln who became an international fugitive. After the assassination, "when he had done his utmost to bring
anarchy and desolation upon his native land" (in the words of Nathaniel Wilson, assistant district attorney and prosecutor at this trial), Surratt fled first
to Montreal, Canada, and then with help to Rome, where he rather bizarrely
joined the papal army as a private.

There, "but by the happening of one of those events which we sometimes call
accidents, but which are indeed the mysterious means by which Omniscient
and Omnipotent justice reveals and punishes the doers of evil," Surratt "was
discovered by an acquaintance of his boyhood," and subsequently he confessed
his crimes. The pope promptly had Surratt arrested before even being requested
to do so by the United States. He announced his willingness to have Surratt extradited irregularly despite the fact that there was no extradition treaty between
the papal state and the United States. The American minister in Italy noted that
Surratt's arrest interested "all civilized commonwealths." Yet before a surrender could be arranged, Surratt escaped into Italy, which surprisingly "declined
to give any assurances for the surrender of Surratt should he be arrested within
their jurisdictions, except upon conditions . . . greatly doubted our government
would accept." In the end, Surratt continued his astounding escape and made it
all the way to Alexandria, Egypt, where he was finally captured and extradited
to the United States.[38] Express treaty requirements clearly would have been a
help in such a bizarre case.

Aside from the political question, the transnationality of anarchist crime posed
a special problem for the governance of criminal questions as an act of foreign
policy. Was, indeed, terrorism a form of illegitimate warfare against the sovereign
state, or should it be approached as a crime against all states or against individuals and especially local communities? Should terrorism be handled by the

Figure 4. "Liberty is not anarchy." The hand of American justice grips anarchist terrorists in this drawing by Thomas Nast. *Harper's Weekly*, September 4, 1886. Library of Congress Prints and Photographs Division, LC-USZ62-135065.

executive foreign policy function, or should crimes committed by terrorists be treated within the judicial system? What happened when the crime was planned in one jurisdiction and executed in another, especially if it were not an ordinary crime but instead a "dynamite crime"? The issue of extradition further muddied these questions because it was an executive function, and the question of including dynamite crime as an extraditable offense had an inherent policy implication. Framing terrorism within an inquiry into the internal operations and balance of American governance triggered a broader consideration of U.S. power in the world system.

Here was a fascinating new challenge to executive control of foreign affairs and criminal definition in extradition. While assassins might not find a friendly environment anywhere they fled, a big question the international law community grappled with in the terrorism issue was determining where the actual crime occurred for jurisdictional purposes. This was not merely a question of defining a new and particularly devious form of crime via international convention but of transcending traditional state–power centered conceptions entirely. Dynamite anarchists ignored all established jurisdictions. Their crimes and their ideology (also termed a crime) were truly transnational. There were no sovereignties they respected, and there were no sovereignties that were secure from their crimes, so how could a single sovereign respond in terms of foreign policy?

New global interconnectedness had made it possible to commit terrorist outrages in a far-flung manner from one jurisdiction to another via letter bomb, for example. It was not uncommon to interpret such transnational crime as a crime not against the state but against all states—a crime against the law of nations and civilization itself. The summer of 1886, when the Senate considered and rejected a new extradition treaty with Great Britain that had a clause covering terrorism, produced a great deal of public discussion on the issue.

On July 21, 1886, the *New Yorker Staats-Zeitung*, a German-language paper, argued it was "confessedly a matter of public interest, to the peace and order of the whole world, that the machinery of dynamiters should be put down, wherever and under whatever mask these infamous malefactors present themselves." A few days later, the *Chicago Times* wrote, "the dynamite business is not civilization. It is barbarism. It is not war. It is murder." The same day, the *Philadelphia Press* said "those who invoke the awful power of dynamite to destroy they know not how much and kill they know not whom are guilty of a crime against humanity, and all civilized people should join hands to bring such offenders to speedy justice." There was a huge array of expressions of the same sentiment in newspapers across the United States with regularity for the last two decades of the nineteenth century.[39]

Writing for a policy-oriented audience in the *North American Review*, Thomas M. Cooley had argued similar points about the globalized threat demanding a globalized response. The nature of terrorism was that any single crime threatened the safety and security and mood of the entire civilized world:

> [M]urders committed in France or Germany do not merely shock the public mind and create a feeling of uneasiness and insecurity in those countries, but they affect, though in a less degree, the public of Great Britain and America, and do something toward rendering life less secure the world over. The interest that murder committed in France or Germany shall be punished, is therefore general; not merely on grounds of theoretical justice, but because immunity to crime in any part of the civilized world has a disquieting and demoralizing effect, which cannot be limited by national boundaries.[40]

This perspective, and the grandiose invocation of civilization and the moral need to unify against terrorism, cut directly against the basic premise and established thrust of U.S. extradition policy, which is that all crime was best handled in a unilateralist, sovereign, and delineated fashion, constrained by treaty and entirely in the realm of foreign relations. The issue of anarchist crime was a threat not just to state security but also to the established system of state governance treasured by the United States. Transnationality in crime potentially bred transnationality in jurisdiction.

What if, for example, terrorist bombings were not even treated as crimes at all but as something akin to interstate commerce, traveling along the routes of international connectivity and delivering terror in the same way that goods and services were being exchanged around the world in rapid-fire and newly interconnected fashion? This would call for an entirely new approach to the governance of crime that deemphasized sovereign foreign relations. George Ticknor Curtis accordingly argued for a criminal law rather than foreign policy approach to dealing with terrorist violence, with an emphasis on congressional rather than executive control of the issue. The crime was the use of dynamite in extraterritorial ways. This meant that "dynamite and every other explosive substance that is carried across the ocean, from any port in the United States to any port in Europe, enters into commerce just as every other commodity does." Therefore, it should be treated as such under the law pertaining to Congress's "plenary power to regulate the mode in which any commodity shall be carried to a foreign country."[41] Fighting terrorism could become as much about redefining the nature of crime and the boundaries of jurisdiction as it was about "fighting" crime. Taxation of the weapon of choice, dynamite, as a commodity rather than a weapon might in fact accomplish the task.

This approach was a bit fanciful to say the least, but it was indicative of a strong drive to gain local ownership over the political ramifications of terrorism that had entered mainstream political and legal thought. The *New York Tribune* wrote on July 26, 1886, that "when a conspiracy is formed in the territory of one government by its own citizens against life and property in another country extradition is out of the question, for the simple reason that the offense is one to be dealt with by local tribunals." In this sense, laws pertaining to dynamite crimes were both a domestic and international concern because of the extraterritorial reverberations of bombings across state lines.

The fear of dynamite bombings was so great that it was used simultaneously to exaggerate the separateness of jurisdictional lines within the United States and to clarify their meaning. Thus, sending dynamite across state lines was also conceived of as creating two separate criminal acts, in the act of sending the bomb as homicide and in the delivery of the mortal blow as homicide. In an influential article on the subject, Francis Wharton argued that the political context of dynamite crimes was muddying the understanding of their jurisdictional complexities. Wharton was one of the most important legal voices of this time on all aspects of foreign relations law and the author of the standard official *Digest of International Law*, which was the basic handbook explaining the source and meaning of all legal decisions in American foreign relations.[42]

On dynamite bombing, Wharton emphasized the local significance of these crimes as a way of exploring their policy significance: "To a citizen of Massachusetts . . . a telegraphic message or a letter containing a libel or a false pretense, or a package containing an explosive compound, comes, when it is forwarded from New Jersey, from a foreign jurisdiction as much as if it came from Russia." This conflation of libel and dynamite killing was a bit fatuous, but Wharton's concern was that globalization had so radically accelerated the threats to order and the public good that extradition law could not keep up.[43]

In a transnational age, accounting for the location of jurisdiction was critical. Wharton said that the problem was a "far greater moment than it is to any European nation" because of the scale of it. The United States had such "criminal attempts made by offenders at the time resident in any of one of more than fifty foreign sovereignties." As Wharton constructed it, the fusion of the national and the international in terrorism had profound implications for deciding jurisdictional lines as well as both sovereign and moral responsibility:

[I]n any country subject to the English common law, an injurious agency to take effect in a foreign land, the country in which the agency is started has jurisdiction over those concerned in the wrong. It is both indictable and actionable to so divert or well a stream of water in Texas is to do injury in Mexico or Louisiana—and Mexico and Louisiana are, in this sense, and to the same extent, foreign states to Texas—then it is both indictable and actionable in New York to propel a stream of dynamite from New York to Liverpool. If it is murder in New York to put a shot into a man, of which he afterwards dies in England, so it is murder in New York to put an explosive into a ship in which he sails, so that he will be destroyed in an English dock. If it is indictable in New York to be, in New York, accessory before the fact to a murder perpetrated in New Jersey, so it is indictable in New York to be, in New York, accessory before the fact to a murder perpetrated in England. If to attempt, in Georgia, to commit an offence in Alabama, is indictable in Georgia, so it is an indictable offence in Georgia to attempt an offence to be committed in Mexico.[44]

Wharton's compression of these jurisdictional quandaries between each of these diverse national and state sovereignties into a singular whole was a fascinating admission that the new nature of transnational crime had transformed existing conceptions entirely. International relations had evolved so that only new and robust jurisdictional assertions could meet the challenge of terrorism.

Wharton felt that concerted, bilateral international action was the solution but that local intervention into prosecution was also essential. It was impossible to meet the unique challenges of dynamite crime through the old model of extraterritorial jurisdiction or through blanket treatment of it as a pure extradition issue in the realm of foreign relations. It was also impossible to meet the challenge constitutionally if the United States tried to assert foreign jurisdiction under current structures. Wharton wrote, "not only would it be unconstitutional in the federal government to assume jurisdiction of attempts at extra-territorial crime, but it would be unwise so to do, as the jurisdiction properly belongs to the states to whose interests and order it is essential that such a jurisdiction should remain in their hands."[45] The globalization of dynamite crime called for the localization of jurisdiction in a new and extreme form of territoriality.

The solution, then, was to expand the system so that all affected local jurisdictions were granted the ability to respond legally. Wharton wanted simultaneously to empower local jurisdictions for prevention and response, restrain national extraterritorial jurisdictional claims, and strengthen the foreign relations power by refocusing it only on issues of purely international impact. Wharton sought to reaffirm the divisions of the domestic and foreign policy spheres but to do so in an uncommon way that empowered local jurisdiction. "They on whom the retaliation would fall . . . should be the parties to ward off the blow," Wharton wrote. "If explosives are permitted in New York to be shipped from New York to Liverpool, it is New York, not the federal government, which must suffer if explosives are to be permitted in Liverpool to be shipped from Liverpool to New York."[46]

Wharton called for practical, local ownership of these issues, and especially for stripping out the political content of them, as the means of stopping the acts. His solution to transnational violence could not be met solely by international agreement or even expansion of a robust federal response in the diplomatic sphere; it had to be local and directed toward criminality itself, not abstractions. "To enable a prosecution for dynamiting to work effectively, therefore, it should be stripped of its political and international incidents. It should be made to appear as a matter of social order, affecting the houses and lives of the whole community from which the jury is drawn," he contended. To bring in foreign issues by raising a pending possibility of extradition to a foreign sovereign "would at once divide the jury according to their national sympathies." On the other hand, a local emphasis would create a surety of solution. This was as much an issue of framing and perspective as of jurisdiction.[47]

Although he stressed "local jurisdiction" in discussing dynamite crime, Wharton expressed broader, strong support for strict territoriality that characterized American policy and with which he was well familiar. He considered the extraterritorial origins of crime within the United States to be an unheralded but very significant area of unexploited jurisdiction. His understanding of extraterritorially sourced crime would today be called transnational crime.

Elsewhere Wharton wrote that the extraterritorial origins of a crime that had territorial effect did not limit national jurisdiction but called for its wide expansion on the basis of "objective territoriality." He referred to this responsibility as the "liability of an extra-territorial principal" in his established *Treatise on Criminal Law*. "Cases can easily be conceived in which a person, whose residence is outside a territory, may make himself, by conspiring extra-territorially to defeat its laws, intra-territorially responsible," wrote Wharton. He used the example of a forger in Mexico forging U.S. securities for distribution in the United States. Clearly, argued Wharton, the forger had to be held liable under American law, or it would "merely expose us to spoliation" and even "bring our government into contempt." Mexico could not be expected to prosecute the forger for a number of reasons:

> First, in *countries of such imperfect civilization* penal justice is uncertain; secondly, because Mexico holds that we have jurisdiction, and that therefore she will not exert it; thirdly, because in cases where, in such countries, the local community gains greatly by the fraud, and suffers by it no loss, the chances of conviction and punishment would be slight; and fourthly, because all that the offender would have to do to escape justice in such a case would be to walk over the boundary line into the United States, where on this hypothesis he would go free.[48]

Thus, Wharton collapsed a huge swath of the logic underlying U.S. territoriality and unilateralism as well as general attitudes toward foreign, and particularly Mexican, justice. No other country could be counted on to have the fortitude and purpose to prosecute such a crime, especially one "of such imperfect civilization." If it did so, such prosecution would be incompetently handled. Most likely, a foreign nation would instead seek to profit from the crime within U.S. territory. International borders clearly could not be allowed to serve as a cover for deficiencies in foreign penal legislation and legal systems. Neither could they be escape hatches. Wharton amassed a great deal of case law that he said proved his point in American law on "intra-territorial" responsibility even, incredibly, in ways that ran suspiciously close to the reasoning of Article 186 of the Mexican Penal Code of Cutting case infamy.[49]

This strident expansion of territoriality in the face of transnational criminality led Wharton to some rather extreme claims. Such a legal philosophy had real-world echoes and consequences. Transnational criminality pushed forward the boundaries of the assertions of American extraterritorial authority and knocked loose some core understandings of the limits of sovereign reach. The extradition of noncitizens for crimes that had territorial effect, such as terrorist bombings, can be viewed as one result of the approach Wharton supported. Terrorism might have changed the complexion of international crime and the status of political crime, but it did not change the imperatives of state power. Indeed, if anything, it ended up enhancing the power of the state. Wharton's push for local and territorial control was filtered through a unilateralist perspective and reshaped into a tool of state policy. In this way, the heightened transnationality of crime required ever-more powerful assertions of sovereign state authority as the sole repository of the security of the nation.

It is important to distinguish that Wharton did not look to the prosecution of all crimes committed anywhere by American citizens (called personal jurisdiction) since he found "this theory has little support in our jurisprudence." But he felt transnational crime with territorial effect was a decidedly different animal and required a flexible response. Importantly, it also invited a much more open-ended response: "Jurisdiction is acquired, not because the criminal was, at the time of the crime within the territory of the offended sovereign, nor because he was at the time a subject of such sovereign, but because his offence was against the rights of that sovereign or of his subjects." The new approach freed the state to consider crime anywhere. Basic territoriality "confine[d] the real theory to attacks upon objects existing within our territorial bounds," while Wharton's enhanced view "expand[ed] this theory so as to include attacks upon our citizens and their property abroad." Wharton did not concede any argument that the United States could not exercise its jurisdiction in this way, though he did admit that there was no arrest or abduction power that could be used to make "unconditional arrests" in violation of "the countervailing principle of the inviolability of the soil of foreign States."[50] If this prohibition of the abduction of fugitives in foreign sovereignties was the last limit on the potential expanse of American jurisdiction, it certainly would not remain so for long.

The State Department did not feel an impulse to push extradition issues in terrorist or other cases into local courts since, obviously, this would have reversed established federal supremacy by empowering state courts in issues of purely foreign policy significance. Throughout the end of the nineteenth century, there had been a movement away from the jurisdictional reach of state courts into any matters of foreign affairs, particularly in regards to keeping lines of jurisdiction unencumbered in all legal matters between states and foreign powers. This exclusion ensured that foreign states were free from what John W. Foster described as "annoyance through the inconsiderate or ignorant action of state courts." In 1899, a New York judge characterized a tort case as not just excessive but "an inadvertence . . . and a nullity."[51] American policymakers also did not rush to recalibrate federal-state jurisdiction in an attempt to localize terrorist prosecution. The federal government did not seek to limit its power to gain control of terrorist fugitives or to surrender them.

Although there was not a particular rush to embrace policy innovations, the United States did begin to introduce clearer and more exacting language into extradition treaties, which reflected an awareness of the danger of anarchist dynamite crimes to life and property at home and abroad. But this was not a rapid response to any specific terrorist bombing or assassination; it was a slow accretion of small policy changes. Indeed, it would be accurate to say that the United States dragged its feet in order to make only the changes it wished to make while preserving its jurisdictional latitude in other significant ways. The two decade–long renegotiation of the treaty with Great Britain signaled this approach, as policymakers demanded changes in extradition relations that were quite apart from any concerns over terrorism or definition of crime. After failing to ratify an 1886 treaty, the United States finally signed a revised extradition convention with Great Britain in 1889 that was ratified a year later, but none of the ten newly added crimes it covered could be construed as terroristic. The two nations were simply more concerned with property and maritime crimes.

The first formal change in a U.S. treaty came in the 1882 revision of the agreement with Belgium, where the new crime appearing in Article II was referred to as "willful and unlawful destruction or obstruction of railroads which endangers human life." This new commitment to treating terrorist activity as an extraditable crime was geared toward crimes that affected both property and people, which was the case in all subsequent inclusions.

The next treaty to include this type of new extraditable crime was the 1886 treaty with Japan, Article II of which had the extremely precise crime quoted earlier: "malicious destruction of or attempt to destroy railways, public edifices, etc., when the act endangers human life." A modernizing nation no stranger to widespread terrorist activity, Japan seemed more concerned with property-related crimes, which constituted seven of the thirteen extraditable crimes in the treaty.[52]

In applauding the new treaty, the *Japan Mail* was particularly enthusiastic about the clause covering terrorist activity: "The thirteenth clause of Article II will be read with special interest. . . . [A]s it stands it is a sufficient protection against the outrages of that increasing class of scoundrels who pervert the discoveries of science into instruments of savage crime." The *Mail* made a point of highlighting that this provision covering extradition for a terrorist act was precisely the one "whose insertion in the new [failed] extradition treaty between

Great Britain and the United States is so much desired by the former." The newspaper's editors were pleased that Japan had in fact pioneered this concept in international extradition relations: "Thus Japan's first extradition treaty has also the honor of being the first to contain a condition clearly necessitated by the state of modern society, but hitherto rejected by international prejudice."[53]

Following the treaty with Japan, the explicit inclusion of terrorist crimes on the list of extraditable offenses became more common, though not always as obviously or wordily. Assassination, which could perhaps be considered solely a terrorist offense, ultimately appeared in eighteen U.S. treaties. The key change came in the wake of the British Extradition Act of 1870, with its clear enumeration and definition of every extraditable crime recognized by the state. Thereafter, other European sovereigns began to craft their own legislation requiring all subsequent—and some existing—treaties to be crafted in line with this document. This was the case with the Netherlands, for example, where the Law of April 6, 1875, governed all extradition agreements and permitted extradition for any attempt on the life of the sovereign, his family, or the head of a republic.[54] It was this kind of language, following foreign insistence, more so than any particular desire on the part of the United States that drove the treaty language for these extraditable terrorist crimes.

The United States clearly cared deeply about the apprehension of terrorist criminals, but it seemed relatively unconcerned about structuring its extradition agreements with clear definitions of crimes in this regard. Nor was there an evident desire in placing anarchist crimes into a unique governance category aside from the international one that separated terrorism from true political crime. The operative part of the system relied on eliminating the political exception as an escape hatch. Terrorism was not an exception to the definition of crime, and it did not warrant access to the political exception that defined extradition as a system.

In September 1892, this approach was formalized in international law by the Institute of International Law in Geneva, which disallowed extradition "for purely political crimes" but made two exceptions directly relevant to anarchist terrorism. According to these guidelines, extradition was appropriate for such "crimes as murder, assassination, poisoning and theft, especially theft perpetrated by violence" and "crimes directed to uproot the fundamental social institutions, irrespective of national divisions or of any given political constitution, or form of government." As sociologist (and later Italian consul in New York and Boston) Gustavo Tosti wrote, in considering murder and theft by anarchists in

1899, it was in "the absence of the minimum of pity and probity required for the normality of the moral type of man, [that] the denomination 'political crime' becomes misleading. There we have crime, pure and simple."[55] The United States rather effortlessly adopted this international interpretation of the political exception, though in so doing, it maintained a great deal of executive latitude in deciding on extradition in all cases of political crime. The issues of extraditable terrorist crime, then, had the potential to obscure the more important use of the exception, which was to create a shifting framework for the definition of appropriate political behavior in a very wide variety of cases.

THE RULE OF DOUBLE CRIMINALITY AND QUESTIONS OF JURISDICTION

Extradition as a system was founded on the principle of "double criminality" (also sometimes called "dual criminality"), which was a seemingly straightforward rule holding that in order for a crime to be extraditable, it had to be considered a crime in both the requesting and receiving countries. The rule functioned in close coordination with the enumeration of crimes in the treaty and could almost be seen as a redundancy in U.S. extradition policy, which so completely adhered to treaty enumerations in the nineteenth century. Double criminality was also generally made explicit in each extradition treaty. If the accused act was not a crime in the state upon which a request was made, there was no legal obligation for the requested nation to extradite the fugitive. This did not mean that the country could not extradite the fugitive, just that there was no requirement. Sovereign executive choice remained the final deciding factor, based on political interest as much as on any notion of justice.

Double criminality had a quiet development, and scholars consider its basic source to be the "principle of reciprocity which underlies the whole structure of extradition." But this reciprocity varied, and the Institute for International Law actually concluded at its 1880 Oxford meeting that "the condition of reciprocity in this matter can be based on a political consideration; it is not required by justice."[56] It was the politically derived, bilateral treaty requirements compelling action and the list of extraditable crimes that mattered most.

The centrality of treaty requirements on double criminality would become relevant for the United States in the very rare instances it requested extradition without a treaty or was asked to surrender a fugitive. In the first instance, the United States generally argued it was not a precedent-setting request. In the latter, it generally refused surrender. In 1887, Secretary of State Bayard wrote that in the absence of clear treaty requirements, "the action of the executive branch of the Government has uniformly been guided by the principle that the expression of one thing is the exclusion of another. An agreement between two nations to comply with demands for extradition for certain enumerated offenses implies that surrender will neither be granted nor asked for others not enumerated."[57] Reciprocity was not enough. Without a treaty, extradition could not exist.

Double criminality was relatively straightforward, but the complexities and inherent malleabilities of jurisdiction and the vagaries of crime made it more complicated in some important situations. In other cases, the many divisions of jurisdiction and criminal definition in federal states like the United States and Mexico acted as additional complicating factors. Some aspects of the U.S. penal code were locally derived or defined, which provided ambiguities in terms of exactly which standards of criminality were to form the basis of double criminality. The debates over these definitions and standards were continual between all partners in extradition relationships. For example, in 1870, Secretary of State Fish suggested to the British minister, Sir Edward Thornton, that the two nations should consider having "different offences for Canada and Great Britain," given the nature of the extradition regimes and geographic realities. Thornton's view four years later about the definition of bankruptcy laws was that they were "municipal and purely local in their theory and in their details. . . . [T]here is much hesitancy to making this class of crimes even as limited to Bankrupts themselves." Fish sounded the same themes, arguing that the country of refuge could not be used to "determine the exemption from prosecution for an offense committed in any other country." The United States had no statute of limitations and all of the states had different standards, so Fish insisted that the "place where the offense was committed was the only standard on which to judge suitability of prosecution."[58]

There were also different graduations among the definitions for crimes such as forgery, theft, larceny, embezzlement, and murder. Some of these differences were detailed by the jurisprudence in each state, some evolved over time, and some were the result of differences in language or emphasis. To resolve these definitional issues, U.S. courts came to rely on not just enumerations of the crimes but also "the essence of the offense" and "the spirit of that treaty" to guide extradition determinations. In the 1893 case *In re Adutt*, the Circuit Court of Illinois had to decide if forgery included the offense of "uttering forged paper" in the extradition treaty with Austria-Hungary. The court decided that the crime was included, although it noted that the treaty language could have been more precise in order to avoid the problem:

> We must look to *the essence of the offense,* and not to its mere denomination in foreign Codes, to ascertain just the offense comprehended in the treaty. And the spirit of that treaty is, as I conceive, that one should be extradited for the commission of the offense known as forgery, by whatever name it may be called in the Criminal Code of Austria-Hungary; and if the charge before the commissioner is that of forgery, as known to our law, and *the evidence is sufficient to hold the prisoner for the action of the executive,* it is, I think, quite immaterial that the offense of forgery, as known to our law, is classified in Austria under the title of "Fraud by Means of Forgery."[59]

Adutt made strong mention of the need for the executive to have the power of setting in motion extradition and final determination of the extradition commissioner's requests: "The danger to individual liberty by the institution of these proceedings, except under the sanction of the executive of the United States, is too grave to be tolerated."[60] It did seem to go against the belief in strict treaty enumeration, but apparently the executive could be relied upon to correctly divine the spirit of the law.

Similarly, in deciding that Charles Cohn could be lawfully extradited from Canada for burning a store in Polk County, Iowa, in *Cohn v. Jones* in 1900, the U.S. District Court of Iowa held that "when an extradition treaty uses general names, such as 'murder,' 'arson,' and the like, in defining the classes of crimes for which persons may be extradited, the question of whether a given offense comes within the treaty must be determined by the law as it exists in the two countries at the time the extradition is applied for."[61] These cases in which an extradited individual disputed the surrendering nation's interpretation of the law also brought questions about double criminality into consideration with issues of specialty, which are discussed in the last section of this chapter.

There were numerous varieties of jurisdiction practiced in the nineteenth century that were relevant to the question of double criminality. Of course, the crime rather than the jurisdiction was the basis for an extradition request. But jurisdiction could certainly be the basis for the *rejection* of a request in the subtleties of double criminality. Not all types of jurisdiction were recognized or endorsed by the United States, and some that seemed to stand counter to U.S. notions of strict territoriality were in fact actively rejected in extradition requests. Such jurisdictional definitions included the core assertions of strict sovereign territoriality and extraterritoriality in "uncivilized" states, along with more slippery concepts of "active nationality or personality principle which relates to the status of the alleged offender; the passive nationality or personality principle which relates to the status of the victim of the offence; [and] the protective principles which relates to the national security of the state affected by the offence." There was, additionally, a less commonly invoked jurisdictional rule called "subjective territoriality," which was "jurisdiction over acts started in the state but completed abroad."[62]

The distribution of these different varieties of jurisdiction was as diverse as the distribution of legal systems around the world, and their application also varied by case and time. The United States relied most heavily on territoriality and extraterritoriality and not infrequently sought to limit jurisdictional overstretch by other nations. Jurisdictional assertions tended to expand and become more complicated over time, and the United States regularly expanded its own jurisdiction when and where possible, all the while claiming perfect coherence and continuity in its policy. This was the expansive approach Wharton presented when arguing for jurisdiction over criminal acts that were planned extraterritorially but executed intra-territorially, within the United States.

By reinforcing reciprocity of some kind, double criminality in extradition served the broader policy utility of extending the reach of national sovereignty into foreign sovereignties for the direct purposes of fugitive capture and surrender. This was the core function of extradition, yet it remained tightly constrained by the incorporation of treaty requirements, limitations, and exceptions. In this sense, extradition-as-extension also served in many fascinating ways as a *limitation* on American jurisdictional assertions as a result of the double criminality rule and the necessity to act within treaty strictures. There were inbuilt practical and legal constraints to jurisdiction in the world system, which extradition regimes directly reflected.

Yet there remained ways around these limits. These became obvious in cases dealing with criminals beyond territorial borders and in jurisdictions that did *not* require reciprocity or extradition strictures. In these spaces, sovereign power was absolute. In extraterritorial criminal cases, the United States demonstrated how freely it structured its power over the accused as best fit unconstrained and unilateral state interest. While extradition might have highlighted the limits of reciprocal exchange (as well as signaling, for a nation like Japan, the attainment of full equal sovereignty), in a converse way, the persistence of extraterritoriality revealed the potential limitlessness of state assertions of authority within the world system.

"THE CONSTITUTION CAN HAVE NO OPERATION IN ANOTHER COUNTRY"

Late nineteenth-century foreign policy and Supreme Court decisions alike sought to significantly liberate the power of the state from constraint in foreign affairs. Two of the best examples of this liberation came in cases dealing with the intensifying projection of American jurisdictional power over criminal acts in different extraterritorial areas, one in the Caribbean and the other in Japan. Though neither of these cases was an extradition case, they serve to clarify how the Supreme Court shaped official conceptualization of state power in criminal jurisdictional cases in the global setting. These cases therefore demonstrate the projective endpoint of sovereign claims of jurisdiction. They guided the creation and application of exceptions in foreign policies such as extradition based upon interlacing jurisdiction, citizenship, sovereignty, and territoriality.

These cases simultaneously affirmed the U.S. embrace of both territoriality and extraterritoriality for its own state ends at the same time it supported defined limits to both of these concepts in extradition relations. These cases determined that external jurisdiction was an outward, unilateral projection of delineated power, not a blanket extension of rights, and that American sovereignty and jurisdictional claims were a function of foreign policy, not law. If extradition relationships were limited, delineated, and structured, pure assertions of extraterritorial jurisdiction freed of treaty constraints were the opposite. As Sarah Cleveland noted in her study of the plenary foreign affairs power of the Constitution, in these extraterritorial cases, "the United States stepped into an extraconstitutional realm governed only by the law of nations" in which unrestrained power beckoned.[63]

The first of these cases involved Henry Jones, who was accused of murdering Thomas N. Foster with "three mortal blows with an axe" during a riot on Navassa Island in the Caribbean on September 14, 1889. Others were involved in the riot-murder but not named in this case. Jones was working for the Navassa Phosphate Company, loading cargo and guano bird-dropping fertilizer in the brutal climate of this obscure corner of the American empire. Navassa is a tiny (two-square-mile) island approximately one hundred miles from Guantanamo

Bay, Cuba, which had been under continuous U.S. control since 1857. Originally claimed by American guano prospector Peter Duncan under the terms of the territorially expansive Guano Act of 1856, Navassa has continued to be the subject of disputed sovereignty and international tension with Haiti and, to a lesser extent, Cuba, Colombia, Jamaica, Mexico, and Honduras. Navassa stood and continues to stand as a geographic exception—neither independent, sovereign, incorporated, nor dependent. Though under the "the possession of the Navassa Phosphate Company, incorporated by the State of New York" at the time of the crime, the island was not private property, a colony, or part of the nation. Administratively, it was only an "anomalous zone," a part of the United States but in a unique jurisdictional and territorial black hole from which only sovereign American power emerged.[64]

There was no need to extradite Jones since Navassa fell jurisdictionally under American authority, specifically under the District of Maryland. On appeal of error, the U.S. Supreme Court was tasked with determining why this jurisdiction (and hence the decision) was constitutionally acceptable. In so doing, on November 24, 1890, the Court clarified sharp divisions of jurisdiction and of judicial and political power. The island, as the Jones decision described it, "was recognized and considered by the United States as appertaining to the United States" under the terms of the Guano Act. Appertaining territories do not appear in the Constitution. This was an invented category of territorial control that had persisted since the brief but intense Guano fertilizer age before the Civil War.

The Guano Act of 1856 was a unilateralist attempt to bypass the monopolistic Peruvian trade in extremely valuable bird-dropping fertilizer as well as the domination of the shipping trade by British interests. The act allowed unclaimed territory with guano deposits anywhere in the world to be secured by American entrepreneurs with federal protection of their monopoly as long as the guano mined was sold only in the U.S. market to citizens at a congressionally mandated price. This was a novel and quirky piece of legislation constructing a state-private monopoly arrangement for public benefit. It allowed the extension of deliberately undefined territorial sovereignty in order to directly extend clearly delineated U.S. law into the commodity trade in guano.

Legal scholars have considered the Guano Act principally in its territorial frame, but in so doing, they have not emphasized the core economic motivations that intensified its impact. In an important article, Christina Duffy Burnett argues that "the guano islands help us to understand that American imperialism is ultimately about the management of national boundaries as much as it is about their expansion." Burnett explains that U.S. expansionism was designed to limit the expansion of full government power and responsibility in order to maintain legal ambiguity in later expansions and to limit the "responsibilities that sovereignty implies."[65]

In other significant respects, the Guano Act was a crystalline assertion of the very marrow of the U.S. approach to unilateral governance of transnational interests. It highlighted a very expansive extraterritorial solution to a sharp supply and transport problem in international trade and indicated the potential limitlessness of federal power beyond borders. The key was that United States jurisdiction was projected into global legal spaces of both territory *and* trade on autarkic terms, an expansion of sovereign power in global systems that necessarily admitted few limits even while sharply constraining actions within the system by controlling source, price, and market.

Some creative legal fictions were required for the establishment of clear and undeniable authority in the territory. Though Navassa Island was obviously not a ship, under the revised statutes, it was governed by "admiralty jurisdiction." The U.S. Supreme Court held that "in the exercise of the power of the United States to preserve peace and punish crime in all regions over which they exercise jurisdiction, it unequivocally extends the provisions of the statutes of the United States for the punishment of offenses committed upon the high seas to like offenses committed upon guano islands which have been determined by the President to appertain to the United States." The key, then, was to determine the definition of these "regions over which they exercise jurisdiction." The Court decided "who is the sovereign, *de jure* or *de facto*, of a territory is not a judicial, but a political, question, the determination of which by the legislative and executive departments of any government conclusively binds the judges, as well as all other officers, citizens, and subjects of that government. This principle has always been upheld by this Court."[66]

The key to the Jones case, then, was that the United States, in its foreign affairs capacity, could determine that it had jurisdiction over an area for whatever reason the executive (the sovereign) saw fit, and the judicial system's role was to reinforce this decision-making process in recognizing this jurisdictional claim. In reaffirming the legitimacy of U.S. jurisdiction over a territorial anomalous zone because it was fictionally considered to be "appertaining" to the United States, the Court also signaled how expansive jurisdictional reach could be when concocted within the foreign affairs power.[67] There were significant implications for the exercise of U.S. jurisdiction in self-constructed anomalous zones. Jurisdiction was always malleable in governing the exceptions. *Jones* served as an important example of how questions of legal spatiality in criminal law cases were used by the Court to clarify the essentially unlimited executive power in nineteenth-century foreign relations. While questions of territorial appurtenance and extradition were different in form, the linkage and promotion of jurisdictional reach, executive power, and exception in the world system were not.

Another case to consider was the far more significant one of John Ross, which began in 1880 and was finally decided by the U.S. Supreme Court on May 25, 1891. It involved many of the same issues as *Jones* but deepened the meaning of assertions of U.S. jurisdiction by drastically limiting the rights associated with this expansion. John Ross was a British sailor working on the American ship *Bullion*. He murdered the second mate, an American named Robert Kelly, onboard the ship while it sat in Yokahama harbor, Japan. This crime fell under the jurisdiction of the U.S. consular court in Japan because of the extraterritorial treaty in force at the time. Ross, from Prince Edward's Island, Canada, tried to claim immunity from American jurisdiction as a British subject but since he was serving on an American ship, this claim was denied. He was sentenced to death by hanging by the U.S. consular court in Japan on May 20, 1880, in front of a four-person panel headed by the consul general. The death verdict was affirmed by U.S. Minister John A. Bingham, but President Rutherford B. Hayes commuted the sentence into "hard labor for the term of his natural life in the Albany Penitentiary in the State of New York." Apparently not relishing either death or hard labor (though he had accepted Hayes's pardon), Ross appealed the decision on the claim that he had been denied his constitutional right to trial by jury.[68]

The Supreme Court opinion, delivered by Justice Stephen Field, provided one of the most important and memorable explanations of U.S. extraterritorial jurisdictional authority in U.S. history. Field explained and defended the now well-established system of extraterritorial consular courts as the modern variant of an ancient European practice. It was recapitulated in the modern era by the United States through its powerful treaty power: "The treatymaking power vested in our government extends to all proper subjects of negotiation with foreign governments. It can, equally with any of the former or present governments of Europe, make treaties providing for the exercise of judicial authority in other countries by its officers appointed to reside therein." The U.S. power to construct systems of extraterritorial power was therefore unquestionable and unlimited when within the scope of the executive treaty-making power. Jurisdiction could in this sense be constructed out of whole cloth when possible or desirable by any treaty. Exceptions to jurisdiction and sovereignty were easily carved.[69]

More importantly, Field explained the ways in which this system of sovereign jurisdiction created within foreign sovereignties was unlimited in terms of power but limited in terms of constitutional governance. The reason for this difference was that the Constitution did not apply abroad. In the most famous lines from this case, Field wrote "by the Constitution, a government is ordained and established 'for the United States of America,' and not for countries outside of their limits. . . . *The Constitution can have no operation in another country.* When, therefore, the representatives or officers of our government are permitted to exercise authority of any kind in another country, it must be on such conditions as the two countries may agree, the laws of neither one being obligatory upon the other."[70] Not addressed at this time was the logical question raised by Kal Raustiala that "how was it possible for the United States to exercise judicial power—or any government power—outside American territory if the Constitution literally 'had no operation' beyond those borders?"[71]

The United States recognized no limits to its assertions of authority, including the core limits in its own founding document. It saw no requirement of reciprocity, just that which it chose to make for specific, limited purposes. *In re Ross* posed a challenge to the governance of systems like extradition because it expressly did not guarantee or even recognize reciprocity. It is ironic to note that this strident defense of American unilateralism and strict territoriality was constructed through an argument utilizing international examples. As Sarah Cleveland has written, "The net effect of his approach, however, was to employ international practice to deny constitutional protections."[72]

How can the *Ross* decision, with this limitless assertion of U.S. authority beyond its borders, be squared with the strong push for extradition relations that so constrained this very authority in international relations? The contradiction was not as great as it seemed if extradition is viewed in terms of governance, power, and exception rather than in terms of attenuation of these forms.

Extradition was the scalpel to the blunt instrument of extraterritoriality. Extradition was not designed to create limits through new bilateral forms but to open up closed jurisdictions in regimes inaccessible to more blunt maneuvers like forcing an extraterritorial relationship. Reciprocity or double criminality was not a mitigation of sovereign authority but a reaffirmation of the central balance on which sovereignty-opening extradition was carefully constructed. It is vital to recognize that through all U.S. policy and assertions of jurisdiction ran a strong reliance on the unrestrained executive foreign affairs power coupled with a facile reversion to the exception whenever it was expedient.

One example of the carving of a new exception when possible came just two years after *Ross*. Field had argued that Ross was properly under U.S. jurisdiction because he was on an American vessel putatively on the "high seas." The basis of his argument was found in a letter from the Secretary of State to the British on June 16, 1881, that read, "That principle is that when a foreigner enters the mercantile marine of any nation and becomes one of the crew of a vessel having undoubtedly a national character, he assumes a temporary allegiance to the flag under which he serves, and in return for the protection afforded him becomes subject to the laws by which that nation, in the exercise of an unquestioned authority, governs its vessels and seamen."[73] This perspective was well established in international law and was not startling, and Field very handily dealt with the complication of the *Bullion* being in harbor at the time of the murder.

It was the broad definition of "high seas" in *United States v. Rodgers* in 1893 that demonstrated how readily U.S. jurisdiction could be unilaterally extended over a transnational issue so as to engage the established machinery of sovereignty. This case examined whether the United States had "jurisdiction . . . to try a person for an assault with a dangerous weapon, committed in a vessel belonging to a citizen of the United States, when such vessel is in the Detroit River, out of the jurisdiction of any particular state, and within the territorial limits of the Dominion of Canada." At issue was a question of jurisdiction more than anything else. On November 20, 1893, Field, against the dissents of Justices Gray and Brown, asserted that the Great Lakes were properly considered "high seas" and that U.S. jurisdiction over its vessels therefore was absolute:

> We do not accept the doctrine that because, by the treaty between the United States and Great Britain, the boundary line between the two countries is run through the center of the lakes, their character as seas is changed, or that the jurisdiction of the United States to regulate vessels belonging to their citizens navigating those waters, and to punish offenses committed upon such vessels, is in any respect impaired. Whatever effect may be given to the boundary line between the two countries, the jurisdiction of the United States over the vessels of their citizens navigating those waters and the persons on board remains unaffected. . . . *So far as vessels on those seas are concerned, there is no limitation named to the authority of the United States.*[74]

When the boundary line posed a problem of limitation, the solution was to redefine the terms of the issue by redefining the lakes themselves. The Great Lakes became seas, and sovereignty thus faced no limits in this foreign policy realm.

Rodgers stood as an important example of the oddities of jurisdiction in American foreign relations. Real limits were placed on reciprocal recognition of other states' jurisdictional claims in extradition cases by express treaty reservation, yet at the same time, the U.S. expanded its own extraterritorial claims with unilateralist ease. This decision represented a very significant assertion of state authority over these individuals and vessels in the transnational setting. Commenting on the Rodgers case, Harry E. Hunt asked, aghast, "why discuss, much less abrogate, a rule of international conduct unless its gross injustice is conclusively proven?"[75] The answer is that the motivation for change simply reflected U.S. unilateralism. By this decision, in keeping with policy interests of the time, the Court sought to unilaterally strip Canada of authority and assert federal control to gain control not just of criminal behavior but of the entire coloration of transnationality and jurisdiction on the Great Lakes.

Expansion of jurisdiction was one extremely effective means of limiting the true transnationality of any relationship or exchange. Double criminality played a similar, though less blatant, role in extradition law by providing an inherent means of limiting foreign jurisdiction. If a crime was not recognized by myriad local or national jurisdiction, then it was not a crime the United States had to respond to for an extradition request, or even to recognize as a criminal act. This policy had the function of limiting the purview of any single treaty to be reflective only of major crimes, U.S.-acknowledged crimes, or crimes that made it through the deliberate, narrowly constrained diplomatic process and into a treaty. U.S. policymakers would not be surprised by the outcome in any specific case because the extraditable list was limited in its very creation.

One interesting controversy that arose from this question of limitations and reciprocity came in the debate over signing an extradition agreement with illiberal tsarist Russia. In opposing it, George Kennan wrote in the *Forum* in 1893 that "it is a well-established principle of international policy, if not of international law, that an extradition treaty ought not to be concluded between nations whose systems of criminal jurisprudence are not in accord, and whose political institutions are based upon mutually contradictory and antagonistic conceptions of the citizen's relation to the State." He was unalterably opposed to the treaty because he viewed it as "not . . . merely valueless and useless" but as "an active and positive agency of evil" because in Russia so "many of the fundamental principles of civilized jurisprudence [were] disregarded," such as trial by jury. Russia's system was simply "archaic and medieval." Kennan argued that the United States should treat Russia as it treated uncivilized countries and no more sign an extradition treaty with the tsar as it would "with the King of Dahomey, nor even with the Emperor of China or the Shah of Persia, because the systems of criminal jurisprudence which prevail in those countries are not at all in accord with the system which prevails in the United States." It followed, then, that if the United States were to be foolish enough to sign a treaty with Russia, it would be emboldened to enter the ranks of civilized nations: "The chief of the Prison and Exile Department will point to this extradition treaty and say . . . '[o]ur penal system has now the countenance and support of the freest, most powerful and most enlightened republic in the world.'" In addition to a fundamental incompatibility on the basis of reciprocal double criminality, Kennan believed there was no way to find a list of acceptable extraditable crimes because of the political offense exception and the different meanings of crimes like assassination and tsaricide.[76]

John Bassett Moore ridiculed this opposition as foolishness disconnected from American policy realities. Moore saw no problem with finding reciprocity with the Russian system since it meant, fundamentally, that "assassins, robbers, forgers, burglars and embezzlers" would not "be shielded from trial and punishment in their own country, under the laws which they have violated." If it were true that the United States could not make treaties with states that were not entirely civilized, Moore argued, "there must be some foundation for the impression of the French journal which not long ago classed 'The Yankee and the Cossack' together as 'two new and pitiless peoples.'" He pointed out that the United States extradited fugitives to Turkey, Japan, Haiti, and San Domingo. "In some respects the most liberal of all our extradition treaties is that with Mexico, where there is no trial by jury," he remarked.

In any case, Moore noted that trial by jury had never been considered a reciprocal requirement for extradition and that the United States as a matter of policy did not (and here he quoted former Secretary of State William L. Marcy) attempt "to reform the jurisprudence of another." As proof, Moore argued that the United States did not even require trial by jury itself! "Nor is trial by jury secured by our own laws to American citizens in all cases. In the various countries in which we exercise extra-territorial jurisdiction, such as China, Turkey, Japan and Corea, American citizens may be convicted and sentenced in our consular courts, according to the methods prescribed by our laws, without presentment by a grand jury or trial by a petit jury. In permitting this to be done, our Government has simply acted on the conditions with which it was confronted," he wrote. Recall that Ross was sentenced to death without a jury. Here it was clear that the unrestrained state freedom created by the *Ross* decision had direct resonance in the determination of extradition relations. Double criminality required reciprocal systems on a basic level, but the United States readily separated issues of justice, jurisdiction, and power in conceiving the overall system of legal spatiality. The treaty with Russia was signed in 1887.[77]

THE RULE OF SPECIALTY

Related to the double criminality issue was the "non-trial" principle, also called "the rule of specialty." This meant that any extradited fugitive could only be tried for the crime enumerated in the original extradition request. In its fullest expression, the rule forbade a government, without consent of the surrendering government, to try a criminal for any crime that occurred *before* the extraditable event. Before having to face any other charge, or to be sent to any third sovereign, the fugitive must first have been released and allowed to return (or perhaps even be transported back) to the place he or she was captured. Occasionally treaties stipulated that the fugitive be given an "ample opportunity" to return to the country from which surrendered.[78] This set up an extremely austere definition of jurisdiction over extraditable crime for nations requesting the surrender of a fugitive and was, like the double criminality provisions, designed to limit any overreach on the part of these foreign powers and reserve the jurisdictional integrity of the surrendering nation. If the United States was to extradite a fugitive, it was to be only for expressly enumerated reasons clarified in a treaty and no more.

Specialty also was meant to prevent trial for a political offense occurring at any time earlier to an extraditable offense. In this way, it prevented an extradition on trumped-up charges as part of a broader political persecution. This view was very clearly expressed in the interesting *R. A. Blandford v. The State* case in 1881, decided by Judge James M. Hurt on the Texas State Court of Appeals. This was an embezzlement case purely built on questions of specialty with no overt political content. Yet Hurt savaged the idea that a person could be extradited for one crime and tried for another because of what he saw as a potential bait-and-switch operation for political oppression through extradition. He declared that

> ... all civilized nations agree on one point, and that is that they will not deliver a fugitive to be tried for political offenses and through great caution with a view to prevent this, the sixth article of the above treaty [with Mexico] provides among other things that "the provisions of the present treaty shall not be applied in any manner to any crime or offense of a purely political character." What supreme nonsense is this if the fugitive can be extradited for one crime and then placed on trial for another—make a prima facie case of murder, extradite, and then try him for rebellion![79]

This decision in *Blandford* was a strong (and very stridently presented) limitation on the ability of the state to add new indictments after extradition, but as will be discussed below, it was out of sync with most others being decided at the same time. Clearly, specialty in extradition cases on the Mexican border, with its numerous administrative authorities and strikingly different tonalities, was seen as a vital concern in ways that would not be duplicated in New York in cases involving Great Britain. *Blandford* also revealed the inherent problems produced by vague definitions of larceny and noninclusion of other crimes in relation to specialty.

In the Blandford case, treasurer of the Austin Home Building Association in Texas, R. A. Blandford, embezzled five thousand one hundred dollars from the business on September 4, 1879, and fled to Mexico under the name of Robert Brown. He lived and worked in Mexico for over a year until being arrested in Bagdad, Mexico, by Gregorio Soto, "extradition agent of the Bravo line between the State of Tamaulipas, in the Republic of Mexico, and the State of Texas" acting on the extradition warrant of James M. Haynes, a Cameron County, Texas, judge and extradition agent. There was no federal extradition request because such requests could be handled by local officials under the border states exception in the 1861 U.S.-Mexico Extradition Treaty. Haynes's warrant was actually written for the theft of fifty dollars because it was an extraditable crime. Alternatively, embezzlement was not an extraditable crime in the treaty with Mexico, and no extradition could therefore have been based on it without being, as the trial transcript noted, "in violation of the constitutions and laws of Texas and of the United States, the law of nations and the treaty between the United States and Mexico, and in bad faith to the Republic of Mexico." Embezzlement was not actually even "the defined name of any offense" in the Texas penal code either, though "a party indicted for theft [could have been] . . . convicted of embezzlement."[80]

After his arrest and before being extradited, Blandford had met with Sutton, the U.S. consul in Matamoros, who mentioned to Blandford that he could only be tried for the specific crime for which he was extradited. Sutton said he "very plainly expressed my opinion," and he clearly both encouraged Blandford to fight the extradition and equipped him to do so successfully. This official help might be surprising since there was little doubt about Blandford's guilt given the amount of evidence in the association's receipt book. Indeed, when Blandford was confronted with the evidence of his embezzlement in false entries, "he admitted its falsity and acknowledged that he had used the money. It appears that he offered certain land by way of restitution, and that his downfall was attributable to habits of intoxication." Blandford was found guilty of embezzlement and given five years in prison, but happily for him, the decision was reversed on appeal by Judge Hurt. The decision stood on a strict textual basis for non-trial. The opinion, quoted as the epigraph of this chapter, was ferocious as it compared the clarity of the treaty language with life itself: "This treaty negatives, by imperative necessity as patent as that there is life in nature, the right to extradite only for crimes named in the treaty, and not then until after an examination into the charge by the authorities of the government upon which the demand is made—the charge named in the treaty or one of them and contained in the requisition." To do otherwise would be "a snare and a delusion, a farce and a solemn fraud."[81] Blandford was allowed to return to Matamoros, where he had been originally arrested, and he soon left for Veracruz, never again to face justice in Texas.

Sutton was extremely pleased with the outcome and told the State Department so. He thought the enumeration of crimes in the extradition treaty had to be followed strictly if law was to prevail. "If a man could be extradited for one offense and then put on trial for another, especially if it be not extraditable, then the recovery of the many fugitives resorting to this [escape into Mexico]— always difficult—would be nearly impossible," he wrote.[82] In Sutton's view, it was the limitations in extradition that allowed its effective operation. Though he wished that more crimes were listed as extraditable, he was so attentive to the letter of the requirements of extradition treaties and their limits that he was pleased to see a criminal got free in order to preserve what he understood to be the integrity of the overall system.

The rule of specialty existed in general practice and intent but was not explicitly included in a U.S. extradition treaty until the treaty with Italy in 1868, Article III of which stated "the provisions of this treaty shall not apply to any crime or offence of a political character, and the person or persons delivered up for the crimes enumerated in the preceding article shall in no case be tried for any ordinary crime, committed previously to that for which his or their surrender is asked."[83] This article explicitly linked the political exception with the stricture on trial for the specifically named extraditable crimes only. But there was an interesting loophole. In 1874, the United States did agree to extradite "Angelo De Giacomo, surnamed Ciccariello," a fugitive from Italy wanted for a murder committed in 1867. This crime had been perpetrated before the treaty was signed, and since it was not a prior crime expressly excluded because of the absence of a treaty or a political exception as other agreements required, specialty was deemed not to apply, and Ciccariello was returned to Italy.[84]

This same non-trial provision appeared in all subsequent treaties signed by the United States except, for reasons that are not clear, in the first treaty with the Orange Free State signed on December 22, 1871.[85] But the full expression of the rule also preventing prosecution for older crimes did not appear in a U.S. treaty until the second treaty with Belgium signed on June 13, 1882 (ratified November 18, 1882). The first treaty with Belgium in 1871 had no such provision, and the change a decade later reflected the hard-fought exchanges with Great Britain over this issue in the hotly contested Lawrence and Winslow cases of the 1870s discussed later in this chapter.

In the 1882 treaty with Belgium, the accused fugitive was granted the right to leave before being prosecuted for any political offense or for any offense committed before the act for which he or she had been extradited. To make it fair, the fugitive was granted "liberty to leave the country for one month after having been tried and, in case of condemnation, for one month after having suffered his punishment or having been pardoned, one month to leave the country after having been discharged."[86] This requirement demanding the release of an accused or convicted criminal before any additional prosecution was a pronounced interdiction on the jurisdiction of foreign countries in the interests of an American emphasis on the rights of the accused. It was also further insurance that the United States could retain control over the definition of political crimes.

The rule of specialty, or rather its explicit absence in the Webster-Ashburton Treaty of 1842 (which was the source of U.S.–Great Britain extradition relations), triggered a massive dispute between the two countries, which mostly shut down extradition for more than a decade starting in 1876. This issue had been simmering for some time before finally reaching a crisis situation after a series of cases. In the 1871 *U.S. v. Caldwell* case, the U.S. Supreme Court decided that additional charges could indeed be tacked onto an indictment of a surrendered fugitive from Great Britain in a criminal case. The Court recognized that this would potentially irritate relations between the two countries but held that this was clearly an executive foreign relations concern. To argue otherwise would be to "permit a person accused of crime to put the government on trial for its dealings with a foreign power." In any case, the Court saw a much simpler issue of "not one of jurisdiction of the court, but rather of privilege from arrest" and decided that a warrant of extradition did not create "legal exemption from prosecution for other crimes by him committed." The Court sidestepped any policy pronouncements in favor of a definite future political-diplomatic discussion that did not, in fact, develop with any clarity at the time.[87]

U.S. v. Caldwell was an irritant, but the crisis really began with the 1876 case of Charles L. Lawrence, who was extradited from England to the United States under the terms of the 1842 treaty to face charges of forging and uttering a bond and an affidavit. Lawrence was actually a citizen of Great Britain, though he had resided in the United States for thirty years. Upon his forcible return to New York on the limited warrant, Lawrence was newly charged with several different counts of forgery, smuggling, and conspiracy. He in turn claimed legal immunity as well as the right to "reasonable time . . . after his trial for the crimes specified in the extradition warrant, that he may have an opportunity to return to her Britannic majesty's dominions." The federal government argued that "no limitation exists as to the number and character of the offences for which a person extradited may be tried." There being no rule of specialty outlined in the 1842 treaty, the New York Circuit Court agreed, holding that U.S. jurisdiction could not be escaped. According to the court, "[a]n offender against the justice of his country can acquire no rights by defrauding that justice. Between him and the justice he has offended no rights accrue to the offender by flight. He remains at all times and everywhere liable to be called to answer to the law for his violation thereof, provided he comes within the reach of its arm."[88]

Here was a case where the vague language in the treaty actually provided a platform for a very large assertion of U.S. latitude. The court argued that the 1842 treaty actually was "calculated to repel the idea" of limits since it had the idea of the offender shall be "delivered up to justice—a significant and comprehensive expression, plainly importing that the delivery is for the purposes of public justice, without qualification." The British might wish that the Act of 1870 applied, but the court rejected this idea with a curt "upon such a question no time need be spent."

In closing, the court also took the significant opportunity of this case to make a broad statement of its jurisdictional and structural autonomy in such decisions: "no order of the president, nor direction of the attorney general, can have any legal effect to restrict or to enlarge the jurisdiction conferred by law upon the courts. The courts, in determining the extent of their jurisdiction, look to the law, and, within that jurisdiction, they are absolutely free from the control of any other department of the government." Thus, the court found itself free to make large jurisdictional assertions in such cases within a state that was even more free in this regard. The combination of judicial enlargements of jurisdiction with marked executive intransigence on the issue of U.S. latitude under the Treaty of 1842 became a major source of friction. But it is important to realize that no aspect of the U.S. governance system saw this as a problem to be fixed; it was interpreted as a British problem for attempting to externalize the Act of 1870.[89]

While this case was brewing, another occurred that acted as the final catalyst for crisis. In this case, Ezra D. Winslow was charged with forgery and utterance of forged paper in the State of Massachusetts, and his extradition was requested from Canada in February 1876. The British refused on the basis of its new Extradition Act of 1870, which stated the rule of specialty very clearly, and also out of a sense that Winslow faced the threat of trial for other crimes, given the negative example of the still-brewing Lawrence case. Winslow was actually released in Great Britain, to the chagrin of the Americans.

What followed was an enormously significant and numbingly long political crisis that fixated diplomats and commentators at the time. Moore wrote that

> . . . general opinion has been that, while Mr. Fish was wrong in his view that the trial of Winslow for an offence other than that for which he was surrendered would have been justified by the principles of international law and the treaty of 1842, yet he was right in refusing to comply with the demand of the British government for a stipulation that Winslow would not be tried for any other offence than that for which he was surrendered. Possessing no power to enforce such a stipulation as against the possibly antagonistic views of the judicial tribunals before which Winslow might have been brought for trial, he would not have been justified in entering into such an agreement.[90]

The interest of the executive and the judicial branches, the core components of the system, in maintaining an expansive understanding of U.S. extradition prevented a quick resolution to the crisis.

It is worth noting that Fish believed in the appropriateness of the rule of specialty, as did the United States generally in its extradition relations. It had, after all, become an explicit part of recent treaties and was a principle that appealed to American policymakers. The controversy with the British must then be viewed within two related contexts. The first was the broader competitive U.S.-British relationship concerning the issue of territoriality and jurisdiction. The second and more relevant context was of U.S. unilateralism. Given the opportunity, the United States stressed national jurisdiction and territoriality within transnational concerns, expanded areas of unilateral jurisdiction, and otherwise shaped relationships for maximum latitude and policy efficacy, even while following the opposite track in other areas. Article X of the treaty of 1842 was beneficially limited in its scope, and the United States moved to exploit this convenient situation even as it worked at truly contradictory purposes in the structuring of its other extradition relations at exactly the same time. The courts followed this same pattern, strongly asserting and extending jurisdiction whenever possible, reaffirming the power of treaties and the autonomy of the executive in foreign affairs, and simultaneously pushing all potential complications of this approach into the political realm for future resolution. These two congruent approaches helped to sustain and bolster U.S. power and interests conveniently and effectively, each side stretching and pulling, fitfully but in the same general direction.

The Lawrence-Winslow dispute was most significant in retrospect because it became folded into negotiations for a new extradition agreement that eventually was signed as the Convention of 1889. There were many attempts to get the problems of extradition, exception, and specialty and definitions of extraditable crime worked out, especially since the personal relationship between these diplomats was quite good and since the two powers were not so terribly far apart in the abstract. In October 1876, Lord Derby said, "I think we can get this satisfactorily arranged; I am not speaking officially; I am only talking to you unofficially." He was off by a dozen years. There were structural constraints and shifting political realities. The United States insisted that all negotiations had to take place in Washington instead of overseas via a minister, and American diplomats were tightly controlled and often chastised for what was perceived as accommodationism. Negotiations proceed slowly.[91]

Britain was constrained most of all by the self-imposed requirements of the

Act of 1870. On August 10, 1877, in language used many times over the subsequent years, F. R. Plunkett wrote to Acting Secretary of State F. W. Seward that Great Britain "regret[s] the unwillingness" to conclude a treaty in line with the others signed, noting that "it must be borne in mind that Her Majesty's Government are precluded by the Act of 1870 from entering into any engagement inconsistent with that Act."[92] Britain also had sharp internal political squabbles over the extradition issue that culminated in a royal commission report on extradition that seemed to threaten the whole treaty structure.[93]

The United States had an equally diverting array of domestic issues, including the contested election of 1876, the end of Reconstruction, and widespread socioeconomic unrest in the sharp downturn after the Panic of 1873.[94] It also had an abiding interest in maintaining an unilateralist policy at the hazard of not completing a new agreement. By 1883, Secretary of State Frederick Frelinghuysen lamented that treaty revisions had "been an almost constantly pending question since 1870."[95] It was in fact an enormously tedious diplomatic discussion, with the same issues discussed at great length by many of the same diplomats for so many years. Fish, for example, was secretary of state from 1869 to 1877 and heavily invested in this case. Nevertheless, this dispute struck on the fundamental issues of sovereignty and jurisdiction that animated U.S. extradition policy and so is worth considering briefly.

Secretary of State Fish stood firm on the U.S. position that the treaty of 1842 did not require limitation on trial after extradition and that the nation could not accept any retroactive revision of the treaty on the basis of the British Act of 1870. Fish also interestingly protested that the federal government actually could not intercede too directly into the Winslow case because it was an offense against state law and needed to be dealt with at that level. Though extradition was a purely federal function, his argument was that the expansive postsurrender indictments were actually beyond federal control. On May 27, 1876, he told Thornton that to allow the Act of 1870 to unilaterally rewrite the treaty and to force the United States to follow British declarations effectively "would be admitting away one of the grounds on which the United States stands." The Act of 1870 was "unequal in its provisions" and "wanting in reciprocal powers and rights." With no solution in sight, he declared the lack of a working extradition relationship a "very serious inconvenience and the great encouragement to crime arising from the failure of the extradition of criminals between two States whose relations of business and of social intercourse are as close and as intimate as those which happily exist."[96]

The unwillingness of the United States to adhere to the Act of 1870 came at least as much from a desire to project an uniquely American-shaped agreement and bend Great Britain to its own will as from a desire to prevent explicit support for the rule of specialty. American diplomats demanded a "non-retroactive" treaty, though many extradition treaties did allow retroactive application in any case. They insisted that the government upon whom demand was made rather than statute would be the sole judge as to the political nature of the offense. The decisions were to remain purely political and open to change. There were a few real differences, but they were more definitional and procedural than philosophical or ideological. The British did not like the U.S. standards on authentication of legal documents or use of depositions and warrants as evidence of criminality. Other issues between the British and the Americans—the political offense exception (both supported one), specialty (also supported), and specific definitions of crime—were ones on which they differed but could find reasonable solutions.[97]

By June 1883, the strong hand of the United States seemed to have prevailed. L. S. Sackville-West said that Great Britain "attached so great an importance to the conclusion of a new and extended Extradition Treaty with the United States, that [it was] of the opinion that the difficulties heretofore found to exist should no longer be allowed to stand in the way." He said he would ask Parliament to amend the act of 1870, allowing for trial of surrendered people: "It would be greatly to be regretted if the negotiations, having reached a stage where the two Governments appear to be in substantial agreement through the diplomatic channel, should now fail." Sackville-West forwarded a list of suggested extraditable offenses from Canada such as murder, assault with intent to commit murder, piracy, arson, robbery, forgery, and utterance of forged taxes as well as embezzlement. This effort stalled, and nothing was accomplished.[98]

The next year, in what was becoming a ritualistic if not actually bizarre exchange, it was Frelinghuysen's turn to tell Sackville-West that "it gives me much pleasure, because promising a speedy and harmonious conclusion of a negotiation now some ten years old—to receive your announcement that her Majesty's Government attach[es] so great an importance to the conclusion of a new and extended Treaty of Extradition with this country that [it is] unwilling to permit the past difficulties to longer stand in the way of an object of such grave national importance." He was now in agreement that there should be "non-trial for other than the surrender offense, for a political offence, or for an offense not enumerated in the treaty." This concession seemed to resolve a major set of problems, though some finer points of conflict remained such as determining a reasonable time for return to the surrendering state before a new charge was tried.[99] Frelinghuysen's anticipation turned out to be wishful; it was still another two years before a final settlement began to emerge.

A full ten years of discussion after the Winslow affair, Secretary of State Bayard looked to conclude the "incomplete negotiations of 1883" by artfully accepting an article with a non-trial provision. He felt the American point had been made sufficiently that the British Act of 1870 could not simply command American adherence in the absence of such a treaty stipulation. Bayard demurred that Fish had "merely held, and rightly" that the United States could not guarantee anything in the absence of a treaty. But, "it is a different thing to stipulate by treaty for the precise guarantee asked," and the mood had shifted, "especially as some of our courts and a majority of our best authorities on international law hold that a moral obligation exists forbidding trial for other than extraditable offenses for which surrender is asked and granted." After a few more wrangles unnecessary to detail here, a new convention was finally signed on July 12, 1889, and ratified shortly thereafter. This agreement furthered but did not supersede Article X of the treaty of 1842 and adhered closely to the U.S. positions argued since 1876. It detailed political exception, nonretroactive indictment, and specialty and reserved determination of any questions raised by extradition requests to the separate nations. In short, it reflected U.S. policy interests (and other treaties) with no explicit concession to the Act of 1870.[100]

The new extradition relationship with Great Britain might have seemed a triumph for a unified and focused State Department pursuing its vision within a coherent global extradition system, but the situation was even more complicated and interesting than that. The development of U.S. policy in the decade after the Winslow case was shaped enormously by a series of court decisions that clarified many of the decisions that had hitherto been left to the political realm and guided the future agreement, as had been acknowledged by Bayard. The slow accretion of decisions finally changed the policy, and they were, in fact, strikingly political. *Blandford* was one of the most significant decisions that stood fast on specialty, but this was in the context of constricting Texas charges in a case that remained local because of the border states exception and the unique borderlands environment. In other areas of the United States, the courts ratified the expansion of jurisdiction but increasingly longed for political clarity from policymakers.[101]

In one of these specialty cases, *United States v. Watts* of 1882, which regarded an individual extradited from Great Britain, Judge Hoffman on the U.S. District Court in California immediately centered the discussion on two questions: "First. What is the true construction of the tenth article of the treaty of 1842 between the United States and Great Britain? Second. How far are the judicial tribunals of the United States and of the states required to take cognizance of, and in proper cases give effect to, treaty stipulations between our own and foreign governments?" The Distict Court plainly stated that it was "incontrovertible" that the United States only extradited on the basis of explicit treaty requirements that became the law of the land, "whatever speculative views may have been taken by jurists of America as to the duty of sovereign states, on grounds of comity or by the laws of nations." The decision not only detailed the intent of the 1842 treaty going back to the language of John Tyler but also considered and quoted the recent diplomatic correspondence between Britain and the United States.[102]

In the end, this long decision stood firm on treaty strictures and on the divisions of jurisdiction within the United States. Once the foreign policy component of a fugitive surrender was completed, the executive could not remain solely in control of a fugitive's trial because of the threat to liberty and because of other "peculiar difficulties" relating to protection for an individual in the system. Federalism also posed constraints: "In cases where the extradition has been obtained for an offense against the laws of the United States the president could easily interfere, by directing the district attorney to abandon the prosecution. But when the criminal has been surrendered for an offense against the laws of a state, (as most frequently happens,) neither he nor the governor of the state has any such power. The latter may pardon, but he cannot control the district attorney or the court." The courts, of course, were required to follow the treaty as it was written and not allow such unsecured specialty claims to "defeat justice" as the case law (*U.S. v. Caldwell* and *United States v. Lawrence* and other cases) had previously warned. The only real way for there to be any flexibility inserted into this situation, said the court, would be through a new agreement: "It would not be difficult to provide for them by new treaty stipulations."[103]

This was a more urgent reminder that a judicial opinion had to be coupled with political moves in order to clarify or restructure the system, a refrain since the days of *U.S. v. Caldwell* but one now given increased urgency and relevance. Virtually the same expression came in another specialty case in 1886, *Ex parte Hibbs*, which dealt with the many crimes of Isaac N. Hibbs in forging dozens of postal money orders in numerous jurisdictions. Though he was only extradited from British Columbia for one act of forgery, he was soon shipped around the country to Idaho, Iowa, and Illinois to face numerous additional charges. The District Court of Oregon declared that though "the law ought not to be forced or stretched to meet this or any other emergency, it would be a reproach to the law of this country if the prisoner could not be punished for his misconduct." The treaty and precedents welcomed this kind of broadening of jurisdiction for the purposes of justice, but in the end, this was "an important and vexed question which must finally be settled by the Supreme Court."[104]

The same year, the Supreme Court finally settled the non-trial issue in the very political decision of *United States v. Rauscher*, decided on December 6, 1886. The case involved William Rauscher, second mate of the American ship *J. F. Chapman*, who "unlawfully inflicted cruel and unusual punishment" upon a man named Janessen on October 9, 1884. Rauscher fled to Britain but was later surrendered on a charge of murder. Upon arriving back in New York, he was instead charged with the cruel and unusual punishment of Janessen, which was not an extraditable crime. By now, the non-trial issues the Court considered were familiar, and the decision barely bothered to cover the case law so ably presented in all of the cases since *U.S. v. Caldwell*. *United States v. Rauscher* instead stressed the primacy of treaties within American sovereignty and considered the meaning and process of the extradition exchange. The Court was bluntly cognizant of the timeliness and contemporary importance of this case:

> Not only has the general subject of the extradition of persons charged with crime in one country who have fled to and sought refuge in another been [a] matter of much consideration of late years by the executive departments and statesmen of the governments of the civilized portion of the world, by various publicists and writers on international law, and by specialists on that subject, as well as by the courts and judicial tribunals of different countries, but the precise questions arising under this treaty, as presented by the certificate of the judges in this case, have recently been very much discussed in this country and in Great Britain.[105]

Accordingly, Justice Samuel F. Miller considered in detail the diplomatic correspondence since the Lawrence-Winslow dispute and noted that it in fact was the point of the trial: "The correspondence is an able one upon both sides, and presents the question which we are now required to decide as to the construction of the treaty and the effect of the acts of Congress already cited and of a statute of Great Britain of 1870 on the same subject." This made the decision an explicitly political one, since the Court was overtly committed to resolving this diplomatic disagreement. Miller also went beyond case law to discuss a wide variety of contemporary writers on extradition offering their opinions of this specific dispute, which lent this decision a more partisan cast.[106]

In the Court's view, modern extradition was not just about securing the transfer of someone from one sovereignty to another; it was about the process itself. It involved the engagement of a complex machinery that was in fact deliberately limited by a treaty: "this right of transfer, the right to demand it, the obligation to grant it, the proceedings under which it takes place, all show that it is for a limited and defined purpose that the transfer is made." Miller relied on U.S. statutes to emphasize that non-trial was clearly indicated in practice and held that "this is undoubtedly a congressional construction of the purpose and meaning of extradition treaties such as the one we have under consideration, and whether it is or not, it is conclusive upon the judiciary of the right conferred upon persons brought from a foreign country into this under such proceeding."[107]

Thus, the court decided, clearly drawing on the wide nonjudicial discussion, that "the weight of authority and of sound principle are in favor of the proposition that a person who has been brought within the jurisdiction of the court, by virtue of proceedings under an extradition treaty, can only be tried for one of the offenses described in that treaty, and for the offense with which he is charged in the proceedings for his extradition, until a reasonable time and opportunity have been given him, after his release or trial upon such charge, to return to the country from whose asylum he had been forcibly taken under those proceedings." Besides the treaty requirements and other questions of law, Miller thought that "the national honor also requires that good faith shall be kept with the country which surrendered him."[108] It was hard to create a much clearer rule than the one detailed here.

The decision claimed to be jurisdictionally neat as well as good policy. Because the treaty was the law of the land and now clearly delineated in full, there would be no reason for internal jurisdictional problems or future confusion on the separation of the domestic and the foreign. This solution "relieve[d] the relations between the executive department of the United States government and the courts of a state before whom such case may be pending of a tension which has more than once become very delicate and very troublesome." The treaty was the key, firmly planting the issues in the realm of foreign relations and the process internally. Surrendered fugitives who did not think they had received their due rights could seek either a writ of error from the Supreme Court or a writ of habeas corpus from one of the federal judges or federal courts. The Court was pleased to claim that "this is a complete answer to the proposition that the rights of persons extradited under the treaty cannot be enforced by the judicial branch of the government, and that they can only appeal to the executive branches of the treaty governments for redress." *United States v. Rauscher* remained an essential case not only for the finality it created on the long-simmering rule of specialty and treaty questions but also for the directness of its division of the political and judicial roles for extradition. As Tim Wu argues, "with *Rauscher* the Supreme Court created the first domain of treaty law enforceable against the Executive."[109]

Though at heart a reciprocal system built on carefully constructed, bilateral surrender agreements, extradition also required the careful nurturing of the distributed reciprocal layers of overlapping and sometimes competing internal U.S. jurisdictions.[110] In the end, however, extradition was regarded by the lightly constrained executive branch as a means of furthering the elaborate goals of U.S. foreign relations. This balanced system of external and internal constraints operated effectively while also allowing spaces to be carved by increasingly assertive U.S. policymakers.

CHAPTER FIVE

Uncertainties of Citizenship and Sovereignty

If I were asked to mention a subject that would clearly illustrate the slowness with which the human mind may rid itself of primitive conceptions that have ceased to have any foundation in existing conditions, I should not hesitate to suggest the subject of extradition. . . . The moment a national boundary line is crossed, a change seems to come over the spirit of our dreams.

John Bassett Moore, "Difficulties of Extradition," 1911

In the violent and heady days of 1877, citizenship served variously as a shield, weapon, and escape hatch, and nowhere more pungently than on the U.S.-Mexico border. Both sides of the Rio Grande were "lawlessly invaded" with regularity, and U.S. generals on the frontier described "the disturbed condition of the frontier [as] in a continual state of anarchy." Extradition exchanges still occurred at this time, but each was heavily larded with jurisdictional conflicts over citizenship.

The citizenship exception in U.S.-Mexico extradition was an increasing oddity in American relations, and its existence was enormously revealing about the U.S. governance of citizenship regimes along the border and beyond. At the border, citizenship had real and valuable clarity unequaled along the often-indistinct geographic line and also surprisingly elusive in global jurisdictional terms. This most imaginary of legal forms had real resonance at the territorial border. The recognition of citizenship on the part of Mexicans and Americans in issues of extradition and fugitive surrender also provided a convenient means of excluding all who were defined as not citizens while sometimes successfully skirting thorny conflicts of sovereignty.[1]

In August 1877, fifteen to twenty men launched a very controversial transboundary assault on the jail in Rio Grande City, Texas, which led to the escape of "two notorious criminals, murderers, and horse-thieves" and the "severe" wounding of the state attorney, Noah Cox, and three jailers. U.S. troops pursued the escapees to the river. Texas governor R. B. Hubbard immediately made a direct extradition demand to Mexico as was authorized by the 1861 treaty. The sheriff of Starr County was ordered to demand the extradition directly from the governor of Tamaulipas. Hubbard later explained to the State Department that "as the executive of a State having over five hundred miles of exposed border, with a shallow stream as the boundary-line between it and a people who cherished a traditional prejudice toward the American people, intensified by the Texas revolution for independence, and the international war of 1846," he wanted extradition of the people "irrespective of nationality" because they were guilty of crime on Texas territory.[2]

Hubbard had also asked for a "simultaneous demand" from President Hayes, decrying the "outrageous violation of our treaty relations and international law." Acting Secretary of State F. W. Seward followed through on Hayes's order and urged Mexico to extradite the perpetrators since the act was "no merely ordinary crime. It partakes of the character of a national injury." If Mexico failed to surrender them, Seward presumed they would be "no longer disposed to maintain the attitude of a friendly power at peace with the United States." Mexico agreed to surrender the jailbreakers because it was sure they were Americans and that no actual invasion had occurred. Mexico did not even require any official "formal or written application for the extradition of the criminals" because the border states clause was enough "as the treaty conferred ample powers upon the authorities of the frontier States to effect the extradition without diplomatic intervention or the action of the central federal government." It seemed as though the system operated smoothly.[3]

The early clarity soon devolved into a sharp dispute over extradition and jurisdiction, fueled by the newly proven fact that the attackers were indeed Mexican. This was the common pattern in the citizenship exclusion extradition cases with Mexico; the requesting state almost always swatted aside concerns about citizenship while on the other hand, it caused everything from friction to full-blown political crisis in the surrendering state. In the Rio Grande City Jail case, it was Mexico that experienced convulsions while the United States harbored its well-worn sense of injured national pride. For a time it seemed that Mexico was "concentrating troops . . . with the evident intention of protecting rather than delivering them" to the United States. General Servando Canales, the governor of Tamaulipas, assured Brigadier General E. O. C. Ord that he doubted "Mexicans crossed to do this [raid], there being plenty to do on that side." But the invaders were soon arrested in Mexico, as promised, and it emerged that despite the earlier claims that they were American criminals who would be immediately extradited, they were actually Mexican citizens. Immediately it seemed the Mexican promises to surrender were forgotten. A crisis predictably ensued.[4]

This crisis appeared during the same contentious period the infamous Ord Order of June 1, 1877, was in effect. This order authorized U.S. troops to invade Mexican territory at will while in pursuit of Indians, bandits, and other illicit border-crossers. Ord was granted astounding powers of incursion and enforcement. The order stated in part that "in case the lawless incursions continue he will be at liberty, in the use of his own discretion, when in pursuit of a band of the marauders, and when his troops are either in sight of them or upon a fresh trail, to follow them across the Rio Grande, and to overtake and punish them, as well as retake stolen property taken from our citizens and found in their hands on the Mexican side of the line." This assertion of extraterritorial authority generated enormous controversy and ill will along the border after numerous American violations of Mexican sovereignty. After Ord was informed by John Weber, U.S. consul at Monterrey, that Mexican troops had been rushed to the border to resist these moves, he wrote a note to an unidentified colonel whom he commanded that "I am hopeful that the efforts of the Mexican Officials on the frontier will when they see were are only working for the Common good cooperate with us in a friendly spirit and without fear that they will lose in position or property by the final result."[5] Mexico was expected to accept or even serve the American law even if the United States had created an exception for itself from any such strictures.

As Mexico wavered on the extradition surrenders, Governor Hubbard was at first interested in keeping the extradition request "a civil one, under extradition treaty" rather than making it a military incident under the Ord order. He ordered his state troops under Lieutenant Lee Hall to limit their "duties solely to the protection of property and citizens on the Texas side of the river." He told them, "*when* time comes to cross, General Ord and myself will act in concert, and you will be advised." At the same time, he told Ord that he was waiting for the extradition process to unfold, but failing that, "then I shall introduce other actors, I hope, but always by consent of the United States Government." Ord, not at all eager to invade Mexico with Texas Rangers at his side, advised the governor that "any unlawful interference of our citizens only [would impede] the efforts."[6]

The potential for violence caused by the state was strong, as Ord was not only being prodded by the governor but also by Gustave Schleicher, the U.S. representative from the Sixth District in Texas. Schleicher believed another revolution was brewing in Mexico and in a letter of mid-September, 1877, seemed to be egging on Ord to action by dangling the likelihood of the Texas troops becoming involved. The representative wrote emphatically, "I am afraid that the fear of having your command disgrace itself might make you *too cautious*." He called that "of course human nature [as well as] the necessary caution of a military man." But he enjoined Ord not to be afraid of conflict: "For us it would make little difference if we would meet with a reverse at first. Perhaps it would be better in the long run. But it would be asking too much of you to sacrifice yourself to such a consideration!"[7]

So Schleicher promised him that "there is another way out of it" through secret dealings. He had "in a private way made an application for arms and ammunition to be sent to San Antonio" and told Ord "if there is an emergency you will be authorized by dispatch to call on the governor of Texas for troops. I have written to Gov. Hubbard and every preparation should be made to have a sufficient force of Texans quietly organized and ready to assemble and start immediately when you call. They will fight, and if your force just brings on a fight you can have as much force as you will need." The representative assured him that he had "accurate information" that "the orders you may receive in certain contingencies *may be determined by that knowledge*." All the evidence indicates that the failed extradition might have been useful to achieve other ends related to Texas's political interests.[8]

But Ord had a stronger interest in restraining the Texas troops then he did in gaining their assistance in a possible raid, especially in this tense atmosphere. He considered them to be a loose force that would produce a wider conflict. It was the federal troops who were maintaining the calm on the border; the state was just agitating the issue. Ord had set up his own careful transborder networks, and he did not wish them to be disturbed. Indeed, in a series of meetings in the previous summer, Ord had cut an informal deal with General Jerónimo Treviño that U.S. troops could cross under the order of June 1 only if they were federal troops, which he told Schleicher in no uncertain terms. A month later, Schleicher was "astonished" that Ord had so strongly responded that the Texas troops "would not be the right material for your present cooperative work." In fact, he rejected this cooperative spirit. "I did not know the value was the conditions [announced to Treviño] of that permission" to cross the border, Schleicher wrote.

He sniffed, "I see that your view on the reliability of the Mexican officers have undergone a change." Ord later wrote William T. Sherman to say he had faced down this pressure from Hubbard and Schleicher, who were mad simply because the Army was not "providing thereby for his and the Governor's friends."[9]

When Mexico did finally decide to surrender the men it had captured so far (including Rudolfo Espronceda, one of the escapees, and Pablo Parra and Brigido Olivares, two of the raiders), Minister of Foreign Relations Vallarta wanted it known this was a novel act of comity and not a change in policy. The surrender would be done on the sole ground that not be taken as a precedent but instead as a remarkable exception to the citizenship exception. Vallarta instructed Mata, citizen minister plenipotentiary in the United States, to tell the State Department

> . . . in the clearest and most explicit manner that in ordering the surrender of said offenders without being obligated to do so by treaties, when the giving up of the Mexicans is solicited, it has only been done on account of the exceptional circumstances of the case, and in order to give incontrovertible proof of the firm and sincere wish which animates the present administration to put an end to the troubles on the frontier; but that this new surrender is not to serve as a foundation for the conduct of Mexico in all the cases which may happen hereafter, nor to be cited as a legal precedent, inasmuch as it has been an entirely voluntary act on the part of the government of the republic, to which it has not been obligated by treaties, but only moved to it by the considerations stated.[10]

Vallarta told the State Department that Mexico could have tried the men, had it chosen to, because the state had the "laws to try and punish crimes committed in foreign territory" in Articles 186 and 187 of the Mexican penal code, which he sent to the United States. This, of course, was another time when the United States had been officially apprised of the language of Article 186, which was supposedly so much of a shock nine years later in the Cutting case.[11]

The eventual surrender of the men launched a huge political controversy in Mexico on the basis that the military had overruled the judicial power and that Mexico had violated Article 6 of the extradition treaty. John C. Russell, the Texas extradition agent, reported to both Hubbard and Ord that "the whole of the frontier is aflame" and the attitude in Mexico was very strongly against the surrender. He characterized the mood as "popular fanaticism against surrender of any more Mexican criminals." There were strong rejections in the press and pronouncements by the *alcalde* of Matamoros that there would be no future surrender of any criminals. Russell reported that Canales had been forced to make the surrender and so had resigned in protest of the surrenders. Ord cautioned later that the few surrenders happened almost entirely because of the direct intervention of General Benavides, "who happened to be at Brownsville" and that the rest of the requests were ignored and "the efforts for the extradition of these criminals [had] caused the resignation of nearly all the Tamaulipas officials applied to."[12]

Russell warned, "the populace along the other side is very much excited, and a revolution is imminent on account of the surrender." Troops were being moved to the area. Meanwhile, the other requested fugitives were released. The issue now became one purely of diplomatic negotiation, as Hubbard told Russell to abandon his efforts to get the surrender and that he would bring his complaint to the State Department. The governor felt Mexican failure to surrender all the fugitives was "conclusive evidence of either inability to observe the treaty or hostility to all Texans and Americans, or perhaps both."[13]

The major question being debated was whether the treaty stipulated that citizens could not be surrendered under *any* circumstances or if it was a matter of sovereign choice in each situation. This question about the exact definitions and application of the citizenship exception remained hotly contested for three decades. There was no doubt that citizens could be excluded from extradition, so the issue was really one of inclusion. Who or what governance or structure was to decide? And how did it fit into the local control of extradition that was the other singular feature of borderlands extradition?

The Mexican Department of Foreign Affairs defended the position it took on surrendering these nationals in the Rio Grande City case in a manner that was certainly very familiar to American diplomatic ears. It declared "the competency of the federal executive to order the extradition of fugitives from justice" and argued that "the character of extradition" was "unquestionably an international matter" and therefore was undeniably a function of executive power: "The extradition of fugitives from the justice of a foreign country is not an act of judicial jurisdiction, but of national sovereignty." Later, this point was repeated and refined: "The extradition of fugitives from the justice of a foreign country is not a judicial but a diplomatic matter." The ministry argued that "the best proof of this is the treaty with the United States," where the judicial authorities were not actually given power as a way to ensure that extradition stayed an executive privilege, even in the decentralized system in the borderlands.[14]

Hubbard complained about the results of this elevated atmosphere to Secretary of State William M. Evarts at great length in October 1877, amplifying extradition issues into broad borderlands conflict. The governor presented a great many other examples of times when Texas extradition agents had been turned away, often without even being able to question people about their citizenship at all. Hubbard reported that his extradition agent was told officially in Tamaulipas that "if the Americans were smart they would get what Mexican prisoners they wanted in some other way." He complained about the "friendless and homeless vagabonds" who were bringing crime to the border and the inability of extradition to have an impact. To continue to request fugitive surrenders within this kind of system "would be to re-enact a solemn farce at the expense of the pride and dignity and honor of Texas." There was no peace or security along the border and would not be as long as the system continued. "Our claims for redress are met with indifference, or our demands for fugitive thieves and murderers laughed to scorn from the opposite shore of a shallow river, and almost within sight of their victims."[15]

This incident was the final catalyst to convince Hubbard that Mexicans were in fact the primary problem. The Mexican state was not helping matters: "a nation *with whom we are at peace* and hold treaty *relations* has answered our demands under the treaty by silence." But Hubbard thought it was the Mexican people who were the problem. As he announced a short time later in a speech to the Texas Legislature, "it cannot be held, of course, that citizens of Texas have *never* been at fault or that Mexican citizens have committed all the thefts, outrages and murders of that border; but . . . I have to state as my predecessors for twenty years in this office have announced before me, that nine-tenths of *all* these past troubles and depredations have been committed by persons from the border states of Mexico on our citizens and their property." He blamed the problems entirely on "the Mexican people of these states, bordering on the Rio Grande—states, whose inhabitants cherish a traditional hatred towards the United States in general, and Texans in particular. I cannot deny that in some sense this feeling on the border is mutual."[16]

Hubbard had a rather sanguine view of the actions of the state forces, claiming that "our State forces, though few in number, have always acted under strictest orders not to violate the laws of neutrality or to provoke bloodshed with our neighbors across the Rio Grande." His solution was partly to continue the supposedly peaceful ways "the United States department commander [Ord] and the Governor of Texas have acted together in harmony" and more importantly for Mexico to obey the extradition treaty requirements as a minimum step toward establishing law and peace.[17]

In the borderlands at this time, extradition was definitely politics by other means. The issues of extradition and surrender were easily conflated with numerous other jurisdictional concerns such as Indian raids. General Ord evidently listened to the complaints of Governor Hubbard about the connections between an inadequate extradition regime with Mexico and the broader issue of national security. Ord reported to Colonel R. C. Drum, assistant adjutant general for the Division of the Missouri, about the same group of murderers who were not surrendered from Mexico who had so disturbed Hubbard. Ord was quite sure nothing would be done: "These failures may, I think be attributed to the strong local feeling in favor of screening offenders seeking refuge from Texas, and to the fact that the treaty provides only for the extradition of persons not citizens of this country."[18]

But Ord argued that the broader insecurity question should actually be separated from the extradition question and put in terms of broad jurisdictional considerations. The problems were both structural and endemic. He pointed out that there was a sharp difference between local, state, and federal policy in Mexico, with the borderlands officials much more likely to be offended by U.S. policy, so even if the federal state wanted to "act the part of a good neighbor, border feuds, and the unrestrainable character of some of its more remote populations may nullify its best efforts." Indians also had a "regular system of depredations" from their Mexican mountain redoubts that had been continuing for two hundred years in "northern Mexico, which is simply a continuation of western Texas so far as concerns the character of the country and the inhabitants."[19]

Ord's solution to the problems of extradition and Indian incursion was not law but calibrated extralegality and military force. He argued that since Indians could not be considered citizens, they should not be protected from extradition under the treaty provisions and instead should be treated as enemy combatants. Texans deserved the protection of the federal government: "During the war and reconstruction, [they] have submitted to the murdering of the frontier inhabitants and plundering of the border settlements . . . but now that they are reconstructed and about as good American citizens as if they had been born in Maine (some of them were), they feel that something should be done to make life and property more secure on the border." Ord believed his orders allowed him to "follow the trails of these marauders to their homes in the mountains south of the Rio Grande, if necessary" and that this power was "sufficient." The violent race hate of Texas might be an effective tool, but Ord did not think it should be unleashed. "Texas volunteers, from the well known animosity existing on the border between the two races, might be very effective in war," but Ord thought regular soldiers were better because of their discipline. Moreover, according to Ord, "the old feuds between the border men of Texas and Mexico have been kept up, and new ones have arisen, so that there would be no more certain way of bringing on a collision than to have two such forces of hostile local troops facing each other, especially on the lower Rio Grande where the river, by changing its course, has made the boundary line uncertain."[20]

He thought applying effective military force on both sides of this boundary line as the need presented itself was the best guarantor of peace and order, not an inherently weak extradition system that excepted the very citizens and others causing unrest. "Few persons, in the well wooded and watered States, have any idea of the self sacrificing character of the service which our officers and men are called upon to perform in order that the border settlers may sleep in peace," Ord wrote in reflecting on this exercise of power.[21]

But as much as Ord embraced power, he was hesitant to allow something like this extradition conflict to spiral into a broader conflict, which he thought was likely given the contentiousness of it, the political pressure from the statehouse and the congressional delegation, the ongoing Indian problems, and the overall aggressive context of the border. Texans tended to view everything in a way that escalated issues. As Ord wrote William T. Sherman, he was "trying to carry out the whole order of the president and no more. If the President wants war, he can get it by calling out the Texas Volunteers. I am of the opinion that neither the President, or the Sec'y of State is disposed to encourage a war until other means fail to obtain the desired end; but I am advised from good sources that the Governor ordered state troopers to concentrate at Laredo, and that they have instructions from the Governor that if a chance occurs to go into Mexico, they should do it."[22]

On the border, wrote Ord, "these Texas frontiersmen would to make money plunge the country in a war with all Europe." Ord's emphasis on not abusing the border-crossing authority he had was in stark contrast to the calls for it from all sides. Nor did it make Ord popular in Texas to oppose offensive movement into Mexico among all but "those who 'fit in the Rebellion' who all say they have 'had all the war they want.'"[23]

Hubbard continued for months to pressure Ord to respond, since the extradition squabbles just seemed to be encouraging escalating levels of chaos. Each successive border outrage could be piled on the earlier ones, and Hubbard complained about the slowness of the federal troops to help "our beleaguered state troops." This was the time of the El Paso Salt War discussed in chapter 1, and Hubbard made a direct, if illogical, connection between this violent episode and the jailbreak the previous summer. He also interpreted the whole thing as a Mexican attack on American sovereignty. "You have doubtless seen the El Paso despatches," he wrote Ord. "It was and is a bloody mob, having with them over one hundred and fifty citizens of Mexico (from Chihuahua) in their number." They were "infuriated and blood-thirsty citizens—who came on Texas (*American*) soil, and plundered and murdered our people." This may have been a mob of private citizens, he wrote, but the Mexican government was responsible:

> Of course the Mexican government as such did not send this mob to San Elizario—neither did their Govt send the Rio Grande City Raiders to break open jails—release murderers and shoot down citizens, nor officially send to Texas the multitudes of Robber-Bands, who for more than twenty years have sacrificed the lives and stolen the property of our Frontier people. Neither is it *necessary* to this question of *international responsibility*—that the *Govt* should be an accessory before the fact of such outrages by every principle of international law and especially of Comity and good—neighborhood.[24]

The ease with which Hubbard fused all of these concerns together into one ranting stream was well within the regional tradition of seeing all issues as interrelated and self-reinforcing. Indeed, these definitional and jurisdictional disputes signaled that a rich vein of controversy was produced when citizenship could be used as a shield from sovereign power. In Hubbard's view, transnationalism meant each nation was inherently an "accessory before the fact" to the acts of their citizens, and neither the government nor the citizens could be shielded from (American) justice.[25]

This idea that transborder action intensified state responsibility was often the view from the American side, but only when Mexican citizens were involved. When U.S. citizens were involved, the approach tended to be completely different, most often stridently opposed to surrender of a citizen under any circumstances. It is almost too obvious to point out that Hubbard's insistence on strict state responsibility and the sanctity of territory occurred precisely at the time it was official U.S. policy to violate the territoriality of Mexico through military incursion under the Ord Order whenever the general thought it was necessary or desirable.

The citizenship exception was especially galling, perhaps because it provided a clear textual exception to *all* such powerful assertions of extraterritorial authority. Here was a treaty stricture that was convenient to use but also a thorn when applied in reverse. There was no Ord order that could countervene the exceptions in the 1861 extradition treaty. Citizens did not have to be extradited if the state did not wish it, and therefore neither state could, in fact, be at all considered an "accessory before the fact," no matter how earnestly Hubbard may have desired it.

The power of the citizenship exception along the most contentious border in North America seems even greater when compared with the major thrust of U.S. argument in all of its other extradition relations against any exception for citizens. Indeed, the United States was the principal power arguing for a global regime of fugitive surrender in which citizenship afforded no shield from the reach of American sovereignty. In the world away from the border with Mexico, the defenses of citizenship were not always recognized.

CITIZENSHIP IN U.S. EXTRADITION RELATIONS

Approximately half of U.S. treaties had citizenship exceptions, following the very common practice among European states and the standard in international law at the time. But these standards were shifting as the Institute of International Law in 1881–1882 had adopted resolutions which called for "the jurisdiction of the *forum delicti commissi* [the forum of the place of the tort] should, so far as possible, be called upon to judge." The United States worked hard to stop this exception in many of these relations and in fact long refused to ratify treaties because of this very exception. The 1850 treaty with Switzerland had no clear citizenship provision, and despite the European standard of the day, the broad American interpretation of it prevailed until finally being codified by the Swiss courts in 1891.[26]

Explicit exception first appeared in the 1853 treaty with Prussia and the other states of the Germanic Confederation like Baden and Bavaria and thereafter the united Germany. In this latter case, Secretary of State James G. Blaine claimed the United States had only capitulated to this exception "in order to avoid the misfortune of a total lack of extradition." He noted that the preamble of the treaty stated that it was "expedient for the better administration of justice" that both nations give up criminals. It made this citizenship exception plain as "strictly reciprocal," and accordingly the United States was free of obligation to surrender its own citizens. A similar preamble was in the treaties with other nations. The United States refused for six years after 1868 to sign a formal agreement with Belgium because it initially included the citizenship exception.[27]

Subsequently, the United States created citizenship exceptions in treaties with Austria-Hungary, the Ottoman Empire, Haiti, Portugal, Spain, the Netherlands, Salvador, Sweden, Norway, Russia, Japan, Peru, and a few smaller states. Brazil did not extradite its citizens; however, it did extradite noncitizens in the absence of a treaty altogether. Some of the U.S. treaties forbade citizen surrenders entirely, such as the one with Salvador, which stipulated "in no case and for no motive shall the high contracting parties be obliged to deliver up their own subjects." Some, such as Mexico, simply reserved the right not to be "bound" to surrender. In the case of Italy, the United States signed a treaty not excluding citizens (at the same time it refused to sign the one with Belgium) in order to replace the 1855 treaties with Sardinia and the Two Sicilies, which did have explicit citizenship exceptions built into them. But profound difference of interpretation still developed, as is discussed later.[28]

There was no presumption of exemption for citizens. If the citizenship exception was not explicitly delineated in the extradition agreement, then American policymakers regularly asserted that "the treaties warrant no distinctions as to nationality," as John Bassett Moore put it. This was the "uniform and unquestioned practice" dating back to the 1842 treaty with Great Britain, which explicitly included "all persons." U.S. treaties increasingly followed this inclusive model of persons, especially as American power grew, and very few of the treaties signed after the Civil War included an exemption for citizens.[29]

Ironically, as the United States dramatically expanded its conception of citizenship and naturalization in the post-1861 era, it stopped including it whenever possible in extradition relations. There were some important reasons for this, starting with the reality that the United States was a major destination for global immigration and thus uniquely interested in controlling the movements of fugitive nationals away from national territory. This search for control of citizens involved in this flow was related to what Barbara Young Welke has called the "borders of belonging" in the sense of connecting "legal individuality" to "the legal relationships of authority and subordination."[30] Citizenship was a bind as well as a protection.

Once within the U.S. borders, all people, citizens or not, were under the sovereign jurisdiction of the state. Both crime and jurisdiction over crime were viewed in territorial terms, so individuals could not evade responsibility merely by leaving the territory, and they certainly could not invoke the protection of a foreign state. The global pursuit of criminals was a function of strict territoriality and therefore included a clear rejection of extraterritoriality. Rather than allow foreign sovereigns to try their citizens for crimes committed extraterritorially, the United States lobbied strongly for territorial jurisdiction and enhanced surrenders. As Moore wrote in considering the exemption, "as the great object of extradition is the trial and punishment of an offender *under the laws which he has violated and at the place of such violation*, an object rendered important by considerations of convenience as well as by the just requirements of the penal law, it may well be questioned whether nations should persist in the general exemption of their citizens from extradition process."[31] Nevertheless, the United States held very strongly to the citizenship exemption in the treaty with Mexico and strongly rejected extraterritoriality on the border, while it attempted to reverse long-standing citizenship and extraterritorial practices elsewhere. The Ross case had proven that citizenship did not matter in the exercise of foreign relations, only jurisdiction and power. This logic was followed in extradition relations—most of the time.

The sharpest and most prolonged conflict that arose over the citizenship exemption came with Italy, where the issue became so heated that extradition completely stopped between the countries as a consequence of Italian intransigence and American frustration. This was in marked contrast to the situation in extradition relations with virtually all of the other states, which featured the exception and where conflict was therefore unusual. In some instances, such as in relations with Mexico, it was embraced. In others, as in extradition with Sweden and Norway, there was essentially no conflict during the same period in the 1880s. The matter was treated simply as a matter of course, and surrenders were not even requested, nor were the promises of Swedish extraterritorial handling of fugitives contested. A man named Risch was extradited from the United States to Germany in 1888 because it was ruled that his declared "intention to become a citizen" was not a shield to surrender.[32] But the issues raised in the conflict with Italy became extremely significant ones in examining citizenship exceptions in foreign relations.

The situation with Italy was analogous in importance to the suspended British-American extradition relations in the controversy over the rule of specialty, only longer, more acrimonious, and more complex. The conflict with Italy was similar to the extradition relationship with Mexico in that policymakers tended to associate both countries with lawlessness and disdain for the strict rule of law and because the movement of nationals led to uncommonly high numbers of fugitive flights. But the role of the citizenship exception in the relations of these states was incomparable in fascinating ways.

There was a very strong transnational movement of Italian citizens traveling for short-term work in the United States in this era (about a million people between 1880 and 1900), coupled with very high rates of remigration of between 20 percent for women to what Thomas Archdeacon has placed precisely at 45.6 percent for men.[33] The scale, size, and ease of movement back to Italy obviously was not comparable to the fluid and regular movement across the boundary with Mexico, but it was significant and the cause of the disputes. A complicating factor in the Italian situation was that citizens were required to serve in the military, which American policymakers belittled as "the Italian theory of the indefeasibility of his allegiance to the Italian Government" or the "concept of perpetual allegiance." U.S. officials noted that "the Italian writers on International Law prefer to express it, 'indelible nationality.'" This was once a common practice across Europe since the belief was that "dual nationality posed the most serious threat to interstate order," but the United States was progressively crafting agreements with the "North-German Confederacy, Baden, Wartemberg, Belgium, Hesse, Austria and England [in which] the right of expatriation [had] been expressly recognized."[34]

Some Italians who were naturalized Americans and had children born back in Italy were claiming that their children were in fact American citizens in order that they could avoid military service. Italy has considered calling on Italians to serve in times of war, but the point had not been pressed at this time, said U.S. Minister in Rome J. B. Stallo, "because the Italians find it to their interest to extend the largest hospitality to Americans whose wealth is a material addition to the resources of their country." Stallo told Italian Minister of Foreign Affairs F. Crispi in April 1889 that "it is clearly impossible for us to concede that an American citizen may owe military service to a foreign country," just as it was also totally unacceptable that Italians could flee to Italy if they had committed a crime, which would allow them to "enjoy privileges not conceded to the ordinary American citizen." If Americans had to serve in a foreign military, it would create "an intolerable anomaly" if they had then to fight against their adopted country. This was a strong fear—precisely the same one expressed at this time over possible consequences of the Mexican matriculation policy.[35]

Crispi indicated that the Italian Code required "express or tacit consent of the person naturalized" while "in America the naturalization of strangers is understood in a much wider sense than in the European States, inasmuch as the stranger might, under certain conditions, be considered an American citizen without the concurrence of his own consent." He either did not or chose not to have a clear understanding of American citizenship, since this lack of consent was only felt by the child born on American soil. Nevertheless, in 1889, Italy began demanding that Italians expressly renounce their citizenship in order to no longer be considered citizens. It was not enough just to have the U.S. Constitution or the revised statutes say they were citizens. Italy had a strong interest in keeping citizens under its exclusive sovereignty.[36]

In this way, remigration produced conflicts of what scholars of migration call reterritorialization. This was an increasingly significant transnational problem because citizenship could be shed so readily by boundary-crossing. It became a global issue for U.S. policymakers, especially with ever-accelerating globalization. Lloyd L. Wong has written that "the deterritorialization of the identity within transnational communities threatens the modern nation-state."[37] Though globalization generally increased calls for extraterritoriality, the United States sought very strongly to reject it and strengthen its unilateral territoriality, especially regarding naturalization. Citizenship was not just social membership but jurisdictional membership in global terms, or what Miles Kahler terms "jurisdictional congruence." The United States had firm views on this congruence. As Moore noted, it was a fully American "doctrine that naturalization in the United States not only clothes the individual with a new allegiance but also absolves him from the obligations of the old."[38]

Conflict over extradition tracked alongside a complex struggle over the meaning and international weight and reach of U.S. naturalization laws when they conflicted with the interests of other sovereignties. Naturalization in a globalizing world economy changed the entire architecture of power relations down to the individual level. The creation of a new citizen was a dual process involving both expatriation and naturalization through, most importantly, the change in allegiance.

The United States had a long conflict with Spain over the definition and portability of American citizenship as well as the rights regime that tracked along with it when citizens were under Spanish jurisdiction, especially in Cuba. At heart, the conflict came down to the fact that the United States refused to accept challenge to its definition of citizenship or Spanish authority over sojourning individuals for any reason. Daniel E. Sickles, U.S. minister to Spain, argued clearly that naturalized citizens retained the full span of U.S. citizenship anywhere they traveled in the world:

> [T]he Government of the United States cannot discriminate between native-born and adopted citizens of the republic in demanding equal and due respect for all alike, whether at home or abroad. When an adopted citizen of the United States returns temporarily to his birth-place, whether called there by ties of affection for parents and kindred, or to give needful attention to business affairs, or by reason of infirmities or bereavement, or for any legitimate purpose, he retains his acquired nationality unimpaired and with it the right to the protection of his adopted country, unless he voluntarily resumes his former allegiance. This principle has been consistently asserted by the Government of the United States from the beginning of its history.[39]

Sickles pointed out that Spain seemed to think that "all persons within Spanish jurisdiction, bearing Spanish names, are Spaniards." But he noted that "there are many thousands of native-born Americans whose names are of Spanish origin." Moreover, many had European names but were Americans, and there were also "persons of Mexican, Peruvian, Chilian, Brazilian, and Columbian birth."[40]

Moore put these ideas rather ungracefully but clearly by writing, "the word expatriation is often employed to denote merely the giving up of one's country, and more particularly one's native country, by a permanent change of abode; but, as used in diplomatic discussions, it signifies the change both of home and of allegiance, and more especially of allegiance." The change in allegiance was fundamental and permanent, and the United States did not recognize other nations' extraterritorial assertions that ran counter to this perspective (fig. 5).[41]

The only exception Moore saw to this rule, which meant that "the right of expatriation [was] only imperfectly realized," was, importantly, the issue of race, on the basis of which some people were "excluded from naturalization." This racial exclusion to naturalization, long in practice in the domestic setting, would be externalized when the United States came into control of foreign territories and people, none of whom were seen as fit for citizenship. Gender was another critical category; women did not have access to the same citizenship and naturalization regime until the early twentieth century. As Linda Kerber has argued, "It is possible that the state *needs* its negation in order to know itself." She found that "statelessness loomed" when American women married foreigners. Astoundingly,

Figure 5. John Bassett Moore of the State Department. Library of
Congress Prints and Photographs Division, LC-USZ62-61240.

"even Ulysses Grant's daughter was denationalized when she married an Eng-lishman in 1874, and it took a special act of Congress to reinstate her citizenship when she was widowed."[42]

But it is important to recognize that these claims on citizenship jurisdic-tion did not serve as the totality of territoriality and could in fact be sacrificed to greater state ends. Building exceptions into this new globalized citizenship regime was one means of limiting this sovereign reach, but reciprocally it also *extended* it. The United States may not have protected its citizens from surren-der in extradition cases, but it did significantly broaden its global reach by in-serting its sovereignty into foreign sovereignties for the same purpose. When a foreign nation claimed a citizenship exception, this in fact could be (and was) interpreted as an attack on sovereign territoriality. It was this fluid reality of mi-gration, global labor flows, and especially the complex jurisdictions of citizen-ship regimes that underlay the conflict over the citizenship exception. At the intersection of the three lay state power.

By 1890, Blaine was complaining (though futilely) to Italian Minister, Fava that "while citizenship is recognized as a ground for refusing extradition, citi-zenship by naturalization can not confer the right to demand it" in exchange. This was not only a rejection of the durability and meaning of U.S. naturaliza-tion but also an easy escape hatch for fugitives wishing to free themselves of obligation to their adopted nation. A naturalized Italian could commit a crime and escape to Italy, and there was no way to demand his extradition.[43]

The U.S.-Italian extradition relationship was already tense before the citizen-ship kerfuffle. In the early 1880s, the United States and Italy had a two-month squabble on the issue of "provisional arrest" of a fugitive suspect before an offi-cial extradition request, which Italy practiced and urged and which the United States saw as a violation of an array of laws. This was eventually resolved in 1885 with the signing of a convention supplementary to the extradition convention that the United States and Italy had signed.[44] But it was citizen surrenders that caused the most problems. Some of the wrangles over extradition went on for more than a year before petering out from sheer exhaustion.

In April 1888, Secretary of State Thomas F. Bayard officially requested the extradition of Italian citizen Salvatore Paladini for passing counterfeit coins in New Jersey but got no response. J. B. Stallo, at the U.S. legation in Rome, was not optimistic about the likelihood of the surrender. He told Bayard a long story of asking for extradition of Paladini and a seven-week delay for a variety of rea-sons that led him to "suspect that the Italian Government would eventually refuse to surrender Paladini on the ground that he was an Italian subject." Italian officials had waited a couple of weeks after the initial extradition request before even asking Paladini's nationality. Minister Crispi "boldly took the ground" that Italy did not have to extradite its citizen nationals, according to the treaty. Stallo said he "informed [Crispi] that I was quite fresh from the reading of the treaty of March 23, 1868, and that he was mistaken." When, after much time and confusion, Paladini was caught, Crispi reported that it was no longer necessary to figure out what the extradition treaty actually said since the courts in Messina, Sicily, were going to figure it out before Paladini could be extradited. Stallo noted that Crispi's "interpretation, as he called it, of the treaty of March 23, 1868" gave Italy extraterritorial jurisdiction over the acts of Italian subjects. Crispi argued that "the law of Italy prohibited the extradition of Italian subject to foreign jurisdictions, crimes committed by said subjects within such jurisdictions being justiciable by the Italian courts as much as if the crimes had been committed in Italy."[45]

The man sent to collect Paladini, Cono Casale, was a U.S. citizen of Italian descent who acted effectively as an "agent of the Government of the United States" authorized to accept the criminal. Ironically, Casale had never done his required Italian military service and suddenly feared being pressed into service. Stallo writes, "if such an attempt should be made a new question would arise of far greater consequence than that relating to the extradition of an Italian counterfeiter." After making Casale wait for two months, Italy finally refused to let him act in any official capacity in the country, though they did not draft him. He was later stabbed by one of Paladini's friends. Italy also claimed for a time that Paladini was back in the United States. Stallo meanwhile reread the extradition treaty and declared himself "able to state with entire confidence" that there was no citizenship exception. He wrote, underlining his words for emphasis, that "I venture to say that since the middle of the present century no state has asserted the right to refuse the extradition of its own subjects charged with the commission of crime abroad, unless the treaty under which the extradition was demanded, contained a clause justifying such refusal."[46]

Paladini was captured by early August 1888 and tried in an Italian court. A. Damiani, the Italian undersecretary of state, rebuked the United States, stating that even if it and Great Britain agreed to extradite citizens because of a core belief in territoriality, Italy believed in "rendering personal to the citizen the penal laws [penal codes 5–7] of the State to which he belongs; thus, then, returning to his own country, by reason of the same (principle) he should be tried and punished likewise for the crimes committed in a foreign territory." It was also illegal for a citizen to be "deprived of [his or her] national judges." Damiani was quick to point out that the United States had signed many treaties that expressly excluded citizens, and he alluded to "the great facility with which the American laws admit foreigners to citizenship" as another source of the problem.[47]

This extradition issue quickly escalated into a conflict over the nature of citizenship and the global meaning of U.S. naturalization as well as the relationship of these concepts to sovereign jurisdiction. The dispute was in part ironic since Paladini was never naturalized, but it revealed how readily the friction of an extradition request could cause sparks. Stallo rejected Italy's citizenship argument as "a novelty, even in Italian diplomacy" and then proffered a very strong defense of American naturalization within growing global interconnections. He agreed that "in the United States rights of citizenship are conferred with great facility. That observation is perfectly just, and can hardly have been meant as a criticism or reproach. Innumerable Europeans and, I am happy to say, numerous Italians, find refuge every year in the United States, seeking fortune under the protection of our laws. Most of them remain with us, if not permanently, at least during long periods. We bid them welcome." The only requirement would be that they follow national laws or face the consequences. "We, therefore, encourage naturalization, and in conferring upon the immigrant the rights, we at the same time devolve upon him the duties of American citizenship," Stallo stated. If an Italian could commit a crime and return to Italy and get state assurance that he was "still an Italian subject and therefore not amenable to the same penalties which are inflicted upon native or other adopted American citizens, it [would] become a very serious question whether or not it is proper to persevere in a policy which confers upon a stranger privileges denied to members of our own household." The Italian exception threatened the stability of the entire system and undermined domestic American naturalization policy.[48]

The Paladini case was but one in a long string that ended unsatisfactorily for the United States when the criminal section of the Court of Appeals of Messina refused his extradition. Each subsequent conflict broadened the scope of the overall conflict. The issues of treaty interpretation and the rejection of extraterritoriality remained the most important. The 1889 request for the surrenders of Giuseppe Bevivino and Vincenzo Villella, who were charged with "most atrocious murders in the United States," dragged on for more than a year. Fava argued that just because the treaty did not explicitly exclude citizens, it was a "universally accepted doctrine and it is not expressly forbidden." He also referred to the newly revised Italian penal code, Article 9 of which recapitulated Articles 5 and 6 of the old code, "solemnly declaring that '*the extradition of a citizen is not admissible.*'" In any case, he assured Blaine that the men would be tried in Italian, "the notorious fact [being] that the Italian magistrate at once recognized his own competency" in the case.[49]

Blaine's rejections of this treaty interpretation and of the extraterritoriality were sharp and clear, and it stood as a firm affirmation of extradition as a foreign policy function governed by the uniformities of delineated state power rather than idiosyncratic legal standards. Blaine "wholly" disagreed with Fava and argued that Italian law simply was not relevant to "an international compact . . . to say nothing of the provisions of the new penal coded adopted 10 years after the conclusion of the treaty." If Italy was going to appeal to municipal code, then the United States could theoretically do the same thing "by which no exception is made in favor of its citizens." The clear language of the treaty had to stand as written. To deny otherwise would be to "violate or refuse to fulfill the treaty." The United States totally rejected the application of (particularly *ex post facto*) national laws to supersede established treaties and was long hostile to attempts by other nations to claim unilateral authority. "It would be a dangerous precedent to admit that a nation may determine its conventional duty by its own statutes," Blaine wrote.[50]

The United States particularly rejected the new Italian penal code, which had two extraterritorial assertions (Articles 5 and 7) that exceeded those of the infamous Mexican penal code (Article 186 of Cutting case fame). The Italian Article 5 indicated that any crime against the Italian state anywhere, including counterfeiting, was punishable by Italy for up to five years, and it allowed for double jeopardy wherein the criminal could "be tried and punished according to Italian law even though he has already been tried and punished in the country where the crime was committed." Article 6 said that someone who committed a crime abroad against foreign law could be tried in Italy. And Article 7 read, "a foreigner who . . . commits a crime in a foreign country to the injury of an Italian citizen or of the State . . . is tried whenever found within the Kingdom and punished according to the milder law of the two States." Italy thus compounded its refusal to extradite even naturalized Americans by asserting extraterritorial jurisdiction over the very crime on which the United States requested surrender. Blaine strongly rejected this broad Italian claim of "very extensive jurisdiction claimed under the Italian statutes to punish foreigners for their conduct outside of the Kingdom" because the United States "[had] always maintained that for acts committed within its jurisdiction its citizens were answerable to no other law than its own. It could not, therefore, make a concession so extraordinary as that suggested."[51]

From the American perspective, the whole issue should only have revolved around the power realities created by the treaty and of the sanctity of these delineated agreements. "Where no treaty exists, the subject is simple," wrote Blaine. "It is generally agreed that, in the absence of a convention, extradition is a matter of comity, and not of positive obligation." But when a treaty was created, "what before was a matter of comity and discretion, becomes a matter of duty, and the measure of that duty is the treaty." The only reason a citizenship exemption was installed was to prevent extradition from working, he said. Europeans have "industriously inserted in their treaties an express stipulation to exempt themselves from that obligation" so "the duty of surrender is avoided." Suffice it to say, nothing in the treaty with Italy had such a clear exception. And Blaine demurred that "what may have been said in the oral discussions can not now be discovered." Blaine ended his sixteen-page letter with the strongly worded caution that "I am unable to discover any ground of reconciliation of the totally opposite views entertained by the United States and Italy in regard to the force and effect of the treaty of 1868."[52]

By the 1890s, despite ongoing negotiations over the meaning of naturalization procedures and amidst simmering complaints over the citizenship exceptions, extradition essentially ended between the United States and Italy. A month after requesting the surrender of Italians Michele Delzoppo and Antonio Rindaldi, wanted for murder in New York, the governor was informed of Italy's refusal. The U.S. response was muted and resigned to the realities, though it did not "acquiesce in the view" of Italy. By June 1894, Secretary of State Walter Q. Gresham made it clear that the president would never sign an extradition treaty and stated that "no good reason is perceived why citizens of the United States who commit crimes in Italy or Italian subjects who commit crimes in the United States, should not, if they take refuge in their own countries be delivered up by its authorities to the country whose laws they have violated. A refusal to surrender them would result in the case of Americans committing crime in Italy, in an utter failure of justice," and in Italy it would be impossible to give a decent and fair trial or even "[ascertain] the truth." The United States rejected the proposed naturalization convention as well, especially since it would prevent women from becoming citizens upon marriage or children becoming citizens when their fathers were naturalized and because the United States could not accept the military service requirement for a naturalized American returning for a time to Italy. The Americans also regularly refused to entertain the expansion of the list of extraditable crimes in their negotiations with Italy. By 1899, Secretary of State John D. Hay indicated to the governor of Massachusetts that he would not even bother asking Italy for extradition of "alleged murderer Di Blassi" because, simply, "the Department is of the opinion that it would be useless to incur the expense of sending an officer to Italy to endeavor to secure his return."[53]

BORDERLANDS CITIZENSHIP AND EXTRADITION

Why, then, given this record of firm and long-standing opposition to the Italian assertion of the citizenship exception, was the United States not only willing to countenance the same "utter failure of justice" on the Mexican border but to *insist* on it? Surely the ease of transborder escape would have created an interest in securing justice in order to prevent a fugitive from going "unwhipped" of it? Here was a sparklingly clear example of the emphasis placed on furthering state power as opposed to instead of abstractions of justice. The citizenship exclusion in the relations with Mexico served other state purposes that trumped considerations of legality and the pursuit of criminals—an interesting emphasis in a region that was so often viewed as violent, lawless, and chaotic.

Order was pursued by other means as the United States emphasized the sanctity of territoriality and unilateralism in transnational questions. The citizenship exclusion worked in support of this territoriality as it directly opposed jurisdictional claims over fugitive nationals. Maintenance of the borderlands citizenship exception served as a key component of the broader effort to assert clear order in the legal spaces on the border. It was seen as a mere cost of attaining unilateralist order in a borderlands so resistant to it. One of these costs was, ironically, accommodating Mexican unilateralism to some degree. This exception to sovereignty allowed for its fullest expression, though it may have worked at cross-purposes to diplomatic arrangements in other regions. The exception was the catalyst to clearer jurisdictional power, even if it meant that the Mexican state gained its own relative autonomy and Mexican criminals gained freedom of escape.

There were important limits to the U.S. willingness to buy its own unilateralism at the cost of allowing a certain modicum of Mexican unilateralism. If both sides had the same exception, it was not a problem. Controversy arose when this unilateralism did not seem (however paradoxically) to be reciprocal. Unsurprisingly, this rang particularly true in economic disputes, as the case of the *Zona Libre* demonstrated so clearly. As discussed in Part 1, the half-century controversy grew from broad fears that the *Zona Libre* locked U.S. business and commercial interests out of the Mexican market, despite the fact that this was consistently proven to be untrue. But the real problem was that it was a truly unilateral policy, which the United States lacked the political will to match in Texas.

Mexico had a strong sovereign interest in protecting its citizens from extradition to the United States, and like Italy it, too, had a tradition of extraterritorial assertions in its penal code. Only the United States categorically refused to recognize extraterritoriality in all civilized and semicivilized areas, a fact that corresponded in policymakers' minds to the need to end the citizenship exception as a factor in global extradition regimes. There were a great many times when Mexican unilateralism in transboundary criminal cases was applauded. This was true even when Mexico made extraterritorial assertions that in other instances the United States rejected with great vigor. Thus, Mexico's punishment, imprisonment, or even execution of the perpetrators in the Avalos, Arvizú, Muñoz, and Jesus Garcia cases, as well as many others, were applauded as suitable solutions. Its assertions of non-surrender on the basis of citizenship were accepted without trouble. But when the northern border states created a smart trade policy in the form of the *Zona Libre* as a purely internal matter, the U.S. response was empurpled.

The U.S. interest in excluding its citizens from surrender to Mexico at the exact same time it was fiercely contesting the issue with Italy was regularized with the case of Alexander Trimble in 1884. A train of the Mexican National Railway had been wrecked at Las Jarita, Nuevo Leon, Mexico, in November 1883, with one American killed and one wounded and eight thousand dollars in silver bullion stolen. Some men were charged and tried in Monterrey, and they in turn implicated others, including the mayor of Nuevo Laredo and Alexander Trimble, an American from Laredo, Texas. Mexico had demanded his surrender for the crimes of murder and complicity in the train robbery, and his case was heard before Judge J. C. Russell in Corpus Christi.

Russell told Consul Warner P. Sutton in Matamoros (who underlined the argument for emphasis) that "there was not sufficient evidence produced before him to warrant Trimble's arrest and commitment for trial had the offense been alleged as committed in Texas. Besides the lack of any reasonable evidence against the man, the papers were fatally defective in at least two other points." Sutton told the State Department that "the Judge informed me that he would not have rendered up a *Mexican on so slight grounds*" but nevertheless, "now the unfortunate Trimble has been charged with the most revolting crimes, accused as the ring leader of the wrecking gang, and a villain of the darkest dye."[54]

Judge Russell believed that he had the power to extradite a citizen to Mexico, but Sutton knew this was not always the case and fought hard to make sure Trimble got into a U.S. court "before he was actually rendered up." Sutton had learned that there was a strong movement to "run him [Trimble] immediately" back to Mexico and even "a special train well armed with state Rangers" for this purpose. Sutton, very concerned that Trimble was not getting "a fair show for his rights as a citizen," intervened with the State Department to get him released. Sutton did not think that the border should be an escape hatch, but the fact remained that the strict language of the law made it one. "Now it is not proper, right, or compatible with the peace or security of this border that any American or Mexican can resort to the neighboring country, there commit crime and then find a safe asylum in his own country," he remarked. He thought the extradition treaty needed to be amended since "such cases may occur any day on either side of the border and the guilty parties are sure to go free." But until such a revision was completed, Sutton was standing firm on the law, which did not require the surrender of citizens just because it was convenient or because they happened to be guilty.[55]

And so, as was typical of these cases, the question of guilt was secondary to the question of power. The Trimble case very rapidly became a federal matter despite the fact that extradition matters could be determined locally. The law held that "before any actual surrender the accused should have full opportunity for a hearing before the Supreme Court of the United States on a writ of habeas corpus and certiorari from a local court, wither Federal or State." And, all things being in order with the request, the final decision about extradition still had to be made by the president, as Secretary of State Frelinghuysen observed.[56]

The most central question, then, was not if the president was "*bound* to extradite an American citizen on a requisition made by the republic of Mexico," since he was clearly not at all so bound by the strict language of the treaty. The question, Frelinghuysen wrote, was *if* a president could even extradite an American citizen under this treaty at all. Some commentators and authorities claimed that comity and the law of nations required a surrender (and there was at least one case to back up this idea), but Frelinghuysen wrote, "I find a long and almost uniform course of decisions, which, while not denying the international doctrine stated, holds that the President, in the absence of legislation and treaty, has not the power to enforce the doctrine." If a treaty did not compel the president to surrender a citizen, he could not do it at all.[57]

And, indeed, the extradition of a citizen was denied by the United States in many instances when policymakers were not compelled by treaties and empowering legislation from Congress. Frelinghuysen provided a lot of examples. In the Carl Vogt case of July 28, 1873, the United States refused to extradite Vogt for robbery, arson, and murder charges in Belgium expressly because of this lack of a treaty obligation (and reciprocal agreement) to extradite citizens. In 1874, Mexico refused to extradite Francisco Perez, a Mexican citizen who murdered Joseph Alexander in Brownsville, Texas. The United States did not press the case strongly, in part because it was unwilling to provide reciprocity in extradition and in part because Secretary Evarts understood readily that Mexico "had a technical right to refuse the request." As Frelinghuysen put it, "by the opinions of several Attorneys-General, by the decisions of our courts, and by the ruling of the Department of State, the President has not, independent of treaty provision, the power of extraditing an American citizen."[58]

The Trimble case was a perfect example of the limits on executive authority in this regard. The treaty with Mexico particularly conferred "upon the President no affirmative power to surrender an American citizen." The treaty merely created "an obligation on the part of the respective Governments, and does no more, and *where the obligation ceases the power falls.*" The United States viewed the treaty in very limited and constrained terms, as "a contract," that only required express fulfillment of its terms. It "must be so construed. . . . It confers upon the President only the power to perform that contract," Frelinghuysen intoned. He viewed the treaty obligations in this austere, limited fashion: "the President shall be bound to surrender any person guilty of crime, unless such person is a citizen of the United States." Better, he thought, that a known criminal were free than that the delineated powers were expanded without an express agreement. In his defense, he claimed "that the time to prevent a violation of the law of extradition was before the citizen left the jurisdiction of the United States." No American citizen could be so held for surrender. In a clear assertion of the baseline interests at stake, Frelinghuysen laid out the choice quite starkly. "It would be a great evil that those guilty of high crime, whether American citizens or not, should go unpunished," he wrote. "But even that result could not justify an usurpation of power."[59] Better a crime went unpunished than sovereignty diminished.

Power was the key. Ironically, once executive power was created in a potentially unlimited treaty, the limitations of the treaty itself could be held up as barriers to additional action. Frelinghuysen stood on the letter of the law, the side of power, and the notion of treaties as limited contracts, but he also understood that the spirit of the times was shifting away from this citizenship exception, particularly in U.S. agreements. And he was candid enough to draw attention to the fourteen treaties at that time in which the United States had accepted a citizenship exception.

Frelinghuysen decided that "safety and peace of society on the frontier would be greatly injured if criminals, because citizens of this country, could here find an asylum and go unpunished." So this question was "of too much importance" not to ask for "judicial determination" in this case. Trimble had already been released and disappeared, so this case would not provide final clarity. Therefore Frelinghuysen urged that the judicial branch somehow soon decide the habeas corpus implications of the presidential power in extradition. Meanwhile, the executive branch would be sure to allow the state extradition system to take the lead in borderlands extradition. The president would no longer simply stop an extradition authorized by the officers in Texas based on citizenship as long as the accused was informed of his habeas rights. Until the court finally decided whether "the President has a discretionary power of extraditing citizens proven guilty of crime, the evil apprehended will not be realized, and should the court hold that the President has the power to extradite only when bound by treaty to do so, Congress can then, if it should be its pleasure, by statute confer the discretionary power."[60] This did not signal the end of the citizenship exception at all, but it was an interesting empowerment of the state authorities and endorsement of the balance of powers.

Though Frelinghuysen signaled a possible change in the place of citizenship in the legal space of the borderlands, this change was slow to come. Calls for reform became a perennial component of state political speeches, press statements, and consular service reports. One of the catalysts for intensified concern with border security, jurisdictional, and citizenship issues was the second inauguration of Texas governor John Ireland on January 20, 1885.

Ireland, who just won the largest popular vote in Texas history, was a very influential champion of using state power to organize rangelands, establish clear jurisdiction, and maintain secure borders. The year previous, he had overseen a solution to the brief but violent fence-cutting war, an enclosure struggle over boundaries, control, and use of public lands, which helped to further the spirit and reality of lawlessness in Texas.[61]

In 1885, the politically emboldened Ireland gave a short, fiery speech that demanded action from the federal government on extradition and border security. He particularly desired a revised and intensified extradition treaty with Mexico. Ireland mentioned "the perpetration of a series of horrible crimes, murders and thefts on Texas soil by incursions of predatory bands from Mexico" and blamed them not on a generalized lawlessness but quite centrally on the citizenship exception: "Since it has become known that neither Mexico nor the United States will surrender one of their own citizens to be taken to the other government to be tried for crime, the people on the right bank of the Rio Grande have become emboldened, and they stand on Mexican soil covered with the blood of our women and children and their booty in sight of our people."[62]

Ireland fretted that though he had "made repeated efforts, through the Secretary of State, to induce a discussion of the propriety of so amending the treaty of 1861 as to permit any one, no matter where his allegiance may be, to be extradited, but no results have followed. Commercial treaties and money affairs seem to be of more importance than the blood of our people." He also complained forcefully about raids over the border and very dramatically called for new state or national military patrols in words that he said were "not intended as a criticism of the commanding officers in Texas, but of the general management of the War Department." Militarization and an end of the exception were the keys to prosperity and peace.[63]

The newspaper response in the state was also supportive of treaty revision. The *Galveston Weekly News* noted that not extraditing citizens simply increased lawlessness and called for reform. The *Mexican Financier* considered Frelinghuysen's nod toward ending the citizenship exemption to extradition and declared both sides of the river to be "exhausted" by the issue. "At present the valley of the Rio Grande on both sides of the river, outside of the towns, is the chosen dwelling space of the most desperate characters. Human life has no value there and property exists there only for the benefit of thieves. Criminals from America make their home on the Mexican side; criminals from Mexico make their home on the American side," the editors observed. Criminals could escape back and forth and take advantage of either side, depending on what looked good, like eating fruit in season. Sutton, approving of the shift in public discussion toward treaty reform and considering the well-entrenched popular support for the pursuit of Mexican fugitives, continued to agitate for reforms of the extradition treaty, promising wishfully that "such changes . . . would, if adopted and enforced, make this border as law-abiding as any portion of the United States."[64]

But for a time, the region remained one where law was easily bypassed by either stepping over the boundary line or seeking refuge in citizenship (or both). In 1888, the State Department reaffirmed the *Trimble* decision to Texas by refusing to consider surrender in the case of Charles Hudson, a citizen wanted in Mexico for robbery. In 1891, after "Dr. Martinez . . . was basely assassinated on the streets of Laredo, Tex., by persons who fled to Mexico," Secretary of State Blaine again denied there was any power to request surrender: "This government is precluded from demanding the extradition of the fugitives in the present instance."[65]

Transboundary extradition proceedings also continued to retain their decidedly local rhythms and idiosyncracies. This was the reality in 1891 in one of the last cases under the old regime of pronounced loose legality and exceptions that were corrosive of justice. On February 13, Mary Inez McCabe was arrested between Alice and Corpus Christi by Patrick Whelan, sheriff of Nueces County, Texas. Everything about McCabe's crime and arrest was a tad strange. She was charged with killing a Mexican judge named Max Stein in Matamoros. When arrested, she was "suffering severely from a badly sprained or broken limb" and fleeing Mexico with the help of a companion who turned out to be a certain Dr. Stedley, an Edinburg customshouse inspector who was at the time on a leave of absence.[66]

E. C. Forto, county judge and extradition agent of Cameron County, Texas, had issued a requisition based on the direct request of Lamon F. Flores, the federal judge and extradition agent of the third district of Tamaulipas. There was no diplomatic request, and the Texas and Tamaulipas governors were not even in the loop on this issue, though this was a requirement of the border states clause. Judge Russell of the District Court of Western Texas had heard McCabe's writ of habeas corpus and gave the decision that she be delivered to the extradition agent at Brownsville.

According to John B. Richardson, the U.S. consul at Matamoros, McCabe's friends thought that the extradition agent favored her extradition and was illegally expediting the process. Indeed, Richardson thought that Mexico was "not anxious for her extradition. The anxiety is felt wholly by her husband's enemies in Texas who are numerous and powerful the most bitter of whom is Judge Russell himself." There was a feeling among her defenders that if she were not legally extradited, some pretense would be found "either under cover of some technicality or by force. All sorts of rumors are in the air." Even if the State Department had made its policy on nonextradition of citizens clear, Richardson thought McCabe faced fast surrender: "Yet this part of Texas is a long way from Washington. These people are a kind of law unto themselves. Might exerts itself more earnestly and with less shame to make right here than in any part of the United States with which I am acquainted. Partisan feeling is strong in these border counties. Outbreaks and bloodshed are possible at anytime and almost imminent in Hidalgo County to-day."[67]

Richardson was sensitive to the existence of McCabe's supposed enemies, and especially to the enemies of her husband. It is possible McCabe had been seeking revenge for her husband, who she and others believed had been properly elected to the office that Stein held but who had subsequently been "deprived of his office, driven from his home and country and, at the time of the Tragedy, lying wounded with a pistol shot in his foot." There was in fact no question Mrs. McCabe was guilty of killing Stein. The question Richardson thought was important was her character. McCabe had admitted to shooting Stein "in defense of her virtue and character" as he had "dogged her steps lying in wait for her and seeking by every means in his power to gain possession of her person—some of his attempts amounting to force." To make the matter even more poignant and bizarre, McCabe had only just recently delivered a child who lived but a few hours, a death that she blamed on Stein for reasons that are not clear. The consul reported that McCabe was in a "delirium of her fever" as a result and was convalescing when the tragedy at Reynosa occurred. Local physicians had assured the consul that McCabe was "suffering from mental aberration resulting from her perpetual fever" and would have been acquitted or lightly sentenced in a fair trial. "Mrs. McCabe is not a criminal in any deep, true sense of the term. She is a young, beautiful and spirited Texas girl whose chief fault—if it be fault—seems to be a ready sympathy with her husband in his struggles and ill luck and whose misfortune it is to possess a person that attracts the eye and awakens the lust of that class of men to which Max Stein was said to belong."[68]

He went on at unusual length to defend McCabe against extradition, and noted so in his dispatches. Perhaps because this crime clearly counted as an "outrage" in that it involved the shooting of a public figure by an American, the consul felt obliged to beg the State Department not to let a citizen be extradited. Since this in fact almost never happened, it was certainly curious how detailed and strident Richardson's defense of McCabe's actions were. Quite clearly, he felt that the need for an exception in this case was so strong that the mere existence of a treaty exception was not insurance enough to save McCabe. He felt compelled to make a case for the treaty provision as a fail-safe: "Now it is proposed to take this young woman 'more sinned against than sinning' after her heroic and painful effort at escape and send her back into Mexico for 13 years of penal service, a service that is at once assumed to mean a most horrible and indescribable degradation of her womanhood." If the United States were to agree to her extradition and the certain bespoilment of her womanhood, "it would be excoriated by every honorable man or woman, Mexican or American on this border."[69]

McCabe fought her case in court, and it was brought on a new writ of habeas corpus before Judge Maxey of the U.S. District Court at Austin. Maxey did not consider the virtues of the criminal accusation since the issue raised by McCabe's lawyers rested on what they saw as the core irregularity of the case. Maxey alternatively found that correct extradition procedure had been followed since the warrant issued by Judge Forto was for McCabe to be at a preliminary hearing. Just because it was done by "an officer who styles himself 'county judge and extradition agent, Cameron County, Texas,' is of no consequence," Maxey wrote. "In performing the act, the function was judicial not executive. No extradition agent, as such, could issue a warrant of that nature." Maxey also swatted aside other claims of the defense of the warrant. But it was the citizenship exception that was the focus of this decision: "The judiciary is rarely called upon to decide questions of more magnitude and importance than those arising under treaty engagements involving the reciprocal rights and duties of independent governments. The court therefore approaches with diffidence the performance of so delicate a duty, and has exercised in this case unusual care and diligence in the endeavor to reach a just conclusion, just to the two high contracting parties, and just to the petitioner, whose liberty is imperiled."[70] This seriousness was suitable since this was the highest decision to treat this issue in this era.

Maxey based his decision on cases such as *Blandford v. The State* (1881), *United States v. Rauscher* (1886), and *Benson v. McMahon* (1888) to find that the "almost unbroken current of American authority and the practice of our own government" proved that there was no requirement to act or an "obligation to surrender" under any circumstance unless a treaty compelled it. Maxey found that the precise phrasing of the 1861 treaty, where neither party "shall be bound to deliver up its own citizens," proved that there had in fact been no explicit command or even a right to surrender citizens. To Maxey, it was "therefore apparent that the purpose of the treaty was to authorize the parties to do something which they had no previous authority to do." Evoking Judge Santos's argument from the *Case of Jose Ferreira dos Santos* in 1835 about the inherent limitations between reciprocity and sovereignty in the process, Maxey wrote, "if power to surrender be not affirmatively given, the right to demand a fugitive can have no existence. The right to demand implies, *ex vi termini*, the corresponding authority and obligation to surrender. But both to exist should be founded upon express stipulations."[71]

Maxey concluded that "extending through a period of 17 years, 4 different administrations of the federal government have invariably held that no authority was conferred upon the executive, by the sixth article of the treaty, either to demand of the Mexican authorities the extradition of their subjects committing crimes in the United States, or to surrender an American citizen upon demand made by the republic of Mexico." Therefore McCabe could not be surrendered. Maxey considered it a pity that the case could not reach the U.S. Supreme Court for a truly final solution, but it was not possible. As solace, he quoted Frelinghuysen's strong words in the Trimble case, and added a few of his own. "'It would be a great evil that those guilty of high crime, whether American citizens or not, should go unpunished; but even that result could not justify an usurpation of power.' Nor is judicial usurpation less reprehensible. Both are wrong; both defy the law, and are repugnant to the genius of our institutions."[72] Frelinghuysen had hoped for a clear judicial determination of the executive power question in the extradition relations, but this case did not yield the clarity or finality he wished. It did, however, skate free of usurpation.

There was one coda to the story worth telling because it is illustrative of how rapidly and readily notions of justice and comity were shifted as new situations arose along the border, as they always did. Before Maxey's trial in Austin, Consul Richardson had experienced a quick change of heart about the wisdom of surrendering this "spirited Texas girl" he had so strongly supported. The catalyst for this change in his view of the inalterable value of American citizenship came when he considered the wisdom of trading her for a couple of train robbers. A Rio Grande Railway train was robbed on January 19, 1891, between Brownsville and Point Isabel in Texas, which resulted in "large losses of three American merchants" of up to seventeen thousand dollars. By March, two of the criminals, Blas Loya and Severiano Loya, were being held in Matamoros and represented by Mrs. McCabe's former lawyer, A. Martinez Cacereo, who had supposedly abandoned her defense once taking all of her money. The consul rather sneeringly rejected the idea that they were really Mexican citizens, as they claimed. "It is probably true that they may have signed some declaration of intention to become American citizens in order to obtain the small pittance usually paid for

Mexican votes in Texas elections," he wrote. The consul wanted them extradited to the United States at all costs.[73]

Richardson noted that there was "a good deal of uneasiness" in Matamoros because of U.S. demands that the thieves be extradited despite Article VI. The authorities in Brownsville were strongly divided on how to proceed, how to arrest the robbers, and where and how to try them. They had in fact arrested and released some and arrested one Severian Jimenez, who escaped. Others arrested were released on lack of evidence. One was killed in a raid. There was a one-thousand-dollar bounty put on the Loyas's heads by the Rio Grande Railway company, which led to exclamations in *El Cronista* newspaper in Matamoros that "never can our National Government sell, at any price, the heads of it citizens to a foreign Government as this deal would be repugnant to civilization."[74]

But there was an idea floating "in the air and as improbable as it may appear in face of all the precedents" that was thoroughly embraced by the consul. Perhaps the thieves could be traded for McCabe! Richardson offered to broker such a swap: "I am inclined to think the exchange would be made if the respective Governments could be induced to wink at it." The consul was not subtle about his motivation or about the stakes. McCabe's honor, so important just a week prior, was forgotten. "There is a great deal of temptation on both sides," the consul wrote before detailing the temptation he felt. "The rewards are large for the conviction of the robbers and the recovery of the money." Richardson also claimed that it would break the logjam in Brownsville and reward the Mexican authorities, who had been "heartily cooperative from the beginning." They, too, would be "willing to engage in an exchange of international courtesies contrary to the usual interpretation of the Treaty of 1861 and glad of an excuse to do so. Since it would be flattering to their pride to gain possession of Mrs. McCabe while being relieved of the trial and conviction of these men under Mexican law."[75]

After the Maxey decision, Richardson was calmer and gladdened to have confirmed that the United States did not extradite citizens. He rather oddly recommended that perhaps the United States should begin to consider extraterritoriality along the border as a way to control crime by American citizens, rather than just to free them by refusing to extradite them. "It is my opinion that the lawlessness of this border would be materially abated if the Texas authorities were as eager to stop it as those of Mexico," he wrote. "The law of Mexico, by which crimes committed in Texas by Mexicans can be punished on Mexican soil, is healthy in its influence."[76] Richardson's suggestions were not followed, not least because they stood so sharply opposed to established practices. But it was increasingly apparent that the citizenship exception in the treaty was perhaps producing more problems than it was solving.

One of the final straws came in a situation that frustrated the United States, which was the hotly contested case of Chester W. Rowe. Skating along the various exceptions that riddled extradition relations on the border to escape a charge of embezzlement of approximately thirty thousand dollars in Iowa in 1895, Rowe and his brother, Richard Rowe, fled for Mexico City. There they renamed themselves "Rose" and cleverly bought an expatriate bar, which was said to be successful. Because of this property ownership and Article 30 of the Mexican Constitution and the related matriculation laws, they automatically became Mexican citizens, which meant they could not be extradited.

There was no doubt that Chester Rowe was now legally Mexican, though the change in citizenship was more readily disputed in the case of Richard for reasons that are unclear. The United States "urged" the view that "citizenship assumed for [the] purpose [of] evading extradition should not be allowed" in either case, but Mexico ignored the plea. It never disputed Rowe's guilt and in fact displayed evidence that he had hidden in a safety deposit box. The fact was that Mexico did not have to surrender him and so refused to do so. All U.S. requests in the summer of 1895 for their surrender were rejected, though Mexico did follow through on its claim of extraterritorial jurisdiction over criminal acts of its citizens (even freshly minted ones), and Rowe spent six years in Belem Prison in Mexico City, where he became known as "the American Consul to Belem."[77]

The American extradition agent sent to Mexico to try to pry out the Rowe brothers was William Farmer Forsee, who in turn hired a Mexican lawyer named Francisco Alfaro to plead the case. This argument that the Rowes should not be allowed to adopt retroactive citizenship immunity ranged from exegesis on asylum that "condemn[ed] the old theory that its territory was an inviolable asylum for crime" to soaring rhetoric claiming that "the tendencies of this are toward erasing the borders to justice, pursuing the criminals, the enemies of mankind." The Mexican foreign ministry was unmoved by this set of arguments and in pointed terms rejected the U.S. request as handily as it rejected the criticism of Mexican naturalization procedures.

Mexican Foreign Minister Ignacio Mariscal argued that there was not a problem of "inexpediency" in the notion of retroactive naturalization due to it conferring immunity on the Rowes. "Such immunity does not exist," he wrote, because the fact was that Mexican extraterritoriality ensured that they would be "tried in Mexico, in accordance with Mexican law which allows for the punishment of crimes committed abroad, especially that of the embezzlement of funds under false pretenses, provided always that the party guilty preserved such funds in his possession, which, according to those who have moved in the extradition, is the case at issue." Since the Rowes had hidden the stolen money in a safety deposit box in Mexico City and were caught red-handed, Mexico believed it had clear jurisdiction. Mariscal noted that "unless a competent tribunal declares that the naturalization of C. W. Rowe is null and void, we shall consider it as valid and of effect (as was really the case) in accordance with the laws of Mexico." Mexico "believed itself in duty bound to consider Rowe a Mexican." Mariscal also sharply observed that the United States also functionally allowed naturalization to act as retroactive immunity when it denied extraterritorial jurisdiction. "There is also impunity inevitably in your country for those who hide the fact that they have committed a crime in another country," he wrote, "for in the United States, as a general rule, crimes committed abroad are not punished."[78]

Mariscal recognized that Mexico could in fact extradite its new citizen if it chose to, but he did not believe that this case was serious enough to warrant such a significant reversal without explicit reciprocity from the United States allowing for similar surrenders in the future. His key emphasis was on the nature of the crime and, perhaps more importantly, on the need for true reciprocity on the border. The citizenship exception quite clearly cut both ways but was only ever appealing to one side at a time in a particular situation. Mariscal quoted Frelinghuysen during the Trimble case that "when the question is one of discretion, the better rule is that wherever by the jurisprudence of a particular country, it is capable of trying one of its subjects for an offense alleged to have been committed by such subject abroad, the extradition in such case should be refused." With the United States unwilling to extradite its own citizens, Mexico saw no reason to be excessively accommodating in this case, no more so than had the United States in Trimble's case and so many others. "What this Government did once, when it sacrificed delicate national sentiments, whether they be just or not, against the delivery of a Mexican, it would do again in like circumstances," he wrote. But this case was not as serious:

> [The Mexican government] can not [extradite] in the present instance for the circumstances are radically different. Not only does it see that it can not obtain reciprocity in action, but this is not a case, as it was then, where a capi-

tal crime is involved, one wholly extraordinary—an assassin menacing the frontier of both territories. Of course, the crime at issue is repugnant, as all crimes are, but it is not of colossal proportions, nor is it a crime such as hor-rorizes [*sic*] humanity. Therefore, there is not sufficient reason to justify a waiver of the general rule which admits of delivery (without reciprocity) of one's own citizens.[79]

If the United States wished to avoid similar troubles in the future, Mariscal wrote rather forcefully, then it could renegotiate the extradition treaty without the citizenship exception: "If the Government of the United States is of the belief that it can remedy the ill results incident to any possible immunity of offenders, who may take out letters of naturalization in Mexico, and that the remedy might be found in a new treaty, this Government, which, on its part, has met with serious difficulties in consequence of procedure observed in extraditions requested by your country, would be disposed to negotiate a new treaty upon this important matter."[80]

Secretary of State Richard Olney stressed the problems of Mexican naturalization much more than he did those of the refusal to surrender the Rowes. This was because he had little choice, as the treaty allowed it and the United States had long defended it: "If Chester W. Rowe is a bona fide citizen of Mexico, the refusal of the Mexican Government to surrender him for extradition is perfectly satisfactory. The United States asks nothing which may not be demanded under the treaty. Nothing is sought upon the ground of favor of comity; for the United States is powerless to reciprocate, the Executive being bound under our law to surrender or to refuse to surrender according as upon facts the case is within or without the obligation of the treaty." The treaty was limited, and the United States appreciated these limitations.

But, Olney argued, "the method of this man's naturalization is peculiar, and when the antecedents, the manifest purpose, and the announced result are considered, is startling." Because of it, "this criminal has escaped unpunished from the people whom he has wronged and is a fellow-citizen of the people against whom his very presence is a wrong." Olney claimed that "Rowe's adoption of Mexican citizenship as a cloak to his crime [was] inconsistent with the spirit if not the letter of the [Mexican] law and subversive of its intent," though this was not the view of the Mexican authorities on the subject. The fact was the United States just could not bear the blatant use of this naturalization escape hatch or the Mexican insistence on the validity of its own interpretation of its laws.[81]

Olney also expressed concerns about the injection of more disorder and muddled jurisdiction in the borderlands, and he used the same ringing phraseology that Warner P. Sutton had been using since the 1870s to express it:

The inevitable consequence of protecting Chester Rowe from extradition will be to induce other criminals in the United States to flee to Mexico as the most accessible and the safest haven for the lawbreaker on the continent. If they have but the price of a bit of land they will flock to the Mexican border like the criminals of old to the city of refuge, and there, *unwhipped of justice and rejoicing in evil*, they will take on the highest honor and privilege the Mexican nation can bestow—its citizenship. The detriment to the peace and good order of both countries which perseverance in the course now threatened by the Mexican Executive would cause is inestimable. The protection of Rowe from extradition would be an invitation to lawlessness in the United States and to an invasion of lawbreakers into Mexico.[82]

Olney insisted that what the United States wanted was not even just retribution or justice but deterrence of future crime: "In our law, the end of punishment judicially administered is not in the nature of atonement or expiation for the crime committed, but it is a precaution against future offenses of the same kind." Territorial jurisdiction was undermined, and the "effect of legally administered punishment is wanting when the crime is committed in one place and the consequent punishment is inflicted at another and a distant place." He wanted to realize this deterrence and allow what the State of Iowa earnestly desired, not to avenge itself upon Rowe, but to "make an example of him for the benefit of those who may otherwise be tempted to do as he has done—embezzle trustfunds and escape to Mexico."[83]

As weak as this argument clearly was, Mexico saw fit to extradite Richard Rowe back to Iowa in November 1895. His naturalization had always been under dispute, and it is not hard to see why Mexico may have done this to partially calm the waters and move negotiations forward on a new extradition agreement. Olney had signaled his willingness to deal. "The suggestion of Mr. Mariscal that a repetition of this disappointment of justice can be avoided by amending the treaty has not escaped attention," he wrote in passive but diplomatically clear language. "The United States is ever ready to annul or to narrow the exemptions contained in its extradition treaties based on the citizenship of the fugitive."[84] The move toward negotiation had begun.

This dispute thus rapidly broadened beyond the extradition of an embezzler to involve a new line of dispute in which the United States questioned the procedures of Mexican naturalization and its effect on the legal spatiality of the borderlands. Here, too, was another unilateralist policy that had within it the power to completely and effortlessly counter U.S. dominance of the bilateral relationship. Citizenship was power along the border, thanks to the exception in extradition, and Mexico had created a system through which this power was readily accessible in ways that challenged U.S. notions of order and jurisdiction.

This broad naturalization policy had long been a concern, but there had been no solution to it, despite various pleadings and promises of reciprocal benefits. In the wake of the Morteritos dispute discussed in the last chapter, Frelinghuysen had attempted, a bit self-servingly, to convince Mexico to make changes on its own for no real reason aside from the U.S. interest in seeing the changes made and before the United States was willing to make reciprocal concessions of its own. Mexico had, as would be expected, not changed its policy and had even extended unilateralist assertions like extending the *Zona Libre*. All such assertions bespoke a concerted Mexican resistance to U.S. dominance of the relationship, or so it seemed to Texas and Washington policymakers. Now the Rowe case revealed that a wily American fugitive could actually *exempt himself* from sovereign authority just by taking advantage of the liberal Mexican naturalization laws. Jurisdiction at the border was not just being challenged here; the seeds of its own dissolution were clearly sewn.

This realization that the citizenship exception was not sustaining sovereignty as designed but actually beginning to undermine it happened to occur just as there was a renewed push to forcibly compel Mexico to revise the *Zona Libre* through the ill-starred attempt to end the bonded routes, as discussed in chapter 3. There was no direct causal relationship between them that was evident, but the borderlands were clearly saturated with a renewed sense of looseness and disorder and the potential for more of both. If Mexico represented not only free movement of goods but readily accessible citizenship protections in a system founded in part on citizenship distinction and exception, then this could easily be viewed as ultimately destructive of U.S. order and sovereignty. The realization soon produced a movement for change in the procedures for fugitive surrender even though the commercial issues remained intractably tilted toward Mexican interests. Extradition was easily addressed, if not actually easily fixed.

In fascinating ways, the Rowe case was something of the mirror image of the U.S. wrangles with Italy in the same era; the issues were all very much the same but the positions were entirely reversed. With Italy, the United States had defended its own liberal naturalization laws as inviolable and absolute and refused to recognize the citizenship exception as a legitimate component of extradition relations. In dealing with Mexico, the United States attempted to argue that liberal naturalization laws should not be unilaterally applied or universally accepted and that independent laws of immigrant states should not be used to diversify global jurisdictional regimes. A change in citizenship could not deny sovereign jurisdiction. And the United States rejected extraterritoriality in both instances, especially since such assertions were corrosive of the idea of inviolable citizenship.

But the general incoherence of this approach soon gave way in elimination of the citizenship exception in U.S.-Mexican extradition. Though Frelinghuysen had called for the Supreme Court to rule on the issue as far back as the Trimble case, it never had. Instead, the cumulative weight of a series of increasingly poor policy choices finally convinced U.S. policymakers that sovereignty perhaps would be better served without this particular exception.

The real push for change came from Mexico, which had finally reached the limits of its patience for the varying standards for extradition. It forced the issue (for this and more important reasons detailed in the next chapter) by exercising its option to terminate the 1861 treaty. A new U.S.-Mexican extradition convention was thereafter signed on February 22, 1899.[85] Designed to solve the problems of the previous four decades, it still managed to be a longer and more convoluted document than many extradition agreements of this era.

The new treaty was reflective of an increasingly sophisticated and fine-tuned system of fugitive exchange that took a large step beyond the limited bilateral agreements of mid-century. Many of the treaty's core features were similar to the American standard, including double criminality, the rule of specialty, and the political exception, which is discussed in the next chapter. The border exception clause was also renewed in this agreement, assuring local input and continued local wrangles.

Interestingly, the new treaty did not in fact eliminate the citizenship exception but rather streamlined it in a way that produced more executive choice. This presumably would yield more surrenders. But citizenship remained a reified category on the border in ways increasingly uncommon across U.S. extradition relations (it was permanently gone by 1905). Article IV of the treaty read, "neither of the contracting parties shall be bound to deliver up its own citizens under the stipulations of this convention, but the executive authority of each shall have the power to deliver them up, if, in its discretion, it be deemed proper to do so." This very carefully delineated construction built upon sovereign discretion was the same as that of the 1886 treaty with Japan and was rapidly becoming the standard in U.S. treaties at the turn of the century. This article resolved the interpretative question about the power of the president to surrender a citizen under any circumstances. This confusion, highlighted in the Trimble case, had been (depending on one's view) either hampering surrenders or serving as a convenient explanation by the United States. Interesting to observe is that since Article XII of the treaty allowed "subsequent surrender to a third Power of a person given up," it was possible that an American citizen surrendered by choice under the new treaty could then be surrendered by Mexico to another nation.[86]

Article III of the treaty forbade extradition "on account of a crime or offense for which the person demanded is undergoing or has undergone punishment in the country from which the extradition is demanded" or if the person had been acquitted of the charge, which signaled on the part of the United States a greater willingness to trust the Mexican justice system in managing the legal regime along the border. And at the same time, the new treaty removed the typical sticking point of this type of territorial punishment by eliminating extraterritorial jurisdiction over "the punishment of crimes committed *exclusively* within the territory of the other." The only crime that was exempted from this exception was "embezzlement or criminal malversation of public funds committed within the jurisdiction of either party by public officers or depositories." Any future Rowe would not go unwhipped of justice.[87]

The new treaty regularized extradition relations for a time. Soon after its signing, there was a quick extradition that proceeded without a hitch despite some potentially profound complications. This was the case of Mattie Rich, who was extradited from Mexico to the United States for shooting and fatally wounding her husband, John D. Rich, in Ciudad Juárez. She had discovered him with a prostitute, whom she hit and gave two black eyes. On the afternoon of April 26, 1899, Mattie Rich then shot and wounded her husband. The complication in the case came when John D. Rich crossed the river to El Paso before he died on April 30, 1899.

The Rich case proceeded on two levels, with the extradition proceedings decided by Extradition Commissioner J. B. Sexton in Texas under the border states clause and the merits and political wisdom of her surrender considered at the federal level under the new guidelines of the 1899 treaty. The Rich case revealed that the new system could work even while every American policy-maker involved in it had numerous caveats. In deciding the case, Sexton noted that his responsibility was not to judge Rich's final guilt or innocence but to de-termine probable cause for her imprisonment and surrender under the terms of the treaty. He went through all of the evidence supplied by Mexico, including some very damning statements from John D. Rich before he died. Sexton noted, approvingly but with a bit of flair, that "of course, to be acceptable and effective a dying declaration should be [made] on the understanding that he will die." As Rich did indeed die, and as the other evidence was overwhelming, Sexton found that there was "sufficient cause to believe" that Mattie Rich had fired the shot and should be extradited.[88]

Since Mattie Rich was an American citizen, and given the express respon-sibility of the executive for such surrenders in the 1899 treaty, this case did not remain a local borderlands affair. Gender was apparently not a mitigating factor as it had been in the McCabe case. But the Rich case did not generate the kind of problems that had become so familiar. President William McKinley was fa-vorably inclined to extradite Rich since this situation seemed tailor-made for the new treaty. Since the executive was now newly empowered with an explicit grant of authority to extradite a citizen, Secretary of State John D. Hay reported that the surrender was done as a result of deliberate political calculation: "With a view to the efficient operation of this clause of the treaty, it is thought desir-able to avert, as far as possible, any occasion for popular agitation and arous-ing a sentiment hostile to the execution of this clause of the treaty in all proper cases." McKinley had faced some strong public pressure not to give up Rich, but as he announced in his annual address,

> . . . the extradition of Mrs. Mattie Rich, a citizen of the United States, charged with homicide committed in Mexico, was after mature consideration directed by me in the conviction that the ends of justice would be thereby subserved. Similar action, on appropriate occasion, by the Mexican Executive will not only tend to accomplish the desire of both Governments that grave crimes go not unpunished, but also to repress lawlessness along the border of the two countries. The new treaty stipulates that neither Government shall assume jurisdiction in the punishment of crimes committed exclusively within the territory of the other. This will obviate in future the embarrassing controver-

sies which have heretofore arisen through Mexico's assertion of a claim to try and punish an American citizen for an offense committed within the jurisdiction of the United States.[89]

McKinley's phrasing was pointed and astute. In the previous paragraph, he had reported the new change to the citizenship exception regime and the injection of executive discretion. He then acknowledged that Rich should be extradited in the interests of justice since she was a murderer and her punishment would help to stop lawlessness on the border. This was due to "mature consideration directed by me," an act of sovereign choice rather than one beholden to the emotions of the border or an unnecessary reliance on past precedent. But at the same time, he implicitly recognized that this kind of surrender to Mexico was a novelty and was, in fact, a small but significant attenuation of U.S. sovereignty. The president followed up his remark about Rich's surrender with approval of the formal end of extraterritorial claims by Mexico under the treaty. Though it had been thirteen years since the Cutting case, McKinley said that the United States would never have to again face "the embarrassing controversies which have heretofore arisen through Mexico's assertion of a claim to try and punish an American citizen for an offence committed within the jurisdiction of the United States."[90] Thus, McKinley mollified critics that this end to the citizenship exception, albeit a partial and heavily contingent end, was mitigated by this small closure to the muddled and contested jurisdictional regime on the border.

CHAPTER SIX

Exception as Metaphor and Practice

The tendency which has been emphasized, to stretch the jurisdiction of
this country beyond the law and the usage, is not one which will stand still.
It must be checked at once or grow greater. Every instance of it will raise a
controversy. . . . Can one imagine this country embarked upon such a sea of
adventure, without dread? . . . Place the burden of responsibilities, involved
in such a position, upon our government, contrast with this the heavy cost,
the empty glory, the nature of the return, a harvest of dislike, distrust, commercial jealousy and discrimination; what has the political headship of this
continent to offer in compensation!

Theodore S. Woolsey, "An Inquiry Concerning Our Foreign Relations," 1892

The reciprocal nature of extradition was at its most elemental in the balance
between the right to request surrender of a fugitive and the right to refuse
that request. This choice was a key attribute of sovereignty, as Judge Maxey had
argued in *Ex parte McCabe* and as was stressed in a variety of other cases. It
was, to be sure, a deeply political choice to invoke the sovereign right of refusing to surrender a fugitive, and so it was not taken lightly. Political exceptions
drew from explicit grants of power *not* to act, called "treaty reservations."[1] This
was separate from powers absent from a treaty, for sovereignty produced its
own exceptions.

Arguably the most interesting cases in which the politics of refusal were laid
bare came through the application of the political offenses exception. Every
one of these decisions was a contingent one based on a broad range of factors
and a shifting array of political interests external to the matter of extradition.
Other refusals to surrender based on non-trial, double criminality, or citizenship grounds were rooted in structural requirements. The elaborate politics of

surrender produced by the malleable political nature of an extraditable act continuously reflected U.S. policy interests and ambitions as they evolved across different regions at different times.

The political offenses exception was among the most fluid components of any extradition treaty and certainly the one most open to divergent interpretation. Since each extradition relationship was bilateral and separate, each also presented the opportunity to create piecemeal zones of sovereign exception. Political offenses mitigated reciprocity and therefore any limitation on sovereignty. Through this exception, many inconsistencies could be resolved, and foreign policy power exercised with nary a limit, if necessary or desirable.

This meant there was no need to define the "political" and the "criminal" in any consistent way. Instead, the definition of a political offense was set upon a sliding scale based on any number of other considerations. Through a range of perspectives on political offenses, the United States crafted new responses to revolution, revolt, and a wide variety of challenges to legal spaces and definitions. In this way, exception served as a linchpin of the disparate parts of the U.S. extradition system. It also served as a laboratory of the U.S. response to revolution and transnational crime in an increasingly revolutionary and violent world at the end of the nineteenth century.

The political offenses exception was a key component of the American system of extradition as a foreign policy because it was the most purely unilateralist element in extradition. Only the surrendering nation could decide on issues of the political nature of any particular crime, according to its own shifting and expedient definitions and interests. The United States created its own definitions of political crime, determined by the judicial system and fulfilled by the executive.

Virtually all definitions of political action remained a matter of choice. The United States alone could define when, how, and where to apply the law. It evaluated the meaning and impact of any particular fugitive's situation and acts on decidedly un-legal grounds and weighed his or her actions in balance with any number of other broad policy aims, ideological traditions, or sovereign interests.

An exception could be a shield, a tool, or a weapon, depending on the case. It was a good example of the intensified contradiction between sovereignty and "the rule of law" mapped by Nasser Hussain, who has described the latter as "a rather fungible category . . . better understood within the large context of changing conceptions of law and sovereignty and specific power relations."[2] The evolving concept of the political directly worked in conjunction with these changing categories of law. Ironically, the invocation of exception significantly intensified the meaning of any individual surrender and clarified the meaning of extradition as governance and policy.

What authority decided if a crime was political or not? This could be a political, legal, philosophical, and even metaphysical question, but the ultimate determination depended on the extradition proceedings of each country. In 1874, Secretary of State Hamilton Fish told the British minister that he "could not consent to refer [such questions] to the judicial officers of either government, and that the decision whether an offense was or was not political was of itself purely a political question and must be decided by a political department of the Government."[3] In the United States, the courts made the determination, but it was the executive who finally decided whether or not to invoke the exception. Criminals, freedom fighters, revolutionaries, assassins, and terrorists all were defined through an evolving understanding of state interest and vantage point. On one side of a boundary line, an act could be viewed entirely differently from another, and usually was.

Nowhere was the line between crime and political act more blurry or complex than in the U.S.-Mexican borderlands. The United States, harboring an aggrieved and well-exercised sensitivity to border incursions and transnational instability, made particularly effective use of the political exception in asserting jurisdiction along the Mexican border. The border states clause in the extradition treaty also made the political exception supremely useful for local assertions of control into the legal and political spaces of the region. Here was a mechanism by which to define an act with clear consequences. If political, it was allowed to stand. If criminal, it could be controlled. Considering transborder acts in this way was a remarkable and very seductive power. There was an evident pattern of this type of sovereign assertion, but no clear standards were established.

There were important governance implications in the determination of political offenses that were side stepped in other extradition surrenders. Consideration of the relative political weight of acts was suddenly directly germane to extradition proceedings that otherwise had focused exclusively on delineated treaty language. This exception thereby injected potentially quite significant regional and domestic political considerations into exchanges that otherwise were centered on prosaic issues of crime and fugitive flight. Judicial extradition hearings did not consider the guilt of a fugitive but only if treaty requirements were being met. But they did have a core responsibility to determine the political significance or intent of an act aside from grappling with the jurisdictional assertions of a foreign sovereign requesting surrender.

Political exceptions generated political repercussions, though they did not necessarily produce a more lawful (or appealing) outcome to extradition proceedings. Crime did not have to be lofty to be political, and political acts were not always progressive ones. They could often be quite odious and even against the existing sense of American ideals and sense of order, justice, or peace. The rights of fugitives were protected because the exception prevented individuals from being targeted by the requesting state. There was also a clear state interest in non-surrender of some fugitives because it provided plausible deniability of passive intervention in another nation's affairs. Questions of criminality were thus embedded in political choice.

Because of the political offenses exception, bilateral fugitive exchange could function smoothly without disrupting core notions of sovereignty or territoriality. It dissolved dangers of foreign jurisdictional overreach and isolated potential snares of ideology. It also allowed a gleam of national autonomy and unilateralism to be maintained within this delineated and reciprocal relationship. It cushioned interstate relations by guaranteeing the preferable default that states simply not extradite political offenders, and each could therefore avoid the appearance of taking sides in another nation's domestic disputes.

But the exact nature of the political crimes that helped to lubricate interstate relations was hard to define. Stephen Schafer has written that "many analysts of the issue of extradition see in the concept of political crime a kind of supralegal category which can be defined only as the analogue of the interests of any given political power, and is therefore beyond the descriptive ability of the law." He quoted nineteenth-century Italian legal scholar F. Carrara in this regard, who called political crime simply "in-definable."[4]

Truly transnational or global crimes (and those considered to be uncivilized or anti-civilized) were more likely to be deemed insufficiently political for exclusion from surrender in global extradition. On the other hand, truly political crimes were functionally considered *not* to be international in character so they could be handled within a single territory and protected from foreign policy exchanges. Since truly political crime by definition did "not violate international public order," the theory was that states were "supposed not to have a mutual interest in the suppression of such crimes."[5] The acts were deemed not criminal and not international precisely because of their political coloration. The irony that sovereign political choice in a foreign relations act could render political actions not international or criminal generally was not emphasized.

Conversely, certain categories of political actions were lumped together as crimes because of a globally accepted standard of isolating them from the political exception. This categorization was "as complicated as it [was] delicate" since the political offenses exception was almost never fully defined. The Institute of International Law spent seven years constructing guidelines for the treatment of political offenses in extradition, and its final product, adopted in 1892, was both long and riddled with exceptions to the main exception. As the editors of the *American Journal of International Law* noted later, "this is not to be wondered at, because it is very difficult to state categorically and in the abstract what is or is not a political offense." The inherent looseness of the political category left it ripe for potential abuse by "questionable characters who have taken advantage of disorder and commotion to commit crime."[6]

The Institute of International Law determination had four articles. Article I pronounced that "extradition is inadmissible for purely political crimes or offenses," which was the tightest global standard given the emphasis on the "purely political." This meant "entirely political" rather than being a value judgment about the purity of the politics. Purely political referred to acts against sovereign power, such as revolution, treason, or uprising, or "opposition to a political, religious, or racial ideology or to its supporting structures (or both) without having any of the elements of a common crime."[7] If something could be proven to be purely political, there was no way it was extraditable. The certainty of this statement did not indicate the incredible difficulty of determining the relatively totality of the politics of any specific action. In this way, the determination of the "purely political" did often come to rest on the very value judgment it skirted in the statement. The purer the act appeared in any context, the greater the likelihood that it could be seen as political. Impure acts such as terrorism or assassination or dynamite crime were easily categorized as crime.

The Institute also voted against extradition "for unlawful acts of a mixed character or connected with political crimes or offenses, also called relative political offenses" unless it crucially involved a very wide array of acts considered "crimes of great gravity from the point of view of morality and of the common law." These included "murder, manslaughter, poisoning, mutilation, grave wounds inflicted willfully with premeditation, attempts at crimes of that kind, outrages to property by arson, explosion or flooding, and serious thefts, especially when committed with weapons and violence." Since it is difficult to conceive of a political crime that would not include one of these (other than perhaps "thought crime" from a later era), Article III made yet another exception "so far as concerns acts committed in the course of an insurrection or of a civil war by one of the parties engaged in the struggle and in the interest of its cause." As long as revolutionists did not engage in "acts of odious barbarity or vandalism forbidden by the laws of war," then they should not be extradited. And if they did, they should not be extradited until after the conflict was over.[8]

Interestingly, Article 4 of the resolution excluded broadly and abstractly directed crimes from consideration as political offenses and therefore allowed extradition for this select group. These were "criminal acts directed against the bases of all social organization, and not only against a certain State or a certain form of government." It was criminal to seek the destruction of the base structures of society but political to fight a state. International anarchist terrorism, as was discussed in chapter 4, was the most obvious example, as were all the various assassination attempts directed at sovereigns for any reason. Christine Van den Wijngaert has called this redefinition of crimes "the legal fiction of depolitization."[9]

Two American treaties had a lower barrier of "depolitization" because they exempted only the "*purely* political" crimes. The phrase only appeared with regard to the United States in the extradition agreements with France and Mexico. Recognition of this exception for the "purely political" allowed yet another level of exception for the United States, which alone could pass judgment not just on the political nature of particular criminal acts but on their essence and meaning vis-à-vis other crimes.

Though the purely political standard had a specific legal meaning, the language and distinction remained open to a wider range of interpretation. Eliminating "purely political" crimes from extradition irrevocably made all extradition decisions that much more political because of the implicit recognition that extraditable crimes could be political, though perhaps just not "purely" enough so to meet uncodified American standards. Matías Romero, Mexican minister to the United States, argued that "the fact [is] that the treaty of extradition between the two countries only excepts from extradition those charged with a crime of a purely political character, which seems to mean that when they are mixed with others of a common character, they can not be considered as political offenders to deny their extradition."[10] In cases of transborder crime involving Mexico in the 1890s, the determination of the purity of the political offense and the nature of this "mixed" character process itself can be questioned, as the end of this chapter explores.

The political offenses exemption could be applied or neutralized in myriad ways. It was applied in some cases that seemed to actually counter professed American political goals. One noticeable case in this regard is the U.S. extradition treaty signed with the Kingdom of the Two Sicilies in 1856, "although the kingdom had a notoriously reactionary government and a corrupt legal system." The political exception in this treaty was rendered essentially meaningless, as a person could be extradited if he or she was also guilty of another enumerated crime, such as murder. Since crime and political actions were not uncommonly connected, this placed a clear emphasis on surrender and sovereign control.[11]

The political exception was inserted often in U.S. treaties but at the lower standard of the simply "political." Often it was coupled with other concepts that have already been considered in this book, such as double criminality, non-trial, non-retroactivity, and the citizenship exception. The non-trial principle was especially key in dealing with political crimes in order to avoid the kind of bait-and-switch extradition request that had so alarmed Judge Hurt on the Texas State Court of Appeals in the 1881 case *R. A. Blandford v. The State.* Hurt had designated any attempt to extradite a fugitive for one crime and try him for another political crime "supreme nonsense." Hurt had announced that "all civilized nations agree on one point, and that is that they will not deliver a fugitive to be tried for political offenses."[12]

This idea of the uniformity of the "civilized" states to exclude political offenses held true in U.S. extradition relations. The U.S. treaty with Belgium, for example, allowed no extradition for political crime and no trial for one unless the accused could leave the country for at least a month before hand. Assassination or poisoning of the head of the government or his family was not considered a political act. The same was true for Luxemburg. The revised U.S.-British Extradition Treaty allowed for no extradition for political crime, especially if it looked like an extradition request was itself political retribution. There was no trial for any political crime committed before extradition. The treaties with Haiti, Italy, Japan, the Netherlands, Sweden, Norway, and Austria-Hungary all had the same provision.[13]

The U.S. approach to the treatment of political offenses in extradition treaties was hoisted as the standard for the hemisphere in April 1890 at the first International American Conference, which took place in Washington, D.C. This meeting was called with the intention to serve the ends of U.S. trade expansionism, particularly the foreign trade policy ambitions of Secretary of State James G. Blaine, which were congruent with U.S. ambitions for extradition. In this conference, Blaine attempted but failed to create an "inter-American customs union." Instead, trade reciprocity remained a decidedly bilateral affair created and governed piecemeal by treaties.[14] Blaine was a visionary in terms of the long-term shifts in U.S. foreign economic policy and market expansionism, but he was insufficiently effective to do much about it at this point. This was the age of strident, seemingly unassailable protectionism and of the 1890 McKinley tariff, the highest tariff in U.S. history (as high as 49.5 percent) but with some reciprocity provisions signaling a new emphasis in American policy. It was, of course, both ironic and typical that the protectionist United States at the same time sought new opportunities abroad with fitful reciprocal market openings and other pursuits. It was this double movement wrapped around the insatiability for ever-expanding new markets in the 1890s that helped to produce imperial expansionism.[15]

Trade policy and extradition policy may not seem related, but they both crucially reflected U.S. interests in the unilateral governance of transnational concerns. American economic supremacy in theory as well as practice during this time (and for the next century) was based on focused expansion into, and dominance of, foreign markets. This was enabled and promoted through the action of the state. In its global economic policy, the United States embraced unilateralism, territoriality, and sovereign choice, just as it did in dealing with questions of ordering and controlling legal spatiality and producing fugitive exchange. Reciprocity was merely an exception carved into a bedrock of protectionism, and both were reflective of a distributed U.S. approach to achieving order. Both trade and extradition required bilateral exchange, and U.S. policymakers saw clearly that defining the terms of both of these exchanges produced dominant governance over the acts themselves. Canada seemed to sense this, such as when an extradition judge in Canada sought "free trade" in criminals between Canada and the United States and offered reciprocity for any exchange for an act that amounted "to nothing more than a standing offer to conclude arrangements for the reciprocal surrender of persons charged with certain specified offences."[16]

As legal scholar John G. Hawley explained it in 1893, the U.S. approach to both trade and extradition was carefully calibrated, practical, and focused. Interest, not abstractions, was the objective. Exceptions were but a key component:

Without an exception, extradition treaties are reciprocal and impose a mutual obligation on the United States and the foreign government with which they are contracted, to surrender persons accused of certain specified crimes. They are, as it were, framed upon the same principles as a cartel for the exchange of prisoners of war. A desire to purge out territories of foreign criminals, a consideration much dwelt upon by writers on the law of nations, does not appear to be a controlling consideration. Existing treaties are framed upon commercial principles, and governments surrender persons charged with certain offenses only to those countries which agree to surrender in turn persons found in their territories charged with like offenses.[17]

Extradition fared marginally better at the conference than did trade reciprocity. Even though extradition relations remained bilateral, a vague but deliberate regional standard of exception for political offenses was reified.

It was in preparation for the International American Conference that John Bassett Moore prepared his cornerstone 1890 *Report on Extradition* to provide guidance on the overall discussion on finding consensus in hemispheric extradition procedures. This report inaugurated the process of creating coherence out of the array of U.S. treaties and actions, and it became the basic collection of materials used to systemize U.S. extradition relations for decades.

At the conference, the Committee on Extradition officially recommended that all Latin American governments adopt the treaty of penal international law drafted by the South American Congress of 1888 to govern relations between them but also that each country should conclude an extradition treaty with the United States "upon bases acceptable to them and as uniform as possible." Recognizing the idiosyncratic nature of U.S. policy, the chairman of the committee, Jeronimo Zelaya recommended that Latin American governments "conclude with the United States special treaties of extradition founded on other principles more suited to the peculiar circumstances and habits of legislation of the latter country, and more in harmony with the other treaties thus far concluded between the United States and many other nations, both of Europe and America." He particularly stressed the U.S. emphasis on the territoriality of the crime rather than the nationality of the criminal.[18]

The U.S. approach was very close to the committee's recommendation. It produced a draft model treaty, which had no citizenship exception, allowed asylum "except upon request for extradition," and gave political refugees "an inviolable asylum." Dueling, adultery, libel, and treason were all non-extraditable unless they were connected with other "common (non-political) offenses." All political offenses "subversive of the internal or external safety of a State" as well as concurrent offenses fell under the exception. The model treaty acknowledged the right of the surrendering nation to determine the political nature of a crime but stipulated that it be done "according to the provisions of the law which shall prove to be most favorable to the accused."[19]

The strongest opposition to the model extradition treaty pertained to the inclusion of treason, which some representatives saw as being connected to the political offenses exception and others saw as separated. J. M. P. Caamaño, the delegate from Ecuador, argued that the exception should be eliminated entirely. "Every offense, from the very fact of being such, is subject to penalty, and every penalty should be made effective under pain of weakening the foundation upon which human society rests," he said. Allowing some crimes (especially treason) to go punished created looseness in the system that threatened the entire edifice of society: "That tolerance, carried to the extreme, is the worst of tyrannies, because, applied to the practices which at bottom affect social tranquility, it either obliges individuals again to exercise the rights of primitive ages, or imposes on society the duty of tolerating crimes which ought to be expiated; and it imposes it in favor of the guilty." Bolet Peraza, the Venezuelan delegate, alternatively separated treason from true political offenses. The latter, he said, "are apt to become some day the aureole of great men, of great patriots, when the judgment of history confronts them and examines their conscience and the motives which prompted them to act. By this path of sublime effort have ascended to glory all the great figures humanity recognizes as liberators of their fellow-men."[20]

The tension between these two poles of prosecuting all crime or allowing political actions to exist in a realm protected from the law animated the question of the political offenses exception and the appropriate state responses to it. The final result of this conference was at best just a move toward a system of definition of political offenses. But this result could hardly have been characterized as clear or definitive, and the approach to this core question was never treated multilaterally. By 1902, there was finally an agreement on eliminating anarchism as a political offense in the Treaty for the Extradition of Criminals and for Protection Against Anarchism signed by Argentina, Bolivia, Colombia, Costa Rica, Chile, the Dominican Republic, Ecuador, El Salvador, the United States, Guatemala, Haiti, Honduras, Mexico, Nicaragua, Paraguay, Peru, and Uruguay. But this came several years after it had been established in trans-Atlantic practice and did not resolve the large question of political exception.[21] Sovereign autonomy remained quite vast. If anything, the question was raised even more in specific instances given the contrast with the treatment of the major transnational political criminal action of the time.

"A PRIVILEGE RESTING ON SUFFERANCE": ASYLUM

The concept of asylum was strongly endorsed by the International American Conference, but it remained a very contested issue in U.S. conceptualization and usage. Like extraterritoriality, with which it was often connected, asylum was a flexible but often misunderstood legal fiction. Moore wrote, "no legal term in common use is perhaps so lacking in uniformity and accuracy of definition as the 'right of asylum'. The word asylum has in its legal relations become to a great extent metaphorical."[22] Asylum became part of a nexus along with extradition, exclusion, and exception.

The political offenses exception triggered the need to carve out spaces for asylum within territorial sovereignties and within the interstate system. Tightly interwoven with extradition, asylum raised a wide array of issues concerning territoriality and the spatiality of jurisdiction and power. Moore, whose views were representative of the fundamental perspective of the State Department in the last two decades of the nineteenth century, argued very forcefully that "the granting of asylum to political offenders was simply the transformation of a decaying abuse, which sprang up in times when the principle of territorial sovereignty was not fully established and when the privileges of ambassadors were greatly exaggerated." He argued that it was only "because of the failure to consider asylum in its true legal aspect as a derogation from the sovereignty of the state, that writers have sometimes seemed to supposed that an exception might be made in favor of one class of offenders as against another."[23] There could be no exception made—unless the state found a reason to apply an exception.

In a theoretical sense, asylum itself was a form of exception. The nature, application, extent, and uses of any of these kinds of asylum, like the political character of a crime, were entirely due to sovereign choice. Scholars have identified numerous kinds of political asylum such as prominent territorial asylum, extraterritorial and diplomatic asylum, and asylum on vessels and in time of war. Sovereign territoriality had inherent in it the right to "exclude the exercise of jurisdiction over that territory by any other sovereign." M. Cherif Bassiouni has identified a "duality" between asylum and extradition. These concepts operated on related but totally separated tracks, and the connection was especially close considering the political offenses exception. However, "the two determinations are made in different legal processes using different legal standards and having different review processes and standards." Granting of asylum did not need to include extradition requests or proceedings, but it was possible to end an extradition request (particularly one with political implications) through the granting of asylum. However, in international law and under basic diplomatic procedures and immunities, there was no right to asylum whatsoever.[24]

Since extraterritorial assertions of jurisdiction involved this exclusion from foreign process, asylum within these areas was a similar exception. The fact that asylum could be a marker of strict territoriality as well as a function of extraterritoriality by the granting of asylum abroad within anomalous zones showed how complicated the applications of it could get. But as one commentator noted, basing extensions of asylum on extraterritoriality was "treating as a matter of fact a mere figure of speech."[25] Generally hostile to the concept, the United States was more open to territorial asylum than to any other form and extremely resistant to extending asylum in legations and on ships. It did happen, however, though rarely and unhappily. All grants of asylum were reflective of a definable policy interest as well as the facts on the ground. It does not seem entirely possible to discern a pattern other than a willingness to allow exceptions when they were convenient or seemed appropriate.

Recognition of a *right* of asylum could be recast as an attack or at least limitation on sovereignty whereas the denial of it could be cast as a reification of sovereignty. Samuel Spear, the nineteenth-century scholar on extradition, saw this strengthening of state sovereignty clearly in the case of the Spanish citizen Arguelles, who had the distinction of being the only person extradited in the absence of a treaty. Secretary of State William S. Seward had surrendered him with the claim that no nation is "bound to furnish asylum to dangerous criminals who are offenders against the human race." Spear caustically noted that "the theory that any person, peacefully coming within the jurisdiction of our laws, and committing no offense against them, may, in the absence of any treaty or law of Congress authorizing his extradition . . . be denied the right of unmolested asylum at the discretion of the President of the United States, assigns to his office the prerogatives of an absolute despot." If a right to asylum did not exist, neither did the right to surrender. Both were not exceptions but rather grants of authority and jurisdiction through a treaty: "The President of the United States is not clothed with the total sovereignty of the United States, but is simply the executive authority thereof." All power, whether it be to arrest, surrender, offer asylum, or assert an exception, was limited by the Constitution, statutes, and treaties, and no president could "lawfully exercise any power with which he is not thus invested."[26]

However, in practice, the executive branch made most of the asylum decisions, usually outside the United States, where it had sole authority in foreign relations. Asylum increasingly became a regular aspect of diplomatic relations in unstable states. The United States only grudgingly recognized asylum "not as a right derived from positive law or from custom, but as a privilege resting on sufferance."[27]

The diplomatic record of the late nineteenth century was punctuated by asylum cases large and small, most of them in Latin America. In 1909, Barry Gilbert considered the special problems posed in each of forty different instances of the invocation of asylum up to 1899 and concluded that "any attempt on the part of our diplomatic representatives to formulate definite rules for the regulation of the practice has met with an indifferent reception at Washington." In fact, he wrote with evident exasperation in considering the record, "how a claim for consistency can be maintained in a record of this sort (no, no, yes, no, yes, no, no, yes, yes, yes, yes, no) is inconceivable."[28]

The pattern that emerged was actually one that can be placed alongside that which existed in extradition relations. The United States chose different responses for different regions, emphasized unilateral sovereign choice, and always maximized its freedom of action both at the time in the specific region and in the future in all other cases. A rare grant of asylum was accompanied by multiple assurances of its unique and limited character. In a case in 1875 in Haiti, Secretary of State William M. Evarts acquiesced to the temporary extension of asylum and referred to it as the "quasi rule of public law in communities where the conspirators of today may be the government of tomorrow."[29] In 1876, Secretary of State Fish described "the universal practice [of the United States] to discountenance the granting of asylum by its diplomatic and consular offices." He believed it "to have no good reason for continuance, to be mischievous in its tendencies, and to tend to political disorder" and to be "a cause of annoyance and embarrassment to the minister and [to] tend to bring about questions of a vexatious and troublesome nature."[30]

The Gamez case in January 1885 involved "Don Jose Dolores Gamez, a Nicaraguan political refugee, having embarked at San Jose, Guatemala, for Punta

Arenas, Costa Rica, on board of the Pacific Mail Company's steamship *Honduras*," a U.S. flagged merchant ship. Nicaraguan authorities sought to arrest Gamez while the steamer was in the port of San Juan del Sur. The captain of the ship refused to surrender Gamez and then disobeyed an order to stay at port, a move that was strongly supported by the U.S. minister there. But Secretary of State Thomas F. Bayard argued that the captain should have handed over Gamez. Bayard wrote, "It may safely be affirmed that when a merchant vessel of one country visits the port of another for the purposes of trade, it owes temporary allegiance and is amenable to the jurisdiction of that country, and is subject to the laws which govern the port it visits, so long as it remains, unless it is otherwise provided by treaty. Any exemption or immunity from local jurisdiction must be derived from the consent of that country." Bayard saw no reason why Gamez should have been protected, especially since there was no exception in the U.S. treaty with Nicaragua. This might have been one of those cases in which U.S. discretion had long-term resonance, as Gamez was later the Nicaraguan ambassador to the United States.[31]

In 1888, Assistant Secretary of State George C. Rives again approved asylum in unrest in Haiti and corrected U.S. Consul Stanislas Goutier, who had written to his consular agents that "in view of the revolutionary state of this country, I deem it my duty to inform you that the United States Government does not recognize the right of asylum in consulates for political refugees; consequently you have no right to receive refugees in your consular agency." Actually, wrote Rives in a statement that was considered definitive, the United States determined each case on its merits:

> The position of this Government, briefly summarized, is this: We do not regard extraterritorial asylum, either in a legation or a consulate, as a right to be claimed under international law. We do not sanction or invite, the exercise of asylum in those countries where it actually exists as a usage, but in such cases we recognize and admit its existence, and should circumstances bring about the uninvited resort of a political refugee for shelter to a consulate or legation of the United States, we should expect equal toleration and privilege in this regard with that allowed by such local usage to any other consulate or legation.[32]

Grover Cleveland, in considering a case involving the Chilean government in 1893, helped to clarify the standard of responding to events as they unfolded in his first annual message: "under no circumstances can the representatives of this

Government be permitted, under the ill-defined fiction of extraterritoriality, to interrupt the administration of criminal justice in the countries to which they are accredited." This approach was reiterated by State Department officials for decades in a wide variety of situations from the procedural to the revolutionary. Consular officers' dwellings were deemed inviolable but were explicitly disallowed from being used for asylum in a wide variety of treaties such as those with Italy, Congo Free State, Korea, Morocco, Romania, Salvador, and Serbia.[33]

In a case of revolution in Ecuador in September 1895, Secretary of State Richard Olney made a distinction between "shelter" and "asylum." The former "was a mere act of humanity, unaccompanied by any assumption of extraterritorial prerogatives by you, or interference with any rights of legitimate government or sovereignty" and could be distinguished from "the so-called right of asylum, which can logically only be exercised in disparagement of the rights of the sovereign power by withdrawing an accused subject from its rightful authority." Asylum was the carving of an exception out of a foreign sovereignty whereas shelter was a temporary enclosure required by a revolutionary or emergency situation. Olney thought that the issue was different when it involved "a member of an overturned titular government," when sovereignty could be violated temporarily until the "empire of law" was restored with the return of "the rightful government, competent to administer law and justice in orderly process." In this sense, "the humane accordance of shelter from lawlessness may be justifiable." But in the absence of emergency, there was no call for sovereign exception: "When the authority of the state is reestablished upon an orderly footing, no disparagement of its powers under the mistaken fiction of extraterritoriality can be countenanced on the part of the representatives of this Government."[34]

In 1899, Secretary of State John D. Hay, responded to another situation in Ecuador in which Minister Archibald J. Sampson regretted that he could have "saved from death the legitimate heads of the Government" had he been authorized to extend asylum. Hay declared that only in "exceptional circumstances" involving political offenders and "extreme circumspection" could asylum be granted. "Its exercise [was] not the exercise of a strictly diplomatic right or prerogative," it was "founded alone in motives of humanity" and applicable almost exclusively in situations involving "lawlessness and mob violence."[35] Like Olney, Hay emphasized the temporary, contingent character of asylum for limited purposes rather than the blanket acceptance of any standard. It could be temporarily extended in response to lawlessness, by the exigencies of political need, and, of course, by the consideration of policy interests in each local situation. The granting of extraterritorial asylum was a peculiar exercise of sovereignty, and the "extreme circumspection" Hay referred to was triggered by a closely calibrated mix of interest and situation.

The only place where asylum was largely assured was on U.S. flagged vessels, but even there it was contested and problematic in numerous instances and rooted closely to the late nineteenth-century precedents on land. Ships had clearer and more durable claims on extraterritorial jurisdiction than did any territory on land. This was described in 1894 as similar to "the fiction of extraterritoriality . . . in fact founded on a metaphor [in that] . . . the ship is conceived as a portion of the floating sovereign State, floating in the high sea or elsewhere." Legal scholar John Norton Pomeroy clarified the different jurisdictional meanings of ships at sea and in port. In the "open sea," no other state had a right to any jurisdiction at all; the ship remained "entirely under the laws and government and empire of its own country." "Every relation which a foreign ship holds with it is purely an international relation," limited only by international agreements, comity, or treaties. However, when a ship arrived "within the territorial waters of a foreign state," there arose "an apparent conflict of jurisdictions." Ships of a state remained "solely governed by the sovereignty of its own country; the laws, the authorities, and the jurisdiction of the state in whose waters it is moored remain foreign to it," but the same was not true for merchant vessels, which came under local control.[36]

The U.S. Navy increasingly grappled with this issue of asylum as both a legal and policy matter. Considering this problem for the U.S. Naval Institute in Annapolis, Lieutenant J. H. Gibbons was very clear about the reason grounded in regional realities and U.S. ambitions: "The instability of governments in the neighboring republics of Central and South America, coupled with the desire of the United States to extend its trade relations with those countries, has of late years placed the interpretation of certain principles of international law with the commanding officers of our public vessels in those waters. Such duty is always a delicate one." Naval regulations were vague on this issue, and the complexities of each specific case created a situation in which some captains were applauded and others were punished for their actions. But the extraterritorial jurisdiction of U.S. vessels provided one example for asylum, particularly for some fugitive political offenders. Gibbons asserted that "[t]his exemption rests on the broad principle of humanity, and the United States, more than any other nation, has always been active in upholding it."[37]

By the end of the nineteenth century, with its scope and responsibilities increasingly globalized, the Navy became stricter about the temptations of granting asylum in unstable regions. Given the hypothetical example of a ship encountering a situation in which "a revolutionary outbreak occurs in a South American state," U.S. naval officers were instructed that "the commander of the ship of war should reply that his Government discountenances the practice of granting asylum on board of ships of war, and also that the regulations of the service allow the grant of asylum *only under extreme and exceptional circumstances.*" Each commander was responsible for individually judging "the actual emergency should such emergency unfortunately arise in regard to the [foreign] President and his cabinet while he remains in port." If asylum was granted in this extreme and exceptional situation, the "commander could in no case promise asylum for a future time of which the conditions could not be foretold." Asylum was a fully contingent possibility rooted in sovereign choice (down to the state's sharp end of the spear), not a requirement or a fact, and certainly not a guarantee of a future such grant.[38]

THE BARRUNDIA CASE

The issue of sovereign choice and asylum on U.S. flagged vessels became a significant challenge in the highly controversial case of the killing of General J. Martín Barrundia in Guatemala. On August 28, 1890, Barrundia was shot in a hail of fifty bullets by Guatemalan military officers while sequestered on the U.S. flagged Pacific Mail steamer *Acapulco* in the port of San José, Guatemala. This case resulted in the firing of the U.S. consul as well as a detailed and extremely unusual public flagellation of him in Benjamin Harrison's second annual message.[39] The Barrundia case motivated the Navy to revise regulations for its commanders and Secretary of State Blaine to provide a definitive clarification of the connections between asylum and political offenses. This determination drew deeply upon the unilateral assertion of U.S. sovereignty into transnational questions.

The Barrundia case was extremely complex, made even more so by the complicity of U.S. Consul Lansing B. Mizner. The consul essentially ran a private diplomacy with the Guatemalan government on the issue of the general's arrest, a misplaced use of authority that invited bloodshed and controversy. Barrundia had once been the Guatemalan Secretary of War with designs on the presidency, but once exiled he had been reduced to organizing failed revolutionary armies of invasion in Mexico. When his invasion was repulsed, Barrundia was eventually disarmed, and Guatemala sought his arrest for "high treason." The government put out a public warning that any ship giving Barrundia passage would be held responsible. Nevertheless, Barrundia was allowed to board the Pacific Mail steamer *Acapulco* heading for Salvador "to continue his machinations," which, in a profound piece of bad luck, stopped in a harbor in Guatemala on the way.[40]

Guatemalan Foreign Minister Augustin Paniagua demanded the surrender of Barrundia off the ship, "according to the law of nations, besides the extradition treaty for criminals, ratified in 1870" even though this was not an extradition request but an extralegal grab. Paniagua said that the government had "the perfect right . . . being in a state of war" to "capture" Barrundia on the ship since in wartime all ships could be inspected. Later, Guatemala justified the arrest by stating, bluntly that "Barrundia was contraband of war. . . . As every one is aware, not only arms and munitions, but also persons—those who go to assist and serve the enemy—are considered contraband of war." U.S. Consul General James R. Hosmer "thought Guatemala had the right to search foreign vessels in her own waters, for persons suspected of hostility to her, during war," which he told Consul Don F. Souza, in Retalhulen, Guatemala, three days before the killing.[41]

Mizner handled the case as a loose cannon, apparently because he misguidedly saw Barrundia's capture as the conclusion of a peace process and general amnesty he had been helping to construct and not because he had chosen sides. Nevertheless, his record in the case was damning and his actions vilified. Barrundia's daughter even tried to shoot Mizner for his responsibility in her father's death. At the very least, Mizner had acted irregularly in a manner that indicated a lackadaisical if not reckless approach to diplomacy. He had sent telegrams to Captain Pitts of the *Acapulco* assuring him the arrest was fine and was going to proceed peacefully. These were not reported to the State Department. Mizner also secretly discussed guarantees of Barrundia's safety with President Barillas and Minister Anguiano in conversations that were not disclosed to the State Department. Some correspondence with the Guatemalan officials was not disclosed to the U.S. government until a month after Barrundia's death. The Guatemalan government later claimed it only even met with Mizner to show "friendly deference." But this meeting in no way implied that it was "necessary to obtain the consent of the American Minister for the exercise of an undisputed and perfect right recognized by everybody. For the exercise of that right there could not be proposed, nor did he [Anguiano] have to accept, any condition whatever."[42]

By the time the *Acapulco* docked on August 27, 1890, in "the port of San Jose, where, it is said, she was commanded by a large Krupp cannon," it seemed unlikely that the event would end peacefully. Commander Reiter from the nearby U.S. gunboat *Ranger* had boarded the *Acapulco* to hear and deny Pitts's request for protection of Barrundia. Reiter refused to extend protection without the approval of the governor of the port or absent direct orders from the Navy (which later removed him for this leadership failure). Several police boarded the ship without a warrant but bearing a letter from Consul General James R. Hosmer authorizing the arrest and telling Captain Pitts to "see that no obstacle is permitted." Barrundia, seeing the men, drew two revolvers, remarked "very good," and started firing. In the following firefight, "probably fifty shots were fired in all before General Barrundia was killed." After the shooting, "the Guatemalans had to wipe their feet a little more on the suffering ship" before letting it leave the port.[43]

There was no aspect of this case or of the actions of Consul Mizner that Secretary of State Blaine did not excoriate on many grounds in a very long letter he wrote removing Mizner from office (fig. 6). This letter stands as among the fullest statements of U.S. policy regarding political offenses, even though the Barrundia case was not exclusively based upon this question. For the sheer outrageousness of Mizner's actions, the secretary could "discover no justification." Blaine was particularly incensed by this outrageous jurisdictional overstretch, the invasion of sovereign U.S. territory on the flagged ship, and, most of all, by the implications of this action for asylum and the treatment of political offenders. Blaine told Mizner that despite all of his excuses after the bungled operation, "the declarations which you report can not, however, fail to deepen the regret here felt that you should have permitted yourself to furnish the warrant and excuse for arbitrary and violent proceedings, without even the semblance of legal forms and authority, on the deck of an American vessel, which thereby became the scene of confusion, of danger, and of assassination."[44]

Barrundia was a revolutionary, and while "it is true that he was said to be 'hostile' and an 'enemy,'" Blaine argued that "those terms were obviously not employed in the sense in which they are understood in public law when we are considering such questions as 'contraband' and the 'right of search.'" Guatemala's appeals to the extradition treaty on the one hand and the appeal to seizing Barrundia as contraband of war under martial law on the other were fallacies. In fact, the extradition treaty had been signed but not yet ratified. Furthermore,

Figure 6. James G. Blaine in 1884. Library of Congress Prints and Photographs Division, LC-DIG-pga-02231.

"the unratified treaty [forbade] the extradition of political offenders—a point of special significance in view of the original ground assumed by Guatemala."[45]

Blaine also found alarming the implications for U.S. maritime authority under the "general principles of international law," even aside from the potential harm to the Pacific Mail Company. Guatemala claimed in part that officials could board the ship because of its contract with the company, but Blaine could not accept that a contract would "limit the rights and duties of the government whose flag such vessels carry, [since it] would destroy the foundation of maritime law and render intercourse between nations altogether uncertain and hazardous." The ships of a nation were considered sovereign territory, and this territorial nature was not at all challenged by entry into a port or subject to foreign jurisdiction. Nor was Blaine aware of any case in Latin America where the U.S. refusal to hand over a fugitive was met with arrest or violence.[46]

The core problems for the United States that were produced by the killing of Barrundia had to do with the invasion of territorial sovereignty and challenge to inviolate jurisdiction as well as the basic U.S. responsibility for the entire affair. Blaine quoted John Marshall from the *Exchange v. McFaddon* decision: the "absolute and complete jurisdiction within their respective territories which sovereignty confers" could only be challenged by consent based on "common usage and by common opinion growing out of that usage." In particular, Blaine saw that this case produced a perfect example of the kind of "common usage" that derived from the political offenses exception "not only in respect to extradition, but also in respect to all matters in which the cooperation of foreign governments is required" and where "the law of nations contains a clear distinction between ordinary criminals and political offenders."[47]

Looking at the American application of the exception, Blaine saw a clear tradition of avoiding the surrender of individuals on political offenses and quoted former Secretary of State William Marcy that it would be "a dishonorable subserviency to a foreign power and an act meriting the reprobation of mankind." Blaine referred less to the subordination of the United States and more to the call of "national independence and of humanity" to allow political offenses "a very considerable abatement of jurisdictional claims." One such example was the 1885 Gamez case. The U.S. minister in that case had argued for this protection, though this may have exceeded the jurisdictional facts on the ground since, following Marshall, "any exemption or immunity from local jurisdiction must be derived from the consent of that country." Blaine jabbed at Mizner that "between the general doctrine as broadly laid down by my predecessor in office and your action in respect to General Barrundia's seizure there is an impassable space."[48]

Blaine might have agreed that there was no standard for the political offenses exception, but he stressed that it was "a very considerable and important exception" in Latin America, both in vessels and in legations. Indeed, the only exception to harboring a fugitive in extraterritorial possessions was on the basis of the political offense. Sounding the central theme of U.S. policy toward the exception, Blaine argued that "it is proper to say that the Government of the United States has never encouraged an extension of this exception, for the reason that it is likely to lead to abuse. But at the same time it has on grounds of humanity frequently found itself obliged to maintain it." The United States felt so obliged to act despite "its indisposition to exercise exceptional privileges." All the while, the nation was regretful that events had "so often caused those in power suddenly to seek a place of refuge from the hot and vindictive pursuit of others who have been able violently to drive them from their positions." Blaine thought most places where asylum was granted were actually grateful, even more so in areas where the need for asylum was felt both keenly and often: "Under these circumstances especially, no nation could acquiesce in the sudden disregard, or heed a demand for the peremptory abandonment, of a privilege sanctioned by so general a usage."[49]

The passive tone here belied the political utility of asylum as an exception. In Blaine's formulation, the United States could and did claim asylum exceptions in foreign sovereignties *only when forced to* by lawlessness and revolution. This supposedly detached, episodic approach could be pitched as respect for foreign sovereignties while also very effectively serving U.S. interests. Here was an example of a usage where, as Giorgio Agamben has written, "the concept of necessity [acted] as the foundation of the state of exception. . . . The theory of necessity [being] none other than a theory of the exception by virtue of which a particular case is released from the obligation to observe the law. Necessity is not a source of law, nor does it properly suspend the law; it merely releases a particular case from the literal application of the norm."[50] There was never a compulsion or a requirement to allow asylum, nor was there a need to explain (rather than announce) its denial. It was asserted when and where possible or desirable, often by U.S. warships that happened to be in the neighborhood of the disruption.

Asylum for political offenders was thus cast as a defensive act produced by the necessities of the situation instead of as a unilateralist, sovereign exclusion coupled with a jurisdictional incursion. It is clear that sovereign exceptions like that produced by asylum or in the determination of political offenses could be carved for any number of state purposes but were balanced neatly upon the political situation and rhetorically draped with the language of immediacy.

Theodore S. Woolsey, commenting in the immediate aftermath of the Barrundia affair, was well attuned to the potentialities of the claims. Unlike those involved, he did not find the situation especially complex. "There is nothing very unusual in this petty tragedy," he wrote. "Nothing is clearer than that a merchant ship within the waters of a foreign state is under that state's jurisdiction." Woolsey was very concerned about calls that the U.S. Navy would have offered asylum or that it should in *any* case: "One of our men of war could have furnished Barrundia an asylum had he reached it, but surely it is not the business of our navy to exert itself actively in rescuing political exiles from the laws of their offended states. Asylum when it ceases to be passive, is rescue, a very different matter."[51]

Unlike Blaine or the Guatemalan authorities, Woolsey determined that Commander Reiter and Mizner had acted appropriately and in line with international law. "And yet . . . their action proved so unacceptable to their government that the one was recalled, and the other removed from his command with a reprimand," he wrote, more than a little disgusted. The Navy castigated Reiter for "remaining inactive" and having "neglected [his] obvious duties, and placed [his] government in the position of renouncing those who had sheltered themselves under its flag." Woolsey warned that this kind of language represented an important shift in U.S. naval policy and foreign relations: "Here . . . we notice a marked extension of the jurisdiction claimed by the United States. It announces to its naval officers the duty of protecting all political refugees sailing under its merchant flag, even when within the waters of the country, to which those refugees belong, by strategy if not by force—the duty of *bringing asylum* to them, instead of permitting them to seek it. This was destined to bear fruit."[52]

This fruit of extended jurisdiction and the assertion of new and ever-greater sovereign exceptions that Woolsey discussed (and he had several other examples from the same period not essential to discuss here) were sure to cause a revolution in the overall exercise of power by the United States and its position in the world. Woolsey saw very clearly that the expansion of jurisdiction meant the end of any semblance of isolationism and noninterference, as the epigraph at the start of this chapter demonstrates. He predicted that expanded jurisdictional assertions could produce revolutionary change at home in the domestic political system and in the nature of society as well as result in newly aggressive and unlawful foreign relations: "It means one collision after another, each with its sulphurous war cloud about it. It means the violation of former precedents, setting up new ones in their stead which may prove awkward, even dangerous. It will encourage aggressions upon weak neighbors." Jurisdictional assertions would also have a negative impact on trade in the Western hemisphere by "throwing trade into other channels than our own" since "international trade is largely based on sentiment" and the United States would produce resentment. New jurisdictional claims would require a larger military, "a reversal of our military and naval policy," and an increase in taxes to support it. He asked, plaintively, "We should have then, also, a much larger admixture of foreign influences and foreign questions in our domestic politics. A presidential campaign might be decided, not by the belief of a party as to questions of currency or the tariff or the civil service, but by its spirited foreign policy. Would this be likely to give us better government?"[53]

Part of Woolsey's point regarding the sour legacy of the Barrundia affair was echoed elsewhere, which is that the determination of jurisdictional claims was profoundly political and reflective of a particular state interest at a particular time, not of some abstract notion of justice. The state determined its own exception based upon a shifting view of interest and objective. Referring to the Trent Affair, which became one of the most controversial diplomatic acts during the Civil War and almost caused a "catastrophic" war with Great Britain, Woolsey, who found the varying assertions of jurisdiction errant, asked, "suppose the *Trent* with Mason and Slidell on board had sailed into New York Harbor, would the right of their seizure have been questioned by any power on earth?"[54]

J. H. Gibbons, writing for the U.S. Naval Institute, asked the same question about the different possible perceptions of the actions in the Trent affair and warned that in a democracy, a Navy captain might take a politically popular move rather than one in conformity to law.

A fancied insult to the American flag will arouse a feeling of indignation that brushes aside legal technicalities. This swift, but often imperfect judgment may encourage a naval commander to take the chance of error, that he may win the plaudits of his fellow citizens. Was Commodore Ingraham right when, at Smyrna, he threatened to destroy the Austrian frigate that held Martin Koszta a prisoner? Was Captain Wilkes right when, on the high seas, he took Mason and Slidell out of the Trent? Congress gave the one a gold medal and the other a sword. The question of might brought these commanders lasting reward, while the question of right was still being discussed by academicians and publicists.[55]

Nevertheless, after the Barrundia surrender, the Department of the Navy did not uphold the conduct of the senior officer present and made two suggestions that also reflected the assertion of sovereign exception. The first was that "when the *Acapulco* was sighted off San Jose, the senior naval officer present should have proceeded at once to meet her outside, to warn the captain of the danger, and to offer the passenger asylum," and failing that, the senior naval officer present should have literally stepped into the situation and helped to resolve it by personally representing U.S. sovereignty. The Navy said the officer "should have then prevented *by his presence*, with such assistance as he might find necessary, any proceedings on board the steamer calculated to endanger the safety of those on board." Once it was clear that he was "a political fugitive, the naval commander should have offered the passenger asylum on his own vessel." Gibbons, a critic of the navy commenting on this change, called the "presence" of its officers in such situations "a radical departure from the theory of the exclusive territorial authority of a government over foreign merchant vessels in its ports."[56]

In response to the confusions of the Barrundia case, the navy added a new paragraph to Article 287 of its Regulations of 1893, stating that "when a political refugee has embarked, in the territory of a third power, on board a merchant vessel of the United States as a passenger for purposes of innocent transit, and it appears upon the entry of such vessel into the territorial waters that his life is in danger, it is the duty of the captain of a ship of the Navy present to extend him an offer of asylum." Gibbons found that this new regulation implied "that the territorial authority over a foreign merchant vessel is not absolute and un-limited . . . [and] cannot grant asylum" whereas the Navy could in certain cir-cumstances. The navy would have to use its discretion, wrote Gibbons, since "we have seen that diplomats, like doctors, sometimes disagree." The navy told captains to base their decisions on "sound judgment" and "all possible care and forbearance."[57]

THE EZETA CASE

Perhaps in no situation was this duality between asylum and the determi-nation of political offenses clearer than in the most famous case of General Antonio Ezeta (alias The Rabbit) and Carlos Ezeta and others, a group John Bassett Moore rather kindly called "the Salvadorean Refugees." In fact, they were deposed revolutionary leaders who led a brutal regime during an unstable time and who used asylum on U.S. ships to escape capture and eventually to dodge extradition for their acts. This case was similar in some respects to sev-eral others involving revolutionaries and the conveniently floating asylums of the U.S. Navy in Latin American waters. On June 22, 1890, the Ezeta brothers had overthrown Antonio's mentor, General Francisco Menendez, and the two held power in various high leadership positions for four bloody years. At the time they were deposed, Antonio Ezeta was commander-in-chief of the armed forces of Salvador, and his brother was president. A revolution swept them from power and out of the capital on June 4, 1894.[58]

The next day, out of the "few hundred" followers left from an original force of one thousand seven hundred who fought, seventeen people, including the Ezeta brothers, arrived at the U.S. man-of-war *Bennington* in port at La Libertad asking for asylum. General Rafael Antonio Gutierrez, now in power, officially requested the surrender of the Ezeta brothers and the others. U.S. Captain Thomas professed to having early intentions to release the requested men as "a courtesy to the new government" and as a way to seek favor for the protection of American citizens in the country, but he ended up neither surrendering the men nor allowing them to get aboard other ships coming into the harbor. In fact, he kept them on his ship under his own authority despite their numerous requests to be let onto other ships. Moore wrote that it was later "contended that the omission or refusal of the government of the United States either to order their transfer to the first mail steamer that called at La Libertad, or to yield to their desire to put ashore at the first neutral port at which the *Bennington* touched, was an outrage upon their rights which required their immediate judicial liberation." However, Captain Thomas was unmovable, and he was soon supported by official orders not to let the men off the ship. The United States officially feared relaunching the revolution or simply turning the fugitives loose as a "a gross breach of neutral duty." The *Bennington* eventually sailed for San Francisco, where it was held in port until extradition warrants were executed on the fugitives on August 23, 1894.[59]

The extradition hearing for Antonio Ezeta, Leon Bolanos, Jacinto Colocho, Juan Cienfuegos, and Florencio Bustamente was heard in U.S. District Court for the Northern District of California. The Salvadoran government demanded surrender for the men based upon a series of crimes including murder, arson, robbery, and rape. Most of these acts were quite brutally done. Juan Cienfuegos was charged with the attempted murder of Andreas Amaya, Ezeta and Cienfuegos were charged with the murder of Tomas Canas, Bolanos and Bustamante (nicknamed Monkey in the Hole) were charged with the hanging murder of four unknown people in Pulgas Ravine on May 29, 1894. All of the accused together were charged with the murder of Casimiro Henriquez. All of the men claimed the United States had no jurisdiction over them or the case, but the proceedings actually ended up focusing on the political context (if not nature) of the crimes.[60]

R. B. Mitchell, counsel for Salvador at the hearing and a colorful speaker attempting to emphasize the brutality of the Ezeta brothers and their men, said "to a gay soldier of fortune like Mr. Cienfuegos, the death of one, more or less, could have made no difference." In the "early days of June, a maddened carnival was taking place in the streets. There was a carnival of blood, and in that throng the figures of Antonio Ezeta and his dusky mistress paraded to the very gallows where the body of this young man was swung into eternity." W. M. Pierson, another attorney for Salvador, argued that the men did not just kill Tomas Canas, they shot him unarmed and in the back, "as cold-blooded and foul an assassination as the record of jurisprudence can furnish." But the main argument of Salvador was that the judge "sitting here as a committing magistrate, [had] no jurisdiction to pass upon the question as to whether these crimes were of a political character." Instead, they tried to claim that "your honor's jurisdiction here in this proceeding is to examine into the question pure and simple of the criminality of the accused." Determining the political nature of the crime was a "purely political question and not a judicial one." Given the foreignness of the state and the procedure, and all other aspects of the case, "must it not be so in the nature of things?" None of the acts were political, Pierson claimed; it was all "a simple act of tyrannous cruelty by a man, at the instance of a lot of lewd and infamous wretches."[61]

The defense turned on the idea that determining a political offense was, in fact, a judicial decision to be made rooted in issues of law and calm, not political passions and vengeance. Salvador was clamoring for blood. The real target was Antonio Ezeta, he said. "I have no doubt we could trade the 'Monkey in the Hole' for the 'Rabbit' at any time with the Government."[62]

U.S. jurisdiction over the case was rapidly dispatched with quite lengthy referrals to *United States v. Rauscher* (discussed in chapter 4) and *Ker v. Illinois* (which is considered in the epilogue). Judge Morrow set as his task deciding upon one of the two poles these cases represented for the operation of sovereign power in this regard—limitless or limited. He found "the question is as to whether or not the principle involved in the Case of Kerr [sic], as distinguished from the Case of Rauscher, is applicable to this case." Morrow saw the United States as not a party to the case at all in any way: "The United States simply furnishes the process, and furnishes the machinery for these proceedings." The court would decide only upon extraditability. The judge did not feel it "proper for [him] to enter into an inquiry as to the conduct of a war vessel of the United States" nor to render a political judgment. The court also made it explicit that it could not obligate the president to act since that was to be a purely executive decision: "Whatever may be the evidence in this case, as interposed in support of this plea, it relates entirely to political matters, or to matters coming within the jurisdiction of the political department of the government."[63]

After long consideration of all of the evidence presented and the relative guilt or involvement of all the men in the killings and other crimes, Morrow at last "reached the most important question to be considered in this examination." While the final surrender was a political and solely executive act, Morrow did not at all limit the power—or "duty"—of the court to determine if extradition was due under the terms of the treaty, which meant determining its political character. In Morrow's estimation, all of the acts (except Cienfuegos's attempted murder of Amaya) were "committed during the progress of actual hostilities between the contending forces, wherein Gen. Ezeta and his companions were seeking to maintain the authority of the then existing government against the active operations of a revolutionary uprising." He announced that "with the merits of this strife I have nothing to do." He was simply investigating "the character of the crimes or offenses charged against these defendants, with respect to that conflict." No matter how "atrocious and inhuman character" these acts were "within the rules of civilized warfare. . . . War, at best, is barbarous, and hence it is said that 'the law is silent during war.'"[64]

Given the politics inherent in all of the murders and the theft, the final dissolution of the Ezeta regime did not change the sovereign, and therefore exempt, nature of its acts. Morrow had no U.S. examples to follow in this line of reasoning, so he drew from British case law, which was more thoroughly developed on this point. He quoted John Stuart Mill in the House of Commons, who had declared a political offense to be "any offense committed in the course of or furthering of civil war, insurrection, or political commotion." In a similar vein, Morrow relied heavily on *In re Castioni*, which was "the first case decided under the United Kingdom's Extradition Act of 1870." This case determined essentially the same definition as supplied by Mill, "acts of violence of a political character with a political object, and as part of the political movement and rising in which [the accused] was taking part." The British judge in this case (Hawkins) held that

> I cannot help thinking that everybody knows there are many acts of a political character done without reason, done against all reason; but at the same time one cannot look too hardly, and weigh in golden scales the acts of men hot in their political excitement. We know that in heat, and in heated blood, men often do things which are against and contrary to reason; but none the

less an act of this description may be done for the purpose of furthering and in furtherance of a political rising, even though it is an act which may be deplored and lamented, as even cruel and against all reason, by those who can calmly reflect upon it after the battle is over.[65]

Morrow applied the same logic to the actions of Ezeta and the others. The "state of siege" in Salvador during which the crimes were committed allowed their acts of murder to be subsumed into independent sovereign action under the exception of martial law. The state of siege was common usage in creating the state of exception, and in this situation it created a double system of exception. There was the sovereign exception produced internally by periods of war or revolution. There was also the portable sovereign exception represented by the political offenses doctrine's shield of fugitives from the justice system in the state from which they fled, whatever the state's relationship to "justice" might have been in that territory.[66]

Morrow used an interesting example as his conclusion that Ezeta and the others could not be extradited because of the political offense exception, which was argued in the 1878 case *Coleman v. Tennessee*. In this case, a U.S. soldier in occupied east Tennessee during the Civil War killed a woman named Mourning Ann Bell on March 7, 1865, for which he was court martialed and sentenced to hang. After the end of federal occupation, the state of Tennessee wished to try him as well and also sentenced him to death. The U.S. Supreme Court found that the Tennessee laws did not apply even after the occupation was over, since the war had suspended the state's sovereign jurisdiction and the soldier was entirely under federal jurisdiction. "It is well settled that a foreign army permitted to march through a friendly country or to be stationed in it by permission of its government or sovereign, is exempt from the civil and criminal jurisdiction of the place," Justice Field wrote, citing *Exchange v. McFaddon*. War created sovereign exception and maintained military jurisdiction in all areas. Morrow believed the same had been the case in Salvador, which strongly indicated that the offenses were entirely political. All the men were discharged except for Cienfuegos, who was extradited for the nonpolitical murder of Andres Amaya.[67]

The Ezeta ruling's definition of a political offense became variously known as the "political-incidence theory" or the "uprising test." Thereafter, any ideologically motivated or violent action in service of a political end during a disturbance was deemed to inherently be a political offense. Historian Christopher H. Pyle bemoaned that "the uprising test was imported from the United Kingdom to become part of U.S. case law solely through Judge Morrow's amoral disregard of General Ezeta's brutality." The results of the ruling were varied. In the aftermath of the ruling, the U.S. Navy issued new, stronger regulations for ship captains to "refuse all application for asylum except when required by the interests of humanity in extreme or exceptional cases." Pyle and Barbara Ann Banoff have argued that "subsequent American cases have continued to apply the *Ezeta-Castioni* uprising test mechanically, whether or not the result is reasonable. If the crime occurred during a violent insurrection, it was political whether the offender was working for the government or against it. If the crime did not occur during an insurrection, it was not political."[68]

The mood was less condemnatory at the time of the decision. For Moore, observing shortly after the decision in 1895, the Ezeta extradition case opened up an interesting space in the law about the question of war and politics in extradition. Political motives were not enough, as, of course, politically motivated anarchists were not exempt. He also did not think the existence of war was "sufficient to invest every act . . . with a political character." The one example he chose was the case of Abraham Lincoln assassination conspirator John H. Surratt, discussed earlier.[69] The clear lesson Moore drew from the Ezeta case was that the political aspects of defining a political offense could not be underestimated and were always reflective of broader policy goals. One certain result was an emphasis on the sovereign exception at home and abroad in cases where political ends were violently pursued. Morrow's reference to *Coleman v. Tennessee* in the Ezeta case in this light seems even more significant. The United States could create areas of sovereign exception through occupation or war, for example, and the new jurisdictional reality would persist.

Moore also saw more abstract ways in which sovereignty and the exception it produced reflected the relative power of the executive and judicial magistrates in extradition questions. Moore contended that the power of the executive necessarily had to become heavily involved in the determination of the political nature of the crimes. While the judiciary may have been empowered via a quite clear treaty grant to decide to extradite, it was the executive who made the final decision. Moore found numerous cases in which this disparity had occurred, with the result being an ever-evolving and subtle balance of authority between the two branches. The executive had plenary authority, but this could not be confused with *total* authority. Moore felt that the divided internal jurisdiction within any single surrender was helpfully protective of both liberty and the overall system. A court could refuse to recommend a person for surrender on the basis of citizenship, for example, and the executive would be left with no effective choice as a result, no matter what the court's position was. "At the end," he concluded, "extradition, whatever may be the character of the offense, is a political act." But "prior to that stage," it was "chiefly a judicial proceeding." The lines between the two were clear, but the actual operations of power had to be viewed separately from the stated structuring of it. Both the courts and the executive had a stated balance between them; however, this system actually created more power in the division since it provided for yet more assertions of the political offenses exception from the separate spheres.

REVOLUTION AND EXCEPTION IN THE BORDERLANDS

In the U.S.-Mexico borderlands, this kind of clarity in defining political acts was only rarely achievable, and with increasing revolutionary activity, it got much harder. A strong example from the U.S. experience of defining the nature of political offense was the 1887 extradition case of Francisco J. Cazo. Along with thirty men he commanded, Cazo had assaulted the town of Agualeguas in the state of Nuevo Leon, Mexico, in July 1880 for three days. During this occupation, the men "had armed encounters with the inhabitants, seized horses and other property, and committed other acts of violence." During the siege, the men shouted, "hurrah for Don Francisco J. Cazo!" and "death to the Garra party!" These statements were later presented as evidence of the political nature of the attack. Cazo left a manifesto to be read in Agualeguas before fleeing to the safety of Texas, an act that was also considered political.[70]

Mexico requested extradition seven years after the attack but gave no reasons for this long delay. In denying the request, the United States treated the matter as a straightforward one. Secretary of State Bayard wrote on February 7, 1887, that since no effort was made to hide Cazo's identity or other aspects of "the character of the outbreak, the kind and quantity of the property taken, and the mode of attack," this was indeed a political crime. The determination that Cazo's raid was "an avowed partisan political conflict" was straightforward and certain. In the Ezeta case, Judge Morrow saw a direct analog of this "political uprising" to the acts of Ezeta.[71]

The Cazo case, in which Mexican revolutionary activity was treated with official notice and therefore some modicum of respect, was a notable exception in the borderlands. Generally at trials of captured revolutionaries, it was local juries that expressed sympathy and understanding of the core political motives of transborder acts.

This was what happened in the case of revolutionary Francisco Ruiz Sandoval, who led an armed expedition of thirty-six men across the border into Mexico near Laredo in a brief raid in June 1890. Sandoval was, according to Warner P. Sutton, U.S. consul general at Nuevo Laredo, "a man of some prominence," though the group that crossed the river was "a band of Mexican malcontents" and "a lot of loafers, ex-convicts, etc, with perhaps one or two of better character." The local press was equally as dismissive, calling them "would be revolutionists" and an "embryo revolutionary party." Only after the raid did Sutton's understanding of Sandoval's politics start to change. He interviewed Sandoval in the Webb County jail with the "opinion that these people were more bandits than revolutionists." But in the conversation, Sandoval showed plainly that he at least "had revolutionary intentions." Sandoval was "very anxious to learn whether he was likely to be extradited to Mexico and seemed much relieved when some doubt was expressed," Sutton reported, though he averred, "I was careful to make no definite statement."[72]

Sandoval and his men were very rapidly tried for violating American neutrality laws in federal court in San Antonio. Mexico was so happy with the swift justice that, according to Sutton, Governor Reyes of Monterrey ordered the instrumental band of the 13th Regiment to play in Laredo, Texas, "to show in part his appreciation of our action." But this exuberance was premature. Sandoval was not to be extradited. As Matías Romero wrote disapprovingly, "notwithstanding that their crime was notorious, and that the proof was conclusive, the jury acquitted them." This was to be expected, Romero thought, given the nature of Mexican-American jury nullification in the region. He wrote that the verdict was "not strange when it is considered that a political character is given to such events, and that their perpetrators are held up to the jury as martyrs and heroes." The problem, he thought, was that such determinations of political exception merely encouraged others to try the same given the sense of latitude projected, unofficially or not.[73]

Revolt, revolution, and transborder attack or flight laden with political meaning were endemic to this section of the U.S.-Mexican border, where the handprint of the federal government was still indistinct and jurisdictional lines still disputed. U.S. Army Captain John G. Bourke claimed, "as long as there are no Railroads in this section, trouble may be looked for unless strong garrisons be maintained on both sides of the Rio Grande at the most eligible points."[74] This was the region most riddled with broad and shifting jurisdictional assertions and a wide variety of exceptions to sovereignty, as has been explored in numerous ways in this book.

The border was also a region in which political offenses and the question of asylum took on especially potent meaning given the easily accessible boundary line and the reality that all acts had inherent transborder effects and amplified meanings as a result. As General John McAllister Schofield, the major general commanding the U.S. Army, wrote in considering the need for borderlands security against raiding groups on both sides, "considering the physical features of the border country between the United States and Mexico, and the character of a large portion of the population inhabiting that country on either side of the boundary line, it is not strange that the general experience of these and other nations should have found no exception there" to the need for firm state power. Schofield was convinced that military force and state action had made "such lawless attempts very dangerous and unprofitable to the criminal whose robber designs have been only thinly veiled under a pretense of political purpose."[75]

Romero was even harsher in his estimation of the borderlands context. His expression is worth quoting at length because of how thoroughly it characterizes the mindset of the policy elites on both sides of the border who were grappling with revolutionary foment:

It is well known that, as a general rule, the least desirable elements of two bordering countries collect on their frontiers. Smugglers, cattle thieves, fugitives from justice, people compelled to leave their country for their country's good, but who usually attribute their flight to political motives, and other persons under more or less similar circumstances, meet on the frontier, and they are ever ready to undertake any kind of enterprise, no matter how illegal it may be. On the border-line between Mexico and the United States, and particularly on that part of the frontier embraced in the State of Texas, these persons are not an exception to that rule. The inhabitants of that section are largely of Mexican origin, who have never amalgamated with their neighbors of that country, many of them ignorant of the English language and having very little in common with the rest of the inhabitants. Under these circumstances they are peculiarly susceptible to pernicious influences, and therefore only too ready to take part in disturbances of the peace. These people are generally ignorant, few being able to read and write, and they are easily influenced by unscrupulous members of their own race, who can appeal to them in their native tongue. When adventurers pose before them as victims of the tyranny of the existing home government, and know how to work upon their feelings, making them believe that they are cooperators in a legitimate, and even laudable, as well as remunerative, undertaking, they readily elicit their sympathies and support.[76]

All actions taken in the borderlands were larded with economic, racial, and ideological meanings that were often as difficult to characterize as to refute in determinations of the political nature of a crime. It was often very difficult if not impossible to separate out the planning and execution of political actions that often occurred in conjunction with violence and crime. And, to be sure, political actions taken by Mexicans and Mexican-Americans were more readily described and dismissed by Texas and U.S. policymakers and observers as banditry or outlaw "depredation" than as legitimate political action in pursuit of a specific objective, however idealistic or unsettling.

Bourke, no stranger to highly racialized readings of borderlands culture and society, decided that "of the population of this part of the Rio Grande Valley not much can be said. There are some few people of education and refinement, but the mass of the inhabitants are saturated with ignorance and superstition which have no parallel this side of the Congo. In thought, habit, speech and dress that are essentially anti-American, but they are also anti-Mexican. They have no sympathy for either Government." A military officer more sympathetic to Mexicans than Bourke named George F. Chase, who was a squadron commander from Fort Sam Houston, characterized the region in terms of its easily shifting jurisdictions: "This entire country is sparsely settled, in the most part by Mexican people, ignorant of law, claiming allegiance to the Mexican Government and at the same time the protection of the American laws."[77]

In no case was the impact of the borderlands' sociopolitical and power systems more obvious than in the situation of the disruptive Garza rebellion, a "perfectly justified democratic and revolutionary movement" that raged fitfully along the border in South Texas from 1891 to 1893.[78] The leader of this movement, overlooked and misunderstood until recently, was Catarino Garza, a stalwart journalist of Brownsville, Texas (born in Matamoros), who had become a popular local figure sharply critical of Mexico and unafraid of conflict or fighting in the pursuit of his goals. After a tumultuous rise (and a period working for the Singer Sewing Machine Company), he led a group of slightly more than one thousand Mexicans and Mexican-Americans in a revolt designed to topple the Porfirio Díaz government. The first of many transborder raids into Tamaulipas occurred on September 15, 1891, which was Mexican Independence Day. Other than the overthrow of Díaz, Garza presented a relatively staid revolutionary plan including free trade, liberalized politics, and a return to the Constitution of 1857. Nevertheless, the movement threw the region into years of turmoil, violence, and controversy that long outlasted Garza's flight from Texas in February 1892.[79]

Garza's revolution triggered a massive military response from the U.S. Army, an effort that vacillated between waging war and seeking to capture and bring Garzistas to face legal charges. President Benjamin Harrison kept the task on a war footing, in part because he concluded that since the army was in the region and being used effectively, there was no reason to use the limited funds available to deploy more U.S. marshals, as had been requested. There was some question about exactly how to treat the captured revolutionaries—as criminal bandits or unlawful combatants. The preference was for the former so that the rebels could be tried in U.S. courts. In December 1891, Bourke, who led the campaign against Garza, stated that he was using "reasonable suspicion" when investigating people and was "careful not to harass innocent parties in violation of the 4th Amendment to the Constitution." He also said he had "insisted upon the presence of U.S. Deputy marshals with proper warrants for the apprehension of 'suspects.'" But a month later, a Captain Wheeler inquired whether the revolutionaries could be arrested with regular warrants or held as prisoners without possession and whether he was "authorized to subsist civilian prisoners." It took several years to defeat the movement, round up many of the major figures in the revolt, and eventually quiet local support, if not actually to defeat it.[80]

The Garza revolution stood out in the long line of disputes and transborder incursions of the era because of its resonance within the development of borderlands culture, racialized politics, and economy and because of the depth of its popular support. This was a truly popular uprising in motivation, execution, and backing rather than an episodic transborder raid by a small group. The rebellion and its violent suppression revealed the connections between the militarization of the frontier; struggles involving racial categorization, identity, and individual agency in the region; and the relations of Mexican-Americans to the apparatus of state power both in Mexico and the United States. As Elliott

Young, the principal historian of Garza and his era, has written, "Garza's story reminds us that even at the height of nineteenth-century imperialism, power did not rest exclusively in the nation-state but rather was to a large degree already transnational, hybrid, and decentered."[81]

The story that has not been told is what happened in the aftermath of the Garza rebellion during the confusing array of mop-up army operations and especially in the subsequent extradition trials that clearly highlighted the American approach to sovereign manipulation of exceptions in such contentious matters. In this instance, the state did not respond in the straightforward way it had in the Cazo or Sandoval cases, which involved action only on the Mexican side of the Rio Grande and did not challenge the power of the state to organize and control the territorial edge of the United States. The explosion of Mexican revolutionary fervor in South Texas starting in 1891 and the persistent and obvious support for Garza in the region clearly changed the political calculations of how the institutions of state power could grapple with rebellion.

Of particular importance was the extradition of Garzista leaders Francisco Benavides, Juan Duque, Inez Ruiz, and Jesus Guerra, which has not received sufficient attention. The standard history of the Garza rebellion does not detail the long-lasting revolutionary reverberations along the border by these small bands of men or the fates of the subsequent extradition cases. Studies of extradition meanwhile generally ignore, mischaracterize, or deliberately minimize the significance of the Benavides case. They do not properly contextualize or characterize the transborder contestation that these late Garzista raids represented. Indeed, the persistence of the label of banditry or of pseudo-revolutionary meaning to the Garza rebellion in some contemporary scholarship on extradition is striking. It stands as evidence of how thoroughly the tenor of the old narrative of American order has persisted and how foreign the nineteenth-century borderlands still remain in so much contemporary scholarship attempting to explain U.S. sovereign power.[82]

In the spring of 1893, Captain Chase was one of the principal cavalry squadron commanders on patrol in South Texas in pursuit of "alleged adherents of Garza and other so-called bandits" as violators of the U.S. neutrality laws. These revolutionaries were, in the army's dehumanizing language of the day, "believed to infest the region south of the Mex. Nat. R.R. and between it and Rio Grande." Chase and his men created a line of camps and daily patrols along the Rio Grande from Laredo to Rio Grande City, "thus preventing the possibility of armed bodies of men crossing the river." There were some problems with the effort, as Chase noted, since his "troops did not speak the Mexican language" and the country was "a perfect hiding place for outlaws." Moreover, the army had little intelligence or support: "[we had] absolutely no means of identification of Revolutionists and should they be arrested and claim to be innocent, we had no means of knowing the persons arrested." It was grueling and often unproductive work. After two years of pursuing the Garza troops and much violence, Chase reported that "six months of hard work with a troop and part of the time with a squadron of cavalry under my command" only turned up six men.[83]

Nevertheless, Chase rode in pursuit, particularly of the dispersed Garza followers who had attacked the town and fought the Mexican troops in San Ygnacio, Mexico, on December 10, 1892. This attack was variously characterized as "a battle fought between the revolutionary forces of Garza and the Mexican forces in the barracks at San Ignacio" (as it was described in the later extradition trial of a participant, Inez Ruiz) or, by Mexican and U.S. authorities, as a criminal raid by a ragtag group of would-be revolutionary border bandits. Plutarco Ornelas, consul of Mexico, did not doubt that the raid was the work of "the Garza bandits," and neither did he think it to be a legitimate act. He called them "murderers" and "bandits" who stole fifty horses. "I have noticed certain inclination on the part of the press to disconnect the barbaric raid upon San Ignacio and the previous raids committed by the followers of Catarino E. Garza," Ornelas wrote to U.S. General Frank Wheaton shortly after the raid. "The simultaneous appearance of this impassioned war call, and the assault on San Ignacio detachment, leaves no doubt in my mind that they are the same thing connected with the same leaders and for the same purpose." Ornelas simply saw all Garza actions as criminal.[84]

The San Ygnacio raid was in fact led by a major Garza revolutionary commander, General Francisco Benavides, and involved at least seventy-one men known to the United States. Ornelas called Benavides a "very well known character among the pretended revolutionists and [he] has been connected with the movement since its incipiency, and is commonly known as Genl. Francisco Benavides. He has performed a prominent part in the re-organization of these disastrous raids." General Frank Wheaton described the "bandit leaders Francisco Benavides, Cecilio Echeverria and Prudencio Gonzales" and told the Adjutant-General that among them, Benavides was "the bandit chief who led the murderous attack."[85]

In addition to leading the men, Benavides was the author of a strident manifesto that was well known among Garza supporters. The fact that this manifesto was taken seriously by the U.S. Army is clear: numerous copies were distributed widely among the troops with specific orders that each copy was meant for further distribution.[86] This was a certain sign that the federal government understood that the manifesto was a political document central to understanding the raid and not a random expression of criminal intent. Written the month before the raid, the Benavides manifesto was typically Garzista in tone and objective, calling for action and an overthrow of Porfirio Díaz in terms that certainly seem politically motivated. It read, in small part,

> Mexicans listen to the cry of our Country that calls us to its aid. The national Banners are rent in pieces and a mass of false evidence has been distributed that like hungry cannibals has swallowed up the remnant of our liberty. . . . Poor Country! Your own sons have auctioned you off: Their blind ambition, their thirst for complacent pleasures, had made them snatch your clothes to dress their Concubines; they have taken your laurels from you and have cast them in the mud, by the side of the infamous Porfirio Díaz. . . . The Tyranny of today is a thousand Times worse than that of 1872. . . . There is no longer any respect to that constitution that has been converted into a plaything for even the most insignificant of those in authorities in the country. All govern with a sabre in their hands and blasphemy on their mouths. May the shadow of Cuaunhtémoc of Morales and of Juárez watch us from their eternal thrones and expect to see us fulfill our duty as they knew how to do theirs, filling with laurels and reknown the humble people among whom they were born. Let us march as faithful soldiers of justice to revenge the tears and the mourning planted all over the country by the unjustifiable atrocity of a despotic and sanguinary government. . . . Forward Mexicans! Let us march to die for liberty. Immortal glory for those who know how to die for it. Shame and degradation for those who prefer being slaves to patriots. Mexico dry your Tears! For our sons are going to die for you before they will see you further abused and vilified. . . . Let us march without halting and strike with our chains the brow of Porfirio Díaz. Hurrah for Liberty!!! Down with Tyrants!!![87]

The purple prose, mixed metaphors, and excited calls to action of this manifesto certainly indicate that if this was not a real revolution, then Benavides definitely made an enormous effort to make it seem real. Benavides and his men also released a "Plan Revolution," which was "conceived and reacted [sic] for the purpose of derogating the tyranny and despotisms of General Porfirio Díaz, and to bring the country to the constitutional order."[88]

Chase, working closely with local officials who, unbeknownst to him, had Garza's sympathies and ties, had negotiated with Benavides on January 2, 1893, for a surrender of as many men as he could muster. It took some doing, and there was quite a bit of confusion. In the end, fewer men surrendered than expected. However, Benavides surrendered and admitted he was the leader of the San Ygnacio raid. Chase believed the next two most important men were Procorpio Guiterez and Tomas Cuellar. By March, they and several others had surrendered to the 7th Cavalry.[89]

The captain had no illusions about the nature of the men he was hunting, and his attitude was less dismissive than simply condemnatory. He definitely did not view them as criminals but as revolutionaries. "These people are born Revolutionist," he wrote in a long report on his progress. "They have little or no respect for constituted authority whether it be vested in President Cleveland or President Díaz and until the present conditions are materially changed we may expect constant trouble from the shiftless, wandering, irresponsible element now occupying our Rio Grande border. Any man among them seems competent to start a revolution." Chase made special note of this seeming revolutionary drive among the leader's men despite the fact that he believed (quite wrongly) that they actually had none: "Catarino Garza was a man of no force of character. He was poorly educated and possessed of no ability to lead men other than as a talker." Further, Chase argued that Francisco Benavides, Garza's successor in command, could hardly read or write (no telling how he created the manifesto) and that his second in command, Prudencio Gonzales, supposedly could not sign his name. "Very few of their followers can read and write," he claimed, and yet "they are one and all possess of a sufficient amount of cunning to hide in the brush, to live off their neighbors and to vote for officers who will do the square thing by them."[90]

Chase was relatively sensitive to the difficulty of this surrender, and he was attuned to the need to handle suspects and prisoners with respect in order to prevent hardened resistance in the area to further arrests. For this reason, he was extremely unhappy to learn that immediately after their arrest, Benavides and Escheverria had been ordered by U.S. marshals to leave Rio Grande City for San Antonio. Ornelas had filed for extradition the day they were captured, and extradition hearings were scheduled before L. F. Price, commissioner of the Circuit Court of the Western District of Texas.[91]

This extradition hearing order was a state matter, and the federal government was neither involved nor, seemingly, apprised of this situation. Ornelas had requested extradition for Benavides, Prudencio Gonzales, and Cecilio Echevarrtia and said he had "consulted with General Wheaton upon the advantage of extraditing these criminals and the general, appreciating the importance and grave need of accomplishing it, offer[ed] me all the cooperation within his power." Wheaton in turn had told the adjutant general that "in the interests of good order and quiet on the Rio Grande border, so long disturbed by these renegades and their sympathizers, I earnestly hope that the application of Consul Ornelas may be favored by the Government." Yet Chase was still surprised and a bit mortified. He felt that he had been assured that since Benavides was facing U.S. trial, he would not face immediate extradition proceedings. But that turned out not to be the case. "I was flooded with questions, telegrams and letters asking me about extradition," he remarked. The result was nothing short of catastrophic for his efforts: "I could not guarantee no extradition. This condition of affairs frightened a great many so that their assistance was withdrawn from us. They were willing to help us so long as the lives of the Insurrectionists were to be spared, but they would not consent to give us any information leading to the arrest of men who they thought might be taken to Mexico."[92]

Chase believed that the army had the system under control and could end the rebellion through the use of state criminal courts without the possibility of extradition being allowed. "We had but one encouragement through all these disagreeable conditions" while tracking down the San Ygnacio people, he wrote. "It was: 'The President has decided that these border troubles shall be settled by the Army.'" Chase noted that so far, seventy-one Garza supporters had been arrested, tried, and convicted in federal court in San Antonio in the May 1893 term. Alongside fourteen arrested and not tried and fifty-two others indicted by a grand jury, Chase had counted an additional eighty-four men who had been killed, captured, or surrendered. Therefore, he did his best to stop the extradition, and in his official report of the incident, he explained why quite clearly:

We have officers on our own side of the river perfectly competent to manage our affairs and who are anxious to protect every interest of the Mexican Republic. I am of the opinion that if no extradition proceedings had been instituted by the Mexican Government we would have had a great many more men behind the bars at the present time for violating our neutrality laws. If extradition be proper and right, Mexico can get these men when we are through with them.

Extradition, as intrusive as it was on U.S. sovereignty and as politically resonant as every surrender was, simply interfered with the smooth operation of military power along the border.

> I knew the temper of the people on our Rio Grande frontier; I had labored with them for days and nights in order to obtain the co-operation of the better element and had partially succeeded in my endeavor believing that our Government would refuse extradition. . . . I knew the disastrous effect which the mere fact of extradition proceedings would have upon our plans on the border; they would alienate all our allies among the people; they would turn against us and our work would be vastly more difficult than it ever had been.[93]

Chase was willing even to concede that extradition would be useful if it was actually "possible, but the law seemed to me so clearly plain that extradition would surely be refused and the agitation of the subject at that time would cause our troops no end of trouble and materially decrease our prospects of full success." Chase was clearly thinking that the political offenses exception would eliminate the possibility for extradition. He left for San Antonio to try "if possible to suspend any extradition proceedings until such time as we have captured a large number of Insurrectionists."[94]

Chase was unsuccessful in trying to stop the extradition proceedings, but his trip away from the frontier did school him in the complicated local wrangles that helped define order, jurisdiction, and the exercise of power in the borderlands. Chase had been disappointed by state actions with regard to extradition but generally found local county officials to be an enormous help, particularly W. W. Shely of Starr County and R. B. Haynes of Zapata County, though both were suspected of having Garza sympathies. John Buckley, the sheriff of Duval County, "could not be prevailed upon to assist us in any way. He was indicted for assisting the Garza men himself and the leading men of the county were so implicated that they had refused us any aid in our efforts in their county." Chase was working a bit unaware amongst all of these overlapping loyalties and interests, and they exploded while he was away.[95]

While Chase was en route to San Antonio for the Benavides extradition trial, one of his scouts, Pablo Longorio, was arrested on February 1, 1893, for horse stealing on a two-and-a-half-month-old warrant by a Ranger. Chase said he "did not believe Pablo Longorio, one of my best scouts, was a horse thief." The man who pushed the arrest, José Angel Hinojosa Peña, had furnished arms to Garza while Pablo Longorio had been Garza's agent. Chase sent a Lieutenant Heard to follow Longorio to San Diego and pay his bail. Longorio was ultimately sentenced to eight years in jail for allegedly stealing Peña's horse, though he was pardoned by the governor.[96]

Meanwhile, another one of Chase's scouts was arrested on February 7, 1893, for murder, this time on a three-year-old charge. The charge was totally spurious, said Chase. The man arrested, Lino Cuellar, was also a U.S. marshal. Cuellar had in fact just arrested Peña and was leading him through the streets of San Diego. Another scout, Juan Morino, was arrested and charged with carrying a pistol and fined the highest possible amount (two hundred dollars) and then jailed for being unable to pay the fine.[97]

Jurisdiction in Texas was clearly cracking under the pressures produced by transborder revolution and local political interests. Chase reported all of this confusion to Assistant Adjutant General J. P. Martin: "it seemed to me that this was open defiance against U.S. Authority to arrest a Deputy Marshal under these circumstances when he was at the time in charge of a United States prisoner, the Marshal being arrested and the prisoner turned loose." "That Longorio, Cuellar and Moreno were arrested for not committing any crime but because they were working in the interest of the United States in suppressing the Garza movement is very apparent to me," Chase decided. Lawlessness reigned, both in terms of widespread Garza supporters and a state making things worse by not contributing to the federal effort. Meanwhile, Chase met with Texas governor Hogg, who expressed no interest in using the Rangers to help the Army round up the remaining Garzistas and said it was the "business of the United States," not Texas.[98]

Texas proceeded with the extradition hearing for Benavides, though it should have been stopped as soon as it was revealed that he was a U.S. citizen, born in Casa Blancas, Texas. "I know what constitutes American citizenship; I consider myself an American citizen," Benavides said at the trial. He had been a "Justice of the Peace and discharged the duties of that office without being able to write English." He had only voted twice, most recently under the Confederacy in 1863, for a judge.[99]

Incredibly, Commissioner L. F. Price elected to proceed anyway. "Although the evidence adduced by the accused is strongly persuasive if not conclusive of the fact that he is a born citizen of the Republic of Texas in 1845 and has remained in Texas ever since, a real estate owner . . . [and] office holder, I decline to pass upon the question of citizenship, leaving it to the tribunal having power to surrender." Price, and the state, clearly had an interest in seeing how far the issue could be pushed. If the extradition could be deemed legitimate and the executive chose to ignore his citizenship, Benavides very well could have been extradited.[100]

Since the citizenship exception was sidestepped, much of the evidence at the trial turned on the political nature of Benavides's acts. Benavides was accused of murdering five people in San Ygnacio on December 10, 1892, as well as burning down a barracks filled with dead and wounded. The question turned on the structural aspects of political offenses. Did the raiders wear hats? Juan Martinez testified that they all had red bands on their hats. Did they have a plan? Pablo Gomez testified, "yes sir. I saw that plan. I read very badly but have read the plan."[101]

Price's attempt notwithstanding, the extradition proceedings could not trump Benavides's citizenship even if they could disrupt Chase's efforts along the border. Benavides was returned to U.S. court for trial for his crimes against the neutrality laws, as Chase had originally desired. The political meaning of Benavides's actions were allowed to fade and be forgotten, one senses deliberately. Unlike the raid by Cazo, who could be seen as a revolutionary because he acted only on the Mexican side of the line, the San Ygnacio raid was loaded with much more profound political and racial complications within the territory of the United States.

Indeed, within a year, the Benavides example was used as a precedent in response to the transborder assaults of Victor L. Ochoa, who led "a band of people armed in the State of Texas for the purpose of invading Mexico" on an attack of the customshouse at Las Palomas. He was freed by the U.S. extradition commissioner under the citizenship exception, which Minister Romero complained was merely "an exception to be alleged in order to place obstacles in the way of extradition." Ochoa then organized thirteen more raiders and went on attacks near El Borracho, Chihuahua. At first, the U.S. State and Justice Departments protested that the federal government was unable to "compel the U.S. commissioner or other judicial officers to act upon its views" in any case. Underscoring the jurisdictional interference, Acting Secretary of State Edwin F. Uhl wrote that the Department had "hope the governor of Texas . . . may be able to take action in the matter." Later the State Department ruled that Ochoa was a common criminal, and Romero indicated that there was a "precedent which sustains the request of the Mexican Government in this case," as he called for the United States to try to imprison Ochoa as a criminal. Romero argued, "a number of persons, led by Francisco Benavides, Maximo Martinez, Pablo Gomez, and Cecilio Echeverria, organized in United States territory an expedition very similar to that which, a year later, was carried into effect by Ochoa, for the purpose of committing depredations in Mexico, and upon their return to the United States they were tried and sentenced by the Federal courts."[102] It had worked well in the Benavides case for both sides of the border not to identify that which was patently political in his political acts. State interests on both sides of the border could often be better served by identifying such movements as purely criminal and therefore diminished in significance, readily punished, and unilaterally controlled.

It was a different matter in the extradition trial of Garzistas Juan Duque, Inez Ruiz, and Jesus Guerra, a controversial case that eventually made it all the way to the U.S. Supreme Court, making it the first case involving political offenders to do so. The extradition process was largely a local border affair, and it reflected the strong push in the region to resolve the residual Garza problem without grappling with its political meaning or motivations. Consul Ornelas directly requested extradition. The case was first heard by the local hard-line extradition commissioner, L. F. Price. This was the same man who had chosen to ignore the clear evidence of Benavides's American citizenship. The trial began in May 1894.

Duque, Guerra, and Ruiz were all involved in the December 1892 raid on San Ygnacio. Like their commander, Benavides, the three men were charged with murder, kidnapping of twenty-two people, arson, robbery, and burning down a house filled with "certain dead and wounded men who names . . . are unknown." Since the political offenses exception was the only way these men could avoid extradition, it became the focus of their defense and was well supported by witnesses. Much of the discussion was on what might be seen as the structural aspects of revolution—the question as to whether banners were evident during the raid, the wording of manifestos, the "Plan Revolution," and other factors. Basilo Martinez of Tamaulipas testified that "there have been so many revolutions in Mexico during the past sixty years that I do not remember the number." Pablo Longoria of Zapato County, Texas, said the Garza movement was called a "revolution" from the beginning.[103]

On the other hand, Damasia Martinez, a rurales (Mexican ranger), testified that "government, rural guards, soldiers and friends" called Ruiz and the gang bandits. When asked the difference between bandits and revolutionaries, he said, "the bandit will steal and the Revolutionist don't." Refuigo Martinez, of Guerrero, Mexico, agreed. Ruiz and the others "were not revolutionists they were bandits." Asked to define the difference between bandits and revolutionaries, he responded, "the revolutionist respects families, the bandit respects nothing." The defense summary by attorney W. N. Brooker essentially argued that it was never proven that Ruiz and the others committed any crime at all and that the extradition warrant was "duplicitous and multitudinous, and an attempt to convict the defendant with some crime." And if these acts "were committed at all," they were committed "in open revolt and in action against the Soldiers and armies of the Republic of Mexico, and in hostile engagement, and the result of war, and the defendant is sought as a political prisoner of that revolution and to be tried and adjudged as such."[104]

Despite all evidence to the contrary, Commissioner Price found that the acts warranted extradition. Duque, Guerra, and Ruiz "applied to the District Court of the United States for the Western District of Texas for writs of habeas corpus, alleging that they were unlawfully restrained of their liberty by the United States marshal for that district, and praying that they be released." In this effort, the men were successful. Judge Thomas S. Maxey found that the men's actions had been "purely political offenses" and ordered them released. The appeal that reached the Supreme Court was, curiously, not on the issue of whether the crimes were purely political but on whether Consul Ornelas had had the authority to request extradition.[105]

Chief Justice Melville Fuller ruled that the consul was indeed appropriate in requesting the extradition: "the official character of this officer must be taken as sufficient evidence of his authority, and, as the government he represented was the real party interested in resisting the discharge, the appeal was properly prosecuted by him on its behalf." It was Maxey who had overstepped his jurisdiction. As many cases had argued for decades, a writ of habeas corpus could not "perform the office of a writ of error." If an extradition magistrate had appropriate jurisdiction over the crime and solid evidence of the fugitive's criminality, and the offense charged was extraditable, the Court saw no way for the ruling to be overturned or revived on habeas corpus grounds. "Whether an extraditable crime has been committed is a question of mixed law and fact, but chiefly of fact, and the judgment of the magistrate, rendered in good faith, on legal evidence, that the accused is guilty of the act charged, and that it constitutes an extraditable crime, cannot be reviewed on the weight of evidence, and is final for the purposes of the preliminary examination unless palpably errone-ous in law," Fuller affirmed.[106]

Fuller did briefly consider the political nature of the acts and dismissed them rather freely. He made note of the nature of the crimes and the speed with which the men had recrossed into the United States and argued flatly "that these men were bandits, without uniforms or flag, but with a red band on their hats, and that Garza was not there, and had nothing to do with the expedition" into San Ygnacio. Apparently, Fuller was unaware that Ornelas, the very consul who requested extradition, had recently identified all of these men as "the Garza bandits" to the U.S. Army fighting for "the same thing connected with the same leaders and for the same purpose." Fuller relied on Secretary of State Walter Q. Gresham's claim that the crimes were "not of such a purely political character as to exclude them from the operation of the treaty." Gresham had argued, a bit fatuously, that "the idea that these acts were perpetrated with *bona fide* political or revolutionary designs is negatived by the fact that, immediately after this oc-currence, though no superior armed force of the Mexican government was in the vicinity to hinder their advance into the country, the bandits withdrew with their booty across the river into Texas." In Gresham's estimation, apparently, purely political revolutionaries always stood and fought.

Though this case really revolved around the question of Ornelas's authority, Fuller asked, "can it be said that the commissioner had no choice, on the evi-dence, but to hold, in view of the character of the foray, the mode of attack, the persons killed or captured, and the kind of property taken or destroyed, that this was a movement in aid of a political revolt, an insurrection, or a civil war, and that acts which contained all the characteristics of crimes under the ordi-nary law were exempt from extradition because of the political intentions of those who committed them? In our opinion, this inquiry must be answered in the negative."[107]

Thus did the Ruiz decision reaffirm the border clauses exception to the extradition treaty. It lent greater authority to the decisions made at the local level by individuals with specific local agendas and empowered them to pur-sue their idiosyncratic interests through acts of foreign policy inaccessible to all but those operating within the borderlands exception. The Maxey decision was reversed, and Ruiz and Duque were extradited on the basis of nonpoliti-cal extraditable crimes. Guerra escaped and was free for a time. Interestingly, Ruiz was extradited and sentenced to death by Mexico for political action in the raid in a violation of the rule of specialty, whereupon he escaped to the United States. The State Department, which had begun broadening its perspective on political crimes, refused to extradite the now doubly fugitive and clearly political Ruiz.[108]

The newly developed (or hardened) stance arrived with the tenure of Secretary of State John Sherman. Guerra was captured in September 1897 in Starr County (by former Garza sympathizer Sheriff Shely), and Mexico immediately requested his extradition. In a notable act of executive discretion in extradition policy, and without even involving the courts, Sherman refused to extradite Guerra. "After mature and careful consideration of the evidence adduced in the case before the extradition commissioner at San Antonio I have the honor to inform you that this Department can find no sufficient ground on which to grant the extradition," he wrote to Romero. Sherman had two reasons: Guerra was not really guilty and, more importantly, the raid had been revolutionary. "From an attentive reading of that evidence it appears that Guerra was a member of the expedition making the attack, but it does not appear that he is implicated, either as an abettor or participant, in the commission of any offenses against private parties," Sherman asserted. "Therefore he is not deemed culpable for those offenses committed without his privity, and as the evidence shows the expedition to have been revolutionary in its origin and purpose the offense of being a member thereof was of a purely political character, outside of the purview of the extradition treaty."[109]

This refusal became the subject of an enormous and deeply aggrieved correspondence, driven by Romero's confusion and unsurprising irritation that Sherman had so thoroughly reversed the established State Department precedents of Secretaries Gresham and Olney as well as the determination of the Supreme Court. To be sure, the new secretary of state did not even interpret Benavides's return to Texas in the same way. From Sherman's perspective, that spoke to both the revolutionary fervor and political will of the raiders since after the fall of San Ygnacio, "the surrounding country lay at the mercy of Benavides and his followers, and pillage was at length within their easy grasp, the evidence fails to show any attempt to pursue and accomplish the very thing which your excellency deems to have been the main or sole object of the assault."[110]

Not only did Sherman not back down on his new policy, he articulated a new rule of defining the purely political and expanding its limits. "To argue that the acts themselves were intrinsically wicked, and therefore demonstrate the presence of the intent characteristic of common crimes, would have the effect in all cases of unsuccessful revolutionary movements, conducted by force and bloodshed, to destroy the right of asylum to political offenders and refugees," he wrote. "It was therefore by no means intended to be decided that since the assault was revolutionary 'crimes committed by a member of the expedition are of a purely political character.' The decision was that as the movement was revolutionary, acts done in aid thereof, are not common crimes." This distinction, fine-grained as it was, made all the difference. Noting the problems with the "purely political," Sherman discussed the concept of exceptions for "absolute political offences" and further claimed that "nonextradition for absolute political offenses is always implied in treaties without making any express exception. When they exclude political offenses, it is precisely connected or complex offenses which are meant."[111]

On January 24, 1898, an exasperated Mexico abrogated the extradition treaty of 1861. It had long complained of problems related to citizenship exceptions, as noted in the last chapter, and the Guerra extradition and the evolving notion of political exception in it served as the final straw for Mexico. Romero identified "the necessity of concluding a new convention in such precise terms as shall not admit of conflicting decisions in analogous cases, and which shall, moreover, embrace other rules of action, the addition of which is suggested by experience."[112]

There may have been a sea change occurring at the level of federal policy, but along the Texas-Mexico boundary, the ability of local officials to operate the levers of extradition themselves continued to perpetuate the most local variant of the exception. Absent the political explosiveness of the Garza revolution's long tail, smaller groups of attempted revolutionaries were dispatched to their fates in Mexico for being insufficiently pure in their political acts. In *The Republic of Mexico vs. Demetrio Cortes and 27 Others*, brought by a local Mexican consul named Francisco Mallen, J. B. Sexton, commissioner of the Circuit Court of the United States for the Western District of Texas, ordered the surrender of a group that testimony variously described as "the revolutionists of Ojinaga" or a gang of "bandits" that had "dedicated themselves to brigandage." This group had organized themselves in Shafter, Texas, in order "to attack El Norte, Ojinaga, and . . . to depose the authorities, establish new ones and then march against Chihuahua or Ciudad Juarez." Demetrio Cortez, Preculiano Gonzales, and Jose Salavzar all pleaded guilty and were sentenced to the penitentiary at Fort Leavenworth for two years and fined one dollar. Other cases were dismissed for a variety of reasons, and eventually the twenty-seven who Sexton judged were whittled down to Tomas Burgues, Simon Rede, and Epifenio Armendariz. Sexton decided that Burgues was not extraditable because his father was an American who had not renounced his citizenship. Sexton (unlike Price) believed "citizenship is always a question of fact."[113]

As for Rede and Armendariz, the remaining border crossers, their lawyers argued that since the Mexican proceedings and all of the witnesses had called the band revolutionists "that the plaintiff was necessarily bound by the use of those terms to the conclusion that the defendants were guilty, if at all, of political offenses, and therefore not extraditable." Sexton disagreed. Even though Governor Ahumada of Chihuahua wrote to Mexico City that "the revolutionists of Ojinaga crossed the American line," Sexton refused to be swayed since all sorts of language was used in the testimony. Witnesses used terms like "'revolutionists, bandits, criminals, malefactors, outlaws,' and applied to them numerous inculpatory epithets without regard to legal definitions or accuracy of language." Though the authorities in Mexico called the raid a revolt, Sexton declared such actions to be "unguarded expressions." He was sure the group was "hostile to the government of Mexico." But, he argued, "Criminal offenders are generally hostile to any government that does not allow them to follow out the dictates of their criminal instincts." With this kind of ironclad logic, few revolutionary acts could be determined to be political.[114]

Sexton did "not think that these loose expressions [could] be held to define the character of the offenses with which the defendants [were] charged." Since Mexico accused the men of murder, intent to murder, arson, and kidnapping rather than revolution or sedition *in the actual extradition request*, Sexton rather surprisingly argued that he could not consider other possibilities beyond the Mexican government's case. He rejected the idea that these crimes were even carried out by an organized political group like the Ezeta brothers. He announced, "the Ezeta case is not this case." The group was small, "only 25 max, sometimes only 7. It is, in fact, a gang. Not intending to use harsh language I cannot regard the expedition, if it be called such, as anything more than one for the purpose of plunder. All of the acts of the defendants, as disclosed by the testimony, were predatory in their complexion. . . . [P]rey, financial and otherwise, was their object."[115]

Sexton certified to the secretary of state that the men should be extradited for their crimes. In doing so, he recognized that the political definition was difficult to make and "pre-eminently circumstantial." But the words he used in his conclusion reflected a much wider range of approaches to legal spatiality in American foreign relations throughout this era than just this case: "as a legal proposition . . . the law is always modified to a greater or less extent by the facts of the case to which it is sought to be applied."[116]

Epilogue

Marco Polo describes a bridge, stone by stone:
"But which is the stone that supports the bridge?" Kublai Khan asks.
"The bridge is not supported by one stone or another," Marco answers,
   "but by the line of the arch that they form."
Kublai Khan remains silent, reflecting. Then he adds: "Why do you speak
   to me of the stones? It is only the arch that matters to me."
Polo answers: "Without stones, there is no arch."
   Italo Calvino, *Invisible Cities*

I began research for this book because I was fascinated by a single case involving an embezzler named Frederick M. Ker who fled Chicago for Lima, Peru, in 1882, where he was kidnapped by an agent of the Pinkerton Detective Agency and returned to the United States for trial. No official extradition request was made to Peru during this process, though there was an existing treaty with the United States dating to 1870. Rather than rejecting this act of forcible extraterritorial abduction, in 1886 the U.S. Supreme Court decided in *Ker v. Illinois* that the Constitution offered no protection for individuals from extraterritorial abduction. This expansive and astonishing decision clarified my understanding of the tenor of late nineteenth-century American sovereignty claims and led me to write this book.

Ironically, *Ker v. Illinois* was decided the same day in 1886 that the court handed down the ruling in *United States v. Rauscher*, which so thoroughly constrained sovereign prerogatives in extradition cases involving the rule of specialty.[1] The bifurcated, seemingly contradictory approach to U.S. sovereignty and legal spatiality represented by these two cases could be thought of as downright bizarre until further study reveals how comfortably they sat among the interpolated assertions, exceptions, and elisions that characterized jurisdictional issues in late nineteenth-century U.S. foreign relations examined throughout this book.

The Ker case perfectly reflected American notions of territoriality, unilateralism, and sovereign freedom and provided a deep challenge to the whole notion of the "rule of law" within U.S. foreign policy. It demonstrated what Nasser Hussain explores as the "persistence of sovereignty even in the normative universe of the rule of law."[2] Moreover, by making extraterritorial abduction entirely legal and legitimizing it as another policy tool, *Ker v. Illinois* created an essentially limitless field of action for the pursuit of both fugitives and state interests wherever they might ferret themselves around the globe. The case established in no uncertain terms that U.S. power was unlimited when asserted abroad in service to the sovereign state or when asserted via sovereign exception within established legal, territorial, or jurisdictional orders.

This epilogue offers a brief exploration of how this breed of sovereign exception was created, implemented, and governed in the Ker case in order to situate it within the broader context of U.S. extradition foreign policy explored throughout this book. *Ker* stands with other exceptions and jurisdictional assertions considered here as a clear example of the core continuities and expansive ambitions of U.S. foreign relations in the late nineteenth century. Similar goals and techniques have continued to animate policymakers and been found to have renewed utility in each successive era since 1877. Exceptions have been especially valued for the slippery latitude they produce in the transnational and imperial relationships in which the United States has sought rationalization or control in so many ways.

BRIEFLY CONSIDERING EXTRATERRITORIAL ABDUCTION AND U.S. FOREIGN RELATIONS

Frederick M. Ker was an unabashed thief who never denied his crimes; he simply did not like the fact that he was caught or the way he was kidnapped and brought to trial. Ker had embezzled money and securities while in his position as the assistant cashier and assistant manager for the Chicago firm Preston, Kean & Co. While on a fast track to promotion, Ker was discovered speculating rather excessively on the Chicago Board of Trade, though he only made eighteen hundred dollars a year and such speculation was not allowed in his position. But when confronted by his bosses, Ker managed to assuage them that he was using his own money. He thereafter left for a supposed vacation to New Orleans. Around the time of his scheduled return, Preston, Kean & Co. received a letter informing the company of his theft of twenty-one thousand dollars in cash and thirty-five thousand dollars in U.S. bonds. According to the amicus brief filed by Illinois Attorney General George Hunt in *Ker v. Illinois*, "the letter contained an intimation that if [Ker were] allowed to take his journey unmolested, the bank would be let alone, but if pursued and brought back, a run would be organized and the bank ruined; and concluded with the cool remark that if successful in future life, he would endeavor to refund the money to those entitled to receive it."[3]

After Ker fled for Lima, Peru, the Illinois governor (who was named, fittingly for a sovereignty case, John Marshall Hamilton) asked President Arthur for an extradition warrant and promptly received it. Embezzlement was an extraditable crime listed in the U.S.-Peru treaty, so it seemed like this should have been a fairly straightforward exchange. Yet, oddly, neither the Peruvian authorities nor the U.S. consular and diplomatic apparatus in the country were notified of Ker's flight, the extradition warrant, or any other matters of the case. Preston, Kean & Co. independently hired a Pinkerton agent named Henry G. Julian to find Ker, and it was Julian who eventually carried (but did not execute) the presidential extradition warrant. This kind of public-private overlap was not unusual. The fact that none of the diplomatic apparatus was engaged was significant and clearly intentional given the nature of overall Pinkerton work. The following digression illustrates.

The Pinkerton Detective Agency was the principal private contractor and strikebreaker used by U.S. business for a variety of tasks which were very often extralegal and better classified as dirty work. The agency was very large, reputedly outnumbering the U.S. Army by the early 1890s and with many branches overseas. As Ethan A. Nadelmann noted in his study of international policing, "so well-known had the name Pinkerton become by then that many Europeans thought it was the title of the U.S. criminal police." Pinkertons were often employed by large international institutions such as the Bank of England to pursue a large array of criminals and fugitives. The private contractor had several advantages, including experience, freedom of movement, and the lessened chance of aggravating foreign sovereignties. Pinkertons were a flexible non-state tool used in transnational affairs.[4]

During the last three decades of the nineteenth century, the Pinkertons followed criminals abroad in countries including Belgium, Hungary, England, France, Switzerland, Austria, Mexico, Canada, Portugal, Peru, and Germany.

Later, between 1901 and 1907, Pinkertons also famously pursued the Wild Bunch to Bolivia. For a brief period after the Civil War, the United States had on occasion officially used the agency for surrenders of foreign fugitives. Founder Allan Pinkerton himself was involved in the extradition of the Reno brothers, train robbers who were ultimately lynched. This episode triggered a major international squabble with Canada and Great Britain in 1868, which marked the end of using private guards for official extraditions. Thereafter, the protection of American fugitives in foreign surrenders became a federal responsibility, though the serving of warrants continued to be outsourced to private contractors. Pinkertons also continued to be used unofficially for transboundary abductions in places like Mexico.[5]

There was no doubt that however hazy his legal status, Henry Julian, the Pinkerton, was good at his job as a detective. He originally tracked Ker to Panama and knew it was a fresh trail when he discovered an overcoat with all the labels cut out except for one that read "Ker." Based on local tips, the agent trailed Ker to Lima, where he "recognized Ker sitting under the shade of a tropical tree, regaling himself with a cigar." Speaking in French, the two men rather unexpectedly ended up becoming friends. Over a couple of weeks, they passed the time in Lima "dreaming and scheming," according to Illinois Attorney General Hunt. During this time, the extradition warrant arrived in Lima specifying larceny as the extraditable offense. Yet no official request was made to Peru. Hunt stated baldly, "there was no Peru" since as part of the War of the Pacific, the capital had been occupied by the Chilean army, and the Peruvian government had fled for Ariquipa. The Circuit Court of Illinois later held that Ker was under the law of Peru and not the extradition treaty of 1870 because of this situation. For reasons that are not entirely clear, Julian decided to forgo any attempt at a formal extradition surrender and enlisted the help of the Chilean military to grab Ker and transport him to the U.S. naval warship *Essex* in Callao harbor.[6]

Ker and Julian floated on the *Essex* off the coast of Peru for a month and then traveled to Honolulu, where a merchant ship took them to San Francisco. During this time, Ker claimed to have been prevented from "communicating with any person, or seeking any advice or assistance in regard to procuring his release by legal process or otherwise." Illinois requested and received interstate rendition of Ker from California, and after his circuitous route back, he was at last brought to trial in the summer of 1883.[7]

In his trial in the Illinois Supreme Court, *Ker v. The People*, Ker argued that the Criminal Court of Cook County had no jurisdiction over him because he was brought into court without due process of law and because his supposed right to asylum had been violated. The court decided that Illinois was not responsible in either case:

> Conceding, as may be done, [that the] defendant was arrested in Peru, and brought into the state of California, without warrant of law, the state now prosecuting defendant was not a party to any violation of any treaty or other public law. The application the state made to the executive department of the general government was for the legal arrest of defendant, and if there was any abuse of the warrant of the federal government, or any treaty obligations with a friendly power violated, it was not done by the state now conducting the prosecution against defendant.

Any issue of extradition was "a national affair" and not a state problem. And, the court noted, Ker was not arrested or extradited in any case but produced "by sheer force, and not under the treaty at all." The use of force actually eliminated any problems. If Peru was unhappy about it (and no complaint had been recorded about this case), it had to seek a diplomatic remedy. Ker received ten years in Joliet prison for embezzlement.[8]

Ker appealed his case all the way to the Supreme Court, and it was finally heard in April 1886. The defense argument turned especially on the spurious claim that extradition treaties included an implicit "personal right of asylum." The defense also complained about violations of the rule of specialty, since the extradition warrant was for larceny rather than embezzlement.[9]

The Supreme Court focused on the question of a writ of error to the Supreme Court of the State of Illinois in terms of the asylum question and Ker's claim that his kidnapping and transfer from Peru to Illinois had constituted multiple violations of due process of law. It handily dismissed Ker's assertion that there was anything illegal or untoward in the rendition from California to Illinois.[10] On the issue of due process of law, though this was guaranteed quite clearly by Article XIV of the Constitution, the Court found an exception to it that "mere irregularities" like kidnapping did not override:

> We do not intend to say that there may not be proceedings previous to the trial in regard to which the prisoner could invoke in some manner the provisions of this clause of the Constitution, but, for mere irregularities in the manner in which he may be brought into custody of the law, we do not think

he is entitled to say that he should not be tried at all for the crime with which he is charged in a regular indictment. He may be arrested for a very heinous offense by persons without any warrant, or without any previous complaint, and brought before a proper officer, and this may be in some sense said to be "without due process of law." But it would hardly be claimed that, after the case had been investigated and the defendant held by the proper authorities to answer for the crime, he could plead that he was first arrested "without due process of law." So here, when found within the jurisdiction of the State of Illinois and liable to answer for a crime against the laws of that state, unless there was some positive provision of the Constitution or of the laws of this country violated in bringing him into court, it is not easy to see how he can say that he is there "without due process of law" within the meaning of the constitutional provision.[11]

As far as the law was concerned, it was as if Ker had suddenly materialized in Illinois, where he was liable for his crimes. How he got there was not a matter for notice or for concern.

The claim of asylum was a key to Ker's defense, and the Court thoroughly annihilated it. Asylum, of course, stood only as a malleable and complex exception to sovereignty. In this case, the opinion of the Court was notably clear and sharp: asylum meant nothing in the face of sovereign choice.

There is no language in this treaty or in any other treaty made by this country on the subject of extradition of which we are aware which says in terms that a party fleeing from the United States to escape punishment for crime becomes thereby entitled to an asylum in the country to which he has fled. *Indeed, the absurdity of such a proposition would at once prevent the making of a treaty of that kind.* It will not be for a moment contended that the government of Peru could not have ordered Ker out of the country on his arrival or at any period of his residence there. If this could be done, what becomes of his right of asylum?[12]

Peru *could* have surrendered Ker even without a treaty as an aspect of its sovereign choice, just as it *could* have chosen to extend asylum out of the same exact power. But it did not, and no fugitive could ever flee and remain in either Peru or the United States with an expectation of asylum.

In any case, the Court decided that the discussions of extradition and the treaty limits and possible protections were moot since this was not at all an extradition case but instead a kidnapping case. And the Court truly had no problem with this question of extraterritorial abduction: "In fact, that treaty was not called into operation, was not relied upon, was not made the pretext of arrest, and the facts show that it was clear case of kidnapping within the dominions of Peru, without any pretense of authority under the treaty or from the government of the United States." The fact that Ker was kidnapped rather than extradited actually simplified the matter, since the rule of specialty did not apply to forcibly abducted fugitives. *Because* of the illegality of his capture, the Court asserted, Ker actually had no rights like those it had just so thoroughly clarified in *United States v. Rauscher*:

> But it is quite a different case when the plaintiff in error comes to this country in the manner in which he was brought here, clothed with no rights which a proceeding under the treaty could have given him, and no duty which this country owes to Peru or to him under the treaty. We think it very clear, therefore, that in invoking the jurisdiction of this Court upon the ground that the prisoner was denied a right conferred upon him by a treaty of the United States, he has failed to establish the existence of any such right.[13]

The Court saw no protections for abducted individuals brought into U.S. jurisdiction. It also saw no real limits to extraterritorial abduction, at least under the Constitution and federal statutes: "The question of how far his forcible seizure in another country and transfer by violence, force, or fraud to this country could be made available to resist trial in the state court for the offense now charged upon him is one which we do not feel called upon to decide, for in that transaction we do not see that the Constitution or laws or treaties of the United States guarantee him any protection."[14]

One suspects it was with a taste for the mischievous that the Court indicated that Ker did have one remedy to his complaint. Since kidnapping was an extraditable crime in the treaty with Peru, it was theoretically possible that Julian could be extradited there on the plain, unchallenged facts of the case. If that were to happen, Justice Miller argued, Ker "could sue Julian in an action of trespass and false imprisonment" in Peruvian court. However, the Court was not able to make a judgment on "whether he could recover a sum sufficient to justify the action" since that "would probably depend upon moral aspects of the case, which we cannot here consider."[15] Any reading of the Ker case confirms that neither morality nor especially stringent notions of legality seemed especially engaged in the decision.

Ker v. Illinois stands as one of the baldest and most profound assertions of U.S. unilateralism and sovereign reach ever uttered by the Court at any time, past or present. In reifying this forcible extraterritorial kidnapping, the Supreme Court indicated that territorially limited jurisdiction could be served by power that was, because it lay beyond the Constitution, treaty constraints, and territorial jurisdiction, essentially limitless. There was no assumption of asylum from jurisdiction by fleeing abroad, and it did not matter how a person was brought into territorial jurisdiction. Ironically, territorial jurisdiction was thus granted an element of global extraterritorial scope in this way. The territorial conception of jurisdiction gained long tentacles of the legal, extralegal, and extraterritorial varieties.

Ker also swept aside the necessity for extradition relations or delineated treaty responsibilities. It accepted and encouraged the extraterritorial acts of private contractors engaged in extralegally kidnapping citizens abroad and returning them to American justice. It signaled a clear division between acts of foreign policy by the executive or by mercenary private interests and the domestic legal system that was structured to protect the rights of the accused in accordance with established principles of jurisprudence. And all the while, it ignored the "massive changes in the application of the Fourth and Fifth Amendments domestically and in the perception of individual human rights internationally."[16]

As a Supreme Court case, *Ker v. Illinois* did not itself mint policy, but it did set the tenor of future policy and indicate the trajectory for sovereign exceptions in foreign relations over the next century. It was not a judicial or federal power grab per se but rather a loosening of the reins. In an era of strict treaty interpretation, tightened jurisdictional regimes, protectionism, and racial and citizenship exclusion, *Ker* introduced an oppositional looseness. Balanced with the strongly limited and treaty-based extradition decisions of this era, *Ker* posited an exercise of power that was beholden to no constraint in application, reach, implementation, or impact. It was what Giorgio Agamben has referred to as a true "state of exception appear[ing] as the legal form of what cannot have legal form" where "the law employs the exception—that is the suspension of law itself."[17]

Accordingly, the *Ker* decision should be viewed as an example of the ways in which the late nineteenth-century state incorporated exception directly into its governance of extradition and international jurisdictional questions. This was an approach already at work in citizenship regimes for African-Americans in the South and Chinese at the borders and would soon be applied on a wider, international scale in the colonial consolidations after the War of 1898. *Ker* signaled the flexible and quite sophisticated expansion of the many folds of the state in an era usually mischaracterized as weak or laissez-faire in terms of governance and control. The exception was hardwired into the structuring of state power on local, national, and global scales.

The fact that the Ker and Rauscher cases were decided on the same day provides a neat way of contrasting the different aspects of the U.S. approach to legal spatiality and the exercise of sovereign power. In *Ker*, the Court recognized no limit to action abroad because there were no acts of extradition and the abduction happened in the realm of state power, where only other states could protest or limit state interests and actions. In contrast, *Rauscher* set up very real limits produced by extradition treaties. The resulting bifurcation was clear: once within a system, constraints mattered. Outside a system, as outside the border, effectively there were none.

Ker v. Illinois could be considered not just expansive but close to nihilistic in the rule and precedents it created for international responsibility and acts of state. The case implied that the rule of law was not relevant to the exercise of U.S. jurisdiction outside national borders. In this way, *Ker* nestled comfortably within the developing understanding of sovereignty, legal spatiality, and exception so evident in increasingly assertive statements of U.S. foreign policy goals and power as well as in the Supreme Court cases previously considered in this book. One exception begat another.

Though unrelated in a direct sense, *Ker* easily sat squarely alongside the increasingly common expressions of unilateral authority and burgeoning U.S. hegemony, such as in the famously strident statement of Secretary of State Richard Olney in the Venezuelan Boundary Dispute of 1895, where he proclaimed "the United States is practically sovereign on this continent, and its fiat is law upon the subjects to which it confines its interposition."[18] The *Ker* embrace of power over law in external relations was also clearly evident in *In re Ross*, when the Court intoned that the "Constitution can have no operation in another country." External affairs existed alongside the outward, unilateral projection of power, not the blanket extension of rights or asylum. *Ker* and *Ross* significantly liberated the power of the state and its designated private contractors from constraint in foreign affairs. These cases offered clear answers on nineteenth-century terms to Gerald L. Neuman's deft question: "the Constitution begins with 'We the People.' Where does it end?"[19]

The same combination of neatly bifurcated domestic and foreign spheres and the recognition of sovereign exception came in the 1897 case *Underhill v. Hernandez*. This case was extraordinarily influential because of the way the Supreme Court firmly rejected extraterritoriality in favor of expanded foreign affairs freedoms by articulating what became known as the "act of state doctrine." American George Underhill, who had been building waterworks in Ciudad Bolivar for the Venezuelan government, complained of having been prevented from leaving the country when General Jose Hernandez took control of the city in 1892. Hernandez was part of the new government that had been recognized by the United States on October 23, 1892. Underhill was pressed into service to keep the waterworks operating in support of the revolution, and once freed, he sued Hernandez in the Second Circuit Court for damages and confinement.[20]

The Court rejected Underhill's ability to sue Hernandez in a strong assertion of territoriality and sovereign freedom: "Every sovereign state is bound to respect the independence of every other sovereign state, and the courts of one country will not sit in judgment on the acts of the government of another done within its own territory." The only way for a state to be held responsible was for another state to seek satisfaction, as an act of foreign policy: "Redress of grievances by reason of such acts must be obtained through the means open to be availed of by sovereign powers as between themselves." Neither did the Court limit this immunity to the recognized government of the state. It extended, in fact, to all competing authorities as well, even if they were at war: "Where a civil war prevails (that is, where the people of a country are divided into two hostile parties, who take up arms and oppose one another by military force), generally speaking, foreign nations do not assume to judge of the merits of the quarrel."[21]

The immunity of the sovereign or would-be sovereign in the acts of state should be viewed as an important form of exception. The Court's broad definition of the legitimacy of all sides in a conflict and of their immunity was a significant assertion of how a sovereign exception could be created and allowed to operate unimpeded. *Underhill* concluded that no sovereign within its territory could be held liable for its actions by another sovereign. *Ker* and *Ross* argued that the sovereign was not responsible for the actions happening outside its jurisdiction and did not have to extend rights into that realm. Power, not law, was the proper realm of dispute beyond territorial borders. The state was liberated both from unsought responsibility abroad and from limitation on action at home.

Ker v. Illinois accepted a willful blindness to illegality in the form of abduction when it occurs in service to legality and territorial jurisdiction over crime. The decision simultaneously constructed a neat division between the foreign (lawless, power-driven, unfixed) and domestic (sovereign, territorial, delineated) spheres of action. There was a very large policy impact in the succeeding two decades, when the United States undertook to construct an overseas colonial empire founded upon similar sharp distinctions and contradictions.[22]

It is important to note that *Ker v. Illinois* was not some forgotten oddity from the woolly days of the Supreme Court; it has been continually upheld and strengthened ever since it was written. *Ker* was expanded in the case *Frisbie v. Collins* in 1952, and since that time, the rule allowing extraterritorial abduction has been called the Ker-Frisbie rule. It was applied most egregiously and memorably in the 1990 transboundary abduction of Humberto Alvarez-Machain in Mexico by bounty hunters hired by the U.S. Drug Enforcement Administration.[23] State-directed extraterritorial abduction and rendition have been reaffirmed and broadened in the twenty-first century in ways familiar to any global citizen observing the contemporary and ongoing U.S. "global war on terror." *Ker* provided a window into the operation of sovereignty and the myriad exceptions that the United States granted and continues to grant itself as both a rising power and a hegemonic one.

Expansive jurisdictional assertions in extradition and interdiction were key means of regularizing and perfecting systems of exception in global interstate relations that were unilateralist in origin, implementation, and effect but that avoided the thorny issues of subordination and invasiveness which characterized extraterritoriality and other jurisdictional fictions. The significance of this system extended far beyond the region and the period. The multifaceted consolidation of order honed in the U.S.-Mexico borderlands was redeployed in diverse ways in other regions and in later insular imperial governance.

All of the issues explored in this book came to prominence at the end of the nineteenth century in the endgame of American consolidation of its territorial empire. Indeed, many of the approaches to sovereign exception that came to define subsequent U.S. imperial spatiality and globalization policy, especially those rooted in building divergent governance systems for each aspect of the empire, were conceived of within this context. As David Kazanjian has written, it is "this interpenetration of the domestic and the foreign that marks the emergence of U.S. imperialism."[24] American hegemonic power, familiar to all scholars of U.S.

foreign relations in the period after 1898, was founded upon many of the lessons drawn (if not necessarily learned) from these late nineteenth-century jurisdictional disputes.

In this context, and by way of conclusion, it is useful to briefly consider the need to engage the concept of empire. Interest in the history and structure of American empire has perhaps never been greater. But the study of the legal underpinnings of American imperial governance stretching back to the late nineteenth century and the relation of conceptions of sovereignty, territoriality, and jurisdiction to empire have not yet received adequate attention from historians of American foreign relations.[25] Yet these legal fictions and jurisdictional assertions formed the sinews of empire long before the United States embarked on a path of overseas conquest and dominion. In pursuit of global empire, the United States combined these malleable assertions with a disposition toward pursuing power and wealth despite the inconsistencies produced or required. This approach was evident most famously in the Insular Cases, which combined formal territorial control with fitful extension of the constitutional rights usually associated with American sovereignty.[26] This fluid and divided approach to legal spatiality was well honed from long practice in a wide variety of forms explored throughout this book.

It is clear that the legal core of the expansive and controversial contemporary global assertions of the hegemonic United States in the twenty first century was in fact created in a much earlier era. In the late nineteenth century, a powerful but developing United States worked from an idiosyncratic but focused understanding of the many utilities of unilateral control of transnational concerns and jurisdictional autonomy. Most lastingly and most importantly, the United States created an archipelago of anomalous zones freed of jurisdictional constraints that continued to be systemically useful long after territorial empire became an albatross. This system, from its origins to its persistence, is worth our unvarnished attention.

NOTES

Abbreviations Used in the Notes

ALJ	*Albany Law Journal*
AHR	*American Historical Review*
AJIL	*American Journal of International Law*
AJLH	*The American Journal of Legal History*
ALR	*The American Law Review*
AQ	*American Quarterly*
BYIL	British Yearbook of International Law
BHR	*Business History Review*
CJTL	*Columbia Journal of Transnational Law*
CR	*Congressional Record*
EPT	El Paso Times
HLR	*Harvard Law Review*
CMPP	James D. Richardson, ed. *A Compilation of the Messages and Papers of the Presidents, 1789–1908*
JAH	*Journal of American History*
JCH	*Journal of Contemporary History*
JCLC	*The Journal of Criminal Law and Criminology*
JPE	*Journal of Political Economy*
FRUS	Foreign Relations of the United States
MLR	*Michigan Law Review*
NARA	National Archives
NRJ	*Natural Resources Journal*
NYJILP	*New York University Journal of International Law & Politics*
NAR	*North American Review*
PSQ	*Political Science Quarterly*
PUSNI	*Proceedings of the United States Naval Institute*
RCUS	*Reports from the Consuls of the United States*
RG	Record Group
SCLR	*Southern California Law Review*
SHQ	*Southwestern Historical Quarterly*

SLR   *Stanford Law Review*
UPLR   *University of Pennsylvania Law Review*
NYUJILP *New York University Journal of International Law & Politics*
TLR   *Texas Law Review*
VLR   *Virginia Law Review*
YJIL   *Yale Journal of International Law*
YLJ   *Yale Law Journal*

Introduction

1. Sutton thought one recent situation reflected the snarled reality of impossibility: "a Mexican soldier deserted to the American side. His return was requested, but a local justice whose sympathies are perhaps largely with this class, had him arrested for bringing stolen property into the state [an extraditable crime], and had the sheriff, who delivered the man in midstream to the Mexican authorities, arrested for conniving at the escape of a prisoner. The sheriff in turn had the justice arrested for interfering with an officer, and both parties are now under bond for trial!" #30 Sutton to William Hunter, 3 July 1879, NARA, RG 59, Despatches from United States Consuls in Matamoros, 1826–1906, roll 6.

2. #30 Sutton to William Hunter, 3 July 1879, NARA, RG 59, Despatches from United States Consuls in Matamoros, 1826–1906, roll 6.

3. Ibid.

4. #153, Sutton to William Wharton, 12 July 1890, NARA, RG 59, Despatches from United States Consuls in Nuevo Laredo, 1871–1906, roll 2.

5. Ibid.

6. Ibid.

7. #231, Sutton to William Wharton, 27 January 1891, ibid. On September 8, 1892, Adee wrote Sutton and said the department was well aware of the problems with the treaty and had even negotiated a treaty with Mexico on February 20, 1885. It was submitted to the senate on March 2, 1885, with a greatly expanded extraditable crimes list, but Mexico ultimately refused to ratify it. This is a rare time when a State Department response is inserted into this consular file—and importantly, it does not address the citizenship issues that Sutton stressed. Attached to #448, Sutton to Wharton, 4 August 1892, ibid.

8. This understanding of legal spatiality was shaped by Raustiala, "Evolution of Territoriality: International Relations and American Law," in *Territoriality and Conflict in an Era of Globalization*, and the richly detailed Raustiala, *Does the Constitution Follow the Flag?* Also Sarat, Douglas, and Umphrey, "Where (or What) Is the Place of Law," in *The Place of Law*, 2–6; Wong, "Rumor of Trafficking: Border Controls, Illegal Migration,

and the Sovereignty of the Nation-State," in *Illicit Flows and Criminal Things*, 69–99; Taylor, "The State as Container," 151–62; Krasner, *Sovereignty*, 152–83.

9. On the application of the Constitution in foreign relations at this time, though not expressly discussing extradition, see Cleveland, "Powers Inherent in Sovereignty," 1–284; Aleinikoff, *Semblances of Sovereignty*; LaFeber, "The Constitution and United States Foreign Policy," 695–717; Lawson and Seidman, *Constitution of Empire*. On foreign relations in this area, among other books cited herein, see Long, *Gold Braid and Foreign Relations*, 338–413, and Pletcher, *The Awkward Years*.

10. On the concept of "legalities," this book follows the work of Christopher L. Tomlins, who emphasizes "legalities" rather than laws. The latter implies "universality of application, singularity of meaning, rightness" while "legality, in contrast, is a condition with social and cultural existence; it has specificity. . . . They are the means of effecting law's discourses, the mechanisms through which law names, blames, and claims. . . . Legalities, so powerful, are also fragile and contingent." Legalities should also be considered in terms of "the appropriation, occupation, and transformation of place." Tomlins, "Introduction," in *The Many Legalities of Early America*, 2–3, 14.

11. For example, extradition is almost wholly absent in the core current bibliographies and historiographical collections on the history of American foreign relations despite the fact that the legal literature on all aspects of extradition is stupendous. The indispensible modern work on extradition is Bassiouni, *International Extradition*, which is focused on current legal procedure. An early bibliography of relevant international works in several languages is "Bibliography on Extradition," 51–65. Numerous works on specific aspects of extradition are cited throughout this book when relevant and not repeated here. The one book that broadly analyzes extradition in foreign policy terms is Pyle, *Extradition, Politics, and Human Rights*, with a specific emphasis on the modern period and rise of human rights regimes rather than the core unilateralism manifest in the policies. Aleinikoff emphasizes unilateralism as a key element of legal spatiality but, oddly, does not focus on extradition in his otherwise excellent *Semblances of Sovereignty*.

12. Fitzpatrick and Joyce, "Normality of the Exception in Democracy's Empire," 70n26. Also, Agamben, *Homo Sacer: Sovereign Power and Bare Life* and *State of Exception*.

13. Sovereignty remains an enormously complex concept that animates whole fields in international relations and has a massive literature that is rendered approachable by Teschke, *Myth of 1648*, and on a smaller scale, by Kratochwil, "Of Systems, Boundaries, and Territoriality," 27–52. On the nineteenth-century political meanings, see Platt, "A Triad of Political Conceptions." On sovereignty and territoriality, see Brenner, "Beyond State-Centrism?"

14. *The Exchange v. McFaddon*, 11 U.S. (7 Cranch) 116, 136–37 (1812).

15. "Letter from the Secretary of State, submitting report on the Citizenship of the United States, Expatriation, and Protection abroad," 59th Cong., 2nd sess., H. Doc. 326,

197; Moore, *Digest of International Law*, 630–31. Emphasis original. Moore was referring specifically to the question of extraterritorial immunity for diplomats.

16. Raustiala, *Does the Constitution Follow the Flag?* 226–27; Kayaoğlu, *Legal Imperialism*, 6. On British extraterritoriality, see Piggott, *Extraterritoriality*. On law of empire, see Anghie, *Imperialism, Sovereignty and the Making of International Law*, 32–114; Benton, *Law and Colonial Cultures*, 210–66; Koskenniemi, *Gentle Civilizer of Nations*, 98–178. On the U.S. view of the system, see *Extraterritoriality: A Letter from the Secretary of State to the Chairman of the Senate Committee on Foreign Relations Concerning the Judicial Exercise of Extraterritorial Rights Conferred upon the United States*; Grover Cleveland, first annual address, 4 December 1893, in CMPP, vol. IX, 435. On the concept of legal fictions, see Fuller, *Legal Fictions*.

17. Raustiala, "Evolution of Territoriality," 221.

18. "Official Opinions of the Attorney-General," 51st Cong., 1st sess., 1890, H. Misc. Doc. 238, 229; "Jurisdiction of the United States in Places Out of Their Territory and Dominion," 48th Cong., sess., 1885, H. Rep. 2250, 1.

19. Scully has closely examined in particular the negotiations regarding rights between sojourner and the state that formed the core focus of this form of extraterritoriality. Scully, *Bargaining with the State from Afar*; Ruskola, "Canton Is not Boston: The Invention of American Imperial Sovereignty," in Dudziak and Volpp, eds., *Legal Borderlands*, 267–92; Ruskola, "Colonialism Without Colonies."

20. Moore, *Report on Extraterritorial Crime and the Cutting Case*, 35.

21. Army Orders, 1868–1881, Correspondence and Papers, 1852–1883, Army orders, accounts, and miscellaneous, Edward Otho Cresap Ord Papers, 1850–1883, box 8, BANC MSS C-B 479, Bancroft Library, University of California, Berkeley. The broad context of the Ord Order is in Gregg, *Influence of Border Troubles on Relations between the United States and Mexico, 1876–1910*, 43–52.

22. Berman, "Globalization of Jurisdiction," 427.

23. Blakesley, "United States Jurisdiction over Extraterritorial Crime," 1109–11. Also see Preuss, "American Conception of Jurisdiction with Respect to Conflicts of Law on Crime"; Akehurst, "Jurisdiction in International Law."

24. Moore, *Report on Extradition*, 3.

25. In the fluid years of the early nineteenth century, American policymakers translated the word extradition from the original French language treaties with the Free Hanseatic Republics of Lubeck, Bremen, and Hamburg as referring merely to the surrender of deserters who committed crimes. "Treaties with Lubeck, Bremen, and Hamburg. Message from the President of the United States, transmitting copies of a convention between the United States and the Free Hanseatic Republics of Lubeck, Bremen, and Hamburg, ratified on the 2d of June last. January 26, 1829," 20th Cong., 2nd sess., H. Doc. 92, 10; Act of Congress, 12 August 1848, c. 167, 9 Stat. 302 (1848), cited by Shearer, *Extradition in International Law*, 12; Moore, *Treatise on Extradition and Interstate Rendition*, vol. 1, 1.

26. Moore, *Treatise on Extradition and Interstate Rendition*, vol. 1, 568 (emphasis added); Billot quoted, ibid., 8n2, 7n2.

27. On individuals, Blumenthal, "The Default Legal Person," 1135–1266, and especially Welke, *Law and the Borders of Belonging in the Long Nineteenth Century United States*. On the political and legal consequences of acceding to "prevailing juridical conceptions of corporate competence," see McCurdy, "Knight Sugar Decision of 1895 and the Modernization of American Corporation Law, 1869–1903," 304–42.

28. Bassiouni, *International Extradition*, 3.

29. Ibid., 8, 49.

30. Moore, *Treatise on Extradition and Interstate Rendition*, vol. 1, vii; Scott, *Law of Interstate Rendition, Erroneously Referred to as Interstate Extradition*, 2–4.

31. *Commonwealth v. Deacon*, 10 Sergeant and Rawle 125 (1823), quoted by Hurd, *Treatise on the Right of Personal Liberty and on the Writ of Habeas Corpus*, 579; Clarke, *Treatise upon the Law of Extradition*, 42–43. As Sir Francis Piggott, the principal British scholar of extradition at the turn of the twentieth century wrote, "extradition is a political question, the law governing it having been created by statute and treaty. There is no law in the sense of recognized legal principles applicable to the subject." Piggott, *Extradition*, 5.

32. Tim Wu argues that "while the judiciary usually defers to Executive constructions in treaty cases, judges have never granted great deference to the Executive in the construction of criminal laws." Wu, "Treaties' Domains," 629. On the treaty implementation, see 571–649, and specifically on extradition, 622–30. Interpretation of the meaning of the treaty power grant is quite varied. For example, see Cleveland, "Powers Inherent in Sovereignty: Indians, Aliens, Territories, and the Nineteenth Century Origins of Plenary Power over Foreign Affairs," 1–284, and Lawson and Seidman, *Constitution of Empire*, passim, but esp. 48–50. William S. Seward was the only secretary of state to give an order to surrender a fugitive in the absence of a treaty, in the 1864 surrender of a man named Arguelles to Spain. Seward later disavowed it. Spear, *Law of Extradition, International and Inter-State*, 13.

33. Title LXVI of the Revised Statutes of the United States, sec. 5270 (1878).

34. An example would be the extradition papers of Guiseppe Exposito, 1881, which took up hundreds of pages for a noncontroversial process, or that of José Castro Garcia, extradited from France to Puerto Rico for embezzlement of public funds on July 30, 1900, whose file notes it required "the original criminal proceedings . . . together with triplicate original warrant of arrest duly issued thereon, and the returns thereto, and triplicate copies of the said warrants, all properly certified by the said Municipal Judge, acting herein as Magistrate, and authenticated (as far as can be) in conformity with the requirements of the extradition laws of the Republic of France." "Extradition Papers: Extradition Case Files, 1836–1906," NARA, RG 59, General Records of the Department of State, boxes 12A, 55.

35. Booth, *British Extradition Law and Procedure*, vol. 1, LI.

36. However political in origins, a model system of extradition is thought to be rooted in "some level of agreement . . . [since] inherent in any such arrangement is the potential for reciprocity." Gilbert, *Aspects of Extradition Law*, 17. Gilbert was wishful when he argued that "extradition should not be viewed as an arm of foreign policy," 19.

37. On reciprocal trade agreements, Healy, *James G. Blaine and Latin America*, 160–79. Also on the overall movements, Wolman, *Most Favored Nation*, 19–153; Lake, "The State and American Trade Strategy in the Pre-Hegemonic Era," in Ikenberry, Lake, and Mastanduno, eds., *The State and American Foreign Economic Policy*, 33–58.

38. Mariscal, quoted in de la Barra, *Estudio sobre la ley Mexicana de Extradicion*, 24–25, 26; Shearer, *Extradition in International Law*, 25–26.

39. "In the matter of the resolution of inquiry touching the proceedings for the extradition of one Vincenzo [i.e., Vicenzo] Rebello, an Italian, &c. . . ." 47th Cong., 1st sess., S. Rep. 82. One of the central studies of habeas issues in nineteenth-century extradition was Hurd, *Treatise on the Right of Personal Liberty*.

40. Federman, *The Body and the State*, 5.

41. *Benson v. McMahon*, 127 U.S. 457, 462, 463 (1888). The *Benson* ruling limiting habeas corpus was intensified two years later with *In re Luis Oteize y Cortes*, 136 U.S. 330 (1890) and again in *Ornelas v. Ruiz*, 161 U.S. 502 (1896).

42. *Reports of Cases Adjudged in the District Court of South Carolina by the Hon. Thomas Bee*, 266. John Marshall's speech to the House about this case was considered so "luminous and convincing" (in Henry Cabot Lodge's words) on the issues of power and jurisdiction that it became a hallmark of assertive unilateralism for the federalist's ideological heirs as far back as the imperialist era of the late nineteenth century. Lodge, "John Marshall," in *Henry Cabot Lodge*, 40. As Ruth Wedgwood argues pointedly, "the dispute of Executive power in foreign affairs in our own century looks back without remembrance that the President is 'the sole organ of the nation in its external relations,' famous as the nostrum of *United States v. Curtiss-Wright Export Co.*, was plucked by Justice Sutherland from Congressman Marshall's defense in the Robbins affair. Executive power's critics have lethely overlooked the ambitious, even radical, character of John Marshall's claim for the Presidency." Wedgwood, "Revolutionary Martyrdom of Jonathan Robbins," 234–35. See also Cress, "The Jonathan Robbins Incident." Others argue that Sutherland deliberately used Marshall's language out of context to enhance the power of the president, whereas Marshall was speaking of "implementing national policy." Devins and Fisher, *Democratic Constitution*, 111.

43. Webster-Ashburton Treaty, *The Avalon Project*, avalon.law.yale.edu/19th_century/br-1842.asp; Gordon, *Treaty of Washington*, 174. On the context of its negotiation, see Jones, *To the Webster-Ashburton Treaty*.

44. Tyler to the Senate of the United States, 11 August 1842, in CMPP, vol. IV, 168–69.

45. Moore, *Treatise on Extradition and Interstate Rendition*, vol. 1, 170.

46. The full text of the treaty with France is in Moore, *Report on Extradition*, 24–25.

47. Hurst, *Law and the Conditions of Freedom in the Nineteenth-Century United States*, 9, 24. Also see Novak, "Law, Capitalism, and the Liberal State," 97–145.

48. As Michael Hardt and Antonio Negri write, "the imperial order is formed not only on the basis of its powers of accumulation and global extension, but also on the basis of its capacity to develop itself more deeply, to be reborn, and to extend itself throughout the biopolitical latticework of world society." The approach here is not as programmatic as their work, however. Hardt and Negri, *Empire*, 41, 164–66.

49. Kahler and Lake, "Globalization and Governance," in *Governance in a Global Economy*, 19.

50. This transformation is not unrelated to the classic "search for order" idea articulated by Wiebe, *Search for Order*, or the changes described by Polanyi, *Great Transformation*. See also Scheiber, "Federalism and Legal Process." On the corporate impact on governance, see Sklar, *Corporate Reconstruction of American Capitalism, 1890–1916*. On managerial structural innovations, see Skowronek, *Building a New American State*, and Reynolds, "Expansion and Integration: Reflections on the History of America's Approach to Globalization," in Mazlish, Chanda, and Weisbrode, eds., *The Paradox of a Global USA*, 57.

51. On these issues relating specifically to foreign relations, Schoonover, *Uncle Sam's War of 1898 and the Origins of Globalization*, and Eckes Jr. and Zeiler, *Globalization and the American Century*. On the U.S. responses to the challenges and opportunities of globalization specifically in terms of global definitions of jurisdiction and enforcement, Nadelmann, *Cops across Borders*. Extradition fit directly into an emerging policy orientation in which divergent and sometimes quite contradictory bilateral legal regimes were created for different policy objectives in a globalizing era. Paul Schiff Berman has demonstrated that the creation of these new regimes has real meaning for future development of legal spaces: "the global legal system is an interlocking web of jurisdictional assertions by state, international, and non-state normative communities. And each type of overlapping jurisdictional assertion (state versus state; state versus international body; state versus non-state entity) creates a potentially hybrid legal space that is not easily eliminated." Berman, "Global Legal Pluralism," 1159.

52. These issues frame contemporary policy toward extradition and sovereign jurisdiction in global frameworks and have shaped historical understanding as well. See William and Sheptycki, "Transnational Crime and Transnational Policing," 485–98; Slaughter, "Disaggregated Sovereignty: Towards the Public Accountability of Global Government Networks," 159–90; Slaughter, *A New World Order*; Sassen, *Territory, Authority, Rights*; Berman, "Globalization of Jurisdiction," 311–529; Banoff and Pyle, "'To Surrender Political Offenders,'" 173–74.

53. Moore, *Treatise on Extradition and Interstate Rendition*, vol. 1, 549.

54. Bassiouni, *International Extradition*, 643.

55. Kerber, "Toward a History of Statelessness in America," 735.

56. Neuman, "Anomalous Zones," 1201.

57. Ford, "Law's Territory (A History of Jurisdiction)," in *Legal Geographies Reader*, ed. Blomley, Delaney, and Ford, 202.

58. Martínez, *Troublesome Border*, 25; Gomez, *Manifest Destinies*, 139.

59. Jacoby, "Between North and South," in *Continental Crossroads*, ed. Truett and Young, 209. For a broad theoretical approach to borderlands, see Zartman, "Identity, Movement, and Response," in Zartman, ed., *Understanding Life in the Borderlands*, 1–18. On critical border disputes, see Littlefield, *Conflict on the Rio Grande*, 16–55; Larralde, *Juan N. Cortina and the Struggle for Justice in Texas*; Kraft, *Gatewood and Geronimo*. The richest array of new approaches is found in Johnson and Graybill, eds., *Bridging National Borders in North America*.

60. Mora-Torres, *Making of the Mexican Border*, 65. See Hart, *Empire and Revolution*, 500, 71–267, for the detailed process of this movement toward dominance. Also see Pletcher, *Diplomacy of Trade and Investment*, 77–113, and Irigoyen, "El Problema Económico de las Fronteras Mexicanas."

61. Novak, "Myth of the 'Weak' American State," 763–67.

62. Ibid., 767.

63. This book considers race to be of fundamental importance in all events in the region but focuses directly upon the jurisdictional questions, as so much other work has been done on the subject in the borderlands context. Gomez, *Manifest Destinies*, 8; Montejano, *Anglos and Mexicans in the Making of Texas, 1836–1986*; De León, *They Called Them Greasers*. On the rich approach to Chinese agency within the judicial and administrative management of immigration and exclusion, see Salyer, *Laws Harsh as Tigers*, especially 33–94.

64. Berman, "From International Law to Law and Globalization," 491, 533 (emphasis in original).

65. *Chae Chan Ping v. United States*, 130 U.S. 581, 605–6 (1889).

ONE. Outrage and Order

1. John W. Foster to William Evarts, 26 September 1879, FRUS 1880, 707.

2. On corridos of the borderlands and their relation to issues of power, the starting place remains Paredes, *With His Pistol in His Hand*. Miguel Ruelas, Minister of Foreign Affairs, to Foster, 29 April 1879, enclosures from the Superior Tribunal of Coahuila, FRUS 1880, 707–8, 714–17.

3. Miguel Ruelas, Minister of Foreign Affairs, to Foster, 29 April 1879, enclosures from the Superior Tribunal of Coahuila, FRUS 1880, 707–8, 714–17.

4. As John Bassett Moore phrased it, "It is true that in the case of an offense com-

mitted within the territory of one state by a person corporeally within the territory of another state, there may sometimes be concurrent jurisdiction." However, "the principle that a man who outside of a country willfully puts in motion a force to take effect in it is answerable at the place where the evil is done, is recognized in the criminal jurisprudence of all countries." Moore, *Report on Extraterritorial Crime and the Cutting Case*, 22.

5. Articulo VI, *Tratado de extradicion entre los Estados-Unidos Mexicanos y Los Estados-Unidos de America*.

6. Transcript in FRUS 1880, 716–18; Foster to Evarts, 26 September 1879, 707.

7. Translation of Article 186 enclosed with Foster to Evarts, 18 December 1879, FRUS 1880, 719.

8. Foster to Evarts, 26 September 1879, 707.

9. Foster to Evarts, 18 December 1879, FRUS 1880, 714.

10. Evarts to Foster, 23 January 1880, FRUS 1880, 729–30.

11. "Report and Accompanying Documents of the Committee on Foreign Affairs on the Relations of the United States with Mexico," 45th Cong., 2nd sess., April 25, 1878, H. Rep. 701; Evarts to Foster, 13 August 1878, quoted in Hershey, "Incursions into Mexico and the Doctrine of Hot Pursuit," 561. The overall diplomatic record of these events is covered in Gregg, *Influence of Border Troubles on Relations between the United States and Mexico, 1876–1910*, especially 11–80; also Thompson, *Cortina: Defending the Mexican Name in Texas*, 200–218; Hatfield, *Chasing Shadows*, 11–54.

12. 45th Cong., 2nd sess., H. Rep. 701, iii.

13. Ibid., xxv.

14. Ibid., i.

15. Ibid., i, iii.

16. Ibid., xxiv–xxv.

17. Ibid., xxvi.

18. Ibid., xxvi (emphasis added).

19. Ibid., ii.

20. *Lone Star* (El Paso, Texas), November 25, 1881; #64, 21 December 1886, NARA, RG 59, Despatches from United States Consuls in Ciudad Juárez (Paso del Norte), 1850–1906 (hereafter Consular Despatches–Ciudad Juárez), roll 3.

21. Adams Jr., *Bordering the Future*, 43; Timmons, *El Paso*, 187, 204–6; Martínez, *Border Boom Town*, 19–22.

22. "Law, Race, and the Border," 948; also phrased a bit differently in Romero, "El Paso Salt War," 119.

23. Gómez, *Most Singular Country*, 99.

24. Adams Jr., *Bordering the Future*, 43.

25. Ortíz-González, *El Paso*, xxxi.

26. Romero, "El Paso Salt War," 136.

27. Neal, *Getting Away with Murder on the Texas Frontier*, 11.

28. "Law, Race, and the Border," 942–47, 961–63. According to Gordon, "Critical Legal Histories," 101, "one approach to this idea of consciousness is legal forms as ideologies and rituals whose 'effects'—effects that include people's ways of sorting out social experience, giving it meaning, grading it as natural, just, and necessary or as contrived, unjust and subject to alteration—are in the realm of consciousness."

29. Matsuda, "Law and Culture in the District Court of Honolulu, 1844–1845," 39–40.

30. On the treatment of Mexicans in the El Paso legal system and complaints of the Mexican consuls, including concerning deserters who were extradited with unusual vigor, Garcia, "Porfirian Diplomacy and the Administration of Justice in Texas, 1877–1900," 14–17. Escobar y Armendariz, quoted on 17.

31. All people arrested in El Paso County were listed in the jail register during the 1880s. There were six hundred and seventy-nine prisoners arrested between 1884 and 1886 (the years for which records exist), which constituted a significant percentage of the total population of the city at the time, though these figures included at least one hundred and nineteen Mexicans. Mexican women were usually separately noted, as were "half breed Mexicans." Also arrested were seven Chinese, five Germans, seven Irish, four French, and one Swede as well as a wide array of deserters and criminals from all over Texas and the rest of the United States. A noticeable percentage of people were arrested for the offense of being "insane," and most were sent to the state asylum by the order of the county judge. Fee book, Register of Prisoners, Foreign Docket, Execution Docket, El Paso County, El Paso County Records, MS 132, C. L. Sonnichsen Special Collections Department, University of Texas at El Paso.

32. Though it would seem logical for Mexican prisoners to escape across the river, in fact there did not seem to be any connections between escape and the prisoners' origins. Andy O'Brian from Ireland, arrested for assault and attempted murder on December 9, 1881, escaped, as did James Jackson from Kentucky, who was in for forgery on January 4, 1882. Fee book, Register of Prisoners, 81–82.

33. McKanna Jr., *Homicide, Race, and Justice in the American West, 1880–1920*, 4–5. On legality and criminality in west Texas and Oklahoma in this regard, see Neal, *Getting Away with Murder on the Texas Frontier*. The understanding of struggle over jurisdiction, territoriality, and extralegal forms in this era should be viewed in the same way that Altina Waller has shown the legendary Hatfield-McCoy Kentucky feuds to be complex political, economic, and partisan struggles rooted in post–Civil War capitalist development rather than ancient family battles rooted in endemic regional pathologies. Waller, *Feud*.

34. Timmons, *El Paso*, 195. Romero, "El Paso Salt War," 122–23, has good coverage of the vastly differing historiographical interpretations of the Salt War. "Law, Race, and the Border," 943, 955–56; "El Paso Troubles in Texas," 45th Cong., 2nd sess., H. Ex. Doc. 93, 2–3; Cool, *Salt Warriors*, 3.

35. #16, 21 October 1877, NARA, Consular Despatches–Ciudad Juárez, roll 2.

36. Ibid. Also #19, 6 March 1878.

37. The full series of events is covered by the War Department investigating board in "El Paso Troubles in Texas," 45th Cong., 2nd sess., H. Ex. Doc. 93, 3–19.

38. "El Paso Troubles in Texas," 45th Cong., 2nd sess., H. Ex. Doc. 93, 16–17.

39. Ibid. The full minority report is on 20–31.

40. #19, 6 March 1878, NARA, Consular Despatches–Ciudad Juárez, roll 2. For follow-up on the Salt War extradition issue, see #21, 3 December 1878, and #29, 19 January 1880.

41. Cool, *Salt Warriors*, 2. The post-1877 conflicts are covered on 258–73.

42. Ibid.

43. "El Paso Troubles in Texas," 45th Cong., 2nd sess., H. Ex. Doc. 93, 18.

44. #19, 6 March 1878, NARA, Consular Despatches–Ciudad Juárez, roll 2.

45. "El Paso Troubles in Texas," 45th Cong., 2nd sess., H. Ex. Doc. 93, 18 (emphasis in original).

46. Warner P. Sutton, "Report of an Inspection of the Rio Grande Consulates," 11–14, enclosed in #57, 24 December 1879, NARA, RG 59, Despatches from United States Consuls in Matamoros, 1826–1906 (hereafter NARA, Consular Despatches–Matamoros), roll 6.

47. Ibid.

48. Ibid., 76–77.

49. Ibid., 77–78.

50. Ibid., 79–96.

51. Ibid.

52. Uglow, *Standing in the Gap*, 11.

53. Descriptive chronology of events and some documents are in "Lists of Letters Sent and Received and Extracts of Letters Relating to the Jurisdiction of the United States over Certain Military Installations, 1883–1891," NARA, RG 393, Records of U.S. Army Continental Commands, 1821–1920; Department of Texas, 1870–1893, entry 4876.

54. "General Orders and Circulars, 1883–1886," NARA, RG 94, General Orders and Circulars; Special Orders, Department of Texas, 1873, entry 44, vol. 540.

55. Ibid.; *United States v. Cornell*, 2 Mason 60 (1819).

56. Wooster, "Fort Davis and the Close of a Military Frontier," 177, 180. Wooster expands exploration of Fort Davis as a tool and catalyst of empire in *Frontier Crossroads*. On the political economic context, see Robbins, *Colony and Empire*, 22–38.

57. Wooster, "Frontier Army and the Occupation of the American West, 1865–1900," in United States, *Army Training and Doctrine Command*, 72–73; Smith, *U.S. Army and the Texas Frontier Economy, 1845–1900*, 179–80; Miller, *Soldiers and Settlers*. Dobak emphasizes army expenditures in local communities as the engines of development, *Fort Riley and Its Neighbors*, 44.

58. Williams, "United States Indian Policy and the Debate over Philippine Annexation," 810–31.

59. *Fort Leavenworth R. R. v. Lowe*, 114 U.S. 525 (1885), 525, 540–42.

60. Ibid., 526–28.

61. "With great respect to the Courts and to State authorities, it is not thought that the government should yield possession pending litigation. . . . [T]he Government cannot submit to be ousted of its possession of property by state authority until its rights have been adversely determined by a court of competent jurisdiction." "Memorandum relating to Cemetery property at Fort Bliss, taken from papers on file in the office of the United States District Attorney" and L. A. Grant to J. S. Hogg, 4 March 1892; "Lists of Letters Sent and received and extracts of Letters Relating to the Jurisdiction of the United States over certain Military Installations, 1883–1891," NARA, RG 393, Department of Texas, 1870–1893, entry 4876.

62. Uglow, *Standing in the Gap*, 18.

63. Brigham, "Growing Importance of Paso del Norte," 281; #64, 21 December 1886, NARA, Consular Despatches–Ciudad Juárez, roll 3. On railroad development, see Hart, *Empire and Revolution*, 106–30, 136; Martínez, *Border Boom Town*, 22.

64. Brigham, "Growing Importance of Paso del Norte," 283.

65. Martínez, *Border Boom Town*, 22. For the establishment of the *Zona Libre*, Pérez, *La Zona Libre*, 16–25, 121–29, 163–328; Romero, *Mexico and the United States*, 434–37. On the counterbalancing intent of the *Zona Libre*, see Riguzzi, "Las Relaciones de Mexico con Estados Unidos, 1878–1888," 299–321; #1, Fitzpatrick to Cass, 5 January 1859, NARA, Consular Despatches–Matamoros, roll 3. On Mexican tariff laws of the era overall, see Sutton's translation, "Tariff Laws of Mexico: Report on the Tariff Laws and Rates of Duty of Mexico, in Force March 1, 1882," enclosed with #234, 22 March 1882, NARA, Consular Despatches–Matamoros, roll 7. On overall early U.S. diplomacy and attitudes toward the *Zona Libre*, see Bell and Smallwood, *Zona Libre, 1858–1905*, 1–21.

66. The announcement of the *Zona Libre* was included with #6, Peter Seuzeneau to Lewis Cass, 21 March 1858; also #7, 4 April 1858; #11, William G. Jones, Consular Agent, Miers, to Cass, 6 September 1858, NARA, Consular Despatches–Matamoros, roll 3.

67. "Treaty with Mexico," 45th Cong., 3d sess., February 13, 1879, H. Rep. 108, 1.

68. #113, Wilson to Hunter, 1 August 1872, NARA, Consular Despatches–Matamoros, roll 4; "Report on the *Zona Libre* and Bonded Routes," enclosed with #67, 10 January 1880, NARA, Consular Despatches–Matamoros, roll 6. Romero, *Mexico and the United States*, 439.

69. #50, John Weber, Consul, to William Hunter, 10 August 1879, NARA, RG 59, Despatches from United States Consuls in Monterrey, Mexico, 1849–1906, roll 3; Foster to Evarts, 26 December 1879, FRUS 1880, 725.

70. Telegram, 4 April 1884, and #150, Sutton to Hunter, 8 April 1884, NARA, Consular Despatches–Matamoros, roll 8. Development of the *Zona Libre* up to this point

was considered in the *Galveston Daily News*, 21 December 1884. For the full text of the act extending the *Zona Libre* (called "A Law Regulating the Traffic and the Clearance at the Custom-Houses, of Goods Transported by the International Railways of the Mexican Republic"), see "Message from the President of the United States Transmitting, In response to Senate Resolution of May 2, 1884, report of the Secretary of State relative to the latest law of the Mexican Republic creating or modifying the *Zona Libre*," 48th Cong., 1st sess., June 13, 1884, S. Ex. Doc. 185, 2–5. For a map of the state of Chihuahua under the *Zona Libre* that clearly shows the zone's convoluted geographic structure, see Pérez, *La Zona Libre*, 158.

71. #13, Brigham to John Davis, 30 March 1884, NARA, Consular Despatches–Ciudad Juárez, roll 2.

72. "Trade and Industries of Northern Mexico, Report by Consul General Sutton of Matamoros," enclosed with #220, 30 September 1884, NARA, Consular Despatches–Matamoros, roll 8; *Lone Star*, 12 April 1884. It is worth noting that outside the narrow border strip, the news of the expansion of the *Zona Libre* was treated with much less excitement, for example, #661, Alexander Willard to William Hunter, 1 December 1884, NARA, RG 59, Despatches from United States Consuls in Guaymas, 1832–1896, roll 3.

73. Bell and Smallwood, *Zona Libre*, 42–43.

74. Memorial enclosed with Coke and Lanham to Frelinghuysen, 17 April 1884, in "A letter of the Secretary of State in Response to Senate Resolution of February 16, 1888, relative to the Mexican *Zona Libre*," 50th Cong., 1st sess., March 27, 1888, S. Ex. Doc. 130, 3–4.

75. Ibid.

76. Ibid.

77. *Lone Star*, June 4, 1884.

78. Responding to Morehead's criticisms and pamphlet, see Romero, *Mexico and the United States*, 443; Morehead to Lanham, 24 April 1884, 50th Cong., 1st sess., March 27, 1888, S. Ex. Doc. 130, 9. Sometimes his name was spelled Moorehead in the documents or the newspapers. It is standardized here.

79. *Lone Star*, April 11, 1885.

80. Quoted in ibid.

81. *Galveston Daily News*, December 13, 1885.

82. *Lone Star*, April 11, 1885; Morehead to Lanham, 24 April 1884, 50th Cong., 1st sess., March 27, 1888, S. Ex. Doc. 130, 9.

83. Salvucci, "Origins and Progress of U.S.-Mexican Trade, 1825–1884," 698.

84. Beatty, "Impact of Foreign Trade on the Mexican Economy," 406–8.

85. Salvucci, "Origins and Progress of U.S.-Mexican Trade, 1825–1884," 698.

86. 49th Cong., 1st sess., 1886, CR XVII (Senate), 697.

87. "Trade and transportation between the United States and Latin America, by William Eleroy Curtis, Executive Officer, International American Conference," 51st Cong., 1st sess., S. Ex. Doc. 54, 31.

88. Pletcher, "Consul Warner P. Sutton and American-Mexican Border Trade during the Early Díaz Period," 382.

89. #23, 5 October 1880, "Return of Trade with the United States," NARA, Despatches from United States Consuls in Nuevo Laredo, 1871–1906, roll 1.

90. "Report on the *Zona Libre* and Bonded Routes," enclosed in #67, 10 January 1880, NARA, Consular Despatches–Matamoros, roll 6.

91. "Report by Consul Sutton on the commerce and industries of the Consular District of Matamoros, for the year ending September 30, 1881," enclosed in #210, 22 December 1881, NARA, Consular Despatches–Matamoros, roll 7.

92. "Report on the *Zona Libre* and Bonded Routes," enclosed in #67, 10 January 1880, NARA, Consular Despatches–Matamoros, roll 6.

93. Ibid.

94. Ibid.

95. "Report by Consul Sutton on the commerce and industries of the Consular District of Matamoros, for the year ending September 30, 1881," enclosed in #210, 22 December 1881, NARA, Consular Despatches–Matamoros, roll 7. Emphasis added to both quotes.

96. 51st Cong., 1st sess., S. Ex. Doc. 54, 31.

97. Ibid.

98. #157, Sutton to Wharton, 28 February 1881; #224, Sutton to Wharton, 27 January 1882, NARA, Consular Despatches–Matamoros, roll 7.

99. #236, Sutton to Wharton, 28 March 1882; #258, Sutton to Wharton, 24 June 1882, ibid.

100. #258, Sutton to Wharton, 24 June 1882, ibid.

101. Ibid.

102. Telegram, 4 April 1884; #180, 24 May 1884, ibid., roll 8.

103. #180, 24 May 1884, ibid.

104. #180, Sutton to William Hunter, 24 May 1888, report titled "The *Zona Libre* at Paso del Norte," ibid. The pages of this report are unnumbered.

105. Ibid.

106. Cameron and Palan, *Imagined Economies of Globalization*, 8.

107. #180, Sutton to Hunter, 24 May 1888, "The *Zona Libre* at Paso del Norte," NARA, Consular Despatches–Matamoros, roll 8.

108. Ibid.

109. Ibid.

110. Ibid.

111. Ibid.

112. Ibid.

113. Pletcher, *Diplomacy of Trade and Investment*, 113; Salvucci, "Origins and Pro-

gress of U.S.-Mexican Trade, 1825–1884," 721–22. On the reciprocity relations broadly see Riguzzi, *Reciprocidad Imposible?*, 26–128.

114. Romero, *Mexico and the United States*, 431; Salvucci, "Origins and Progress of U.S.-Mexican Trade, 1825–1884," 725–26.

115. The official Mexican case in support of reciprocity, with related documents, is printed in *Reciprocidad comercial entre México y los Estados Unidos*.

116. Chester Arthur, third annual message, CMPP, vol. XI, 4759.

117. W. Jett Lauck emphasizes political expediency, territorial expansionism, and global politics as motivating forces for American reciprocity negotiations in "Political Significance of Reciprocity," 495–524; *Report of the Secretary of Finance of the United States of Mexico on the 15th of January, 1879 on the Actual Condition of Mexico, and the Increase of Commerce with the United States*, 1.

118. Lauck, "Political Significance of Reciprocity," 495. The logic is detailed in Wharton, ed., *Digest of International Law of the United States*, vol. 2, 39–41; *Report of the Secretary of Finance of the United States of Mexico on the 15th of January, 1879*, 169.

119. *Report of the Secretary of Finance of the United States of Mexico on the 15th of January, 1879*, 172, 175.

120. Romero, *Mexico and the United States*, 658.

121. Ibid.

122. Pletcher covers the failure of the treaty well in *Diplomacy of Trade and Investment*, 110–12.

123. Evoking the emphasis on "the limits of hegemony" applied with a different emphasis in Schell Jr., "American Investment in Tropical Mexico," 218.

124. Romero, *Mexico and the United States*, 440.

125. *San Francisco Daily Evening Bulletin*, May 30, 1881.

126. Romero to Bayard, 4 January 1886, 50th Cong., 1st sess., S. Ex. Doc. 130, 9–25.

127. Romero, *Mexico and the United States*, 443–44, 452.

128. Ibid., 449.

129. *El Paso Daily Times*, May 29; June 22, 30, 1886.

130. León, *They Called Them Greasers*, 89–93.

131. Palacios, *La Prision del Americano A. K. Cutting en Paso Del Norte*, 7; Moore, *Report on Extraterritorial Crime and the Cutting Case*, 3–4.

132. Moore, *Report on Extraterritorial Crime and the Cutting Case*, 4. Cutting's card was enclosed with #45, Brigham to James D. Porter, 1 July 1886, NARA, Consular Despatches–Ciudad Juárez, roll 3.

133. #45, Brigham to James D. Porter, 1 July 1886, NARA, Consular Despatches–Ciudad Juárez, roll 3.

134. Enclosure from the court, included in #46, Brigham to Porter, 3 July 1886, NARA, Consular Despatches–Ciudad Juárez, roll 3.

135. *El Paso Daily Times*, August 20, 1886.

136. Blakesley, "Jurisdictional Issues and Conflicts of Jurisdictions," in Bassiouni, ed., *Legal Responses to International Terrorism*, 174.

137. *El Paso Daily Times*, June 24, 1886. The next month the paper covered "Another Outrage" when an American was killed in Tres Jacales, *El Paso Daily Times*, July 17, 1886. Long quote is from August 19, 1886.

138. *El Paso Daily Times*, August 10, 17, 1886.

139. Secretaría de Relaciones Exteriores, *Case of the American, A. K. Cutting* and *Correspondencia diplomática sobre el caso del ciudando de los Estados-Unidos de America A. K. Cutting*.

140. Romero to Bayard, 7 August 1886, *Correspondencia diplomática cambiada entre gobierno de los Estados Unidos Mexicanos y los de varias potencias extranjeras desde el 30 de Junio de 1881 a 30 de Junio de 1886*, 1112–13; Ignacio Mariscal to Jackson, 21 July 1886, *Correspondencia diplomática sobre el caso del ciudando de los Estados-Unidos de America A. K. Cutting*, 8.

141. Bayard to Jackson, 20 July 1886, "Imprisonment of A. K. Cutting in Mexico," 49th Cong., 1st sess., H. Ex. Doc. 371, 13.

142. Ibid.

143. Ibid.; Romero to Bayard, 7 August 1886, *Correspondencia diplomática cambiada entre gobierno de los Estados Unidos Mexicanos y los de varias potencias extranjeras desde el 30 de Junio de 1881 a 30 de Junio de 1886*, tomo III, 1113.

144. *The Independent*, September 2, 1886, 17.

145. *El Paso Daily Times*, July, 21, 22, 1886; *New York Times*, July 24, 1886.

146. *Galveston Daily News*, August 4, 1886.

147. Quoted in Moore, *Report on Extraterritorial Crime*, 7.

148. *El Paso Daily Times*, August 25, 1886.

149. Raustiala, "Geography of Justice," University of California, Los Angeles School of Law Public Law & Legal Theory Research Paper Series Research Paper No. 05-7 available at ssrn.com/abstract=693924. The Cutting case is not discussed in the classic W. W. Mills, *Forty Years at El Paso, 1858–1898* or in Timmons, *El Paso*. The only recent work that considers it focuses on José Mart Martí's view of the case. See Sarracino, *José Mart Martí y el Caso Cutting*, 1–120. For Martí's own writings on the case, see "Cutting case," Martí, *Selected Writings*, 176–82. The Cutting case is discussed in the standard international law texts from around the time, such as Snow, *Cases and Opinions on International Law with Notes and a Syllabus*, 172–74; Taylor, *Treatise of International Public Law*, 241–42; Stowell and Munro, *International Cases*, 386–89.

150. Davis, *Elements of International Law*, 172.

151. Moore, *Report on Extraterritorial Crime and the Cutting Case*, 22.

152. Ibid.

153. Taylor, *Treatise of International Public Law*, 242.

154. Moore, *Report on Extraterritorial Crime and the Cutting Case*, 124.

155. Ibid., 124.

156. Ibid., 125.

157. "Message from the President of the United States, transmitting in Response to Senate resolution of July 26, 1886, report of the Secretary of State relative to the A. K. Cutting case," 49th Cong., 1st sess., S. Ex. Doc. 224, 3.

TWO. Jurisdiction, Sovereignty, and Space

1. John Sherman to Romero, 22 September 1897, "Notes to Mexican Embassy, Wash. from State Department, 1849–1906," NARA, RG 76, Records of Boundary and Claims Commissions and Arbitrations, International Boundaries U.S.-Mexico Border (hereafter NARA, RG 76, Records of Boundary and Claims), entry 486, envelope 32, box 51.

2. John J. Gosper to S. J. Kirkwood, 30 June 1881, envelope no. 29. Typewritten copies of miscellaneous letters to the Department of State, 1849–1911, 1802, 1819, 1836, box 50; #826, P. H. Morgan to Frelinghuysen, 7 June 1884, "Dispatches from American Embassy, Mexico City to State Department, 1856–1906," envelope 32, box 52; Cleveland speech to the Senate, 4 February 1886, envelope 29, box 50; Blaine to Phillip H. Morgan, 18 July 1881 (enclosing Kirkwood to Blaine 9, 14 July 1881), "Typewritten copies of, Instructions from the State Department to the American Embassy, Mexico City," envelope 35, box 531. All from NARA, RG 76, Records of Boundary and Claims, entry 486.

3. Arthur, Message to the Senate and House of Representatives, 1 December 1884. Message concerning the boundary between the United States and Mexico, *State Papers, Etc., Etc., Etc., of Chester A. Arthur, President of the United States*, 303, 89.

4. #34, Delos H. Smith to William F. Wharton, 25 April 1890, NARA, RG 59, Despatches from United States Consuls in Nogales, 1889–1906 (hereafter NARA, RG 59, Despatches–Nogales), roll 1.

5. The fact that it was a uniquely Mexican beverage with cultural resonance might have also intensified the fear of it. Mitchell, *Intoxicated Identities*, 93–94.

6. *Commercial Relations of the United States with Foreign Countries during the Years 1894 and 1895*, vol. 1, 336; #81, Delos H. Smith to William Wharton, 17 February 1891, NARA, RG 59, Despatches–Nogales. This was the period when tequila first began to spread across the country, and "in 1893, 'Mezcal brandy' won an award at the Columbian Exposition in Chicago," Blocker, Fahey, and Tyrrell, eds., *Alcohol and Temperance in Modern History*, 618.

7. Lowell H. Jerome to Daniel Manning [secretary of the treasury], 17 February 1887, "Letters Received, Special Agents (Letters Received from Special Agents of the Treasury, 1858–95)," NARA, RG 206, PI-171, entry 36, box 82.

8. "Annual report for year Ending September 30, 1878 Consular District of Guaymas, Mexico," 16, NARA, RG 59, Despatches–Guaymas, roll 2; #70, Delos H. Smith to

Wharton, 9 December 1890. Also #5, Smith to Thos. Ryan, 1 October 1890, NARA, RG 59, Despatches–Nogales, roll 1.

9. Cridler [?] to Delos H. Smith, 23 December 1890. The following are all Smith to Wharton: #73, 15 January 1891; #84, 14 March 1891; #94, 13 May 1891; #95, 4 June 1891; #1024, Willard to Wharton, 1 January 1891; Mexican Republic Fiscal Guards telegram (enclosure), NARA, RG 59, Despatches–Guaymas, roll 5; #38, J. F. Darnall to David J. Hill, 12 May 1899, NARA, RG 59, Despatches–Nogales, roll 3; Gresham to Grey, 17 January 1894; Gresham to Romero, 17 January 1894; Romero to Gresham, FRUS 1894, 415–16.

10. #17, Edwin F. Uhl to Romero, 3, 13 May 3, 1895, dealing with seizure of cattle and compensation for them and whether the cattle were seized on U.S. or Mexican soil in 1891. The cattle were owned by J. Nepomuceno Ornelas and had been an issue of correspondence for years. Ornelas and the Mexican government wanted a payment of $8,362; W. W. Rockhill to Romero, 29 March 1897; Sherman to Romero, 10 September 1897; #287, John Sherman to Romero, 22 September 1897 (re. horses that wandered over the line and were impounded by customs but then clandestinely driven back into Mexico by owner were left alone, issue left to slide); "Domestic Letters from State Department," NARA, RG 76, Records of Boundary and Claims, entry 486, envelope 31, no. 2; Evarts to Carl Schurz, Secretary of the Interior, 10 December 1878; Zamacona to Blaine, 13 April 1881, "Letters Received Relating to Disturbances Along Mexican Border, December 13, 1878–January 25, 1884 and Miscellaneous Subjects, February 14, 1868–January 24, 1888," NARA, RG 48, Records of the Office of the Secretary of the Interior, United States Department of the Interior, Territorial Papers, Arizona, 1868–1913 (hereafter NARA, Territorial Papers, Arizona, 1868–1913), folder 1878–1881, roll 3.

11. "Consular Report for the District of Guaymas, México"; J. C. Fremont to Evart, 6 January 1879; Joseph Boyer to Gosper, 17 September 1881, NARA, RG 59, Despatches–Guaymas, roll 5.

12. Moore had many other cases in Texas not cited here. R. U. Moore to Kenneth Rayner, 3 July 1880; Moore to Chas. J. Folger, 30 January 1882, "Letters Received, Special Agents (Letters Received from Special Agents of the Treasury, 1858–95)," NARA, RG 206, PI-171, entry 36, box 82.

13. Eugene H. Hathaway to Kirkwood, 30 August 1881, ibid.

14. A story recently well synthesized and contextualized by Benton-Cohen, Borderline Americans, 50–63. She wrote, "'Cowboy' and 'Lawman' often translated into 'Democrat' and 'Republican' in southern Arizona, but not always," 55.

15. Gospers to S. J. Kirkwood, 8 December 1881, NARA, Territorial Papers, Arizona, 1868–1913, roll 3.

16. Report of the Acting Governor of Arizona made to the Secretary of the Interior for the Year 1881, ibid.

17. Tate, Frontier Army in the Settlement of the West, 96–97; Gosper to Kirkwood, 5 May 1881; Arthur's proclamation about the use of military force, 3 May 1882, NARA,

RG 48, Territorial Papers, Arizona, 1868–1913, roll 3; CMPP vol. VIII, 101–2; Zagaris and Peralta, "Mexico–United States Extradition and Alternatives," 525; Calhoun, *Lawmen*, 196. On the *Posse Comitatus* doctrine and its relationship to the large, new expanded use of state power, see Rao, "Federal Posse Comitatus Doctrine," 46–56.

18. Blaine to S. J. Kirkwood, 15 November 1881; Gosper to S. J. Kirkwood, 8 December 1881; J. W. Evans, U.S. Marshall for Arizona Territory from 12 October 1881, to Luis E. Torres, Gov. of Sonora, NARA RG 48, Territorial Papers, Arizona, 1868–1913, roll 3.

19. See Hatfield, *Chasing Shadows*, 47, 40–54, for the broader story involved with the series of reciprocal crossing agreements. On hot pursuit, see Hershey, "Incursions into Mexico and the Doctrine of Hot Pursuit," 557–69, and E. D. D., "The 'Hot Trail' into Mexico and Extradition Analogies," 536–37.

20. Frelinghuysen and Mexican Minister Romero exchange, forwarded to Interior Department on 20 July 1882, NARA, Territorial Papers, Arizona, 1868–1913, roll 3.

21. Gov. Tritle to Interior Secretary H. M. Teller, 10 March 1884; Frelinghuysen to Teller, 28 March 1884, asserting that Daniels had support of Mexican government via "Mexican judicial authorities," ibid.

22. *Journals of the Thirteenth Legislative Assembly of the Territory of Arizona*, 125.

23. #875, Willard to Rives, 12 June 1888; #877, Willard to Rives, 20 June 1888, NARA, RG 59, Despatches from United States Consuls in Guaymas, 1832–1896, roll 4.

24. "Chinese immigration. March 2, 1891," 51st Cong., 2nd sess., H. Rep. 4048, II; *El Paso Daily Times*, August 18, 1886.

25. Lee, *At America's Gates*, 10, 179. Though she concentrates most on the twentieth century, Lee has an excellent section on border-crossing, 151–87; Truett, *Fugitive Landscapes*, 120. On the Chinese in the West, see Dirlik, ed., *Chinese on the American Frontier*.

26. Neuman, *Strangers to the Constitution*, 19–112.

27. *Chae Chan Ping v. United States*, 130 U.S. 581, 603–4 (1889) (emphasis added). On the contextual meaning of this case, see the essential Cleveland, "Powers Inherent in Sovereignty," 1–284. Chin, "Chae Chan Ping and Fong Yue Ting: The Origins of Plenary Power," in Martin and Schuck, eds., *Immigration Stories*, 7–29.

28. *Chae Chan Ping v. United States*, 606.

29. Aleinikoff, *Semblances of Sovereignty*, 16–23, 6 (emphasis in original).

30. #15, Delos H. Smith to William F. Wharton, 28 January 1890; #19, 8 February 1890, NARA, RG 59, Despatches–Nogales, roll 1.

31. The finest and most thorough account of federal attempts at interdiction during this time is Ettinger, *Imaginary Lines*, particularly 55–66, in dealing with Chinese on the Mexican border.

32. #977, Willard to Wharton, 18 April 1890; #983, 8 May 1890, NARA, RG 59, Despatches–Nogales, roll 5. On the demographics and economic roles of the Chinese in Mexico at this time and a bit later, after the large change resulting from the 1899

Mexican-Chinese treaty, see Hu-DeHart, "Latin America in Asia-Pacific Perspective," 262–70. This important book expands and complicates the notion of territorial national development and state and regional formation by applying the Asian rim idea, as does Dirlik, "Asia-Pacific in Asian–American Perspective," 283–308.

33. #130, Sutton to Wharton, 14 June 1890, NARA, RG 59, Despatches from United States Consuls in Nuevo Laredo, 1871–1906 (hereafter NARA, RG 59, Despatches–Nuevo Laredo), roll 2.

34. Lee cites six thousand Chinese crossing from Mexico between 1882 and 1910. Lee, *At America's Gates*, 158; "Chinese immigration. March 2, 1891," 51st Cong., 2nd sess., H. Rep. 4048, II, 329.

35. #93, Joseph G. Donnelly to Uhl, 6 December 1895, NARA, RG 59, Despatches–Nuevo Laredo, roll 3; #46, Charles W. Kindrick to David J. Hill, 28 December 1896, NARA, RG 59, Despatches from United States Consuls in Ciudad Juárez (Paso del Norte), 1850–1906 (hereafter NARA, RG 59, Despatches–Ciudad Juárez), roll 5.

36. *Reports of the Industrial Commission on Immigration*, vol. XV, 406–7.

37. Ibid., 133.

38. Ibid., 797–98.

39. For an overview of surveillance in Chinese exclusion, see Parenti, *Soft Cage*, 61–76, and more exactingly, Torpey, *Invention of the Passport*, 96–102.

40. *Reports of the Industrial Commission on Immigration*, vol. XV, 798.

41. #131, Sutton to Wharton, 14 June 1890; #351, Sutton to Wharton, 7 December 1891, NARA, RG 59, Despatches–Nuevo Laredo, roll 2; #994, Willard to Wharton, 21 June 1890; #983, 8 May 1890, NARA, RG 59, Despatches–Nogales, roll 5.

42. "In the midst of conditions favoring smuggling across the southern border in 1890, only a skeletal force of Chinese inspectors patrolled the vast space." Ettinger, *Imaginary Lines*, 61. The Arizona political climate was less hostile than that of California. Among other essays in this collection, see Fong, "Sojourners and Settlers," 39–54.

43. "Chinese immigration. March 2, 1891," 51st Cong., 2nd sess., H. Rep. 4048, 409.

44. Rosenberger, "Free Zone," 622.

45. "Chinese immigration. March 2, 1891," 51st Cong., 2nd sess., H. Rep. 4048, 328–29.

46. #939, Willard to Wharton, 18 September 1889, NARA, RG 59, Despatches–Nogales, roll 1.

47. #110, Stone to Wharton, 11 February 1892, and several enclosures, NARA, RG 59, Despatches–Nogales, roll 1.

48. Ibid.

49. On Chinese businesses in Sonoras, see Hu-DeHart, "Latin America in Asia-Pacific Perspective," 269.

50. J. F. Darnall to J. B. Moore, 12 May; 31 October 1898, NARA, RG 59, Despatches–Nogales, roll 3.

51. Korea, another nation with which the United States maintained extraterritorial relations, made one request, in February 1886. Denby letter printed in Moore, *Report on Extradition*, 85; "List of requisitions by foreign governments upon the Government of the United States," Moore, *Report on Extradition*, 195.

52. #18, George to Quincy, 4 December 1893, NARA, RG 59, Despatches–Nogales, roll 2; #13, Long to W. W. Rockhill, 10 November 1896, NARA, RG 59, Despatches–Nogales, roll 3.

53. #13, Long to W. W. Rockhill, 10 November 1896, and enclosures; Reuben D. George to Manuel Moscareñas [Mexican consul in Nogales, Arizona], 6 March 1894, NARA, RG 59, Despatches–Nogales, roll 3.

54. #18, George to Quincy, 4 December 1893, NARA, RG 59, Despatches–Nogales, roll 2.

55. Romero to Gresham, 6 September 1893, FRUS 1893, 439–41.

56. Gresham to Romero, 12 October 1893, "Notes to Mexican Embassy, Wash. From State Department, 1849–1906," NARA, RG 76, Records of Boundary and Claims, entry 486, envelope 31, box 51.

57. Olney to Covarrubias, 9 June 1896, affidavit of Deputy Sheriff Roberts; Covarrubias to Olney, 15 July 1896; Covarrubias to Olney, 15 July 1896, FRUS 1893, 444–45.

58. #13, Long to W. W. Rockhill, 10 November 1896, NARA, RG 59, Despatches–Nogales, roll 3. Contrast the archival report and enclosures to the report printed in FRUS 1896, 448–53.

59. #13, Long to W. W. Rockhill, 10 November 1896, NARA, RG 59, Despatches–Nogales, roll 3; Romero to Olney, 25 January 1897, FRUS 1896, 454.

60. Telegram and #32, Darnell to J. B. Moore, 8 November 1898, NARA, RG 59, Despatches–Nogales, roll 3.

61. Darnall to David J. Hill, 9 November 1898; telegram enclosure, Ramon Corral to Darnall, NARA, RG 59, Despatches–Nogales, roll 3.

62. "Caso de Extradición de James Temple," vol. VII, 195–96; vol. VIII, 15.

63. Another odd example was the fist fight between an American and a Mexican after a baseball game in the border town of Naco in October 1899 that led to shootings and the deployment of troops on both sides of the border. #51, J. F. Darnall to David J. Hall, 30 October 1899; Jas. Welsch [deputy collector of customs at Bisbee, Arizona] to Darnall, 27 October 1899, NARA, RG 59, Despatches–Nogales, roll 3; #59, John Hay to Don Manuel de Azpiroz, 5 December 1899, "Notes to Mexican Embassy, Wash. from State Department, 1849–1906," NARA, RG 76, Records of Boundary and Claims, entry 486, envelope 31, box 51.

64. Werne, *Imaginary Line*, 152, 223–24. Dating back to the surveying done under the treaty of 1848, the real problems always seemed to be on the U.S. side for the surveyors: "the American Section appeared to be rent by personal jealousies and, more especially, by a clear-cut difference of opinion between the commissioner and the surveyor in

regard to the initial point on the Rio Grande above El Paso." Timm, *International Boundary Commission United States and Mexico*, 23.

65. The treaty also "described the boundary as it would run from east to west" and actually "began offshore" even though "at the time of the treaty, as now, the offshore waters or marginal sea were considered to be part of the national territory of a coastal nation." This has been a disputed concept, however. Rebert, *La Gran Línea*, 3.

66. All of the many treaties, conventions, and extensions are in "Treaties and Conventions," NARA, RG 76, Records of the Boundary and Claims Commissions and Arbitrations, International Boundaries U.S.-Mexican Border, entry 487.

67. #25, Evarts to Phillip H. Morgan, 12 June 1880, "Typewritten copies of, Instructions from the State Department to the American Embassy, Mexico City," NARA, RG 76, Records of Boundary and Claims, entry 486, envelope 35, box 53.

68. Stanley, quoted in "Irrigation of Arid Lands; International Boundary; Mexican Relations," 51st Cong., 1st sess., H. Rep. 490, 3. There could possibly have been a role for the military in managing the water issue in Texas, arguably "the most professional part of the nineteenth-century American state." Klyza, "United States Army, Natural Resources, and Political Development in the Nineteenth Century," 26.

69. H.R. 9710, March 19, 1900, and supporting testimony in *El Paso Dam and Elephant Butte Dam*.

70. J. J. Cocke to W. H. Crain, 31 December 1887; Enrique Vizcaya to Geo. W. Lume [U.S. customs inspector, Roma, Texas], 31 May 1884; 30 December 1884, "Typewritten copies of miscellaneous letters to the Department of State, 1849–1911, 1802, 1819, 1836," NARA, RG 76, Records of Boundary and Claims, entry 486, envelope 29, folder 50.

71. Mills, *My Story*, 278–79.

72. Hill Jr., "El Chamizal," 510n1. El Chamizal *banco* in El Paso was the biggest and most important in diplomatic terms. Its status was not resolved until 1964. For documentation on the El Chamizal tract and many questions raised about jurisdiction exercised there during this time period, see among other collections, "Typewritten copies of 1) Weller-Conde Journal of the Commission, 2) Journal of Emory Commission, 3) Water Boundary Commission, Anson Mills," NARA, RG 76, Records of Boundary and Claims, entry 486, envelope 30, folder 50. The entire dispute raised an interesting jurisdictional question, as the U.S. courts "[had] refused to take jurisdiction of cases involving title to lands within the Chamizal tract owing to the attitude taken by our national executive which was in turn based upon the position adopted by the Mexican Government that the matter was not a national but an international one, and that, therefore, until finally adjudicated, the courts of neither country were authorized to pass upon the merits of titles derived from either government." "'El Chamizal' Dispute between the United States and Mexico," 929. The overall story is told broadly in Mueller, *Restless River*, and directly in Liss, *Century of Disagreement*.

73. #221, Sutton to William Hunter, 30 December 1884, NARA, RG 59, Despatches from United States Consuls in Matamoros, 1826–1906 (hereafter NARA, Consular Despatches–Matamoros), roll 8; Telegram, Fechet to State, 30 March 1885, NARA, RG 59, Despatches–Ciudad Juárez, roll 3.

74. Juan Armendariz to Anson Mills, 18 May 1899, NARA, RG 76, Records of Boundary and Claims, entry 486, box 36.

75. His second point was to expect that the Mexicans "will be misleading." W. W. Follett to Anson Mills, 3 November 1899, NARA, RG 76, Records of Boundary and Claims, entry 486, box 36; #221, Sutton to William Hunter, 30 December 1884, NARA, RG 59, Despatches–Matamoros, roll 8.

76. A. D. McCabe to John Hay, 2 April 1900 [maybe 1901], NARA, RG 76, Records of Boundary and Claims, entry 486, box 36.

77. "International Commission with Mexico," 50th Cong., 1st sess., H. Rep. 1008, 2.

78. John Hay to Powell Clayton, 15 November 1899, "International Commission with Mexico," 50th Cong., 1st sess., H. Rep. 1008, 2; Convention for the Elimination of the Bancos in the Rio Grande from the Effects of Article II of the Treaty of November 12, 1884, concluded 20 March 1905, ratified 31 March 1907, in "Treaties, Conventions, International Acts, Protocols and Agreements between the United States of America and Other Powers, 1776–1909," vol. 1, 61st Cong., 2nd sess., S. Doc. 357, 1199–1202.

79. Congressional Record., 47th Cong., 1st sess., March 23, 1882, 2191.

80. Ibid., 2191–92.

81. Ibid., 2192.

82. José M. Quiñoines [Mexican consul at Roma, Texas] to Romero, 3 March 1884, *Chamizal Arbitration*, vol. II, 582; Juan Gójon, 23 February 1884; M. Fernandez, "Ministerio de Fomento, Colonizacion, Industria y Commercio—México—Seccion 3—Número 2, 782," and miscellaneous Ciudad Mier documents, in *Correspondencia diplomatica cambiada entre el gobierno de los Estados Unidos Mexicanis y los de varias potencias extranjeras desde 30 de Junio de 1881 a 30 de Junio de 1886*, vol. IV, 232–43; Frelinghuysen to Phillip H. Morgan, 23 April 1884; 17 June 1884, "Typewritten copies of, Instructions from the State Department to the American Embassy, Mexico City," NARA, RG 76, Records of Boundary and Claims, entry 486, envelope 35, box 53.

83. Frelinghuysen to Phillip H. Morgan, 23 April 1884; 17 June 1884, NARA, RG 76, Records of Boundary and Claims, entry 486, envelope 35, box 53; Haynes to French, 26 March 1884, *Chamizal Arbitration*, 585–86.

84. There had been an 1875 Fish-Mariscal negotiation on this, especially since the presumption was that no shifts in channel would change the actual boundary fixed by the survey.

85. #609, Frelinghuysen to Phillip H. Morgan, 11 July 1884, "Typewritten copies of, Instructions from the State Department to the American Embassy, Mexico City," enve-

lope 35, box 53; Frelinghuysen to Matias Romero, 10 July 1884, "Notes to Mexican Embassy, Wash. from State Department, 1849–1906," envelope 31, box 51. Both in NARA, RG 76, Records of Boundary and Claims, entry 486.

86. #633, Frelinghuysen to Phillip H. Morgan, 14 August, ibid.

87. Frelinghuysen to Phillip H. Morgan, 16 October 1884; 10 April 1884; #645, John Davis to Phillip H. Morgan, 14 August 1884, ibid. Romero to Frelinghuysen, 5 June 1884, *Chamizal Arbitration*, 595.

88. Hart, *Empire and Revolution*, 129.

89. Frelinghuysen to Morgan, 4 November 1884, NARA, RG 76, Records of Boundary and Claims, entry 486, envelope 35, box 53.

90. Ibid.

91. Ibid.

92. Hamilton, *Border States of Mexico*, 222. On the law of the matriculation system in Mexico and its meaning for U.S. policymaking and citizens at the time, see Webster, *Treatise on the Law of Citizenship in the United States*, 263–69; Wharton, ed., *Digest of International Law*, vol. 2, 331–38; and "Matriculation," in Hamilton, *Hamilton's Mexican Law*. In 1882, Mexico had terminated the Convention Regulating Citizenship of Emigrants signed in 1868. In 1886, there was "a new law on alienage and nationality . . . known as the Ley Vallarta," named after the president of the Supreme Court, Ignacio L. Vallarta. Articles 30–40 "recognized the principle of equality with Mexican nationals in regard to constitutional rights and individual guarantees." For discussion of how this worked practically over time and regarding the Mexican treatment of "foreign legal entities," see Bayitch and Siqueiros, *Conflict of Laws*, 41–53.

93. Frelinghuysen to Morgan, 24 July 1882, FRUS 1882–83, 395.

94. Mariscal to Morgan, 21 May 1883; Morgan to Frelinghuysen, 23, 28 May 1883, FRUS 1883, 651–54 (emphasis in original).

95. Frelinghuysen to Morgan, 4 November 1884, NARA, RG 76, Records of Boundary and Claims, entry 486, envelope 35, box 53.

96. Ibid.

97. J. J. Cocke to W. H. Crain, 31 December 1887, "Typewritten copies of miscellaneous letters to the Department of State, 1849–1911, 1802, 1819, 1836," NARA, RG 76, Records of Boundary and Claims, entry 486, envelope 29, folder 50.

98. Ibid.

99. Famhill to State, 24 January 1888; Bayard to Thos. C Manning, 16, 26 January 1888; Bayard to Connerty, 15 February 1888, ibid.

100. James G. Blaine to Romero, 21 March 1890, "Notes to Mexican Embassy, Wash. from State Department, 1849–1906," ibid., envelope 31, box 51; Isaac P. Gray to Ignacio Mariscal, 5 July 1893, "Dispatches from American Embassy, Mexico City to State Department, 1856–1906," ibid., envelope 32, box 52.

101. Anson Mills to Edwin F. Uhl, 7 November 1895, ibid.; Banco Vela correspondence and enclosures, FRUS 1894, 391–95.

102. Mills, *My Story*, 279.

103. McCaffrey, "Harmon Doctrine One Hundred Years Later," 449–590. There has been a lot of effort to explain how the Harmon decision was bad law. "[A]n incorrect statement of international law," according to Waite, "International Law Affecting Water Rights," 119. "The Harmon doctrine has never won complete acceptance because it violates the concept of justice. Even countries that benefit from the rule have conceded rights to the lower riparian users." Shiva, *Water Wars*, 77.

104. Guarneros to Romero, 4 October 1894; Romero to Gresham, 12 October 1894; Gresham to Romero, 1 November 1894, FRUS 1894, 395–97.

105. *Official Opinions of the Attorneys General of the United States*, vol. XXI, 275–77.

106. Ibid., 278.

107. Ibid., 281–83.

108. McCaffrey, *Law of International Watercourses*, 76–111 (quote on 90); McCaffrey, "Harmon Doctrine One Hundred Years Later," 570.

109. Mills, *My Story*, 264.

110. For example, the United States took the opposite position in the Trail Smelter case, "where Canada's sovereignty implied the right to exploit its natural resources as it willed, that same sovereign norm protected the United States' right to the inviolability of its national territory." Bratspies and Miller, eds., *Transboundary Harm in International Law: Lessons from the Trail Smelter Arbitration*, 3.

THREE. Borderlands Exceptions

1. *Eagle Pass Press Telegram* clipping enclosed with #470, Sutton to George L. Rives, 10 March 1888, NARA, RG 59, Despatches from United States Consuls in Matamoros, 1826–1906 (hereafter NARA, RG 59, Despatches–Matamoros), roll 10.

2. Agamben, *Homo Sacer*, 15.

3. Smith, *Civic Ideals*, 347–48.

4. Affidavit of Atanacio Luis, FRUS 1889, 592; William F. Wharton to Thomas Ryan, 8 July 1889, FRUS 1889, 591. After the affair was over, James A. Ware, the lawyer to Shadrack White, described the Mexican soldier's "defiance of the law, in contempt of the sovereignty and in violation of the right of sanctuary." Ware to James G. Blaine, 20 June 1889, FRUS 1889, 592.

5. #470, Sutton to George L. Rives, 10 March 1888, NARA, RG 59, Despatches–Matamoros, roll 10; also Consul Allen to Sutton [enclosure with no. 470], 10 March 1888, ibid. Sutton, for his part, thought that Allen described the affair in excessive verbiage. Coming from the inexhaustible Sutton, this was quite a charge! He noted to the

State Department in a handwritten addendum that "Consul Allen has used 320 words at a great expense and entirely without reason to say what might have been better said in 50 words." This criticism might have rung a bit hollowly coming from Sutton, who was no stranger to long missives.

6. White, who said he was fluent in Spanish ("I understand and speak [it] well"), still very politely translated the phrase as "equivalent to damn the law" in his affidavit. FRUS 1889, 597.

7. Affidavit of Shad White, FRUS 1889, 597–98; #470, NARA, RG 59, Despatches–Matamoros, roll 10.

8. Articulo VI, *Tratado de Extradicion entre los Estados-Unidos Mexicanos y Los Estados-Unidos de America.*

9. Quoted in H. Remsen Whitehouse to Bayard, 28 February 1889, 51st Cong., 1st sess., H. Ex. Doc. 1, 551–52.

10. Ware to Blaine, 20 June 1889, FRUS 1889, 592; Thomas Ryan to Wharton, 17 August 1889, FRUS 1889, 606; Ryan to Blaine, 20 May 1890; affidavit of Shadrack White, 24 April 1890; Fechét to Ryan, 11 May 1890, FRUS 1890, 635–36, 640.

11. #470, NARA, RG 59, Despatches–Matamoros, roll 10.

12. Willard and Manning both called it an "outrage" at different times in these documents. #841, A. Willard to Adee, 5 November 1887, NARA, RG 59, Despatches from United States Consuls in Guaymas, 1832–1896, (hereafter NARA, RG 59, Despatches–Guaymas), roll 4; Manning to Mariscal, 21 March 1887; Captain H. W. Lawton to the Adjutant General, 7 March 1887, FRUS 1887, 698, 700–701.

13. Bayard to T. C. Manning, 7 March 1887; Manning to Bayard, 9, 12 March 1887; Manning to Mariscal, 21 March 1887, FRUS 1887, 692–98.

14. Mariscal to Manning, 11 March 1887; Manning to Mariscal, 21 March 1887, FRUS 1887, 697–98.

15. Bayard to Manning, 19 March; 9 April 1887; Manning to Bayard, 21, 28 March; 6, 14 April 1887; Mariscal to Manning, 14 April 1887, FRUS 1887, 695–98, 709–10, 714.

16. Invitation quoted in Manning to Bayard, 7, 11 May; 19 September 1887; Mariscal to Manning, 21 May 1887; Bayard to Manning, 24 May 1887, FRUS 1887, 719, 723, 725–29, 742–43; Willard to Adee, 5 November 1887, NARA, RG 59, Despatches–Guaymas, roll 4.

17. #4, Sutton to Alory Adee, 2 November 1887, NARA, RG 59, Despatches–Matamoros, roll 10.

18. #470, Sutton to George L. Rives, 10 March 1888, NARA, RG 59, Despatches–Matamoros, roll 10.

19. Indeed, U.S. and Texas courts threw out all cases from these *bancos*, in everything from murder to smuggling. "If the alleged act is committed anywhere near the line, which is often a mere depression or hollow of dry ground, the offender is likely to get clear because of the doubt," Sutton fretted to the State Department. The same was

true for "offences against the peace." #475, Sutton to Rives, 19 March 1888, NARA, RG 59, Despatches–Matamoros, roll 10.

20. #475, Sutton to Rives, 19 March 1888, NARA, RG 59, Despatches–Matamoros, roll 10.

21. Ibid.

22. Ibid.

23. Castel, *Extraterritoriality in International Trade*, 9.

24. Moore, *Treatise on Extradition and Interstate Rendition*, vol. 1, 75.

25. Articulo II, *Tratado de Extradicion entre los Estados-Unidos Mexicanos y Los Estados-Unidos de America.*

26. *Ex parte McCabe*, 46 F. 363, 366 (1891).

27. Bayard to Cayetano Romero, 29 August 1888, FRUS 1888, vol. 2, 1315–17. For all materials related to the Preciado case, see 1308–17.

28. Moore, *Report on Extradition, with Returns of all Cases from August 9, 1942 to January 1, 1890 and an Index*, 7. An example of a case "based solely upon the accusation of the grand jury of the State of Texas" and handled purely between Texas and Mexico under this clause was that of William F. Brice in December 1897 in "Caso de Extradición de William F. Brice," 271–76.

29. "Constitutional Amendments, March 10, 1881," and "Initial Message to the Eighteenth Legislature," 20 January 1883, *Collections of the Archive & History Department of the Texas State Library*, 381, 448.

30. For example, Silas H. Jennison, the governor of Vermont, was essentially practicing a private foreign policy of extradition in cases along the Canadian borderland. This was not unknown at the time among northern border states. New York was another that allowed governors great leeway in extraditing fugitives to foreign countries for charges of murder, forgery, larceny, or other crimes punishable by death or imprisonment. *Holmes v. Jennison*, 39 U.S. 14 Pet. 540, 561–78 (1840); also Hurd, *Treatise on the Right of Personal Liberty and on the Writ of Habeas Corpus*, 582.

31. "Provided, that if such requisition be made by any such justice of the Supreme Court, it may be under the seal of the district court, which, by law, he is assigned to hold." Quoted in Moore, *Treatise on Extradition and Interstate Rendition*, vol. 1, 75–76.

32. Benton-Cohen, *Borderline Americans*, 50.

33. Zamacona to Blaine, 25 July 1881; Blaine to S. J. Kirkwood, 2 August 1881, "Letters Received Relating to Disturbances Along Mexican Border, December 13, 1878–January 25, 1884 and Miscellaneous Subjects, February 14, 1868–January 24, 1888," NARA, Territorial Papers, Arizona, 1868–1913, folder 1878–1881, roll 3.

34. Gosper to Blaine, 30 September 1881, ibid.

35. Ibid.

36. Ibid. Also see Gosper to Kirkwood, 5 May 1881, ibid.

37. *Message of Gov. Lionel A. Sheldon to the Legislative Assembly of New Mexico at its*

session commencing January 2nd, 1882, NARA, RG 48, Records of the Office of the Secretary of the Interior, Interior Department Territorial Papers: New Mexico, 1851–1914 (hereafter NARA, Territorial Papers, New Mexico, 1851–1914), roll 1.

38. For example, see the list of extradition requisitions to and from New Mexico in the years 1886–88 (the available records), which indicate only one case with Chihuahua. "Executive Proceedings, Oct. 8, 1874–Dec 31, 1888," NARA, Territorial Papers, New Mexico, 1851–1914, roll 1. Ten years later, there were regular requests for fugitive surrender from Mexico, "Executive Proceedings, July 1, 1889–December 31, 1899," ibid., roll 2.

39. #95, Robert C. Campbell to James D. Porter, 24 August 1885, NARA, RG 59, Despatches from United States Consuls in Monterrey, Mexico, 1849–1906, roll 4.

40. "Case of John H. Aufdemorte, Report by Consul Campbell of Monterey," in ibid.

41. Henry R. Jackson to Bayard, 10 August 1886; San Antonio *Daily Express* clipping, FRUS 1886, 709–10, 717; *Galveston Daily News*, August 12, 1886.

42. Sutton was apparently investigating the local circumstances months later. #436, Sutton to Rives, 9 December 1887, NARA, RG 59, Despatches–Matamoros, roll 10; Garza Galan testimony in Mariscal to Jackson, 10 August 1886, FRUS 1886, 710. The most detailed account is in Consul Linn's report and its supporting documents, Linn to Porter, 3 August 1886, FRUS 1886, 713–18.

43. #436, Sutton to Rives, 9 December 1887, NARA, RG 59, Despatches–Matamoros, roll 10.

44. Ibid.

45. Bayard to Jackson, 14 August 1886, FRUS 1886, 711

46. Bayard to Jackson, 12 August 1886, FRUS 1886, 710.

47. #436, Sutton to Rives, 9 December 1887, NARA, RG 59, Despatches–Matamoros, roll 10; Mariscal to Jackson, 25 August 1886, FRUS 1886, 720. The legality of killing was contextual, and American officials were much less exercised when it was an American doing it. A year after this event, Sutton defended an American citizen for killing someone in Mexico on no greater evidence than that he was a naturalist with impressive credentials (he had been a collector for the American Museum of Natural History in New York) and because he claimed to be acting in self-defense: "A reputable person has no incentive to kill a man on the road in this country, *but when he has to do it* he has no time to call in witnesses to prove that he was acting in self defense." #509, Sutton to Rives, 18 July 1888, NARA, RG 59, Despatches–Matamoros, roll 11.

48. Attached to #436, Sutton to Rives, 9 December 1887, NARA, RG 59, Despatches–Matamoros, roll 10.

49. Joseph G. Donnelly to Matias Guerra, 23 September 1894; #59, Donnelly to Uhl, 24 September 1894, NARA, RG 59, Despatches from United States Consuls in Nuevo Laredo, 1871–1906 (hereafter NARA, RG 59, Consular Despatches–Nuevo Laredo), roll 4.

50. Summary of events by Donnelly in #62, Donnelly to Uhl, 6 October 1894, ibid.

51. #60, Donnelly to Uhl, 27 September 1894, ibid. Affidavit enclosed by Donnelly, #62, Donnelly to Uhl, 6 October 1894, ibid.

52. #60, Donnelly to Uhl, 27 September 1894; #67, Donnelly to Uhl, 25 January 1895, ibid.

53. #95, Donnelly to Uhl, 18 January 1896; Franco P. Villasenor to Donnelly, 26 January 1896, ibid.

54. Charles W. Kindrick to Powell Clayton, 10 May 1899; Charles W. Kindrick to David J. Hill, 12 May 1899; Powell Clayton to Kindrick, 10 May 1899; [Governor] Joseph D. Savers, 11 May 1899 ("will ask at once his extradition of Mexican government"). Powell Clayton, the ambassador, made the formal request. Powell Clayton to Kindrick, 11 May 1899, NARA, RG 59, Despatches from United States Consuls in Ciudad Juárez (Paso del Norte), 1850–1906, roll 5.

55. *El Paso Herald*, January 25, 1890.

56. "Letter from the Secretary of the Treasury in response to the Senate Resolution of February 16, 1888, relative to smuggling in the Free Zone of Mexico," 50th Cong., 1st sess., S. Ex. Doc. 108, 1 (emphasis added).

57. At first, Sutton declined to translate the pamphlet because he said that the budget cuts and inability to hire a clerk made it impossible for him to do it, but he rapidly sent it and his own typically long-winded report. #81, Sutton to William F. Wharton, 14 March 1890, NARA, RG 59, Despatches–Nuevo Laredo, roll 2.

58. #108, Sutton to Wharton, 25 April 1890, ibid.

59. Ibid. The importance of the border town railroad trade and its agitation for the *Zona Libre* is emphasized in Bell and Smallwood, *Zona Libre, 1858–1905,* 49–54.

60. #162, Sutton to Wharton, 29 July 1890, NARA, RG 59, Despatches–Nuevo Laredo, roll 2.

61. "[T]the foreign trading zone is a necessary tool of the seaport in a protectionist country if it desires to act as middleman handling traffic moving between foreign lands." Clapp, "Foreign Trading Zones in our Seaports," 262.

62. #69, John F. Valls to Edwin F. Uhl, 28 February 1895, NARA, RG 59, Despatches–Nuevo Laredo, roll 4. On the regulated operation of the bonded routes, see Morgan, Masson, and Morgan, *Digest of the United States Tariff and Customs Laws,* 72–76.

63. "Negotiations with Mexico," 51st Cong., 1st sess., H. Rep. 1967, 1–2.

64. Pérez, *La Zona Libre,* 260.

65. Ibid.

66. "The Mexican *Zona Libre*," *Reports from the Consuls of the United States vol. XXXVIII: Consular Reports on Commerce, Manufactures, etc. No. 133 October, 1891,* 52nd Cong., 1st sess., H. Mis. Doc 154, 206–8; Fisk, *International Commercial Policies, with Special Reference to the United States,* 123; "Change in the Mexican Tariff," *Department of State, Consular Reports: Commerce, Manufacturers, etc.,* vol. LII, nos. 192, 193, 194, 195, September–December, 1896, 618.

67. *El Paso Herald*, February 25, 27, 1890.

68. 22 January; 8 February 1895, *Journal of the House of Representatives, 24th legislature, City of Austin*, started Jan 8, 1895, 90, 253–54.

69. "The people in the *Zona Libre* are not people of wealth who buy imported China Silks or revel in Brussell's laces and Carpet." Instead they buy "necessities of life, flour, corn, lard, oats, dry goods, groceries, bacon, bleached cotton's [sic] prints, harts, shoes, canned goods, tobacco, willowware, hardware, blankets, oils, &c, all from the United States, and given us in exchange, their horses, mules, hides, leather, silver, sugar &c., all the merchandise bought is American, and thousands of other articles unenumerated." J. B. Gorman [consul] to Uhl, 30 January 1895, NARA, RG 59, Despatches–Matamoros, roll 11.

70. Joseph G. Connelly, 7 February 1895, attached to Gorman to Uhl, ibid.

71. This long speech was so ringing and so thorough a devastation that it was quoted in full by Matías Romero in an appendix to his book, *Mexico and the United States*, 487–91. This 1890s debate over the *Zona Libre* led Romero to publish his explanation of the history of the policy and its faults as "The Free Zone in Mexico," 459–71.

72. "Goods in Bond for the Free Zone," *Consular Reports, Commerce, Manufacturers, Etc.*, vol. XLVII nos. 172–175 (January–April, 1895) United States Bureau of Foreign Commerce, United States Department of Commerce and Labor, 601–2.

73. Interview and a reprint of Sutton's *Zona Libre* report enclosed with Gorman to Uhl, 13 May 1895, NARA, RG 59, Despatches–Matamoros, roll 11.

74. Ibid.

75. #69, John F. Valls to Edwin F. Uhl, 28 February 1895, NARA, RG 59, Despatches–Nuevo Laredo, roll 4.

76. *Sacramento Record-Union*, quoted in *El Paso Times*, January 9, 1890; also *El Paso Times*, January 14, 1890.

77. Pérez, *La Zona Libre*, 263–64.

78. Bell and Smallwood, *Zona Libre, 1858–1905*, 56.

FOUR. **Crime, Pure and Simple**

1. Shearer, *Extradition in International Law*, 16; Clarke, *Treatise upon the Law of Extradition*, 28.

2. Fish to Colonel Hoffman, 31 March 1876, quoted in Hudson, "The Factor Case and Double Criminality in Extradition," 278n16. On the details and application of the Act of 1870, Stanbrook and Stanbrook, *Extradition: Law and Practice*, 8; Jones, *Jones on Extradition*, 9–11.

3. "Her Majesty's Government are precluded by the Act of 1870 from entering into any arrangement inconsistent with that Act," F. R. Plunkett told Secretary of State Evarts in 1877 in what was soon to become a rather constant refrain. F. R. Plunkett to Evarts,

2 August 1877, NARA, RG 59, Extradition Papers: Correspondence Concerning the Extradition Treaty with Great Britain, 1870–1890 (hereafter Extradition Papers–GB), entry 863. This entry is contained in only one box and volume, but the documents are not in chronological order. The markings of some of the documents that are duplicates of those in other RG 59 collections have been retained. These are noted in brackets.

4. Fish to Sir Edward Thornton, 27 January 1871, NARA, RG 59, Extradition Papers–GB.

5. Brilmayer, "Extraterritorial Application of American Law," 11–38; "Papers Relating to the Foreign Relations of the United States Transmitted to Congress with the Annual Message of the President, December 6, 1880," 46th Cong., 3d sess., H. Ex. Doc. 1, part 1, xi.

6. W. Q. Gresham to Charles D. Pierce [consul general of OFS], 22 January 1894; Edwin F. Uhl to Pierce, 16 May 1894; John Sherman to Pierce, 11 January 1898, NARA, RG 59, Consular Correspondence, 1785–1906: Notes to Foreign Consuls, 1853–1906, vol. 4, 12-1-1881–2-21-1906. Dating back to the Grant administration, the United States had thought the situation of the two countries was similar, as they were both surrounded by contiguous nations. Grant's message to the Senate, 19 March 1872, in Simon, ed., *Papers of Ulysses S. Grant*, vol. 23, 360–61.

7. The survey and the answers are in NARA, RG 59, Extradition Papers: Printed Report on Extradition Cases, 1842–1890, entry 862, 68–166. The most important of these Supreme Court cases include *United States v. Rauscher*, 119 U.S. 407 (1886); *Ker v. Illinois*, 119 U.S. 436 (1886); *Benson v. McMahon*, 127 U.S. 457, 462, 463 (1888); *In re Ross*, 140 U.S. 453 (1891); *Ornelas v. Ruiz*, 161 U.S. 502 (1896); *In re Luis Oteize y Cortes*, 136 U.S. 330 (1890); *Underhill v. Hernandez*, 168 U.S. 250, 252 (1897).

8. List taken from Moore, *Report on Extradition, with Returns of all Cases from August 9, 1942 to January 1, 1890 and an Index*, 6. The text of each treaty is in appendix B, 13–67.

9. Bassiouni, *International Extradition*, 490; Moore, "Russian Extradition Treaty," 641.

10. The full list of crimes is in Moore, *Report on Extradition*, 65–67.

11. On the nineteenth-century expansion of counterfeiting, see Johnson, *Illegal Tender*.

12. *Japan Mail*, 3 September 1886, enclosed with Richard B. Hubbard to Bayard, 11 October 1886, FRUS 1886–87, 566;

13. #143, E. J. Phelps to Bayard, 23 November 1885, NARA, RG 59, Extradition Papers–GB. This critique formed part of a twenty-four-page analysis of the proposed treaty revisions.

14. #143, E. J. Phelps to Bayard, 23 November 1885, NARA, RG 59, Extradition Papers–GB.

15. "Unlike the word 'murder,' the word 'fraud' does not in itself connote a crime or an offense," argued Manley O. Hudson, and it was exactly this ambiguity that drove

the British desire for "the qualification on fraud in the Extradition Act of 1870, in the British-French treaty of 1876, and in the United States convention of 1889," which expanded the list of extraditable crimes from 1842 by ten. Hudson, "The Factor Case and Double Criminality in Extradition," 294; Clark, Marshall, and Lazell, *Treatise on the Law of Crimes*, 504. The latter was a standard text for tracing the distinctions and the relevant case law during the late nineteenth century.

16. Bayard to Phelps, Minister, London, 3 March 1886, [Instructions–Great Britain, vol. 27 no. 329], NARA, RG 59, Extradition Papers–GB.

17. *Proceedings of the Convention of the American Bankers Association*, 157.

18. Ibid., 162.

19. Ibid., 155–56.

20. Ibid., 163.

21. Adams quoted in, and other quotes from, "Extradition Treaty," *The Nation*, July–December 1886, 130.

22. Moore, *Report on Extradition*, 65–67.

23. Ibid.

24. Ibid., and 5.

25. W. W. Rockhill [acting secretary] to Pierce, 19 August 1894, NARA, RG 59, Consular Correspondence, 1785–1906: Notes to Foreign Consuls, 1853–1906, vol. 4, 12-1-1881–2-21-1906.

26. "Extradition Treaty," *The Nation*, July–December 1886, 130.

27. *Reform Government in the Dominion*, 79, 145–46.

28. Sutton had detailed his early critique in #125, 19 February 1884; #220, 29 December 1884; #233, 19 February 1885; #300, 10 December 1885, NARA, RG 59, Despatches from United States Consuls in Matamoros, 1826–1906 (hereafter NARA, Consular Despatches–Matamoros), roll 8–9.

29. #475, 19 March 1888, ibid., roll 10.

30. Leiker, *Racial Borders*, 82–83.

31. #475, 19 March 1888, NARA, Consular Despatches–Matamoros, roll 10.

32. Woolsey, *Introduction to the Study of International Law*, 114.

33. *The Nation*, 12 August 1886, 128; *Treaties and Conventions between the Empire of Japan and Other Powers Compiled by the Foreign Office*, 359–63.

34. Jensen, "United States, International Policing and the War Against Anarchist Terrorism, 1900–1914," in Rapoport, *Terrorism*, 370; Jensen, "Evolution of Anarchist Terrorism in Europe and the United States from the Nineteenth Century to World War I," in Bowden and Davis, eds., *Terror*, 140. On the rise of international anarchism in the late nineteenth century through 1900 and the use of violence generally, see 136–48. On the role of anarchism in shaping general American attitudes, see Fine, "Anarchism and the Assassination of McKinley," 787–89.

35. Angell, Curtis, and Cooley, "Extradition of Dynamite Criminals," 47.

36. Ibid., 47–48, 51.

37. Ibid., 57.

38. Harris, *History of the Great Conspiracy*, 248; Marsh to Visconti Venosta, 16 November 1866, FRUS 1866, 124; Rufus King to William H. Seward, 1 March 1867, FRUS 1867, 704. Seward was extremely happy with the "friendly and prompt proceedings of the Papal government." FRUS 1866–67, 148.

39. *New Yorker Staats-Zeitung*, July 21, 1886; *Chicago Times*, July 24, 1886; *Philadelphia Press*, July 24, 1886; *Public Opinion*, April–October 1886, 308–10.

40. Angell, Curtis, and Cooley, "Extradition of Dynamite Criminals," 55.

41. Ibid., 53.

42. Wharton, ed., *Digest of International Law Taken from Documents*. This three-volume digest was later taken over by John Bassett Moore.

43. Wharton, *Dynamiting and Extra-Territorial Crime*, 155.

44. Ibid., 178.

45. Ibid., 179.

46. Ibid., 179–80.

47. Ibid.

48. Wharton, *Treatise on Criminal Law*, 301–2 (emphasis added).

49. The full accounting of the cases is in ibid., 302–6.

50. Ibid., 309, 310–11n5.

51. Foster, "Foreign Sovereign in an American Court," 283–86; Wolfman, "Sovereigns as Defendants," 373–83.

52. The property crimes were "2. Counterfeiting or altering money, or uttering or bringing into circulation counterfeit or altered money; counterfeiting certificates or coupons of public indebtedness, bank notes, or other instruments of public credit of either of the parties, and the utterance or circulation of the same. 3. Forgery or altering, and uttering what is forged or altered. 4. Embezzlement or criminal malversation of the public funds, committed within the jurisdiction of either party, by public officers or depositaries. . . . 5. Larceny, of the value of fifty dollars and upwards, and robbery. 6. Burglary, defined to be the breaking and entering by night time into the house of another person with the intent to commit a felony therein; and the act of breaking and entering the house of another, whether in the day or night-time, with the intent to commit a felony therein. 7. The act of entering, or of breaking and entering, the offices of the Government and public authorities, or the offices of banks, banking-houses, savings-banks, trust companies, insurance or other companies, with the intent to commit a felony therein. . . . 11. Piracy by the law of nations." *Treaties and Conventions between the Empire of Japan and Other Powers Compiled by the Foreign Office*, 359–60.

53. Ibid., 359–62; *Japan Mail*, September 3, 1886, enclosed with Richard B. Hubbard to Bayard 11 October 1886, FRUS 1886–87, 567; Moore, *Report on Extradition*, 26–27; Hudson, "The Factor Case and Double Criminality in Extradition," 299n102.

54. R. B. Roosevelt to State Dept., 5 January 1889, with Law of April 6, 1875 enclosure, in Moore, *Report on Extradition*, 137.

55. Tosti, "Anarchistic Crimes," 408, quote on 415.

56. Institute for International Law, quoted in Bassiouni, *International Extradition*, 494–96. Bedi writes, "It is true, as the resolution of the Institute for International Law declared in 1880, that justice does not require reciprocity, but politics and the exorbitant doctrine of sovereignty do." Bedi, *Extradition*, 78.

57. Quoted in Devlin, *Treaty Power under the Constitution of the United States*, 343–44.

58. 6 October 1870; 19 January 1874, "Memorandum from Mr. Fish's notes of substance of various interviews with Sir Edward Thornton" and "Thornton, March 1874, Memorandum of Objections and of proposed changes to the draft of an Extradition Treaty . . ." NARA, RG 59, Extradition Papers–GB.

59. *In re Adutt*, 55 F. 376, 379–80 (1893) (emphasis added).

60. Ibid.

61. *Cohn v. Jones*, 100 F. 639, 645 (1900).

62. Universal jurisdiction, familiar in prominent twentieth-century extradition cases like that of General Pinochet, was not applicable in the nineteenth century. Castel, *Extraterritoriality in International Trade*, 9–20.

63. Cleveland, "Powers Inherent in Sovereignty," 206.

64. *Jones v. United States*, 137 U.S. 202, 204 (1890). On Navassa, see U.S. General Accounting Office, "U.S. Insular Areas," 47; Neuman, "Anomalous Zones," 1197–1234.

65. Burnett, "Edges of Empire and the Limits of Sovereignty," 187–211. Yet it is essential to emphasize the centrality of autarkic reshaping of the guano market, which was the most important component of the act, albeit the most fleeting one. Burnett's argument is effective in the ways it provides support for her other work on "territorial deannexation." Burnett, "'Untied' States," 797–879.

66. *Jones v. United States*, 211–12.

67. Recently, the Jones case has been minimized as "a trivial chapter in the history of American overseas expansionism." But this assessment is really only in comparison with the major determinations of the shape of empire in later cases like the Insular Cases. Raustiala, *Does the Constitution Follow the Flag?*, 75.

68. *In re Ross*, 454–60 (1891).

69. Ibid., 462–63.

70. Ibid., 465 (emphasis added).

71. Raustiala, *Does the Constitution Follow the Flag?*, 67.

72. Cleveland, "Our International Constitution," 16.

73. *In re Ross*, 473.

74. *United States v. Rodgers*, 150 U.S. 249, 265–66 (1893) (emphasis added).

75. Hunt, "How the Great Lakes Became 'High Seas,'" 310. Also see Gregory, "Jurisdiction over Foreign Ships in Territorial Waters," 333–57.

76. Kennan, "Russian Extradition Treaty," 283–84, 294, 297.

77. Moore, "Russian Extradition Treaty," 635–37. On broader opposition to the treaty, see Griffin, "Protesting Despotism," 91–99.

78. Austria-Hungary insisted on an "ample opportunity." Moore, *Report on Extradition*, 72.

79. *R. A. Blandford v. The State*, 10 Tex. Ct. App. 627, 639 (1881).

80. Ibid., 634.

81. Ibid., 637–38.

82. #206, 30 November 1881; #210, 22 December 1881, NARA, Consular Despatches–Matamoros, roll 7.

83. Moore, *Report on Extradition*, 32.

84. Clarke, *Treatise upon the Law of Extradition*, 81–82.

85. Moore, *Treatise on Extradition and Interstate Rendition*, vol. 1, 196.

86. Text of the treaty with Belgium in Moore, *Report on Extradition*, 20.

87. *U.S. v. Caldwell*, 25 F. Cas. 237, 237–38 (1871).

88. *United States v. Lawrence*, 26 F. Cas. 879, 881–83 (1876).

89. Ibid.

90. J. B. Moore has the best synthesis. See Moore, *Treatise on Extradition*, vol. 1, 196–216, quoted from 212–13.

91. Pierrepont to Fish, 4 October 1876. In the "memorandum of a conversation between Sir Edward Thornton and Mr. Fish at the Department of State, Saturday May 27, 1876," Thornton told Fish that [Minister] Hoffman had offered to negotiate the treaty of 1842 and allow for fugitives to be set free for a certain period of time before facing new charges. Fish said that Hoffman "had no authority from his Government to make or to entertain any such proposition or suggestion and in fact asked in the future that all discussions with Hoffman would be based on written instructions." Fish later instructed U.S. minister Pierrepont to tell Lord Derby, "you say 'to which I replied that I was not yet authorized to enter upon such negotiation'" and thereafter forbade him to negotiate repeatedly. Fish to Pierrepont, 2 August 1876; Pierrepont to Fish, 22 August 1876 [no. 23], NARA, RG 59, Extradition Papers–GB.

92. F. R. Plunkett to F. W. Seward, 10 August 1877 [Despatches, GB, vol. 131, no. 46], NARA, RG 59, Extradition Papers–GB.

93. There were also wider diversions such as the "Eastern Question" and other imperial issues that derailed treaty negotiation periodically. "Royal Commission on Extradition–Report of the Commissioners," FRUS 1878–79, vol. 1, 268–78. An important American analysis of the report, later cited in the Rauscher case, was Lawrence, "Hon. William Beach Lawrence on Extradition," 329–35.

94. The thematic connection of these issues to questions of governance is in Richardson, *West from Appomattox*.

95. To get an idea of the span of non-activity bridged by correspondence, see Pierrepoint to Fish, 29 December 1876; Frelinghuysen to James Russell Lowell, 15 July 1884 [Instruction–GB, vol. 27, no. 915], NARA, RG 59, Extradition Papers–GB.

96. Fish to Thornton, 23 February 1877 [Notes–GB, vol. 17], NARA, RG 59, Extradition Papers–GB.

97. L. S. Sackville West to Bancroft Davis, 16 February 1882, NARA, RG 59, Extradition Papers–GB.

98. L. S. Sackville West to State, 11 March 1882. A full retrospective report of the negotiations up to this point since the 1870s is in Frelinghuysen to James Russell Lowell, 15 July 1884 [Instruction–GB vol. 27, no. 915]. As stated in L. S. Sackville West to Frelinghuysen, 9 May 1883, nothing that "the minister is of opinion that Canada has followed the wiser course in not raising any question as to the violation of the Sovereignty of British Soil [sic] in these [older extradition] cases, where the only result would have been to have assisted Criminals to escape trial or punishment and to have offered them a safe asylum in this Country, and, situated as the United States and Canada are, it is in the interest of a healthy administration of Justice that each Country give to the other the utmost support and assistance in the arrest and bringing to trial of Criminals." "Certified Copy of a Report of a Committee of the Honorable the Privy Council for Canada, approved by H. E. the Governor General on the 4th Day of May/83," NARA, RG 59, Extradition Papers–GB.

99. West wanted to know if the United States could allow a surrendered person who had been extradited a chance to "quit the country before bringing any other charge against him that that for which he was surrendered." Adee said that Frelinghuysen would not negotiate this point at all as "since 1876 it had been consistently the view of this government that the privilege of trial for *any treaty offense* should not be given up." Conversation notes between West and Adee, 12 June 1883, NARA, RG 59, Extradition Papers–GB.

100. Frelinghuysen to L. S. Sackville West, 7 July 1883; Bayard to Phelps, Minister, London, 3 March 1886 [Instructions–Great Britain, vol. 27 no. 329]; James G. Blaine to Julien Pauncefote, 19 November 1888 [GB Notes, vol. 31], NARA, RG 59, Extradition Papers–GB.

101. For an example of another significant state decision, see *Commonwealth v. Hawes*, 76 Ky. (13 Bush) 697 (1878), which upheld specialty and the autonomy of the courts but also called for a reasonable time of return to the surrendering state. It also noted that further indictments could be issued in certain circumstances in which the fugitive came into local jurisdiction. See also *State v. Vanderpool*, 39 Ohio St. 273 (1883).

102. *United States v. Watts*, 14 F. 130, 131 (1882).

103. Ibid., 139–41.

104. *Ex parte Hibbs*, 26 F. 421, 434 (1886).

105. *United States v. Rauscher*, 411.

106. Ibid., 416.

107. Ibid., 408, 424.

108. Ibid., 424–30.

109. Ibid., 431–32; Wu, "Treaties' Domains," 629.

110. For example, the U.S. attorney general later argued that surrendered fugitives should invoke their treaty rights to non-trial themselves and not rely on the surrendering state. A person named Acosta, who was extradited from Mexico to Florida and was then convicted and imprisoned, was upon release arrested for another crime before being allowed to return to Mexico. The Mexican government demanded his release through the State Department, but because Acosta himself did not "attempt to invoke his right to return to Mexico," the attorney general decided that his release would have been "premature." Also, in Texas in 1897, an American named Underwood was extradited from Canada, charged for murder, and acquitted and thereafter rearrested for robbery, found guilty, and sentenced to sixteen years in prison. Though Great Britain demanded his release, since the prisoner did not specifically invoke this treaty right himself, it was held that "no international obligation exists on the part of the United States to secure, on demand of the British Government, the release of Underwood." *Digest of Official Opinions of the Attorneys-General of the United States*, 184, 212.

FIVE. Uncertainties of Citizenship and Sovereignty

1. On the idea of "embeddedness, political membership, and social inclusion," see Somers, *Genealogies of Citizenship*, 5–7.

2. R. B. Hubbard to the President [Hayes], 13 August 1877; Hubbard to Evarts, 10 October 1877, "Mexican Border Troubles," 45th Cong., 1st sess., H. Ex. Doc. 13, 43, 77–79; E. O. C. Ord to Hubbard, 12 August 1877, "Report and Accompanying Documents of the Committee on Foreign Affairs on the Relations of the United States with Mexico (April 25, 1878)," 45th Cong., 2nd sess., H. Rep. 701, 337.

3. Sweitzer to A. A. General, 15 August, 1877; F. W. Seward to R. B. Hubbard, 14 August 1877; Seward to Foster, 15 August 1877; Foster to Evarts, 23 August 1877; Seward to Foster, 15 August 1877; Foster to Evarts, 23, 30 August 1877, "Mexican Border Troubles," 45th Cong., 1st sess., H. Ex. Doc. 13, 43–47.

4. J. L. Hall [lieutenant commanding state troops] to Hubbard, 22 August 1877; Ord to Adjutant-General, 16 August 1877; Foster to Evarts, 11 September 1877, ibid., 46–47, 86.

5. Army Orders, 1868–81, Correspondence and Papers, 1852–83, Army orders, accounts, and miscellaneous, box 8; John Weber [U.S. consul at Monterrey] to Ord, 11 November 1877, box 6: "Incoming Letters, U.S. C–Z, folder: U.S. Consulate, Monterrey,

Mexico," Edward Otho Cresap Ord Papers, 1850–83, BANC MSS C–B 479, Bancroft Library, University of California, Berkeley (hereafter Ord Papers).

6. Hubbard to Hall, 24 August 1877; Hubbard to Ord, 24 August 1877; Ord to Hubbard, 27 August 1877; "Mexican Border Troubles," 45th Cong., 1st sess., H. Ex. Doc. 13, 91.

7. Schleicher to Ord, 16 September 1877, "Correspondence and Papers, 1852–1883, Incoming Letters, S–U.S.," box 5, Ord Papers (emphasis in original).

8. Ibid.

9. Schleicher to Ord, 7 October 1877, ibid. On Ord's dealings the previous summer with Treviño, see Gregg, *Influence of Border Troubles*, 58.

10. Vallarta to Mata [translation], 10 September 1877; John C. Russell [extradition agent] to Hubbard, 12 September 1877, "Report and Accompanying Documents of the Committee on Foreign Affairs on the Relations of the United States with Mexico (April 25, 1878)," 45th Cong., 2nd sess., H. Rep. 701, 333–34.

11. Enclosure with ibid.

12. Russell to Hubbard, 26 September 1877, "Correspondence and papers, 1852–1883, Incoming Letters, I–R; R Miscellany folder," box 4; Ord Report to Colonel R. C. Drum, assistant adjutant general, Division of the Missouri, 1 October 1877, "Outgoing letters, 1872–1881," box 1, Ord Papers.

13. Russell to Hubbard, 26 September 1877, "Correspondence and papers, 1852–1883, Incoming Letters, I–R; R Miscellany folder," box 4, Ord Papers; Hubbard to Russell, 8 October 1877, ibid., 339; Foster to Evarts, 6 October 1877, "Mexican Border Troubles," 45th Cong., 1st sess., H. Ex. Doc. 13, 48.

14. Vallarta, "Mexican Republic, Department of Foreign Affairs, Section of America," translation enclosed in Foster to Evarts, 12 October 1877. Commentary from several newspapers follows. Also, more Mexican Department of Foreign Affairs commentary is enclosed with Foster to Evarts, 18 October 1877, ibid., 50–55.

15. Hubbard to Evarts, 10 October 1877, ibid., 77–81.

16. "Governor Hubbard's Initial Message to the Sixteenth Legislature," *Collections of the Archive & History Department of the Texas State Library*, 759–61.

17. Ibid.

18. Ord Report to Colonel R. C. Drum, assistant adjutant general, Division of the Missouri, 1 October 1877, "Outgoing letters, 1872–1881," box 1, Ord Papers.

19. Ibid.

20. Ibid.

21. Ibid.

22. Ord to Sherman, 25 October 1877, "Outgoing letters, 1872–1881," box 1, Ord Papers.

23. Ibid.

24. Hubbard to Ord, 21 December 1877, "Correspondence and papers, 1852–1883, Incoming Letters, S–U.S.," box 5, Ord Papers (emphasis in original).

25. Ibid.

26. Blaine to Baron de Fava, 23 June 1890, NARA, RG 59, Record of Requests Made to Italy for the Punishment of Italian Fugitives from U.S. Justice 1869–1910 NARS A–1 (hereafter NARA, RG 59, Italian Fugitives Requests), entry 864; Institute of International Law, quoted in ibid.; Hyde, "Notes on the Extradition Treaties of the United States," 497.

27. Blaine to Baron de Fava, 23 June 1890, NARA, RG 59, Italian Fugitives Requests; text of the treaties in Moore, *Report on Extradition*, 13–65. The United States finally signed an extradition treaty with Brazil on May 14, 1897. McKinley, annual address, 5 December 1899, CMPP, vol. X, 139.

28. Moore, *Report on Extradition*, 13–65.

29. Moore, *Treatise on Extradition and Interstate Rendition*, vol. 1, 170–77.

30. Welke, "Law, Personhood, and Citizenship in the Long Nineteenth Century," 346.

31. Moore, *Report on Extradition*, 5 (emphasis added).

32. Moore, *Treatise on Extradition and Interstate Rendition*, vol. 1, 168–69.

33. Archdeacon, *Becoming American*, 122, 137–39.

34. Stallo to Comm. F. Crispi, 17 May 1888, NARA, RG 59, Italian Fugitives Requests; "Letter from the Secretary of State Submitting Report on the Subject of Citizenship of the United States, Expatriation, and Protection Abroad, December 20, 1906—Referred to the Committee on Foreign Affairs and Ordered to be Printed," 59th Cong., 2nd sess., H. Doc. 326, 523. On dual citizenship and the state system, see Spiro, "Mandated Membership, Diluted Identity," 89–90.

35. Stallo to Crispi, 30 April 1889, NARA, RG 59, Italian Fugitives Requests.

36. "Verbal note" from the Ministry of Foreign Affairs dated 27 April 1889, ibid.

37. Dealing with more contemporary issues but very relevant and insightful on the theoretical quandaries is Wong, "Home Away From Home?" 174–75.

38. Kahler, "Territoriality and Conflict in an Era of Globalization," in Kahler and Walter, eds., *Territoriality and Conflict in an Era of Globalization*, 16; Moore, *American Diplomacy*, 173.

39. Sickles to Praxedes Mo. Sagasta, 14 October 1870, NARA, RG 59, Diplomatic Correspondence Regarding Judicial Procedures in Spain, June 9, 1870–June 28, 1877.

40. Ibid.

41. Moore, *American Diplomacy*, 169–70.

42. Ibid., and 192–93; Kerber, "Toward a History of Statelessness in America," 731–35.

43. Blaine to Fava, 18 November 1890, NARA, RG 59, Italian Fugitives Requests.

44. A. Dalle Valle to Secretary of State, 6 November 1882; Frelinghuysen to Marquis A. Dalle Valle, 18 September 1883; Bayard to Baron de Fava, 14 March 1885, ibid.

45. Bayard to Stallo, 26 April 1888; #223, Stallo to Bayard, 4 August 1888; Damiani to U.S. minister [Stallo], 1 June 1888, ibid.

46. Stallo to Crispi, 17 May 1888; Stallo to Crispi, 14, 27 July 1888; Dougherty to Crispi, 6, 24 September 1888, ibid.

47. Damiani to Stallo, 24 August 1888, ibid.

48. Ibid.

49. Blaine to Baron de Fava, 21 March; 13 June 1890; Fava to Blaine, 20 April; 16 June 1890, ibid.

50. Blaine to Fava, 23 June 1890, ibid.

51. Italian Penal Code adopted June 30, 1889; Blaine to Fava, 23 June; 18 November 1890, ibid.

52. Ibid.

53. Uhl to Potter, 22 January 1894; MacVeagh to Gresham, 10 April 1894; Edwin F. Uhl to Wayne MacVeagh, 24 April 1894; Gresham to Fava, 13 June 1894; Alvey A. Adee to Fava, 29 August 1895; John Hay to Governor of Mass, 11 February 1899, ibid.

54. #134, Sutton to William Hunter, 27 February 1884; "'Trade and Industries of Northern Mexico,' Report by Consul General Sutton of Matamoros," part of his annual report for year ended 30 September 1884, enclosed with #220, Sutton to Hunter, 30 September 1884, NARA, RG 59, Despatches from United States Consuls in Matamoros, 1826–1906 (hereafter NARA, RG 59, Despatches–Matamoros), roll 8.

55. "'Trade and Industries of Northern Mexico,'" ibid.

56. "A Communication from the Secretary of State in Response to Senate Resolution of February 11, 1884, relative to the case of Alexander Trimble, whose extradition has been demanded by Mexico," 48th Cong., 1st sess., S. Ex. Doc. 98, 2.

57. Ibid.

58. Ibid., 4–5.

59. Ibid., 5 (emphasis added).

60. Ibid., 6.

61. Short biography of Governor Ireland in *Collections of the Archive & History Department of the Texas State Library*, 470. On the legislation of the fence-cutting war signed on February 7, 1884, see Spaw, *Texas Senate*, 326–27; Gard, "Fence-Cutters," 1–15; Green, *Grass Roots Socialism*, 2.

62. "Governor Ireland's Second Inaugural Address," *Collections of the Archive & History Department of the Texas State Library*, 517–18.

63. Ibid.

64. *Mexican Financier*, January 31, 1885; *Galveston Weekly News*, January 29, 1885: #233, Sutton to Hunter, 19 February 1885 (with clippings enclosed), NARA, RG 59, Despatches–Matamoros, roll 8.

65. The State Department–Texas correspondence and Blaine letter are quoted in *Ex parte McCabe*, 46 F. 363, 378–79 (1891).

66. The narrative of Mary Inez McCabe's arrest and crime are drawn from *Ex parte McCabe*, 46 F. 363 (1891) and #39, John B. Richardson to William F. Wharton, 23 February 1891, NARA, RG 59, Despatches–Matamoros, roll 10.

67. #46, John B. Richardson to William F. Wharton, 13 March 1891, NARA, RG 59, Despatches–Matamoros, roll 10.

68. Ibid.

69. Ibid. His use of the phrase "more sinned against than sinning" is interesting because it is the end of the phrase from *King Lear* in which the phrase "unwhipped of justice" appears—a favorite phrase of the previous consul in Matamoros, Warner P. Sutton in discussing extradition.

70. *Ex parte McCabe*, 46 F. 363, 368–69 (1891).

71. Ibid., 372–74.

72. Ibid., 381.

73. #47, John B. Richardson to William F. Wharton, 17 March 1891, NARA, RG 59, Despatches–Matamoros, roll 10.

74. *El Cronista*, March 13, 1891; clipping included with ibid.

75. Ibid.

76. Richardson to State, 13 April 1891, ibid.

77. On the bar and Belem prison, see Schell Jr., *Integral Outsiders*, 55. On the surrender request and rejection, Butler to Ignacio Mariscal, 18 July 1895; Pedro Rincon, Sección 5 Número 3, 844; Ignacio Mariscal to E. C. Butler [U.S. Chargé in Mexico City], 22 July 1895, "Demanda y resoluciones sobre extradición de los hermanos Rowe," 65–69. On U.S. urgings, Adee to Butler, 19 July 1895; Butler to Olney, 26 July 1895, and other procedural exchanges, FRUS 1895, part 2, 997–1001.

78. "Demanda y resoluciones sobre extradición de los hermanos Rowe," 75–78. Spanish text of Mariscal's letter is in ibid., 79–84. U.S. translation is in Mariscal to Butler, 29 July 1895, FRUS 1895, part 2, 1004–6. In this FRUS volume, the date of the extradition treaty mentioned by Mariscal is misprinted as 1851 (it should be 1861), and there are grammatical mistakes.

79. Mariscal to Butler, 29 July 1895, FRUS 1895, part 2, 1007.

80. Ibid.

81. Olney argued that the Mexican naturalization law "was doubtless intended as an invitation to immigrants of probity and industry who desired to own homes. It guaranties them, without any period of long waiting as strangers in the land of their adoption, the rights and privileges accorded to native-born Mexicans as soon as they shall manifest their intent to abide and cast their lot with the Mexican people by acquiring real estate in Mexico with intent to become citizens of Mexico." Olney to Matt W. Ransom, 13 December 1895, ibid., 1008.

82. Ibid., 1009.

83. Ibid. The Mexican citizenship and naturalization procedures are presented in Ransom to Olney, 9 November 1895, FRUS 1895, part 2, 1011–18.

84. Secretaría de estado y del Despacho de Relacíones Exteríores Número 319, Mariscal, 7 November 1895; Mariscal to Matt W. Ransom, 7 November 1895, "Demanda y resoluciones sobre extradición de los hermanos Rowe," 91–92; Olney to Matt W. Ransom, 13 December 1895, FRUS 1895, part 2, 1008.

85. González, *Secuestrar para juzgar pasado y presente de la justicia extraterritorial*, 37.

86. Text of the treaty is in "Treaties, Conventions, International Acts, Protocols and Agreements between the United States of America and Other Powers, 1776–1909," 61st Cong., 2nd sess., S. Doc. 357, vol. 1, 1184–90; Hyde, "Notes on the Extradition Treaties of the United States," 499n39. For comparison with other and later treaties, see "Non-Extradition of Nationals," 525–27.

87. "Treaties, Conventions, International Acts, Protocols and Agreements between the United States of America and Other Powers, 1776–1909," 61st Cong., 2nd sess., S. Doc. 357, vol. 1, 1184–90.

88. "Caso de Extradición de Mattie Rich (documentos oficiales)," 264–73.

89. McKinley, annual address, 5 December 1899, in CMPP, vol. X, 149.

90. Ibid.

six. Exception as Metaphor and Practice

1. *Ex parte McCabe*, 46 F. 363 (1891); Van den Wijngaert, *Political Offence Exception to Extradition*, 1n1.

2. Hussain, *Jurisprudence of Emergency*, 133.

3. Fish to Thornton, 15 January 1874. Fish wrote the same phrase repeatedly. For example, on 19 January, he wrote again, "we cannot consent under any circumstances to refer the decision of the question of the political character of the crime to the decision of the courts, and that it belongs properly to the political department which ought not to be allowed to shield itself behind an alleged judicial decision and the therefore insists peremptorily upon it." In September 1874, the same. "Memorandum from Mr. Fish's notes of substance of various interviews with Sir Edward Thornton," NARA, RG 59, Extradition Papers: Correspondence Concerning the Extradition Treaty with Great Britain, 1870–1890, entry 863.

4. Schafer, "Concept of the Political Criminal," 382; Carrara, quoted in Schafer.

5. Van den Wijngaert, *Political Offence Exception to Extradition*, 3.

6. "'Political Offence' in Extradition Treaties," 459–61.

7. Scott, ed., *Resolutions of the Institute of International Law*, 103; Malik, "Comment: Unraveling the Gordian Knot," 154; Bassiouni, *International Extradition*, 660.

8. Scott, ed., *Resolutions of the Institute of International Law*, 103.

9. Ibid.; Van den Wijngaert, *Political Offence Exception to Extradition*, 15. See also how these issues were reflected politically in Jensen, "The International Anti-Anarchist Conference of 1898 and the Origins of Interpol," 323–47.

10. Romero to Olney, 14 November 1895, FRUS 1896, 494.

11. Pyle, *Extradition, Politics, and Human Rights*, 104; Moore, *Treatise on Extradition and Interstate Rendition*, vol. 1, 306n2.

12. *R. A. Blandford v. The State*, 10 Tex. Ct. App. 627, 639 (1881).

13. Moore, *Report on Extradition*, 20–76.

14. Lake, "State and American Trade Strategy in the Pre-Hegemonic Era," 43–45.

15. On Blaine and the conference, see Healy, *James G. Blaine and Latin America*, 138–59. On the McKinley Tariff, see Terrill, *Tariff Politics, and American Foreign Policy*, 159–83. On the paradoxes and drives of market expansionism in this era, see LaFeber, *New Empire*; McCormick, *China Market*; Schoonover, *Uncle Sam's War of 1898 and the Origins of Globalization* and *United States in Central America*; Williams, *Contours of American History* and *Roots of the Modern American Empire*; and Lipson, *Standing Guard*.

16. Justice Osler was the judge in the case *In Re Parker*, 9 P.R. 332, 335, quoted in Moore, "Extradition," in Moore, *Collected Papers of John Bassett Moore*, vol. 1, 276–77.

17. Hawley, *Law and Practice International Extradition between the United States and Those Foreign Countries*, 3–4.

18. See "Report on Extradition Prepared by the Third Assistant Secretary of State for the Use of the International American Conference, February 13, 1890," 51st Cong., 2nd sess., S. Ex. Doc. 55; "Message from the President of the United States, Transmitting a Report of the International American Conference on the Extradition of Criminals," 51st Cong., 2nd sess., S. Ex. Doc. 187, 1; *International American Conference*, vol. II, 570, 580–82.

19. *International American Conference*, vol. II, 570–74.

20. Ibid., 606.

21. "Second International Conference of American States, Message from the President of the United States, transmitting a Communication from the Secretary of State, submitting, the Report, with accompanying Papers, of the Delegates of the United States to the Second International Conference of American States, held at the City of Mexico from October 22, 1901 to January 22, 1902," 57th Cong., 1st sess., S. Doc. 330, 186–94.

22. Moore, "Asylum in Legations in Consulates and in Vessels," in Moore, *Collected Papers of John Bassett Moore*, vol. 1, 141.

23. Ibid., 205.

24. Bassiouni, *International Extradition*, 167–68; Morgenstern, "'Extra-Territorial' Asylum," 239.

25. Evans, "Observations on the Practice of Territorial Asylum in the United States,"

149–50; Bassiouni, *International Extradition*, 172–73; Gilbert, "Practice of Asylum in Legations and Consulates of the United States," 581. On asylum and immunity, see Frey and Frey, *History of Diplomatic Immunity*, 345–74.

26. Spear, *Law of Extradition, International and Inter-State*, 13.

27. Moore, "Asylum in Legations and Consulates and in Vessels. III," 403.

28. Gilbert, "Practice of Asylum in Legations and Consulates of the United States," 588, 591.

29. Quoted in ibid., 569.

30. Quoted in Moore, "Asylum in Legations and Consulates and in Vessels. II," 209.

31. Quoted in Gibbons, "Extraterritoriality and Asylum," 303–4; Moncada, *Imperialism and the Monroe Doctrine*, 4.

32. Goutier to Dupuy, 16 August 1888; Rives to Goutier, 31 October 1888, FRUS 1888, part 1, 937–38.

33. Cleveland, first annual address, 4 December 1893, in CMPP, vol. IX, 435; *Regulations Prescribed for the Use of the Consular Service of the United States*, 31.

34. Olney to Tillman, 25 November 1895, FRUS 1895, 245–46.

35. Hay to Archibald J. Sampson, 5 June 1899, FRUS 1899, 258–59.

36. Morse, "International Status of a Public Vessel in Foreign Waters," 205; Woolsey, ed., *Lectures on International Law in Time of Peace by John Norton Pomeroy*, 215.

37. Gibbons, "Extraterritoriality and Asylum," 302.

38. This case was prepared in 1902, but all of the examples are drawn from the period under discussion in the 1880s and 1890s, including many of the same cases quoted from the FRUS series. Naval War College, *International Law Situations with Solutions and Notes, 1902*, 21–27. See also Wilson, "Insurgency and International Maritime Law," 46–60.

39. Harrison, second annual address, in CMPP vol. IX, 109.

40. *Report Transmitted from the Office of the Secretary of Foreign Relations of the Republic of Guatemala to the National Legislative Assembly, Concerning the Capture and Death of General J. Martín Barrundia*, 3–16.

41. Also Angiano to Hosmer, 25, 26 August 1890; Hosmer to Wharton, 29 August 1890; Hosmer to Souza, 25 August 1890, "The Barrundia Case. The Message from the President of the United States, Transmitting, In response to a resolution of the House of Representatives, a report of the Secretary of State and Accompanying Correspondence in Relation to the Killing of General J. Martin Barrundia," 51st Cong., 2nd sess., H. Ex. Doc. 51, 4–6. On Barrundia as contraband, *Report Transmitted from the Office of the Secretary of Foreign Relations of the Republic of Guatemala to the National Legislative Assembly*, 37.

42. *Report Transmitted from the Office of the Secretary of Foreign Relations of the Republic of Guatemala to the National Legislative Assembly*, 17–23. The event from the U.S. perspective is recounted with many but not all relevant documents in Blaine to Mizner,

18 November 1890, FRUS 1890, 123–29. The attempted shooting is mentioned in Woolsey, "Inquiry Concerning our Foreign Relations," 167.

43. *Report Transmitted from the Office of the Secretary of Foreign Relations of the Republic of Guatemala to the National Legislative Assembly,* 17–23; Barrundia quoted in Brooks, "Legal Aspects of the Killing of General Barrundia," 569; Woolsey, "Inquiry Concerning our Foreign Relations," 167.

44. Blaine mentions deepened regret several times in this letter: "The more the question is examined in the light of important facts tardily disclosed the deeper becomes the regret that you so far exceeded your legitimate authority as to sign the paper which, in the hands of the officers of Guatemala, became their warrant for the capture of General Barrundia." Blaine to Mizner, 18 November 1890, FRUS 1890, 123–42. This long letter/treatise so thoroughly encapsulated this complicated case that it was also printed as most of "The Barrundia Case," 51st Cong., 2nd sess., H. Ex. Doc. 51, 26–45.

45. Blaine to Mizner, 18 November 1890, FRUS 1890, 124, 129.

46. Ibid., 131, 133–34.

47. Ibid., 135.

48. Ibid., 138.

49. Ibid.

50. Agemben, *State of Exception,* 24–25.

51. Woolsey, "Inquiry Concerning our Foreign Relations," 167.

52. Navy, quoted in ibid., 168.

53. Ibid., 173.

54. Ibid. On the *Trent* Affair, see Symonds, *Lincoln and His Admirals: Abraham Lincoln, the U.S. Navy and the Civil War,* 71–97.

55. Gibbons, "Extraterritoriality and Asylum," 312.

56. Ibid., 309–10.

57. Ibid.

58. *In re Ezeta,* 62 F. 972 (N.D. Cal. 1894). Full case, with additional introduction, was *In re Ezeta, In Re Bolanos, In re Colocho, In re Cienfuegos, In re Bustamante* (District Court, N.D. California, September 4, 1894), nos. 11,095–99, *Federal Reporter 62,* 964 (henceforth *In re Ezeta*); Moore, "Case of the Salvadorean Refugees," in Moore, *Collected Papers of John Bassett Moore,* vol. 1, 347–48.

59. *In re Ezeta,* 964, and for more detail of the revolt and asylum seeking, 976–79; Moore, "Case of the Salvadorean Refugees," 348, 351.

60. The detailed list of the crimes is in *In re Ezeta,* 972–74, and further detailed at 972–95. Testimony is printed in "Message from the President of the United States, in response to Senate Resolution of December 19, 1894, transmitting the record of the Extradition Proceedings in the Case of General Ezeta." Feb 11, 1895, 53rd Cong., 3rd sess., S. Ex. Doc. 64, 2–4.

61. 53rd Cong., 3rd sess., S. Ex. Doc. 64, 11–13, 17–20, 24–25.

62. Ibid., 64.

63. *In re Ezeta*, 965–71.

64. Ibid., 997–98.

65. Ibid., 998–99.

66. Ibid., 1002–3.

67. Ibid., 1004–5; *Coleman v. Tennessee*, 97 U.S. 509, 515 (1878).

68. Bassiouni, *International Extradition*, 666–67; Pyle, *Extradition, Politics, and Human Rights*, 111; Navy regulation quoted in Moore, "Case of the Salvadorean Refugees," 362. The international standard in the French, Italian, and German navies was "immediate danger," Morgenstern, "'Extra-Territorial' Asylum," 255; Banoff and Pyle, "To Surrender Political Offender," 184.

69. Moore, "Case of the Salvadorean Refugees," 360.

70. In Snow, *Cases and Opinions on International Law with Notes and a Syllabus*, 161–62, and Moore, *Treatise on Extradition and Interstate Rendition*, vol. 1, 324–25.

71. Ibid.; *In re Ezeta*, 1001–2.

72. #138, Warner P. Sutton to William F. Wharton, 24 June 1890; #144, Sutton to Wharton, 27 June 1890, including *Daily Times* clippings, NARA, RG 59, Despatches from United States Consuls in Nuevo Laredo, 1871–1906 (hereafter, NARA, RG 59, Consular Despatches–Nuevo Laredo), roll 2. The contextual background of Sandoval's raid is in Young, *Catarino Garza's Revolution on the Texas-Mexico Border*, 78–81.

73. #148, Warner P. Sutton to William F. Wharton, 3 July 1890, NARA, RG 59, Consular Despatches–Nuevo Laredo, roll 2; Romero, "Garza Raid and Its Lessons," 326. Details of the trial testimony, some of which are hilarious, are in Young, *Catarino Garza's Revolution on the Texas-Mexico Border*, 81–84. Young also discusses the astounding, unexecuted Mexican plot to kidnap Sandoval, 84–85.

74. John G. Bourke to Assistant Adjutant General, 10 December 1891, NARA, RG 393, Records of U.S. Army Continental Commands, 1821–1920, box 1; Department of Texas, 1870–1893, Letters and Reports received Relating to the Garza Revolution, 1891–93, entry 4877 (hereafter NARA, RG 393, Garza Revolution).

75. FRUS 1893–94, vol. 1, 439–40.

76. Romero, "Garza Raid and Its Lessons," 324.

77. John G. Bourke to Assistant Adjutant General, 10 December 1891, box 1; Report of George F. Chase, Commander of Squadron, Fort Sam Houston, to Assistant Adjutant General J. P. Martin, 31 May 1893, box 2, NARA, RG 393, Garza Revolution. On the cultural significance of Bourke's racial constructions, see Limon, *Dancing With the Devil*, 21–42. On their temporal meaning, see Young, *Catarino Garza's Revolution on the Texas-Mexico Border*, 240–43.

78. Some of the documentation of Garza's revolt is printed in Saldivar, ed., *Documentos de la Rebelion de Catarino E. Garza*; quote is on 10.

79. "Plan Revolucionario de Catarino Garza," in ibid., 13–16. Catarino Garza "Procla-

mation" and partial list of the Garza revolutionaries, "List de los Bandidos," T. B. Dugan, Post Adjutant, Fort McIntosh, 2 January 1892, NARA, RG 393, Garza Revolution, box 1. Young, "Remembering Catarino Garza's 1891 Revolution," 231–72, offers the most concise discussion. A more detailed narrative and analysis of the revolt is Young, *Catarino Garza's Revolution on the Texas-Mexico Border*, especially 98–130, 155–208, 268–70.

80. Blaine to Secretary of War, 11 January 1892; W. H. H. Miller [attorney general] to Blaine, 4 January 1892; John G. Bourke to Assistant Adjutant General, 10 December 1891; telegram of 10 January 1892, NARA, RG 393, Garza Revolution, box 1.

81. Young, *Catarino Garza's Revolution on the Texas-Mexico Border*, 10–11.

82. An example of this mischaracterization is in Pyle, *Extradition, Politics, and Human Rights*, 110–11, where he writes that Benavides and his men "supposedly signed" the manifesto, and then includes the fatuous and loaded remark that "most ranchers, marshals, and sheriffs in the area did not take the political ambitions of Garza's men seriously and characterized them as mere cattle rustlers, smugglers, and robbers." While this was true, it said far more about the ranchers, marshals, and sheriffs than it did about the actual political nature of the Garzistas' actions. Pyle also bases his discussion on an uncomplicated reading of Chief Justice Fuller's argument in *Ornelas v. Ruiz*, 161 U.S. 502 (1896), including approvingly quoting Secretary of State Gresham's facile dismissal of the Garzistas.

83. Special Orders no. 134; Report of George F. Chase, Commander of Squadron, Fort Sam Houston, to Assistant Adjutant General J. P. Martin, 31 May 1893, NARA, RG 393, Garza Revolution, box 2, 5–6.

84. Examination of Enlogio J. Martinez, *In Re Ynez Ruiz*, U.S. Western District of Texas, San Antonio, NARA, RG 59, Extradition Papers: Extradition Case Files, 1836–1906 (hereafter NARA, RG 59, Extradition Case Files), box 39, entry 857; Ornelas to General Frank Wheaton, 20 December 1892, NARA, RG 393, Garza Revolution, box 2. Young, citing Bourke, writes erroneously that Maximo Martínez led the raid (*Catarino Garza's Revolution on the Texas-Mexico Border*, 126–27). However, Captain Chase, General Frank Wheaton, Mexican Consul Ornelas, and the Texas and U.S. courts (including the Supreme Court in 1896) all identified Benavides as the leader of the raid, as discussed variously in this chapter.

85. Ornelas to General Frank Wheaton, 20 December 1892, NARA, RG 393, Garza Revolution, box 2; "Names of men who crossed at San Ygnacio, December 10th, 1892," compiled by A. S. B. Keyes, 9 February 1893, NARA, RG 393, Garza Revolution, box 2; two telegrams, General Frank Wheaton to the Adjutant-General, 23 January 1893, FRUS 1893–94, vol. 1, 440.

86. List of names for distribution of Benavides's manifesto, NARA, RG 393, Garza Revolution, box 2.

87. This is from the official translation of the manifesto from the Benavides trial. There was an alternative translation in the Ruiz trial, which was very close to the origi-

nal. "The Proclamation" and "In the Matter of Francisco Benavides: Application for Extradition," NARA, RG 59, Extradition Case Files, box 36.

88. *In re Ynez Ruiz*, U.S. Western District of Texas, San Antonio. Also see "Manifesto of Procopio Gutierez," ibid.

89. W. Q. Gresham to the Secretary of War, 23 March 1893, sending along the note from Romero to Gresham, 16 March 1893, noting all who had participated in the raid on San Ygnacio and surrendered to Captain Jackson of the 7th Cavalry, including Julian Flores, Librado Guiterrez, Dionisio Salazar, Gregorio Jueborro, Clements Guiterrez, Jose Maria Morales, Auceto Trevino, Tomas Cuellar, Procepio Guiterrez, and Amando Garcia. See also Fernano Salinas, private secretary to Garza, NARA, RG 393, Garza Revolution, box 2.

90. Report of George F. Chase, 31 May 1893, box 2, 21; also Chase to Adjutant General, 12 March 1893, ibid.

91. Report of George F. Chase, 31 May 1893, ibid., 6–8.

92. Ibid., 9–11; Ornelas to Romero, 25 January 1893, ibid.; telegram, Wheaton to the Adjutant-General, 23 January 1893, FRUS 1893–94, vol. 1, 440.

93. Report of George F. Chase, 31 May 1893, NARA, RG 393, Garza Revolution, box 2, 10, 21.

94. Ibid.

95. Ibid., 16.

96. Ibid. On some of the local loyalties, see Young, *Catarino Garza's Revolution on the Texas-Mexico Border*, 172–82.

97. Report of George F. Chase, 31 May 1893, NARA, RG 393, Garza Revolution, box 2, 19.

98. Ibid., 19–20.

99. Benavides file, NARA, RG 59, Extradition Case Files, box 36.

100. Ibid.

101. Ibid.

102. Romero to Gresham, 9 January; 13 March 1894; Uhl to Mr. Romero, 11 January; 12 March; 29 June 1894, FRUS 1894, 426–29. For a discussion of the entire affair, 426–32.

103. This is just a small sample of the 137 pages of testimony. *In Re. Ynez Ruiz*, U.S. Western District of Texas, San Antonio, NARA, RG 59, Extradition Case Files, 1836–1906, box 39, entry 857.

104. Ibid.

105. *Ornelas v. Ruiz*, 504 (1896); Romero to Gresham, 22 May 1894, FRUS 1896, 491.

106. *Ornelas v. Ruiz*, 508–9.

107. Ibid., 510–12.

108. Pyle, *Extradition, Politics, and Human Rights*, 354n30. It is interesting that Pyle

cites this fact and yet still discounts the political nature of the Garzista acts in the body of the text.

109. Romero to Sherman, 28 September 1897; Sherman to Romero, 13 November 1897, FRUS 1896, 498–99.

110. Romero to Sherman, 15 November 1897; Sherman to Romero, 17 December 1897, ibid., 499–502.

111. Sherman to Romero, 17 December 1897; 6 January 1898, ibid., 503–9.

112. Romero to Sherman, 24 January 1898, ibid., 510.

113. The complaint alleged that on August 7, 1896, near Peguis [Peguez?] in Chihuahua, the following men were involved in a raid across the border: Demetrio Cortez, Romualdo Carrzco [maybe Carrasco, as a later Mexican document has it], Jorge Lugo, Crispin Beltran, Mauro Cortez, Gregorio Cortez, Antonio Rodriguez, Tomas Burgues, Francisco Salas, Primo Onzures, Felipe Rubio, Antonio Rubio, Simon Rede, Nabor Rede, Perfecto Baca, Felope Frias, Nieves Jaso, Cosme N. [?], Jesús Zepeda, Epifanio Armendariz, Desiderio Muñoz, Pablo Muñoz, Teodore Sanchez, Albino Saenz, Domingo Luna, Agapito Cortez, Canuto Carrazco, and Preciliano Tarrango. This allegation was based upon the testimony of Eleuterio Franco, including a statement by Luciano Ontiveros (Ontiveros did not sign his statement "because of not knowing how"), Pedro Marquez, and Jenaro [or Genaro] Forzan (Jr.). *Republic of Mexico vs. Demetrio Cortes and 27 Others*, NARA, RG 59, Extradition Case Files, box 47.

114. *Republic of Mexico vs. Demetrio Cortes and 27 Others*, NARA, RG 59, Extradition Case Files, box 47.

115. Ibid.

116. Ibid.

Epilogue

1. *Ker v. Illinois*, 119 U.S. 436 (1886); *United States v. Rauscher*, 119 U.S. 407 (1886). Both were decided on December 6, 1886.

2. Hussain, *Jurisprudence of Emergency*, 7. He dissects the meaning of "rule of law," (see 9–11). Also very useful on these concepts is Sarat, "At the Boundaries of Law: Executive Clemency, Sovereign Prerogative, and the Dilemma of American Legality," in Dudziak and Volpp, eds., *Legal Borderlands*, 19–39.

3. The finer details of Ker's embezzlement came out in another case, *Gray v. Merriam*, in the Supreme Court of Illinois, November 29, 1893. See *Northeastern Reporter*, 811–14. The story of Ker's crimes, flight, and return to the United States can be found in the text of *Ker v. The People*, 110 Ill. 627 (1884) in Gibbons, ed., *American Criminal Reports*, vol. IV, 214–29. Quotations here are drawn from the full text of the Illinois attorney general's brief, which is reprinted in Fairman, "*Ker v. Illinois* Revisited," 684–85.

Fairman notes, the story was so good, "it might be entitled 'The Attorney General's Detective Story,'" 684.

4. On Pinkerton activity on behalf of corporations, see Smith, *From Blackjacks to Briefcases*, 3–21. On Pinkerton numbers and repressiveness, see Chacón and Davis, *No One Is Illegal*, 16. On international work following counterfeiters, see Nadelmann, *Cops across Borders*, 55–60; Andreas and Nadelmann, *Policing the Globe*, 116. Examples of the Pinkertons' international work are listed in "Binders List Crimes A–Z," Pinkerton National Detective Agency Records, Manuscript Division, Library of Congress, Washington, D.C. (hereafter LOC-Pinkerton), box 38. The LOC files are not exhaustive, and many of the materials hint at a much wider range of action. Allan Pinkerton was no stranger to expansive self-promotion, as demonstrated by a long series of self-glorifying books. For his take on the pursuit of criminals in Peru, see Pinkerton, "Don Pedro and the Detectives" in *Mississippi Outlaws and the Detectives*, 125–265.

5. Reno Brothers files, Criminal Case File, 1861–1992, LOC-Pinkerton, folders 7–11, box 153. See also Moffett, "Destruction of the Reno Gang," 549–54, which called the final lynching "swift justice at last." Pinkerton, "Highwaymen of the Railroad," 530–31. The Canadian events are covered in Williams, *Call in the Pinkertons*, 47–56. In February 1890, U.S. consul general at Nuevo Laredo, Warner P. Sutton, reported that a Pinkerton got a fugitive named J. T. Lattner arrested with the help of an American named Charles W. Zaremba in San Luis Potosí, Mexico. Sutton seemed far more concerned about Zaremba's long experience with Mexican justice as a result of the "illegal extradition" than he was about the illegality of Lattner's abduction. #72, Warner P. Sutton to William F. Wharton, 10 February 1890, NARA, RG 59, Despatches from United States Consuls in Nuevo Laredo, 1871–1906, roll 2. On Zaremba's fate, which unfolded over a long period, see #190, 8 October 1890; #213, 29 November 1890; #215, 20 December 1890; #245, 25 February 1891; #266, 10 April 1891; #267, 18 April 1891; #279, 7 May 1891, NARA, RG 59, Despatches from United States Consuls in Nuevo Laredo, 1871–1906, roll 2. Ironically, given his fate, Zaremba was the author of *The Merchants' and Tourists' Guide to Mexico*.

6. Details of Julian's pursuit and the situation in Lima in the Illinois Attorney General brief is reprinted in Fairman, "*Ker v. Illinois* Revisited," 684–85, and in "*Ex Parte Ker* (Circuit Court, N.D. Illinois, October 8, 1883)" in *Federal Reporter* 18: 167–72. On Lima in the War of the Pacific, see Farcau, *Ten Cents War*, 157–70.

7. *Ker v. Illinois*, 438–39 (1886). Once Ker was back in Chicago, however, he refused to talk to reporters when he had the opportunity. *Milwaukee Sentinel*, August 28, 1883.

8. *Ker v. The People*, in Gibbons, ed., *American Criminal Reports*, vol. IV, 217–22.

9. The case was first heard by the U.S. Circuit Court for the Northern District of Illinois in October 1883 in *Ex Parte Ker*, 18 F. 167 (1883). See Spear, *Law of Extradition, International and Inter-State*, 181–86; Fairman, "*Ker v. Illinois* Revisited," 681.

10. "It is sufficient to say in regard to that part of this case that when the governor

of one state voluntarily surrenders a fugitive from the justice of another state to answer for his alleged offenses, it is hardly a proper subject of inquiry on the trial of the case to examine into the details of the proceedings by which the demand was made by the one state and the manner in which it was responded to by the other. The case does not stand, when a party is in court and required to plead to an indictment, as it would have stood upon a writ of habeas corpus in California, or in any of the states through which he was carried in the progress of his extradition, to test the authority by which he was held, and we can see in the mere fact that the papers under which he was taken into custody in California were prepared and ready for him on his arrival from Peru, no sufficient reason for an abatement of the indictment against him in Cook County, or why he should be discharged from custody without a trial." *Ker v. Illinois*, 440–41 (1886).

11. Ibid., 440.

12. Ibid., 442.

13. Ibid., 443.

14. Ibid., 444.

15. Ibid.

16. Lowenfeld, "U.S. Law Enforcement Abroad," 467.

17. Agamben, *State of Exception*, 1. In the same vein in his earlier work, Agamben wrote, "if the exception is the structure of sovereignty, then sovereignty is not an exclusively political concept, an exclusively juridical category, a power external to law . . . or the supreme rule of the juridical order. . . . {I}t is the originary structure in which law refers to life and includes it in itself by suspending it." Agamben, *Homo Sacer*, 28. For the theoretical approaches to the notion of exception, also see Fitzpatrick and Joyce, "The Normality of the Exception in Democracy's Empire," 65–76.

18. Olney, quoted in *Official History of the Discussion between Venezuela and Great Britain on Their Guiana Boundaries*, 404. For the context for the statement, see FRUS, 1895, vol. 1, 545–67; LaFeber, *Cambridge History of American Foreign Relations*, 123–25; Pletcher, *Diplomacy of Trade and Investment*, 313–21.

19. *In re Ross*, 140 U.S. 453, 464 (1891); Neuman, "Whose Constitution," 910.

20. *Underhill v. Hernandez*, 168 U.S. 250, 250–52 (1897).

21. Ibid., 253.

22. The richest array of new approaches to the imperial implementation of this divide is found in McCoy and Scarano, eds., *Colonial Crucible*.

23. *Frisbie v. Collins*, 342 U.S. 519 (1952); *United States v. Alvarez-Machain*, 504 U.S. 655 (1992). There was one exception in 1974, when the abduction also happened to be coupled with three weeks of torture. The abduction-torture case was *United States v. Toscanino*, 504 F.2d 1380 (1974). The literature on modern extraterritorial abduction since World War II is enormous, but, incredibly, there are essentially no historical studies of abduction in U.S. foreign policy. For a brief contextual account of the context, see Gibney, *Five Uneasy Pieces*, 41–44. A few of the best legal studies are Ward, "Forc-

ible Abduction Made Fashionable," 477–504; Abramschmitt, "Neighboring Countries," 122–43; Lonner, "Official Government Abductions in the Presence of Extradition Treaties," 998–1023; Bush, "How Did We Get Here?" 939–83; Matorin, "Unchaining the Law," 907–32; and importantly, Lowenfeld, "U.S. Law Enforcement Abroad: The Constitution and International Law," 880–93, and "U.S. Law Enforcement Abroad: The Constitution and International Law, Continued," 444–93.

24. Kazanjian, *Colonizing Trick*, 223. On the domestic and regional resonance of empire, see Margolies, *Henry Watterson and the New South*, and Fry, *Dixie Looks Abroad* and *John Tyler Morgan and the Search for Southern Autonomy*. In terms of constitutional and ideological aspects of this linkage, see LaFeber, "The Constitution and United States Foreign Policy," 695–717, and "The 'Lion in the Path,'" and Henkin, *Constitutionalism, Democracy, and Foreign Affairs*.

25. On critical aspects of American imperial power, see LaFeber, *New Empire*; McCormick, *China Market*; Williams, *Contours of American History*; Healy, *Drive to Hegemony*; Pletcher, *Diplomacy of Involvement*; Kramer, *Blood of Government*; Gobat, *Confronting the American Dream*; and Jacobson, *Barbarian Virtues*. For conceptualizing legal aspects of empire broadly, see Anghie, *Imperialism, Sovereignty and the Making of International Law*; Koskenniemi, *Gentle Civilizer of Nations*; and Benton, "Constitutions and Empires," *Law and Colonial Cultures: Legal Regimes in World History*, "Legal Spaces of Empire," and "Spatial Geographies of Empire." On international law and hegemony, see Byers and Nolte, eds., *United States Hegemony and the Foundations of International Law*.

26. In the Insular Cases, the United States legitimated the exclusion of the new colonies from open-door equal access to the continental common market via tariff barriers and denied or curtailed the extension of American rights to the colonized. Sparrow, *Insular Cases and the Emergence of American Empire*, 79–211; Kerr, Insular Cases; Burnett and Marshall, eds., *Foreign in a Domestic Sense*.

BIBLIOGRAPHY

Archival and Manuscript Collections

Bancroft Library, University of California, Berkeley.
  Edward Otho Cresap Ord Papers, 1850–83, BANC MSS C–B, 479.
C. L. Sonnichsen Special Collections, University of Texas at El Paso.
  Ciudad Juárez (Mexico) Municipal archives: Documentos históricos/Archivo Municipal de Ciudad Juárez. 1750–1939.
  El Archivo Judicial: Distrito Hidalgo, Parral, Chihuahua, Mexico, 1828–1920, MF 546.
  El Paso County Records, MS 132.
  El Paso del Norte Consular Letters, 1885–86.
  El Paso Herald–Post Records.
  Record of Inspection of Animals and Hides, by the Inspector of El Paso County, Texas, 1889–93.
El Paso Public Library Special Collections.
  A. K. Cutting vertical file.
Library of Congress Manuscript Division, Washington, D.C.
  Grover Cleveland Papers
  Philander C. Knox Papers
  Pinkerton National Detective Agency Records
  Theodore Roosevelt Papers
  Elihu Root Papers
  George Sutherland Papers
National Archives and Records Administration, Washington, D.C.
  Record Group 94: Records of the Adjutant General's Office, ca. 1775–ca. 1928.
    General Orders and Circulars; Special Orders, Department of Texas, 1873, entry 44.
  Record Group 393: Records of U.S. Army Continental Commands, 1821–1920
    Department of Arizona, Letters received, 1886, entry 181.
    Department of Texas, 1870–1893.
    Letters and Reports Received Relating to the Garza Revolution, 1891–93, entry 4877.
    Letters Received Relating to Difficulties with Indians ("Indian File"), 1870–76, entry 4875.

Lists of Letters Sent and received and extracts of Letters Relating to the Jurisdiction of the United States over certain Military Installations, 1883–1891, entry 4876.

Records, Cards and Correspondence Relating to Various Subjects, 1909–12, entry 4882.

National Archives and Records Administration (Archives II), College Park, Md.

Record Group 48: Records of the Office of the Secretary of the Interior, 1826–1981.

Records of the Office of the Secretary of the Interior, United States Department of the Interior, Territorial Papers, Arizona, 1868–1913, microcopy 429, roll 3.

U.S. Department of the Interior, Interior Department Territorial Papers: New Mexico, 1851–1914. Record Group 48 (Records of the Office of the Secretary of the Interior) (15 rolls) Executive Proceedings, Oct. 8, 1874–Dec. 31, 1888, microcopy M-364, roll 1.

Record Group 59: General Records of the Department of State.

Consular Correspondence, 1785–1906: Notes to Foreign Consuls, 1853–1906.

Consular Courts Returns of fines, fees, etc.

Correspondence Regarding the Canadian–Alaskan Boundary.

Despatches from United States Consuls in Ciudad Juárez (Paso del Norte), 1850–1906, M-184.

Despatches from United States Consuls in Durango, 1886–1906, M-290.

Despatches from United States Consuls in Guaymas, 1832–1896, M-284.

Despatches from United States Consuls in Matamoros, 1826–1906, M-281.

Despatches from United States Consuls in Monterrey, 1849–1906, M-165.

Despatches from United States Consuls in Nogales, 1889–1906, M-283.

Despatches from United States Consuls in Nuevo Laredo, 1871–1906, M-280.

Despatches from United States Consuls in Piedras Negras (Ciudad Porfirio Díaz), M-299.

Despatches from U.S. Ministers to Mexico, 1823–1906.

Diplomatic Correspondence Regarding Judicial Procedures in Spain, June 9, 1870–June 28, 1877.

Extradition Papers Correspondence Concerning the Extradition Treaty with Great Britain, 1870–1890.

Extradition Papers: Extradition Case Files, 1836–1906.

Extradition Papers: Printed Report on Extradition Cases, 1842–1890.

Record of Requests made to Italy for the Punishment of Italian Fugitives from U.S. Justice 1869–1910.

Records Relating to Consular Protection in Morocco, 1836–1909.

Returns of Fees, Expenditures, and Balances, compiled 1908–1911.

Special Series of Domestic and Miscellaneous Letters: Misc. Memorandums of conversations of the Secretary of State, 1893–1898.

Record Group 76: Records of the Boundary and Claims Commissions and Arbitrations.

U.S. and Mexican Claims Commission, entries 47, 51, 53, 56, 57, 64, 65, 76, 79, 82, 83, 87–90, 97, 442–44, 479, 486.

Record Group 206: Records of the Solicitor of the Treasury, 1791–1934.

Letters Received, Special Agents (Letters Received from Special Agents of the Treasury, 1858–95), PI-171, entry 36.

Rare Books and Manuscripts, Benson Latin American Collection, University of Texas–Austin.

Catarino Garza manuscript collection: Garza, C. E., "La logica de los hechos o sea, observaciones sobre las circunstancias de los Mexicanos en Texas desde el ano de 1877 Hasta 1889, tomo I," Corpus Christi.

Documentos relativos al establecimiento de la Zona Libre en la frontera de Tamaulipas. Mexico: Imprenta del Gobierno, en Palacio A Cargo de Jose Maria Sandoval, 1869.

Jiménez, Pedro. "Breves Observaciones hechas á las 'Ligeras aclaraciones' publicadas por el General Carlos Ezeta, ex-presidente del Salvador, con motivo del incidente ocurrido en el hotel 'Mariachi Niel' en San Francisco California entre el mismo General Exeta y el." 1896.

Periodicals

Brownsville *Daily Ranchero and Republican*

Brownsville *Sentinel*

The Daily New Mexican (Santa Fe)

El Paso Herald

El Paso Times

Galveston Daily News

Galveston Star

Harper's Weekly

The Independent

The Lone Star (El Paso, Texas)

The Nation

New York Times

San Francisco Daily Evening Bulletin

Two Republics (Mexico City), 1868–99

Washington Post

Government Documents

A Digest of International Law as Embodied in Diplomatic Discussions, Treaties and other International Agreements, International Awards, the Decisions of Municipal Courts, and the Writings of Jurists, and Especially in Documents, Published and Unpublished, Issued by Presidents and Secretaries of State of the United States, the Opinions of the Attorneys-General, and the Decisions of Courts, Federal and State. 8 vols. Washington, D.C.: GPO, 1906.

Boletin Oficial de la Secretaría de Relaciones Exteriores. I, no. 2 (Diciembre 1, 1895). Mexico: Imprenta del Gobierno el el Ex-Arzobispado, 1895.

Boletin Oficial de la Secretaría de Relaciones Exteriores. VII, no. 4 (Febrero 15, 1899). Mexico: Salvador Gutiérrez, 1899.

Boletin Oficial de la Secretaría de Relaciones Exteriores. VIII, no. 5 (Septiembre 15, 1899). Mexico: Salvador Gutiérrez, 1899.

Brigham, J. Harvey. "Growing Importance of Paso del Norte." *Reports from the Consuls of the United States.* XXIII (July–September 1887): 281–84.

"Caso de Extradición de James Temple." *Boletin Oficial de la Secretaría de Relaciones Exteriores.* VII, núm. 4 (Febrero 15, 1899). Mexico: Salvador Gutiérrez, 1899, 195–97.

"Caso de Extradición de Mattie Rich (documentos oficiales)." *Boletin Oficial de la Secretaría de Relaciones Exteriores.* VIII, núm. 5 (Septiembre 15, 1899). Mexico: Salvador Gutiérrez, 1899, 264–73.

"Caso de Extradición de William F. Brice." *Boletin oficial de la Secretaría de Relaciones Exteriores.* V, núm. 5 (Marzo 15, 1898). Mexico: Salvador Gutiérrez, 1899, 271–76.

Chamizal Arbitration: Appendix to the Case of the United States before the International Boundary Commission, United States–Mexico. Vol II. Washington, D.C.: GPO, 1911.

Commercial Relations of the United States with Foreign Countries during the Years 1894 and 1895. 2 vols. Washington, D.C.: GPO, 1896.

Correspondencia diplomatica cambiada entre el gobierno de los Estados Unidos Mexicanos y los de varias potencias extranjeras desde el 30 de Junio de 1881 a 30 de Junio de 1886 (edicion oficial). Tomo III–IV. Mexico: Tipografia "La Luz," 1887.

Correspondencia diplomática sobre el caso del ciudano de los Estados-Unidos de America A. K. Cutting. México: Imprenta del Gobierno Federal, 1886.

"Demanda y resoluciones sobre extradiciéón de los hermanos Rowe." *Boletin oficial de la Secretaría de Relaciones Exteriores.* I, núm. 2 (Diciembre 1, 1895). Mexico: Imprenta del Gobierno el Ex-Arzobispado, 1895, 65–69.

Digest of Official Opinions of the Attorneys-General of the United States covering Volumes 17 to 25, inclusive, 1881–1906. Washington, D.C.: GPO, 1908.

Extraterritoriality: A Letter from the Secretary of State to the Chairman of the Senate Committee on Foreign Relations Concerning the Judicial Exercise of Extraterritorial Rights Conferred Upon the United States. Washington, D.C.: GPO, 1882.

Journal of the House of Representatives, 48th Cong., 1st sess.

Journals of the Thirteenth Legislative Assembly of the Territory of Arizona. San Francisco: H. S. Crocker and Co., 1885.

Mexico, Guaymas, Report of Consul Willard, *Reports from the Consuls of the United States*. XXIII (July–September 1887): 274–80.

Moore, John Bassett. *A Digest of International Law as Embodied in Diplomatic Discussions, Treaties and other International Agreements, International Awards, the Decisions of Municipal Courts, and the Writings of Jurists, and Especially in Documents, Published and Unpublished, Issued by Presidents and Secretaries of State of the United States, the Opinions of the Attorneys-General, and the Decisions of Courts, Federal and State*. Vol. IV. Washington: GPO, 1906.

———. *Report on Extradition, with Returns of all Cases from August 9, 1842 to January 1, 1890 and an Index*. Washington, D.C.: GPO, 1890.

———. *Report on Extraterritorial Crime and the Cutting Case*. Washington, D.C.: GPO, 1887.

Naval War College, *International Law Situations with Solutions and Notes, 1902*. Washington, D.C.: GPO, 1903.

Official History of the Discussion between Venezuela and Great Britain on Their Guiana Boundaries. Atlanta: Franklin Printing and Publishing Company, 1896.

Official Opinions of the Attorneys General of the United States XXI. Washington, D.C.: GPO, 1898.

Regulations prescribed for the Use of the Consular Service of the United States. Washington, D.C.: GPO, 1896.

Report Transmitted from the Office of the Secretary of Foreign Relations of the Republic of Guatemala to the National Legislative Assembly, Concerning the Capture and Death of General J. Martín Barrundia. Guatemala: Tipografia y Encuadernación El Modelo, 1891.

Reports of the Industrial Commission on Immigration, including Testimony, with Review and Digest, and Special Reports and on Education, including Testimony, with Review and Digest. Vol. XV. Washington, D.C.: GPO, 1901.

Roberts, O. M. "Constitutional Amendments, March 10, 1881." *Collections of the Archive & History Department of the Texas State Library, Executive Series: Governors' Messages, Coke to Ross (Inclusive), 1874–1891*. [Austin]: Texas State Library, 1916, 379–82.

———. "Initial Message to the Eighteenth Legislature, January 20, 1883." *Collections of the Archive & History Department of the Texas State Library, Executive Series: Governors' Messages, Coke to Ross (Inclusive), 1874–1891*. [Austin]: Texas State Library, 1916, 430–67.

Rosenberger, José. "The Free Zone." *Consular Reports: Commerce, Manufactures, Etc.* LVIII, nos. 212, 213, 214, 215. May, June, July, August 1898. Washington, D.C.: GPO, 1898.

Texas. *Journal of the House of Representatives.* 24th Legislature, City of Austin, started January 8, 1895. Austin: Ben C. Jones and Co., 1895.

U.S. Congress. House. "Treaties with Lubeck, Bremen, and Hamburg. Message from the President of the United States, transmitting copies of a convention between the United States and the Free Hanseatic Republics of Lubeck, Bremen, and Hamburg, ratified on the 2d of June last. January 26, 1829." 20th Cong., 2nd sess., H. Doc. 92.

U.S. Congress. House. "Affairs on the Texas Frontier: Letter from the Secretary of War Relative to the Political Complexion of Affairs on the Texas Frontier." 42nd Cong., 2nd sess., H. Ex. Doc. 216.

U.S. Congress. House. "Texas Frontier Troubles." 44th Cong., 1st sess., H. Rep. 343.

U.S. Congress. House. "Depredations on the Texas Frontier." 44th Cong., 1st sess., H. Misc. Doc. 37.

U.S. Congress. House. "Mexican Border Troubles." 45th Cong., 1st sess., H. Ex. Doc. 13.

U.S. Congress. House. "El Paso Troubles in Texas." 45th Cong., 2nd sess., H. Ex. Doc. 93.

U.S. Congress. House. "Report and Accompanying Documents of the Committee on Foreign Affairs on the Relations of the United States with Mexico." 45th Cong., 2nd sess., H. Rep. 701.

U.S. Congress. House. "Treaty With Mexico." 45th Cong., 3rd sess., H. Rep. 108.

U.S. Congress. House. "Lawlessness in Parts of Arizona." 47th Cong., 1st sess., H. Ex. Doc. 58.

U.S. Congress. House. "Imprisonment of A. K. Cutting in Mexico." 49th Cong., 1st sess., H. Ex. Doc. 371.

U.S. Congress. House. "Irrigation of Arid Lands; International Boundary; Mexican Relations." 51st Cong., 1st sess., H. Rep. 490.

U.S. Congress. House. "Negotiations with Mexico." 51st Cong., 1st sesss, H. Rep. 1967.

U.S. Congress. House. "The Barrundia Case. The Message from the President of the United States, Transmitting, In response to a resolution of the House of Representatives, a report of the Secretary of State and Accompanying Correspondence in Relation to the Killing of General J. Martin Barrundia." 51st Cong., 2nd sess., H. Ex. Doc. 51.

U.S. Congress. House. "The Mexican Zona Libre." Reports from the Consuls of the United States, vol. XXXVIII: Consular Reports on Commerce, Manufactures, etc. 52nd Cong., 1st sess., H. Misc. Doc. 154.

U.S. Congress. House. "Certain Correspondence between the United States and Mexico." 53rd Cong., 2nd sess. H. Misc. Doc. 152.

U.S. Congress. House. "Mexican Free Zone." 53rd Cong., 3rd sess., H. Rep. 1850.

U.S. Congress. House. "*International Bureau of the American Republics, Mexico: Geographical Sketch, Natural Resources, Laws, Economic Conditions, Actual Development, Prospects of Future Growth.*" 58th Cong., 3rd sess., H. Doc. 145.

U.S. Congress. House. "Letter from the Secretary of State Submitting Report on the Subject of Citizenship of the United States, Expatriation, and Protection Abroad, December 20, 1906—Referred to the Committee on Foreign Affairs and Ordered to Be Printed." 59th Cong., 2nd sess., H. Doc. 326.

U.S. Congress. Senate. "In the Senate of the United States. January 24, 1882. Ordered to be printed. Mr. Garland, from the Committee on the Judiciary, submitted the following report (to accompany Bill S. 979). In the matter of the resolution of inquiry touching the proceedings for the extradition of one Vincenzo [i.e., Vicenzo] Rebello, an Italian, &c." 47th Cong., 1st sess., S. Rep. 82.

U.S. Congress. Senate. "Message from the President of the United States Transmitting, In response to Senate Resolution of May 2, 1884, report of the Secretary of State relative to the latest law of the Mexican Republic creating or modifying the Zona Libre." 48th Cong., 1st sess., S. Ex. Doc. 185.

U.S. Congress. Senate. "Letter from the Secretary of the Treasury in response to the Senate Resolution of February 16, 1888, relative to Smuggling in the Free Zone of Mexico." 50th Cong., 1st sess., S. Ex. Doc. 108.

U.S. Congress. Senate. "A letter of the Secretary of State in Response to Senate Resolution of February 16, 1888, relative to the Mexican Zona Libre." 50th Cong., 1st sess., S. Ex. Doc. 130.

U.S. Congress. Senate. "Trade and transportation between the United States and Latin America, by William Eleroy Curtis, Executive Officer, International American Conference," 51st Cong., 1st sess., S. Exec. Doc. 54.

U.S. Congress. Senate. "Report on Extradition Prepared by the Third Assistant Secretary of State for the Use of the International American Conference, February 13, 1890." 51st Cong., 2nd sess., S. Ex. Doc. 55.

U.S. Congress. Senate. "Message from the President of the United States, Transmitting a Report of the International American Conference on the Extradition of Criminals." 51st Cong., 2nd sess., S. Ex. Doc. 187.

U.S. Congress. Senate. "Second International Conference of American States, Message from the President of the United States, transmitting a Communication from the Secretary of State, submitting, the Report, with accompanying Papers, of the Delegates of the United States to the Second International Conference of American States, held at the City of Mexico from October 22, 1901 to January 22, 1902." 57th Cong., 1st sess., S. Doc. 330.

U.S. Congress. Senate. "Treaties, Conventions, International Acts, Protocols and Agreements between the United States of America and Other Powers, 1776–1909," 2 vols. 61st Cong., 2nd sess., S. Doc. 357.

U.S. Department of State. *Consular Reports, Commerce, Manufacturers, etc.,* 1895–98.

U.S. Department of State. *Papers relating to the Foreign Relations of the United States* (FRUS), 1865–1900.

U.S. General Accounting Office, Office of the General Counsel. *U.S. Insular Areas: Ap-*

plication of the U.S. Constitution, Report to the Chairman, Committee on Resources, House of Representatives (November 1997).

Wharton, Francis, ed. A Digest of International Law taken from Documents, Issued by Presidents and Secretaries of State and from the Decisions of Federal Courts and Opinions of the Attorneys–General. 3 vols. Washington, D.C.: GPO, 1887.

Primary Sources

Angell, James B., George Ticknor Curtis, Thomas M. Cooley, "The Extradition of Dynamite Criminals." North American Review 141, no. 344 (July 1885): 47–59.

Baker, Sir Sherston. Halleck's International Law or Rules Regulating the Intercourse of States in Peace and War. 3rd ed. Vol. 1. London: Kegan Paul, Trench, Trübner, and Co., 1893.

Barra, Francisco L., de la. Estudio sobre la Ley Mexicana de Extradicion. Mexico: Imprenta del Gobierno Federal, 1897.

Bourke, John G. Apache Campaign in the Sierra Madre: An Account of the Expedition in Pursuit of the Hostile Chiricahua Apaches in the Spring of 1883. New York: Charles Scribner's Sons, 1958.

Brooks, William Gray. "Legal Aspects of the Killing of General Barrundia." United Service: A Monthly Review of Military and Naval Affairs 5, new series (June 1): 568–76.

Clark, William L., William L. Marshall, and Herschel Bouton Lazell. Treatise on the Law of Crimes. 2nd ed. St. Paul: Keefe-Davidson Corp., 1905.

Clarke, Sir Edward. Treatise upon the Law of Extradition with the Conventions upon the Subject Existing between England and Foreign Nations and the Cases Decided Thereon. London: Steven and Haynes, 1888.

Collections of the Archive & History Department of the Texas State Library, Executive Series: Governors' Messages, Coke to Ross (Inclusive), 1874–1891. [Austin]: Texas State Library, 1916.

Davis, George B. Elements of International Law with an Account of Its Origin, Sources and Historical Development. New York: Harper's Brothers, 1900.

Devlin, Robert T. The Treaty Power Under the Constitution of the United States: Commentaries on the Treaty Clauses of the Constitution; Construction of Treaties; Event of Treaty-Making Power; Conflict between Treaties and Acts of Congress, State Constitutions and Statutes; International Extradition; Acquisition of Territory; Ambassadors, Consuls and Foreign Judgments; Naturalization and Expatriation; Responsibility of Government for Mob Violence, and Claims Against Governments. San Francisco: Bancroft-Whitney Company, 1908.

Federal Reporter 62: Cases Argued and Determined in the Circuit and District Courts of the United States, June–August, 1894. St. Paul: West Publishing Company, 1894.

Foster, John W. "A Foreign Sovereign in an American Court: A Novel Case in International Practice." Yale Law Journal 9, no. 7 (May 1900): 283–86.

Gibbons, J. H. "Extraterritoriality and Asylum." *Proceedings of the United States Naval Institute* 20, no. 2 (whole no. 70) (1894): 301–12.

Gibbons, John, ed., *American Criminal Reports: A Series Designed to Contain the Latest and Most Important Criminal Cases Determined in the Federal and State Courts in the United States, as well as Selected Cases, Important to American Lawyers, from the English, Irish, Scotch and Canadian Law Reports with Notes and References.* Vol. IV. Chicago: Callaghan and Company, 1885.

Hall, William Edward. *Treatise on International Law.* 2nd ed. Oxford: Clarendon Press, 1884.

Hamilton, Leonidas. *Border States of Mexico: Sonora, Sinaloa, Chihuahua and Durango, with a General Sketch of the Republic of Mexico, and Lower California, Coahuila, New Leon and Tamaulipas, A Complete Description of the Best Regions for the Settler, Miner and the Advance Guard of American Civilization.* 4th ed. New York, 1883.

———. *Hamilton's Mexican Law: A Compilation of Mexican Legislation Affecting Foreigners, Rights of Foreigners, Commercial Law, Property Real and Personal, Rights Pertaining to the Inhabitants of the Republic, Sales, Prescription, Mortgages, Insovency, Liens, Rights of Husband and Wife, Donations, Dower, Quit-rent, Leases, Inheritance, Commercial Companies, Partnership, Agency, Corporations, etc., etc., Procedure, Attachment, Levy under Execution, Property Exempt, Registry, etc., Land Laws and Water Rights—Mexican Constitution—Jurisdiction of Courts—Writ of Amparo—Extracts from Treaties—Mexican Decisions of Federal and State Courts and Mexican Mining Law Annotated.* San Francisco, 1882.

Harris, T. M. *History of the Great Conspiracy: Trial of the Conspirators by a Military Commission and a Review of the Trial of John H. Surratt.* Boston: American Citizen Company, 1892.

Hawley, John G. *Inter-State Extradition.* Detroit: John G. Hawley, 1890.

———. *Law and Practice International Extradition between the United States and Those Foreign Countries with Which It Has Treaties of Extradition.* Chicago: Callaghan and Company, 1893.

Hurd, Rollin C. *Treatise on the Right of Personal Liberty and on the Writ of Habeas Corpus and the Practice Connected with It and a View of the Law of Extradition of Fugitives.* 2nd ed. Albany: W. C. Little & Co., 1876.

International American Conference: Reports of Committees and Discussions Thereon. Washington, D.C., 1890.

Lawrence, William Beach. "Hon. William Beach Lawrence on Extradition." *Albany Law Journal* 19 (1879): 329–35.

Lodge, Henry Cabot. *A Fighting Frigate and Other Essays and Addresses.* New York: Charles Scribner's Sons, 1902.

Martí, Jose, *Selected Writings.* Edited and translated by Esther Allen. New York: Penguin, 2002.

"Mexican Outrages on the Texas Border." Speech of Hon. Richard Coke of Texas in the Senate of the United States November 14, 1877. Washington, D.C.; Austin: Center for American History, University of Texas–Austin, 1877.

Mills, Anson. *My Story.* 2nd ed. Washington, D.C.: Bryon S. Adams, 1921.

Moncada, J. M. *Imperialism and the Monroe Doctrine (Their Influence in Central America).* New York, 1911.

Moore, John Bassett. *American Diplomacy: Its Spirit and Achievements.* New York: Harper & Brothers, 1905.

———. "Asylum in Legations and Consulates and in Vessels. I." *Political Science Quarterly* 7, no. 1 (March 1892): 1–37.

———. "Asylum in Legations and Consulates and in Vessels. II." *Political Science Quarterly* 7, no. 2 (June 1892): 197–231.

———. "Asylum in Legations and Consulates and in Vessels. III." *Political Science Quarterly* 7, no. 3 (September 1892): 397–418.

———. *Collected Papers of John Bassett Moore.* 7 vols. New Haven: Yale University Press, 1944.

———. "Difficulties of Extradition." *Proceedings of the Academy of Political Science in the City of New York* 1, no. 4 (July 1911): 625–34.

———. *Four Phases of American Development: Federalism—Democracy—Imperialism—Expansion.* Baltimore: Johns Hopkins Press, 1912.

———. "The Russian Extradition Treaty." *The Forum* 15 (1893): 629–46.

———. *Treatise on Extradition and Interstate Rendition.* 2 vols. Boston: Boston Book Company, 1891.

Morgan, John T. "Mexico." *North American Review* 136, no. 318 (May 1883): 409–18.

Morgan, Samuel T., William H. Masson, and Charles H. Morgan. *Digest of the United States Tariff and Customs Laws, with a Schedule of Duties on Imports.* 8th ed. Baltimore: Samuel T. Morgan and Co., 1895.

Morse, Alexander Porter. "The International Status of a Public Vessel in Foreign Waters." *Albany Law Journal; A Weekly Record of the Law and the Lawyers* 50, no. 13 (September 29, 1894): 204–6.

Northeastern Reporter, volume 35, Containing All the Current Decisions of the Supreme Courts of Massachusetts, Ohio, Illinois, Indiana, Appellate Court of Indiana, and the Court of Appeals of New York. Permanent Edition, November 24, 1893–February 9, 1894. St. Paul: West Publishing Co., 1894.

Palacios, Jesus M. *La Prision del Americano A. K. Cutting en Paso Del Norte: Estudio sobre el Articulo 186 del Código Penal del Estado de Chihuahua.* Chihuahua: Imprenta Goméz del Campo, 1886.

Piggott, Francis Taylor. *Extradition: A Treatise on the Law Relating to Fugitive Offenders.* London: Butterworth & Co., 1910.

————. *Extraterritoriality: The Law Relating to Consular Jurisdiction and to Residence in Oriental Countries.* London: William Clowes and Sons, 1892.

Platt, Charles Malcom. "A Triad of Political Conceptions: State, Sovereign, Government." *Political Science Quarterly* 10, no. 2 (June 1895): 292–323.

Proceedings of the Convention of the American Banker's Association Held at Saratoga Springs, N.Y. August 16th and 17th, 1882 with Constitution and By-Laws and an Appendix. 2nd ed. New York: Banker's Publishing Association, 1882.

Reciprocidad Comercial entre México y los Estados Unidos. México: Oficina Tip. De la Secretaría de Fomento, 1890.

Reform Government in the Dominion: Pic-Nic Speeches Delivered in the Province of Ontario during the Summer of 1877 by the Hon. A. MacKenzie, Hon. E. Blake, Hon. R. J. Cartwright, Hon. L. S. Huntington, Hon. D. Mills. Toronto: Globe Printing and Publishing Company, 1878.

Report of the Secretary of Finance of the United States of Mexico on the 15th of January, 1879 on the Actual Condition of Mexico, and the Increase of Commerce with the United States, Rectifying the Report of the Hon. John W. Foster, Envoy Extraordinary and Minister Plenipotentiary of the United States of Mexico, the 9th of October, 1878. New York: N. Ponce De Leon Publisher and Printer, 1880.

Reports of Cases Adjudged in the District Court of South Carolina by the Hon. Thomas Bee, Judge of that Court, to Which is Added an Appendix Containing Decisions in the Admiralty Court of Pennsylvania by the late Francis Hopkinson, Esquire and Cases Determined in other Districts of the United States. Philadelphia: William P. Farrand and Co., 1810.

Richardson, James D., ed. *Compilation of the Messages and Papers of the Presidents, 1789– 1908.* Washington, D.C.: Bureau of National Literature and Art, 1908.

Romero, Matías. "The Free Zone in Mexico." *North American Review* 154, no. 425 (April 1892): 459–71.

————. "The Garza Raid and Its Lessons." *North American Review*, 155, no. 430 (September 1892): 324–37.

————. *Mexico and the United States: A Study of Subjects Affecting Their Political, Commercial, and Social Relations, Made with a View to Their Promotion.* New York and London: G. P. Putnam's Sons, 1898.

Saldivar, Gabriel, ed., *Documentos de la Rebelion de Catarino E. Garza en la Frontera de Tamaulipas y Sur de Texas, 1891–1892.* Mexico D.F., 1943.

Scott, James A. *The Law of Interstate Rendition, Erroneously Referred to as Interstate Extradition.* Chicago: Sherman Hight, 1917.

Scott, James Brown, ed. *Resolutions of the Institute of International Law Dealing with the Law of Nations, with an Historical Introduction and Explanatory Notes.* New York: Oxford University Press, 1916.

Secretaría de Relaciones Exteriores, *Case of the American, A. K. Cutting: Latest Notes*

Exchanged Between the Legation of the United States of America and the Minister of Foreign Relations of the Republic of Mexico. Washington, D.C.: Judd and Detweiler, Printers, 1888.

Snow, Freeman. *Cases and Opinions on International Law with Notes and a Syllabus*. Boston: Boston Book Company, 1893.

Spear, Samuel Thayer. *Law of Extradition, International and Inter-State: With an Appendix Containing the Extradition Treaties and Laws of the United States, the Extradition Laws of the States, Several Sections of the English Extradition Act of 1870, and the Opinion of Governor Cullom*. 3rd ed. Albany: Weed, Parsons & Company, 1885.

State Papers, etc., etc., etc., of Chester A. Arthur, President of the United States. Washington, D.C., 1885.

Sutherland, George. "Internal and External Powers of the National Government." *North American Review* CXCI (1910): 373–89.

Taylor, Hannis. *Treatise of International Public Law*. Chicago: Callaghan & Company, 1901.

Tosti, Gustavo. "Anarchistic Crimes." *Political Science Quarterly* 14, no. 3 (September 1899): 404–17.

Tratado de Extradicion entre los Estados-Unidos Mexicanos y los Estados-Unidos de America. Mexico: Imprenta de Vincente Garcia Torres, 1862.

Treaties and Conventions between the Empire of Japan and Other Powers Compiled by the Foreign Office. Tokio: Z. P. Maruya and Co. Ltd., 1899.

Webster, Prentiss. *A Treatise on the Law of Citizenship in the United States*. Albany: Matthew Bender, 1891.

Wharton, Francis. *Dynamiting and Extra-Territorial Crime*. Jersey City, N.J.: Frederick D. Linn & Co., 1885.

———. *Treatise on Criminal Law*. 8th ed. 2 vols. Philadelphia: Kay and Brother, 1880.

Woolsey, Theodore Salisbury, ed. "An Inquiry Concerning Our Foreign Relations." *Yale Review* 1 (August 1892): 162–74.

———. *Introduction to the Study of International Law*. 6th rev. ed. New York: Charles Scribner's Sons, 1901.

———. *Lectures on International Law in Time of Peace by John Norton Pomeroy*. Boston: Houghton, Mifflin and Company, 1886.

Zaremba, Charles W. *Merchants' and Tourists' Guide to Mexico*. Chicago: Althrop Publishing House, 1883.

Secondary Works

Abramschmitt, Dea. "Neighboring Countries; Un-Neighborly Acts: A Look at the Extradition Relationships among the United States, Mexico, and Canada." *Journal of Transnational Law and Policy* 4 (1995): 122–43.

Adams, John A., Jr. *Bordering the Future: The Impact of Mexico on the United States.* Westport: Praeger, 2006.

Agamben, Giorgio. *Homo Sacer: Sovereign Power and Bare Life.* Stanford: Stanford University Press, 1998.

———. *State of Exception.* Translated by Kevin Attell. Chicago: University of Chicago Press, 2005.

Akehurst, Michael. "Jurisdiction in International Law." *British Yearbook of International Law* 46 (1972–73): 145–257.

Aleinikoff, T. Alexander. *Semblances of Sovereignty: The Constitution, the State, and American Citizenship.* Cambridge: Harvard University Press, 2002.

Andreas, Peter, and Ethan Nadelmann. *Policing the Globe: Criminalization and Crime Control in International Relations.* Oxford: Oxford University Press, 2006.

Anghie, Antony. *Imperialism, Sovereignty and the Making of International Law.* Cambridge: Cambridge University Press, 2005.

Archdeacon, Thomas. *Becoming American: An Ethnic History.* New York: The Free Press, 1983.

Banoff, Barbara Ann, and Christopher H. Pyle. "'To Surrender Political Offenders': The Political Offence Exception to Extradition in United States Law." *New York University Journal of International Law & Politics* 16, no. 2 (1984): 169–210.

Bassiouni, M. Cherif. *International Extradition: United States Law and Practice.* 5th ed. Oxford: Oxford University Press, 2007.

Bayitch, S. A., and José Luis Siqueiros. *Conflict of Laws: Mexico and the United States, A Bilateral Study.* Coral Gables: University of Miami Press, 1968.

Beatty, Edward. "Impact of Foreign Trade on the Mexican Economy: Terms of Trade and the Rise of Industry 1880–1923." *Journal of Latin American Studies* 32, no. 2 (May 2000): 399–433.

Bedi, Satyadeva. *Extradition: A Treatise on the Laws Relevant to the Fugitive Offenders within and with the Commonwealth Countries.* Buffalo: William S. Hein & Co., 2002.

Bell, Samuel E., and James M. Smallwood. *The Zona Libre, 1858–1905: A Problem in American Diplomacy.* El Paso: Texas Western Press, 1982.

Benton, Lauren. "Constitutions and Empires." *Law & Social Inquiry* 31, no. 1 (2006): 177–98.

———. *Law and Colonial Cultures: Legal Regimes in World History, 1400–1900.* Cambridge: Cambridge University Press, 2002.

———. "Legal Regime of the South Atlantic World: Jurisdictional Politics as Institutional Order." *Journal of World History* 11, no. 1 (2000): 27–56.

———. "Legal Spaces of Empire: Piracy and the Origins of Ocean Regionalism." *Comparative Studies in Society and History,* 47, no. 4 (October 2005): 700–724.

———. "Spatial Geographies of Empire." *Itinerario* 30, no. 3 (2006): 19–34.

Benton–Cohen, Katherine. *Borderline Americans: Racial Division and Labor War in the Arizona Borderlands.* Cambridge: Harvard University Press, 2009.

Berman, Paul Schiff. "From International Law to Law and Globalization." *Columbia Journal of Transnational Law* 43 (2005): 485–556.

———. "Global Legal Pluralism." *Southern California Law Review* 80 (September 2007): 1155–1238.

———. "The Globalization of Jurisdiction." *University of Pennsylvania Law Review* 151, no. 2 (December 2002): 311–529.

"Bibliography on Extradition." *American Journal of International Law* 29, supplement, *Research in International Law* (1935): 51–65.

Blakesley, Christopher L. "Jurisdictional Issues and Conflicts of Jurisdictions." In *Legal Responses to International Terrorism: U.S. Procedural Aspects*, edited by M. Cherif Bassiouni, 181–202. Dordrecht: Martin Nijhoff Publishers, 1988.

———. "United States Jurisdiction over Extraterritorial Crime." *Journal of Criminal Law and Criminology* 73, no. 3 (Autumn 1982): 1109–63.

Blocker, Jack S., David M. Fahey, and Ian R. Tyrrell, eds. *Alcohol and Temperance in Modern History.* Santa Barbara: ABC-CLIO, 2003.

Blomley, Nicholas, David Delaney, and Richard T. Ford, eds. *Legal Geographies Reader.* Oxford: Blackwell Publishers, 2001.

Blumenthal, Susanna L. "The Default Legal Person." *UCLA Law Review* 54, no. 5 (2007): 1135–1266.

Booth, V. E. Hartley. *British Extradition Law and Procedure.* Alphen aan den Rijn: Sijthoff & Noordhoff, 1980.

Bratspies, Rebecca M., and Russell A. Miller, eds. *Transboundary Harm in International Law: Lessons from the Trail Smelter Arbitration.* Cambridge: Cambridge University Press, 2006.

Brenner, Neil. "Beyond State-Centrism? Space, Territoriality, and Geographical Scale in Globalization Studies." *Theory and Society* 28, no. 1 (February 1999): 39–78.

Brilmayer, Lea. "The Extraterritorial Application of American Law: A Methodological and Constitutional Appraisal." *Law and Contemporary Problems* 50, no. 3 (1987): 11–38.

Burnett, Christina Duffy. "The Edges of Empire and the Limits of Sovereignty: American Guano Islands." In *Legal Borderlands: Law and the Construction of American Borders*, edited by Mary L. Dudziak and Leti Volpp, 187–211. Baltimore: Johns Hopkins University Press, 2006.

———. "'Untied' States: American Expansion and Territorial Deannexation." *University of Chicago Law Review* 72, no. 3 (Summer 2005): 797–879.

Burnett, Christina Duffy, and Burke Marshall, eds. *Foreign in a Domestic Sense: Puerto Rico, American Expansion, and the Constitution.* Durham, N.C.: Duke University Press, 2001.

Bush, Jonathan A. "How Did We Get Here? Foreign Abduction after Alvarez-Machain." *Stanford Law Review* 45, no. 4 (April 1993): 939–83.

Calhoun, Frederick A. *The Lawmen: United States Marshals and Their Deputies, 1789–1989.* Washington: Smithsonian Institution Press, 1989.

Cameron, Angus, and Ronen Palan. *The Imagined Economies of Globalization.* London: Sage Publications, 2004.

Castel, J. G. *Extraterritoriality in International Trade: Canada and the United States of America Practices Compared.* Toronto: Butterworths, 1988.

Chacón, Justin Akers, and Mike Davis. *No One Is Illegal: Fighting Racism and State Violence on the U.S.-Mexico Border.* Chicago: Haymarket Books, 2006.

Chin, Gabriel J. "Chae Chan Ping and Fong Yue Ting: The Origins of Plenary Power." In *Immigration Stories*, edited by David Martin and Peter Schuck, 7–30. New York: Foundation Press 2005.

Clapp, Edwin J. "Foreign Trading Zones in Our Seaports." *American Economic Review* 12, no. 2 (June 1922): 262–71.

Cleveland, Sarah H. "Our International Constitution." *Yale Journal of International Law* 31, no. 1 (2006): 1–125.

———. "Powers Inherent in Sovereignty: Indians, Aliens, Territories, and the Nineteenth Century Origins of Plenary Power over Foreign Affairs." *Texas Law Review* 81 (November 2002): 1–284.

Cool, Paul. *Salt Warriors: Insurgency on the Rio Grande.* College Station: Texas A & M University Press, 2008.

Crapol, Edward. *James G. Blaine: Architect of Empire.* Wilmington: Scholarly Resources, 2000.

Cress, Larry D. "The Jonathan Robbins Incident: Extradition and the Separation of Powers in the Adams Administration." *Essex Institute Historical Collections* 111, no. 2 (1975): 99–121.

Davids, Jules. *American Political and Economic Penetration of Mexico, 1877–1920.* Reprint. New York: Arno Press, 1976.

De León, Arnoldo. *They Called Them Greasers: Anglo Attitudes toward Mexicans in Texas, 1821–1900.* Austin: University of Texas Press, 1983.

Devins, Neal, and Louis Fisher. *The Democratic Constitution.* New York: Oxford University Press, 2004.

Dirlik, Arif. "The Asia-Pacific in Asian–American Perspective." In *What Is in a Rim? Critical Perspectives on the Pacific Region Idea*, edited by Arif Dirlik, 283–308. Lanham: Rowan and Littlefield, 1998.

———, ed. *Chinese on the American Frontier.* Lanham: Rowman and Littlefield, 2001.

Dobak, William A. *Fort Riley and Its Neighbors: Military Money and Economic Growth, 1853–1895.* Norman: University of Oklahoma Press. 1998.

Dudziak, Mary L., and Ledi Volpp, eds. *Legal Borderlands: Law and the Construction of American Borders*. Baltimore: Johns Hopkins University Press, 2006.

Eckes Jr., Alfred E., and Thomas W. Zeiler. *Globalization and the American Century*. Cambridge: Cambridge University Press, 2003.

E. D. D., "The 'Hot Trail' into Mexico and Extradition Analogies." *Michigan Law Review* 20, no. 5 (March 1922): 536–37.

"'El Chamizal' Dispute between the United States and Mexico." *American Journal of International Law* 4, no. 4 (October 1910): 925–30.

Ettinger, Patrick. *Imaginary Lines: Border Enforcement and the Origins of Undocumented Immigration, 1882–1930*. Austin: University of Texas Press, 2009.

Evans, Alona E. "Observations on the Practice of Territorial Asylum in the United States." *American Journal of International Law* 56, no. 1 (January 1962): 148–57.

Fairman, Charles. "*Ker v. Illinois* Revisited." *American Journal of International Law* 47, no. 4 (October 1953): 678–86.

Farcau, Bruce W. *The Ten Cents War: Chile, Peru, and Bolivia in the War of the Pacific, 1879–1884*. Westport: Praeger, 2000.

Federman, Cary. *The Body and the State: Habeas Corpus and American Jurisprudence*. Albany: State University of New York Press, 2006.

Fine, Sidney. "Anarchism and the Assassination of McKinley." *American Historical Review* 60, no. 4 (July 1955): 777–99.

Fisk, George Mygatt. *International Commercial Policies, with Special Reference to the United States*. New York: MacMillan, 1921.

Fitzpatrick, Peter, and Richard Joyce. "The Normality of the Exception in Democracy's Empire." *Journal of Law and Society* 34, no. 1 (March 2007): 65–76.

Fong, Lawrence Michael. "Sojourners and Settlers: The Chinese Experience in Arizona." In *Chinese on the American Frontier*, edited by Arif Dirlik, 39–54. Lanham: Rowman and Littlefield, 2001.

Ford, Richard T. "Law's Territory (A History of Jurisdiction)." In *The Legal Geographies Reader*, edited by Nicholas Blomley, David Delaney, and Richard T. Ford, 200–217. Oxford: Blackwell Publishers, 2001.

Frey, Linda S., and Marsha L. Frey. *History of Diplomatic Immunity*. Columbus: Ohio State University Press, 1999.

Friedman, Lawrence M. *History of American Law*. 3rd ed. New York: Touchstone, 2005.

Fry, Joseph A. *Dixie Looks Abroad: The South and U.S. Foreign Relations, 1789–1973*. Baton Rouge: Louisiana State University Press, 2002.

———. *John Tyler Morgan and the Search for Southern Autonomy*. Knoxville: University of Tennessee Press, 1992.

Fuller, Lon L. *Legal Fictions*. Stanford: Stanford University Press, 1967.

Garcia, Mario T. "Porfirian Diplomacy and the Administration of Justice in Texas, 1877–1900." *Aztlán: A Journal of Chicano Studies* 16, nos. 1–2 (1985): 1–25.

Gard, Wayne. "The Fence-Cutters." *Southwestern Historical Quarterly* 51, no. 1 (July 1947): 1–15.

Gibney, Mark. *Five Uneasy Pieces: American Ethics in a Globalized World.* New York: Rowman and Littlefield, 2005.

Gilbert, Barry. "The Practice of Asylum in Legations and Consulates of the United States." *American Journal of International Law* 3, no. 3 (July 1909): 562–95.

Gilbert, Geoff. *Aspects of Extradition Law.* Dordecht: Martinus Nijhoff Publishers, 1991.

———. *Transnational Fugitive Offenders in International Law: Extradition and Other Mechanisms.* The Hague: Kluwer Law International, 1998.

Gobat, Michel. *Confronting the American Dream: Nicaragua under U.S. Imperial Rule.* Durham: Duke University Press, 2005.

Goldstein, Judith. *Ideas, Interests, and American Trade Policy.* Ithaca and London: Cornell University Press, 1993.

Gómez, Arthur. *A Most Singular Country: A History of Occupation in the Big Bend.* Salt Lake City: Signature Books, 1990.

Gomez, Laura E. *Manifest Destinies: The Making of the Mexican American Race.* New York: New York University Press, 2007.

González Oropeza, Manuel. *Secuestrar para Juzgar Pasado y Presente de la Justicia Extraterritorial.* Mexico: Universidad Nacional Autónoma de México, 1998.

Gordon, Hugh Taylor. *The Treaty of Washington, Concluded August 9, 1842, by Daniel Webster and Lord Ashburton.* Berkeley: The University Press, 1908.

Gordon, Robert W. "Critical Legal Histories." *Stanford Law Review* 36 (January 1984): 57–125.

Green, James R. *Grass Roots Socialism: Radical Movements in the Southwest, 1895–1943.* Baton Rouge: Louisiana State University Press, 1978.

Gregg, Robert D. *The Influence of Border Troubles on Relations Between the United States and Mexico, 1876–1910.* Baltimore: Johns Hopkins Press, 1937.

Gregory, Charles Noble. "Jurisdiction over Foreign Ships in Territorial Waters." *Michigan Law Review* 2, no. 5 (February 1904): 333–57.

Gregory, Gladys. "The Chamizal Settlement: A View from El Paso." *Southwestern Studies* 1, no. 2 (Summer 1963): 3–52.

Griffin, Frederick C. "Protesting Despotism: American Opposition to the U.S.-Russian Extradition Treaty of 1887." *Mid-America* 70 (April–July 1988): 91–99.

H., L. "International Law: Extraterritorial Criminal Jurisdiction." *Michigan Law Review* 26, no. 4 (February 1928): 429–34.

Hardt, Michael, and Antonio Negri. *Empire.* Cambridge: Harvard University Press, 2001.

Haring, Sidney. *Crow Dog's Case: American Indian Sovereignty, Tribal Law, and United States Law in the Nineteenth Century.* New York: Cambridge University Press, 1994.

Hart, John Mason. *Empire and Revolution: The Americans in Mexico since the Civil War.* Berkeley: University of California Press, 2002.

Hatfield, Shelley Bowen. *Chasing Shadows: Apaches and Yaquis along the United States–Mexico Border, 1876–1911*. Albuquerque: University of New Mexico Press, 1998.

Healy, David. *Drive to Hegemony: The United States in the Caribbean, 1898–1917*. Madison: University of Wisconsin Press, 1988.

———. *James G. Blaine and Latin America*. Columbia: University of Missouri Press, 2001.

Henkin, Louis. *Constitutionalism, Democracy, and Foreign Affairs*. New York: Columbia University Press, 1990.

Hershey, Amos S. "Incursions into Mexico and the Doctrine of Hot Pursuit." *American Journal of International Law* 13, no. 3 (July 1919): 557–69.

Hill, James E, Jr. "El Chamizal: A Century-Old Boundary Dispute." *Geographical Review* 55, no. 4 (October 1965): 510–22.

Hu-DeHart, Evelyn. "Latin America in Asia-Pacific Perspective," in *What Is in a Rim? Critical Perspectives on the Pacific Region Idea*, edited by Arif Dirlik, 262–70. Lanham: Rowan and Littlefield, 1998.

Hudson, Manley O. "The Factor Case and Double Criminality in Extradition." *American Journal of International Law* 28, no. 2 (April 1934): 274–306.

Hunt, Harry E. "How the Great Lakes Became 'High Seas,' and Their Status Viewed from the Standpoint of International Law." *American Journal of International Law* 4, no. 2 (April 1910): 285–313.

Hurst, James Willard. *Law and the Conditions of Freedom in the Nineteenth-Century United States*. Madison: University of Wisconsin Press, 1967.

Hussain, Nasser. *The Jurisprudence of Emergency: Colonialism and the Rule of Law*. Ann Arbor: University of Michigan Press, 2003.

Hyde, Charles Cheney. "Notes on the Extradition Treaties of the United States." *American Journal of International Law* 8, no. 3 (July 1914): 487–514.

Ikenberry, G. John, David A. Lake, and Michael Mastanduno, eds. *State and American Foreign Economic Policy*. Ithaca: Cornell University Press, 1988.

Irigoyen, Ulises. *El Problema Económico de las Fronteras Mexicanas; Tres Monografías: Zona Libre, Puerto Libres y Perímetros Libres*. Mexico D.F., 1936.

Jacobson, Matthew Frye. *Barbarian Virtues: The United States Encounters Foreign Peoples at Home and Abroad, 1876–1917*. New York: Hill and Wang, 2000.

Jacoby, Karl. "Between North and South: The Alternative Borderlands of William E. Ellis and the African American Colony of 1895." In *Continental Crossroads: Remapping U.S.-Mexico Borderlands History*, edited by Samuel Truett and Elliot Young, 209–40. Durham: Duke University Press, 2004.

Jensen, Richard Bach. "The Evolution of Anarchist Terrorism in Europe and the United States from the Nineteenth Century to World War I." In *Terror: From Tyrannicide to Terrorism*, edited by Brett Bowden and Michael T. Davis, 134–60. Queensland: Queensland University Press, 2008.

——. "The International Anti-Anarchist Conference of 1898 and the Origins of Interpol." *Journal of Contemporary History* 16, no. 2 (April 1981): 323–47.

——. "The United States, International Policing and the War Against Anarchist Terrorism, 1900–1914." In *Terrorism*. Vol. 1, *The First or Anarchist Wave*, edited by David C. Rapoport, 369–400. New York: Routledge, 2006.

Johnson, Benjamin H. and Andrew R. Graybill, eds. *Bridging National Borders in North America: Transnational and Comparative Histories*. Durham: Duke University Press, 2010.

Johnson, David R. *Illegal Tender: Counterfeiting and the Secret Service in Nineteenth-Century America*. Washington, D.C.: Smithsonian Institution Press, 1995.

Jones, Alun. *Jones on Extradition*. London: Sweet & Maxwell, 1995.

Jones, Howard. *To the Webster-Ashburton Treaty: A Study in Anglo-American Relations, 1783–1843*. Chapel Hill: University of North Carolina Press, 1977.

Kahler, Miles. "Territoriality and Conflict in an Era of Globalization." In *Territoriality and Conflict in an Era of Globalization*, edited by Miles Kahler and Barbara F. Walter, 1–24. Cambridge: University Press, 2006.

Kahler, Miles, and David A. Lake, eds. *Governance in a Global Economy: Political Authority in Transition*. Princeton and Oxford: Princeton University Press, 2003.

Kahler, Miles, and Barbara F. Walter, eds. *Territoriality and Conflict in an Era of Globalization*. Cambridge: Cambridge University Press, 2006.

Kayaoğlu, Turan. *Legal Imperialism: Sovereignty and Extraterritoriality in Japan, the Ottoman Empire, and China*. Cambridge: Cambridge University Press, 2010.

Kazanjian, David. *The Colonizing Trick: National Culture and Imperial Citizenship in Early America*. Minneapolis: University of Minnesota Press, 2003.

Kennan, George. "The Russian Extradition Treaty." *The Forum* 15 (1893): 283–97.

Kerber, Linda K. "Toward a History of Statelessness in America." *American Quarterly* 57, no. 3 (September 2005): 727–49.

Kerr, James Edward. *The Insular Cases: The Role of the Judiciary in American Expansionism*. Port Washington, N.Y.: Kennikat Press, 1982.

Klyza, Christopher McGrory. "The United States Army, Natural Resources, and Political Development in the Nineteenth Century." *Polity* 35, no. 1 (Autumn 2002): 1–28.

Koskenniemi, Martti. *The Gentle Civilizer of Nations: The Rise and Fall of International Law, 1870–1960*. Cambridge: Cambridge University Press, 2001.

Kraft, Louis. *Gatewood and Geronimo*. Albuquerque: University of New Mexico Press, 2000.

Kramer, Paul A. *The Blood of Government: Race, Empire, the United States, and the Philippines*. Chapel Hill: University of North Carolina Press, 2006.

Krasner, Stephen D. *Sovereignty: Organized Hypocrisy*. Princeton: Princeton University Press, 1999.

Kratochwil, Friedrich. "Of Systems, Boundaries, and Territoriality: An Inquiry into the Formation of the State System." *World Politics* 39, no. 1 (October 1986): 27–52.

Lacher, Hannes. *Beyond Globalization: Capitalism, Territoriality, and the International Relations of Modernity*. London: Routledge, 2006.

LaFeber, Walter. *The Cambridge History of American Foreign Relations: The American Search for Opportunity, 1865–1913*. Cambridge: University Press, 1993.

———. "The Constitution and United States Foreign Policy: An Interpretation." *Journal of American History* 74, no. 3 (December 1987): 695–717.

———. "The 'Lion in the Path': The U.S. Emergence as a World Power." *Political Science Quarterly* 101, no. 5 (1986): 705–18.

———. *The New Empire: An Interpretation of American Expansion, 1865–1898*. Ithaca: Cornell University Press, 1963.

Lake, David A. "The State and American Trade Strategy in the Pre-Hegemonic Era." In *The State and American Foreign Economic Policy*, edited by G. John Ikenberry, David A. Lake, and Michael Mastanduno, 43–45. Ithaca: Cornell University Press, 1988.

Larralde, Carlos, and Jose Rodolfo Jacobo. *Juan N. Cortina and the Struggle for Justice in Texas*. Dubuque: Kendall/Hunt Publishing Company, 2000.

Lauck, W. Jett. "The Political Significance of Reciprocity," *The Journal of Political Economy*, 12:4 (Sep., 1904): 495–524.

"Law, Race, and the Border: The El Paso Salt War of 1877." *Harvard Law Review* 117, no. 3 (January 2004): 941–63.

Lawson, Gary, and Guy Seidman. *The Constitution of Empire: Territorial Expansion and American Legal History*. New Haven: Yale University Press, 2004.

Lee, Erika. *At America's Gates: Chinese Immigration During the Exclusion Era, 1882–1943*. Chapel Hill: University of North Carolina Press, 2003.

Leiker, James N. *Racial Borders: Black Soldiers Along the Rio Grande*. College Station: Texas A & M University Press, 2002.

Limon, José. *Dancing with the Devil: Society and Cultural Poetics in Mexican-American South Texas*. Madison: University of Wisconsin Press, 1994.

Lipson, Charles. *Standing Guard: Protecting Foreign Capital in the Nineteenth and Twentieth Centuries*. Berkeley: University of California, 1985.

Liss, Sheldon B. *A Century of Disagreement: The Chamizal Conflict, 1864–1964*. Washington, D.C.: The University Press, 1965.

Littlefield, Douglas R. *Conflict on the Rio Grande: Water and the Law, 1879–1939*. Norman: University of Oklahoma Press, 2008.

Long, David Foster. *Gold Braid and Foreign Relations: Diplomatic Activities of U.S. Naval Officers, 1798–1883*. Annapolis: Naval Institute, 1988.

Lonner, Jonathan A. "Official Government Abductions in the Presence of Extradition

Treaties." *Journal of Criminal Law and Criminology* 83, no. 4 (Winter 1993): 998–1023.

Lowenfeld, Andreas F. "U.S. Law Enforcement Abroad: The Constitution and International Law." *American Journal of International Law* 83, no. 4 (October 1989): 880–93.

———. "U.S. Law Enforcement Abroad: The Constitution and International Law, Continued." *American Journal of International Law* 84, no. 2 (April 1990): 444–93.

Malik, Marcell Daly. "Comment: Unraveling the Gordian Knot: The United States Law of International Extradition and the Political Offender Exception." *Fordham International Law Forum* 3, no. 14 (1979–80): 141–66.

Margolies, Daniel S. *Henry Watterson and the New South: The Politics of Empire, Free Trade, and Globalization.* Lexington: University Press of Kentucky, 2006.

Martínez, Oscar J. *Border Boom Town: Ciudad Juárez since 1848.* Austin: University of Texas Press, 1978.

———. *Troublesome Border.* Tucson: University of Arizona Press, 1988.

Matorin, Mitchell J. "Unchaining the Law: The Legality of Extraterritorial Abduction in Lieu of Extradition." *Duke Law Journal* 41, no. 4 (February 1992): 907–32.

Matsuda, Mari J. "Law and Culture in the District Court of Honolulu, 1844–1845: A Case Study of the Rise of Legal Consciousness." *American Journal of Legal History* 32, no. 1 (January 1988): 16–41.

Mazlish, Bruce, Nayan Chanda, and Kenneth Weisbrode, eds. *The Paradox of a Global USA.* Stanford: Stanford University Press, 2007.

McCaffrey, Stephen C. "The Harmon Doctrine One Hundred Years Later: Buried, Not Praised." *Natural Resources Journal* 36 (1996): 449–590.

———. *The Law of International Watercourses: Non-Navigational Uses.* Oxford: Oxford University Press, 2001.

McCormick, Thomas J. *China Market: America's Quest for Informal Empire, 1893–1901.* Chicago: Quadrangle Books, 1967.

McCoy, Alfred W., and Francisco A. Scarano, eds. *Colonial Crucible: Empire in the Making of the Modern American State.* Madison: University of Wisconsin Press, 2009.

McCurdy, Charles W. "The Knight Sugar Decision of 1895 and the Modernization of American Corporation Law, 1869 –1903." *Business History Review* 53, no. 3 (Autumn 1979): 304–42.

McKanna, Clare V., Jr. *Homicide, Race, and Justice in the American West, 1880–1920.* Tucson: The University of Arizona Press, 1997.

Miller, Darlis A. *Soldiers and Settlers: Military Supply in the Southwest, 1861–1885.* Albuquerque: University of New Mexico Press, 1989.

Mills, W. W. *Forty Years at El Paso, 1858–1898: Recollections of War, Politics, Adventure, Events, Narratives, Sketches, etc.,* 1901.

Mitchell, Timothy J. *Intoxicated Identities: Alcohol's Power in Mexican History and Culture*. New York: Routledge, 2004.

Moffett, Cleveland. "The Destruction of the Reno Gang: Stories from the Archives of the Pinkerton Detective Agency." *McClure's Magazine* IV (December 1894–May 1895): 549–54.

Montejano, David. *Anglos and Mexicans in the Making of Texas, 1836–1986*. Austin: University of Texas Press, 1987.

Mora-Torres, Juan. *The Making of the Mexican Border: The State, Capitalism, and Society in Nuevo León, 1848–1910*. Austin: University of Texas Press, 2001.

Morgenstern, Felice. "'Extra-Territorial' Asylum." *British Yearbook of International Law* 25 (1948): 236–61.

Mueller, Jerry E. *Restless River: International Law and the Behavior of the Rio Grande*. El Paso: Texas Western Press, 1975.

Nadelmann, Ethan. *Cops across Borders: The Internationalization of U.S. Criminal Law Enforcement*. University Park: Pennsylvania State University Press, 1993.

Neal, Bill. *Getting Away with Murder on the Texas Frontier: Notorious Killings and Celebrated Trials*. Lubbock: Texas Tech University Press, 2006.

Neuman, Gerald L. "Anomalous Zones." *Stanford Law Review* 48, no. 5 (May 1996): 1197–1234.

———. "Whose Constitution." *Yale Law Journal* 100, no. 4 (January 1991): 909–91.

"Non-Extradition of Nationals." *Yale Law Journal* 46, no. 3 (January 1937): 525–27.

Novak, William. "Law, Capitalism, and the Liberal State: The Historical Sociology of James Willard Hurst." *Law and History Review* 18 (2000): 97–145.

———. "The Myth of the 'Weak' American State." *American Historical Review* 113 (June 2008): 752–72.

Ortíz–González, Victor M. *El Paso: Local Frontiers at a Global Crossroads*. Minneapolis: University of Minnesota Press, 2004.

Paredes, Américo. *With His Pistol in His Hand: A Border Ballad and Its Hero*. Austin: University of Texas Press, 1990.

Parenti, Christian. *The Soft Cage: Surveillance in America from Slavery to the War on Terror*. New York: Basic Books, 2003.

Pérez, Octavio Herrera. *La Zona Libre: Excepción Fiscal y Conformación Histórica de la Frontera Norte de Mexico*. Mexico: Secretaría de Relaciones Exteriores, Acervo Histórico Diplomático, 2004.

Pinkerton, Allan. "Don Pedro and the Detectives." In *Mississippi Outlaws and the Detectives*, 125–265. New York: G. W. Carleton & Co., 1879.

Pinkerton, William A. "Highwaymen of the Railroad." *North American Review* 157, no. 444 (November 1893): 530–31.

Platt, Charles Malcom. "A Triad of Political Conceptions: State, Sovereign, Government." *Political Science Quarterly* 10, no. 2 (June 1895): 292–323.

Pletcher, David M. *The Awkward Years: American Foreign Relations under Garfield and Arthur*. Columbia: University of Missouri Press, 1962.

———. "Consul Warner P. Sutton and American-Mexican Border Trade during the Early Díaz Period." *Southwestern Historical Quarterly* 79, no. 4 (July 1975–April 1976): 373–99.

———. *The Diplomacy of Involvement: American Economic Expansion across the Pacific, 1784–1900*. Columbia and London: University of Missouri Press, 2001.

———. *The Diplomacy of Trade and Investment: American Economic Expansion in the Hemisphere, 1865–1900*. Columbia and London: University of Missouri Press, 1998.

Polanyi, Karl. *The Great Transformation: The Political and Economic Origins of Our Time*. Boston: Beacon, 2001.

"'Political Offence' in Extradition Treaties between the United States and Other Countries." *American Journal of International Law* 3, no. 2 supplement, *Official Documents* (April 1909): 144–52.

"'Political Offence' in Extradition Treaties." *American Journal of International Law* 3, no. 2 (April 1909): 459–61.

Preuss, Lawrence. "American Conception of Jurisdiction with Respect to Conflicts of Law on Crime." *Transactions of the Grotius Society* 30 (1944): 188–91.

Pyle, Christopher H. *Extradition, Politics, and Human Rights*. Philadelphia: Temple University Press, 2001.

Rao, Gautham. "The Federal Posse Comitatus Doctrine: Slavery, Compulsion, and Statecraft in Mid-Nineteenth-Century America." *Law and History Review* 26, no. 1 (Spring 2008): 1–56.

Raustiala, Kal. *Does the Constitution Follow the Flag? The Evolution of Territoriality in American Law*. Oxford: Oxford University Press, 2009.

———. "The Evolution of Territoriality: International Relations and American Law." In *Territoriality and Conflict in an Era of Globalization*, edited by Miles Kahler and Barbara F. Walter, 219–50. Cambridge: Cambridge University Press, 2006.

Rebert, Paula. *La Gran Línea: Mapping the United States–Mexico Boundary, 1849–1857*. Austin: University of Texas Press, 2001.

Reinhardt, Frederick. "Rectification of the Rio Grande in the El Paso–Juarez Valley." *American Journal of International Law* 31, no. 1 (January 1937): 44–54.

Reynolds, David. "Expansion and Integration: Reflections on the History of America's Approach to Globalization." In *The Paradox of a Global USA*, edited by Bruce Mazlish, Nayan Chanda, and Kenneth Weisbrode, 49–63. Stanford: Stanford University Press, 2007.

Richardson, Heather Cox. *West from Appomattax: The Reconstruction of America after the Civil War*. New Haven: Yale University Press, 2007.

Riguzzi, Paolo. *Reciprocidad Imposible? La Política del Comercio entre México y Estados*

Unidos, 1857–1938. Zinacantepec, Estado de México: El Colegio Mexiquense el Colegio Mexiquense, Instituto de Investigaciones Dr. José María Mora, 2003.

———. "Las Relaciones de Mexico con Estados Unidos, 1878–1888: Apertura Economica y Politicas de Seguridad." *Jahrbuch fur Geschichte Lateinamerikas* 39 (2002): 299–321.

Robbins, William G. *Colony and Empire: The Capitalist Transformation of the American West.* Lawrence: University Press of Kansas, 1984.

Romero, Mary. El Paso Salt War: Mob Action or Political Struggle? *Aztlán: A Journal of Chicano Studies* 16, nos. 1–2 (1985): 119–43.

Rosenberg, Emily. *Financial Missionaries to the World: The Politics and Culture of Dollar Diplomacy, 1900–30.* Cambridge: Harvard University Press, 1999.

Ruskola, Teemu. "Canton Is Not Boston: The Invention of American Imperial Sovereignty." In *Legal Borderlands: Law and the Construction of American Borders,* edited by Mary L. Dudziak and Ledi Volpp, 267–92. Baltimore: Johns Hopkins University Press, 2006.

———. "Colonialism without Colonies: On the Extraterritorial Jurisprudence of the U.S. Court for China." *Law & Contemporary Problems* 71 (2008): 217–42.

Salvucci, Richard J. "The Origins and Progress of U.S.-Mexican Trade, 1825–1884: 'Hoc opus, hic labor est.'" *Hispanic American Historical Review* 71, no. 4 (November 1991): 697–735.

Salyer, Lucy E. *Laws Harsh as Tigers: Chinese Immigrants and the Shaping of Modern Immigration Law.* Chapel Hill: University of North Carolina Press, 1995.

Sarat, Austin. "At the Boundaries of Law: Executive Clemency, Sovereign Prerogative, and the Dilemma of American Legality." In *Legal Borderlands: Law and the Construction of American Borders,* edited by Mary L. Dudziak and Ledi Volpp, 19–39. Baltimore: Johns Hopkins University Press, 2006.

Sarat, Austin, Lawrence Douglas, and Martha Merrill Umphrey, eds. *The Place of Law.* Ann Arbor: University of Michigan Press, 2003.

Sarracino, Rodolfo. *José Martí y el Caso Cutting: ¿Extraterritorialidad o annexionismo?* La Habana: Centro de Estudios Martianos, 2004.

Sassen, Saskia. *Territory, Authority, Rights: From Medieval to Global Assemblages.* Princeton: Princeton University Press, 2006.

Schafer, Stephen. "The Concept of the Political Criminal." *Journal of Criminal Law, Criminology, and Police Science* 62, no. 3 (September 1971): 380–87.

Scheiber, Harry N. "Federalism and Legal Process: Historical and Contemporary Analysis of the American System." *Law & Society Review* 14, no. 3 (Spring 1980): 663–722.

Schell, William, Jr. "American Investment in Tropical Mexico: Rubber Plantations, Fraud, and Dollar Diplomacy, 1897–1913." *Business History Review* 64, no. 2 (Summer 1990): 217–54.

———. *Integral Outsiders: The American Colony in Mexico City, 1876–1911*. Wilmington: Scholarly Resources, 2001.

Schoonover, Thomas. *Uncle Sam's War of 1898 and the Origins of Globalization*. Lexington: University Press of Kentucky, 2003.

———. *The United States in Central America, 1860–1911: Episodes of Social Imperialism and Imperial Rivalry in the World System*. Durham: Duke University Press, 1991.

Scully, Eileen P. *Bargaining with the State from Afar: American Treaty Citizenship in Treaty Port China, 1844–1942*. New York: Columbia University Press, 2001.

Shearer, I. A. *Extradition in International Law*. Manchester: University of Manchester Press, 1971.

Shiva, Vandana. *Water Wars: Privatization, Pollution, and Profit*. Cambridge: South End Press, 2002.

Simon, John Y., ed. *The Papers of Ulysses S. Grant*. Vol. 23, February 1–December 31, 1872. Carbondale: Southern Illinois University Press, 2000.

Sklar, Martin J. *The Corporate Reconstruction of American Capitalism, 1890–1916: The Markets, the Law, and Politics*. Cambridge: Cambridge University Press, 1988.

Skowronek, Stephen. *Building a New American State: The Expansion of National Administrative Capacities, 1877–1920*. Cambridge: Cambridge University Press, 1982.

Slaughter, Anne-Marie. "Disaggregated Sovereignty: Towards the Public Accountability of Global Government Networks." *Government and Opposition* 39, no. 2 (April 2004): 159–90.

———. *A New World Order*. Princeton: Princeton University Press, 2004.

Smith, Robert Michael. *From Blackjacks to Briefcases: A History of Commercialized Strikebreaking in the United States*. Athens: Ohio University Press, 2003.

Smith, Rogers. *Civic Ideals: Conflicting Visions of Citizenship in U.S. History*. New Haven: Yale University Press, 1997.

Smith, Thomas T. *The U.S. Army and the Texas Frontier Economy, 1845–1900*. College Station: Texas A & M Press, 1999.

Somers, Margaret R. *Genealogies of Citizenship: Markets, Statelessness, and the Right to Have Rights*. Cambridge: Cambridge University Press, 2008.

Sparrow, Bartholomew H. *The Insular Cases and the Emergence of American Empire*. Lawrence: University of Kansas Press, 2006.

Spaw, Patsy McDonald. *The Texas Senate: Civil War to the Eve of Reform, 1861–1889*. Austin: Texas State Senate, 1999.

Spiro, Peter J. "Mandated Membership, Diluted Identity: Citizenship, Globalization, and International Law." In *People Out of Place: Globalization, Human Rights, and the Citizenship Gap*, edited by Alison Brysk and Gershon Shafir, 87–108. London: Routledge, 2004.

Stanbrook, Ivor, and Clive Stanbrook. *Extradition: Law and Practice*. 2nd ed. Oxford: Oxford University Press, 2000.

Stowell, Ellery C., and Henry F. Munro. *International Cases: Arbitrations and Incidents Illustrative of International Law as Practised by Independent States.* Boston: Houghton Mifflin, 1916.

Symonds, Craig L. *Lincoln and His Admirals: Abraham Lincoln, the U.S. Navy and the Civil War.* Oxford: University Press, 2008.

Tate, Michael L. *The Frontier Army in the Settlement of the West.* Norman: University of Oklahoma Press, 1999.

Taylor, Peter J. "The State as Container: Territoriality in the Modern World-System." *Progress in Human Geography* 18, no. 2 (1994): 151–62.

Terrill, Tom E. *The Tariff, Politics, and American Foreign Policy.* Westport, Conn.: Greenwood, 1973.

Teschke, Benno. *The Myth of 1648: Class, Geopolitics and the Making of Modern International Relations.* London: Verso, 2009.

Thompson, Jerry. *Cortina: Defending the Mexican Name in Texas.* College Station: Texas A & M University Press, 2007.

Timm, Charles A. *The International Boundary Commission: United States and Mexico.* Austin: University of Texas Press, 1941.

Timmons, W. H. *El Paso: A Borderlands History.* El Paso: Texas Western Press, 2004.

Tomlins, Christopher L., and Bruce H. Mann, eds. *The Many Legalities of Early America.* Chapel Hill: University of North Carolina Press, 2001.

Torpey, John C. *Invention of the Passport: Surveillance, Citizenship, and the State.* Cambridge: Cambridge University Press, 2000.

Truett, Samuel. *Fugitive Landscapes: The Forgotten History of the U.S.-Mexico Borderlands.* New Haven: Yale University Press, 2006.

Truett, Samuel, and Elliot Young, eds. *Continental Crossroads: Remapping U.S.-Mexico Borderlands History.* Durham: Duke University Press, 2004.

Uglow, Loyd M. *Standing in the Gap: Army Outposts, Picket Stations, and the Pacification of the Texas Frontier, 1866–1886.* Fort Worth: Texas Christian University Press, 2001.

United States. *Army Training and Doctrine Command, ed., Armed Diplomacy: Two Centuries of American Campaigning.* Fort Leavenworth, Kans.: Combat Studies Institute Press, 2003.

Van den Wijngaert, Christine. *The Political Offence Exception to Extradition: The Delicate Problem of Balancing the Rights of the Individual and the International Public Order.* Deventer: Kluwer, 1980.

Van Schendel, Willem, and Itty Abraham, eds. *Illicit Flows and Criminal Things: States, Borders, and the Other Side of Globalization.* Bloomington: Indiana University Press, 2005.

Waite, G. Graham. "International Law Affecting Water Rights." In *Water Rights Laws in the Nineteen Western States,* edited by Wells A. Hutchins, 116–40. Clark, N.J.: Lawbook Exchange Ltd., 2004.

Waller, Altina. *Feud: Hatfields, McCoys, and Social Change in Appalachia, 1860–1900.* Chapel Hill: University of North Carolina Press, 1988.

Ward, Linda C. "Forcible Abduction Made Fashionable: *United States v. Alvarez-Machain*'s Extension of the Ker-Frisbie Doctrine." *Arkansas Law Review* 47 (1994): 477–504.

Wedgwood, Ruth. "The Revolutionary Martyrdom of Jonathan Robbins." *Yale Law Journal* 100, no. 2 (November 1990): 229–368.

Welke, Barbara Young. *Law and the Borders of Belonging in the Long Nineteenth Century United States.* Cambridge: Cambridge University Press, 2010.

———. "Law, Personhood, and Citizenship in the Long Nineteenth Century: The Borders of Belonging." In *The Cambridge History of Law in America.* Vol. II, *The Long Nineteenth Century (1789–1920),* edited by Michael Grossberg and Christopher Tomlins, 345–86. Cambridge: Cambridge University Press, 2008.

Werne, Joseph Richard. *The Imaginary Line: A History of the United States and Mexican Boundary Survey, 1848–1857.* Fort Worth: Texas Christian University Press, 2007.

Wiebe, Robert H. *The Search for Order, 1877–1920.* New York: Hill and Wang, 1967.

William, James, and Edward Sheptycki. "Transnational Crime and Transnational Policing." *Sociology Compass* 1, no. 2 (November 2007): 485–98.

Williams, David Ricardo. *Call in the Pinkerton's: American Detectives at Work for Canada.* Toronto: Dundurn Press, 1998.

Williams, Walter L. "United States Indian Policy and the Debate over Philippine Annexation: Implications for the Origins of American Imperialism." *Journal of American History* 66, no. 4 (March 1980): 810–31.

Williams, William Appleman. *The Contours of American History.* New York: W. W. Norton Company, 1988.

———. *The Roots of the Modern American Empire: A Study of the Growth and Shaping of Social Consciousness in a Marketplace Society.* New York: Vintage, 1969.

Wilson, George Grafton. "Insurgency and International Maritime Law." *American Journal of International Law* 1, no. 1 (January–April 1907): 46–60.

Wolfman, Nathan. "Sovereigns as Defendants." *American Journal of International Law* 4, no. 2 (April 1910): 373–83.

Wolman, Paul. *Most Favored Nation: The Republican Revisionists and U.S. Tariff Policy, 1897–1912.* Chapel Hill: University of North Carolina Press, 1992.

Wong, Diana. "The Rumor of Trafficking: Border Controls, Illegal Migration, and the Sovereignty of the Nation-State." In *Illicit Flows and Criminal Things: States, Borders, and the Other Side of Globalization,* edited by Willem Van Schendel and Itty Abraham, 69–99. Bloomington: Indiana University Press, 2005.

Wong, Lloyd L. "Home Away from Home? Transnationalism and the Canadian Citizenship Regime." In *Communities across Borders: New Immigrants and Transnational Cultures,* edited by Paul T. Kennedy and Victor Roudometof, 169–81. London: Routledge, 2002.

Wooster, Robert. "Fort Davis and the Close of a Military Frontier." *Southwestern Historical Quarterly* 110, no. 2 (2006): 172–91.

————. *Frontier Crossroads: Fort Davis and the West*. College Station: Texas A & M University Press, 2006.

Wu, Tim. "Treaties' Domains." *Virginia Law Review* 93, no. 3 (May 2007): 571–649.

Young, Elliott. *Catarino Garza's Revolution on the Texas-Mexico Border*. Durham: Duke University Press, 2004.

————. "Remembering Catarino Garza's 1891 Revolution: An Aborted Border Insurrection." *Mexican Studies/Estudios Mexicanos* 12, no. 2 (July 1996): 231–72.

Zagaris, Bruce, and Julia Padierna Peralta. "Mexico–United States Extradition and Alternatives: From Fugitive Slaves to Drug Traffickers—150 Years and Beyond the Rio Grande's Winding Courses." *American University Journal of International Law and Policy* 12 (1997): 521–627.

Zartman, I. William, ed. *Understanding Life in the Borderlands: Boundaries in Depth and in Motion*. Athens: University of Georgia Press, 2010.

INDEX

9 780820 338871